D0007242

MELANIE
KLEIN

MELANIE KLEIN

Her World and Her Work

Phyllis Grosskurth

JASON ARONSON INC.
Northvale, New Jersey
London

THE MASTER WORK SERIES

1995 softcover edition

Copyright © 1986 by Phyllis Grosskurth

Published by arrangement with Alfred A. Knopf, Inc.

Grateful acknowledgment is made to Basic Books, Inc., for permission to reprint excerpts from *Bloomsbury/Freud: The Letters of James and Alix Strachey, 1924–1925,* edited by Walter Kendrick and Perry Meisel. Copyright © 1985 by The Strachey Trust and copyright © 1985 by Walter Kendrick and Perry Meisel for selection and editorial matter. Reprinted by permission of Basic Books, Inc., Publishers.

All rights reserved. Printed in the United States of America. No part of this book may be used or reproduced in any manner whatsoever without written permission from Jason Aronson Inc. except in the case of brief quotations in reviews for inclusion in a magazine, newspaper, or broadcast.

Library of Congress Cataloging-in-Publication Data

Grosskurth, Phyllis.
    Melanie Klein : her world and her work / by Phyllis Grosskurth.
        p.   cm.
    Previously published: New York : Knopf, 1986.
    Includes bibliographical references and index.
    ISBN 1-56821-445-6
    1. Klein, Melanie. 2. Psychoanalysts — Austria — Biography.
  3. Psychoanalysis — History. I. Title.
RC339.52.K43G76 1995
150.19′5′092 — dc20
    [B]   94-42683

Manufactured in the United States of America. Jason Aronson Inc. offers books and cassettes. For information and catalog write to Jason Aronson Inc., 230 Livingston Street, Northvale, New Jersey 07647.

FOR MY SON BRIAN
WITH LOVE AND GRATITUDE

We have never prided ourselves on the completeness and finality of our knowledge and capacity. We are just as ready now as we were earlier to admit the imperfections of our understanding, to learn new things and to alter our methods in any way that can improve them.

SIGMUND FREUD, Lines of Advance in Psycho-Analytic Therapy (1919).

These were the first words Melanie Klein ever heard Freud utter.

Contents

FOREWORD ix

PART ONE: VIENNA TO BUDAPEST, 1882–1920 1
1. *Early Memories* 3
2. *Emanuel* 21
3. *Marriage* 40
4. *Crisis* 60

PART TWO: BERLIN, 1920–1926 87
1. *The Protégée* 89
2. *Limbo* 114
3. *Ostracism* 130

PART THREE: LONDON, 1926–1939 151
1. *The British Psycho-Analytical Society* 153
2. *Cock of the Walk* 183
3. *Mourning* 212
4. *The Arrival of the Freuds* 232

PART FOUR: CAMBRIDGE AND PITLOCHRY, 1940–1941 247
1. *Moratorium* 249
2. *Richard* 262

Contents

PART FIVE: THE CONTROVERSIAL DISCUSSIONS, 1942–1944   279
1. *Resumption of Hostilities*   281
2. *Warring Women*   310
3. *The Ladies' Agreement*   334

PART SIX: THE POSTWAR WORLD, 1945–1960   363
1. *Mothers and Daughters*   365
2. *The Matriarch*   386
3. *Envy*   408
4. *Political Infighting*   424
5. *Last Years*   435

CHRONOLOGY   463
APPENDIXES   467
REFERENCES   471
BIBLIOGRAPHY:
   Works of Melanie Klein   483
   General Bibliography   485
ACKNOWLEDGMENTS   499
INDEX   501

Foreword

It has generally been assumed that Melanie Klein left little documentation about her life. In actuality there is an abundance of material, largely in the keeping of the Melanie Klein Trust. Inevitably I have encountered the frustration of penetrating the total silence concerning certain episodes and relationships, but from the wealth of evidence that is available I think we are now in a position to evaluate the connection between the woman and her work. The Melanie Klein Trust has deposited the Klein papers in the Wellcome Institute for the History of Medicine, where other scholars will be able to examine and evaluate them for themselves.

I could not have embarked upon this book without the theoretical and biographical foundations laid by Dr. Hanna Segal in *Introduction to the Work of Melanie Klein* (1978) and in *Klein* (Fontana Modern Masters Series, 1979). Edna O'Shaughnessy's Notes to the *Collected Works* have been invaluable. Dr. Segal and the Melanie Klein Trust have given me unrestricted access to Klein's papers, and in innumerable ways have endeavored to assist me in my task. Klein's son, Eric Clyne, has allowed me to examine family papers, has suggested possible sources of information, and has patiently answered persistent questions. Fortunately, he has a phenomenal memory for what he describes as "trivia"; but what might seem trivial to him is invaluable to the biographer. His relatives have also been extremely helpful. Scattered to the far ends of the earth by pogrom, war, and revolution, their history represents a miniature Diaspora.

I am also greatly indebted to the members of the British Psycho-Analytical Society. Dozens of analysts have given me hours of their time, and I shall take pleasure in acknowledging them by name, in addition to the many other people who have assisted me, at the end of the book. Dr. Dennis Duncan, former

Archivist of the British Institute of Psycho-Analysis, kindly allowed me to use its archives. Pearl King, former President of the British Psycho-Analytical Society and its present Archivist, has guided me through its history and given me generous permission to quote from unpublished material. Both John Jarrett, Administrator of the Institute, and Jill Duncan, its Librarian, have given me cheerful and unstinting help.

A number of people have been involved in the translation of German material, but the great bulk has been the work of Bruni Schling, whose sensitive translating has been invaluable, particularly in the chapters on Melanie Klein's early years.

I wish also to thank my students in Women's Studies at New College, University of Toronto, for discussion and encouragement.

No biography is definitive. Other scholars will correct and elaborate my interpretation of Melanie Klein. This book would have been enriched if I had been given access to the correspondence between Freud and Karl Abraham and Freud and Joan Riviere, which is deposited in the Library of Congress with an embargo until 2000; but this was denied to me by Dr. K. R. Eissler, then Secretary of the Sigmund Freud Archives. His attitude has been a dramatic exception to the cooperation I have received elsewhere.

A biographer can create only an approximate composite of a sentient being; and if the woman who has emerged is not the one some people remember, I ask the reader to ponder on the fact that each of us presents multiple personae in our commerce with others during the course of our lives.

I have ended the book with Melanie Klein's death in 1960, but the story by no means ends there. Elizabeth Bott Spillius has written on the elaborations in Kleinian thought within the British Society ("Some Developments from the Work of Melanie Klein," *International Journal of Psycho-Analysis* [1983] 64, Part 3, 321–32). Many books remain to be written on the dissemination and development of Kleinian ideas throughout the world.

Few professional women have been subjected to as much distilled malice and rumor accepted as fact as Klein endured both during her lifetime and since her death. I hope that I have in some measure presented a more balanced evaluation.

PHYLLIS GROSSKURTH
Toronto, 1985

PART ONE

1882-1920
VIENNA TO
BUDAPEST

CHAPTER ONE

Early Memories

Melanie Klein was the stuff of which myths are made. Seemingly secretive about her past, indomitably self-assured about her present, her very being aroused speculation and suspicion. In a sense, she sought this enigmatic role; in another, it was thrust upon her by enemies and friends alike. Her enemies—who were numerous during her lifetime and after—spread scurrilous gossip about her. Her supporters, tenderly protective, assured the world that she was extremely discreet about her private life. She was more transparent than any of them realized, but in the course of her turbulent passage she learned the caution necessary to safeguard her work, and for most of her career the woman and her work were indistinguishable.

Melanie Klein was a woman with a mission. From the moment she read Freud's paper *On Dreams* (1901)* in 1914 she was enraptured, converted, and dedicated to psychoanalysis. Captivated by the concept of the unconscious, she followed its seductive lure into speculative depths from which even Freud had retreated. This was her offense: for daring to branch out on her own paths of investigation, she was branded, vilified, and mocked. Her detractors, by attacking the woman herself, sought to devalue her contribution to the knowledge of the mind. The innuendos about a shadowy past have been so widespread that a whole subliterature about the woman, her family, and her early work has proliferated. The truth is both simpler and more complex—and certainly more elusive—than her defamers have imagined.

During the last decade of her life, Melanie Klein began to receive numerous inquiries, particularly from America, about the history and development of

* *Über den Traum.*

her concepts. She was delighted by the interest, particularly as she feared that her work might not survive, an anxiety her colleagues often heard her voice. To the queries from abroad, she listed the facts of her life in virtually formulaic fashion: the information that her father had been a doctor and that she also had intended to study medicine but was prevented by an early marriage; her introduction to psychoanalysis through reading Freud's work while living in Budapest and her subsequent analysis by Ferenczi; the latter's encouragement to pursue investigations into child analysis; her joining Karl Abraham's group in Berlin in 1921; the invitation by Ernest Jones to give a course of lectures in child analysis to the British Psycho-Analytical Society in 1925; and her subsequent decision the following year to settle in England. To this was appended a bibliography of her major works: *The Psycho-Analysis of Children* (1932), *Contributions to Psycho-Analysis, 1921–1945* (1948), *Developments in Psycho-Analysis* (1952), *New Directions in Psycho-Analysis* (1955),* and *Envy and Gratitude* (1957). *Narrative of a Child Analysis* was to be published a year after her death, in 1961.

In 1953 she began work on a brief autobiography, which she continued at intermittent intervals until 1959, the year before her death. It is cautious, repetitious, ingenuous, and evasive—and invaluable to an understanding of the woman. There are also various fragmentary pages, as though she were attempting to rework the document until it reached its final, acceptable form. Similarly, all through her life she tended to write initial drafts of her most important letters. Aware of her position in the psychoanalytic movement, she realized the importance of setting down selected facts of her early life. Both a childlike vulnerability and a mature self-knowledge shine through the implacable façade of the public image.

Melanie Klein was the first European psychoanalyst to become a member of the British Psycho-Analytical Society, and ultimately she became its dominant influence. A somewhat exotic figure when she settled in England in 1926, rumored to be at odds with the Freuds, father and daughter, in disrepute with the Berlin Society of which she had been a member, a divorcee in the days when divorce still carried an aura of scandal, she inevitably became the subject of gossip. What, it was asked, had she done with her husband? To this day a ribald story makes the rounds that she ate him up.

The unpublished Autobiography is in the possession of the Melanie Klein Trust. Her story, as she relates it, is the "official" record. However, in 1983 a large collection of early family letters was discovered in her son's loft. These letters reveal information very much at variance with some of the facts related

---

* *Developments in Psycho-Analysis* and *New Directions in Psycho-Analysis* also included papers by her colleagues.

in the Autobiography. Why, then, did she not destroy them, since she must have been aware that they would ultimately be discovered? Several explanations are possible. Perhaps certain letters are not destroyed because the subject wants the truth ultimately to be told, even in its unpalatable aspects; yet naturally one is ambivalent about exposing desires, fears, and embarrassment to public scrutiny.

In Klein's case, it is possible that she simply could not bear to part with some of the most important areas of her past. Most of the letters from her mother and her brother seem to have been preserved, whereas only a single letter from her husband survives. The letters kept her relatives alive in a very concrete way. To the distanced biographer, her mother and her brother emerge from the letters as very different people from the portraits in the Autobiography; and it is conceivable that Klein idealized them to the point where the real and the official figures merged indissolubly.

In her Autobiography she moves back and forth in time and, in reflecting on time past and time present, she has created a family romance. Just as much as an analyst, a biographer finds self-mythologies revealing in their revelations of displacements, condensations, and evasions. Yet how can one encompass her turbulent life in a single telling, how give the allotted weight to each event and person who helped shape the course of that life?

Her background was one of both conventionality and rebellion. Her father's early life fascinated her, but the details she gives are scrappy and inconsequential. She does not even mention his date of birth (1828), but explains that Moriz Reizes came from a rigidly orthodox family, somewhere in Poland—the exact location she apparently regarded as irrelevant. It actually was Lemberg (now Lvov), Galicia, the site of one of the oldest and most distinguished universities in Europe.* Her grandfather she describes as a "businessman," possibly a small shopkeeper, or a dealer in cattle or lumber. For years her own father was known as a *bocher*—a student of the Talmud, the ancient, many-volumed codification of Jewish law and tradition. Yet Moriz Reizes must have had a very private inner world where he nursed his own hopes and dreams, probably influenced by the Haskalah, the Jewish emancipation movement that met strong opposition from both the orthodox rabbinate and the Hasidim in Galicia. One day he announced to his pious, simple parents that he had passed the general matriculation examinations and, worse still, intended to study medicine. He supported himself while in medical school (presumably in Lvov) by tutoring. Many years later he told his daughter that when he was taking his first examinations he knew that his mother was at home

---

* At the time Galicia was part of the Austro-Hungarian Empire. Poland, as a separate entity, was formed after the First World War. After World War II Lvov was taken by the Russians and is now part of the Ukraine.

praying that he would fail. By the time he passed all his examinations he had broken away completely from his orthodox tradition, although he never cut the ties with his family.

As a child, Melanie loved hearing about her father's courage during a cholera epidemic. In answer to an appeal for doctors to go out to the Polish villages, he not only went but, unlike the other doctors who would stand at the windows telling the victims what to do, Moriz Reizes boldly entered the cottages and treated the patients as he would have done if they had been suffering from any other complaint. When he returned, he found a letter from his mother imploring him not to risk his life. Whether this act of heroism actually happened or not is immaterial; Klein believed that it had.

He was married twice, but Klein is vague about the details of the first marriage. It probably took place prior to his medical studies, because he was married in Jewish rites to a girl he had never seen prior to the wedding. The marriage was unsuccessful and was "soon dissolved"—in Klein's reckoning, when her father was about thirty-seven. No reason is given, but it is an indication of his independence and rebelliousness.

He was in his mid-forties when, on a visit to Vienna, he met a black-haired beauty, Libussa Deutsch, who was staying at the same boardinghouse. He immediately fell in love with this "educated, witty, and interesting" young woman, with her fair complexion, fine features, and expressive eyes. Her death certificate indicates that she was born in 1852, twenty-four years after her future husband. If she was such a beauty and the daughter of a rabbi, why did she marry this Polish stranger with whom there are no signs that she was infatuated?

In actual fact, Reizes was a general practitioner in Deutsch-Kreutz, a small town (which later became Burgenland, Austria) about seventy miles from Vienna, two or three miles inside the Hungarian border. Libussa, on the other hand, lived not in Deutsch-Kreutz (where Klein situates her) but in Warbotz (Verbotz) in Slovakia. She was named after Libussa, the mythical founder of Prague who in the nineteenth century became the symbol of Czech national identity. Klein's failure to give her mother's real birthplace could be accounted for if she despised the Slovaks, particularly as Slovakian Jews spoke Yiddish. Her mother, however, was proud of her origins and in a letter of 1911, written to Melanie who was staying in a resort on the Baltic, quoted their new Slovakian housemaid: "You will see what a loyal maid you will have in me, for only a Slovak girl can be so loyal and devoted when she gets such good treatment as I do. The Hungarians are all treacherous, slovenly, thievish, and irresponsible."

Melanie was much attracted to the cultural ambience of Libussa's family, in which both the father and grandfather were widely respected for their scholarship and tolerance. (Libussa's brother, Hermann, who was to play an important part in their lives, attended a Jesuit school.) Melanie's great-grandfather,

Rabbi Mandel Deutsch, was noted for his gentle disposition. One of the longings of Melanie's childhood was to have known her maternal grandmother: "I longed for her to be living, because I never had a grandmother, and I knew this was a nice, kind, and pleasant woman." This is an interesting statement from a woman who herself was apparently far more successful as a grandmother than as a mother. It is also interesting that she never knew or showed any interest in her maternal grandfather. Perhaps she imbibed this lack of interest from her own mother. There was certainly a pattern of matriarchy in the family. But she never formed even an image of her father's mother, and was patently scornful of all his family. She says of the Deutsch family: "The whole impression I got, in contrast to my father's family, was one of a good family life, very simple, in restricted circumstances but full of knowledge and education." Seventy years later, Klein still shuddered at the memory of her revulsion towards her father's sister and her husband on the occasions when they appeared, dressed in the ritual kaftan that Polish Jews had adopted from eighteenth-century aristocrats.

According to Klein, Libussa and her two sisters were consumed with a passion for learning, and these determined young autodidacts gained knowledge by reading and discussions with their father. Melanie admired the way her mother had taught herself to play the piano. She had a vivid recollection of Libussa pacing up and down the wide veranda of a summer flat they rented in Dornbach, on the outskirts of Vienna, totally absorbed in a book of French idioms she was memorizing. For Klein this was a demonstration of intellectual passion, since opportunities for her mother to put these idioms to practical use were almost nonexistent. There is evidence that as a young woman Libussa did have some respect for learning: she was attracted to her future husband partly because of his command of ten languages. Other relatives recalled Karoline as the clever sister, while Libussa was known as the beauty of the family. In any event, Libussa's later letters are written in a German that indicates the language did not come easily to her.

The letters exchanged between the engaged couple in 1874 put a slightly different emphasis on Melanie's image of her mother. Libussa freely admits in her letters to her fiancé that she composed them very carefully, sometimes writing them out twice. Moriz was very eager for them to exchange letters in French—a suggestion Libussa stubbornly resisted, giving as an excuse that she did not want to deprive the other members of her family of the pleasure of reading his letters. When she did include a phrase in French it was awkwardly expressed. Moriz writes with flowery ardor, Libussa with self-conscious restraint. "I feel only too clearly," she wrote on one occasion, "that I will not be able to follow your lofty and enthusiastic flights which keep you in the highest heights, in ever growing, enthusiastic distances. My wings are tied. I am too earthbound even to dare to dream of following you."

After their marriage in 1875 the couple settled in Deutsch-Kreutz. Here three children were born in quick succession: Emilie in 1876, Emanuel in 1877, and Sidonie in 1878. At some point, probably between the birth of Sidonie and the birth of Melanie on March 30, 1882, the family moved to Vienna,* undoubtedly in the hope of improving their straitened financial circumstances. They could not have been so naïve as to harbor any expectation that a middle-aged Jewish doctor of Polish origin could achieve professional success.† Dr. Reizes was forced to take on a dental practice (indeed, he seems at first to have been a dentist's assistant) and to supplement his income by acting as medical consultant to a vaudeville theater.

Their difficult financial circumstances made it necessary for Libussa to open a shop—not only in itself a humiliation for a doctor's wife, but also personally distasteful because in addition to plants she sold reptiles, from which she cringed in horror. Melanie does not speculate on her mother's choice of a somewhat bizarre type of shop, but notes that such was the power of her mother's beauty that customers loved to drop in to chat with her. She adds that Libussa's customers "understood" that she was a "lady," not a common shopkeeper—a rather curious disclaimer for her to feel obliged to make. One of Melanie's earliest memories was of being taken to visit this place into which her mother disappeared every day. The shop was an integral part of their lives until 1907, when Libussa was finally relieved of this burden.

A change in their fortunes occurred with the appearance of Moriz Reizes' father in their midst (when, Klein does not say). Since the death of his wife he had been living with a daughter, who one day turned him out of the house. Melanie's mother "readily" agreed to take him in, and apparently he lived with them peacefully until his death—an event that changed their lives, for he not only left them with some savings, she says, but with a winning sweepstakes ticket worth 10,000 florins.

As far as Melanie was concerned, their new apartment in the middle-class Martinstrasse seemed luxurious. The Martinstrasse was in Wachring, then a suburb of Vienna. She blocked out the details of the first, rather squalid fifth-floor flat in Borsegasse where they had been living,‡ while she delighted in everything about the new one—the balcony, the gleaming silver, the fact that she had new clothes and that her father gave her mother diamond earrings to mark the occasion. At the same time, her father bought the house in which he conducted his dental practice. "It seemed to me an enormous thing that my parents should actually own a house. The pride and happiness that I felt about these changes made it clear to me that I had been worried about the financial difficulties, I would say poverty, which preceded the move."

---

* Melanie was born at Tiefer Graben 8.
† It was in 1882, the year of Melanie Klein's birth, that the German-Austrian student fraternities passed the infamous Waidhofer Resolution, which declared that "every son of a Jewish mother, every human being with Jewish blood in its veins, is born without honor and must therefore lack in every decent human feeling."
‡ This must have been their second home in Vienna.

Now at this point Klein seems to have enmeshed herself totally within the family romance. The money was actually lent to them by Libussa's younger brother Hermann, a successful lawyer who had lived with them while a student.* In a letter of September 9, 1906, Libussa wrote to Melanie and Arthur Klein that Uncle Hermann "considered it the best deed in his life that he had stepped in for us and thus enabled us to live free of any worries about rent for nineteen years—which at the end brought us even into the possession of property. On that occasion he reminded me of his having to raise money before each time the rent was due; he did not at all profit from it. At that time, he said, he had got 20,000 gulden,† of which he invested 9,000 in the house. The furniture had cost him another few thousands, and the remaining thousands he needed for his business. If he had at the time bought that house in Brigittenau, it would by now have trebled in value. Yet he did not wish to burden me with all this now, he said, he was just indulging in melancholy thoughts. Now he really cares very much that he will be paid—for our sake as well as his."

Hermann never let them forget their indebtedness to him, and in a letter of October 10, 1902, written from Venice, Melanie's brother, Emanuel, voiced his resentment at the news that Libussa had to borrow the money from Hermann to pay for Melanie's trousseau: "That Uncle had to help out once again is very disagreeable to me! To the devil with him for that! Whenever I hear the name of this good, weak, and conceited man I have to think of those twelve years of my childhood and youth which he darkened and destroyed irreparably for me—and each time I feel something that chokes me rising up in my throat, and my heart gets black with gall." Klein, on the other hand, is disinclined to say anything disagreeable about him because she basked in the knowledge of being her uncle's favorite. In her Autobiography she recalls: "I was very fond of him and he too spoilt me very much. I heard him say many things, among them that, being so beautiful, a young Rothschild would come to marry me. He also had a lovely big dog, on which I rode."

Melanie was five at the time of the change in the family fortunes, and the move coincided with her starting at the local state school in the Alsenstrasse. From the beginning she was very happy there. Until then there had been no children of her own age with whom to play, and she enjoyed their company immensely. She had also inherited the family passion for knowledge and soon became an ambitious student, very conscious of her marks; it was particularly important for her to receive a report with the words *wurde belobt* (commended).

An early photograph of Melanie aged about six shows her standing confi-

---

* It could not have been for very long, since he was born in 1856.
† According to Dr. Michael Wagner of the Institut für Wirtschafts-und-Sozialforschung Wien, in 1900 10,000 gulden was about three times the annual income of a senior civil servant in his early fifties. Where did Hermann get the money? Probably from an investment. According to his daughter, Trude Feigl, it would have been totally out of character for her father to have bought a lottery ticket.

dently beside Emanuel and her older sister Emilie. Her whole demeanor exhibits a remarkable self-assurance. In old age she told people, "I absolutely was not shy." She was fond of telling friends about an incident that occurred on her first day at school. The teacher, in order to draw out the shy children, asked them, "Who is Marie?" so that all the little Maries would put up their hands and reply, "I am Marie." While many of the other children were crouching timidly behind their desks, Melanie, bursting with impatience to speak, put up her hand. The teacher said kindly, "Now say nicely 'My name is Marie,'" to which she replied, "My name is Melanie." Regarding the child a little reproachfully, the teacher chided her, "Your turn hasn't come yet." Melanie felt a little embarrassed, but she knew she had to make the gesture because she was the only Melanie and her turn would not have come. Melanie would never let herself be overlooked in life.

Her ambition was clearly stimulated by the fact that she was the youngest of four children, and very much in competition with her older siblings. The eldest, Emilie, was six years old when Melanie was born, her only brother, Emanuel, five, and Sidonie four, so that the first three always seemed to her a much older, integrated unit. Not only was she the youngest and the most helpless, but she had other causes for grievance. Her mother at some point— "later on"—told her that she was unexpected, but Melanie seems to have sensed this almost from the beginning. "I have no particular feeling that I resented this," she reflects, "because there was a great deal of love towards me." These words were written when she was in her mid-seventies, and they must be considered later in connection with her theories about infantile emotion.

Another possible grievance was that her mother had breast-fed the three older children but Melanie had a wet nurse "who fed me any time I asked for it." How did she know? She does not say whether her mother was unable to nurse her or whether she was too busy tending the shop. The next sentence, following the statement about the fecundity of the wet nurse, reads: "At this time Truby King* had not yet done his devastating work." She then abruptly drops the subject of breast-feeding and continues, within the same paragraph, an account of the attention Uncle Hermann lavished on her. The juxtaposition is very revealing.

In other words, far from being helpless and neglected, she was a beautiful Jewish princess, obviously the favorite of her mother's brother, and also—a fact not mentioned in her memoir—her mother's favorite daughter. Again, it must be remembered that this account was written at the end of a career in psychoanalysis in which her own technique became famous for its multiple and deep interpretations; but in her recollections she uses none of her own concepts to further an understanding of herself as a child. There is none of the transfixed

---

* A New Zealand pediatrician who advocated a strict regimen for babies.

attention that she would apply to one of her own patients. She seems utterly remote from the child she was, nervously pulling away whenever she encounters a memory that might be painful or disturbing to her image of her childhood. This could be interpreted as a failure of nerve, yet in the analytic situation she had always insisted that the analyst must maintain a distance from the analysand, never allowing any glimpse into his own private life. How, then, could she break down that barrier between herself and the putative reader when she had spent most of a lifetime building a remote image of herself? As with Freud, we have to turn to Melanie Klein's theoretical papers to find her real turbulence reflected in the conclusions she drew from patients in case studies. The very fact that she seized upon psychoanalysis with such passion indicates that the anxieties which beset the young Melanie were far deeper than her bland account would suggest. Freud had already created a model of a public autobiography for other analysts to emulate. *An Autobiographical Study* disappointed many with its self-protectiveness, whereas *The Interpretation of Dreams* contains the inner Freud—although here, too, the author masked any traces that would lead back to himself.

In Klein's autobiographical memoir, immediately following the passage about the admiration her uncle felt for her, she turns again to reflections about her father: "I don't think I sufficiently understood my father, because he had aged so much by this time." The image of her father weaves in and out of the narrative—his temperament, his interests, his gifts, and, above all, his relative neglect of her. Here was perhaps her greatest grievance. Not only was her conception a mistake, but her presence scarcely intruded itself upon his consciousness. He was an "old fifty" when she was born. "I have no memories of his ever playing with me. It was a painful thought to me that my father could openly state, and without consideration for my feelings, that he preferred my older sister, his first-born."

She longed for some sign of approval from this man who always struck her as immensely learned. Whenever Melanie asked him for the meaning of a French or German expression, he never had to consult a dictionary. With time she realized that his French was a little quaint and outdated, as it was bound to be, having been learned from perusing Molière and Racine. Nevertheless, this did not diminish her admiration for his knowledge.

One wonders about her feelings—and Libussa's—about his inability to establish himself professionally. He despised the music hall where he served as medical consultant, not only because of its boredom but because he scorned the morals of the English *artistes*. He loathed being tied down to attending the performances night after night, but the stipend was necessary to supplement the family income.

This music hall figures in Melanie's earliest memory of her father, an incident that took place when she was about three. Her mother was still at the

shop, and the servant was handing him the little rissoles he had every night before leaving for the Orpheum. The child clambered up on his knee and he
pushed her abruptly away. "That," she recalled laconically, "is a painful memory." Her one fond memory was of his holding her hand as they walked up the
hill to the house where they spent the summer at Dornbach.

Yet she says that every day, on her way back from school, she would fetch
her father from work and they would proceed home together for their midday
meal. Again, this detail is puzzling: his working space was in the family flat, so
that it would appear to be the father, not the daughter, who did the fetching.
(Probably she transposed her facts because she wanted to suggest that her father had his office in a separate location.*) She fails to mention whether this
strange, shut-away man ever said anything to her on these daily walks. On only
one occasion was he moved to strike her, an incident she clearly provoked.
When she refused some food, he remarked that in his day children ate what
was given to them. Melanie replied cheekily that what was done a hundred
years ago did not apply today—knowing full well what the consequences
would be. On the other hand, when she was thirteen she overheard him boast
to a patient† that his youngest daughter would go to the gymnasium, an assertion that awakened her resolve to do just that. Who knows if her ambition was
stimulated by her anxiety to have her father pay her some notice? In retrospect,
she believed that she did not sufficiently understand him. Perhaps, she rationalized, he did not pay much attention to her because he was so old when she was
born.

The family's good fortune did not continue long. Certainly before the end
of the century they had fallen on bad times again—this Melanie largely attributes to her father's "senility"—and her mother assumed responsibility for
holding things together. They even had to take in a permanent boarder.

With her mother it is a different story. "Up to the present day," Klein
recalls, "I still think a great deal about her, wondering what she would have
said or thought, and particularly regretting that she was not able to see some
of my achievements." According to Klein, Libussa was a gentle, unassuming
woman. "She has in many ways remained my example and I remember the
tolerance she had towards people and how she did not like it when my
brother and I, being intellectual and therefore arrogant, criticized people."
This is an astounding description in light of the tough, domineering
woman who emerges from Libussa's letters. At the age at which Klein was
writing, it was particularly painful for her to write about a mother-daughter
relationship, so it is difficult to know—even after the passage of time—to
what degree she was indulging in remorse or idealization. She seemed,

---

* An old photograph shows the building at 1 Martinstrasse bearing a plaque that a dental practice had been
established there in 1849. The house has since been demolished.
† Here she inadvertently gives away the fact that patients came to the family dwelling.

too, to continue to be troubled by the nature of her parents' marriage.

Moriz Reizes was obviously in love with his wife and extremely jealous of her, but Melanie, while aware that her mother was completely devoted to her family, suspected that she still pined for a young student in her hometown who had died of tuberculosis. Certainly Melanie often detected dissatisfaction in her mother—and possibly contempt. "I have never been able to get to the bottom of this," Klein muses, "whether she was simply not passionate or not passionate as far as my father was concerned, but I do believe that occasionally I saw a slight aversion against sexual passion in her, which might have been the expression of her own feeling or upbringing, etc." She says nothing about whether she was an affectionate, loving mother; and the correspondence reveals that Libussa found it very difficult to express her feelings.

Klein could never recall an occasion when her parents went out alone together. She evokes a united Jewish family; while not rigidly orthodox, Melanie's childhood was steeped in Jewish ceremonial, and she was always deeply aware of her Hebraic background. Both parents maintained a strong feeling for the Jewish people, "though," she remarks cryptically, "I am fully aware of their faults and shortcomings." She would never have been able to live in Israel, she asserts. At one point her mother tried to keep a kosher household but soon abandoned the attempt, particularly as she was opposed by her strong-minded children. Klein describes the circle in which they grew up in Vienna as "anti-Orthodox."

However, certain ritual celebrations were always maintained. Melanie had a lasting attachment to the first evening of Passover, particularly because she, as the youngest child, took part in the traditional service. "Since I was very keen to get some attention and to be more important than the older ones, I am afraid this attitude influenced my liking of that occasion. But there is more to it. I liked the candles, I liked the whole atmosphere, and I liked the family sitting round the table and being together in that way."

The ceremonies connected with the Day of Atonement also left her with pleasant memories. Every detail was interesting to her: the black coffee preceding the festive meal, the day of fasting which she spent with her mother at the synagogue. Like the other children, Melanie was dressed in her best clothes and was keenly aware of being scrutinized by their mothers, although her own mother was too deeply engrossed in her prayers for such frivolity.* On Friday evenings, too, Libussa would recite short prayers from a lilac velvet-bound prayer book her husband had given her as a wedding present. After only a few minutes she would close it and return it to the wardrobe; in Klein's view, these religious observances were an expression of family tradition rather than true piety. She felt this impression to be confirmed when her mother told her

---

* Another astonishing detail, since Libussa's letters reveal her to have been obsessional about clothes.

admiringly of the doomed student in her hometown who, on his deathbed, declared, "I shall die very soon and I repeat that I do not believe in any god." The tone in which her mother related this story convinced Melanie that she had been in love with him.

During the period of family affluence Melanie had what she describes as "French governesses." Since she was attending school at the same time, it would appear that they were more like nannies—or possibly maids-of-all-work—than proper governesses. The term "governess" is indicative of the snobbish fantasies that pervade the Autobiography. Undoubtedly the young women contributed to Melanie's knowledge of French, which she learned early. The first one, Mlle Chapuis, was hired from a convent, but did not stay long because she was so homesick. The second governess, Constance Sylvester, came from the same convent.*

When Melanie was eight or nine, she was "tortured" by the belief that one day she would turn Catholic, which she knew would torment her parents. What is puzzling is how these middle-class Jewish parents could have exposed her to such a temptation. When she poured out her heart to the gentle Constance, the latter would reply, "Well, if you have to do it, you can't help it." At school she felt deprived when she saw the Catholic children running to the priest and kissing his hand, receiving in return a pat on the head. Once she plucked up courage to do the same, a guilty secret that she at long last revealed in her autobiography.

While always feeling "Jewish," she was never a Zionist, and her way of life was in no way distinguishable from that of a Gentile. Yet as a Jewish child in Catholic Vienna she must have been acutely conscious that she was an outsider and a member of an often persecuted minority. Psychoanalysis became for many Jews a religion with its own rites, secrets, and demands of unswerving loyalty. Melanie Klein, when she eventually discovered psychoanalysis, embraced it as ardently as any convert to the Catholic Church.

Melanie's education in the broadest sense—accumulation of information, training in analytic thought, understanding of human beings—is difficult to gauge. Her detractors dismiss her as "an uneducated woman." Her admirers regard this lack as an asset, emphasizing that she was unencumbered by conventional patterns of organizing and assessing data and that her strength lay in her fresh and original insights. While there is truth in both views, she was by no means lacking in education in a conventional sense.

At the lyceum she learned French, English, "and all the things that a girl of good family [sic!] was expected to know." She also learned much from her brother and sisters, who were very proud of her precocity; while they often teased her, they repeated to each other the clever things she would say.

---

* Does she actually mean an orphanage from which they were able to obtain cheap help?

Her relationship with Emilie—their father's favorite—seems to have been ambivalent from the beginning. "I think [sic] that I had an attachment for my eldest sister and that she was very fond and proud of me. I remember that between ten and twelve I felt unhappy before going to sleep* and Emilie was kind enough to move her couch near to mine and I went to sleep holding her hand." But as Melanie developed intellectually, it was clear that there was no rapport between them; and from the family letters, Melanie encouraged malevolent feelings in her mother toward her envied older sister.

The debt Melanie felt she owed her other sister deserves reflection. Sidonie died of scrofula in 1886, when she was eight and Melanie four. This was the first of a long series of deaths that punctuated Klein's life, each reactivating the original fear, grief, and bewilderment. It is not clear how long Sidonie was ill before her death, but since the disease was a form of tuberculosis it is probable that it was at least a year or two. At that time tuberculosis was highly infectious (and there was also a belief that it was hereditary), so Melanie is clearly repressing a deep fear of illness that was implanted in her from early childhood. Her memories of Sidonie date from her sister's return from hospital.† "She was, I have no doubt, the best-looking of us," Klein says; "I don't believe it was just idealization when, after her death, my mother maintained that. I remember her violet-blue eyes, her black curls, and her angelic face." No wonder Melanie was "absolutely never shy." She had to assert herself in view of the fact that her mother told her that she had been unwanted, Sidonie was the best-looking in the family, her father openly expressed his preference for Emilie, and Emanuel was considered something of a genius. Sidonie must have been the center of family attention as she lay in bed wasting away; yet what Melanie remembers is her sister's kindness to her. Emilie and Emanuel took great pleasure in teasing little Melanie, coming up with difficult geographical names like Popocatepetl, while the bewildered child had no idea whether they were genuine or not. The ailing girl took pity on her sister and taught her the fundamentals of arithmetic and reading. "It is quite possible that I idealize her a little," Melanie reflects, "but my feeling is that, had she lived, we would have been the greatest friends and I still have a feeling of gratitude to her for satisfying my mental needs, all the greater because I think she was very ill at the time." She continues: "I have a feeling that I never entirely got over the feeling of grief for her death. I also suffered under the grief my mother showed, whereas my father was more controlled. I remember that I felt that my mother needed me all the more now that Sidonie was gone, and it is probable that some of the spoiling was due to my having to replace that child."

* One would like to know the reason for this. The onset of menstruation?
† There is no official record of Sidonie's death in Vienna. Is it possible that Melanie fantasized her memories of her and that she died before Melanie's birth? In that case, Melanie would have felt that her own birth was in some sense a replacement of her sister.

Emanuel was undoubtedly the major influence on Melanie's early development.

> He seemed to me superior in every way to myself, not only because at nine or ten years of age, he seemed quite grown-up, but also because his gifts were so unusual that I feel that whatever I have achieved is nothing in comparison to what he would have done. From a very early age I heard the most beautiful piano-playing, because he was deeply musical, and I have seen him sitting at the piano and just composing what came into his mind. He was a self-willed and rebellious child and, I think, not sufficiently understood. He seemed at loggerheads with his teachers at the gymnasium, or contemptuous of them, and there were many controversial talks with my father. . . . My brother was deeply fond of my mother, but gave her a good deal of anxiety.

Melanie dated her deep attachment to Emanuel from her ninth year, when she wrote a patriotic poem with which he was greatly impressed and which he helped her to correct.

> From at least this time onwards, he was my confidant, my friend, my teacher. He took the greatest interest in my development, and I knew that, until his death, he always expected me to do something great, although there was really nothing on which to base it.

When she was sixteen she wrote a little play that he thought was a harbinger of her latent literary capacities but, although she went on to try her hand at novels and poems (which she claimed that she later unfortunately destroyed), she very early realized that her bent was not artistic; yet Emanuel was not wrong when he recognized her creative potential. Freud spoke of the confidence imparted to a male child by a mother who has absolute belief in his destiny. Melanie would undoubtedly have preferred her father to express this kind of faith in her, but Emanuel served as an inspiring surrogate.

Yet her father's boast that she would attend the gymnasium while she was still only a student at the lyceum instilled in her the determination to enter the gymnasium even though it was the middle of the year. Her brother, thoroughly approving, coached her in Greek and Latin, although he was an impatient teacher. When she muddled up her Latin conjugations he would exclaim sharply, "*You* a scholar! You must become a shop assistant!" Nevertheless, she managed to pass the entrance examinations, and "life took on an entirely new aspect for me."

She was fired by ambition. Not only did she intend to study medicine, she asserted, but she planned to specialize in psychiatry—an extraordinary ambition for a middle-class Jewish girl when one thinks of the vicissitudes Freud was encountering in his profession at that very time in Vienna. About this time, Moriz Reizes' health began to deterioriate rapidly, and the household was held together by the indomitable Libussa. Melanie seldom had a new dress; the theater or a concert was a rare event; but she felt gloriously alive, infused with that deepest of all the passions, intellectual fervor. Unknown to her mother, she read far into the night—an indication that her mother did not encourage her intellectual interests. Her homework she did on the tram between home and school. Her brother proudly introduced her to his friends, and Melanie blossomed into a vibrant young woman.

The idols of this group were the playwright Arthur Schnitzler, the philosopher Friedrich Wilhelm Nietzsche, and the journalist Karl Kraus, editor of *Die Fackel* (torch), which made its first appearance in 1899. It was an immediate success with Vienna's progressive youth, who identified with its voice of protest against the corruption and spiritual and intellectual lethargy of the Austrian Empire. They delighted in Kraus's idiosyncratic prose style. One of his most quoted aphorisms was: "Psychoanalysis is the mental illness [*Geisteskrankheit*] of which it purports to be the cure." According to George Clare, in *Last Waltz in Vienna*, Kraus hated the Jew in himself, and longed for the disappearance of his race through assimilation and intermarriage. Emanuel was impressed by Nietzsche's affirmation that the superman must abandon conventional morality and live at a level of intense passion and creativity. His own writing was modeled on Nietzsche's aphoristic style, infused with Kraus's caustic wit. Melanie was drawn to Schnitzler's themes of love and sexual (in)fidelity, upon which she focused her own later fictional writings.

It was only to be expected that father and son would disagree. Klein remembered a fierce argument between them as to whether Goethe or Schiller was the better poet. Emanuel maintained that there was nothing in Schiller, whereas his father declared that Goethe was a charlatan who dabbled in science, and quoted a long passage from his favorite poet to prove his superiority.

The family affiliations can be reconstructed partially from the Autobiography and, more reliably, from the recently recovered correspondence. The picture of Emanuel that emerges from Klein's account is that of a willful, restless, angry youth, at odds with his father and a source of perpetual worry to his mother, to whom he was nevertheless attached. When he was twelve he had scarlet fever followed by rheumatic fever, which affected his heart. What Klein fails to mention is that he also developed tuberculosis. It probably preceded the rheumatic fever, which would have produced subacute bacterial endocarditis.* Melanie knew that her mother was filled with self-reproach because she had allowed him, while he was still convalescing, to join a family excursion to

---

* I am indebted for this explanation to Dr. Ronald Mavor, who was trained as a specialist in tuberculosis. That Emanuel had tuberculosis I have on the understanding of Eric Clyne (Klein's son) and Emilie's daughter-in-law, Hertha Pick.

the Prater. As a result he suffered a relapse from which he never fully recovered; and his sister was always bitter that "the family" had forced him to go with them.

In many little ways, Libussa conveyed to the rest of the family the contempt she felt for her husband. Scholarly, withdrawn, inept at business, he left the management of the household in the hands of his wife. The only way he could assert his superiority was by his intellectual prowess, and it was particularly galling to be challenged by his clever, conceited son. Libussa did not hide her pride in Emanuel and in Melanie, whose beauty was bound to catch a good husband. Emilie, on the other hand, is something of a cipher—not very pretty and not at all clever. Nevertheless, her father befriended her, preferring her to the assertive Melanie. It was made clear to father and daughter, in the subtle ways families express such things, that they were excluded from the humid, symbiotic entanglement of Libussa, Emanuel, and Melanie.

Klein later claimed that Emanuel entered medical school despite the objections of his parents, who were concerned about his health. However, his letters do not give the slightest indication that he had any interest in medicine; he fancied himself as an artist, a writer, a musician—he wasn't exactly sure which. In any event, his lack of practical ambition filled his mother with impatience. He stuck out medical school until October 1900, when he transferred to the Faculty of Arts. In her Autobiography, Klein says that Emanuel, knowing that he had not long to live, "stopped his studies, and got permission to do some travelling, because he felt that he wanted to use his gifts as a writer as much as possible." She then adds a cryptic comment: "I know another factor which might have driven him from home, but I will speak of that later on." She never reverts to the subject. She is probably referring to her resentment that Emilie and her husband seemed to be taking over the family home so that there was no room for her brother.

Emanuel convinced himself that his main motive for abandoning his medical studies and leaving Vienna was his certainty that he was doomed to an early death; he intended to live life to the full in the time left to him. His mother shared his view that the climate of Vienna was detrimental to his health, and she settled a small allowance on him to enable him to seek lands of sun and beauty in the traditional pattern of the dying artist. It was in this role that Emanuel saw himself, and he dramatized the situation to the full. His letters for the next couple of years are full of complaints about the meagerness of his allowance. The knowledge of his mortality, Klein says, "of which he never spoke [sic!] must have had a great deal to do with his being rebellious and at times difficult." Quite clearly, the whole family was so terrified of tuberculosis that the dread word was never used.

In the meantime Moriz Reizes gradually faded away until one day people realized that he was actually dead. The cause of his death on April 6, 1900, is listed officially as pneumonia; but since Klein has been describing him as "senile" for some years, it is likely that he was suffering from Alzheimer's disease or some comparable disorder. There is no photograph of him among the numerous family mementos.

In any event, his death precipitated a crisis; and the ensuing events reveal something of the complex family dynamics. In the first place, Emanuel was not told of his father's death until two months later—when he returned to Vienna in June. This might suggest that he and Moriz Reizes had parted on bad terms. Apart from his romantic aspirations, which were focused on the Mediterranean, he was irritated by his mother's constant fretting. A deeper and more disturbing element seems to have been Melanie's impending marriage.

Family circumstances may have been extremely stringent, but somehow enough money was found for a number of photographs of Melanie to have been taken during this period. She is a voluptuous dark beauty with heavy-lidded eyes, and already fully aware of her striking profile. She was aware, too, of her desirability, as all her brother's friends seemed to be falling in love with her. When she was only seventeen she met her future husband (then twenty-one), a second cousin on her mother's side, who was visiting Vienna from his home in what was then the Slovak part of Hungary.

Arthur Stevan Klein was a serious young man who was studying to be a chemical engineer at the elite Swiss Federal Technical High School in Zurich (a kind of M.I.T.). His unpretentious looks—small head and slight frame—were unimportant in comparison with his intellectual gifts. Emanuel was impressed by him, a fact that would weigh heavily with Melanie. Very soon after he met Melanie, Arthur proposed, or so she implies. What on earth made this ambitious young woman so ready to accept him, when clearly it meant the end of her professional ambitions? In later years she told some of those close to her that it was her "passionate temperament." She admits that she was not in love with him at first, but claims that "it did not take very long for me to fall in love with him." She then adds: "From that time I was so loyal that I refrained from any entertainment where I might have met other young men and never expressed a feeling that I already had in my mind, that we were not really suited to one another. Both loyalty to my fiancé, with whom I was up to a point in love, and circumstances, prevented me from mentioning this to my mother or my brother." There is no reference to what they did together, what they talked about—no sense of the nature of their relationship. And there it was, this first great mistake of her life. What were the "circumstances" that prevented her from expressing her misgivings to her mother and brother, who, she suspected, realized that her future husband was a very "difficult" person? Not only was she not in love with him, but she sensed in Arthur a certain rigid inflexibility and a will as strong as her own.

Melanie is terse about the degree to which the economic situation affected her choice: ". . . it would not have been easy for me to return to my studies, which I was longing to do. Whether or not this was the main factor in my doing something which I knew was wrong—my marriage—I cannot say, but it must have been an important reason." While marriage to Arthur had to be postponed for several years, at least he had prospects, just as Moriz Reizes had seemed to have to Libussa's family. In worldly terms, he was by far the most suitable of her admirers.

Emilie, while not as pretty or clever as her younger sister, attracted just as many suitors by her gentle, passive femininity. One young doctor, Leo Pick, fell madly in love with her. With Moriz's death, their marriage seemed eminently suitable to Libussa. As Libussa planned it, Leo could take over his late father-in-law's practice, and the flat would be renovated so that Libussa would have her own quarters and share the kitchen with the young couple. All this Leo acceded to reluctantly, and the marriage took place on December 25, 1900.

Melanie was encouraged to pay an extended visit to her prospective in-laws while Arthur was on a training tour in America. Libussa fitted her out like a desirable commodity and sent her off to Rosenberg to give the engagement some firm reinforcement. Libussa felt compelled to arrange her children's lives like pawns on a chessboard, but when one is an indigent widow one is not left with many options.

Emanuel, in his quest for sun and creativity, brooded constantly on the pittance he was given for an allowance—the money allotted him was, unfortunately, inadequate to sustain his delusions of artistic grandeur. His dead father's clothes were made over for him, another of the grievances he was accumulating, particularly as he saw the finery bestowed upon his sisters. Emilie's trousseau must have cost Libussa a certain amount, and now Melanie had to be outfitted so that she would make a good impression in Rosenberg. Grumbling Uncle Hermann (now with a family of his own) was called upon for help to pay for the renovation of the flat and the two dowries. There was not much left for Emanuel, who felt deprived, banished, and forgotten.

It was a family riddled with guilt, envy, and occasionally explosive rages, and infused with strong incestuous overtones. Melanie's impending marriage was the prelude to Emanuel's death through disease, malnutrition, alcohol, drugs, poverty, and a will to self-destruction. Melanie Klein was made to feel responsible for his death and she carried the guilt with her for the rest of her days—just as Emanuel had probably intended she should.

CHAPTER TWO

Emanuel

In January 1901, Emanuel returned to Italy, apparently under rather suspicious circumstances. A young woman, Irma Schonfeld, who had known both Melanie and Emanuel for years, was desperately trying to escape from an arranged marriage. Not only that, she seems to have been very much in love with Emanuel, whose feeling for her was apparently never more than indulgent affection. However, his letters suggest that he had encouraged and abetted the girl in her flight from Vienna—even accompanying her to Rome—thus putting her in a compromising situation that made her the object of scandal among their circle of friends in Vienna. In a letter of February 1, Emanuel informed his sister that she must communicate with Irma only through him. The following month he wrote a rather cheeky letter to Irma's father admitting equably that Irma's reputation in Vienna was "damaged beyond repair." In addition, he described her as having the kind of temperament that chafed within the limitations of family life, and proposed that her father submit to her desire to settle in Berlin. He also added the suggestion that Herr Schonfeld visit his sister Melanie, a young woman of nineteen, for advice. "If nothing else," he pontificated to the older man, "you will see a reflection of the situation in the mirror of her eyes and her grand vision which, I feel, is becoming more and more clear-sighted. And you will, if you are lucky, catch a glimpse of a great work of art." Like Libussa and Melanie, Emanuel clearly had a compulsion to run other people's lives.

But to his "sweet darling,"* Melanie, he had far more important things on his mind than Irma's welfare. First, he was in "a fit of barbaric rage" at the news that he was to receive an allowance from his mother of only eighty gulden

---

* He used the word *schatz*, a very tender form of endearment.

a month.* He kept his hopes alive with the expectation of soon seeing the sea. In an incoherent letter he told her: "You have no idea what a self-violation my stay in Rome has been, and I have a deadly yearning for this creature of the night and she does for me too—and for you. I embrace you with boundless love and warmth—you and Mum." In a postscript he asked when she was planning to visit Rosenberg, adding a casual question about Arthur's welfare.

Melanie's life had also reached a crucial point. In her Autobiography she makes no reference to Arthur's sister, Jolanthe (Jolan), two years her junior. On several occasions in her late teens Jolan visited her future relatives in Vienna. She was beautiful, cultivated, and talented; and while the two young women became fast, lifelong friends, there was always intense rivalry between them. It is possible that Melanie's engagement to Arthur was motivated as much by competition with Jolan as by her avowed interest in Arthur because her beloved brother admired his intellect. Emanuel viewed both Arthur and Leo as sterling characters, presumably because they were taking over the financial responsibility for his sisters that would otherwise have been his. Arthur could be tolerated so long as the marriage was postponed into the indefinite future. The letters found in Eric Clyne's loft indicate that Jolan attended various lectures while staying with the Reizes family in Vienna in April 1901, but there is no indication that Melanie ever did so or even felt a twinge of frustration at being deprived of the career in medicine that later in life she always said she had desired. This is not to say that she did not harbor such ambitions secretly.

A long engagement was necessary, since the highly ambitious Arthur had to complete his professional training in order to establish himself as a chemical engineer in the paper industry. The letters from every member of the family attest to Melanie's apparent impatience at the delay in the attainment of her one goal in life—marriage to Arthur. Such single-mindedness suggests the desperation that there simply seemed no other alternative. Her life was in a state of moratorium. Completely under the domination of her mother, she would have found it virtually impossible to adopt Irma Schonfeld's bid for freedom. Marriage offered the only solution; but what was she to do with herself in the intervening period?

On April 9 Libussa wrote to Emanuel that Melanie's projected visit to Rosenberg where she would spend the summer with Jolan marked the beginning of a solitary life for her. As though the idea had suddenly occurred to her, she sent him feelers about having Leo and Emilie move in with them. After all, Leo was already practicing in the dental office all day and Emilie stayed until late in the evening because their flat in Dornbach was "uncomfortable, cold

---

* According to Dr. Michael Wagner of Vienna's Institut für Wirtschafts-und-Sozialforschung, Emanuel's allowance must have held him close to the poverty line.

and damp." The details of this proposal had been so carefully worked out that it was clearly not the impulsive idea she claimed it to be:

> Our dining room we do not use at all. We are actually only in the bedroom and drawing room. . . . I shall put the dining room furniture into the drawing room and sell the green drawing-room suite. Emilie will get our dining room, and your small room will become the consulting room. . . . When you, my dear child, come home, you can again have your small room. You would have more peace there than in the past as there is no adjoining kitchen anymore and thus one does not have to pass through it so often. If you want to have absolute peace then you can perhaps rent another small room in the house, or you can study during the day in the small room and sleep in the bedroom. I will sleep in the drawing room.
>
> Leo would pay 400 fl for their flat here, and—as long as Melanie is still living at home or if you come home—we would share the household costs in equal parts. When I live alone we must calculate the expenses very precisely. We could keep only one maid.

Emilie was expecting a baby, and Libussa was completely preoccupied with the renovation of the flat, complaining constantly about money, particularly as the shop was bringing in very little. She expressed satisfaction that Melanie's health seemed to be flourishing in Rosenberg and that she was getting along so well with her future in-laws while Arthur was in Italy on a training course prior to setting off on a longer journey of six months through the United States. In June, prior to his departure, the engagement was finally announced formally, much to everyone's relief. Libussa emphasized to her daughter that a visit to Vienna would not be feasible until after the birth of Emilie's first child in October.

In the meantime Emanuel had tired of Irma, whom he left behind in Rome while he set off for Santa Margherita, where he planned to spend a few contented months on his own. "I have a terrible fear of her letters," he confessed to Melanie in a letter of early June 1901:

> they come across like a gooey flow which sticks to my wings and drags me down. . . . If only I could tell you what I have suffered in these two months! *Right from the first day!* . . . Do write to me often and always about yourself. I count your love among the most precious and unambiguous possessions in my life.

His mood swings are dramatic, in keeping with the hypomanic states characteristic of his disease. Within a fortnight of his arrival at Santa Margherita, he was writing to Melanie from Grotto del Nino on Lake Como, complaining of an "aching for home, a longing for you, Mother, the square in front of the town hall, St. Stephen's Square by night and an old beech forest. All this myrtle, olive tree and oleander stuff, that which is so persistently green, is but a simile of dead life." And this was the southern clime where he was supposed to find true inspiration! In what was clearly an attempt to make his sister jealous, he described his various encounters with women, and then launched into a puzzling, incoherent passage which seems to refer to Melanie and her intended husband:

> The feminine!—Perhaps it is dawning on you how deeply I have drunk from this cup and drowned myself in it in order to reap my pleasures from its gay and foamy brim. Only one other person knows about it, and what he knows is wrong, for he has treacherously expelled it from me with his own loving ways. Therefore I have to get him out of the way. . . . Do not think ill of me because of my life; spread all the tolerance which could prepare you for your seventieth year on this my short life. I am not allowed to live till seventy, so permit me to invent it in poetry. . . . Adieu, my most beautiful, both in essence and appearance! I wish you to live the thousand days of which fate so thievishly deprives me in years. And in return for that you tell me all about Rosenberg's high society. Will you?

This last question was a malicious dig at Rosenberg's provincialism.

Emanuel was discouraged by his mother from returning to Vienna, ostensibly because Vienna in the summer would be bad for his health. On May 16, 1901, Libussa wrote him an extraordinary letter:

> My dear and beloved child,
>
> I must tell you that your relationship with Melanie has often filled me with jealousy. Yet in the course of time I just got used to it and resigned myself to it as I always do. I believe, my dear child, that there is no bond, be it that of friendship or of love, that is as strong and powerful as that of mother-love.
>
> I have experienced, witnessed and watched the most loyal and devoted friendships crumbling into nothing when it came to self-love. Even the love between brother and sister cools down and slackens if one or both enter into different circumstances, or if they live far away from each other. By that I do not mean to say that Melanie loves you less now. But how much your Mum loves you, loves you all, I surely need not tell you. Actually, I never indulged you and your sisters too much in external manifestations of my love. Well, that's the way I am. Thus you can, my beloved child, tell me everything without reservation that is in your heart, what you feel and what you need to talk about. It will be well hidden and kept in me. You

need not fear any indiscretion. Whoever tries to tap me about you will be coolly rejected. As regards Emilie and Leo, the former is well trained by Melanie, and Leo is too noble and too subtle to ask questions. . . .

I must stop now because I still want this letter to be off today. Please write soon and write a lot.

A thousand hugs from your

tenderly loving

Mama Libussa

Emilie and Leo send their regards.

The renovation of the flat almost drove Libussa to distraction. "If I keep my five senses together this summer," she wailed, "I will be immune to anything. These builders, joiners, plumbers, locksmiths and other workers are making me totally confused. And this mess! And even more the great expenses! . . . How glad we would be if this ghastly summer was over! Yet it is all one and the same: then comes the winter, and who knows what that brings."

On May 17 (the day Leo left for a month's military service in the medical corps) Emilie moved in with her mother. On June 26 she started a letter to "Dearest Melachild, You will see that I have courage and strength, for I have decided to write you a long letter." She told her that on the day she and Libussa set up a joint household she had acquired an accounts book: "So you know how meticulous I am—each Kreuzer is accounted for." Her own expenses were carefully differentiated from those of Libussa. She then proceeded to give a "painstakingly precise" itemized list of the gas bill and other necessary expenditures. "Does that meet with your satisfaction, Your Honor?" she concluded. Apparently Melanie had expected such an accounting. In a later letter (June 2), Emilie assured Melanie that if the month turned out well, Libussa would start putting money aside for her sister's trousseau. Each member of this family kept a close eye out to make sure their mother wasn't giving more to one than another. (Emilie, less aggressive than the others, always came out low man on the totem pole.) From the envy, aggression, and sibling rivalry within her own family, Melanie Klein had abundant material from which to formulate her later theories.

Libussa encouraged Emanuel to stay with Melanie in Rosenberg during the summer of 1901. He grudgingly complied, and at the beginning of August she wrote to him: "How are you feeling there, Emanuel? Perhaps it would be good—so that the Klein family will not be inconvenienced too much—if you would look for a boardinghouse in the area in which you can stay till the end of September or middle of October. I expect a lot more of the climate there than from Italy. It is also a lot cheaper for us." When Emanuel objected to this, she replied, on August 17, "If you, Emanuel, think that being in the area is not doing you any good—although I had expected a lot of it—then come to Vienna. I hope the weather will be cooler then. . . . Also, your clothes will need to be seen to and your underwear needs some mending. . . ." He apparently returned on the double; and shortly after his arrival, in a letter of early September, Libussa reported to Melanie: "As far as Emanuel is concerned, the result of his traveling is not very satisfactory. He is in high spirits and a good mood but he does not spend the nights very well. He sleeps in the same room with me, and frequently I have to wake him up because he has cramps. He maintains that he never has cramps in Italy. But Leo thinks that he probably did not notice them in his sleep because nobody woke him up. . . ." After the near-starvation of the preceding months, it is little wonder that he had stomach cramps with the rich food Libussa forced on him. The family continued to pretend that he was not suffering from a fatal disease. Now that Emilie was pregnant, subtle pressure was exerted on him to resume his travels.

But the flat was finally in order, and Emanuel was enjoying his lethargic leisure with his old cronies. He casually refused to reply to Irma's letters from Rome. The family teased him about his infatuation with his sister. There was undoubtedly, besides, an oedipal relationship between mother and son, although Emanuel also harbored feelings of hatred and resentment toward Libussa. To Melanie he was full of complaints about their mother's insensitivity to his real needs: "For me and my aspirations she has not a spark of interest. Not a single word about my aspirations, except for remarks about 'the young people of today with their delusions of grandeur.' She also repeats her joke about the financial exploitation through my travels as a 'commis voyageur' more and more often." Emanuel was outraged at the irritation she expressed when he refused Leo's offer to try to get him a job on a local newspaper. He vaguely considered enrolling in the university again.

In September, Melanie complained of being very homesick, but Libussa tried to dissuade her from returning before the birth of Emilie's baby in mid-October. "There are many other things which I cannot tell you in favor of your staying where you are." In the margin Melanie has written "financial!" She asked her mother plaintively if she did not miss her, to which Libussa replied on October 4: "To tell you the truth I do miss you! Only I do not know what to do about it. Emilie is still not showing any signs. . . . So it depends on you now: if you want to come, write to me and I will send you the money. Or do you want to wait until after the 15th of October? There are no prospects of Emanuel's departure yet. We have to wait to see how this month will turn out. Anyhow, the stay in Vienna seems to be doing him good. He is looking much better than he did when he came. He wants to register again. But I fear that means money down the drain again. And business is not going well." Emanuel added a postscript to the letter:

My darling,

I am longing for you immensely. We would spend a beautiful few weeks together. I like it here and would like it even better if my weakness did not only persist but get worse. Emmy is still not giving any signs. Please write—better come!

1000 affectionate greetings to you, darling,

Yours

Emanuel

It was made quite clear that it would be very inconvenient for Melanie to return home so long as Emanuel was there. In early 1902 he resumed his itinerant life, moving restlessly from place to place in Switzerland. He reacted cheerfully to the news of the repeated postponements of Melanie's wedding; and while he would make an occasional flattering remark about Arthur, he was clearly not at all interested in him. Why should he speak glowingly of the man who was robbing him of the jewel among women, his confidante, his friend? This paragon, he declared, was "a work of art I will never again be able to behold anywhere else, neither in nature nor in imitation."

Otto, Libussa's first grandson, was born on October 16. Melanie was finally permitted to return to Vienna just before Christmas, and stayed for the first five months of 1902, before making another extended visit to Rosenberg. The wedding was set for July, then postponed until August, and later delayed until the following year as Arthur's American tour became more protracted (almost a year longer than originally planned); this extension, it was repeatedly emphasized, was absolutely imperative for his career. He does not sound like a pining prospective bridegroom. Melanie managed to make the best of things in Rosenberg, referring to how rosy her cheeks were becoming in the mountain air and the pride her future in-laws took in this beautiful girl from the big city.

On May 21, Emanuel advised Melanie to become "round and healthy" in Rosenberg, "and do not get thee to a nunnery. Just remember there are only a few months to go!" Arthur's extended American tour seemed to him a splendid idea: "Given his character, his American tour will have put the last polish on a practical and energetic personality, which guarantees him sooner or later a high-ranking position in the industrial hierarchy." Libussa did not take so sanguine a view of the situation, as she indicates to Emanuel in a letter of May 11 to him:

I fitted Melanie out very beautifully. Also I have needed a lot of money since Jolan's departure. If only the summer months would be good! Then I could get straight, that is put something on the side to be able to start with Melanie's trousseau. Now I cannot even think of it. I would rather spare you these things, but you have been demanding detailed letters—also about the shop. . . . Arthur has been traveling from Erie to Chicago. I am curious to know what the outcome of all this traveling will be. The best would be if he came back to Rosenberg, even if his salary here would not be so big—and if they married.

She then shifted to a more personal note:

How are you, dear child? Now since I have been sleeping alone in the room [rest of sentence torn]. And often when I do not sleep I think of you a lot—whether you are well, whether you will not catch a cold without a winter coat in this bad weather. For if it is cold and rainy here, it will be even colder in Switzerland.

Melanie's dowry must take priority over everything else. Melanie seemed as obsessional about her trousseau as her mother was, and was clearly enjoying the role of prospective bride, although she too was very anxious about asking her mother for any pocket money:

Dearest Mum, although I find it most unpleasant, I must ask you for a little money for myself. I bought myself a pair of attractive fingerless kid gloves for four gulden. I gave a tip, and then I bought some equipment for mending my clothes. I need to have a small amount of money in my purse, e.g., for stamps. I did not want to ask you for it last month as I knew how hard up you were. All in all I would need twelve gulden. If you can spare them, please, send them to me. However, if you find it hard in any way, it does not matter if you send the money next month.

Yesterday, I realized how useful my batiste dress will be to me here. In the morning we all went visiting. I was expected to look very elegant, which, of course, I did in my batiste dress. In the afternoon we attended a garden party; everybody was most elegantly dressed, yet my batiste dress was the prettiest of all.

Rosenberg's latest sensation is that Arthur's mama introduces me now to everybody as her future daughter-in-law so that they have nothing to speculate about anymore. By the way, my parents-in-law are rather proud of me. Yesterday there was a gentleman who has been living in New York for twelve years. I conversed with him in English and he was very delighted with how well and finely I spoke English, and he also mentioned this in Rosenberg, so there is a lot of talk now of how educated I am, how beautiful, and God knows what else.

Libussa felt consumed by her family. Her only real joy seems to have been her new grandson; but every penny spent in the Vienna household was as carefully itemized as Melanie's sheets and underwear. Libussa's anxiety over Emanuel's health was subordinated to her nagging worry about the money he was costing her, particularly as she had to go back to Uncle Hermann to borrow the money to pay for Melanie's dowry. Her letters are filled with descriptions of her stomach complaints and diminishing strength caused by all the burdens she had to carry. Careful as she was about expenses, she seemed willfully ignorant about Emanuel's living costs. "After raising his allowance from eighty to one hundred florins," she told Melanie, "I don't want him to suffer hardship, but if he has too much money he can invest it." Then, in an act of self-destructive folly, Emanuel gambled away all his money at Montreux, which elicited the anticipated reproaches of his distraught mother. "It is not surprising that I have lost all my energy, all my mental stability," she cried in desperation. "These eternal worries and troubles undermine my strength." In the meantime, after dunning his mother for money, Emanuel wrote to Melanie:

I do not think that you have a lot to spare from the money you get from home. But no sum can be too big or too small in my present circumstances. If you are in a position to help me, please send me something in a registered letter. It goes without saying that Mama and also poor Leo are out of the question. As regards Mama, I would only like to ask you to remind her in time of my monthly allowance.

Emanuel's single, short-lived, idea for making some money was to write the libretto for an opera. To Melanie he poured out his complaints about Libussa's miserliness: "The soles of my shoes are getting completely transparent. The day of the last blow is drawing close." Melanie, shamed into sending him what money she could, at the same time was being reminded by her mother that Emanuel's allowance was draining off the money allotted for her dowry. Emanuel not only made her feel parsimonious and selfish, but was constantly reminding her of her neglect in not writing to him more frequently. Each member of this narcissistic family seemed compelled to impose guilt upon the others.

In July, Emanuel heard that Arthur had obtained a job in Rosenberg in a paper mill (in which his father held a part interest), so that the wedding was now possible. He wrote to congratulate his sister in a letter infused with envy, malevolence, and hypocrisy.

If your news were not so extremely joyful, I would have to grit my teeth because I feel compelled to interpret the greatest happiness (that has befallen us and that could serve us all) as a part repayment of the overgreat debt I have run up with Mother's patience and willingness to make sacrifices. Most immediately, however, I rejoice in the awareness that Mother will be relieved now of the heaviest burden among her loving concerns, which she has always hidden with her pride and secrecy. I am almost as grateful to you for her sake as I am for mine!

So Melanie had been the greatest burden on poor, dear Mother's shoulders! And while it was going to be an awful bore to have to live in a backwater like Rosenberg, at least Arthur would have an annual salary of 2,200 gulden a year. As for himself, against his will Emanuel had accepted his mother's *offer* to increase his monthly allowance. He was forced to make this sacrifice, he declared, because he realized that his life would be in jeopardy if he could not make a trip to Corfu. He viewed his sufferings as truly heroic:

These sufferings give me the chance to transform them—by living through them—into something great and meaningful. And in spite of everything, I still hope to give the shape of greatness and importance to them, even though their bitter consequences oppose this wish by putting inch for inch further physical pain in my path. I love this pain as my suffering, as my fate, as my life—as Life. But to examine night after night my shoes for further holes—my other pair being already beyond repair—lest a serious defect in them cause a catastrophe that would force me to stay in bed!! that I may have to avoid the concerts in the assembly hall because I cannot afford the obligatory glass of beer there!!—these things are just too petty for me to bear with equanimity! But the most exasperating thing is that I cannot live a single hour of the day without fear of unexpected expenses—and that while I live most parsimoniously! There is an objection that would silence me at once, but you do not want to silence me. Do you?

Presumably his suffering could be alleviated if the pampered princess were to share some of her largesse with him, thus sparing their beloved mother further anxiety. For all his exalted talk about her as a work of art, he could itemize the family expenses with the same obsessional fidelity as Libussa. A calculation of the living expenses of each person in the Vienna household is juxtaposed with descriptions of his physical sufferings. He was particularly alarmed by the ugly tremor that had developed in his hands. If only Mama would let him come home for a couple of months, then he would be able to save enough to stave off death by another flight to the sun. This self-serving letter, with its pages of complaints, ends on a menacing note: either help me, my girl, or you will be responsible for the consequences:

However, you are not to decide what may be good for me. I ask you to weigh up, with as little love for me as possible, what it is that will unburden

Mother. Be hard on me and have consideration for me only to that extent that my burden must not become heavier than I can carry: two months— no matter what they will be like—I can bear, but no more. Remember the "no more."

A letter of Libussa's to Melanie reveals that she had no inkling of Emanuel's plans. In other words, Emanuel had passed over to Melanie the task of dunning their mother on his behalf. References to his imminent death appear with frequent regularity in his letters. At twenty-three he saw his life as essentially completed. In late July he had a tooth extraction in Grotto del Nino. Afterwards, to deaden the pain, he gave himself morphine injections, "which I deemed necessary for the sedation of my heart." As a medical student he must have realized the seriousness of his condition. Exhausted, morbidly depressed, spending more money on cigars, gambling, and drugs than on food, his handwriting during 1902 shows a marked shakiness, and during the year became almost minuscule in size, as though he were trying to erase his being.* His physical symptoms were undoubtedly exacerbated by the emotional stress of Melanie's impending marriage.

Arthur finally set sail from America on September 9, 1902; and Melanie timidly asked her mother if she might return home after a visit of four months in Rosenberg, since Arthur was planning to spend a few days with the family in Vienna before starting his new job on October 1. The wedding was again postponed (at Arthur's suggestion?), this time until January. Emanuel renewed his attempts to stir up Melanie's fears. "I will welcome Arthur as soon as he comes on shore," he announced hypocritically from Grotto del Nino. "By pursuing his American tour, malgré tout, to the end, my deeply founded respect for his masculine—I am writing this word in full awareness of its strong impact—virtues, which I have always had for him, has increased." He was a master at twisting the knife inch by inch into the heart of this basically frightened, sensitive girl. He implies that Arthur was enjoying himself so much in America that he stretched out the trip as long as possible. His harping on Arthur's "masculinity" was also a form of refined cruelty. Melanie might already have had a notion that Arthur was something of a roué; and the reference to "masculinity" could have been a euphemism for the sexual act. Emanuel might have deliberately been reminding her that she would be required to copulate with this man, to submit completely to him in the conjugal bed, a prospect that would have preyed on her mind and intensified her basic dread of the marriage. In this family, so quick to detect emotional nuances, Emanuel suspected that Melanie was terrified by the thought of marriage, just as much as he seemed to loathe the thought of her being possessed by another man. In order to

---

* Melanie retraced the faint writing in ink in order to preserve the letters.

increase her misery, he goes on to tell her of a married woman from his past who has turned up again in his life. She had tried to commit suicide, and was then in Milan recovering from a coma. "Should chance," Emanuel mused, "as is easily possible, lead to an encounter with her, which I do not fear and half wish, then you will know that I am humane enough for any tenderness and man enough to remove any obstacle that might cross my path." This last piece of news elicited an unusually long letter from Melanie, and it conveys better than anything else the quality of her feeling for him. Both of them were desperately trying to find some middle ground between brother and sister, and something more than friends.

Rosenberg, 31, 8, 1902

Dear friend, what you wrote about this woman makes me apprehensive! In order not to lie to you I must own that my first reaction to you was a reproachful feeling of such kind as your unscrupulous behavior towards women has aroused several times in me in the past. I do not judge you from any kind of hidden moral point of view but out of a human concern that makes any mind with interesting features look precious to me. Yet I know a lot could be said against it. Also, one can never form a proper judgment without knowing the ins and outs of all the circumstances. At any rate, I am suspicious of my own judgment when there is something in me that cries for condemnation. I have found that I was usually much less capable of condemning the more I matured, and many things just require personal experience and feeling in order to become understandable. Therefore it is no punishment when I say that "good" and "evil" (and not only in theory) do not exist for me because I am getting to know in myself and through observation how inextricable and undefinable these two concepts are, and because they are present in equal quantities perhaps, yet in different forms, manifestations and relations to each other in the noblest and the basest of human beings. My shattered sense of security manifests itself in my striving for the "tout comprenez." Then I feel this distrust whenever I want to condemn something severely: that the fault may really be mine, and I am lacking the necessary basis for any kind of judgment, that is, understanding.

Nevertheless I cannot apply this fully to you, for it is not understanding that I lack to be in no doubt about the fact that brutality is a constituent part in the makeup of a man, and (of course in the right mixture) essentially belongs to masculinity—just as inertia lies dormant even in the best woman.

But now to what I really wanted to say: I am alarmed at the thought that you half wish for an encounter with this woman. Be convinced, you would probably only hurt her and yourself. I beg you therefore with all my heart: avoid a meeting and leave Como! I implore you to take my advice, just this one time, I beg you most sincerely! However much your desire compels you, it is to a large extent only thirst for excitement, curiosity and pity, and the consequences could be fatal if you give in to this wish. Be that as it may, I beg you to tell me everything about it. I have a peculiar feeling in me which protects me from fearing for my beloved ones as long as they let me participate in everything that concerns them. Therefore, understand me. However much you have assured me of your trust in me, you have not told me anything, dear friend, about precisely the most important and significant events in your life. And what I know, I know from intuition and observation. I never could be more to you—however much I have been longing to be more to you!—I have never reproached you with it, although you have been complaining, with far less reason, about my reserve. But perhaps it is because you are so far away now that I feel so desperately driven to ask you for your confidence. I would, with regard to you, be so much calmer, if I knew that I could share everything with you that concerns you. I think I am worthy of your trust. I need not assure you that everything you write to me will be buried inside me. But apart from this, I believe you will never find a more loyal friend and person who understands you better than I. Let me be your confidante, and be convinced it will be reciprocal!

That you could imagine—even if only for a moment—that my (as you call it) businesslike card, my and Mama's alleged silence could be, though not a result of a premeditated intention, the expression of our resenting you, that you could think that, hurts and surprises me! Neither Mama, especially after her previous letter, nor I deserve such impudence! It is absolutely incomprehensible to me how you could conceive of such a mad idea. I had explained everything so clearly in my letter to you that I have nothing to add to the fact that Mama will send you the money, which I told you on my card. . . .

We shall discuss it no further! I am convinced that you could express these thoughts only in a moment of passing bad temper and overexcitement. . . .

Jolan's genuine great love for me is very beneficial to me. It is certainly a sign of great love if such feelings make a woman forget her own vanity. And this I have noticed quite often with her; also in Losonez, where she receded, completely without jealousy, into the background and rejoiced with me in my triumphs. Her enthusiastic admiration goes so far that recently she got seriously worked up about the thought that any person might have such bad taste as to compare her to me and not notice the difference—she really spoke in earnest, for she is a sincere person as well. Me too, I am really fond of her and I love her as if she were my sister.

Dearest Emanuel, I wish this week were behind me! Tomorrow week I shall leave, and in a fortnight from tomorrow Arthur will probably arrive. . . .

Look after yourself, dear friend, and write to me soon!

With most affectionate hugs

your old

Mela

Emanuel had elicited the response he wanted from her. It was he who was her eternal love, and Arthur was a necessary adjunct who they could pretend did not exist. From St. Mark's Square, he assured her:

You really must love me if you have such sensitive intuition about me. I do not know how I can return this love. . . Do I need to repeat to you that I have concentrated all the love and tenderness I am capable of, and which I need to cherish in myself, on you and Mother. . . And that no greater and devastating disaster could befall me than to lose one of you in any way.

In his next letter, written from Como on October 10, he told her that "during the short time which you and Arthur are allowed to enjoy together I do not wish to distract you and draw your attention to other things that can well wait." He then proceeded to give her a long list of chores that would do precisely that. On October 24 he claimed that he felt "vexed" to hear that the marriage had been postponed yet again—now until February. He then launched into a long plea for her never to address him again as "friend."

Stop it, my girl, "brother" says so much more! If, as in my case, this tie from blood to blood is fortified by admiration, respect and gratitude, then it makes for a relationship that needs no other name than that of brother and sister.

He had decided that in a week he would leave for Rome and Sicily. "These places mean nothing to me except that they are familiar and stimulating environments—and that I need!" He was the Wandering Jew, roaming restlessly for his appointment with death, which he had come to speak of quite calmly. Such sentences are interspersed with angry denunciations of friends who had let him down in the past. His feeling for his mother and his sister was not simply affection, but possession. He was being slung out of the universe because the only two people who meant anything to him were actually capable of continuing their lives without him. He suddenly remembered the existence of Emilie's child, and asked Melanie to buy the child a gift for him—really a good-bye present. The enforced calmness was imposed in the knowledge that he knew that he was losing his grip.

Beryl Gilbertson, a psychologist who specializes in the diagnosis of handwriting, has examined Emanuel's letters in the year preceding his death. She is convinced that he was on cocaine, which was widely used from the 1880s until the early part of this century. Cocaine-based tonics were sold to cure everything, especially fatigue, as army doctors had found that troops operated more energetically on the drug. Cocaine was used pandemically for pain and for morphine addiction. Freud, for example, gave the wonder drug to Fleishl to cure his morphine addiction. In his last paper on cocaine, written in 1887, in answer to criticism he contended that no one became addicted to cocaine unless he was a morphine addict—and all the evidence points to the fact that Emanuel was a morphine addict. He makes frequent reference to his need of money to buy cigars—presumably coca-leaf cigars, which were prescribed for the treatment of respiratory ailments in the nineteenth century. Cocaine was the last thing in the world Emanuel should have been taking—especially as it exacerbates any existing manic tendencies, and even small doses can cause sudden death from cardiac arrest.* As for morphine, it causes drowsiness, mood changes, and mental clouding; it also depresses respiratory centers in the brainstem, causing breathing to become slow and irregular. All these symptoms are part of Emanuel's regular litany of complaints. Photographs taken of him during this period reveal a tormented, self-indulgent face, the full lips suggesting more than a hint of cruelty. The hands, of which he had always been very proud, are languidly passive. Tall and raven-haired, he conveyed something of the air of a bird of prey.

There are no extant letters between October and December 1902—a curious hiatus. One strongly suspects that Klein destroyed them because their contents were particularly painful. All his other letters are preserved in scrupulous chronological order, whereas those from Libussa were left in complete chaos. The missing letters may well have given some indication as to why he changed his destination from Sicily to Spain. Dragging himself from place to place, unable to go home to die, it is probable that these letters were totally heartbreaking. If he took a great many drugs towards the end, the interaction of morphine

---

* See *Cocaine—The Mystique and the Reality*, by Joel L. Phillips and Ronald D. Wynne (New York: Avon Books, 1980), and *A Primer of Drug Action*, by Robert M. Julien (San Francisco: W. H. Freeman, 3d ed. 1981).

and cocaine may have made him psychotic and abusive. The change of plan from Sicily to Spain may have been very sudden. And did the destination matter?

He arrived in Genoa on December 1 in a blinding rainstorm and was planning to sail for Valencia on the first smooth day. In his last card to Melanie, written only a few hours before his death, he complained bitterly of the brief note from her that was waiting for him: "This scantiness has put me very much out of humor and still does so."

The next day, Uncle Hermann received a telegram:

REIZES DIED OF HEART FAILURE—FUNERAL WILL TAKE PLACE ON
THURSDAY MORNING AT THE ISRAELITE CEMETERY—BUNSCHEN
HOTEL GERMANIA

This was followed by an explanatory letter from the hotelkeeper in Genoa:

Lloyd-Hotel Germania
Münchener Bierhaus
von
C. O. Bünsche-Genoa
Via Carlo Alberto.39 – Salita S. Paolo, 38
Telephon 1221

Genoa, 4.12.1902

To Dr. Deutsch,
    In confirmation of your telegram of the third and my cable, I take it upon myself to inform you in the following of the particular circumstances of the decease of Herr Em. Reizes.
    . . . Reizes retired as early as nine o'clock having drunk a cup of hot milk and written several letters. He did not say that anything was wrong.
    Since the above-mentioned gentleman had slept till midday the previous day, it was not taken as odd when he had not appeared by midday on this day.
    In the afternoon someone knocked on his door to ask whether he wanted anything, yet there was no reply. It was now decided to ascertain whether R. had gone out or something else had happened, and for this purpose the door was opened. And Reizes' dead body, already cold, was found. The doctor who was called immediately stated that death must have occurred as long ago as shortly after midnight, and he diagnosed heart failure.
    I informed the local authorities and the Austrian Consulate at once, and after everything had been taken down in writing Reizes' personal effects were sealed and handed over to the Consulate.

R. had no suitcase with him and no baggage ticket was found, only a small handbag. The money that was found consisted of:

French franc notes: 150.—
   "   "   gold: 8o.—
Spanish pesetas: 100.—
Italian lira notes: 15.—
   "   "   copper: 2.—

Furthermore there was a watch and a revolver.

After all the formalities and yet another examination by the municipal doctor were finished, the body was dressed, and the funeral took place this morning. It was not permitted to keep the body any longer because of its rapid deterioration.

As you will understand I have suffered great damages through this sad incident since the room needs complete redecoration and refurnishing, etc.

I shall take the liberty to submit to you shortly an account of my expenses. Meanwhile, expressing my sympathy to you and the family of the deceased, I remain
faithfully yours

C. Otto Bünsche

P.S. For everything to be correct I should like to mention that I had to call three doctors to satisfy the regulations of the law here.

The brusqueness of this curt, irritated communication from the hotel-keeper was softened by a consolatory letter from his wife, in the sincere voice of one grieving mother to another.

Lloyd-Hotel Germania
Münchener Bierhaus
C. O. Bünsche-Genoa
Via Carlo Alberto, 39–Salita S. Paolo, 38

Genoa, 4.12.1902

Dear Mrs. Reizes,

The sad case, the sudden death of your son occasions me to express my deeply felt sympathy. It must be the more painful to you as you could not be at the repose of your beloved child and the hard blow surely came totally unexpectedly to you. It is very sad if one loses one's dearest in a foreign country among strange people. But you may take solace in the fact, dear Madam, that also in foreign countries there are people who feel with you. Take trust in God and consider that He in His Wisdom will always serve our best interests. However, it is easier said than done to submit oneself to the inevitable, a mother's heart will feel and grieve more than any other. I am a mother as well and I too have buried a beloved child, so I can understand your deep grief and appreciate your great loss. . . .

Perhaps it will console you a little to hear that your son passed away completely without pain. He was lying in his bed as if he were asleep, death throes can absolutely not have occurred; he had not even stretched himself. He was lying on one side, the eyes closed, the right hand near the face, the left one under the blanket, exactly as one does when one makes oneself comfortable in bed to go to sleep. Had he not been cold and stiff, one would never have believed that anybody could look so peaceful in death. The authorities sent two more doctors round, but all three were agreed that heart failure had brought his life to an end. After the authorities and the Consulate had been called here by telephone, everything was organized that is necessary in a case of death. This morning at four o'clock, the body was collected from the hotel and at seven was laid to rest. Now that all the excitement a sudden death brings—particularly in a hotel—has subsided, I considered it to be my duty, dear Madam, to give you a most extensive report about the last hours of your son, God bless him, and I do hope it will help you to put your mind a bit more at rest.

Expressing my deepest sympathy,

I am your faithful servant,

Frau M. Bünsche

The fact that the landlord mentions the revolver in such a matter-of-fact way rules out the possibility of suicide. At that time travelers were fair game for footpads because they were assumed to be carrying cash—and Emanuel, who was very reckless with money, frequented low-class gambling casinos. Moreover, he would have been susceptible to attack in many non-Jewish areas in an age when anti-Semitism was overtly rampant. The revolver may even have been insurance against an undignified end.

The landlord's expenses seem callous and calculating. However, it is quite possible that Emanuel purged himself at the time of death (a very common phenomenon), which would have necessitated a new mattress and bedding. Also, superstition could have played a part in the redecoration of the room; and the landlord seems the sort of man who would be excessively careful to avoid a scandal.

According to Dr. Ronald Mavor, a tuberculosis specialist, victims of the disease sometimes die of massive haemoptysis when a substantial artery has eroded, but a very quiet death is far more common. Chekhov, for example, died of progressive exhaustion. One evening, after a performance of one of his plays, he sipped a glass of champagne and passed away. The coughing of blood has largely been a part of the mythology associated with tuberculosis—as is the enhanced sexuality of the sufferer. In Dr. Mavor's view, the doctors who examined the corpse would have recognized the presence of tuberculosis from its advanced state of emaciation. (In that case, extensive renovations of the room would have indeed been necessary.) However, they would not necessarily have perjured themselves on the death certificate; it seems likely that Emanuel's heart simply gave up its long weary struggle.

He may even have killed himself accidentally. He had been deeply distressed to find only a short note from Melanie upon his arrival. In his great dependency on her, he seemed to be losing the last link with his lifeline. He was a physical wreck, prescribing drugs for himself, and he could have had wine with his dinner—a combination that might well have killed him in the early hours of the morning, when the body's metabolism is at its lowest. Without modern methods of chemical analysis, it would have been impossible for anyone to assess his death as anything but heart failure, even had he been overdosed with drugs.

In her Autobiography, Klein wrote:

He was twenty-five when he died. Here again [as with Sidonie] I have the feeling that, had one known more about medicine, one might have been able to do something to keep him alive longer, but I have been told that even now rheumatic heart diseases are not always curable. I don't know whether this is true or not, but it left me with the same feeling that I had about my little sister, that many things could have been done to prevent his illness and early death. ... In my memory he remains a young, strong-minded man, as I knew him, strong in his opinions, not minding if they were unpopular, with a deep understanding of art and a passion for it in many ways, and the best friend I ever had.

This is in a sense an apologia: he died because medicine was not sufficiently advanced, not because he was a manic-depressive with a death wish or because he was neglected or malnourished. Brother and sister, they were twin souls, sharing the same sorts of moods and reactions. He was her surrogate father, close companion, phantom lover—and no one in her life was ever able to replace him.

CHAPTER THREE

Marriage

From the day of Emanuel's death in 1902, all references to him disappear from the family letters—apart from allusions to Melanie's efforts to publish a collection of his work, a goal she finally achieved in 1906. In her Autobiography she carefully omits the details connected with his death, but she does relate the part Arthur played in the retrieval of her brother's papers. According to her account, a postcard addressed to Arthur was found on the table in the hotel room. Upon receiving the tragic news, Arthur immediately traveled to Genoa to fetch Emanuel's luggage, which was already deposited for shipping. Since the baggage ticket could not be found, he had to wander through an enormous hall until his eye caught sight of a suitcase from which a copy of *Die Fackel* protruded—one that Emanuel had requested Melanie to send him. Arthur knew how much Emanuel admired Kraus; and when the suitcase was opened it was found to be filled with miscellaneous manuscripts. As Melanie later read through these semifictional jottings, she became filled with determination to publish them—the only act of reparation she could make to her brother. Despite the ill feeling between husband and wife in later years, Melanie always retained a feeling of immense gratitude to Arthur for going to so much trouble to retrieve the manuscripts.

And so she was finally married, while still in a state of mourning, on March 31, 1903, the day after her twenty-first birthday. Nothing is known about the ceremony. The wedding took place in Rosenberg and the young couple traveled to Zurich by way of Constanza on their wedding journey. Despite their long engagement, she and Arthur scarcely knew each other.

In an undated (c. 1913), undoubtedly autobiographical story, "Life Calls," Klein writes about the shock experienced by a young woman, Anna, on her wedding night: "And does it therefore have to be like this, that motherhood begins with disgust?" Anna makes every effort to accept her husband's conventional view that a chaste and decent woman has a natural dislike for "these things," but is tormented by an indefinable longing for unknown fulfillment. It is highly possible that her revulsion to sex was connected with a sense of having betrayed Emanuel. "I often wonder," she later mused, "whether my brother, with whom I had such a deep and close connection, did not realize that I was doing the wrong thing, and whether he did not unconsciously know that I was going to make myself unhappy."

Returning from their wedding journey, the newlyweds settled in Rosenberg. With a population of about 8,000, of diverse nationalities, it was the principal town of the then Hungarian province of Liptau. The Hungarians dominated the civil service, the Jews were engaged in commerce, and the Slovaks were represented by the peasants and minor gentry. The Klein family seems to have been thoroughly assimilated. While Jakob Klein was a nominal member of the synagogue, Arthur had attended a Jesuit school. Something of a domestic tyrant, Jakob oppressed his family with his irascible temper. Within his small community, he was a highly respected figure, for many years both the town's mayor and manager of the local bank. He was also senator for his town, then unusual for a Jew, and was decorated with the Franz Josef order. He was very proud of his brother, who had run away to join the Austro-Hungarian army and eventually became a regular officer—again, almost unheard of for a Jew at that time. German was the lingua franca of the town, and was largely spoken by the Jews. Arthur could speak Hungarian, Slovak, and German; his father, Hungarian and Slovak; and his mother, Hungarian and German. Melanie, always quick at learning languages, set about learning Slovak.

On their return to Rosenberg, Melanie and Arthur moved to an attractive apartment (it seems to have been above the bank), furnished largely with things sent from the Vienna household. Libussa made suggestions for the decorations—"if you can manage until I come." There were still outstanding bills for the trousseau; and in reply to Melanie's inquiries about the family finances, on May 28, Emilie assured her sister that she and Leo intended to contribute something when possible. Within two months of the wedding Melanie discovered that she was pregnant. For some weeks she felt miserably nauseated. When Libussa heard that she could expect another grandchild, she responded delightedly in a letter replete with maternal advice.

Since I know the sweet secret now, I wish you, my dear child, such a sweet boy as Otto. It can also be a girl and become like you—only less nervous. I am very pleased you will take Somatose; but you must drink at least 1½ liters of milk as Emilie did; and you must take, twice a day, two level teaspoonsful of Somatose. Drink half a liter of milk in the mornings and eat two eggs and a butter bun. In the afternoons drink half a liter of milk with

Somatose and another half a liter of milk with Somatose before going to bed. If you have an aversion for meat, eat poultry, many eggs and especially nourishing food. You must force yourself even if it goes against your stomach. But what is most important is that you must not upset yourself, allow yourself to be diverted, be cheerful and never melancholic or agitated, because that is not only bad for your state but also, as you well know, for your baby. For his sake you must exercise self-control. The mind is like the eye that should have only beautiful impressions. It is my firm conviction that, thank God, Emilie's pregnancy was so successful only because she was relaxed, cheerful and in good spirits and because she consistently fed herself well. At the end of next month I will visit you and I can then continue with my admonitions in person.

There are some features of this letter that deserve comment. In the first place, a boy would be desirable; and if the child turned out to be a girl, she should be someone more placid than Melanie. Secondly, Emilie's pregnancy—which had produced a boy—was so successful because she had had Libussa's watchful eye on her during the whole period. True, she shows a mother's concern, but it is an oversolicitous concern.

In a letter of June 18, 1903, Libussa's only reference to the pregnancy was that Melanie should not hang a certain picture of nymphs and fauns. Apparently the subject might have been unsettling—for its sexual connotations? "Altogether you ought to look only at beautiful pictures and you should not get a fright from anything." She then turned to more immediate concerns such as the purchase of a tablecloth for Melanie, and then proceeded to an even more pressing piece of news: Uncle Hermann had just bought a beautiful villa with a large park in Gersthof which had cost him 290,000 florins, and he appeared very worried about the cost. He and his family planned to move into it in September. The change in his life-style was to have considerable repercussions on the Martinstrasse household—and on the Klein marriage as well.

A baby girl, Melitta, was born on January 19, 1904; and Melanie claimed that she enjoyed motherhood, particularly as she had an excellent Slovak peasant woman, "Dada," as nanny. However, her Autobiography contains an ominous passage: "I threw myself as much as I could into motherhood and interest in my child. I knew all the time that I was not happy, but saw no way out." The letters reveal that Melitta was breast-fed for seven months, but Klein makes no reference to this in her Autobiography. In view of the subsequent relationship between mother and daughter, it would be interesting to know how mother and child responded to the experience.

In August 1904, Emilie visited Rosenberg, while Libussa took herself off to a spa, Bad Reichenhall, near Salzburg, where she was prescribed carbonic acid baths and inhalations for her apparent angina and palpitations. Her sojourn there seems to have been more of a holiday—although she assured her daughters that it was the doctor's wish that she stay a full month for the sake of her health. Yet within a week she was able to climb the mountain paths and delight in the fragrance of the pine forests. Arthur's stepsister, Iren,* and her husband, Karl Kurtz, took Libussa on an enjoyable excursion to Salzburg and its environs, and she would have accompanied them to Berchtesgaden as well had it not interfered with her treatment.

The letters, addressed jointly to both daughters, are an interesting contrast to those written solely to Melanie. In her remarks to Emilie, Libussa seems more relaxed than with her younger daughter. She gives sensible advice without smothering her: "You, my dear Emmy, ought to consider that you have only a short period in which to enjoy the country. So leave your silly embroidery and make use of the time." However, the tranquillity was short-lived.

In the first few months of 1905, Libussa began to bombard Melanie and Arthur with her financial worries. According to her, Uncle Hermann was demanding full payment for the house; if he did not receive this by April or May, she would be left homeless. "To tell you the truth," she assured them, "I am a real mess" ("*Shlesmastik*"). From her description of these negotiations, both brother and sister seem ruthlessly hard bargainers. Since there are so many indications in her correspondence that Libussa habitually twisted the truth, a more likely explanation would be that now that Arthur was in a good position, Libussa was determined to rid herself of her financial burdens. Undoubtedly there were ugly quarrels, but one passage suggests that Libussa did not want Arthur to hear Hermann's side of the story.

> Dear Arthur, I hope it will not occur to you to write anything about this matter to Uncle—or to hurt him in any way. This noble and kind person does not at all deserve to be hurt. He certainly has his eccentricities yet he is next to you (including Leo and Emmy) the dearest person in the world to me.

She showed only the slightest interest in the baby, and her recital of her problems would have disturbed any possibility of Melanie's serenity while looking after her little girl.

Still, there were occasional pleasant distractions. In 1905, when Melitta was a year old, husband and wife traveled to the Adriatic coast, visiting Trieste, Venice, and Abbazia (now Opatija), a popular resort in what is now Yugoslavia. In February 1906 Arthur was informed that he was to be sent in the spring

---

* Iren was the daughter of Jakob Klein by a previous marriage. She had married a successful criminal lawyer. They lived in a town about fifty miles from Vienna.

to a congress in Rome and that Melanie could accompany him. They also planned to go to Naples and Florence, and to visit Emanuel's grave in Genoa. Jolan had been there the previous spring, sending back herbs from the site. Libussa's response to the news of the trip, in a letter to Melanie written on February 10, 1906, is possibly more revealing of her character than anything else she ever wrote:

> Arthur knows where his advantage lies and how to get it. That this journey to Rome means the fulfillment of your most fervent wish is self-evident. But what surprises me is that in the excess of your pleasure you have completely forgotten about me. You write quite correctly that there will hardly be another opportunity to travel to Genoa. I say, for me it is completely out of the question that I will ever get there. For twenty-four years now I have been wanting to go to visit my father's grave, and I never got around to it. And it will be the same for me with Genoa. I cannot make such a journey by myself, and I will not. I believe that this would be my sole opportunity if I could travel with you.
>
> If I consider that I will be fifty-six this month* and that the years pass by so quickly and with them comes infirmity which will perhaps hinder my making this so ardently longed for journey, then I see it as a heavenly dispensation that I could succeed now. Money is no object to me in this case. If I did not have it I would borrow it. But by then I will have enough as I have already saved over 300 crowns. If you want to combine this journey with a holiday you are welcome to do so, and who knows whether some time spent at the seaside would not restore me completely. . . . Having to spend a larger sum of money does not at all deter me. I only tell myself that Uncle will just be paid out half a year later. It is also possible that I as a person who is traveling to the congress will get the journey more cheaply.
>
> Arthur need not fear anything. I shall not inconvenience him. I shall take only a little luggage: a smarter dress, a dressing gown and my travel dress. And as far as other things are concerned you will not any longer be on honeymoon and I shall not inconvenience you in any way.
>
> As far as Meta [Melitta] is concerned, neither Leo nor Emilie would raise any objections if I leave four weeks earlier. Yet I must tell you that you are really overdoing it by still being so fussy with the child. At the age of two Otto ate everything. Now you need not fear anymore that she will get stomach upsets, especially since you have Dada. . . . Dada cooks for her, bathes her, and takes her to bed etc. etc. You can safely entrust her to Dada.

---

* This would make 1850 her date of birth, which is at odds with the date of birth given on her death certificate, 1852. The discrepancy is unresolved.

It is odd that Libussa had never visited her father's grave; also that she had managed to save 300 crowns when her previous letters had been filled with complaints about her penury. It never seems to have occurred to her that the young couple might prefer to be on their own. Melanie was concerned that the trip would be too exhausting for her, and proposed that she make a shorter journey to Abbazia. "Upon careful consideration," Libussa replied, "I have come to see that you are right and I would not be able to cope with the overexertion of the journey. So many sleepless nights and perpetual traveling would not be good for my condition." By April, Libussa had decided that she was really not up to meeting them in Genoa. "I think if I am going to live I will certainly get another opportunity to go to Genoa," she informed them. Eventually even Abbazia was ruled out, and a compromise was reached whereby she visited Rosenberg in their absence. Perhaps she capitulated because she realized she was pushing her luck too far.

In Italy, visions of a more expansive life contributed in a subtle way to Melanie's general discontent. However, she and Arthur were equally indefatigable sightseers, and these seem to have been the happiest times they shared during their marriage. In her Autobiography, Klein fails to mention the visit to Emanuel's grave. As Jolan had described it, it was covered with a green patch of lawn with a small marble plate inscribed simply: Reizes Emanuel. Melanie picked some herbs covering it and tucked them into the bundle of Emanuel's letters which she kept for the rest of her life.

To Emilie, in Vienna, Melanie's life seemed full of glamour in contrast to her own constricted one of petty economies and overwork. A somewhat pathetic letter reveals some envy of her sister's good fortune, but also an acceptance that her younger, brilliant sister was destined for a richer life than she could expect:

When I read your vivid letter I could hardly suppress a certain sadness. Not that I am jealous; you know that I have no strong inclination for traveling, although I would not object to it if the opportunity for it offered itself. . . . And I do get almost jealous of your talent for expressing so beautifully everything that you have seen. Well, that's an old story, and it tells you that there is hardly anybody else who loves you as much as I do. . . . How is our dear Mama? Is she looking well? I long for her enormously. She has been away now for such a long time that her features are sometimes blurred in my recollection. When is she coming? How long will she stay with us? Then it's the spring again, and it draws her to her beloved Rosenberg with her sweet Meta, Mela and Arthur. And it is over with Emilie, Leo and Otto! Why does she neglect us so?

Emilie, too, seems to have been caught up in the family pattern of guilt-inducement. If one of them had good fortune, the other had to pay for it.

From Rosenberg, where Libussa was looking after Melitta, her grand-mother reported to the absent Melanie that the child was "merry and cheerful, laughs and sings like a little bird all day long. She seems to miss you very much. Several times a day she looks into the bedroom and says: 'Papa, Mama, bed,' and quite often without being prompted she says: 'Mama, sweet, nice, good, beautiful.' She has a very good appetite and needs no enemas." Libussa tried to assure herself that the marriage was absolute perfection, and that any little problems were due to Melanie's unfortunate "nerves," which were more and more frequently alluded to as the years passed. In a letter of April 25, 1906 (presumably addressed to Naples), Libussa expressed her satisfaction about Melanie's good health and added, "But it grieves me, dear Melanie, that you are never spared a bitter drop of wormwood—even in raptures of joy! It is your fate or, unfortunately, your disposition that there is always something that tortures you."

Libussa was determined to make Melanie aware of how her own health had suffered as a result of her sacrifice in not sharing their travels. Back in Vienna on May 17, she reported that she had been given a checkup by Professor Schlesinger. She had no heart complaint and so did not need carbonic acid baths, and her bronchial catarrh had disappeared. However, "I need a change of scenery, fresh air—rich in ozone—daily pine-needle baths—and he guarantees me a perfect cure." This she found in a spa at Karetnitza—an excursion presumably paid for by Arthur.

The year 1906 was important in that it saw the long-awaited publication of Emanuel's book. In her Autobiography, Klein describes how

after his death, when I was twenty, I collected his writings together, with a great friend of his and mine, Irma Schonfeld, and managed to publish them. By then I was married and expecting my first child, and I traveled quite a distance to meet Georg Brandes, the literary historian, whom my brother admired, to get the preface from him for this book, since he had refused by letter. Actually, he had already left the house from which he had replied to me that he was too old and tired to give any more prefaces or read any more books, but the friends with whom he had been staying, whose name I cannot remember, a woman writer and her sculptor daughter, seem to have been so impressed with me that their letter to Brandes produced the preface. Actually he used nearly all of what I had written about my brother in this preface. After a long struggle, I managed to get a good publisher for him. . . . This book does not really give any idea of what my brother might have achieved, because we used every scrap in his note-books, some of it quite immature, to put the book together, and it is a feeble picture of what might have come, although there are some beautiful things in it.

The vagueness of where Klein went in quest of Brandes is puzzling, especially as there is no indication of such a journey in the family correspondence. There is, however, a later reference in one of Libussa's letters to a trip Melanie once made to Berlin when Arthur ordered her to return to Rosenberg. By then Irma was living in Berlin, apparently happily married, and letters from her suggest that it was she who was actually responsible for the tedious work of seeing the book through the press. *Aus meinem Leben* ("From My Life"), published by Wiener Verlag, was reviewed with great reservations on April 22, 1906, by an eminent Viennese critic, Sevacse, in the *Neue Freie Presse*—ironically, one of the central butts of Karl Kraus's salvos. Characteristically, Libussa could not bear to be left out of the drama: when, during Melanie's trip to Italy, the publication of the book was delayed because of the publisher's financial difficulties, Libussa took it upon herself to write to Sevacse to ask if he could postpone his review.

The reviewer described the author as somewhat decadent, decidedly so in his relationships with women. "Particularly repulsive is the motif that he is so outraged by a few indifferent words from Thea, by which she means to do no harm, that he breaks with her and subsequently enjoys her suffering." Sevacse was puzzled by the young man's enforced coldness to his mother, although he became more genuinely humane at the end of his life when he adjured her not to weep: "Mother, you must forgive my death since I have forgiven you my life." If Emanuel actually left such a note for his mother, it would almost suggest that he intended suicide.

The physical object—the book—seemed more important to Libussa than her son. She was immensely proud of the review—to the point where she believed everyone in Rosenberg was so impressed as to be reduced to silence. Nevertheless, on her return to Vienna she was disturbed that the book was not stocked in any of the shops. Another (anonymous) review appeared in November: "We are so excited that even after having read it several times we do not know whether it is favorable or unfavorable," Libussa reported. At least Uncle Hermann's wife was impressed with it. Shattered by its contents, she dissolved in tears, a reaction that seemed to puzzle Libussa. Emilie, at Libussa's request, asked Melanie if she would send her a copy of Emanuel's book to give a doctor who was treating her for cystitis in lieu of payment.*

Emilie wrote to congratulate her sister on the fruits of her labors:

Now that the book has been published, and we, at long last, have reached our long desired, long wished for goal, I must tell you how much I admire

---

* This is the only time Emanuel's name actually appears in the correspondence after his death.

you. You know that I am usually not very forthcoming with praise, but now I am simply overwhelmed! Only you could have achieved this, you with your intellect, your iron willpower and perseverance. Do believe me, even if I have been unapproachable at times, that in secret I have always appreciated and admired your strong will! Now, let's hope the best for the book! Those who are worthy of reading it will also appreciate it! . . . Irma told me how much she admires you for having fought so hard for the book. She would never have been able to carry out the task, for her willpower would have slackened. She would have given up long ago.

If Melanie's depression became more marked after the publication of the book, the event itself might have precipitated her morose feelings. After four years of apparently exhorting Irma, the task was completed—and she was intelligent enough to sense the restraint in the review. Moreover, the visit to the grave in Genoa must have had a traumatic effect upon her.

Her second child, Hans, was born on March 2, 1907; and letters reveal that she was in a state of deep depression during the pregnancy. She recalled Hans as showing unusually precocious intelligence as an infant. It seems significant that she should mention this in her Autobiography, since he always retained a very childlike manner and in some ways seemed almost retarded.

In the Autobiography, Klein refers to an event that was ultimately to spell disaster for her marriage: Late in 1907 Arthur accepted a well-paid job as director of one of Count Henkel-Donnersmarck's paper mills in upper Silesia. As a result, they had to move to Krappitz, a small, dreary provincial town without a single congenial soul with whom Melanie could converse. Even Rosenberg had seemed unbearably confining after Jolan moved to Budapest upon her marriage in 1906. At this point Libussa, with little reluctance, was persuaded to come and stay with them. Libussa was only too happy to do so because Arthur was now in a position to pay off Uncle Hermann for his investment in the house, and Libussa could finally give up the shop, which she rented out to a coffeehouse. That Melanie was able to afford adequate household help and Emilie could not was of no consideration. Emilie's second son, Wilhelm Emanuel Pick, had been born on December 18, 1905, and she was overwhelmed with household chores.

While the negotiations for the sale of the house were taking place, Libussa informed Arthur that the house, according to Uncle, would have to be put in Melanie's name. In a private communication Eric Clyne writes: "With regard to the house in Vienna, I believe that my mother purchased her sister's share in it from her, and although it had several apartments she never had an income from it. Eventually, about two years before her death, she sold it, and when I visited the Martinstrasse some years ago I found it had been pulled down and a petrol station built on its site." There is great confusion and contradiction in various people's perceptions of the arrangements connected with the house— as there often is in family factions concerning property. Walter Pick, a son of Otto Pick, believes it possible that his father leased Melanie's portion of the house beginning about 1927. Here his family lived and here Otto conducted a successful dental practice. One of his most distinguished patients was Sigmund Freud.* The house had to be abandoned forever when the family fled to England in 1938. According to Hermann's daughter, Trude Feigel, both daughters inherited the house on Libussa's death and Emilie eventually sold her share (she disputes that the house was bought by Otto). She does not know what Melanie did with hers; Mrs. Feigel confirms that there would have been little income from the house since rents were controlled.

From the moment Libussa moved to Krappitz, she assumed command of the household, filling a void created by Melanie's increasing irritability, depressive exhaustion, and despondency. She was encouraged to spend much time away from home in quiet, restful places visiting friends and relatives, as her anxiety was affecting even Libussa. "It was no surprise that I went down like that," Libussa wrote to her daughter in February 1908, while Melanie was away on a visit to Budapest, "when I had to witness your intense suffering and could not help you." Photographs taken of Klein during this period reveal the paralyzing depression in which she was entrapped. In her Autobiography she describes Arthur as "difficult." There is hardly a letter from Libussa during this period that does not refer to his "nerves," insomnia, and stomach complaints. Often he was too tired, too overworked, or too miserable to write to his wife, and Libussa conveyed messages from one to the other. But Libussa wanted to have a very special place in her daughter's life, and she proposed a curiously oblique way in which Melanie might communicate with her so that Arthur would not read the letter: simply by addressing it to Frau Melanie Klein.

In the two and a half years they lived in Krappitz, Melanie seems to have been away almost as much as she was at home. In 1908, when Hans was less than a year old, from the end of January until mid-April she visited Rosenberg and Budapest, and spent a week in Abbazia. In Rosenberg her mother-in-law gave her hot packs, which she had applied to Arthur in the past. "I believe his mother and I are still the best doctors," Libussa complacently informed her daughter. On the visit to Abbazia, Melanie was accompanied by Klara Vágó, the sister of Jolan's husband, Gyula. This is the first suggestion that Klara, a divorced woman some years older than Melanie, was becoming a close friend. Libussa seems to have had mixed feelings about this turn of events when she heard the news prior to their departure: "As regards Klara, you will certainly be pleased to have a traveling companion. But I would consider it very unwise for

* Presumably Otto was involved in making Freud's prosthesis. Freud wrote a testimonial for Otto Pick in 1938 to enable him to move to England.

you to share a room with her in Abbazia. I think you can tell her that it would not be good for your nerves, that you need complete quiet, and that you must not be under any pressure to comply with anybody." At the resort Melanie underwent a treatment of carbonic acid baths and other current remedies for nerves.

During these absences Libussa bombarded Melanie with letters about the impeccable way the household was being managed, and with advice on the smallest details of her life, as though she were trying to reinforce the dependency of her neurasthenic daughter, even at a distance. Melanie was told what to wear, whom to see, how long to stay in each place. In the morning she was to wear a loose dressing-gown so that she would not be constricted and was *definitely* not to play the piano or to frequent stimulating company. Every piece of advice her mother gave her reinforced Melanie's view of herself as a permanent semi-invalid.

Unfortunately Melanie's letters during this period have not survived, but from her mother's replies it is apparent that she felt worried and guilty about her children's welfare. Her anxiety must have increased on hearing that Hans turned frequently to the door and called, "Mama, Mama!" She was away when each of his teeth appeared—and she was absent for his first birthday. And what could Melanie's maternal reaction have been upon reading that her little girl would say, "What will Mama say when she hears that I am so good?" "Why do you torture yourself so much because of the children?" Libussa demanded. "Why do you make every minute of your life a misery and forbid yourself any joy because of them? You can completely rest assured! The children could not be any healthier and look better than they do now." In other words, they were much better off without their own mother.

To reinforce her point, Libussa chided her daughter that her own physical complaints had been caused by worry over Melanie's condition. And why should Melanie feel so grateful to her? After all, she was doing what any decent mother would do.

What is all this nonsense about my great maternal love and sacrifice? Do you think I could have acted differently from the way I did? . . . You must concentrate on one thing only: that you want to come home as a completely well and strong person! Do not allow homesickness and longing for your children to get hold of you! You know that Arthur, your children, and your home are in good hands—so you can rest assured as far as that is concerned. And by the time you come back—healthy, refreshed, and strong—Arthur will have recovered completely, so I confidently hope. And just think of the new life that lies ahead of you! What more could any person ask of life? Is not everything yours for which most people have to fight and struggle, and for which they envy you?

Libussa also seems to have had Arthur under her thumb, although from time to time he displayed sullen resistance. On February 2, 1908, Libussa gave him a good lecture, which she duly reported to Melanie in Budapest:

I told him: "I hope it has not occurred to you to make Melanie come from Pest to Vienna. You did that when she was in Berlin, you called her back then! You should be glad that she is feeling better now and need not go to a sanatorium. It is better for you if she comes back completely cured and in a cheerful frame of mind. Then you will also lose your nervousness. What use is it to you if she comes back and cries again and is ill again?" . . . He has had second thoughts: you are to stay in Budapest as long as you like. He said, he had anyway to attend many conferences in Vienna and would be very busy. So you see, as Arthur has asked me to write this to you, that you can stay in Budapest as long as you please. And I should like to add: it is your duty to stay there for your sake as well as for the children's and Arthur's sake! For I really need it very much that both of you get well. Therefore I repeat it once again: Stay, stay, stay—and get well!

Libussa wanted Melanie out of the way. She tried to create situations in which husband and wife saw each other as seldom as possible. Her reports of what Arthur or the doctor had said were quite clearly words she put into their mouths. The detail that Arthur would be too busy in Vienna anyway to have much time for Melanie is a diabolical touch. It infuriated her to think that Arthur was making private plans with his wife, and in subtle ways she discouraged him from writing to her. Melanie constantly complained about not hearing from him more often.

In her consuming need to mother (smother?) her daughter, Libussa lost sight of, or was too obtuse to understand, what she really wanted. In her eyes, it was imperative for Melanie to stay as long as possible in Abbazia. If she and Arthur met before her departure, it would interfere with Libussa's plans to get her daughter to the sea air quickly. Arthur must wait to join her in Abbazia. Libussa's motives were probably mixed: she may have had an unrecognized fear that Melanie was susceptible to tuberculosis, but on the other hand she could not bear her daughter to have pleasures that were denied to her. As for the cost of a prolonged stay in Abbazia, money was no object. After years of scrimping and worrying about her own money, she was extremely liberal about the way Arthur should spend his:

This morning I went to Arthur in his bedroom and asked him whether he will comply with your wish and go to Rosenberg. He said it would be impossible for him this week and, in addition, it would wear him out. I agreed with him and put my plan for Abbazia to him. He was quite excited with joy at first. Then he said, it would be impossible for him as he would then get no holiday in the summer. I said to him: "You only need to apply for eight days off your summer holiday. You and Melanie will have only three weeks then for your journey to the Harz Mountains. But by that time the two of you will have recovered your strength. What does one do if one gets influenza and has to stay in bed for two weeks?"

Well, you know what Arthur is like if one talks insistently to him for a while: "It cannot be done! Leave me in peace! Leave me in peace!" Admittedly, I was in a better position than he since he was lying in bed and could not run away. So I have initiated this thing! He will certainly think about it, the rest is for you to do! I think that will be the best solution. Your separation will not be so long, and you will both recuperate. And then you can, on your return journey, stay as long in Budapest as you please, divert yourself, do your shopping, and perhaps have your taffeta suit made. And you can also stay three to four days in Vienna. You can do all this in leisure and comfort and need not rush the journey. Since you will have been together for ten days you will not find a separation of two weeks too hard then. I think you will like my plan.

However, Arthur was not as willing to comply with her plans as she assumed—she was outraged two days later, when he told her she had a completely wrong impression of what Abbazia was really like and that the long train journey would be exhausting for his wife (and himself!). In his view, what Melanie needed was the diversion offered by a big city, where, moreover, he would be able to visit her more easily. Libussa threw up her hands in indignant self-justification:

I listened till he had finished. I am completely shattered by his change of mind! Then I said: "All right, if you take the responsibility, I can't do anything about it." Yet I do see that men love only themselves—I wanted to tell him: "You only love yourself," but in view of the fact that a separation of 6–7 weeks would be unbearable to him and he believes that he has made the greatest sacrifice by putting up with 4 weeks' separation, I remained silent. He was, of course, beside himself about my words, but I couldn't care less!

Without telling Libussa, Arthur then made plans for his wife to meet him in Breslau before she proceeded to Abbazia. When Libussa heard his news on April 4, she was beside herself with rage:

I kept my composure and replied (although I was boiling inside): "This journey will be just as bad for you as for Melanie. If she sees you like that, looking so miserable, she may get a fright and suffer a relapse. And for yourself it would be better if you went back to bed and had a rest." "Do not talk big" was his reply—and so I shut up. Well, what good would it have done me if I had gone on talking? But I must tell you, my dear child, do not dare to break off your cure and come home as has been usual so far when the end was in sight and he lost his patience. Your whole cure, all that money, would be wasted!—and you will, for the rest of your life, remain miserable and ill. And you must become healthy, for your sake as well as for his.

Within a week she had accepted the situation to the point of being able to extract some consolation: "Be so kind as to give your skunk collar to Arthur to bring back with him. You really can do without it for a week, and I need it in Rosenberg since my long fox coat is so very shabby." Apparently the children were not in such desperate straits without her that it was impossible for her to go off to Rosenberg for a few days on her own. This seems to have been an act of reprisal on her part for their parents' defiance.

I asked Meta whether she wanted to go with me to Rosenberg, but I got no reply apart from a deep blush. When she insisted on her refusal to give me an answer, I said to her: "But surely, you will come along if Dada is coming, won't you?" and then she did reply: "But Mama and the boy must come too!" So you see, she would not go with me at all.

This is only one of several hints that Melitta may have disliked and distrusted her grandmother, and Libussa apparently did not hide her preference for Hans. On the other hand, it was constantly drummed into Melitta that her mother was an emotional cripple—so ill that she constantly had to desert her daughter. The bewildered child was accumulating resentments that were to have tragic consequences in later life.

Libussa closed her eyes to the possibility that these separations were undermining the marriage. Everything had to accord with her conception of a conflict-free family situation. In old age Melanie Klein told Hanna Segal that Arthur had been unfaithful to her from the first year of her marriage. Did it not occur to her that her mother had prevented the marriage from developing into a mature relationship? It is even possible that Libussa, with her streak of envy and malice, could vindictively have put the idea in her daughter's mind if Arthur was increasingly resentful of her interference. At any rate, Arthur had to take frequent business trips and had plenty of opportunities for illicit amours if so inclined—and he might have been so inclined, considering that his wife was separated from him for weeks at a time and found sex distasteful even at the best of times. It is doubtful that we will ever know the truth about the marriage.

Only one letter from Arthur survives, written before he set off to join Melanie in Abbazia—because, of course, Libussa did get her own way in the end. The letter was written in the spring of 1908 from a café in Vienna, and is mostly concerned with his plans for the week preceding their meeting. The expressions of affection seem conventional and preoccupied. While voicing only a perfunctory concern for his wife's welfare, he is full of complaints about his own disorders.

> I cannot tell you anything new, darling. I just want to tell you how I am and that I am sure the pain stems from neuralgia. The pain is relenting by occurring less and less spasmically. I hope the journey will do me good, the change refresh me. My only love, I am very, very fond of you and, my dear, I beg you to look after yourself carefully.

After a few more details, he ended:

> And now, my darling, good night, sleep well and be very old and sweet to yourself, whom I love so much—be like that to me too whom you also love a little.
> I kiss you tenderly,
> my only one,
> Yours

When Melanie returned from Abbazia, she found that Melitta had been ill for some time—news her mother had neglected to tell her. Melanie then took Melitta to Rosenberg in an attempt to restore her to health. In her absence Libussa had become the chatelaine of the household, in *loco uxoris*. She was hostess at a luncheon, the success of which she recounted with great gusto to her daughter. But "surely" Arthur had told her about it? The guests expressed astonishment that she was able to produce an elaborate meal at short notice—proof of the household skills she had neglected to teach her daughter.* With wifely pride, she recounted how the general manager of the chain of paper mills praised Arthur's transformation of the dilapidated Krappitz factory into a thriving business. "When he left G. [the manager] said to Arthur that he found it difficult to part from a place where he had enjoyed himself so much."

Meanwhile, Libussa prescribed the daily regimen for Melitta by post. For the first time there are indications that her care had not been as perfect as she had boasted. "Give her nourishing food so that the poor child will recover her strength. If we had applied this treatment systematically her illness would not have lasted so long, and she would not have gone downhill like that."

Despite her avowals of not wishing to spoil a minute of her daughter's visit,

---

* Libussa describes the "simple lunch" she prepared as consisting of "chicken fricassee with small dumplings, lung pot-roast with artichokes, baby carrots, beans, rice, cucumber salad, three different kinds of compote and strudel."

Libussa, within four days of Melanie's arrival in Rosenberg, sent her a hysterical outpouring of hatred against Emilie. It would appear that Leo, until now regarded by the family as the ideal of manhood, had accused his wife of plunging their family into financial ruin by her extravagance. Worse still, Emilie was conducting an adulterous affair with a young man whom she met on her occasional visits to Arthur's stepsister, Iren Kurtz, and her husband. (The Kurtzes, too, according to Leo, were on the brink of disaster because of Iren's extravagance.) Forgetting the kindness Iren had shown her in the summer of 1904, Libussa immediately accepted Leo's version of events without even giving her daughter a chance to defend herself. Emilie pleaded that she could not bear becoming the object of Libussa's and Melanie's hatred, but Libussa was inflexible. How dare Emilie create a situation that disturbed the serene family network she had so assiduously established?

Libussa then gave her younger daughter instructions about the letter she should write to Emilie: Melanie must urge her to break off her friendship with a woman who was encouraging her in her extravagances, and leading her into "moral and financial ruin." Her mother advised Melanie to quote from a letter she was supposed to have received from her, Libussa: "Is it possible that peace and quiet will establish itself in a marriage where there are so many accusations, so much indifference and hatred, and so little respect for each other?" She must emphasize that Mama had no intention of setting foot in Emilie's house again until she was assured that Emilie had made a real effort to mend her ways. Libussa was by now so carried away that she dictated the exact words Melanie must write: "Unfortunately I can only agree with Mama, as I share her view. And you do know that I have always been an upright person and have never known lies and disingenuousness. May our ways part forever: the life and peace of my mother is, next to my husband and children, the most important thing to me on earth. Hence I will no longer have her exposed to such excitement, and consequently I cannot encourage her to write to you."

Libussa then calmly returned to the basic facts of domestic life with which she felt most comfortable: "There is nothing new with us. I have nearly finished potting the eggs. You can bring with you raspberry juice, apricots and other fruit as we have nothing here for jams." In her own eyes, she had no need to feel anything but self-righteous, as the statement that immediately follows this passage indicates: "It just occurred to me that for everybody there will be his punishment. I am becoming religious again."

Completely dominated as Melanie was by her mother, she probably did send some such letter to her sister. In a letter of late August 1908, Libussa wrote:

That I got those letters to Vienna done—after that, you know what I mean, exchange—I owe only to your support. May God grant that everything will take a turn for the better—including the shop—so that I will, finally, be relieved from these great worries. I am very curious what you will be like when you come back!—whether you will be relaxed and not tense and nervous, whether the children will look well. Arthur is in good spirits. The time he spent in the Engadine* has done wonders for him.

In view of later events, Melanie Klein must have felt profoundly uneasy—even though at the time she believed her mother's story—at having allowed herself to be manipulated into condemning her sister.

In late September a morally superior Libussa condescended to visit the unhappy household in Vienna. She described the drudgery of Emilie's life, concluding smugly: "On principle, I will not help her—I think to myself: Well, let her toil." Her indifference to one daughter in contrast to her indulgent concern for her favorite is astounding. Even the penny-pinching details of their life failed to alert Libussa to the possibility of her having been mistaken in her interpretation of the facts. Leo was withdrawn and taciturn, Emilie economizing to the point of poverty.

Finally, at the beginning of October, Libussa reported to Melanie that she and Emilie had had a conversation in which the true facts of the relationship began to emerge: Leo completely ignored his wife and spent his leisure time reading, often refusing to reply to her remarks. After the drudgery of the week, all Emilie wanted was rest and change on Sunday, which she sought in visits to her married friends. But without, it would seem, absorbing the implications of what Emilie had told her, Libussa then returned to matters that she clearly found of greater interest: "The day before yesterday I went with your muff into town. This season one wears smooth and larger muffs, made of one type of fur only."

As for Melanie, she was becoming more entrapped than ever in her depressions, especially when her mother was visiting her. By May 1909 her fits of weeping and despair had reached such a point that she went to a sanatorium in Chur, Switzerland, for two and a half months in order to have a complete rest and change of scene. Libussa, again in charge of the situation, described Arthur as finding the situation "unbearable" until he would be able to join Melanie during his holiday in July. Significantly, however, all news of Arthur's feelings and activities was transmitted to Melanie through Libussa, not by Arthur himself.

From Chur, Melanie reported that her appetite had improved and that she was eating well. In June she moved to St. Moritz; and her mother became extremely concerned over the dramatic deterioration in her condition. Melanie had a bladder complaint and wanted to be examined only by a woman doctor.

---

* Apparently he went off on a holiday (or a "cure") on his own while Melanie was in Rosenberg with the children.

On June 6, 1909, Libussa wrote her a letter that throws some light on the situation:

> What on earth is it that makes you again so despondent and nervous? Is it the weather? . . . Or is it your bladder? Or rather your fear of another pregnancy? . . . You must not lose courage! Just remember the mental state you were in when you were pregnant with Hans, what had gone on before and what you went through—and what a marvelous child he has become! Everything concerning Arthur has changed for the better now so that you will be the happiest wife and mother when your nerves are cured. One has to put up with all those little mosquito bites and vexations of life without getting upset. We should look upon them as the darkness without which there can be no light. Look how much Arthur has changed! I, myself, would not believe it if I did not see it with my own eyes. I always knew that his love for you is boundless and that he is totally absorbed in you. But it is the very nature of his love that makes a completely different man out of him—in other words: that changes him entirely and makes him into what you have always longed for. . . . Real rest and relaxation come only if one can live without any excitement, even pleasant excitement, in complete solitude and spend the day equably—although in boredom. Living with other people, even with one's nearest and dearest such as husband, child, and mother, always brings excitement with it. Dr. Lear said laughingly: "If I had a say in the matter, I would prescribe that Dr. Klein go anywhere but where his wife is. The best cure for afflicted nerves is some weeks of solitude." I am, however, very astonished if you are really pregnant and have not been sick yet. I seem to remember that, right from the beginning, you suffered badly with Melitta and Hans. Can it be that it is only anemia, after all?

Quite clearly, Melanie dreaded pregnancy; and her mother used this fear to separate her from Arthur as much as possible. Melanie could not have been altogether blind to Libussa's machinations. Was her mother going to punish her through the instrument of Arthur's penis? By becoming pregnant, her nerves would disintegrate, Libussa's stomach complaints would return, and her guilt at robbing her mother of something that did not rightfully belong to her would be intensified. It is a chilling conclusion that Libussa did not want her daughter to be happy, that she did not want her to find fulfillment, that she begrudged her the enjoyments of which she herself was deprived when she was young. One remembers that when Melanie was a small girl her mother had told her that she was a surprise—that is, unwanted. It is not at all unlikely that she was subtly emphasizing that no man could love her, either her father, her husband, or anyone else. Perhaps it was Libussa herself who had told her that Emilie was her father's favorite. Libussa had been in fierce competition with Melanie over Emanuel. According to Libussa, Arthur blossomed when she was away, the children were much better off without her, and her own mother needed the absence in order to achieve serenity. Melanie was a pampered object, not a loved daughter, but a lap dog who had been taught to sit up and beg and to lie down passively.

Toward the end of the summer of 1909, Arthur was transferred to another small Silesian town, Hermanetz. By now, however, Melanie's complaints had become so vociferous that he realized his wife would be totally incapacitated if she were confined for the rest of her life to a small town. With his excellent professional record, Arthur had no difficulty in obtaining a transfer to Budapest. At this point it seems to have been decided that Libussa would come to live with them permanently. In a letter dated November 3, 1909, on the eve of Libussa's departure from Vienna, she complains of being totally exhausted after supervising the removal of her belongings. At the time Melanie was with the children in Rosenberg. Incidentally, there is a suggestion in one of Libussa's letters that she hated small towns as well, so she may have contributed to the unhappy situation.

There are no extant letters from 1910. Libussa may have been with them in Budapest, or the letters simply may have been lost; but it is also possible that Klein destroyed them because she wanted to erase the year from her life. The Kleins took a flat in Svabhegy, a smart suburb of Budapest, until they found a more suitable place. In the summers of 1910 and 1911 Melanie and Klara went off on holiday to Rügen, a Baltic resort north of Berlin. On August 8, 1911, Libussa wrote to Melanie, who was staying in Hermanetz with Klara on their return from Rügen during the renovation of a larger apartment to which the Kleins were moving. Libussa assured her daughter of the wisdom of what she was doing: "Did I not see with my own eyes that the nerve-wracking excitements caused by the troublesome servants, every day and every hour, made you really sick? The usual outcome of this is that you have to withdraw for months, if not longer." That Melanie had real cause for worry when the children were left with Libussa is reflected in the fact that Hans suffered from pustules, rashes, and eczema, and even his doting grandmother could not control him when he displayed "an itching for squeezing, pinching, biting and hitting."

The combination of Libussa and Melanie in the same house created disaster. Two strong wills were pitted against each other; and it is not inconceivable that by now Klara was giving Melanie the confidence to assert herself. Mother and daughter were constantly at odds over the upbringing of the children and the management of the household. Melanie disapproved of her mother's easygoing ways with the domestic help. "If only I need not fear that you will be standing there and watching and will get terribly worked up about every little thing that is not to your taste," Libussa remarked in the same letter. Melanie was beginning to assert her dominance in the household. Apparently this time it was Libussa who had the more serious breakdown and was sent to Karlsbad for the "cure." There would certainly have been letters exchanged between mother and daughter during this period; and they may not have survived because Melanie felt responsible for her mother's collapse.

While Melanie Klein eventually faced the force of her own phantasy* life, she could never come to terms with the reality of her mother. She never experienced what she probably needed: a woman analyst capable of interpreting her fear, hatred, and guilt about her mother. Years later, shortly before her death, she said to her analysand Clare Winnicott, "There's no use your talking about your mother. She's dead, and there's nothing you can do about it." At the time she made this remark she was writing her Autobiography, in which Libussa is idealized beyond recognition. Was this Melanie's defense against the metaphysical despair she felt at having no way now to make reparation to the long-dead Libussa? And yet, the last sentence of "Love, Guilt and Reparation" (1937) reads: "If we have become able, deep in our unconscious minds, to clear our feelings to some extent towards our parents of grievances, and have forgiven them for the frustrations we had to bear, then we can be at peace with ourselves and are able to love others in the true sense of the word."

In 1910 Melanie's defense was to find a mentor with whom Libussa could not compete. She had also found a woman in whom she could confide the secrets of her heart. Klara, ten years older than Melanie, was the sort of person who invited confidences as she was the soul of discretion. She was renowned for her excellent housekeeping and gourmet cooking, and Jolan's daughter, Maria Fazekas, remembers her as having "an exceptionally sweet disposition, always good-humored, ready for a joke and a good laugh." She was a beautiful woman with jet-black hair, large blue eyes, and a heart-shaped face. She could have understood Melanie's fixation on Emanuel, as she and her own brother Gyula were unusually close. To Melanie she also represented emancipation, because she had actually been divorced.

On September 18, 1911, in a letter to Melanie, Libussa expressed relief that Melanie's health seemed much improved. She also proposed to ask Klara to go shoppiing with her to advise her on purchases for the children. Libussa was beginning to realize that she was no longer indispensable.

---

* In Kleinian terminology, "phantasy" denotes an unconscious process, while "fantasy" refers to a conscious (or pre-conscious) daydream.

CHAPTER FOUR

Crisis

One of the most persuasive arguments Melanie used to induce Arthur to settle in Budapest was the presence there of his charming relatives: Uncle Samu and Aunt Riza (his mother's sister); his own sister, Jolanthe; her husband, Gyula Vágó; and his sister Klara and his eight other brothers and sisters. Jolan had married Gyula in 1906 and moved to the capital, where Vágó was manager of a factory that made hats and exported fezzes to Montenegro. Arthur knew that Melanie blossomed in Jolan's stimulating company and in the serenity imparted to her by Klara. A close-knit group, the Vágós symbolized for Melanie Klein the ideal family she had always fantasized.

In the middle of August 1911 the family moved to a prosperous area of the city known as Rozsdamb ("hill of roses"). Budapest seemed more glamorous than staid Vienna. It was pervaded with intellectual vitality—café life, concerts, theater, opera, and bookstores. In 1909 Sergei Diaghilev had taken what was to be his Ballets Russes out of Russia for the first time, and his dancers appeared in Budapest before proceeding to Paris. All this world lay ahead for Melanie Klein, but her problems were too deep-rooted to be improved suddenly by a mere change of scene.

During a visit to Vienna at the beginning of 1911, Libussa continued her attempts to enmesh Melanie and Arthur in the problems of their Viennese relatives. Naturally there was a stream of reports on what seemed marital chaos in contrast to the Kleins' idealized marriage. The misconception had been partly invented by Libussa herself, who had put leading questions to her grandson, Otto: she extracted from him an account of family rows that she then embroidered with sordid implications.

Libussa finally acknowledged that she and Melanie had been misjudging Emilie, whose life had been a silent martyrdom for years and whose occasional visits to Iren and her husband provided her only escape from the morose Leo. Emilie's "mad passion" for their friend had been entirely platonic. Leo was so morbidly jealous that once, years before, upon catching a glimpse of Emilie and Emanuel playing with Otto in his cradle, he had begun to harbor a suspicion that Emanuel was the child's father. He would not allow his wife to help him in his dental surgery, out of fear that her presence might encourage an affair with his assistant. Everyone except Libussa's sister, Karoline, had accepted Leo's version of the story, especially as they had been taken in by "his patient look and martyred expression," as Libussa described it. Despite Leo's prospering dental practice, the Picks were living in straitened circumstances, and everyone had blamed this on Emilie's supposedly wild and impulsive spending, even though there seemed to be little to show for her inexplicable extravagance. Arthur had on this account been persuaded to lend Leo money. However, Libussa now learned that since 1905 Leo had been a compulsive gambler and had run up immense debts. As she had spent a large part of the past nine and a half years in the same household, it seems incredible that she could have so blinded herself to the true state of affairs. The shock of Emanuel's gambling away all his money at Montreux had, it would seem, rendered her incapable of facing the situation, until it became so critical that Leo had to confess to her when faced with repaying some of his loans. She was also extremely angry because he had written a play depicting the family situation, and apparently she was not assigned the role of heroine. She ignored Emilie's cries that she should not have been made to marry such a monster; and it never occurred to Libussa that she was the instigator of the family's problems by having persuaded a reluctant Leo to take over the dental practice, a profession in which he had not the slightest interest.

"One thing I do know," Libussa wrote to Melanie and Arthur on February 6, 1911,

we have done Emilie a grave injustice. Although she is guilty on the one hand because of her pleasure-seeking and because of her shallow character and her indolence, she has been, on the other hand, the victim of a person who is malicious to the point of cruelty. His behavior springs from a pathological jealousy that often works itself up into sheer madness. What he says and communicates are the delusions of his morbid fantasies. Thus he knows no limits, and he cannot distinguish between right and wrong, truth and slander—and with that he tortures his victim to death and ruins her reputation, mercilessly gloating over her torments, and the reason for that is that he still loves her as intensely as in their first years of marriage.

You will be beside yourself because I have changed my opinion of Emilie, and you will not believe me as there are also other witnesses, like Otto, who have spoken against her—and also because she did not want to give up that friendship. But all these events were so entangled at the time! Leo had made terrible scenes which were overheard by the child and the maid. In the presence of the child and the maid he had talked about a lover and divorce, as he still does.

Why did Melanie adopt such an intransigently judgmental attitude toward her sister, unless she envied Emilie for seeming to have the fulfilled emotional life that she herself craved, as well as—in the face of all her troubles—a certain serenity? More fundamentally, she still retained the envy of a powerless baby sister. Melanie Klein was an embodiment of her own later theories: the world is not an objective reality, but a phantasmagoria peopled with our own fears and desires.

In 1911 and 1912 elaborate renovations were made to the house in Vienna—all of which had to be supervised by Libussa, whose letters refer plaintively to the confusion and exhaustion she was experiencing. On May 29, 1912, Libussa wrote from Vienna that she was glad that Arthur and the children were well, but "as far as you are concerned I read a lot of tiredness and exhaustion between your lines. I can easily understand because you are so absorbed in the housework and also have to devote your time to your guests. It makes me worry to think how much work you still have to do with putting away the winter things and the carpets—and that you have to do all that alone, for I cannot yet see an end of the work on the house here. And I do not know either when I can come back." Could Arthur possibly give her two months' advance on her allowance as the money was dwindling away? And was Melanie still playing tennis?

On June 10, 1912, Melanie sent her mother directions for Libussa's return to Budapest—to look after the children while she and Klara went on holiday to Rügen—in a remarkably calm letter from a woman whose mother depicted her as a permanent neurasthenic.

Dear Mama,

Do not be cross with me because I am not writing more, but I really have a lot to do. Although I have simplified my shopping very much there is still plenty that keeps me busy. With Klara I bought a lovely little voile dress and a dressing gown in white and red, both ready-made, and everything very good and cheap. I have packed away all the winter things apart from the carpets. This week I am having a go at the carpets, and it is also time that I started on my preparations for the journey. We have fixed the 24th for our departure and we must stick by it because we have to book the sleeping car tickets in advance. So, dear Mama, you must make your arrangements accordingly so that you can be here at the latest 2–3 days before our departure.

We have already had quite hot days here. I am now in the habit of going for walks with Arthur every evening, which I find very pleasant. Arthur is going on the 19th or 20th to Braila, so he will not be back when we leave.

We will go directly to Berlin and from there to the Baltic Sea. On my return journey at the end of August I want to stop for a few weeks in Rosenberg.

I shall send you in the next few days the 300 crowns for Emilie and the 70 crowns for you which were still in Pest.

We are all fine. Melitta's school finishes on the 15th, which means that we still can make a few outings with them. I will have finished my treatment in twelve days. I feel actually quite healthy and now I must keep it up and, I hope, I will.

To all of you, affectionate kisses.

Yours

Melanie

A letter of Libussa's dated August 22, 1911, written just before the Kleins moved into the large flat in Budapest, had expressed her relief at Arthur and Melanie's agreeing with her at last that Melanie's health problems stemmed from nerves. "If you have finally arrived at the insight that attaining your health is the most important thing, everything else is of secondary importance and your illness can really be tackled. . . . [In Budapest] we will ask the best and most noted specialist for nerves to come to us for a house visit so that everything can be discussed and he can examine you thoroughly (not like that doctor who made the ten telephone calls during one consultation). And what he says should be done will be followed precisely." Melanie's letter of 1912 suggests that she had been receiving treatment from someone. A confidence— even contentment—infuses the letter. Her "treatment" was apparently doing her good; but the fact that she seemed to be running her household without any panic suggests that in Libussa's presence she reverted to being a little girl again, totally dependent upon mama, a state that left her demoralized and suffocated in depression.

Evening walks with Arthur indicate the possibility of an amiable relationship; but with the return of Libussa, both of them sank back into their self-absorbed neuroses, in the hands of the seemingly indestructible woman who continued to shuttle between the two households—which, in her view, were incapable of functioning without her controlling hand. With the outbreak of war in 1914, Libussa was permanently confined to the Klein household in Budapest.

The war actually made little difference in the Hungarian capital, where the well-to-do were still able to obtain all the necessities, even luxuries, of life. When Arthur was called up to serve in the Austro-Hungarian Army in late 1914, life continued much as before. However, it was a totally different situation in Vienna, where Emilie suffered great deprivations after Leo was conscripted. In her Autobiography, Klein seems irritated by the recollection of her mother's anxiety over Leo's safety while he was stationed in the Premsyl fortress. Libussa had reason to be worried, because when the fortress fell, Leo was captured by the Russians and taken as a prisoner of war to Siberia, where he remained for four years.

According to Hertha Pick, who married Emilie's younger son, Willy Pick, her mother-in-law was wont to say that this was the happiest period of her life. Emilie demonstrated that she was a very resourceful woman—with both Libussa and Leo out of the way. She hired a dental assistant to look after the patients and, instead of charging them money for work done, established a barter system of clothes and groceries, although she still had to find cash to pay for utilities. All the women in the family proved extremely resilient when the circumstances warranted it.

Melanie's recovery of 1912 was short-lived; 1913 and 1914 were years of incredible tension. By Christmas of 1913 she realized that she was pregnant. Considering her panic when she feared she was pregnant in 1909, she could hardly have reacted with pleasure to having another child when she was over thirty. And now Libussa was no longer the tower of strength upon whom she could always count. Erich was born on July 1, 1914. Libussa obviously enjoyed the baby, but she was growing thin and listless. Melanie had a wet nurse "due to circumstances which I might mention later"—which she fails to do. The woman "behaved very badly and terrorized the whole house." Her mother advised her to accept the whole situation silently and have the baby fed for only nine or ten months!

In late October, Arthur and Melanie took Libussa to a clinic to be X-rayed. The room in which she was examined was icy-cold. One of the assistants assured them that there was no sign of cancer, but suggested that they return in a few months for another examination. In Klein's later view, her mother's dramatic loss of weight was an unmistakable sign that she indeed had cancer. Klein never forgot their return to the flat, Libussa and Arthur plodding up the hill in front, herself slightly behind, choking back tears. Libussa almost immediately came down with bronchitis, which she attributed to the cold room in which she had been examined. They soon realized that she was dying, and Klein recalled being tormented "with a certain feeling of guilt that I might have done more for her, and we know that such feelings exist. I knelt down by her bed and asked her forgiveness. She replied that I should have at least as much to forgive her as she to forgive me. Then she said, 'Don't grieve, don't mourn, but remember me with love.' " On November 6th she was dead.

I did not imagine that one could die in such a serene way, completely without anxiety and regret, no accusations against anyone, and friendliness towards my sister, though there she did actually have cause for complaint. But I never heard her complain about my sister in the preceding years and everything she had left from the pocket money my husband gave her she sent to my sister, who needed it. She has in many ways remained my example and I remember the tolerance she had towards people. . . .

This description in her Autobiography of her mother's last days is so out of keeping with the bossy, pedestrian, petite bourgeoise of the correspondence that one is inclined to speculate whether the touching death-bed scene was fantasized reparation on Klein's part.

Melanie nursed her mother for the first couple of weeks of her illness, but during the last week they called in a nurse. Libussa's only complaint was that she was too strict. Seeing how it distressed Melanie that she was becoming so weak, Libussa told her that she would take some gruel, and, writes Melanie, "being an excellent cook, she told me how to make a chicken broth and forced herself to eat it. It was quite obvious that she attempted to go on living for my sake."

At last the spoiled darling of the family had to look after her oversolicitous mother, and she was incapable of the task. Libussa had assigned her the role of pampered baby, and Melanie had paid a terrible price for it. She could be given the world so long as she did exactly what her mother told her. Libussa reinforced her infantile fear of abandonment by emphasizing that without her mother she was not viable, and this terror was confirmed by her mother's death. Was she now being punished because her mother had overworked herself on her behalf? Rather than face the implications of her grief, in her Autobiography Melanie turns immediately to a peevish diatribe about her sister's ignoble death in contrast to that of their mother. Until her dying day, Melanie could not forgive Emilie for being their father's favorite.

Until 1914 most of our information about Melanie Klein comes from Libussa's letters, written either from Vienna or when she was supervising the Klein household while her daughter was away on her frequent and fruitless quests for serenity. Klein's state of mind in the six years following her mother's death is contained in a collection of some thirty poems, various prose fragments and sketches, and four completed narratives. Since few of these literary works are dated, it is impossible to establish a chronological order for them. However, we can assume that they were written in the seven years between

1913 (the earliest dated one) and the summer of 1920 (the last). Both poetry and prose are variations on a single theme: the longing of a woman for a richer and fuller life, particularly for sexual gratification, and the conflict that is stirred up by these forbidden wishes. The poetry is derivative, and the prose long-winded; but Klein's translator, Bruni Schling, believes that her writings exhibit considerable creative sensitivity, and their echoes from various poets are a reflection of her wide reading. According to Schling, "In spite of their confessional character they are never embarrassing and they never ring false. What lifts the stories and poems above the level of woman's magazine stuff is their absolute sincerity, their soul-searching honesty, and the genuine expression of a tortured mind."

Schling finds Klein's expressionist erotic poetry reminiscent of that of Else Lasker-Schüler (1869–1954), the high priestess of love poetry in the German language, whose first volume of poetry, Styx, was published in 1902 in Berlin, where she lived until fleeing to Switzerland in 1934 (she eventually emigrated to Israel). Incidentally, one of her greatest admirers was Karl Kraus. It is not at all unlikely that Klein modeled her poetry on that of Lasker-Schüler.

The family correspondence between 1901 and 1912 records Klein's increasing depression, the cause of which baffled her obtuse mother and her rigid husband, to whom she once tried to open her heart when he visited her in Abbazia. Klein's literary experiments undoubtedly served as an expression of her frustrated oscillation between a longing for a fuller life and a constant endeavor to come to terms with the reality of her existence. They are written in a stream-of-consciousness narrative, not unlike that of Arthur Schnitzler and James Joyce, who were writing at the same time. The death wish is often as strong as her hunger for life, offering a release from her sufferings. One undated draft describes a woman's state of mind when she wakes up in a hospital from a deep coma, the implication being that she had attempted to take her life.* Her intense sexuality is experienced as something both precious and forbidden, the cause of her suffering: ". . . you live through your desire and die of the disgust at fulfillment." Sublimation is an alternative to fulfillment as she describes it in an allegory, "Spring" (1916). Spring is personified as a cheerful, harmless companion during the day, but at night he is transformed into a demonic and sensuous seducer from whom the poetic persona flees, seeking rescue from her own desires in the arms of Night, who turns out to be in collusion with Spring. "When a Garden Gate Opens," a brief, undated story, is also the account of a spring evening in which a strolling woman encounters a man who gazes ardently at her, but after turning away from him coldly, she is filled with an undefinable sadness, "as if something beautiful which I had lost and found again, was lost once more."

---

* The model for this would have been Emanuel's former lover who tried to take her life in Milan in 1902.

Schling is convinced from the graphic sexual detail of the poems written in 1914 (and typed out in 1920)* that she did find love outside marriage in 1913 or 1914. One, specifically dated 1914, is typical of the descriptions of passionate lovemaking:

> You are close to me, my hand shelters
> In yours. My body firmly pressed against yours.
> My mouth sucked on to yours—
> We are one inseparable being.
>
> Is it your heartbeat, is it mine, which I feel?
> Is that which sounds and surges in my blood
> Not an echo from your blood?
> There is no me, no you. Blessed are the borders.
>
> Deeply sunk away like the entire world
> Is what has ever separated us.—And until
> The sweet miracle renews itself, and dreaming
> Is devoured too by the fire—flood of lust,
> I dream that we are, were and will be—forever one.

Another, dated March 1914, is about a dream of her dead brother. She pleads with him to stay with her, but the wraith vanishes and she is left with emptiness. The four completed stories describe the disappointment the protagonist experiences from life and marriage, and either the agony of denial or the guilt of fulfillment. The only dated story, "Finale" (1913), is presumably written by a woman on her deathbed to a man to whom she confesses her desire and begs for one last hour together. Her longing for him is not only sexual but the yearning for a kind and understanding being who will respond to the needs of her heart, unlike her husband, who has killed her budding love for him by his insensitivity.

The longest story, "Life Calls," is the story of a frustrated, guilt-ridden wife who is reflecting upon her life from a Riviera resort where she has been sent to recover from her nerves. She tries to pour out her innermost feelings to her husband when he visits her, but he rebuffs her; and, trying to repress the pain of their lack of communication, she determines to return and take up the role of dutiful wife. However, her tranquillity is short-lived when her husband commissions a young artist, Georg, to paint her portrait. Georg understands her secret longings and they become lovers. In his arms she experiences all that she has ever fantasized. She feels no guilt, but rather defiance now that she realizes that her husband has cheated her of life itself. The completed portrait is of a woman awakened to life.

* The fact that they were later typed out neatly may indicate that she had contemplated having them published.

However, art is more important to Georg than any relationship, and he deserts her. She would have been prepared to sacrifice everything in life for him except her child, Gerti (who is four, exactly Melitta's age when Melanie stayed in Abbazia in 1908). She even contemplates ways of committing suicide, but life asserts itself too strongly. Georg's "energetic lips that are not at all ugly" are remarkably similar to those of Emanuel, who also sacrificed human relationships to his "art," and for whom the Mediterranean was idealized as the great source of inspiration. Moreover, the narrator addresses her lover as "dear friend" in the way Melanie addressed Emanuel in her last letters to him—a form of address to which he took great umbrage.

There is another personal reference. In her Autobiography, Klein speaks of a friend of her brother's who helped tutor her in geometry, a subject she did not like. "He fell deeply in love with me and at the time I also had opportunities of meeting a few other young men, and when I was seventeen, I met my future fiancé. At that time, there were actually four young men in love with me, all of whom I know would have wished to marry me." In the story the narrator recalls attending a Wagner performance in her teens. She feels the eyes of one of her admirers, Wilsky, resting longingly on her, and as he moves towards her, because she feels incapable of "cutting off this incomprehensible, frighteningly sweet contact," she determinedly moves away from him. Soon afterwards her father dies, so that she has to withdraw from social life. When she meets Wilsky again she is engaged to be married, and she remembers the thrill it gave her to see the suffering in his eyes. Then there is the incident of a young officer watching her on a tram. She recalls, too, her first ball, where she was a sensational success (Emanuel had made a jealous reference to the cavalry officers stationed in Rosenberg). The narrator of the story has a recurrent dream: she is kidnapped half-naked by masked men, who turn out to be Wilsky and the officer:

> Then the dream got blurred. And suddenly she was standing before the Tsar, accused of revolutionary activities—together with Wilsky. They were accused of having committed a serious crime together. And they were sentenced to terrible tortures from which she was saved by waking up.

The last story, untitled and lacking a date, has as its theme the unfaithful wife from the perspective of the abandoned husband. Alfred (=Arthur) Weber did nothing to prevent his wife from leaving him for another man. Yet, after three chance encounters, Alfred begins at last to understand why Marianne (=Melanie) fled. He suddenly remembers the agonized expression that she so often turned to him. Too late he realizes that he cannot face life without her and shoots himself.

A little sketch of 1916 describes the feelings of a woman keeping vigil by her dead husband's side. Instead of grief, she experiences, to her great surprise, triumph. His death has liberated her from a life of enslavement. A poem, "Dirge," obviously based on this sketch, is even more intense in its tone of hatred. In another undated poem, a woman resolves to leave her husband for another man. After persistent entreaties, she returns to see her child. She allows herself to be seduced by her husband, and on awakening is overwhelmed by the realization that she has destroyed her future: "never again will she find the courage to go—now that he is perhaps the father of a child conceived." One wonders if Klein ever made any attempt to leave Arthur while they were living in Budapest. There would have been no way she could have managed financially, but undoubtedly she wanted to break away from the marriage.

In these semifictional outpourings, Melanie's feelings of hostility towards Arthur are indisputable, and seem to be fused with unconscious hatred towards Libussa. It is possible that she found herself incapable of mourning Libussa's death and in consequence her emotional state became even more alarming. Idealization was a defense in repressing true feelings. It is extraordinary that in her seventies she could write: "My relation to my mother has been one of the great standbys of my life. I loved her deeply, admired her beauty, her intellect, her deep wish for knowledge, no doubt with some of the envy which exists in every daughter." And yet this was probably true of her ambivalent attitude.

"About 1914" she read Freud's 1901 paper on dreams (*Über den Traum*), and realized immediately that "that was what I was aiming at, at least during those years when I was so very keen to find what would satisfy me intellectually and emotionally. I entered into analysis with Ferenczi, who was the most outstanding Hungarian analyst." She gives no indication as to who advised her to read Freud or how she happened to meet Sándor Ferenczi. There is one known connection with Ferenczi: When Arthur moved to Budapest, among the numerous enterprises with which he became involved was a trade publication for the paper industry, *Deutsche Papierzeitung*, based in Berlin. This was edited by one of Ferenczi's brothers, from whom Arthur took over the editorship some years later.

On the other hand, it was in no way remarkable that she encountered Freud's work in Budapest, for from the beginning an enthusiastic group of Hungarian intellectuals were receptive to psychoanalysis. Budapest was the small capital of a small country, and ideas that were the *dernier cri* were discussed in circles where people were constantly meeting each other.

When Melanie Klein met Ferenczi, he had for some years been the closest of Freud's associates and held a distinguished position in Budapest society. His father, Moriz, like Melanie's, had emigrated from Galicia. In Hungary he established a bookstore and lending library. Ferenczi studied medicine in Vienna (born in 1873, he had just missed Emanuel at medical school). He became greatly interested in nervous diseases and, like the early Freud, fascinated by the possibility of using hypnosis to relieve hysterical symptoms. In 1905 he was appointed psychiatric expert to the Royal Court of Justice in Budapest.

When he first read Freud's *Interpretation of Dreams* he was repelled, but a further reading convinced him that here was a great breakthrough in an understanding of psychic forces, and in 1908 he wrote to Freud asking if he might come to Vienna to meet him.

Freud was captivated by Ferenczi's spontaneous charm and was soon referring to him as "my dear son." Ferenczi began to accompany him on his annual holidays, mountain-climbing and mushroom-picking, all the time engaged in endless discussions which Freud, in his obituary of Ferenczi, generously acknowledged as the germs from which their later papers developed. According to Ernest Jones, Freud would have liked Ferenczi to have married his daughter Anna. Freud admired the quickness and enthusiasm with which his disciple grasped his concepts and the tenacity with which he used his position to disseminate them. In 1908 Ferenczi gave a series of lectures on psychoanalysis to the Budapest Medical Association. During one lecture a colleague stood up and shouted that Freud's ideas were sheer pornography and that he should be under police surveillance.

In 1909 Ferenczi and Carl Jung accompanied Freud to America, where Freud lectured at Clark University. Each morning Ferenczi would accompany Freud on his walk, making suggestions for the lecture of the day. However, Ferenczi began to be regarded with suspicion by Freud's other associates, particularly by Ernest Jones, as the power behind the throne. At the Second International Congress for Psycho-Analysis in Nuremberg in 1910, Ferenczi proposed that the analysts organize themselves into an international association with centers in London, Vienna, Budapest, and Berlin, a scheme he and Freud had devised together. On May 19, 1913, he founded the Hungarian Psychoanalytical Society. Prior to this Sándor Radó (then only twenty) recalled joining Ferenczi every two or three weeks in group discussions on Freud's work. Freud sent every manuscript to Ferenczi before publishing it, so that to be a member of the colloquium was an enormous privilege. "This group got together almost like the early Christians in the catacombs. Nobody in the city knew what psychoanalysis was," Radó recalled years later.[2] As Radó describes his own supervisory sessions, they could not have been more casual, usually held in a café or coffeehouse.

The group at first consisted of only five charter members: Ferenczi as president; Radó as secretary; Dr. Stefan Hollós; Hugo Ignatus, a well-known writer; and Lajos Levy, the editor of the Hungarian medical journal, *Therapy*. From the beginning the meetings were extremely informal, and wives and other guests attended regularly. It is not improbable that Melanie Klein attended these meetings during 1914. (Perhaps Ferenczi was "the best nerve specialist" in Budapest whom she had begun to see regularly in 1912.)

During the summer of 1913, Jones, on the advice of Freud, stayed in Budapest to have the first training analysis under Ferenczi.* He returned to England to found the British Psycho-Analytical Society in October; and Ferenczi was later made an honorary member of the British Society because of his primacy in the field. On Jones's return to England, Ferenczi went to Vienna to be analyzed by Freud, just after the termination of Freud's analysis of the Wolf Man. The analysis was interrupted by the outbreak of war. In October 1914 Ferenczi was called up to serve as a doctor in the Hungarian Hussars, and for two years was stationed in Pápá, a small military town about eighty miles from the capital. The analysis continued by post, and Freud once visited him in Pápá. Ferenczi was able to send occasional parcels of cigars and food to the hungry Freud family in Vienna. In Pápá Ferenczi analyzed the company commander, who was suffering from shell shock—the first analysis on horseback, as he reported jokingly to Freud. He also spent his leisure time in translating Freud's *Three Essays on the Theory of Sexuality* into Hungarian. According to Weston La Barre, Géza Róheim was analyzed by Ferenczi in 1915 and 1916, which suggests that he visited Budapest occasionally and continued sporadic analyses while still stationed in Pápá. In 1916 he was transferred back to Budapest, where he was given charge of a neurological clinic.

On September 28 and 29, 1918, the Fifth Psycho-Analytic Congress was held in the hall of the Hungarian Academy of Sciences. All the men except Freud (accompanied by his daughter Anna) were in uniform. This wartime congress engendered great excitement and was attended not only by forty-two analysts, but by representatives of the Austrian, German, and Hungarian governments. Ferenczi, Karl Abraham, Max Eitingon, and Ernst Simmel had all done impressive work on war neuroses, and the authorities were interested in establishing clinics for veterans. It was a strangely festive affair when one considers the stage the war had reached, and an index of the isolated position of Budapest, which on this occasion Freud declared to be the center of the psychoanalytic movement. The plenary meetings were held at the new hotel, Gellert-furudo, the participants were overwhelmed with hospitality, and a Danube steamer was placed at their disposal. For the first time Melanie Klein saw Freud in person, when he presented "Lines of Advance in Psycho-Analytic Therapy" (the only time he was known to read a paper rather than deliver it extemporaneously). "I remember vividly," she recalled, "how impressed I was and how the wish to devote myself to psychoanalysis was strengthened by this impression."

Ferenczi was elected president of the International Psycho-Analytic Association, and the following month the students petitioned the rector of the university to invite him to give a course of lectures on psychoanalysis. The ground

---

* It is possible that Jones and Klein were being analyzed by Ferenczi at the same time.

floor of a house was donated as the headquarters for an institute by Mrs. Vilma Kóvacs, the mother of Alice Kóvacs, who later married Michael Balint. Most of the early Hungarian analysts grouped themselves in an analytic nest on a hill in Buda, Naphagy ("mountain of the sun"), just as the English analysts were to settle near one another in Hampstead. A wealthy benefactor, a brewer, Anton von Freund, endowed the new Society liberally as well as putting the Verlag, Freud's publishing house, on a solid basis. Freund's premature death in 1920 was a grievous blow to Freud.

Melanie Klein was a member of the Budapest Society during its brief period of splendor. The fact that her daughter Melitta at fifteen was allowed to attend meetings is an indication of its relaxed atmosphere. It is doubtful that Arthur Klein ever attended; his attitude towards psychoanalysis from the outset was critical. Invalided back to Budapest with a leg wound in 1916, he was put in charge of a depot. Klein had savored freedom for a year and a half, and she could no longer maintain the façade of the marriage.

At meetings Ferenczi was patriarchal in manner and would draw everyone into the discussion. Unlike Klein's practice in later life, there was no strict barrier between Ferenczi's private and public life, and his long courtship of a married woman was common knowledge. As for Klein's own analysis with Ferenczi, she says:

> Technique at this time was extremely different from what it is at present and the analysis of negative transference did not enter. I had a very strong positive transference and I feel that one should not underrate the effect of that, though, as we know, it can never do the whole job.

Klein entered analysis initially because of acute depression, intensified by the death of her mother. Ferenczi, according to Michael Balint, was "essentially a child all his life," and was "accepted as an equal, as a matter of course, by every child and the same was true with those unhappy children, his patients."[3] Ferenczi came increasingly to believe that if a patient was experiencing persecutory anxiety, it was the result of early deprivation of love. He later accused Freud of neglecting the negative transference in his own analysis, and in his 1919 paper,* Ferenczi is alert to the dangers of the positive transference. Those who were analyzed by Ferenczi—such as Sándor Lorand—have testified to his constant alertness to his patient—"his awareness of the bodily movements, positions, gesticulations, modulations of voice, and the like."[4] He treated his patient with gentleness and tenderness, as a deprived child craving attention. Ferenczi was the first analyst to observe and comment on an analysand's tendency to fall asleep during a session or to feel dizzy at its end. Such

---

* "Technical Difficulties in Analysis of a Case of Hysteria."

transfixed attention was undoubtedly craved by Klein after the long years in which she had had no one to whom to pour out her heart, and she in turn brought Ferenczi valuable material. Ferenczi sought within the analytic situation to duplicate the original trauma so that an identical emotional tension would be created. However, in Klein's case he seems to have been incapable of dealing with her positive transference. It would appear that her resistances were so strong that he was unable to penetrate her implacable defenses.

Freud was to admonish Ferenczi about the dangers of hugging and kissing his patients. At the Budapest Congress in 1918, Freud warned about the kind of analyst who "out of the fullness of his heart, perhaps, and his readiness to help, extends to the patient all that one human being may hope to receive from another."

> Their one aim is to make everything as pleasant as possible for the patient, so that he may feel well and be glad to take refuge there again from the trials of life. In so doing they make no attempt to give him more strength for facing life, and more capacity for carrying out his actual tasks in it.[5]

Freud was referring specifically to the Jungians, but it seems probable that he was already voicing unease about Ferenczi's "active" technique. In his pioneering days Freud socialized with his patients; but with the passing of the years he developed a more austere view of the patient-analyst relationship (with some exceptions, like the relationship with Marie Bonaparte). Ferenczi (and later Winnicott) accompanied patients on walks and on one occasion when he went on holiday, a patient followed him by car. ("It was a terrible holiday," comments Dr. T. F. Main.)[6]

Ferenczi's defenders contend that his use of the "active technique" has been greatly exaggerated. In his famous 1913 paper, "Stages in the Development of the Sense of Reality," which undoubtedly left a lasting impact on Klein's thought, Ferenczi argues that the child gains a sense of reality through the frustration of his omnipotent desires. The stage of omnipotence he termed the "introjection stage" and the reality stage the "projection stage," terminology and concepts Klein later borrowed, modified, and elaborated. In her theoretical papers she cites Abraham more frequently than Ferenczi, yet in her autobiographical notes she has far more to say about her first mentor.

> There is much that I have to thank Ferenczi for. One thing that he conveyed to me, and strengthened in me, was the conviction in the existence of the unconscious and its importance for mental life. I also enjoyed being in touch with somebody who was a man of unusual gifts. He had a streak of genius.

She was also indebted to Ferenczi for the importance he attached to primitive emotional life and for his description of symbolic activity in which the child "sees in the world nothing but images of his corporeality, on the other hand he learns to represent by means of his body the whole multifariousness of the outer world."[7] Freud was still speculating on the date of the termination of the pleasure principle in which the child achieves his final psychical detachment from his parents. This varies, according to Ferenczi, with the individual child, and he was not ready to commit himself to a sexual explanation. For Freud it was to be ultimately with the resolution of the Oedipus complex and the establishment of the superego at about the age of five. Klein eventually situated it at the age of four months, when the child works through what she was to call the depressive position. For all three, at whatever age it occurs, it means the beginning of the acceptance of the "otherness" of the parent, which in effect is the acceptance of reality.

In her Autobiography, Melanie Klein explained the origin of her lifework:

> During this analysis with Ferenczi, he drew my attention to my great gift for understanding children and my interest in them, and he very much encouraged my idea of devoting myself to analysis, particularly child-analysis. I had, of course, three children of my own at the time. . . . I had not found . . . that education . . . could cover the whole understanding of the personality and therefore have the influence one might wish it to have. I had always the feeling that behind was something with which I could not come to grips.

Ferenczi also encouraged other female colleagues to concentrate on child analysis—Ada Schott, and even Anna Freud. It seemed a suitable endeavor for a woman; and in Klein's case, it is possible that Ferenczi suggested the close observation of children to her as a means of approaching the heart of her own problems.

Ferenczi himself indicated the possibility of learning more about adult neuroses through the analysis of children when he published the case of a five-year-old boy, Arpád, whose case was reported to him by a former female patient. This he published in "A Little Chanticleer" in 1913. The child had developed a phobia about cocks after being reprimanded for masturbating. He exhibited sadistic behavior towards a slaughtered cock in the kitchen; after mutilating the pictures of birds in books, he would be very upset and want to bring the creatures back to life.

> If such symptoms were observed in an adult patient [Ferenczi concluded], the psycho-analyst would not hesitate to interpret the excessive love and hate concerning poultry as a transference of unconscious affects that really

referred to human beings, probably near relatives, but which were repressed and could only manifest themselves in this displaced, distorted way. He would further interpret the desire to pluck and blind the animals as symbolising castration intentions, and regard the whole syndrome as a reaction to the patient's fear of the idea of his own castration. The ambivalent attitude would then arouse in the analyst the suspicion that mutually contradictory feelings in the patient's mind were balancing each other, and on the basis of numerous experiential facts would have to surmise that this ambivalence probably referred to the father, who—although otherwise honoured and loved—had at the same time to be also hated on account of the sexual restrictions sternly imposed on him.[8]

Klein was still in analysis with Ferenczi in 1919.* Michael Balint recalled sitting in his reception room waiting to discuss a lecture he had heard him deliver at the university when the door of his private office opened and Klein emerged in tears. In a letter dated June 26, 1919, in which Ferenczi informed Freud that he was employing Anton von Freund in his clinic as well as privately, he introduced Melanie:

> The latest task I have assigned to him is to organize the psychoanalytical teaching in the "Association for Child-Research" which had turned to me with the request of finding them a psychoanalytical assistant. A woman, Frau Klein (not a medical doctor), who recently made some very good observations with children, after she had been taught by me for several years, is to assist him.[9]

Klein presented a case study of the "analysis" of a child to the Hungarian Society in July 1919,† after which she was immediately given membership—and without supervision, she later stressed. This paper was published the following year in the *Internationale Zeitschrift für Psychoanalyse* under the title "Der Familienroman in statu nascendi." The unusual aspect of the paper was that it was the analysis of her own son, Erich, whose identity was suppressed in later versions of the paper.

Melitta and Hans had been brought up largely under the supervision of Libussa; but once Klein discovered psychoanalysis, Erich was subjected to the most intense scrutiny from at least the age of three. There is no reference to his infancy, a curious omission in view of her later theories. This first paper sets out to illustrate the miraculous results obtained when a mother trains her child

---

* That year he gave her a photograph of himself inscribed "To Mela—my dear student."
† Freund was the only member of the Hungarian Society, besides Ferenczi, to whom Klein made any reference. She lamented his early death in her Autobiography: "I am sorry he died young—of cancer—I always felt that we would have been friends and he remains one of the good figures in my life." How the other members regarded her we do not know, apart from Balint's recollection that she was renowned as "the black beauty."

according to enlightened psychoanalytic views. The boy was obviously rather backward, a slow developer, although he had a phenomenal memory. At the time of the analysis he was five. He had always been healthy and strong, but had not started to talk until he was two and could not express himself coherently until he was three and a half. He did not recognize colors until he was four, and it was another six months before he could differentiate between yesterday, today, and tomorrow. At four and a half, his curiosity showed a marked increase and he asked persistent questions. He was reluctant to give up his belief in the Easter rabbit, and he was convinced that he had seen the devil in a field, even though his mother pointed out to him that it was a foal. (In later life she would have seized on the significance of his thinking that he had seen the devil.)

He also began to want to stay out in the garden all night with the neighboring "S. children." Sexual curiosity seemed to be aroused by his older brother and sister talking about events that had happened before his birth. "Where was I born?" he suddenly asked his mother. Klein explained to him that the child stays inside the mother until he is strong enough to exist on his own. The explanation of the process of birth did not interest him so much as the fact that he had apparently always existed. This having been settled, he then asked, "How is a person made?" Klein says that she gave him a detailed, fundamental explanation and told him that there were forty little eggs in the mother, and that such an egg developed into the embryo, etc. Does that mean that she described coitus to him? She continues:

> He seemed to understand and asked no more questions, behaving, however, oddly. As soon as I had started with the detailed explanation, he became distracted and somewhat embarrassed and started immediately to talk about something else; he was clearly eager to change the subject he himself had raised.[10]

He then tried a new tack. "And doesn't a child ever grow inside Papa?" This was the first time he had referred to the participation of the father, which would suggest that Klein had avoided a description of the sexual act. Erich did not pursue this line of inquiry with his mother, but later questioned his nanny, who told him that the stork brought children. Klein had given strict instructions that she was not to tell such stories, and as a result the nanny was dismissed.

A day or so later Erich told her that he was going to move to the landlady's and be a brother to the S. children, who believed in the Easter rabbit, Father Christmas, and angels. (He had already run away when he was two and a half, and was discovered looking into a clock shop.) His mother than asked him if she should take his friend Grete as her child instead, and after a struggle he replied affirmatively, something that surprised her very much, "since the extremely tender and loving child is normally very taken aback when there is only the threat that he might be loved less." He also told her that if she tried to prevent his leaving, he would run away and that he was sure that Frau S. would love him more than his mother did. Klein then told the S. family to make it clear to him that he could not stay with them. Consequently, when he turned up at suppertime, his mother acted as though she were very much surprised.

> "I do want to live only here," he said.
> "Have the S.s said anything?"
> "The children have said it was only a joke," replied Erich. I did not want to make the whole thing too easy for him and said mercilessly that I was going to talk to Frau S. myself—maybe she would then keep him. He had big tears in his eyes and said: "Even if she agrees, I don't want to live there." "Why?" I asked.—"Because I love you so much, Mama."
>
> Then I kissed and hugged him and he was very happy and said afterwards to the maid: "Mama was very sweet. You did not see it, but we kissed each other and are friends again." This seemed to be the end of the episode for him.

When an amended version of this paper appeared in *Imago* 7, 1921 (it was the translation of this version that appeared as the first paper in *Contributions to Psycho-Analysis*, 1948) she wrongly describes it as "a lecture delivered to the Hungarian Psycho-Analytic Society, July 1919. This paper was prepared for the press at that time, and I have left the remarks and inferences unchanged as they occurred to me then." She is quite clearly trying to divert attention from the original paper.

Both papers are amateurish, attempts to prove psychoanalysis an educational panacea. By not allowing the child to share the parental bedroom, by not imposing overstrict rules upon him and allowing him to develop at his own pace, and, above all, by answering all his questions, particularly those related to sex, the child, we are supposed to assume, developed into a "normal" five-year-old. Klein was particularly certain that she had overcome his omnipotent feelings by explaining to him that there was no God, no magic, no world of fairies—hence enabling him to accept reality. Such training laid "the foundations for a perfect uninhibited development of one's mind in every direction." "New vistas open before me," she exclaimed ecstatically, "when I compare my observations of this child's greatly enhanced mental powers under the influence of his newly acquired knowledge with previous observations and experiences in cases of more or less unfavourable developments."[11] This was probably the high point in Klein's own optimistic sense of omnipotence.

Anton von Freund was unimpressed. He told her that she had not in any

way touched the child's unconscious, and suggested that she set aside a prescribed time every day to analyze the boy. She then began interpreting his
dreams, his play, and his fantasies in as daring a way as she would have done
with an adult. Instead of the improvement she had claimed to have achieved
with the child, she now discovered that she had a very troubled little boy on
her hands—one who no longer questioned her constantly, who played fitfully,
and had lost interest in stories, particularly Grimm's frightening tales. He became increasingly withdrawn. Klein extracted from the child that he was voraciously curious about the contents of her belly. He told her of a game he played
with three motors, two large ones and a small one. One of the larger motors
gets on top of the other and the little one pushes itself between them. She then
interpreted this that "he has put himself between papa and mamma because
he would so much like to put papa away altogether and to remain alone with
his mamma and do with her what only papa is allowed to do."[12]

She was gradually beginning to realize that some primal anxiety, probably
but not necessarily connected with sex, was the problem to be uncovered. In
one of the notes pertaining to Erich, there is an account of the boy's reaction to
a fish that is very similar to Ferenczi's report of Arpád's fear of the cock in "A
Little Chanticleer."

> A child whom I knew showed at the age of fourteen months anxiety for the
> first time. It happened when he saw a fish with its head cut off hanging
> from the kitchen table. At first he regarded the fish with keen interest, but
> suddenly he showed signs of anxiety, screamed and ran out of the room.
> Yet soon after he came back, looked at the fish again, started screaming
> again and repeated the previous action. Since then it has been his first re-
> sponse upon entering the shop, when he accompanies his mother on her
> shopping trips, to run to the barrel of fish where he displays the same plea-
> surable interest that changes into anxiety as had happened before. Once he
> is in the shop he runs outside in order to return soon after and look at the
> fish again. Thus the fish, which he calls guish, has become his first anxiety
> object—and ever since then he has called everything that causes him anxi-
> ety by this name. He said for instance a few months ago when the noise of
> the shutters going down made him anxious: "Guish." The word also serves
> to discipline the lively and spoilt child on the spot. While his mother tells
> him: "The guish is coming," he immediately behaves well and settles to
> sleep—at other occasions too the word turns him at once into a good
> boy.[13]*

Both Ferenczi and Klein were on the verge of linking sex to some more en-
compassing primordial fear. Ferenczi, indeed, had told her that in his view the

* This incident is relegated to a footnote of a case "taken from direct observation" in *The Psycho-Analysis of
Children*, pp. 149–150.

sexual explanations she had given Erich had satisfied on the one hand his curiosity but on the other hand brought on some sort of internal conflict.

In the second version of the original paper, in which Erich is transformed into Fritz, the disguise is so feeble that it is incredible that anyone could ever have been taken in by it. Several commentators have already detected the parallels, yet when I mentioned the identity of Erich-Fritz to a number of English Kleinians, they expressed shock and dismay. One said that she had always had the impression that "the mother" in the background left something to be desired. Another said that he didn't know what name to apply to this kind of analysis, but it had nothing to do with mothering. A third confessed rather poignantly that the revelation would make him reexamine the work he had been doing for thirty years since he now saw in a new light why Melanie Klein had underestimated the role of the mother. Many analysts had heard for years a rumor that she had analyzed her own children, but they had not linked this with actual case histories she had recorded. Elliott Jaques seems to take a sensible view: the exploration of the roots of anxiety could have been conducted initially in the only way open to her, and it is hindsight that queries its value. Pearl King (not a Kleinian) feels that it could have established "a pathological transference"; but adds, "to be fair, everyone was doing it at that time."[14]

Was it analysis or wasn't it? The account in "The Development of a Child" does not suggest a regular hour of analysis, but prolonged observation of the boy's behavior in the course of the day, rather in the way the psychologist Jean Piaget observed his children. There are no references to Erich's playing with toys, behavior that she later used as the equivalent of free association. Eric Clyne remembers that when they went to Rosenberg—now Ružomberok, in the postwar republic of Czechoslovakia—in 1919, his mother set aside an hour every night before he went to sleep to analyze him and that she continued to do this after they moved to Berlin in 1920. He remarks dryly that he did not find the experience pleasurable, but he holds no grudge against her for it.

An interesting observation occurs in a letter written from Berlin by Alix Strachey to her husband, James (February 1, 1925), during a period in which she was becoming fascinated by Melanie Klein's work. Mrs. Strachey describes Hermine Hug-Hellmuth's recent book* as

a mess of sentimentality covering the old intention of dominating at least one human being—one's own child. I really believe a book like hers might do more harm than good. It gives parents and teachers a new leverage.

* *Neue Wege zum Verständnis der Jugend. Psychoanalytische Vorlesungen für Eltern, Lehrer, Enzieher, Kindergartnerinnen und Fürsorgerinnen (New Paths to the Understanding of Youth. Psychoanalytic Lectures for Parents, Teachers, Educators, Kindergarten Teachers, and Social Workers)*, Leipzig-Wein, Franz Deuticke, 1924.

Now they know that all children masturbate and have phantasies, and so on they'll be much sharper in detecting them and in general interfering (all for the best) with their private lives. Thank god Melanie is absolutely firm on this subject. She absolutely insists on keeping parental and educative influence apart from analysis and in reducing the former to its minimum, because the most she thinks it can do is to keep the child from actually poisoning itself on mushrooms, and to keep it reasonably clean, and teach it its lessons.[15]

It could be argued that Klein was more therapist than mother to Erich. He has no recollection of her playing with him, but she did hug him. The only toy he remembers is a harlequin doll Melitta once made for him. When asked what books his mother read to him, he replied, "I have no recollection of stories being read to me but do have a recollection of being familiar with Grimm,* Anderson, and the old-fashioned books like Strawwelpeter. When I started to read I read everything voraciously. However you must bear in mind that I am ancient and it is a very long time ago."[17]

He does have three very vivid early memories. The first is of being ill with scarlet fever in a darkened room, with everyone whispering and moving around as silently as possible. The second is of running away from home. Hans, his brother, caught sight of him from a tram and very kindly led him home. The third, when he was about three, is of soiling his pants at the dinner table and being absolutely terrified. His mother and Melitta made a great joke of it, and, he recalls, "the extremeness of my relief made it so memorable."

With time Klein seems almost to have come to believe that the child she analyzed was not her own son. In "The Psycho-Analytic Play Technique: Its History and Significance," which she contributed to *New Directions in Psycho-Analysis* (1955), she describes the case with clinical detachment:

My first patient was a five-year-old boy. I referred to him under the name "Fritz" in my earliest published paper. To begin with I thought it would be sufficient to influence the mother's attitude. I suggested that she should encourage the child to discuss freely with her the many unspoken questions which were obviously at the back of his mind and were impeding his intellectual development. This had a good effect, but his neurotic difficulties were not sufficiently alleviated and it was soon decided that I should psycho-analyse him. In doing so, I deviated from some of the rules so far established, for I interpreted what I thought to be most urgent in the material the child presented to me and found my interest focusing on his

---

* In a footnote to "The Development of a Child," Klein comments: "Before the analysis was started he had a strong dislike to Grimm's fairy-tales, which, when the change for the better set in, became a marked preference."[16]

anxieties and the defences against them. This new approach soon confronted me with serious problems. The anxieties I encountered when analysing this first case were very acute, and although I was strengthened in the belief that I was working on the right lines by observing the alleviation of anxiety again and again produced by my interpretations, I was at times perturbed by the intensity of the fresh anxieties which were being brought into the open.[18]

Undoubtedly Erich supplied her some insight into the origin and nature of anxiety, although, in keeping with accepted psychoanalytic thinking, she emphasizes his repression, not his anxiety. Freud did not reverse his view that repression causes anxiety until *Inhibitions, Symptoms, and Anxiety* in 1926. As a mother Klein probably found it difficult to come to the root of her child's anxiety, and was faced with the problem of deciding just how she was going to convey a fictional persona for herself. That she was concerned about her self-image is apparent in the second version when she omits the fact that the nanny had been dismissed for telling the child that storks brought babies. She also omits the reassuring hug she gave the boy after he returned from his experimental move to the other family. Had she already begun to make up her mind that there was some constitutional basis for his problems? In "The Development of a Child" she writes:

> . . . we learn from the analysis of neurotics that only a part of the injuries resulting from repression can be traced to wrong environmental or other prejudicial external conditions. Another and very important part is due to an attitude on the part of the child, present from the very tenderest years. The child frequently develops, on the basis of repression of a strong sexual curiosity, an unconquerable disinclination to everything sexual that only a thorough analysis can later overcome.[19]

Whatever judgments one may form about Melanie Klein's analysis of her own child, it should be remembered that Freud provided her with a prototype in the "Analysis of a Phobia in a Five-Year-Old Boy" (1909), the first published case of a child analysis. According to Freud, he saw the child only once, but supervised the case through the father. This man and his wife (who had been treated by Freud in the past) were firm adherents of Freud's views. Hans had always been a cheerful little boy until the age of three and three-quarters, when he developed a sudden fear of horses after seeing one fall down in the street. This phobia developed about nine months after the birth of a baby sister.

In the course of repeated questioning by his father, it emerged that the child exhibited all the manifestations of an Oedipus complex, suffered from castration fears, and was quite clearly aware of extragenital erotogenic zones in his body—aspects of infantile sexuality that Freud had adumbrated in *Three Essays on the Theory of Sexuality* in 1905. By bringing repressed material to light and by relating his phobia to his castration fear, the child's anxiety was alleviated; and far from viewing it as questionable procedure, Freud believed that the child would speak as freely as he did only because it was his father who was questioning him.

It was only because the authority of a father and of a physician were united in a single person, and because in him both affectionate care and scientific interest were combined, that it was possible in this one instance to apply the method to a use to which it would not otherwise have lent itself.[20]

It is impossible to speculate how Klein's thinking would have developed had she continued working with Freund and Ferenczi. In midsummer 1919, with the support of these two powerful figures behind her, her future within the Hungarian Society must have seemed assured. But then, with bewildering rapidity, everything changed. With the defeat of the Austro-Hungarian Empire, and the downfall of Count Michael Karolyi's government, Béla Kun, who had been converted to communism while a prisoner of war in Russia, set up a dictatorship of the proletariat in Hungary. The Bolsheviks, not yet recognizing psychoanalysis as a bourgeois deviation, installed Ferenczi as the first university professor of psychoanalysis. When Kun invaded Slovakia, a counterrevolution broke out, and a Rumanian army of intervention marched into the country. The Red Terror was followed by the violently anti-Semitic White Terror. The position of professional Jews became intolerable. Géza Róheim had to resign from the staff of the Ethnological Department of the Hungarian National Museum; for some time Ferenczi was afraid to venture into the street, and was expelled from the Medical Society of Budapest, of which he had been a distinguished member. Jews were barred from entering the universities, and they could not join the army's elite regiments except as quartermasters or doctors.

The political situation touched the Klein family as well. Twelve-year-old Hans found a cartridge case in the garden and, while examining it, was accosted by a soldier who tried to arrest him, releasing him only after expostulations by the cook. Arthur Klein could no longer continue in his managerial job in Budapest. In the autumn of 1919 he left for Sweden, where he soon found comparable employment as technical consultant of a paper mill in Säffle and was able to obtain Swedish citizenship. Melanie and the children took refuge with her in-laws in Rosenberg. But this is all that Klein has to say about how the political situation affected her family:

When the short-lived but very stringent Communist regime started in 1919 at the end of the war, we left Budapest and I went to live for a year in Slovakia with my parents-in-law, with whom I had always been on very good terms, especially my mother-in-law, and my husband found a position in Sweden. Having been by birth an Austrian subject, I had now become a Czecho-Slovakian subject. My husband, having settled in Sweden, soon managed to become a Swedish subject since he was not keen on being a Czecho-Slovakian. In this way I became a Swedish subject, which, at a later date, was very useful to me.

The confusion over nationality is compounded by the fact that Moriz Reizes was born in Galicia, settled in Hungary, and moved to Vienna; Libussa was born in Slovakia, moved to Vienna, and died in Budapest; Arthur considered himself an Austrian, became a Swedish citizen, and died in Switzerland; and Klein was born in Vienna and, after moving around a large part of central Europe, settled in England.

Jews were cosmopolitans held together by a shared religious background. There were many Jews like Melanie Klein who had no religious faith, and yet regarded themselves as Jews; and, like others, were forced to make compromises in order to exist in an anti-Semitic society. Hungary had always been latently anti-Semitic. Ferenczi's family had Magyarized their name from Fraenkel when they moved from eastern Europe to Hungary. The Klein children were given instruction in Hungarian in 1912. Arthur's sister, Jolan, became a devout Roman Catholic like the rest of the Vágó family.* Melanie never divulged that in Budapest the Klein family joined the Unitarian Church and that all her children were baptized. (Eric Clyne describes his siblings as the "walking baptized" at the time of his birth.) Some Jews found the Unitarian Church the easiest to accept, since it rejected the concept of the Trinity. According to Eric Clyne, his father was the instigator of the conversion, but his mother must have acquiesced in it. Her Autobiography deals at length with her guilt as a child in Vienna when she was attracted to the Roman Catholic Church; but she seems to be displacing her later guilt, over action taken when she was an adult, to an earlier situation where the feelings of an impressionable child could be deflected to the influence of her governess. The very fact that she refrains from comment on the turbulent political times is an indication of her uneasiness about behavior that could elicit strong moral condemnation. In light of this, a passage in her autobiographical notes bears some reflection:

I have always hated that some Jews, quite irrespective of their religious principles, were ashamed of their Jewish origin, and, whenever the question

* Even Emanuel's hero, Karl Kraus, converted to Catholicism—not from expediency, but because he saw it as a defense against threatened ethical and spiritual values.

arose, I was glad to confirm my own Jewish origin, though I am afraid that I have no religious beliefs whatever.

In my attitude of sympathy with Israel also enters a feeling which, though it may have originated in the state of persecution of the Jews, extends to all minorities and to all people persecuted by stronger forces. Who knows! This might have given me strength always to be a minority about my scientific work and not to mind, and to be quite willing to stand up against a majority for which I had some contempt, which in time has been mitigated by tolerance.

In the second version of her early paper on Erich, written in the winter of 1919–20, she added a long section on the evils of religion, which she links to the views of Freud and Ferenczi on omnipotence feelings.

It is conceivable that while living in Budapest, Klein was strongly tempted—particularly through her association with the Vágó family—to become a Roman Catholic. Her later theories on constitutional envy, the primary importance of the mother, and reparation bear close parallels to the doctrines of original sin, the Immaculate Conception, and Christian atonement.*

Klein would have been particularly attracted to the Catholic faith if she were very much under the influence of someone whom she loved and respected. She had clearly found this in Constance Sylvester in Vienna when she was a child; and I am inclined to believe that she found another such person in her close friend, Klara Vágó. In 1908 they were intimate enough to share a room in Abbazia and to go on holidays together to the Baltic. In August 1911, when Klara stayed with her in Hermanetz while Libussa supervised the move to the large flat in Budapest, her mother commented:

> It is indeed obvious that your nerves need only peace and tranquillity and nothing to upset them in order to become stronger and gradually healthy. I am immensely happy that dear Frau Klara with her calmness, softness, her lovable and kind character can only have the best influence on your agitated mind. Even though I did not have the opportunity of getting to know Frau Klara as well as you are getting to know her now, I have liked her tremendously from the first moment of our acquaintance. In the course of our acquaintance she has constantly become dearer to me.

Among Klein's poems is one that implies that she might have had a relationship with a woman while living in Budapest. It is undated; and the preamble, which seems to have been intended as a letter, reads: "Eva! Yesterday's reminiscence caused me to gather in my head those stanzas with which I had

* I am indebted to Dr. Hans Thorner for pointing out this analogy to me.

tried at the time to bury these memories solemnly—although they have never been more truly alive." There follows a poem infused with the passion of the Song of Solomon. Melanie had been conditioned to be dependent, worshipful of men and of ideal love. Her upbringing had taught her to repress her own sexual energy. It is possible that through Klara she began to question whether her fantasies of romance were false, inimical to her true nature and development, and hence a marriage mistakenly founded on such misconceptions a travesty. From Klara she may have received the tenderness she had longed for but which had been withheld by her father, her mother, her husband, and even her narcissistic brother.

That the relationship with the mysterious woman had a tumultuous aspect is evident in the poem, in which the eyes of the beloved are "dreams of dark distances, deep consuming, cruel like the night!" In the story "Life Calls" the protagonist is at first accompanied by her sister-in-law on her visits to a painter. Later she goes on her own, thus creating a situation for a love affair to develop (this could have been as early as shortly after Jolan's marriage and move to Budapest in 1906). Klara's portrait by a prominent artist hung in her drawing room, and Melanie could have created an imaginary relationship out of these elements.

Klara was divorced sometime during these years, and after the first war remarried a stockbroker, Sándor Klein (no relation), who lost all his money in the 1929 crash. She died in Budapest in 1945. In that strange hiatus of 1920 in Rosenberg, Klein wrote a poem in which the final stanza reads (in free translation):

> Shall I never again, hand in hand with you,
> Walk over green and flowery meadows
> In the sunshine?

> Shall I never again, hand in hand with you,
> Endure life's burdens willingly
> Because we are together?

> One more time, hand in hand with you,
> On your shoulder let me lament to you
> How bitterly alone I am.

PART
TWO

1920-1926
BERLIN

CHAPTER ONE

The Protégée

The only place Melanie Klein ever recorded anything about her divorce was in her Autobiography, where she says that in 1919 Arthur Klein went to live and work in Sweden, and that she moved back from Budapest to Rosenberg with the children. Hungary was in turmoil; and she could see her own future only in negative terms: as she describes it, there seemed no possibility that she and Arthur could ever get together again.

> This was the preliminary of our actually parting from one another, and lasted until 1922, when we were divorced. I took with me my youngest son, who was then only eight, and nominally I also had the right to have my other two children, but that was not practicable, at the time, as I was still financially dependent on my husband.

A few pages later she continues:

> So I arrived at the beginning of 1921 in Berlin. My daughter, who had passed her matric in that Slovakian town where I had lived with my parents-in-law, joined me and my three children were with me. She went to Berlin University to study medicine, and I began slowly to gain ground as a psycho-analyst.

No dates are given as to when all three children were actually living with her again. The implication is that the separation from them was of very short duration, although, in Eric Clyne's recollection, Hans remained in boarding school until the whole family was reunited in 1923. This may be explainable as an old woman's telescoping of events, but what she says is misleading in another way as well. She seemed to feel guilty because all the children did not accompany her, the same guilt she had experienced in earlier years when she left Hans and Melitta for weeks at a time with her mother. During 1921 Melitta stayed behind in what was now known as Ružomberok to take her matriculation examination. She had to take it in Slovak, a language she had never learned. This regulation was imposed by the new Czechoslovakian state in reprisal for the years when Slovaks had been forced to use German as the official language. Melitta, faced with such an extraordinarily difficult challenge, might have felt this to be yet one more abandonment. Hans was put into a boarding school in the Tatra Mountains. It was planned that both the older children would join their mother in Berlin at the end of the school year, but there was no way they could manage without Arthur's financial support. The family spent Christmas of 1920 in the Hotel Praha in Somnitz, a resort in the Tatra Mountains, and early in January Klein, accompanied by Erich, made the momentous move to Berlin, where they settled temporarily in a pension not far from Karl Abraham's home in Grunewald.* Later they moved to a furnished flat in Cunostrasse, a very bleak area in a city that was unspeakably bleak in general in those years immediately after the war.

For the second time Klein dates the divorce as having taken place in 1922:

> From 1922, when the divorce became effective, my practice in Berlin grew, and I had opportunities of analysing children, also some of my colleagues, and some of the fundamental approach which I used has remained true until today.

Why did Melanie Klein insist that the divorce took place in 1922 (in another place she gives the date as 1923), when, according to Eric Clyne's evidence, it could not have been effective before 1925 or 1926?† The date she assigned to the divorce was not a lapse of memory on her part, but a deliberate attempt to draw a veil over intermediate events. As she wanted to remember it, Berlin represented a completely fresh start in her life; yet in reality, it was an extraordinarily unhappy period. This remarkable woman was able to surmount personal and professional difficulties and embark on fearless, creative paths of her own, even if at great cost to some of those close to her.

Before leaving for Berlin, she must have had to do some hard thinking about her life. The Hungarian psychoanalytic movement had come to an abortive end because of the anti-Semitic counterrevolution, and her future must have looked very dark. She acknowledges that she was always highly ambitious,

---

* One of Eric Clyne's earliest memories of Berlin was of telling a playmate that his mother was a psychoanalyst, to which the boy replied that he had an uncle named Paul Federn who was also an analyst.
† It is impossible to check the actual date, as the records were destroyed in the Second World War.

and the prospect of spending the rest of her life in Ružomberok was intolerable. If she was ever to establish herself in the psychoanalytic community, it was necessary to make her mark. She must make a name for herself by publishing papers; and the subsequent recognition would give her freedom to move to other centers. This may have been her rationale for analyzing Erich in earnest—there were no other prospective analysands in Ružomberok—and publishing the results. And it was while she was in Ružomberok that she decided, very prudently, to disguise Erich's identity.

On December 14, 1920, she wrote to Ferenczi:

Dear Doctor,
    After our last conversation an idea crossed my mind which I should like to discuss with you. As I told you, with regard to the more intimate details I think it necessary to conceal that the subject of the second study is my son. This will, however, sever the connection with the first study, which is perhaps a shame. Even if the two studies were not published simultaneously or consecutively, it would perhaps be interesting and plausible to see how the same child, whose rapid intellectual development through sexual enlightenment is portrayed in the first study, offers, in the second study, resistance to more sexual enlightenment—and that this can be treated only analytically and has been done so.
    Perhaps the unity could still be established if the first study, "On the Influence of Sexual Enlightenment on the Intellect," was glossed over in the same way. To achieve this, it would be necessary to make corresponding changes in the introduction (which so far is identical with the announcement made in the July issue), so that in the announcement the identity of the child with that in the first study is obliterated. Further, I would like to change my son Erich into little Fritz, the son of relations of mine, whose mother had been faithfully following my instructions and whom I had often the opportunity to see informally. If the change from "Erich" to "Fritz," and from "I" to "the mother" is applied throughout the study, I think the disguise will be perfect and I can treat the second study in the same way. This unity is the more desirable as I have not finished the observations of my boy yet, and studies based on continuous experience with one child will certainly be more instructive than a number of unconnected observations.[1]

In the same letter she mentioned that she had not yet received copies she had ordered of *On the Psychopathology of Everyday Life* or the latest editions of *The Interpretation of Dreams* and *Three Essays on the Theory of Sexuality*, which she was eagerly awaiting.

Prior to making this decision she attended the first postwar International Congress, held in The Hague in September 1920. Ernest Jones has recorded that the currency problem was solved by the Dutch analysts' subscribing 50,000 crowns to pay the traveling expenses of their colleagues from central Europe; and they also agreed to house twenty of them during their stay in Holland—seven from Austria, seven from Germany, and six from Hungary. This could be the only explanation for Melanie Klein's appearance there on this occasion. Erich was left with her sister Emilie in Vienna.

Karl Abraham, not realizing the intensity of anti-German feeling, had originally wanted the congress to be held in Berlin. On January 16, 1920, Jones, supported by Rank, wrote to plead with him about his intransigence against holding the congress in The Hague:

> Ask yourself how Germans would feel spending some days in Paris in hotels, restaurants, etc., and remember that Berlin is to us what Paris doubtless is to you. There are very few Jewish Internationals in American Ps.A, and none in England. It is hard to say how far this feeling would operate in fact, but it exists. . . . The greater expense and trouble of the journey would also keep some English from going to Berlin, so I am told. . . . The chief point made [by English members] was that to hold the first congress after the war in Berlin would do much harm to the movement in England, where there is enough opposition to psycho-analysis itself without increasing this by linking it with a national prejudice. It has been largely condemned for its German associations and I think it highly desirable to make the whole movement and Association as international as possible, which would be well served by holding our congress in a neutral country.[2]

Grudgingly, Abraham capitulated. Freud, alerted by Ernest Jones, was more sensitive to the highly charged atmosphere, and only about an hour before the proceedings were to commence he asked Abraham, then secretary of the Psychoanalytical Association and well known as a gifted linguist, to give the welcoming speech in Latin. Abraham, to everyone's amazement, rattled off the speech with great ease.

It was at this congress that Melanie Klein first met Hermine Hug-Hellmuth,* who had already started analyzing children in Vienna by watching them at play, a method she described in a paper, "On the Technique of Child Analysis." Klein tried to engage her in discussion, but was given a very cool reception. She later attributed this to Hug-Hellmuth's view of her as a competitive threat, and any references Klein made to her tended to be extremely condescending. In her Autobiography Klein wrote:

* Her full name was actually Hermine von Hugh-Hellmuth.

Dr. Hug-Hellmuth was doing child analysis at this time in Vienna, but in a very restricted way. She completely avoided interpretations, though she used some play material and drawings, and I could never get an impression of what she was actually doing, nor was she analysing children under six or seven years. I do not think it too conceited to say that I introduced into Berlin the beginnings of child analysis.

It seems likely that Melanie Klein asked Ferenczi if he would speak to Abraham at The Hague about the work she was doing. She was still a nobody, although she can be seen standing, her bearing distinctly assertive, in the second row of a group photograph. It was Hug-Hellmuth, not she, who was giving a paper, so it could only have been through Ferenczi's endorsement that she was drawn to Abraham's attention. Again, it is typical of her not to give one of the principal reasons why she could not return to the Budapest group—namely, the eruption of anti-Semitism in Hungary.

Abraham is often spoken of as the most stalwart of Freud's early colleagues, and he would have been a worthy successor to Freud. Why, then, did Freud not regard him as such, unless it was that he was never attracted to Abraham's aloof, self-contained manner? Ernest Jones described him as "the most normal" of the men around Freud. He was born into an old established Jewish family in Hamburg in 1877. After finishing his medical studies, he spent six years in intensive training in mental hospitals, three of them at Burghölzli with C. G. Jung's group. Abraham and Freud became good, if not intimate, friends from their first meeting in 1907; and Abraham was a member of the inner circle, "The Committee of the Seven Rings," those entitled to wear the precious intaglios. The other members were Sándor Ferenczi, Ernest Jones, Hanns Sachs, Otto Rank, and Max Eitingon.

Abraham was very important to Freud because he was the first German physician with a psychoanalytic practice. Abraham wanted to become a professor of psychoanalysis at the University of Berlin under Karl Bonhoeffer, but conservative opinion was against him; and so in 1910 he founded the Berlin Psychoanalytic Society and Institute. In February 1920, with financial assistance from the immensely rich Max Eitingon, a clinic was opened in Potsdamerstrasse, now part of East Berlin. This was to serve as the model for all future clinics.* With the return of shell-shocked veterans, it was overwhelmed with patients, although in inflation-torn Berlin few could pay more than a nominal amount for treatment.

Abraham was a skilled diplomatist; and it is indicative of his tact that he managed to remain friends with both Wilhelm Fliess and Freud after the rupture in their relationship. But however loyal he may have been to Freud, he

---

* Because of Freud's resistance to the idea of a clinic, one wasn't founded in Vienna until May 1922.

had a strong mind of his own; and the latter part of their correspondence (expurgated though it is) reveals a man treading on delicate ground, determined to develop his own ideas, yet careful not to offend Freud's touchy ego. At the clinic he put into practice his emerging realization that professional standards must be enforced: an analyst had no right to practice until he had been analyzed himself. Ferenczi, on the other hand, saw no difference between a training and a therapeutic analysis; but Abraham, Eitingon, and Ernst Simmel, with Germanic tenacity, made the control analysis an integral part of the Berlin Institute, a procedure attacked by Ferenczi in *Entwicklungsziele der Psychoanalyse* in 1924. The very existence of the clinic put Berlin in a position of some rivalry to Vienna; and it immediately attracted promising analysts to its doors. Hanns Sachs moved from Vienna in 1920, and Sándor Radó* and Franz Alexander fled the anti-Semitic climate in Budapest in 1921. Others in the early group included Alix Strachey and the brothers James and Edward Glover from Britain, Theodor Reik from Vienna, Karen Horney, Ernst Simmel, Therese Benedek, and, for a brief time, Helene Deutsch. The Berlin Society seemed to have an even more dazzling future ahead of it than Freud had predicted for Budapest in 1918.

What is puzzling is the arrangements preceding Klein's move to Berlin. In the letter from Klein to Ferenczi dated December 14, 1920, she tells him that she plans to stay with her children in the Tatra Mountains until the end of December, and concludes: "At the beginning of January I shall be back in Berlin and would therefore like to ask you to send any further letters and messages from the 24th of December onwards to my address at the Poliklinik." This letter is a strong indication that between September and December 1920 she had made some temporary connection with the Berlin Society, and that Ferenczi was fully aware of her movements. In her Autobiography she says that Abraham invited her to join his group when they met at the Hague Congress. Yet there is an extant letter from Ferenczi to Jones, dated June 12, 1921, in which Ferenczi writes: "Frau Klein ought to have informed us too about her resignation from the Budapest group and given more detailed reasons. With regard to this I consulted Dr. Radó, by the way."[3] This is curious in view of the clear evidence in Klein's letter to Ferenczi of December 1920 that he did know of her intentions. Moreover, on November 14, 1920, Jones wrote to Dr. E. G. von Emden, president of the Dutch Society, that while the Budapest group was in great trouble, the Berlin Society was thriving and was "installing two doctors there (I believe) Hungarians. Frau Klein of Budapest is also going there to analyse children; she is a pedagogue."[4] As Jones suggests, other Hungarians were joining the Berlin group. But if Ferenczi felt offended by Klein, this was

* Radó explained to Bluma Swerdloff in an interview March 16, 1963, that he moved to Berlin because he had become too close to Ferenczi, and Abraham was the only clinically oriented analyst he knew (Oral History Research Library, Columbia University).

not apparent at the Berlin Congress in 1922, when they were seen walking arm in arm engaged in animated conversation. Immediately after the Salzburg Congress in 1924, Ferenczi wrote to Freud expressing his satisfaction with the papers at the congress and adding, "Frau Klein was good!"[5]

There was intense envy and rivalry among these early psychoanalytic pioneers. Jones, who held strongly ambivalent feelings towards Ferenczi, might have been trying to stir up trouble, aware that Abraham had replaced Ferenczi as Klein's mentor.

Many years later (1965), one of Klein's English colleagues, Elliott Jaques, in an epoch-making paper, "Death and the Mid-Life Crisis," described various ways in which a creative crisis may occur around the age of thirty-five. Klein's career belonged in the category of those whose "creative capacity may begin to show and express itself for the first time."[6] She was thirty-eight when she arrived in Berlin. Her creative potential, stifled for so many years, was finally unleashed, but she had to fight opposition every step of the way. For the historical record Klein claimed that once she arrived in Berlin, she soon widened her practice, but the fact of the matter is that she aroused misgivings among some of her colleagues. There was unease about the advisability of probing too deeply into a child's unconscious (Budapest colleagues like Radó, Alexander, and Ada Schott would already have heard her paper on the analysis of Erich). Apart from the consideration shown her by Abraham, she was always bitter about the way she was treated by the Berlin Society. Gradually some of her colleagues allowed her to analyze their children in what were known as "prophylactic analyses." In later life she complained that the only patients sent to her were children and the deeply disturbed relatives or patients of other analysts. Yet if it had not been for this, she might never have had the opportunity for intense observation of children.

On one occasion a colleague who wanted to go off on holiday left her with a twelve-year-old patient who, she later realized, was schizophrenic. She was undoubtedly frightened, but she realized that he was frightened too, and she asked him if he were afraid that she would put him back in the asylum. Her verbal expression of his terror allayed his anxiety. Forty years later she recalled: "He was one of my first cases, and looking back I see what a well of information he could have been had I understood more. But even so I learnt a great deal from him."[7]

The children whom she analyzed in Berlin are those described later in *The Psycho-Analysis of Children* (1932). However, her two key cases (not mentioned in *The Psycho-Analysis of Children*) were her own sons, "Fritz" and "Felix" (Erich and Hans), to whom more space is devoted than to any other children in *Love, Guilt, and Reparation, and Other Works, 1921–1945*. A seventeen-year-old girl, Lisa (a protagonist in "The Development of a Child"), to whom less attention is paid than to the boys, is also omitted from *The*

Psycho-Analysis of Children. This appears to be Melitta. One can only speculate that these cases were omitted from the 1932 volume lest awkward questions be raised about the advisability of a mother's analyzing her own children.

The identity of Erich is certain, and the ages and information about the other children accord too closely to Hans and Melitta to be coincidental. Extensive case notes on Erich and Melitta still survive. Fritz's brother, "Felix," appears at the age of thirteen (that is, in 1920, the year they spent in Ružomberok).* Eric Clyne was not aware that his siblings were also analyzed by his mother.

The crucial letter to Ferenczi (December 14, 1920) indicates that Klein intended to continue Erich's analysis even before they reached Berlin, although in "Early Analysis" she says only that she resumed it because "Fritz's" intense anxiety reappeared (true). "The boy had had a relapse, which was due in part to the fact that, in my desire to be careful, I had not taken the analysis deep enough. Part of the result obtained, however, had proved to be lasting."[8] This time she endeavored to penetrate to the heart of his problems, but became alarmed when not only did he resist the analysis, but his nervous condition worsened. Abraham knew that she was analyzing her son,† and when she told him that the boy's condition had deteriorated, he urged her to persevere in uncovering repressed material because he believed that this approach would relieve the child's anxiety—and it appeared to do so, according to Klein. Fritz also had "a mild phobia" about going on the streets, where he complained of being tormented by rough boys. Klein brushes this aside to concentrate on the route he took to school, in which the road was lined with trees—a route she sees as symbolically expressing a desire for coitus, which is then followed by castration anxiety.

Still very much under the influence of Freud, Klein attributed her son's problems to his repressed incestuous desires towards herself. Was she so bewitched that she could not see the forest for the trees? There were other important features of Erich's life which she ignores. He had been an unwanted child and his mother was extremely depressed while carrying him. His grandmother had died shortly after his birth; and Klein was in a state of such intense anxiety that she had sought help from Ferenczi. Also, the child must have sensed the continual tension between his parents. When Erich was three his father went off to the war for a year, and on his return the child showed an exaggerated affection for him. When he was five his father disappeared again—this time to Sweden—and the rest of the family moved to Ružomberok. Here

* "Inhibitions and Difficulties of Puberty" (1922) would seem to be based on her observations of Hans. "Fritz" might very well be the same child as "Ernst" in "The Role of the School in the Libidinal Development of the Child" (1923) and "Grete" could be Melitta.
† Apparently Abraham, following Freud's recommendations, sometimes "analyzed" his own daughter. See "Little Hilda: Daydreams and a Symptom in a Seven-Year-Old Girl," *Int. Rev. Psycho-Anal* (1974), I, 5–14.

his mother was disturbed by the fact that he became withdrawn after the move, and took no interest in his surroundings. The following year they moved to Berlin, where boys in the street taunted him for being a Jew. (This is not mentioned by Melanie Klein.) According to Eric Clyne, it was his brother who revealed to him why the boys were treating him so cruelly. Indeed, he did not realize that he was Jewish until an incident that occurred when he was ten: He and his nurse entered the Kaiser Wilhelmsgedächtniskirche, and a young man told them that Jews must sit at the back. The nurse, who was a Gentile, protested indignantly that they were not Jews.

For the five years they were in Berlin they changed their domicile almost every year. In 1923 or 1924 Arthur Klein returned to Berlin. Within a year Melanie Klein moved out permanently, taking Erich with her. First he was sent to a boarding school in southern Germany, then to Frankfurt in order to be analyzed by Clara Happel.* Here he boarded with a schoolmaster and his family, and was grievously unhappy. "It must be nice to be part of a normal family," Eric Clyne remarked years later; and added, philosophically, "but I doubt if there are many normal families." It is little wonder that the child was disturbed, but Melanie Klein takes none of these external factors into consideration, and in writing up the case history ascribes his anxiety to repressed libidinal wishes.

The case of "Felix" (Hans), a boy suffering from a nervous tic, presents equally disturbing evidence. Klein's early opponents objected to the dangers of delving into a small child's unconscious, but surely the dangers of a mother analyzing an adolescent boy were even greater? She uses Franz Alexander's phrase "a neurotic character" to describe Felix at the time she started to analyze him. She feels it necessary to emphasize the first significant stage in his development.

> At the age of three a stretching of the foreskin was performed on him, and the connection between this stretching and masturbation was specially impressed on him. His father, too, had repeatedly given warning and even threatened the boy; as a result of these threats Felix was determined to give up masturbation.[9]

Felix's analysis took place three times a week, but as it was repeatedly interrupted it had to be extended over three and a quarter years, and lasted 370 hours in all. This would suggest that it took place during school holidays and in the year the family lived in a house they built in Dahlem. His problems originated from the fact that until he was six he occupied a cot in his parents' bedroom and consequently developed a fear of the act he repeatedly overheard

* Happel wrote on pederasty, homosexuality, masturbation, and the Oedipus complex.

occurring in the large bed.* We also learn that when his father returned from the war he used to beat the boy for his cowardice in games. Felix was driven to focus on sports to the point where he lost all interest in school. His inertia was exacerbated by his father's insistence on supervising his homework. The father also lay in wait to detect the boy masturbating, and whenever he was caught Felix was beaten. These details suggest that Melanie Klein resented her husband's treatment of the boy; and that she was attributing many of his difficulties to his father.

Felix began to develop a critical interest in music and composers. "His analysis showed me," Klein concludes, "what other analyses confirmed: that criticism always has its origin in the observation of paternal genital activities."[10] Always believing in complete frankness, she repeatedly analyzed his masturbation phantasies.

This analysis is important, as it indicates that Klein was turning more to Abraham than to Ferenczi for intellectual direction. She agrees with a point made by Ferenczi in "Psycho-Analytical Observations on Tic" (1921) that the tic is equivalent to masturbation, but disagrees that it is a primary narcissistic symptom because by then she was convinced that "the tic is not accessible to therapeutic influence as long as the analysis has not succeeded in uncovering the object relations on which it is based."[11] (This seems to have been her first reference to object relations.) Her observations of Felix confirmed the anal-sadistic connections that Abraham pointed out in his paper, "Contributions to the Theory of the Anal Character," read to the Berlin Society in 1921.

The account of the analysis of Lisa is much shorter, and based largely on the girl's attitude to numbers and letters. She praised the letter "A" as being serious and dignified; it impressed her and the associations led to a clear father-imago whose name also began with an "A." Her lack of proficiency at mathematics Klein ascribed to the girl's castration complex. History for her was essentially "the study of the relations of the parents to one another and to the child, wherein of course the infantile phantasies of battles, slaughters, etc., also played an important part, according to the sadistic conception of coitus."[12]

Any modern analyst, of course, is horrified by the notion of a mother analyzing her own offspring. Since Klein was the real mother, she could exercise the prerogatives of a mother. At one point, for example, she forbade Felix to see a girl older than himself because of the identification he was making with the phantasy of his mother as a prostitute. "The transference," she says,

---

* It may seem bizarre for a mother to discuss this sexual situation with her son. However, in 1912 (Zbl. Psychoanal., 2, p. 680) Freud had made this request: "I should be glad if those of my colleagues who are practicing analysts would collect and analyze carefully any of their patients' dreams whose interpretation justifies the conclusion that the dreamers had been witnesses of sexual intercourse in their early years."

"proved strong enough for me to impose a temporary break in this relation"; yet she unwittingly gives away their real relationship:

> This object choice served the purpose of a flight from the phantasies and wishes directed towards me (*sic*), and which only at this stage came more fully to the fore in the analysis. It could now be seen that the turning away from the originally loved but forbidden mother had participated in the strengthening of the homosexual attitude and the phantasies about the dreaded castrating mother.[13]

On another occasion she made him break off a homosexual relationship with a school friend. It must have seemed to the boy that he had no area of privacy from his mother, who knew the innermost secrets of his soul. There was a further problem. His tic and related homosexual problems she repeatedly links to his sense of inferiority to his father. Arthur Klein was deeply suspicious of psychoanalysis, which he saw as driving a wedge between him and his son, and his wife's obsession with it as a disruptive intrusion in the family.

One may ask how a transference could be established in such a situation.* Most of the objections are related to a deep, primitive level, namely the fear of incest. Such penetration of a child's mind is not only a misuse of power, but an intrusion into the area of taboo. It could be argued that a transference could occur when the child imposed on the mother his phantasized internal perception of her. But how would the analyst/mother be able to distinguish between the reality of the child's perception of her and her own perception of herself?

One wonders if Melanie Klein ever experienced misgivings about the wisdom of what she was doing. At first she truly believed that she could perhaps alleviate some of the intensity of the depression she herself had experienced ever since childhood. With all three children, through her enlightening explanations of their problems, she leaves the impression that there was great improvement, if not the total recovery Freud attributed to little Hans. Nevertheless, the fact that her children later went on to other analysts—Melitta to Horney, Sharpe, and Glover; Hans to Simmel; and Eric to Happel, Searl, Winnicott, and Joseph—could have given her pause for reflection. Whenever she was not satisfied with an analysis, she rationalized that it had been terminated too soon. In the dark hours of the night it might have occurred to her that in the case of her children she could actually have caused irreparable damage either to their psyches or to their relationships with her. The fact is, however, that all her future work was based not only upon her in-

---

* Many Freudians have clearly experienced grave embarrassment over the revelation that Freud analyzed Anna. It is seldom discussed, and some people wish the information had never seen the light of day. On the other hand, Freud never seems to have published the analysis as a case history.

sights into her children's anxiety but on her realization of the mistakes she had made while analyzing them.

The problems of these three children are narrated with distanced, clinical detachment. In "Fragment of an Analysis of Hysteria" (1905), Freud said: "It is possible for a man to talk to girls and women upon sexual matters of every kind without doing them harm and without bringing suspicion upon himself, so long as, in the first place, he adopts a particular way of doing it, and, in the second place, can make them feel convinced that it is unavoidable. . . . The best way of speaking about such things is to be dry and direct; and that is at the same time the method furthest removed from the prurience with which the same subjects are handled in 'society.' . . . J'appelle un chat un chat."[14] Melanie Klein quoted this passage in a footnote in "The Technique of Early Analysis," and added: "This attitude is, mutatis mutandis, the one I adopt in analysing children. I talk of sexual matters in the simple words best suited to their way of thought."[15] And this, undoubtedly, was the method she used with her own sons.

Let us suppose that she did use these children as guinea pigs. Through her close observation of their behavior she learned much about the origins of anxiety and how it impeded development, knowledge that undoubtedly contributed to her understanding of other young patients—Rita, Trude, Dick, Richard—tormented children whom she undoubtedly helped.

During those years in Berlin, Klein refined her technique and elaborated her concepts. She did not at that time regard her views as in any way unorthodox; and one can trace her ideas developing in tandem with the preoccupations of Freud and Abraham. Freud, it will be remembered, made his last major statement on anxiety in "Inhibitions, Symptoms, and Anxiety" (1926), in which he reversed his earlier view that repression leads to anxiety; and from his 1925 paper on negation ("I will take this in; I will spit that out") Melanie Klein developed her concepts of introjection and projection.* Depression, anxiety, guilt, the compulsive nature of phantasy—these were the problems to which she would increasingly address herself. Aggression, not libido, began to assume the central force in anxiety, and gradually she recognized the interplay between reality and phantasy.

Abraham taught her how to write up case histories. Unlike the shadowy descriptions of her own children, the children whom she analyzed in Berlin (described in The Psycho-Analysis of Children) are unforgettable. They are inhibited at play, morose, silent, incontinent, exceedingly "naughty." They suffer from obsessionalism, nightmares, temper tantrums. Trude, aged three years and nine months, is filled with the most terrifying sense of destructiveness.

* Introjection" is the process whereby an external object is internalized. In "projection," internal objects are imagined to be located in some object external to oneself (see Charles Rycroft, A Critical Dictionary of Psychoanalysis, Penguin, 1979).

Rita, from the age of eighteen months, experienced severe anxiety attacks, the expression of guilt over her oedipal feelings. At this point Klein—while still subscribing to the orthodox Freudian position that the Oedipus complex reaches its zenith during the fourth year, and that the superego emerges as the end result—began to see, from her observations of these children, that the working through of the Oedipus complex in young children takes years, and that an infantile superego is far more punitive than the one a mature adult is better equipped to deal with.

With these small patients, mostly the children of colleagues, Melanie Klein gradually developed a technique arising out of specific situations. In the case of Rita, hovering in the background were a watchful aunt and mother, creating a tension inimical to the analysis. Consequently Klein insisted that the analysis could not be conducted in the child's own home, a point on which she agreed with Hug-Hellmuth. On one occasion Rita, then seven years old, blackened a piece of paper, tore it up, threw the scraps into a glass of water and, as if drinking from it, muttered under her breath "dead woman." Klein saw at that moment how revealing drawing, paper, and water could be in the symbolic expression of anxiety. Rita, who disliked school intensely, had shown no interest in drawing; but when Klein, on impulse, fetched her some of her own child's toys—cars, little figures, a train, some bricks—the girl immediately began to play, and from the various catastrophes to which she subjected the cars Klein interpreted that she had been engaged in some sort of sexual activity with another child at school. Rita became alarmed by this interpretation, but after the first onset of anxiety subsided into a state of relief.

This experience, supplemented by others, convinced Klein that it was essential to have small toys, nonmechanical, varying only in color and size, and that the human figure should represent no particular profession. The very simplicity of the toys enabled the child to express a wide range of phantasy or evocation of actual experiences. The equipment she gradually began to assemble for each session consisted of wooden men and women in two sizes, cars, wheelbarrows, swings, trains, airplanes, animals, trees, bricks, houses, fences, paper, scissors, a knife, pencils, chalks or paints, balls and marbles, modeling clay, and string. In addition, the child could bring some of his own toys, although she preferred that he concentrate on those that were locked away in his own individual drawer.

As a young girl of eight or nine, Melanie Klein had been fascinated by the play of younger children. When she had children of her own, her observation of them gave her some basis from which to develop her theories. Her recognition that a transference could be established was immeasurably important for the development of her more refined technique. While experiencing a negative transference, the child might assign the role of a child to Klein while he would assume the role of an authority figure, thereby giving himself the power to punish or hurt her. This aggressiveness was restrained only to the degree that Klein insisted that it be kept within the bounds of physical abuse:

> This attitude not only protects the psycho-analyst but is of importance for the analysis as well. For such assaults, if not kept within bounds, are apt to stir up excessive guilt and persecutory anxiety in the child and therefore add to the difficulties of the treatment. I have sometimes been asked by what method I prevented physical attacks, and I think the answer is that I was very careful not to inhibit the child's aggressive phantasies; in fact he was given opportunity to act out in other ways, including the verbal attacks on myself. The more I was able to interpret in time the motives of the child's aggressiveness the more the situation could be kept under control.[16]

Scanning the faces of her patients, she noticed a remarkable range of expressions pass over them; and she found that if she consistently interpreted their play to them, their anxiety decreased. She came to recognize "the knowing look," the moment of perception, and it was one of her surprising discoveries that in very small children there was often a capacity for greater insight than in adults. To some extent she believed that this could be explained by the fact that the connections between the conscious and the unconscious are much closer in children and that, at a preverbal stage, play can reveal even more than free association.

She was particularly interested in the child's attitude towards a damaged toy. The toy often represented a parent or sibling. The child, in the grip of persecutory fear, would shut it away in a drawer, afraid of retaliatory action. Anxiety could be so intense that his sense of guilt would be stifled. Then one day he would open the drawer and rummage around for the damaged toy. This act of restitution (or reparation, as she was later to describe it) would enable Klein to interpret the child's attitude to a particular relative. "This change confirms our impression that persecutory anxiety has diminished and that, together with the sense of guilt and the wish to make reparation, feelings of love which had been impaired by excessive anxiety have come to the fore."[17] In these situations it was essential that the analyst refrain from voicing any disapproval over the broken toy or suggest that it should be mended. Freud had noted in *Beyond the Pleasure Principle* that the child experienced far greater pleasure in the retrieval of a wooden reel than in making it disappear. From these pioneering analyses in Berlin she knew that her role was not to be an educative or moral influence, but to give the child freedom to express his emotions and phantasies, and it was her job to interpret these to him.

One child, Peter, three and a half years old, displayed intense anxiety after the birth of a baby brother. He had shared his parents' bedroom at the time of the baby's conception, during a holiday. In his first session with Klein, he became absorbed in a repetitive pattern of play. He made two horses bump into each other, and repeated this process with all the toys he picked up. When he was informed that they represented people, he at first rejected the idea, but after a little reflection agreed with the suggestion. Further progress was made in the second session. The smashing of toys continued, and this time Klein suggested that he was reenacting his parents banging their genitals together, thus producing the baby brother for whom he had such ambivalent feelings. Peter's subsequent treatment of the toys was even more explicit. He laid a toy man on a brick that he called a bed and declared him "dead and done for." He then did the same thing with two toy men, choosing figures he had already damaged. In this case Klein interpreted that one of the two figures was his father, the other himself, whom his father in turn would have damaged. It was extraordinary insight on her part to realize that the reason Peter had chosen two damaged figures was because the child felt that both he and his father would be damaged if he attacked his father; and the fact that the child was enabled to play in an uninhibited manner confirmed for her that she was on the right track.

In the analysis of Rita, she was particularly struck by the harshness of the child's superego, very active at a much earlier stage than Freud had assumed. Having accepted this fact, she then realized that the superego operates internally in a child in a concrete way: that is, the superego assumes the guise of a variety of figures built up from experiences and phantasies derived from the stages at which the child has internalized (introjected) his parents.

She noticed that in little girls the most acute anxiety occurred when the mother was felt to be the persecutor, both as an external figure and internalized object, whose aim it was to attack her daughter's body and rob it of its imaginary children. These persecutory feelings of depression and guilt led to a desire to make reparation—not in Freud's sense of "undoing" in the obsessional neurotic,[18] but in the variety of processes by which the ego undoes harm committed in phantasy by restoring, preserving, and reviving objects. This impulse, bound up with a sense of guilt, contributes to all forms of sublimation and, ultimately, to mental health.

Other important discoveries were made with these early patients. For example, she realized that Trude, in tearing up and soiling bits of paper, was recreating fears of retaliatory attacks of a specifically anal-urethral-sadistic nature. Such observations confirmed Abraham's speculations in "A Short History of the Development of the Libido, Viewed in the Light of Mental Disorders" (1924) on the nature of sadism. In one child whom she analyzed between 1924 and 1925, who was far more disturbed than either Rita or Trude, she witnessed the oral and anal nature of the child's introjective processes. The child was tormented by internal and external persecutors, the latter an image of her own projection, and derived from her oral-sadistic relation to her mother's breast phantasies interwoven with the beginning of her Oedipus complex. More and more Klein perceived the symbolic complexities of the small child's world. For instance, when she remarked to Peter that his damaging a toy represented an attack on his brother, he protested that he would never do such a thing to his *real* brother. She in turn pointed out to him that this symbolic act was the only way he could express his destructive feelings towards his brother. Finally, by analyzing adults at the same time as she was seeing children, she was able to observe how infantile phantasies and anxieties remained operative in the adult.

Melanie Klein never lost any time in making her presence felt. On February 3, 1921, shortly after her arrival in Berlin, she delivered a paper on child analysis (based on Felix's learning inhibitions), which was followed a week later by a general discussion by members of the Society on points raised in her paper. On May 19 she read another paper, never published, "Über die Orientierungssinnes" (Disturbances of Orientation in Children). Here she was beginning to enunciate her view that the growth of the epistemological instinct develops from a curiosity about the contents of the mother's body, an interest that has been repressed because in the unconscious the exploration takes place by way of coitus. Abraham objected that the interest in the mother's body is preceded by a concentration on the child's own body. She was not convinced, recalling Erich ("Fritz") exploring her own body with a tiny dog which he slid along it, phantasizing as he did so that he was traveling through countries of which her breasts were mountains and the genital area a great river. All these observations were tentative explorations into the sources of infantile anxiety.

It should be emphasized that most of the cases reported in *The Psycho-Analysis of Children* (1932) were written up some years later in the hindsight of the development of her theories. The recollections of Karen Horney's daughter, Dr. Marianne Horney Eckhardt, are interesting as evidence of her actual procedure at the time. In 1923, at the age of ten, Marianne began an analysis with Klein that lasted two years. She visited Klein twice a week at her home in Dahlem, and remembers the newness of the upper-income house, the Bauhaus-type furniture, comfortable though not elegant. The analysis took place in two stages: the first part during the last year of Klein's marriage, and the second part after she had left her husband. Marianne had no idea why Klein had suddenly moved; and the young girl much preferred riding her bicycle through the pretty streets of Dahlem to going to the dark flat she was subsequently forced to visit.

In retrospect Dr. Eckhardt finds the idea of a "prophylactic" analysis ridiculous. At the time most of the analysts seemed to subscribe to the idea that it was important to children's healthy development.* The procedure, as she recalls it, was extremely mechanical. She would lie on the couch relating all that had happened to her during the week, and in the final ten minutes Klein would summarize and interpret what had been said. There was no discussion between them, and no sense of warmth. She has no recollection of Klein's ever smiling or asking how she was. When Eckhardt saw photographs of her years later, she found her far more elegant and attractive than the woman she had known. Dr. Eckhardt believes that she came alive when she moved to England.

In 1922, Klein was made an associate member of the Berlin Society. She continued to deliver papers and commentary on anxiety in children to the members of the Society, and a more fully developed paper to the Seventh Psychoanalytic Congress held in Berlin in September.† This was the last congress Freud ever attended. It is unlikely that he was present when Klein delivered her paper, but he was undoubtedly aware of the contents of all the papers being produced. Quick to detect any heresy, he would have realized that this woman was showing uneasiness about the Oedipus complex as the seat of neurosis. Analysis had shown, she declared, that inhibitions described by Freud arise out of an infantile conception of the birth of a baby through the anus, a fixation that sets in long before the child reaches the genital level.

In February 1923, Klein was elected to full membership in the Berlin Society, and that year "The Development of a Child" was the first of her papers to be published by Ernest Jones in the *International Journal of Psycho-Analysis*. That same year, in *The Ego and the Id*, Freud posited a structural theory of the mind, composed of ego, id, and superego, and advanced a theory of guilt deriving from a death instinct. This work was to have a profound effect in giving Melanie Klein confidence in the conclusions she was drawing from her observations. Abraham, describing the activities of the Berlin group in a letter to Freud of November 7, 1923, announced that Frau Klein would be giving a course to kindergarten teachers on infantile sexuality; and went on to discuss his paper "A Short Study of the Development of the Libido, Viewed in the Light of Mental Disorders," which would be published the following year.

I have assumed the presence of an early depression in infancy as a prototype for later melancholia. In the last few months Mrs. Klein has skilfully conducted the psycho-analysis of a three-year-old with good therapeutic results. The child presented a true picture of the basic depression which I

* In 1922, in Budapest, Peter Lambda (then eleven) was "analyzed" by Stephen Hollos, who tried to make him associate words. There were no games or playing; and Lambda was totally bewildered by the whole experience.
† The original paper was "Infant Analysis; or, The Development and Inhibition of Natural Gifts." When it was published in 1923 as "Early Analysis" in *Imago* 9, it incorporated several other unpublished papers.

postulated in close combination with oral eroticism. The case offers amazing insights into an infantile instinctual life.[19]

At the Hague Congress, Abraham had refused to give a paper on manic-depressive psychosis because of lack of evidence. Now Klein seemed to be providing him with it. Not unnaturally, Freud did not take kindly to his disciples' finding new objects of admiration; or indeed to any idea he had not thought of first, as he explained in a somewhat self-amused way to Ferenczi in February 1924:

I know that I am not very accessible and find it hard to assimilate alien thoughts that do not quite lie in my path. It takes quite a time before I can form a judgment about them, so that in the interval I have to suspend judgment. If you were to wait so long each time there would be an end of your productivity.[20]

Both Abraham and Freud had been working for many years on the problem of the origin of depression. Abraham's 1911 paper, "Notes on the Psychoanalytic Investigation and Treatment of Manic-Depressive Insanity and Allied Conditions," made a new connection between neurotic and psychotic depression. In the former, the sufferer "feels himself unloved and incapable of loving" and therefore despairs of his life and his future.[21] Freud had been struck by the ambivalence in the obsessional neurotic (1909), and Abraham found also that in both psychotic and neurotically depressed patients, they were so much in the grip of hatred that their capacity for love was stifled. Projecting such hatred, they felt that they in turn were despised. In their unconscious they were convinced that they actually carried out the destructive acts they phantasized. This is what Freud described as the "omnipotence of thought," a term and concept Melanie Klein was to borrow from him.

Then in 1916 Abraham published his further investigations into the hypotheses postulated by Freud in *Three Essays on Sexuality* (1905) about an oral pregenital stage of sexual life.* Abraham had found that a frequent symptom among deeply disturbed patients was the simultaneous refusal to take food and the fear of starvation. Freud's classic paper *Mourning and Melancholia* (1917) distinguished melancholia from the normal process of sorrow for the loss of a loved one. "The distinguishing mental features of melancholia are a profoundly painful dejection, abrogation of interest in the outside world, loss

* "The First Pregenital Stage of the Libido."

of capacity to love, inhibition of all activity, and a lowering of the self-regarding feelings to a degree that finds utterance in self-reproaches and self-revilings, and culminates in a delusional expectation of punishment."[22] One of the interesting observations Freud had made from witnessing this self-punishing phenomenon was that melancholia occurred in specially predisposed people. What the melancholic is grieving for is not so much the loss of a loved person, as a damaged ego that he reproaches and abases, a self-directed rather than an external reality–directed activity. Abraham had suggested that the melancholic's self-reproaches were a reflection of the projection of his hatred, but for Freud "the self-reproaches are reproaches against a loved object which has been shifted onto the patient's own ego. The woman who loudly pities her husband for being bound to such a poor creature as herself is really accusing her husband of being a poor creature in some sense or another."[23] This kind of identification Freud sees as a regression to the narcissistic oral phase of the libido. Freud regards it as narcissistic, in that the sufferer's only relation to the external world is formed from objects he places in his mouth, incorporating or "introjecting" them. Freud differs from Abraham in his view that it is introjection rather than projection that is the important element in melancholia, but admits that a great deal of further investigation must be applied to the problem.

Then, in 1924, appeared Abraham's major paper "A Short Study of the Libido, Viewed in the Light of Mental Disorders." Abraham was beginning to find increasing similarities between obsessional neurosis and manic-depressive psychosis. The loss of an object is a reenactment of the anal stage of psychosexual development, in which in the unconscious the mechanism is comparable to the "expulsion of that object in the sense of a physical expulsion of faeces."[24] Further, the melancholic may regress even further back than the anal-sadistic to the earlier oral phase in his cannibalistic phantasies. One patient, for instance, had a phantasy of eating excrement. Such examples provided clinical corroboration of Freud's view that introjection occurs by way of an oral mechanism. Abraham tended more than Freud to the view that melancholia was based on a constitutional overaccentuation of oral eroticism and that problems occur at a much earlier stage than the crisis presented in the resolution of the Oedipus complex. The melancholic's highly ambivalent attitude to the loss of a love object can be seen when he is so overwhelmed by hate that he abandons the object as though it were feces, only to reintroject it into his ego so that he becomes narcissistically identified with it. At a crucial stage of Klein's career, she came under the influence of Abraham's ideas, particularly of the conflict engendered in the psychic life by the functions of projection and introjection.

It is a curious fact that Abraham makes no reference to *Beyond the Plea-*

sure Principle (1920), which he had read in manuscript in 1919.* Here Freud, by his postulation of a death instinct, inaugurated, according to Ernest Jones, "his remodeling of psychoanalytical theory" (*Life*, III, p. 33). In a key passage Freud writes:

> We started out from the great opposition between the life and death instincts. Now object-love itself presents us with a second example of a similar polarity—that between love (or affection) and hate (aggressiveness). If only we could succeed in relating these two polarities to each other and in deriving one from the other! From the very first we recognized the presence of a sadistic component in the sexual instinct. As we know, it can make itself independent and can, in the form of a perversion, dominate an individual's entire sexual activity. It also emerges as a predominant component instinct in one of the "pregenital organizations," as I have named them. But how can the sadistic instinct, whose aim it is to injure the object, be derived from Eros, the preserver of life? Is it not plausible to suppose that this sadism is in fact a death instinct which, under the influence of the narcissistic libido, has been forced away from the ego and has consequently emerged only in relation to the object?[25]

For Freud, this dualistic conception was as yet "a provisional one." Melanie Klein took up the challenge posed by Freud, although she did not fully work out its implications until after her arrival in England. Lacking a biological background, she interpreted the death instinct strictly in psychological terms;† she had no conception of behavior that was not purposeful. She was talking about constellations of mental impulses, the destruction of the object by incorporation or some other means. In the infant, the death instinct operates as a projection of aggression in fear of annihilation, whereas for Freud the infant is unaware of death as such. She always believed that she was following a lead suggested by Freud, but, unlike Freud, she was not the product of a mechanistic nineteenth-century biology, and had no real understanding of instinct in the sense Freud meant. What Klein saw was that the children she was treating were engaged in destructive activity, and she termed this the operation of the death instinct. For her a drive was not a directionless, tension-producing stimulus only secondarily attached to an object. Both libido and aggression she viewed as inherently directional longings, and the drives were in effect relationships.

---

* However, as early as 1911 Abraham was talking about "a tendency to deny life," "negation of life," and "symbolic dying."
† Her view of "Trieb" was that of Bruno Bettelheim and Hanna Segal, who considers the most appropriate translation of the word to be the French *pulsion*, or, in its nearest equivalent in English, "drive." Charles Rycroft believes that "no useful purpose is served by trying to distinguish between an instinct and a drive."

Among Melanie Klein's unpublished papers is the following rough note:

Abraham has never been thought to be a heretic. His work accepted in the classical part of the theory. But it has never been fully made use of in psycho-analysis. Abraham, who had discovered the first anal phase and linked it up with some work done by Ophuijsen, came near to the conception of the internal objects. His work on the oral impulses and phantasies goes beyond F's work. It did not by any means go as far as my own, but it is on the same line and here is another person who has made use of certain thoughts and findings of F. taking them up and conducting them further. I should say that A. represents the link between my own work and F's. Of course his views do not lead so far and were still so much nearer some of the conclusions of F's that they did not strike people as a deviation, as it now seems with my work.[26]

Klein's observations of children seemed to confirm Abraham's theories. This was also a time when she was deeply depressed over a crisis in her own life. In 1923, according to her Autobiography, she approached Abraham with the plea that he take her into analysis.

When I approached Abraham with the request for an analysis, he told me that it had become a principle with him not to analyse anyone remaining in Berlin. He was referring to some very unhappy situations which had resulted from broken-off analyses with colleagues who had become hostile to him. I don't know where I found the courage, but my answer was "Can you tell me of anyone in Berlin whom I could look to in such a way that I could go to them for analysis?" He never replied to that question, but he accepted me for analysis. I had to wait a few months and then analysis started at the beginning of 1924 and came to an end when Abraham fell very ill in the summer of 1925 and died at Christmas of that year; a great pain to me and a very painful situation to come through.[27]

According to the fiction created in her Autobiography her divorce had already taken place when she approached Abraham. The facts were otherwise. After Arthur Klein moved to Sweden (presumably temporarily), Erich was told by his mother that his father had formed "an emotional attachment" from which he found it difficult to extricate himself. In any event, it was decided that husband and wife would attempt a reconciliation for the sake of the children. Melanie probably consented to this for financial reasons; she wanted to have her children with her, but she could not possibly support them without Arthur's help. The very fact that Arthur was willing to return to Berlin indicates his wish to preserve the marriage. He had no difficulty finding consulting work in Berlin after his association with the prestigious Billeruds AB in Säffle. He also now became part owner and editor of the *Deutsche Papierzeitung*. They decided to build a house in the fashionable area of Dahlem, but owing to the rampant inflation and scarcity of building materials in postwar Berlin, it was almost two years before the family was able to move into a very impressive dwelling, Auf dem Grat 19.* A degree of normality was established, and Eric Clyne remembers his excited anticipation while waiting outside the dining room until Melitta finished decorating the Christmas tree. According to him, "I would say that my mother was part of the entire family living there in Dahlem for something like two years. It was when the Dahlem house had been built that my father rejoined the family. He retained the house after the divorce and it was sold later for the benefit of the three children."†

Whatever the hopes the family initially brought to their new home, it soon became clear that nearly four years of separation had not diminished the tensions between husband and wife. Arthur, anxious to regain the authority he feared he had lost during his absence in Sweden, became more of a household tyrant than ever. His bullying of Hans is documented in painful detail in "A Contribution to the Psychogenesis of a Tic." (When Simmel began to analyze Hans is not certain, but Eric Clyne thinks about 1925.) For Melanie, the time she lived in the Dahlem house—the time during which she sought analysis with Abraham—must have been one of the most turbulent of her life. In addition to Arthur's renewed tyranny, both his "emotional attachment" in Sweden and her new career were incentives to attain the independence she had always half-consciously been seeking. She soon realized that a permanent separation was imperative. Yet to walk out on her husband was financially hazardous, and she risked losing custody of Erich. There were ugly quarrels. One day Erich saw a document lying on his father's desk and could not resist reading it. It appeared that Arthur was going to seek to obtain custody of the boy on the grounds that his mother had used him as a guinea pig for her psychoanalytic experiments. When Erich told his mother about this, she said that Arthur had deliberately put the paper on the table where he knew Erich would see it.

There were problems with Melitta as well. By then she had entered Berlin University as a medical student. Whatever their later differences, at this point she supported her mother against her father. Exacerbating the rancor between father and daughter was Arthur's disapproval of her suitor, Walter Schmideberg, a man fourteen years her senior. The rows particularly concerned Schmideberg's drinking problem—and, Arthur claimed, drug addiction as well. Eric remembers being taken to visit Schmideberg in 1924 or 1925 at the Sanatorium Schloss Tegel, where he was being treated for addiction.

---

* Now the Department of Egyptology of Berlin University.
† By this account, the family would have moved into the house in Dahlem before the end of 1923 and Melanie Klein moved out sometime in late 1924. My reckoning is that she lived there for only about a year.

A cultivated Viennese, Schmideberg had been educated at Karlsburg, an exclusive Jesuit school reserved for the sons of wealthy and aristocratic families. Destined to become a permanent officer in the Austro-Hungarian Army, he rose to the rank of *Reitmaster* (captain) in a crack regiment. But he was an unusual young man in that he was deeply interested in psychology; and in 1907 his Jesuit teachers seized his books on hypnosis as "works of the devil" and burned them in front of the entire school.

Consequently, when during the war he met Max Eitingon, then an army psychiatrist in a small town in Hungary, it was inevitable that he would be drawn to psychoanalysis. Eitingon in turn introduced him to Freud and put him in touch with Ferenczi. These were days of hardship in Vienna, when the Freud family was suffering from malnutrition; and Schmideberg acted as courier between Ferenczi and Freud, bringing welcome parcels of food. After the war, he became a regular visitor to the Freud household and attended meetings of the Viennese Psychoanalytic Society.

In 1921 he moved to Berlin, where he stayed with the Eitingons in their exquisite apartment. Serving for a time as secretary of the Berlin Society, he helped Eitingon to set up the Poliklinik. He also played a major part in organizing the International Psycho-Analytic Congress that was held in Berlin in 1922. It was at this congress that he first met Melitta, a beautiful dark-eyed medical student of eighteen.

Melanie Klein's feelings about her daughter's romance were complex. She was still a handsome woman, who felt that her youth had been wasted. She was still a relative unknown in the psychoanalytic movement and was quite openly resented by contemporaries who were far more firmly established than she. And here was Melitta, a slip of a girl, training to be the doctor she had always craved to be. Moreover, she was in a training analysis with Eitingon, and later with Karen Horney, herself a qualified doctor. Finally, her daughter was romantically involved with a handsome, charming man who was on intimate terms both with the wealthy Eitingons and with the Ur-Family in Vienna. In later life Klein was to write much about a daughter's envy of her mother. Given Klein's own rich phantasy life, the seeds of a mother's envy of her daughter were probably already sown with her early fear that Melitta might have been usurping Melanie's place with her mother and her husband; and while she may have encouraged the marriage for the reflected prestige it would give her, it is probable that she did not react with unalloyed pleasure.

The relationship between Melanie Klein and her daughter is puzzling and disturbing. In Klein's paper "The Development of a Child" (the story of Felix), she also discusses, by implication, another child altogether, who had been helped by prophylactic analysis. This child also has a brother and sister, "in a family with which I am well acquainted, so that I have a detailed knowledge of their development." She draws an idealized portrait of their background:

> The children concerned are very well disposed and very sensibly and lovingly brought up. For instance, it was a principle of their upbringing that all questions were permitted and were gladly answered; in other respects, too, a greater degree of naturalness and freedom of opinion was allowed them than is generally the case, but, though tenderly, they were yet firmly guided.[28]

She considers briefly the daughter, now fifteen years old (exactly Melitta's age when the paper was written), who had been unusually gifted as a small child.

> From about her fifth year, however, the child's impulse for investigation weakened very much and she gradually became superficial, had no zest for learning and no depth of interest, even though good intellectual capacities were undoubtedly present and she has, so far at least (she is now in her fifteenth year), shown only an average intelligence.[29]

This condescending statement is extraordinary, considering that in 1921 Melitta did her matriculation in Slovak, a language she had not learned as a child, so the pressure on her must have been intense; and her success was remarkable under those difficult conditions. Was she trying to succeed in order to please her mother? In the autumn of 1921 she entered Berlin University to study philosophy and subsequently transferred to medicine. At Easter 1922 she supplemented her studies with a course in speech difficulties and graduated with distinction in 1927.

After Melitta's arrival in Berlin, her mother resumed taking her to psychoanalytic functions—hence her meeting with Schmideberg at the Berlin Congress. There was a close bond between mother and daughter, but it is possible that ever since she was very small, Melitta had not been sure of the consistency of her mother's love, particularly in view of Klein's frequent absences. The history of their relationship indicates that Melanie Klein was repeating the pattern of her own mother in attempting to confine the young woman to a state of emotional thralldom.

In April 1924 Melitta married Walter Schmideberg in Vienna. Were her motives comparable to those of Melanie when she married Arthur? Hans was now fifteen and about to embark on a course in chemical engineering. It would appear that Melanie Klein finally moved out, taking Erich with her, at about the same time as the wedding, indicating that she stayed only as long as the children needed her. She first moved briefly into the Pension Stossinger in

Augbwigerstrasse 17.* Late in 1924 she moved again, this time to the apartment of an elderly lady in Jeanerstrasse, where she had three furnished rooms. There is a widespread belief that Arthur Klein disappeared into Sweden, never to return. In actual fact he continued to live in the Dahlem house until 1937, when he moved to Switzerland, where he died in 1939. He remarried not long after the divorce ("disastrously," according to Eric Clyne, since he was again divorced within a few years), and there was a daughter by the marriage. According to his son, Arthur Klein was subsequently looked after by a series of housekeepers.

Erich was not with his mother for long after the final separation. He was sent away to school, first to southern Germany, then to Frankfurt. When Klein moved permanently to England in 1926, Erich did not join her until the details of the divorce were worked out. Arthur was given custody of Hans, and the situation was so acrimonious that Erich understood that if his father obtained custody of him, his mother had arranged with a friend to have him spirited out of the country and brought to her in England. The divorce, then, did not take place at the beginning of her sojourn in Berlin, as she indicated in her autobiographical record, but on the eve of her departure for England.

* It is probably this period Helene Deutsch refers to in *Confrontations with Myself* (New York: W. W. Norton, 1973), p. 141: "My personal contact with Melanie Klein was quite active in the period when both of us were analysands of Karl Abraham in Berlin. I think that Abraham achieved therapeutic success in treating Mrs. Klein's neurotic problems, but her analysis did not have a lasting influence on her extremely speculative thinking in child analysis. I was often a listener to her speculations, since during our analysis we lived in the same *pension* near Abraham's office."

CHAPTER TWO

Limbo

Ernest Jones regarded Karl Abraham and Sándor Ferenczi as the best clinical analysts among his contemporaries. Alix Strachey, whose first analyst had been Freud, found Abraham superior to Freud. Melanie Klein, then, had the privilege of contact with two outstanding men.

According to Klein's reckoning, her analysis with Abraham began early in 1924 and came to an end in May 1925 when he became ill. This would make the duration of Klein's analysis at least fifteen months. On the other hand, the arguments for a longer analysis should not be dismissed; her own testimony is not altogether reliable. She resumed the analysis of Erich in 1922; and in her distress about his increasing anxiety as a result of her interpretations, she turned to Abraham for reassurance, an action that would suggest she confided in him within the privacy of the analytic situation.

By general report Abraham, as a clinician, was cool and detached. British analyst Edward Glover praised his "high degree of stability and objectivity. . . . He was a good example of the so-called normal analyst who can tackle any disorder."[1] He was probably exactly the right person for Melanie Klein during this crisis in her life, whereas Ferenczi had provided the warmth she craved after the death of her mother. She never commented on their respective techniques beyond the remark that Ferenczi did not analyze her negative transference; by implication, Abraham presumably did. Grant Allan, Abraham's son, had the impression that it was a training rather than a therapeutic analysis. He cites as evidence the fact that, unlike the secrecy surrounding Abraham's other patients, Melanie Klein came and went in a very open way. He describes her manner with him as stilted and condescending. (For that matter, he also found Anna Freud "aloof.")[2] Clearly Abraham gave her an altogether different approach and theoretical framework from that which she had received from Ferenczi, and her early papers reflect the tension of her divided loyalties.

Grant Allan recalls an incident that tells a good deal about his father. In 1921, Edward Glover, in analysis with Abraham, accompanied him on his holiday to the Austrian Alps. During the night a mountaineer, his leg broken in an avalanche, was brought into their chalet. Abraham and Glover, who was a surgeon, immediately set about amputating the leg. Abraham allowed his son—then fourteen—to witness the operation, warning him that if he fainted he would have to pick himself up.

Dr. Herbert Rosenfeld tells an interesting anecdote that illuminates a side of Abraham not generally known. In 1946, when Dr. Rosenfeld was in analysis with Klein, she asked him to postpone publishing the paper he was working on, "Analysis of a Schizophrenic State with Depersonalization," until after the appearance of her record-making "Notes on Some Schizoid Mechanisms." In making this request she told him that when she was in analysis with Abraham, he would deliberately withhold interpretations lest she make use of them before he published his findings.* (It is sometimes said that Abraham regarded orality as his own private preserve.) Klein implied that she was more generous than Abraham because she at least would not begrudge Rosenfeld her interpretations. Dr. Rosenfeld was not at all offended; he looks back at the incident with some amusement, mixed with enormous respect for the elaborate evidence presented in "Notes on Some Schizoid Mechanisms."

Abraham undoubtedly helped Melanie Klein to surmount the most difficult period of her life. Her activities in 1924 testify both to the effectiveness of Abraham's analysis and to her own resilience. While she had produced relatively little the previous year when her emotional life was in a turmoil, 1924 was something of an *annus mirabilis.*

On April 22, at the Eighth International Congress at Salzburg, she presented a highly controversial paper on the technique of early analysis, which was eventually to appear in more thought-out form as the second chapter in *The Psycho-Analysis of Children.* The paper aroused uneasiness because she was beginning to question the dating of the Oedipus complex, the cornerstone of Freud's sexual theories. She asserted that in her analyses of children she had seen a marked preference for the parent of the other sex as early as the beginning of the second year. With the girl the onset of the Oedipus complex appears as a result of weaning and toilet training. When deprivation loosens the bond with the mother, the girl then turns to the father as a love-object. With boys the development of the Oedipus complex is both inhibitory and promotive. Inhibition is manifested in the trauma experienced when the boy tries

---

* If she was referring to "The Influence of Oral Eroticism on Character Formation" or "A Short Study of the Libido, Viewed in the Light of Mental Disorders" (both published in 1924), papers that had immense influence on her work, this too would suggest that her analysis began earlier than 1924.

to escape from his mother fixation; but in the oral deprivation of weaning, the boy is also forced to change his libido position in the developing desire for his mother as a genital love-object. Constitutional gender development is triggered by these early traumas. Gender identity is ultimately the acceptance of one's own reality. The sexual act is conceived by both sides in oral terms; and at the deepest level the mother is viewed as the dreaded castrator. Here was heresy indeed: the mother was replacing the father as the seat of the neuroses.

If these observations made some members of the audience restless, not so Ernest Jones, who listened with transfixed attention. While chairing the Symposium on Psycho-Analytical Technique held during the congress, Jones was to make a plea that he would later advance to Freud to give Melanie Klein a fair hearing: "In all these fundamental matters, therefore, both of theory and practice, my plea would be essentially for moderation and balance, rejecting nothing that experience has shown to be useful, while ever expectant of further increases in our knowledge and power."[3] Undeterred by adverse criticism in Salzburg, Klein delivered one of the most gripping papers of her life to the First Conference of German Psychoanalysts at Würzburg in October. This was the story of Erna, upon which the third chapter of *The Psycho-Analysis of Children*, "An Obsessional Neurosis in a Six-Year-Old Girl," is based.

In her observations of the severely disturbed Erna, brought to her when the child was six for an analysis that extended over two and a half years, Melanie Klein reached a level of understanding not touched in her previous papers. If Freud was led to an understanding of the development of the libido through the behavior of a hysteric, so Melanie Klein was led to an understanding of early psychic conflict through the observation of a cruelly disturbed child. More than in any of her previous cases, one senses her determination to ease the sufferings of a child old beyond her years, a child who complained that "There's something about life I don't like." There was an expression of visible suffering on her face, and in a photograph taken when she was only three the same expression was apparent. Erna was originally brought to Klein because of her severe inhibitions in learning. Indeed, the child realized she was ill and at the beginning of the treatment begged Klein to help her. She saw every act of her mother's as intended to harm her in some way, and in the transference to Klein it was soon clear that Erna was redirecting her fits of hatred and depression against her mother. From the beginning of the sessions she exhibited curious play patterns in which three people figured. Usually one of them would be destroyed. She frequently pretended she was the mother, and ordered Klein to take the role of a thumb-sucking child. On one occasion she ordered her to put into her mouth an engine with gilded lamps that she had admired: "They're so lovely, all red and burning." In the case of Erna's reaction to the engine, Klein made one of those sudden leaps of intuition that her critics have found disconcerting. The lamps that the child admired and sucked "stood to her for her mother's breast and her father's penis."[4] Similarly, in Erna's phantasies, coitus represented her mother's incorporation of her father's penis, and in turn her father incorporated the mother's breast and milk, acts that aroused envy and hatred in the child. Her fierce reaction was to cut up paper, stuff it in her mouth, chew it, and then pretend she was defecating or vomiting. The consulting room would look like a battlefield after Erna had vented her fury on her surroundings. Following these cannibalistic, aggressive acts, she would sink into states of deep depression.

Melanie Klein is often accused of dwelling exclusively on a child's inner life and attributing to it unbelievably complex and sophisticated perceptions. She is also charged with overemphasizing the aggressive impulses of a very small child. Again and again one hears that she ignored environmental factors. Yet for two years Melanie Klein strove to free Erna from her internal tormentors and to bring her into the real world, where she would encounter a loving mother who bore no resemblance to the avenging fury of her phantasies.

Erna had been toilet-trained without any severity, but had remained fixated at this point and had never recovered from her weaning. One factor in this failure, Melanie Klein contended, was that she had "a constitutionally strong oral- and anal-sadistic disposition." Like the Wolf Man's, Erna's phantasies had been activated by witnessing her parents copulate, in her case when she was two and a half. (In other words, her neurosis pre-dated Freud's Oedipus complex.) Freud had also seen the superego as the introjection of the parental figures, coincident with the resolution of the Oedipus complex; but in this case Klein witnessed an unbelievably cruel superego which projected its hostility onto an external figure. The object of Erna's hatred often appeared as an imaginary sister (she was an only child), and she feared her mother's body as a container of unborn children.

In this paper Melanie Klein began to speculate on the etiology of homosexuality, a phenomenon she had treated only glancingly in the analysis of Felix. Erna's anal love-desires towards her mother manifested themselves in her play, but at the same time it was clear that she experienced great hatred towards her. Here Klein agreed with Abraham's argument in "A Short Study of the Development of the Libido"—that in paranoia the persecutor can be traced back to the patient's unconscious images of the feces in his intestine, which he identifies with the penis of the persecutor, who is really the person of his own sex whom he originally loved.

Melanie Klein would not have had the confidence to pursue her work as she did without Abraham's encouragement.

He was very cautious [she recalled], the real scientist, who would weigh carefully the pros and cons, uninfluenced by emotions, but who seemed to feel that something here was growing which might be of great importance.

It was unforgettable that, when I participated in 1924 in a congress,* he said, at the end of the paper I read (Erna's History), which later made one chapter in "The Psycho-Analysis of Children," that the future of psychoanalysis rested with child analysis. He had never before expressed his opinion so strongly to me and, since I was really in those first years unaware of the importance of the contribution to psycho-analysis that I was making, his saying so came as a surprise to me.[5]

It should be emphasized that both "The Technique of Early Analysis" (Salzburg) and "An Obsessional Neurosis in a Six-Year-Old Girl" were written while she was in analysis with Abraham.

At the time she believed that she was treating children in the only way that could be based on psychoanalytic principles. Drawing her conclusions from what she observed (as Freud had advised), and reading Freud's papers closely as they appeared during these years, she was unaware that she was in fact departing radically from some of the fundamental tenets of psychoanalysis. With hindsight—by the time she finally published Erna's case in *The Psycho-Analysis of Children* in 1932—she saw that even then she had been moving away from Freud. This is apparent in some of the footnotes:

> In his *Inhibitions, Symptoms and Anxiety* (1926) Freud states that it is the quantity of anxiety present which determines the outbreak of a neurosis. In my opinion anxiety is liberated by the destructive tendencies, so that the outbreak of a neurosis would, in fact, be a consequence of an excessive increase of those destructive tendencies. In Erna's case it was *her hatred heightened by witnessing the primal scene* that brought on anxiety, and led to her illness.[6]

The fact that Abraham approved of this paper did not bode well for his future relationship with Freud. It is part of the mythology surrounding the early members of the movement that Abraham was Freud's most loyal disciple. Freud did not have for Abraham anything like the personal affection he felt for Ferenczi, and he initially resented Abraham's criticism of Jung and early warnings about Rank. Edward Glover once made a perceptive remark about the difference between the two men:

> Freud was a very timid man, just like a postgraduate really, most unsure of himself. His followers were not so timid. In the correspondence between Abraham and Freud, for example, Abraham was much more definite and convinced about Freud's findings than Freud was himself.[7]

* At Würzburg.

Freud objected strongly to Abraham's cooperation with a pioneering film-maker, G. W. Pabst, on a film depicting the course of a neurosis, *Geheimnisse einer Seelen* ("The Secrets of a Soul").* It is significant that the Freud-Abraham correspondence contains no reference to Melanie Klein's appearance before the Vienna Society in December 1924. It seems highly likely that differences between them would have widened had Abraham lived longer.

One can gain something of an impression of what Melanie Klein was like during these years from the recollections of her colleagues. One of these was Nelly Wollfheim, a child therapist who was in analysis with Abraham at the same time as Klein. She eventually came to England in 1939, and not long after Melanie Klein's death wrote a memoir of Klein that she took to Donald Winnicott, who was reluctant to see it published because he considered it rather scurrilous.[8]

Shortly after Klein's arrival in Berlin, Abraham suggested that she visit Wollfheim's kindergarten. It was immediately apparent that Klein was unlike previous visitors: she did not come to learn about Wollfheim's method of working with children, but quite clearly wanted to use the nursery for her own research. Nevertheless, Wollfheim was deeply impressed by this woman who was already an analyst as well as a favored analysand of Abraham's.† She was dumbfounded by the pretty, intelligent, and confident creature sitting bolt upright on the sofa, talking nonstop about her views on child psychology. In astonishment Wollfheim heard her say, "When a child, in his play, makes two vehicles crash into each other, he is making a symbolic representation of the coitus of his parents." She did not dare voice her skepticism because she regarded her visitor as an authority figure, a "transferred transference," an attitude that marked the whole course of their relationship.

The next time they met was at the Berlin Congress in 1922. Here Wollfheim watched in envy as Klein walked arm in arm with Ferenczi, her former analyst. Nevertheless, she accepted Klein's invitation to visit her at her home. Again she found herself a captive audience as theories poured out pell-mell. Suddenly Klein jumped up and announced that she had to go out, behavior which her guest found offensive.

They seem to have had little contact for the next couple of years, until 1924 when Otto Fenichel (recently arrived in Berlin from Vienna) suggested that a group, including Wollfheim and Berta Bornstein, approach Melanie Klein about giving a public course in child analysis.‡ Fenichel was responsible for advertising the course, but the posters he put up in shop windows were so

---

* This was *not* the film originally suggested to Freud by Sam Goldwyn. After Abraham became too ill to play any influential part in its development, Hanns Sachs took over. It was shown in Berlin in January 1926, just after Abraham's death.
† This also would suggest that the analysis began before 1924.
‡ This seems to have been a different course from the one referred to by Abraham in his letter to Freud of November 7, 1923, that was sponsored by the Institute.

amateurish that they had to be taken down. Nevertheless, the first lecture was well attended. Soon, however, the course had to be canceled because Klein both shocked and bewildered her listeners by refusing to put psychoanalytic terminology into language a lay audience could understand. But walking to the underground station with her after the lectures, the organizers bombarded her with questions, and Nelly Wollfheim felt that she was now beginning to understand what Klein was talking about. She and Klein then began to meet fairly regularly for Sunday walks in Grunewald to continue their discussions.

Nelly Wollfheim in turn invited her friend to hear her lecture on "Manual Skills as an Aid in the Treatment of Nervous Children" at the Berliner Psychologische Gesellschaft. Nelly was not allowed to have her hour of glory. In the discussion following the lecture, Melanie Klein jumped up and launched into a long outline of her own theories, finally broken into by the chairman, Dr. Albert Moll, a famous neurosurgeon. Embarking on a furious diatribe against psychoanalysis, he suddenly seized the handbag of the woman in front of him and shouted, "And this is described by Freud as the symbol of the female sexual organ!" The audience was in an uproar, and Klein was continually frustrated in her attempts to reply.

The two women were to come into even closer personal contact. Several children whom Klein was analyzing attended Wollfheim's kindergarten. One of these was Erna. Melanie Klein was constantly on the telephone asking about changes in the patterns of Erna's behavior during the course of the analysis. Wollfheim was offended when no reference to Erna's life in the nursery appeared in the published history of the case. She felt this was a glaring omission because the life of the kindergarten and Erna's relationship to the other children seemed enormously important.

> It become more and more clear to me that Melanie Klein was mainly interested in the unconscious proceedings and connections, and paid little attention to the real, everyday life of the children.

Before the beginning of the analysis, Erna was quiet and well behaved in the kindergarten. Then, about two weeks after her analysis started, Wollfheim found that she suddenly became very aggressive, hitting out at the other children without any apparent reason, and becoming highly irritated over mere trifles. She had always masturbated quite openly, but now the masturbation decreased. She had generally avoided the other children, and on walks always wanted to be with her teacher, engaged in intimate, grown-up conversations. She began to slip away from Wollfheim, evincing for the first time an interest in the other children, particularly in attaching herself to one little girl, whom she set out to dominate. This unusually well-behaved child became downright naughty, and Nelly Wollfheim felt that she was losing all her influence over her.

Wollfheim seemed torn between admiration and disapproval of Klein. She thoroughly opposed Klein's idea of prophylactic analyses for all children, about which she confided her uneasiness to Abraham.* Abraham reassured her: "You don't need to worry your head about it. There will never be enough child analysts to carry out this challenge."

Further insight into Klein at this time is provided by Nelly Wollfheim in another context. For two and a half years she acted as Klein's secretary after Melanie's separation from Arthur. Three evenings a week, at the end of the day's work, Klein would make a habit of going to Wollfheim's flat to dictate to her. They would begin by having a cup of tea and a chat about everyday matters, Klein meanwhile consuming the cakes provided by her "secretary." Later, as she marched up and down dictating, she would pause momentarily to seize every remaining edible morsel. The following morning the sullen maid was faced with cleaning up the crumbs she had ground into the carpet.

Klein dictated without notes, her thoughts pouring out of her. She stopped only when a new idea occurred to her, which she would immediately term a "discovery." (Donald Winnicott was later to describe her as a "Eureka shrieker.") To Wollfheim, the way Klein worked could not in any sense be described as scientific, but rather as artistically creative. These lectures were eventually to form the basis of the material incorporated into *The Psycho-Analysis of Children.*

During these sessions Wolltheim saw another, more personal side of Melanie Klein. In addition to the lectures, she dictated personal letters, some concerned with the final breakdown of her marriage. She never discussed these matters, but it was clear to Wollfheim that she was consumed with all kinds of worries and fears.

According to Wollfheim, after Abraham's death Melanie Klein's opponents attacked her far more openly. She recalled one meeting in particular where Klein was criticized so savagely and, she felt, so unfairly by Sándor Radó that Wollfheim could not help feeling pity for her. "It was high time [1926] for her to leave Berlin and follow the call of Ernest Jones to England."

Klein was always regarded by some members of the Berlin group as an outsider. It was also generally known that her father had been a Pole, and Poles were low on the scale of the rigid Jewish social stratification. Eitingon was accepted since he had money; but he always showed kindness to Klein because of his recognition of their shared Polish background.

* She later found Freud supporting the idea of prophylactic analyses in *New Introductory Lectures* (1933), S.E., p. 148: "The question may be raised whether it would not be expedient to come to a child's help with an analysis even if he shows no sign of disturbance, as a measure for safe-guarding his health, jsut as today we inoculate children against diphtheria without waiting to see if they fall ill of it."

The growing hostility towards her within the Berlin Society is attested to by Michael Balint, who, with his wife Alice, was among those who left Budapest for Berlin in 1921 to escape the anti-Semitism in Hungary. Balint, who was being analyzed by Hanns Sachs (Ferenczi was to be his second analyst), lived only a few doors away from Melanie Klein. He describes her in Berlin as

> already an analyst of repute who was listened to attentively, even though at times ironically. She still had an uphill fight to face, being the only non-academic and the only child analyst in the midst of a very "learned" German society. Time and again she brought her clinical material, using very courageously and for the sake of greater faithfulness the naive expressions of the nursery as her child patients did, often causing her learned and even reluctant audience embarrassment, incredulity and even sardonic laughter. [9]

The Berlin Society was composed of energetic, confident people, many of them attracted there after the opening of the Poliklinic in 1920. At the weekly meetings the leading luminaries sat around the long refectory table, the lesser figures ranged behind them against the wall, although there was no sense of rigid hierarchy. The silent but enthusiastic Eitingon was a marked contrast to the loquacious Hanns Sachs, who was almost repellently ugly—so unattractive that his appearance caused difficulties for Sylvia Payne when she was analyzed by him. Despite this he was a notorious womanizer, who managed, to everyone's astonishment, to gain a series of extraordinarily pretty mistresses. There was Otto Fenichel, noted for his encyclopedic knowledge of psychoanalytic literature. To escape from anti-Semitism in Hungary, Sándor Radó and Franz Alexander had joined the group. Both men were volatile and emotional, but possessed first-class minds. Alexander always reminded Paula Heimann of a gangster, but his appearance belied his brilliant intellect. Many of the members were to go on to make remarkable creative contributions, such as Felix Boehm's investigations into the feminine component in men. Karen Horney was already advancing the view that penis envy was simply a cultural phenomenon. This was both a reflection of her own courage and an example of the freedom of the group; the direction of her thinking had begun as a reaction to Abraham's paper given at the Hague Congress in 1920, "Manifestations of the Female Castration Complex." Hans Liebermann was regarded as an expert on obsessive compulsions, and Ernst Simmel a specialist on war neuroses, although at the time he was so obsessed with anal eroticism that he interpreted every paper from this particular angle. The early child analysts were represented by Ada Schott,* Josine Müller, and Melanie Klein. Heinz Hartmann (who was being analyzed by Radó at the time) recalls Klein as standing out

---

* Also from Budapest.

from the others in that she was beginning to develop her own theories. In later years, Edward Glover recollects Klein as "quite a type" when he first saw her at the Berlin meetings in 1921. "Someone should have made a drawing of her sitting at the table brooding over her own ideas . . . she had a personality, although it was not a personality that she put across to me. That's the reason she managed to get such a hold over the British Society."[10]

In addition to Edward Glover, the British contingent included his brother, James Glover, Sylvia Payne, and Ella Sharpe. They found the Berlin discussions free and animated, while tendentiousness was avoided through the serene composure with which Abraham conducted the meetings. On one occasion Simmel read a paper far below his usual standard. When he had finished, Abraham took him aside and had a few whispered words with him, and on returning to the table, Abraham announced that Dr. Simmel would prefer no discussion to follow his paper. As long as Abraham presided at the meetings, there was little overt hostility to Melanie Klein's ideas. Michael Balint described Abraham as "the very best president I ever met in my life. He was simply magnificent. Fair and absolutely firm. No nonsense. And kept the thing very well in hand. Again, he had his limitations. He didn't like fantasy very much. He didn't have much fantasy himself, but he was very much down to earth, excellent clinician, perfect chairman, and really a fair man."[11] Since Abraham was actually very much interested in phantasy, one wonders if Balint made these statements in order to undercut his association with Klein.

There does not seem to have been opposition to child analysis as such among the Berliners. For example, on June 14, 1924, Melanie Klein, Josine Müller, and Ada Schott gave a joint interpretation of children's drawings to the Society. But in September Hermine Hug-Hellmuth, the director of the Child Guidance Center in Vienna, was murdered by her eighteen-year-old nephew, whom she had brought up. The trial and its attendant publicity were very damaging to the early movement; and when the youth was finally released from prison he went to Paul Federn demanding money for having been used systematically by his aunt as raw material for her work. Now even the presence of Abraham could not restrain Klein's critics from giving vent to their nervousness about the dangers of probing a child's unconscious too deeply. Alix Strachey arrived from England at this crucial moment.* She and her husband, James, had been analyzed by Freud; but feeling that she needed further analysis, Alix became Abraham's patient in September 1924. Her letters to her husband give an incomparable account of the atmosphere of the Society at the time. On December 13 Alix heard Klein give a paper on the psychological principles of analysis in childhood:

---

* The former Alix Sargent-Florence was married to James Strachey, brother of Lytton Strachey. A graduate of Newnham, she was an elusive member of the Bloomsbury group.

... at last the opposition showed its hoary head—and it really was *too* hoary. The *words* used were, of course, psycho-analytical: danger of weakening the Ich ideal, etc. But the *sense* was, I thought, purely anti-analysis: We mustn't tell children the terrible truth about their repressed tendencies, etc. And this, altho' die Klein demonstrated absolutely clearly that these children (from 2¾ upwards) were already wrecked by the repression of their desires and the most appalling *Schuld bewusstsein* [excessive or unwarranted oppression by the Ueberich]. The opposition consisted of Drs. Alexander & Rado, and was purely affective and 'theoretical,' since apparently no one knows anything about the subject outside die Melanie and Frl Schott, who is too retiring to speak, but who agrees with her. Abraham spoke sharply to Alexander, and Dr. Boehm ... (possibly a very clever analyst, youngish and birdlike in manner) rushed in too to defend die Klein. In fact, everyone rallied to her and attacked the 2 swarthy Hungarians.[12]

The fact that the major thrust of the opposition came from the Hungarians raises interesting questions. The problem was compounded by Klein's rushed, breathless delivery—probably due to nervousness and inexperience, for in later years she spoke in a slow, measured way.

Alix Strachey was impressed by the examples she gave of small children suffering from acute anxiety. She felt that "die Klein" demolished Alexander's argument that children couldn't understand or would faint with horror at sexual explanations, by her account of one child with whom she could make no contact or create a transference until finally, in desperation, she told him that when he broke all his toys he was really trying to break his brother's "widdler." The general discussion following her paper was important in that it gave Klein an opportunity to emphasize that the only way genuine understanding of a child's mentality could be achieved was by proceeding from direct data gained from the actual analysis of children, rather than by making deductions based on existing knowledge of the structure of the *adult* mind. Alix continued to keep James *au fait* with events:

She's going to Vienna to read her paper, and it is expected that she will be opposed by Bernfeld and Aichhorn, those hopeless pedagogues, and, I fear, by Anna Freud, that open or secret sentimentalist. Two more women backed Mélanie.* One was Horney and the other a Frau Müller, who said something rather interesting, which was that children often *projected* their

* Alix Strachey often gave her name in the French form.

already-formed Ueberichs [which] . . . did not develop slowly in the individual child (I mean ontogenetically) from weakness to strength . . . but that it set in in different parts, in a not yet organized way (i.e. as relates to cleanliness, then as relates to cruelty, and so on) with full strength, so that tho' the child may be uninhibited in some tendencies its wretched Ich may already be ground down beyond endurance in another direction. Mélanie agreed to both these points. Well, it was most stimulating, and much more feeling was displayed than usual.

Meanwhile in London, on October 25, 1924, Nina Searl had given a paper to the British Society entitled "A Question of Technique in Child Analysis in Relation to the Oedipus Complex," in which she pursued the question of what was conscious and what unconscious in the child's mind while the Oedipus complex was being worked through. Sylvia Payne pointed out the difficulties in ascertaining anything specific because of the inactivity of the child's instinct-impulse and the impossibility of establishing a transference. Joan Riviere believed that the strength of inherited inhibition was sufficient to ensure a moderate control of oedipal wishes; and that in a balanced environment the child would be capable of adequate analysis. This and subsequent discussions seemed to be going off in all directions, and Ernest Jones pounced on any talk of archaic inheritance as suspiciously Jungian. Nevertheless, the meetings in which the possibility of child analysis were discussed were so lively that James Strachey, encouraged by John Rickman, wrote to Alix asking her if she could obtain a copy of Melanie Klein's paper for him to read at the next meeting of the British Society on January 7. Klein had already asked her about the situation of child analysis in England. Alix replied that she felt that she could make a five- or six-page summary without any difficulty, but would have to get Klein to write down the actual examples for her lest she get them muddled.

Unfortunately Melanie Klein had left for Vienna. Abraham had her address and volunteered, if she could not be reached, to supply the necessary corrections since he had seen the original paper.* In the meantime James was bombarding Alix with questions.

In what sense can we say that the Oedipus situation is present in the mind of a child of 3? In what sense is it true that a little boy of 3 wants to insert his penis into his mother's vagina? The wish is certainly not present in his consciousness.

Freud's most recent papers had suggested that a boy of three in the phallic stage, believing everyone had a penis, is unaware of such a thing as a vagina. Accepting Freud's hypothesis as self-evident fact, Strachey was puzzled as to

* The fact that Abraham had allowed her to present the paper in Vienna implies his approval of her ideas.

how Klein could claim that the male child wanted in his unconscious to insert his penis into his mother's vagina. With Klein away, Alix could only attempt her own understanding of Klein's concepts. She replied that in the child's unconscious there was "a hostile and sadistic-aggressive-libidinal attitude towards the parent." This would be the outcome of a sadistic image of copulation.

> Melanie is inclined to give great importance to this sadistic sexual theory, by which copulation involves doing damage to the female, castrating her, etc. And probably to the male too (losing his penis). She lays great stress on the importance of the [primal scene], either, I imagine, some real observation of the act of copulation on the part of the infant, or some substitute for it, which sets these sadistic phantasies in motion and encourages the child's aesthetic Triebregungen (sadistic impulses) with all its consequences as well as its intellectual theories.

Alix Strachey was a highly intelligent woman, and it is remarkable how she grasped the essence of Melanie Klein's theories in such short order. It is also an indication that Klein's theories were not so garbled and extreme as her critics described them, if Alix Strachey had no difficulty in hypothesizing an active pregenital period in a child's psychic life.

If Melanie Klein showed courage in discussing her theories before a skeptical Berlin audience, she was a veritable Daniel entering the lion's den in daring to address the Viennese. "I absolutely was not shy," she had said about her first day at school. In some ways she was extraordinarily naive in her touching belief that if she simply explained her theories to Freud, he would immediately perceive in them a logical development of his own postulations.

Anna Freud has said laconically that the response of the Viennese Society to Melanie Klein's paper was very critical. One can imagine the atmosphere at that meeting on December 17, 1924. Hug-Hellmuth's murder was on everyone's mind; there was jittery agitation over Rank's apparent heresy in the publication of The Trauma of Birth; and Anna Freud had recently entered the field of child analysis, unquestioningly accepting all her father's views.

Melanie Klein's unpublished Autobiography makes no reference to her appearance before the Vienna Society or to any meeting with Freud, and contains only a few bitter comments about her relationship with Anna Freud. Yet in 1958 she talked to Dr. James Gammill over tea at the Connaught Hotel about her first meeting with Freud—probably at the Berlin Congress in 1922. She could only approach Freud through the protective screen erected by his vigilant secretary, Otto Rank, she told Gammill. She found this a humiliating experience, "a narcissistic wound," Gammill described it. She was bitterly disappointed when she was finally given the chance to pour out her theories about the infantile psyche to the great man. He seemed uninterested in what she was telling him, and gave her the impression that his mind was occupied elsewhere.

Klein was closer to Rank than she probably recognized. She told Dr. Gammill that she never held a very high opinion of him; yet in her early papers there are footnote references to his works—prior to the 1924 publication of *The Trauma of Birth*. Both Rank and Klein were seeking a prototype of anxiety: Rank found it in the separation from the womb, Melanie Klein in the infant's ambivalent relation to the breast. Melanie Klein's opponents have accused her of never being willing to learn from anyone. It is unlikely that, at a stage when she was completely obsessed by her own adventure in thinking, in her concentration on the infant's early world, she would be willing to modify her views in any significant way; and it is unlikely that she continued to read Rank's work after his fall from grace. Rank's situation was a subject of constant discussion within the Berlin Society, according to Alix Strachey's letters. Abraham recognized Rank's theory as a threat to the core of the theory of neurosis. It is not surprising, then, that Klein no longer quoted him in her papers. Rank served, too, as an object lesson to her in later years. If one broke away from the institution, the price to be paid for such isolation would be the loss of a platform for one's voice, of a journal for one's publications, and of students to propagate one's ideas.

Nevertheless, had she continued to read Rank, she might have discovered that their views were closer than she realized. They were the first figures in the psychoanalytic movement to emphasize the importance of the mother-child relationship. Freud himself had said that the infant's separation from the mother served as a paradigm for all future anxiety situations, but Freud was speaking literally, in physical terms. His hesitancy in recognizing the implications of *The Trauma of Birth* is accountable in that Rank himself first saw it literally, and only gradually came to describe it in psychological terms as the beginning of a lifelong process of separation. For Freud the individual was propelled toward the formation of an ego basically by the need for the reduction of energic tension, namely by way of the pleasure principle and its modification, the reality principle. Neither Rank nor Klein diverged in any significant *psychological* way from the concept of persistent tension, and both saw early parental identifications as modifying the ego nucleus. Nevertheless, they departed from Freud's concept of conscience as self-criticism measured against socially determined concepts of morality. For Rank and Klein, guilt was not the legacy of the oedipal triangle, but arose in the earliest oral stage of development when the child's hostile feelings toward its mother are turned against itself. Rank never traced the process through the developmental phases of infancy and childhood as Melanie Klein was to do, but it should be pointed out that at this stage their thinking was closer to each other's than it was to Freud's.

What is remarkable is that Klein ventured into the Vienna Society. Whatever happened—and there is evidence that it must have been an unpleasant experience—she eventually received Alix Strachey's letter begging for clarification so that she could send a report to the British Society. Such a request would have been sweet music indeed, as she must have been smarting from her humiliation in Vienna. She replied immediately.

December 24, 1924

Dear Mrs. Strachey,

I am replying at once to your letter which I received today. Above all I thank you for having taken the trouble to comment about my lecture and certainly—as I gather from the formulation of the questions—in a most knowing way.

Point 1) I was explaining that initially the child does not consciously digest the interpretation—although at the same time the effects of the interpretation are clearly noticeable, for instance in the changed manner of playing. This is identical with the emergence of new material and makes access to subconscious layers possible, whereby at the same time a consolidation of the positive transference goes hand in hand.

After some time, however, the child begins to show indications of conscious digestion. For that I quoted as an example the child (a 4-year-old boy) who says: he is doing that to the little brother made of wood, not to the real one whom he loves. Or: a 4-year-old girl says, she had done that to the little woman in play, not to the real mother. There is still a need for the child to surmount great resistance before it recognizes that it is a question of *real* objects.

In this way a conscious recognition of a gradually changing *emotional* relationship to the parents follows before the child is capable of digesting the knowledge.

A 4-year-old girl said (this is the example you were asking about): "But that would be terrible if I really bit off Papa's penis." I often hear such remarks.

The 6-year-old Erna said repeatedly after she had again and again described her jealousy of her mother's oral pleasure while copulating: "But Mummy could not really give me that."

Point 2) This is the same child (remark of Frau Dr. Müller) who repeatedly said, quite surprised, after she had portrayed the cruel mother who had tortured her:* "But my real mother has never done that to me."

Such remarks, even if not so precisely formulated, I also hear from quite small children, three-, four- and five-year-olds.

Point 3) A four-year-old patient who, in the presence of an escort came for analysis for three weeks, ignored me in spite of all my endeavors.

---

* The mother in play beat and taunted the child, gave her bad food, locked her in the cellar, and often killed her in the end.

1) She rummaged through the handbag of the escort, then closed it, she said, so that nothing should fall out.

2) She did the same thing with the purse and the money in it.

3) She drew a glass jar in which there were marbles (small colored glass balls, etc.); on top of which she drew a lid, in order to close the glass jar so that the marbles would not fall out.

When, at this point, I gave my first interpretation that these were feces which she did not want her mother to produce and also not the other children, a changed relationship between us was established. Naturally with that only an *analytical contact* had been initiated. Later I still had to struggle with the most severe resistance, and fits of panic still took place when the escort discontinued accompanying the child, and only after having analyzed them was a proper analytical situation established.

I hope I have given you the clarification you asked for.

I shall arrive in Berlin on the third of January, late evening. If you wish to phone me on the fourth between 9 and 9:30 a.m. I shall be at your disposal with pleasure. (Telephone Pfalzburg 96–46.)

With kind regards

yours sincerely

signed:

Melanie Klein

CHAPTER THREE

Ostracism

Fortunately the mail was good in those days. Alix Strachey received the letter on January 1, 1925, sent off her report to James Strachey immediately, and the following day added some emendations after a further perusal of Melanie Klein's letter. James Strachey received it on January 3: "It is exactly what was wanted."[1] On January 5 he complained: "Her writing gave me a shock. What an awful woman she must be. I pity the poor kiddies who fall into her clutches." Despite Klein's awkward writing, Alix's précis allowed Strachey to present an abstract of the paper to the British Society on January 7. With the exception of Ernest Jones, almost all the members (even those who had known her in Berlin) were ignorant of the revolutionary progress of her work until that evening. The British meeting was well attended—about forty people, a large gathering in those days. Strachey reported to Alix that the response was good (a complete antithesis to the reaction of the Viennese to Klein's theories):

> What people said behind the scenes about Melanie was that they couldn't help thinking she *might* be doing it all by suggestion. (I gather that Ferenczi originally said this.) But of course no one had any grounds for believing so, and in the public discussion she was universally acclaimed. Jones, of course, is absolutely heart-and-soul whole-hogging pro-Melanie. . . . Mrs. Riviere, Glover, Rickman, and Tansley* seem to me to have internal reservations.

According to the minutes of the meeting, there seemed to be general agreement that reliable conclusions about the validity of child analysis could

---

* Known as the founder of ecology, Professor A. G. Tansley (1871–1955) published in 1921 *The New Psychology and Its Relation to Life*, in which he interpreted Freud's theories in biological terms.

be reached only by collecting further firsthand data rather than by relying on theoretical deductions. Whatever inner reservations Strachey sensed in Glover, the minutes record his criticism of the contention that the making conscious of the repressed, at any stage of development, could have deleterious results—though he did see a possible exception in any child who was destined to develop along psychotic lines. This original reservation was to have important consequences in his later relationship with Klein.

In Berlin at the next weekly meeting on January 10, 1925, Alix Strachey reported the news to Klein, who told her delightedly that she had "designs" on England. She proposed that they discuss these the following evening, which Alix anticipated with mixed feelings.

> Mélanie is rather tiresome as a person—a sort of ex-beauty and charmer—and she's unpopular with a certain section of the [Society] who pretend she's quite sound in practice, but feebleminded about theory.

The opposition now appeared to Alix to be headed by Hans Lampl, a Viennese.

Alix Strachey's reaction here was typical of her entire relationship with Melanie—by turns affectionate, amused, and irritated, but increasingly captivated by her ideas. Melanie assured her that she (Melanie) was absolutely first in the field, and that Hug-Hellmuth had only dabbled in pedagogical analysis and had never succeeded in unearthing the Oedipus complex. As for her own excursion to Vienna,

> Apparently she's had much more encouragement than she expected in Vienna, and Anna was practically converted, and the Prof. most affable (he appears to be entirely well). Of course M. is a bit expansive, so one doesn't quite know what those wily Austrians really thought.

Was Melanie giving Alix Strachey a prettified account of her visit in order to impress her? Klein told her that she would like to give a course of lectures in England in July, as she was planning to deliver a series in Switzerland in August.* She proposed presenting a general introduction to the subject, one detailed case history, a lecture on her play technique, one on analysis of children three to five, one on the latency period six to eight, and the final one on children nine to twelve.

When Alix raised the problem of Klein's English, she replied confidently that she thought it would be adequate if she brushed up a little. "She asked a number of questions: was there sufficient interest among the English analysts? Would Ernest Jones be supportive? She was anxious to know what she might

---

* These apparently never materialized.

be paid?" (Alix had the impression that she was rather hard up.) Carried away by enthusiasm, Alix promised to persuade her husband to speak to Jones on Klein's behalf:

> Will you? I'm really convinced it'ld be a great thing. For some reason or other, she's a bit sniffed at by some other people here, and has not I *gather* (but I'm not quite certain) been encouraged to give a Kurs here; so that it wd. be rather a score if we got her first. . . .

From now until Alix Strachey left Berlin for good in October 1925, her thoughts seem to have been as much centered on Melanie Klein as on her own analysis. Yet while they endlessly discussed psychoanalysis, attended art galleries, concerts, plays, and masked balls together, Alix Strachey showed no interest in Melanie's private life, nor did Klein venture any information about it. In her letters to James Strachey in England, there is not a single reference to Klein's estranged husband or to her children.* Klein seems to have been determined to put her past behind her.

Despite Alix's enthusiasm, James Strachey was still doubtful about Klein's ability to lecture in English: "What seems to me so awful is the lingo. Could she really do it well enough to be tolerable for six whole lectures?" Alix rose to the challenge and announced on January 25 that she was going to teach Melanie English. They planned to meet every Thursday evening to read "Little Hans" aloud in English, followed by a discussion of the case. Alix was pleased to find that Melanie also found Freud's account *"sehr lückenhaft"* (very incomplete). Alix regarded Melanie as a walking advertisement for the benefits of psychoanalysis: she would have been intolerable without it. She found Klein somewhat rambling in her conversation, but eager to be pleasant and reasonable. Alix realized that her support of Melanie might antagonize the male members of the Berlin Society; what she could not make out was whether their hostility stemmed from opposition to child analysis as such or from a personal dislike of Klein herself.

The English lessons proceeded according to plan. Alix was impressed by Melanie's understanding of the language, but her accent was so atrocious that they decided she should go to a proper teacher to learn conversational English. Alix felt that she herself was getting a private course in child analysis.

> I asked her about the question of transference, and she said that 1. it was as marked and as important in children as in adults 2. she 'deutet' [explains] it before taking it back to the original relation to the parents. The only difference was that 3. children resolved their transference easier at the end of

---

* In a letter of 1926, Alix's friend Carrington remarked on her indifference to people (see Michael Holroyd, *Lytton Strachey*, I, London: Heinemann, 1968, p. 522).

an analysis than grown-ups. Whether because "the world was all before them": or because they were in a state of continuous change themselves, she didn't say.

On January 31 Melanie dragged a reluctant Alix off to a masked ball sponsored by a group of Socialists. After her years of invalidism, she was determined to taste life to the full. Despite Alix's description of her friend as dancing "like an elephant," they whirled through the night until six the following morning. Alix evoked Melanie's appearance in a tone of Bloomsbury amusement:

> She was most elaborately got up as a kind of Cleopatra—terrifically décolleté—and covered in bangles and rouge—exactly as I imagine Cleopatra did look in the late Anthonies. She was frightfully excited and determined to have a thousand adventures, and soon infected me with some of her spirits. . . . She's really a very good sort and makes no secret of her hopes, fears, and pleasures, which are of the simplest sort.

As they circled the dance floor, every now and then Alix would catch a glimpse of a blissful, grinning Melanie. The social activities of the Berlin group were a marked contrast to those of the Viennese Society, under the puritanical eye of Freud, or of London, which was dominated by serious bluestockings. At the ball Ernst Simmel was dressed as a tiny night watchman, and at the end of the evening he appeared hand in hand with a young woman, announcing solemnly, "*Wir sind verlobt*" (We are engaged). Alix spied the flirtatious Sachs in the distance but, intent on his own business, he kept far apart from the other analysts.

On February 14, 1925, the Poliklinik celebrated its fifth anniversary. Eitingon, "the All-Mother of the place," provided "*almost* Russian food," there were toasts, and a general feeling that the Berlin Society was well and truly launched. A few nights later, after attending a film together, Melanie and Alix adjourned to a café, where Alix's admiration continued to grow as she listened to her unlikely little friend rattle on:

> She's not only got vast hoards of data, but a great many ideas, all rather formless and mixed, but clearly capable of crystallizing in her mind. She's got a creative mind, and that's the main thing.

The two incongruous companions, one tall, angular, and Bloomsbury, the other squat, Jewish, and déclassée, must have made a curious pair. Alix was becoming thoroughly caught up in the frenzied life of postwar Berlin and, instead of worrying about Melanie's English, reported that they were attending three more balls the following week.

On Saturday I'm again in Cleopatra's tow, who's got a rage for 'em. It's a Kunst Akademie dance, very large and official. Tomorrow's affair is connected with the Romanisches Cafe and altogether cheap, Communistic and perhaps low. . . . My God, when I look back on conversations in Bloomsbury—Virginia, Charly [Sanger], Lytton—What have I been brought to!

Alix escaped to a ball on her own, and was relieved to be free of Melanie's company for one night. While Melanie was extremely perspicacious about analysis, Alix found her limited as a person:

I was glad not to be with Melanie for she takes the high conventional line—a sort of ultra heterosexual Semiramis in slap-up fancy dress waiting to be pounced on, etc etc and not stooping to amateur behaviour and conversation. . . .

Meanwhile, James Strachey reported from London on Society matters such as the plan to open a clinic and the discussions over the feasibility of lay analysts, a question that was becoming a source of major disagreement within the Psycho-Analytic Association. On January 14 he approached the president of the British Society, Ernest Jones, to sound him out on Melanie's suggestion that she give a course of lectures to the London group. Jones seemed very much in favor of the idea, raising only the objection that he didn't think she should be paid as much as Hanns Sachs, who had received one and a half guineas a lecture the previous year; in his view one guinea would be sufficient. Strachey found other members greeting the idea of the lectures with "unanimous rapture." He suggested that Klein write to Jones herself.

Alix's letters continued to overflow with the remarkable things she was learning from Melanie. James Strachey was particularly fascinated by Klein's idea of the mother as the original castrator; he had, indeed, himself thought of raising the subject at a meeting.

On March 1, Alix had a discussion with Melanie about a case of "tic" (apparently totally unaware that Klein was discussing her own son!). Melanie was "all agog to capture England for her cause"; but by the end of April, having received no reply from Jones, complained vociferously to Alix at the weekly session. "I do think it's rather rude of him," Alix wrote to James. "After all, the damned English Society ought to be properly grateful for any small mercies from over here." Klein refused to prepare the lectures until she received a definite offer from London. While Jones was enthusiastic about her work, his first "invitation" was in fact a response to her suggestion (relayed through the Stracheys), and she was in a state of anxiety until it finally arrived.

At the British meeting on May 6, Jones finally announced that he had received a letter from Frau Melanie Klein offering to give a series of lectures on child analysis at the beginning of July. Very haltingly, he read out the letter to the members, then muttered, "Very interesting programme." James reported: "But on the whole he was extremely unenthusiastic and tentative. I had the impression, which afterwards turned out to be true, that he himself was very anxious that it should be put through, but felt doubtful of what other people would think." However, when all those attending the meeting—a small one on this occasion—raised their hands to signify that they would attend, Jones was wreathed in smiles. Ella Sharpe offered her rooms as accommodation for the lectures. Strachey misinterpreted this as meaning that she was offering to put Melanie up, which was to lead to a good deal of confusion. Now that the issue was settled, he was more worried than ever about her English, especially as her visit was arousing so much interest.

> Melanie need really have had no anxiety. She bids fair to becoming a succès fou. My only dread now is that she may disgrace herself and incidentally us, as the public now identify us beyond hope of recovery.

At this point Alix didn't yet share his concern. Alix's allegiance to Melanie was strengthened after reading Hug-Hellmuth—"a mass of sentimentality"— and particularly after a conversation in February with Lou Andreas-Salomé (reputedly Anna Freud's second analyst), who was staying with the Eitingons.

> Of course the subject drifted to Frühanalyse, and she had the most antiquated ideas got from Freud at the time of "little Hans." When she said that the parents were the only proper people to analyse the child a shudder ran down my spine. It seems to me to be the last stronghold of the desire of adults to have power over others.

This last sentence is chillingly ironical.

At last, on the morning of May 9, Alix intercepted Melanie on her way home from her analysis, to relate the good news from London. Alix had at first planned to translate the lectures—but after only three days of initial effort began to despair of the task. Words like "ghastly" and "horror" begin to appear in her letters as she contemplated the necessity of having the lectures ready by the time die Klein was supposed to deliver them beginning in early July. "I don't believe I'm up to it," she complained. She suggested that James undertake the first one—"for one ought to make a good impression"—and wondered if Joan Riviere, Marjorie Brierley, or Ella Sharpe would consider taking on two more.

James agreed to translate the first one, but reported that Joan Riviere was too busy translating Volume IV of Freud's works to take on any other assignments. In the meantime, Alix was deep in the translation of the second lecture

on the compulsion neurosis of a six-year-old (Erna). One of her major difficul-
ties was the lack of proper English equivalents for the terms used by Melanie
Klein in child analysis. On some days, nonetheless, she felt a little more opti-
mistic: "I don't believe the actual translation ought to be so excruciating as
Freud's, for one can be a little less awe-some; and lots of it is pure anecdote."
(In the midst of all this, James discovered that Miss Sharpe had offered her
rooms only for the lecture; there was no question of her accommodating Frau
Klein herself.)

In retrospect, the task of translating "little Hans" (done by the Stracheys
earlier that year) would seem to have been clear sailing in comparison with
these lectures. Nina Searl agreed to take on one (the fourth). Dr. Rickman announced that the duplicating of the synopsis of the lectures would have to be
deducted from the overall fee of 31/6. And then Klein produced the hat she
had bought for the lectures. Alix predicted that it would knock her audience
dead:

> It's a vasty, voluminous affair in bright yellow with a huge brim and a clus-
> ter, a whole garden, of mixed flowers somewhere up the back, side or
> front—The total effect is that of an overblown tea-rose with a slightly
> roug'd core (her phiz): and the ψ's will shudder. She looks like a whore run
> mad—or, no—she really *is* Cleopatra (40 years on) for through it all,
> there's something very handsome and attractive in her face. She's a dotty
> woman. But there's no doubt whatever that her mind is stored with things
> of thrilling interest. And she's a nice character.

Both women were so busy thinking about the translation of the lectures
and the imminent trip to England that they remained unaware of the seriousness of Abraham's condition when he took ill in the middle of May. They assumed that their analyses were interrupted only temporarily. No one would
have believed it at the time, but on May 9 he made his last appearance at a
meeting of the Society. Abraham and his wife belonged to a health club that
went on periodic excursions in the countryside. On one of these, Abraham
choked on an eel bone. Complications set in: a constant fever, double pneumonia, the necessity for a gall bladder operation, and the discomfort of persistent
hiccups. Frau Abraham or the maid would give daily reports to the stream of
worried callers. Klein realized that there was no possibility of her analysis being
resumed before her departure for England; and Alix's plans were consequently
changed at the last minute so that instead of staying in Berlin during July as
she had originally planned, she left for England in late June within a few days
of Klein's departure.

The final lecture was handed over to Alix on June 17. She instructed James
to shorten the lectures where he felt necessary ("she's a damned lazy little

bitch," Alix snapped wearily). In the end, James Strachey translated lectures one, three, and five, Nina Searl number four, and Alix two and six.

In London, Klein did not stay with the Stracheys at 40 Gordon Square, where they occupied the two top floors of the house, letting off rooms to other members of the Bloomsbury group, but in a small hotel off Bloomsbury Square. At the time the British Society had twenty-seven members and twenty-seven associates, but guests were allowed to attend the meetings; and so many people indicated a desire to attend the lectures that the locale was changed from Ella Sharpe's room to the drawing room of Karin and Adrian Stephen (Virginia Woolf's brother) at 50 Gordon Square. Karin Stephen stipulated that she must have a charwoman to clean up after each lecture, for which a shilling was deducted from Melanie Klein's payment.

These three weeks in July were among the happiest of Klein's life. At last she was the center of attention, listened to with respect. In her Autobiography she wrote:

In 1925 I had the wonderful experience of speaking to an interested and appreciative audience in London—all members were present at Dr. Stephen's house because at that time there was not yet an institute where I could give these lectures. Ernest Jones asked me whether I would answer in the discussion. Although I had learnt a lot of English privately and at school, my English was still not good and I remember well that I was half guessing what I was asked, but it seemed that I could satisfy my audience that way. The three weeks that I spent in London, giving two lectures a week, were one of the happiest times of my life. I found such friendliness, hospitality and interest, and I also had an opportunity of seeing something of England and I developed a great liking for the English. It is true that later on things did not always go easily, but those three weeks were very important in my decision to live in England.[2]

Among those who attended her lectures were figures who were to play an important part in her future life—Ernest Glover, Sylvia Payne, John Rickman, Joan Riviere, Ella Sharpe, and, of course, the Stracheys. During those three weeks she also came into contact with Susan Isaacs, a remarkable woman who was later to become one of her closest colleagues. Three years younger than Melanie Klein, Isaacs already had a distinguished career in child psychology. She had been educated at Manchester and Cambridge, and was now tutor in psychology at the University of London, where she remained until 1933. In 1924 she became the first principal of the Malting House School at Cambridge. This was a short-lived experimental school devoted to children between two and a half and seven. The founder of this school, Geoffrey Pyke, believed in the importance of fantasy as a psychical experience of great importance in the developing mind of the child, but that fantasy should be controlled by interesting the child in objective reality. The school endeavored to give the child scope for imaginative play, and the teacher's task was to record his observations of the children unobtrusively. During her visit to England Melanie Klein was taken to visit the Malting House School; and she and Susan Isaacs, who was already a member of the British Psycho-Analytic Society, recognized then that they had much to learn from each other. The only member of the Society who seemed predisposed against her was Barbara Low,* later to be one of her most spirited opponents during the Controversial Discussions in 1942–44. The reason was not hard to find: In *Beyond the Pleasure Principle* Freud had approvingly borrowed Low's "Nirvana principle": "the effort to reduce, to keep constant or remove internal tension due to stimuli"—that is, to return to a state of tranquillity—from her *Psycho-Analysis: A Brief Account of the Freudian Theory* (1920). In other words, Low believed completely in Freud's instinct theory.

Ernest Jones was aware that Freud would not look favorably on Melanie Klein's appearance in England. Nevertheless, as soon as the course ended, he sent off a straightforward account to Vienna, making no attempt to disguise his enthusiasm for her work. On July 17 he wrote:

> Melanie Klein has just given a course of six lectures in English before our Society on "Frühanalyse." She made an extraordinarily deep impression on all of us and won the highest praise both by her personality and her work. I myself have from the beginning supported her views about early analysis and although I have no direct experience of play analysis I am inclined to account her development of it as extremely valuable.[3]

On July 31, in response to objections raised by Freud, Jones replied briefly, firmly, and diplomatically:

> I know that Melanie Klein's work has met with considerable opposition in Vienna and also in Berlin, though more at first than later. I regard the fact as indicating nothing but resistance against accepting the reality of ~~her~~† your conclusions concerning infantile life. Prophylactic child analysis appears to me to be the logical outcome of psycho-analysis.[4]

Nelly Wollfheim was amazed by the transformation in Klein when they met during their holidays in August. On the way to the Engadine (chosen be-

---

* Low had first been analyzed by Sachs, then by Jones. She was a friend of D. H. Lawrence, who had given her the manuscript of *Sea and Sardinia* to pay for her training analysis with Jones. (See Barbara Guest, *Herself Defined, The Poet H.D. and Her World*, Garden City, N.Y.: Doubleday, 1984, p. 203.)
† The crossed-out word is a revealing slip.

cause Abraham loved it) Wollfheim stopped off in the Walensee between trains to visit Klein, who was staying in a hotel with Erich. It had been cold and wet when she left Berlin and she stepped off the train into brilliant sunlight, still wearing her heavy, unbecoming rain clothes. Dazed, she walked past an elegant lady on the platform, not recognizing her as the Frau Klein of everyday life in Berlin. She was probably already beginning to change her image. Wollfheim discovered that her friend had booked a room for her at the hotel. Dinner was excruciatingly embarrassing. Not only was Frau Klein beautifully dressed, but so were the other guests, most of whom were English. Erich, by then eleven, knew Wollfheim well. He had visited her often in her kindergarten during school holidays, and once had made his way across Berlin to see her without telling his mother. He was in a very mischievous mood, and paid her compliments with the intention of embarrassing his mother. "Aunt Nelly dresses much better than you," he would say; and again, "She looks much prettier than you. Is she much younger?" Klein's face remained an expressionless mask. "For the sake of decency she could not contradict him in my presence," Wollfheim writes. "She was the perfect analysed mother, and Erich was in a typical 'opposition' in a psychoanalytic sense. I cannot explain more about the circumstances on grounds of discretion." This would certainly suggest that she knew about Erich's analysis. The incident is also an insight into difficulties encountered when a woman combines the roles of mother and analyst for her own child.

Melanie Klein was not as composed as she appeared. When she returned to Berlin in late July, she discovered that Abraham's condition had deteriorated. As concern mounted, Felix Deutsch made several trips from Vienna to examine him, although Wilhelm Fliess was his regular physician. There were days when Abraham was well enough to see his patients; and in September 1925 Alix Strachey returned to Berlin assuming that her analysis would be resumed. Immediately after her arrival, die Klein rang her up to suggest that they do something together. Grudgingly, Alix suggested that she join her at *Così fan Tutte* at the Opera Königsplatz. Melanie was habitually late, so Alix told her the opera was due to begin fifteen minutes earlier than it actually was, and this ploy succeeded—Klein arrived only five minutes late, thereby saving herself from experiencing Alix's scathing tongue. However, the chatterbox could not remain quiet for long:

> She was in a flood of conversation from the moment the lights went out,—all about her plans for a social life during the winter. Then, after a momentary pause, just as a hush fell on the audience and the conductor raised his stick, she turned to me and took a fresh start (Und wie geht es ihrem Mann [And how is your husband?]) . . . Then followed a succession of remarks of psycho-analytic nature on the development of the plot, and so on. Never again. But she's an engaging character all the same.

Later they dropped in at the Romanisches for coffee, and Melanie was enormously impressed by a dull Englishman who had been a member of the 1917 Club. Did one dance at the 1917 Club?* "Oh dear, her heart is too nice for the likes of me," Alix sighed.

Now that the first excitement and fervor were over, Alix had to admit that they had very little in common.

> However, I like her, and she's very impressive in her line, there's no doubt of it. (I now think that Anna Freud simply hates her on personal grounds because she thinks she's a "low" woman. Someone ought to speak to her about her general sniffiness, don't you think?)

In the time that was left free because of Abraham's illness, the two women wandered around art galleries together. At first, Alix was inclined to be somewhat condescending about Klein's indiscriminate taste, but she came to see that she had a real love of Cézanne, which spoke well for her in the eyes of Bloomsbury.

Abraham was well enough to attend the Bad Homburg Congress early in September, but as the autumn days deepened, it became increasingly apparent that he was not going to recover. On October 1 Alix Strachey finally departed for England, where James Glover became her analyst the following year. On Christmas Day, Abraham was dead. His death, Melanie Klein recalled in her Autobiography, was

> a great pain to me and a very painful situation to come through. When I abruptly finished my analysis with Abraham there was much that had not been analysed, and I have continually proceeded along the lines of knowing more about my deepest anxieties and defences.

Klein always maintained that if Abraham had lived, her kind of child analysis would have become firmly established in Berlin. It is a moot point: Abraham's continuing support would probably have led to an even sharper confrontation with Vienna than Jones was faced with from England. In any event, the opposition against her which had been held in check by Abraham's presence erupted in full force after his death. On March 2, 1926, she gave a dual paper to the Berlin Society—on two corresponding mistakes in a school exercise and ideas that a five-year-old boy associated with the methods by

---

* The 1917 Club, founded by Leonard Woolf, was named after the February Revolution in Russia, and was intended to provide "a meeting place for people interested in peace and democracy; it soon attracted a membership of unpopular radical politicians and intellectuals" (*The Diary of Virginia Woolf*, Vol. II, London: Hogarth, 1977, p. 57).

which he was educated. The open scorn which greeted this paper convinced her that there was no longer any place for her in Berlin. Simmel, the new president, was sympathetic to her, but he lacked the authority to keep Radó in check. Radó considered himself one of Freud's sons, because Ferenczi passed on all Freud's papers to him to read. After Rank's downfall, Freud had appointed Radó editor of the *Zeitschrift* (Eitingon and Ferenczi were simply "decorative," according to Radó), as well as of *Imago*, a supplementary journal concerned with the application of psychoanalysis to the humanities. Radó refused to accept Klein's papers for publication in the *Zeitschrift*, and became increasingly abusive of her when she spoke at meetings. He reveled in his power as the new secretary of the Berlin Society, and was fiercely opposed to lay analysis. The humiliation Klein experienced at his hands was so intense that other members were moved to pity.

Melanie Klein's life was never free of complexity. In the early spring of 1925, a time when she was supposed to be totally involved in preparing the lectures she was to give in England, she had started attending a dancing class. The masked balls and the dancing class were expressions of her romantic longing for "adventures," and it is not surprising that she soon became romantically involved with her partner. C. Z. (Chezkel Zvi) Kloetzel was a journalist on the *Berliner Tageblatt* who specialized in travel articles and wrote children's books for his own amusement. Nine years younger than Klein, he was married and had a daughter. He was also a confirmed Lothario. He bore an amazing physical likeness both to Emanuel and to the demon lover of her fiction. An affair seems to have started immediately. In May he presented her with a book for lovers, in which he inscribed "Everywhere there is a Rheinsberg for us!" The lovers' secret name for him was Hans. (The choice of the name of her older son is curious.)

Kloetzel then went off on a holiday to Bohemia with his family. From Trautenau (where he had told her to write him Poste Restante) Kloetzel asked in his first brief note, "How are you and the Psychoanalysis à l'anglaise?"[5] He also assured her of his love, wished her courage and "a minimum of disturbing thoughts!" It appears from his next letter that she had reproached him for the coolness of his first note.

> Melchen, it's like this [he replied], to write letters is a stupid thing when one cannot express things verbally.... You know, that in one important respect I am more reticent with words than women on the whole prefer; please forgive me also that writing is even more difficult. Please read between the lines, will you? Let me tell you, dear Mel, that here each Austrian word, each "have the honor," and "kiss your hand," reminds me of you, which, of course, should not be necessary; memory technique is not

required. I am thinking of you often, dearest, and believe sometimes that you are feeling likewise. Especially when working I am aware of you, ambitious muse that you are!

Apparently Klein's colleague, Ada Schott, was her only confidante; and Kloetzel was curious to know how much Klein had told her of "our petit secret." As for the "ethics" of the situation, he was willing to postpone such a discussion indefinitely. He complained of boredom. In order to share her English interests, he was reading Shaw's *Back to Methuselah*. On May 23 he finally heard from her:

For granting me an extra kiss, many thanks. It shall be paid back in full measure. After all, Mel, the best part of a journey is the homecoming. And this will take place in about two weeks at the most, half of it has passed today, dieu soit benit! Perhaps some reason can be found to relieve me, which would enable me to escape earlier. For today, darling, think of everything which has not been put down in black and white. Solicitors only accept what is written down into the document—it is almost the reverse for us. All the best, and as many kisses as you can momentarily manage
    from your

Hans

Klein's pocket diary records that Kloetzel managed to return to Berlin on May 29. However, in a curt note of June 4, he informs her that he is rejoining his wife.

Dear Mel,
    Just arrived home. I found letters from my wife with the news that she is not feeling well. She suffers from nervous exhaustion, etc.
    For reasons that will be as clear to you as they are to me, I am very agitated and depressed. You will understand when I beg you to leave me to myself until I have somehow regained my equilibrium and have more pleasant news. If necessary, I shall depart the day after tomorrow for Trautenau. I will, however, keep you informed.
    Until then
    most sincerely
    yours

H.

Her diary for June—headed "Depression!"—records the disintegration of the relationship, although Kloetzel returned from the holiday earlier than his wife and the lovers saw each other almost every other day. On the thirteenth they made an excursion to Dahlem, but usually they met at Klein's flat, where they had a last rendezvous on June 27, the day before her departure for England.

Kloetzel himself was about to leave for an assignment in South Africa. On July 4 he sent her a few lines, reminding her that he knew that she had already given her first lectures in London, "and I am sure that they will have been a success. You will become more assured with each success, all London will speak of your fame and the Lord Mayor will invite you to dinner." Just before leaving, he sent her a long letter. He wrote again three days later:

Dear Mel,

Received, about an hour ago, your two dear letters of the second and third, and first and foremost I am more than proud of you. Not for one moment did I doubt that you would be a success in London. But it appears that this success even surpassed our expectations; and I am very happy about it. Because you, my dear human child, have richly earned what you now harvest. I know only a few people, and among them hardly any women, who are so deeply involved in their work. And the nicest thing is that, when in the not too distant future all sorts of people talk about you and your achievements, I can say, "I know all about it." And for that firstly a kiss to congratulate and then a kiss in admiration. . . .

I am extremely pleased that they are so nice to you over there and that you have so many pleasurable hours; human nature plays a large part on such occasions. I hope you will have a few happy weekends (without lame excuses) and allow your vitality full steam. With dress, hat and shoes as frame to your attractive personality, you will have no mean success, as with your [illegible; observations?] about the childish play.

Well, dear Mel, without a lot of words but with my whole heart—farewell. A *final* farewell will be said when I get to Lisbon. The few months to Christmas will soon pass and we are both in the good position to know how best to use our time till then.

Meanwhile, for London, lots of luck, success and enjoyment.

And a very very loving kiss for the beloved woman and the wonderful human being from your

Hans.

In late July, after her return from England, Klein took Erich on holiday to Switzerland. Here she received a letter from Kloetzel, mailed at Teneriffe, which must have been absolutely devastating to her—especially following the very loving one she had received in London.

S.S. Tanganyika
20 July

Dear Mel,

Your letter addressed to Lisbon arrived yesterday on board, and if I did not answer it by return, it was because there was a revolution and we left immediately.

I must now finally express something that should have been said a long time ago. We must part, Mel, not only physically but also in our spiritual relationship. You are far too intelligent not to have foreseen this. It is not only that my fears of obligational ties have increased. I have to add that I have fallen madly in love, here on board, more insanely as there is no possible future in it. But one does not think about that. I am in an uproar and cannot bear to keep this from you. I am not sure what the future will bring. I am not made for attachments and would only reproach myself if I allowed it to happen.

Dear Mel, we do not need to go into long explanations. I am *very* grateful to you. I am sure I do not have to beg you to give me my freedom.

I wish you, with all my heart, the very best,

Hans.

Already involved in a shipboard romance, Kloetzel was trying to let her down as lightly as he could. The corrections (shown here) in the draft copies of Klein's reply reveal her hurt.

Weeten, 9.8.25

Dear Hans,

Yesterday I received your letter which you posted at Teneriffe. It does not perhaps call for an answer—but I will follow my feeling—which tells me to say a few words of farewell.

You are at the beginning of a long journey, Hans, and many a lonely and difficult hour lies before you. If you were to think of me then ~~I know that I was also a person~~ of ~~value to you~~ it should not depress you. You write: "I am not made for attachments and would only reproach myself if I allowed it to happen." Well, ~~your memory of me should not be clouded by any reproach~~ You have done nothing to reproach yourself for. And—let me say this for our farewell—I do *not* regret ~~not even now, since I formed an attachment to you~~ What we had together, will always remain with me as something very beautiful. ~~And nothing, not even this way of ending, has changed that.~~

And something else remains unchanged: that is the warm feeling which I extended to you as a *person*.

Do not misunderstand me, Hans. I am entirely accepting your letter in the way it is meant. So far as a person can take and return freedom from the other, I am returning your freedom fully to you. I too will and shall cut the bonds which tied me to you, and I shall find sufficient strength to carry it through. But beyond this relationship, and perhaps I may say it now, ~~there was also a very rich relationship, person to person, which will remain with me forever.~~ That is what I wanted to say to you, Hans, for our farewell. I want you to know that I shall always be a good friend to you ~~who takes an interest in your well being.~~ You ought to know that we could remain friends, and if you wish it to be so.

I am enclosing a previously written letter ~~which I wrote earlier.~~ I was undecided about sending it to you because of the changed situation. But again I followed my intuition ~~which told me~~ and hope you will not misunderstand this gesture. I wrote these lines a few days before receiving your farewell letter. They do not contain anything which I would wish to change, even now. They were meant only for you when I wrote them—accept them as a greeting from a time now past.

If you want to write to me from Cape Town, that is if nothing inside you tells you otherwise, as a good friend from one to another, and if other chances arise, then I would be very happy. ~~If, however, your inner voice tells you not to, then do not force yourself to do otherwise—I will not misunderstand.~~

~~Do you wish to know anything about my future plans? England.~~ London, although completely satisfactory, was not a holiday. ~~The 2 ½ weeks were too short.~~ I shall therefore take a holiday after the congress and return to Berlin at the beginning of September. I may, after leaving Erich in the Oldenwald School, remain in the Taunus and shall perhaps meet up with my friends there.

Something else: as I only have a few copies of my brother's book, I would like you to return the one which is in your possession. There is, of course, no hurry for this, you can wait until your return to Berlin.

~~When this letter reaches you, then the journey through Africa is ahead of you. I hope this trip will be to your satisfaction. The interesting new things, which will take all your attention, will surely form a counterbalance for you against any pain, however strong.~~

~~And now farewell, dear Hans, with all my heart, all the best.~~

~~Mel~~

Kloetzel wrote to her again a few days after his return to Berlin.

Berlin
Sunday, 17.1.26

Dear Mel,

. . . I had intended quite some time ago to come to you, to speak to you, but, Mel,—I cannot. Do not be angry. . . . I cannot live like this.

We must find another way. I propose the following: We will not meet again for a little while until I feel more sure of myself. Then we will go carefully and meet on neutral territory. Everything depends on my learning to remain free in your presence, as my reticence towards binding relationships demands. If this is not possible—it will succeed if we are both sensible—then we must give up.

I know that you are the stronger of the two of us, and that too makes me feel sad. I am very much given to equilibrium in a spiritual relationship, and any will stronger than mine throws me out of balance. I cannot tie myself, but at the same time cannot tolerate other people tying themselves to me. This has been the same even where my mother was concerned although, in spite of everything, she was the only person in the world to whom I was very close.* Dear Mel, I know it is crazy, but this is how I feel: the day on which you were to tell me that you had a lover, I would be closer to you than ever.

When all is said and done, I am sure you have better things to do than to burden your thoughts with my pathology, especially as they are not scientifically of interest. Let us stick to my proposal. I am sure we shall meet again.

I kiss your hands.

Hans.

A draft of her reply indicates her turmoil.

Berlin, 18.1.26

Dear Hans,

At the outset of ~~these~~ my lines I would like to give the assurance that they ~~do not intend~~ are not meant to bring us together again if you do not desire this, nor to contain anything unpleasant for you.

My letter is meant to answer a question, which you did not actually ask me, but which, perhaps, you sometimes asked yourself—the question ~~how things are with me / what happened with me / how I coped / how I am~~ what happened to me. I was not very well last time we met. No one, not even you yourself, could make me believe that you are heartless and that you did not care ~~how I coped~~ what happened to me. ~~Arising from this sen-~~

* Klein later told Erich that Kloetzel had been brought up in a Jewish orphanage.

~~timent~~ I therefore think that what I can tell you about myself ~~will~~ may give you some pleasure.

~~I am well, dear Hans, and have totally mastered the pain from which I suffered. I have risen above it.~~ I am well, dear Hans—I have battled through it, but this does not, however, mean that I ~~have resigned~~ escaped into resignation. ~~This does not~~ No—I have totally risen above it, I am happy and am facing life ~~fully~~ as in my happy days ~~and full of confidence that it will bring me many pleasures in various forms. I am again full of confidence / full of confidence also towards myself~~ What you called my "vitality" ~~in the good days~~ has come back to me and ~~with that~~ also the ~~sure and happy~~ trust in myself and my life, and the sure expectation that it will bring me lots of happiness in various forms.

Fortunately personal circumstances give me the opportunity to use this reborn vitality. I am going to London in August ~~after my summer trip with . . . till the next winter, spring,~~ where I shall find lots of work with favorable material, scientific and personal prospects. ~~Teaching~~ In addition to teaching the children of Professor Jones, I have been asked to analyze several other children of colleagues. ~~Awaiting me is an especially attractive teaching post with my colleagues—in addition to an assortment of scientific work.~~

~~Also an~~ In addition I can also bank on intensive scientific and teaching activities within the framework of our agreement, ~~and also, perhaps, outside this agreement.~~ An invitation to give a talk to the British Psychological Society has been received—also a request from a New York Medical Journal to publish a book by me. My real book—which means a lot to me—is beginning to take definite ~~shape, outline and~~ shape, and may, perhaps, be written in London.

~~It is a / A very difficult but very promising job lies ahead of me / If it is a success~~ If successful—and I hope so—I shall, without doubt ~~go forward quite a bit~~ advance further. My newly awakened spirit will ensure that I shall enjoy life and not just drown in work.

I ~~am enclosing~~ send you my last work, which is purely analytical, but may be of interest to you.

~~Finally, dear Hans, permit me to say~~ Something else, dear Hans—permit me to say that the final sentence in your letter: "so we shall think of each other without bitterness" does not quite apply in my opinion as it does not say enough. ~~Without bitterness, of course—but more than that—with much friendship and sincerity / An~~ Our relationship, which was so beautiful that I would not have wanted to miss it from my life, in spite of the pain ~~it demanded~~ it inflicted ~~especially as the pain has now disappeared~~ has only left ~~friendly, beautiful~~ friendly and sincere feelings for you. . . .

~~I hope and wish with all my heart that your path will also lead upward.~~
~~Farewell,~~
~~Sincere greetings, Mel.~~

I wish with my heart, dear Hans, that your path will lead more and more upwards and that you remain happy and well.

Sincere greetings,

Mel.

The winter of 1925–26 was a particularly cruel one for her. Not surprisingly, Alix Strachey had found her relatively subdued, in contrast to her former exuberance. With Abraham ill, she felt totally isolated, and the excursions with Alix helped to relieve her loneliness. Alix returned to England at the beginning of October. Abraham died on Christmas Day; and Kloetzel's rejection was the final twist of the knife. Klein could not resist seizing on his birthday in February 1926 as an excuse to get in touch with him once more; and after succumbing to her pleas for a meeting, Kloetzel realized that he must take a harsh line in order to make her face the truth of the situation.

Berlin, 19.2.26

Dear Mel,

You will realize yourself that it is best to part for good. It was my mistake to give up a resolution twice made.

Very many thanks and do not be too angry. I do not think I need to say that I wish you all the best from my heart. It is better to be tough than to carry on an unbearable situation. We shall then remember each other without bitterness.

Farewell!

Hans

In desperation she telephoned him again, and the curtness of his next note left her no shred of hope.

. . . A discussion cannot alter things and would be, for both of us, a useless nervous strain.

I beg you, in the interests of us both, to abstain from a further attempt to speak to me again.

Please inform Frau Herz that I would have to have another partner if you intend continuing with the dancing lessons. . . . If you intend to continue, I shall withdraw.

Please let things rest.

Hans.

She drafted two letters before deciding to send the following:

Melanie at eight years.

Melanie, Emanuel, and Emilie Reizes, 1888.

Melanie in 1902.

Libussa Reizes in 1900.

Emanuel Reizes in 1901.

Melanie in 1920.

Melitta in 1924.

C. Z. Kloetzel in 1925.

Melanie in 1912.

Melanie with Libussa on the steps of their house in Budapest, 1914.

Melanie's husband, Arthur, as a student.

Hans and Erich Klein in 1916.

Alix Strachey.

James Strachey.

Ernest Jones.

Sándor Ferenczi.

Max Eitingon.

The Bad Homburg Congress of 1925. Melanie is at the middle of the parapet, Melitta is second from her left.

Karl Abraham with his family, summer of 1925.

Anna and Sigmund Freud at Tegel,
near Berlin, 1928.

Melanie and Hans in Brittany, summer of
1930.

Berlin, 21.2.26

Dear Hans,

As my request for a discussion has, apparently, been misunderstood by you (of course, it was wrong of me to ring you instead of writing), I am first and foremost concerned to assure you that I will not, *in any shape or form*, try to bring about an opportunity to meet, which you do not want. If I add that you will not receive any *further* written communications from me, may I assume that you will accept, without impatience, what I am writing today.

This letter shall partly take the place of the discussion which I so much desired but which I asked for in vain. Need I say—just as in the past, these lines are also no coercion of any kind, but explanation and change of views.

Dear Hans, I want to say to you that you have acted correctly and well to change our relationship to one of friendship, because this was the proper way to remodel and retain something valuable for both of us. But it was also kind of you from a personal point of view, because through this help you lessened the unavoidable pain I had to go through, brought about by this process. Your repeated conclusion, quite recently, that the entire phase, for both of us, was well on the way, was *no delusion.* Some small wavering, the rather large relapse when we last met, do not contradict this conclusion. This relapse especially and its quick recovery (my depression, by the way, had also other causes) have shown, in comparison with previous months, how much I have advanced. You yourself have noticed that I am slowly getting calmer and happier. You are right, dear Hans, one should not prolong an untenable situation. But was our situation thus? Till our last meeting you did not feel it as such, and the conclusions you drew from my depression were mistaken. I am, as always, honest towards myself, and you when I say: the process of parting from you in the way you wished was, with your help, going well. And it was good and soothing, dear Hans, to be able to be grateful to you for this help—it was a solace and substitution to put personal affection in place of our previous relationship.

According to news from London, there is a possibility for developing my English plans. Your departure for Sweden means perhaps farewell for an indefinite time—in which much may change. I am sure it would have been easier and more comforting if I could have seen you now and then during these few remaining weeks before your departure. It would be a gentler, friendlier way of saying good-bye to a beautiful, rich relationship—the chance of retaining something completely wonderful in one's memory, which would be a great help in facing what is happening without bitterness and in a more gentle manner. It is very hard, and to my mind unnecessary pain, to be crossed out of your life and not matter anymore.

I have never asked you for anything which you yourself did not want—

neither during the most beautiful time, nor during the present difficult time. If you cannot give me the opportunity of a gentler farewell, and thus be of great help and relief, then I will not press you, even now. But one thing I beg of you. I would like to see you at least before your departure. Must I tell you, after all you know of me and the situations you have seen me in, that it will not be a tearful farewell, nothing which would burden you. No, a serious, but calm and hopeful farewell between two people who loved one another, and understood each other sufficiently well not to have to separate without a farewell . . . before the parting of the ways a sincere and warm farewell after one has shared a short but beautiful and meaningful part of the way together. Please do not let me beg in vain, dear Hans.

Mel.

Regarding the question of the dancing classes. As Mrs. Herz was quite openly hurt by the cancellation of Mrs. Munk, I would not like to hurt her further, on my part, by a cancellation which can only be misunderstood. I shall therefore continue with the dancing lessons. I would advise you, in order to make the situation less obvious, to make some sort of excuse immediately prior to the next lesson, and then see how you can make it less obvious than by a general final cancellation. I am to tell you from Mrs. Munk that she is awaiting your telephone call. If you have no further need of the *Imago* please return it to me presently.

Melanie Klein was too intense, too serious, too depressed for the kind of light-hearted liaison Kloetzel had in mind. She seems, however, to have continued to exert a strong sexual attraction for him since, according to Eric Clyne, he made periodic trips to England to visit her. She was an intelligent woman who was capable of losing her head. The man whom she always considered the love of her life seems to have regarded the relationship as one of a series of trifling flings.

Help was at hand—this time in the form of a real invitation from Ernest Jones to come to England for a year to analyze his children. She never saw Berlin or Vienna again.

PART
THREE

1926-1939
LONDON

CHAPTER ONE

The British Psycho-Analytical Society

In September 1926, Melanie Klein arrived in England. During the first months in what was to become her adopted country, she stayed, as she had done in Berlin, in a number of temporary quarters. The first was a furnished flat in the Temple, owned by a reporter on the *Times*. Before the end of the year she had found a slightly larger place, a two-floor maisonette at 129 Crawford Street (later renumbered 96), not far from the Institute of Psycho-Analysis in Gloucester Place. Here Erich joined her three months later on December 27.* He stayed with a family in Swiss Cottage during the week and returned to his mother on weekends. When asked recently if he had felt homesick in England, he replied no, that he had never had a real home "so to speak." He felt himself Austrian, if anything; and it was a year before he could speak English with any degree of fluency. Klein regarded the Crawford Street maisonette as a stopgap until she could find a place spacious enough to contain consulting rooms and living quarters. This she shortly found at 63 Linden Gardens, Notting Hill, which also had the advantage of a pleasant garden. Its disadvantage, as she later learned, was the high density of prostitutes in the area.

Klein's first appearance at a meeting of the British Society is recorded in the minutes of November 17, 1926, where she is described as "a visitor." On this occasion she gave a paper on the analysis of a five-year-old child, Peter, whose castration complex was traced both to anal-sadistic phantasies connected with toilet training and to the trauma of witnessing coitus between his parents. She also reported on the Bad Homburg conference the previous year, at which the crucial question of minimal and consistent requirements for the training of analysts had been discussed.

* Klein told Erich that Kloetzel was going to bring him to England if his father was granted custody of him. Given the nature of her relationship with Kloetzel at this point, this seems to have been sheer fantasy.

The London Clinic for Psycho-Analysis had opened officially on Freud's birthday, May 6, 1926. The British Society's growing pains were more or less over when Klein arrived, and her presence was to be inextricably linked to its fortunes. In the bitterness of old age, Edward Glover in 1965 told Bluma Swerdloff that at first the British Society "suffered a good deal from inferiority feelings." In contrast to Vienna, Berlin, and Budapest, little active work was being done. But after the arrival of Klein, from 1926 to 1931,

> the Society felt fairly cock-a-hoop about really developing new ideas, and so they accepted her views. The members were impressed by the strength of the recommendation of Jones, but at that time her own opinions weren't so exaggerated. Actually they were derivative. . . . Some people have said that it was totally derivative. I don't think so, I think she had quite a number of bright ideas along the same lines [as Abraham]. [1]

That the British group had succeeded in reaching this stage of confidence was due to the indefatigable efforts of Ernest Jones, a strong-willed, tenacious Welshman, who was the dragoman of the psychoanalytic movement in the English-speaking world. On November 20, 1926, Freud wrote to Jones:

> Is it really twenty years since you have been in the cause? It has really become altogether your own, since you have achieved everything there was to be got from it: a Society, a Journal, and an Institute. What you have meant to it we will leave the historians to establish. [2]

This last was a rather ambiguous remark, and Freud had reason to be skeptical about the duration of Jones's allegiance.*

Jones was born into a middle-class Welsh family in 1879. His father, a self-made man, worked his way up from a clerk to colliery manager and then chief accountant in the steel mills in the village of Gowerton. Encouraged by the example of his father, Jones in turn had a brilliant career as a medical student at University College Hospital, London. In 1903 he first encountered Freud's work through the recommendation of his future brother-in-law, Wilfred Trotter, who brought to his attention Mitchell Clark's review of *Studies in Hysteria* published in *Brain* in 1898; and he then went on to read Frederic Myers's account in *Human Personality* and Havelock Ellis's discussion in the first volume of *Studies in the Psychology of Sex*. The Dora analysis was actually the first of Freud's works that he read; and (according to his own account) he immediately

---

* Jones was extremely offended when Freud described David Eder as "the first, and for a time the only doctor to practise the new therapy in England" in the Foreword to *David Eder, Memoirs of a Modern Pioneer*, ed. J. B. Hobman (London: Victor Gollancz, 1945). On August 26, 1945, Anna Freud had to remind Jones that Eder was the sole representative of psychoanalysis in England while Jones was in Toronto (JA).

set about learning German in order to read Freud in the original. In September 1907 he met Jung at the International Congress of Neurology in Amsterdam. In November he visited Jung at the Burgholzli Hospital after attending a special two-month postgraduate course in psychiatry at Emil Kraepelin's clinic in Munich. (He also visited the Kraepelin Clinic the following year.) On November 30 Jung wrote enthusiastically to Freud:

> Dr. Jones of London, an extremely gifted and active young man, was with me for the last five days chiefly to talk with me about your researches. Because of his "splendid isolation" in London he has not yet penetrated very deeply into your problems but is convinced of the theoretical necessity of your views. He will be a staunch supporter of our cause, for besides his intellectual gifts he is full of enthusiasm.[3]

Freud, who was happy to spot the possibility of a new convert, particularly if he was British and a Gentile, replied: "Your Englishman appeals to me because of his nationality; I believe that once the English have become acquainted with our ideas they will never let them go."[4] Freud's optimism seems ironic in view of Jones's long struggle with the British medical establishment, which it required all his considerable diplomatic skills to resolve.

The following year, Freud and Jones met at the Salzburg Congress, and Jones visited Freud in Vienna in May 1908. Their relationship was always to be one of wary fencing. While Freud reported to Jung that he found Jones "very clever," he was suspicious of the motives behind the Welshman's interest in psychoanalysis. Freud described him to Jung as both a fanatic and an enigma: "I find the racial mixture of our group most interesting; he is a Celt and consequently not quite accessible to us, the Teuton and the Mediterranean man."[5]

Nevertheless, Jones became increasingly important to Freud after the defection of Jung in 1911, since he was then the only remaining Gentile in the group; and fortuitous circumstances would lead to his becoming the chief spokesman for Freudian ideas in America. His medical career in England had come to a halt when two child patients reported that he had used indecent language to them. In 1908, fearing a scandal, he went into voluntary exile in Canada where, he claimed in his autobiography, *Free Associations,* he was offered a post as associate professor of psychiatry at the University of Toronto. Jones's own account of his activities in Canada is highly suspect. He claimed that C. K. Clarke, the medical superintendent of the Toronto Asylum for the Insane, hired him to be director of a new psychiatric hospital.* For various

---

* A. A. Paskauskas has pointed out in an unpublished paper, "C. K. Clarke and Ernest Jones: The Rise and Fall of a Kraepelin Clinic in Toronto, 1907–1909,"[6] that both men at this stage were enthusiastic adherents of the Kraepelin system (a fact later airily overlooked by Jones); and Clarke saw that the energetic young man could be of help to him in establishing a hospital devised on the Kraepelin model, in which there was a sharp dividing line between neurosis and psychosis.

reasons, however, mainly political, Clarke was never able to put his ambitious scheme into effect. It is also highly doubtful that Clarke intended to give such responsibility to a man totally lacking in administrative experience. In fact, after Jones arrived in Toronto in 1908 he became a sort of jack-of-all-trades: a part-time pathologist and clinical assistant at the Toronto Asylum; a sessional demonstrator in applied physiology and psychiatry at the University of Toronto; and an assistant in the Department of Psychiatry at the Toronto General Hospital.

The myth Jones built up about his own importance in Toronto has been accepted as fact—based only on Jones's own exaggerations. He arrived in the city assuming that his knowledge of Kraepelin techniques would help his advancement. However, he recognized a dead end when he saw one. By January 1910, Jones had published "The Oedipus Complex as an Explanation of Hamlet's Mystery" in the *American Journal of Psychology*. (Incidentally, this paper was revised in 1949 in *Hamlet and Oedipus* to incorporate Klein's research into the deeper layers of the unconscious.)

Jones had already started to make important contacts in the American medical community. In December 1908 he accepted an invitation from Dr. Morton Prince, a prominent American psychotherapist, to go to Boston to discuss recent developments in psychology; and here he persuaded Dr. James J. Putnam, professor of neurology at Harvard, that an American symposium on psychotherapy should be held in New Haven in May 1909.

Jones wrote glowingly to Freud that he had given the first paper on psychoanalysis in America, yet he also added: "A man who writes always on the same subject is apt to be regarded here as a crank . . . if the subject is sexual he is simply tabooed as a sexual neurasthenic. Hence I shall dilute my sex articles with articles on other subjects."[7] Freud was nervous, concerned that Jones might be watering down the sexual elements in psychoanalytic theory in order to make it palatable to American audiences. (In view of Jones's own past history, Freud may also have suspected him of a general disposition to avoid controversy.) Jung agreed: "By nature he is not a prophet, not a herald of truth, but a compromiser with occasional bendings of conscience that can put off his friends."[8]

In September 1909, Jones joined Jung, Ferenczi, and Freud in Worcester, Massachusetts, where Freud was given an honorary degree by Clark University. At this time Freud forced a polite confrontation between them, as Jones records in his biography of Freud:

> During the Worcester time, Freud formed an exaggerated idea of my independence and feared, quite unwarrantably, that I might not become a close adherent. So he made the special gesture of coming to the station to see me off to Toronto at the end of the stay and expressing the warm hope that I

would keep together with them. His last words were, "You will find it worthwhile." Naturally I was able to give him full assurance and he never doubted me again.[9]

As a matter of fact, tension was subsequently to develop between them—chiefly over Jones's sponsorship of Melanie Klein. However, that rift lay many years ahead, and at this point Freud had reason to believe that Jones was becoming an adherent to the cause.*

Jones's Canadian colleagues were suspicious from the outset of the brash young man from London, but he energetically pursued his initial conquest of Putnam and other American physicians. In 1910 Freud stressed to him the importance of establishing in America a branch society of the International Psycho-Analytic Association, which had been founded at the Nuremberg Congress in March. Jones subsequently played an important part in the formation of the American Psychoanalytic Association in 1911, when Putnam became president and Jones secretary-treasurer, a post he held until he returned to England in 1913. He continued to make regular trips to Europe during this period; and in 1912 it was he who proposed the formation of "a small group of trustworthy analysts as a sort of 'Old Guard' around Freud."[10]

For a man of Jones's temperament, Ontario was an inhibiting milieu. His abrasive manner, and the fact that he lived openly with his mistress, made him something of an *enfant terrible* to the medical community at the University of Toronto. Soon he was in trouble again. One of his women patients went to the university's president, Sir Robert Falconer, and accused Jones of assaulting her sexually. Jones told Putnam that the woman had made "unmistakable overtures" to him; but Putnam must have been astonished that a man who professed his total innocence "paid the woman $500 blackmail to prevent a scandal which would be almost equally harmful either way. . . . You may imagine that I am very worried indeed and dreadfully tired."[11] The affair was hushed up by Falconer, but it has never been fully investigated or clarified.

This was apparently not the only scandal in which Jones became involved in Toronto, and the sheer number of such incidents makes it difficult to accept the explanations of coincidence and hard luck. According to Jones, he and the university parted company in 1913 because the latter could no longer tolerate his prolonged absences in Europe, but his presence promised only future embarrassment to the administration. An uneasy Freud suggested an analysis with Ferenczi as a *sine qua non* for his acceptance into the official circles of psychoanalysis.

Soon after Jones's return to London on October 30, 1913, at a gathering of like-minded colleagues at his home, he founded the London Psycho-Analytical

---

* Jones always preferred the word "cause" to "movement," the latter term having in his view distinctly religious connotations.

Society. David Eder, the first practitioner of analysis in England, was appointed secretary and Jones himself became president. (Havelock Ellis declined Jones's invitation to become a member.) It was not the most propitious moment to launch such a revolutionary movement, and during the war that broke out less than a year later, communication with the continental analysts was intermittent at best. Severe doctrinal differences began to develop between Jones and Eder, who was expressing markedly Jungian views. Consequently, Jones dissolved the original Society, and on February 20, 1919, inaugurated a new group of twelve members, with more stringent requirements for admission—that is, every member had to be fully endorsed by Jones. This body was to become the seventh component society within the International Psycho-Analytic Association.* The following year, he founded the *International Journal of Psycho-Analysis* as the official organ of the Association.

Jones's dedication to psychoanalysis displayed an element of a survivor's desperation. As D. W. Winnicott remarked in his memorial address on February 28, 1958, in the early twenties the British medical profession was so hostile to him that there was an almost indefinite delay in his election to Fellowship of the Royal College of Physicians. By 1923 the membership of the Society already included such figures from the British intelligentsia as Edward Glover, Sylvia Payne, John Rickman, Joan Riviere, Ella Sharpe, James and Alix Strachey, and Susan Isaacs; Eder also returned to the fold in 1923, after an analysis with Ferenczi. Through the efforts of Rickman, a Quaker with a strong social conscience, an Institute was established in 1924, and in this same year Leonard Woolf's Hogarth Press became joint publishers with the Institute of the International Psycho-Analytical Library series. The London Society also had a benefactor in the figure of a wealthy American, Pryns Hopkins, who donated sufficient money for a clinic in Gloucester Place, to be used mainly for the benefit of needy patients and also as a training center for future analysts.

All these developments promised well for the institutional future of psychoanalysis, but very early in his career Jones began to show marked divergences from Freud regarding the origin of anxiety. For Freud, anxiety, the result of frustration, was the expression of a discharge of ungratified sexual desire. As early as 1911, in a paper Jones delivered in the United States ("The Pathology of Early Anxiety"), he was already beginning to speculate about the relationship between anxiety and fear:

> Desire that can find no direct expression is introverted and the dread that arises is really the patient's dread of an outburst of his own buried desire. In

---

* The difference between the two words was explained in 1949 in the amended Statutes of the International Psycho-Analytic(al) Association: "Brackets have been inserted here to give members who so desire the choice of discriminating between the two forms. In literary usage the suffix -ic connotes 'of the nature of,' the suffix -al 'pertaining to it.' Thus we speak of 'an historical play,' one with an historical content. So one might speak of 'psycho-analytic therapy' and of a 'psycho-analytical society.' "

other words, morbid anxiety serves the same biological function as normal fear in that it protects the organism against mental processes of which it is afraid.[12]

In 1926, Jones published "The Origin and Structure of the Super-Ego," which Elizabeth Zetzel (an analysand of his) described as "a landmark in his career."*[13] In this paper, which he described as purely tentative in its speculations, he attempted to reconcile his early supposition of innate aggressive impulses with Freud's formulation of the part played by environmental factors contributing to the postoedipal superego. Jones now suggested that harsh pregenital impulses are ultimately incorporated into the definitive superego: "The concept of the super-ego is a nodal point where we may expect all the obscure problems of the oedipal complex and narcissism on the one hand, and hate and sadism on the other, to meet."[14]

He had already heard Melanie Klein describe children tormented by a punitive pregenital superego. He and his Austrian wife, Katherine, believed that two of their children (Mervyn, born in 1923, and Gwenith, in 1921) would benefit from analysis, and he began to envisage London as a pioneering center for child analysis. As early as 1920, Jones had asked members for psychoanalytic commentary on their observations of young children; and a series of papers and discussions on child analysis, particularly on the question of how far analytic methods could be applied to children, were initiated in the Society. Jones was particularly interested in the matter because his own wife was experiencing great difficulties in mothering, and part of the arrangement for Klein to come to England was that she was to analyze Mrs. Jones as well as the two children.

Melanie Klein's pocket diaries indicate that Mervyn Jones's analysis began on September 15, Gwenith started on September 27, and Mrs. Jones on October 4, 1926. Klein reported to Jones on his wife's progress on October 24, 1926:†

> The first analytic session after that critical evening, did not give me the impression that the analysis would *really* come to a stop. I had the impression that Mrs. Jones was rather playing . . . with the idea but would not, if only for reasons of self-esteem (that means failing in this point), break off the analysis! In this session she was already accessible to my reasoning. In the two sessions after that we were already hard at work again—and yesterday's session especially offered the opportunity for elucidating her reactions of Wednesday and, on the whole, her relationship with her children. I see no

---

* We may assume that Freud disapproved of the paper from the fact that in a letter Jones quotes from Freud, dated Nov. 20, 1926, Jones omits a passage in which Freud comments on the paper (Jones, *The Life and Work of Sigmund Freud*, III, p. 130). It was written after he had heard Melanie Klein's paper on the technique of early analysis at the Salzburg Congess in 1924.

† Translation by Bruni Schling. All Klein's letters to Jones before 1930 were written in German.

reason for being pessimistic in this respect. The analysis of Mrs. Jones is
certainly not easy: it requires great discretion and tact and constantly I have
to reckon with great ambivalences. Yet I find that the transference shows
sufficient signs of viability and I am satisfied with the progress and development of the analysis. I have the same impression as you that her relationship with the children would have led later on to severe problems and
that—for various reasons—analysis is altogether quite necessary for Mrs.
Jones. I need your help very much on that point which we have already discussed several times. It can lead to severe disturbances if Mrs. Jones hears
you say anything which she could interpret as criticism of her and praise of
me—I mean everything that relates to the children, their development and
analyses, etc. It would be best if you left me entirely out of your conversations, for praise and criticism will be received by her in a completely different way. I also think it advisable not to say anything at present to your wife
about my plans, which I shall deal with in the second part of my letter. I
believe the prospect of my staying here for good could, at present, have a
very negative effect on her.

In the meantime Klein, desperate to leave Berlin, had been discussing with
Joan Riviere, now a firm ally, the possibility of settling permanently in
England. Riviere in turn put the idea to Jones, who responded favorably. In
light of these events, Klein continued:

It is very important to me that you do not misunderstand why it was not
you to whom I talked about it in the first place. In the course of my conversation with Mrs. Riviere I complained about the worries I have about
the difficulties in bringing up my son. It was a burning question for just at
that time I had received two further pieces of evidence of the very disturbing and damaging influence of his father. I expressed my concern that I
would be unable to continue in the way I have done so far, that I would
have to look for an opportunity to keep the boy permanently with me, but
this opportunity would have, of course, to be compatible with the possibility of my doing my work. Mrs. Riviere went into my worries with great
warmth and thus it happened that in the course of our conversation the
idea of my settling down permanently in London emerged. However, I
stated at once that this could be considered only after I had found out what
you would think of such a possibility. I would have approached you in the
very near future with a request for a frank discussion of this question. Yet
in the meantime Mrs. Riviere has taken the opportunity of raising this
question with you.

I should like to give you a more precise account of my attitude: With
regard to professional prospects, London could prove to be a complete

substitute for Berlin. A viable analytical basis, not only for my work but also for working for the establishment and expansion of child analysis, seems to me to be given here. That which I was able to begin in Berlin, with the fervent and active support of Abraham, could in the most beautiful way be continued and completed in London, if you will stand by me. I could make my contribution to the psychoanalytical movement, which I fervently desire, in London just as well as in Berlin. I am surely walking on safer ground in Berlin—yet I think it would only be a question of time till I established myself in London too. It is obvious that nobody can give a guarantee for such success, one just has to take certain risks in an undertaking of this nature. Yet I have a lot of faith in my work and its success, and if I know that you will support me, I shall be confident enough to dare it. The great warmth with which you, dear Dr. Jones, assure me of your assistance strengthens this confidence and pleases me in my heart of hearts . . .—in my mind I am decided to make London my new home.

The points in favor on a personal level are my very great sympathy for the country and the people, which I have felt already clearly in these last few months, that is, at a time when I was, if anything, rather burdened by initial difficulties. Nowhere else but in England have I experienced this feeling of a very strong sympathy and an ability in me to adapt to the strange and unknown. Neither do I think that the adjustment to a different climate will be a problem at all; in this respect I am neither physically nor psychologically very sensitive. The thought of bringing up my son in England is very attractive to me. He is good at languages and I have the feeling that he will readily acclimatize himself here. Thus, if I have to make a decision to give up Berlin in the interest of my son's upbringing, everything in me speaks for London, indeed, very much more speaks for it than all the other possibilities I discussed with Mrs. Riviere.

It would be essential for me, until I have found enough patients for child analysis, also to get adults for treatment. I very much hope that Dr. Glover will support me too, and I should like to inform him of my plans.

For many reasons I think it better that at present nothing of these plans be spread about and that nobody except Dr. Glover be told about them. Do you think that, if the Home Office creates difficulties, these could be easily overcome?

. . . I cannot finish this very long letter without thanking you once again, dear Dr. Jones, for the valuable support you have given me so far and for the kindness with which you promise me further assistance in the future.

Yours

Melanie Klein[15]

By the end of 1926 Klein had, in addition to the Jones family, six other patients, including an adult. Gwenith died tragically in February 1928 and her mother's last appointment was on March 12, after which her husband sent her to Vienna for a time to escape from the familiarities of home which deepened her grief. Mervyn's analysis was discontinued at the end of 1928 but resumed on October 5, 1931, through 1932 and possibly 1933 (although the diary for that year is missing).

By July 3, 1927, Klein had overcome her initial obsequiousness toward Jones and felt secure enough to offer him suggestions about his paper, "The Origin and Structure of the Super-Ego":

> . . . perhaps you ought to refer, in a few words, to the fact that your finding about the ego of the young child and the conclusions that follow from this, apply also to the older child. Self-evident though it may seem, a direct reference to it may perhaps not come amiss in this case. As a matter of fact, the widespread resistance against child analysis is, indeed, not only put up against the real and deeper analysis of the older child. However, your arguments seem to me to refute these misconceptions for it is obvious that that which the ego of the small child is capable of enduring, cannot be too much for the ego of the older child. It appears to me that a more explicit statement to this effect could easily be added.

Her subsequent remarks indicate that they were necessary to each other:

> I know it is a good and important cause and posterity will acknowledge the validity of your insight and judgment. I too have never, at any moment, doubts about the final success. Yet there can be no doubt either that it will be accelerated by your very effective support, and in the meantime this support will strengthen my enthusiasm toward you, and I shall never forget that you have been espousing my cause.[16]

She still felt apprehensive about arousing Mrs. Jones's jealousy and added a postscript. "I think it would be better—in order to avoid a disturbance in your wife's analysis—not to tell her the exact content of this letter at present."

After visiting London in June 1927, Ferenczi wrote to Freud of his consternation at discovering

> the domineering influence which Frau Melanie Klein has on the whole group. Jones is not only adopting Frau Klein's method but also her personal relationships with the Berlin group. Apart from the scientific value of her work, I find it an influence directed at Vienna. Even in this question

Jones urged me to take sides, but I refused and said that this was a scientific and not a party affair; one should wait for the development.[17]

Jones later told Freud that prior to Melanie Klein's arrival in London, he had taken "a benevolent interest in the matter" of child analysis.[18] His behavior indicated more than benevolence: to invite Melanie Klein to settle in England was in effect a political act, and the political repercussions surfaced less than a year later, early in 1927, with the publication of Anna Freud's *Einführung in die Technik der Kinderanalyse.*

Born in 1895, the last of Freud's children, Anna had never received from her father the affection he bestowed on her beautiful sister Sophie, his "Sunday child" as he described her, whose sudden death in January 1920 devastated him. Anna, although highly intelligent, did not even graduate from the *gymnasium.* Work with children, regarded as less demanding than adult analysis, was considered a suitable occupation for women. Anna, the unmarried daughter, was placed under the guidance of Hug-Hellmuth, whose views she absorbed.

She was also involved with Siegfried Bernfeld's Kinderheim Baumgarten, a camp school for homeless Jewish children which the Americans supported as relief work after the First World War, and she was subsequently attached to two child guidance clinics, one for young children and the other for adolescents, sponsored by the Vienna Psychoanalytic Society.

In June 1922 she became a member of the Vienna Society, after reading her membership paper, "The Relation of Beating-Phantasies to a Day-Dream," although she had attended meetings prior to this date. By then Freud had developed cancer and Anna began her professional life as his solace, his nurse, and his protector. By 1926, after the death of Abraham, the defection of Rank, and the disturbing "unreliability" of the last of Freud's surrogate sons, Ferenczi, his prospective successors* had disappeared from the scene, and none of his flesh-and blood sons seemed remotely interested in psychoanalysis. Moreover, no particular attraction developed between Anna and any of Freud's followers, much as her father tried to promote such a match.

With Freud's deteriorating condition, the relationship between father and daughter became increasingly symbiotic. Analyzed by Freud,[19] she also received referrals from him, and she had no alternative but to assume the role of his alter ego. For an inexperienced young woman to take on such overwhelming responsibilities at a crucial point in her life accounts for her hesitancy to venture into deep waters, her insistence on manageable situations within which work with children could be carried out, and her espousal of a structured ego psychology. This caution was a defense against the chaos that otherwise threat-

---

* Jones never seems to have been considered.

ened to engulf her. Also, her jealousy of Sophie and her fear of her father's death might have motivated her rejection of the death instinct, first postulated by Freud in *Beyond the Pleasure Principle* in 1920 after his daughter's death.*

Anna's reputation had to be established rapidly. In the Preface to the 1946 English edition of her first book, *The Psycho-Analytical Treatment of Children*, she speaks with some bitterness of the fact that the book had originally been rejected for English publication when offered to the International Psycho-Analytical Library. "It is not the author's fault," she states caustically, "that the early material contained in this publication is presented to the English reader at such a late date."†[20] She also says that Part I of the book comprises a course of lectures given before the Vienna Institute of Psychoanalysis in 1926, and that Part II was read as a paper at the Tenth International Psycho-Analytic Congress in Innsbruck in September 1927. She might have added that on March 19, 1927, she addressed the Berlin Society on the technique of child analysis, in what was in effect an attack on Melanie Klein. Klein, by then in England, was still a member of the Berlin Society, and she sent a written contribution to be read at the Berlin meeting, but it was not circulated.

In London, on May 14, Barbara Low gave an abstract of Anna Freud's book—"an excellent and comprehensive review, almost a translation," Jones assured Freud. The minutes record that "Mrs. Klein made some critical comments"; and Eder, Glover, Riviere, Searl, and Sharpe—a group whom Jones described to Freud as "dissimilar and independent of one another"—unanimously deprecated "the check that Anna's attitude was felt to impose on the development of early analysis." In response to Freud's expostulations, Jones voiced his regret "that Anna had been so hasty as to publish her first lectures in such an uncompromising form and on such a slender basis of experience—I felt she might regret it later and that taking so decided a step would make it harder to adopt later on a more advanced position."

Melanie Klein, distressed by the attack on her, pleaded with Jones for an opportunity to answer Anna's charges. He responded by organizing a symposium on child analysis by members of the British Society. When Freud later wrote to protest, Jones explained to him that he had previously written to Radó, the editor of the *Zeitschrift*, requesting that

> Anna's book could be simultaneously reviewed, as has been done before, by two people from different points of view, and his reply indicated that only a favourable view of it could be published. There remained only the "Journal." I should, of course, publish the "Zeitschrift" review in translation in the "Journal," but I promised Mrs. Klein that our pages would also be

---

* I am grateful to one of my students, Ruth Fox, for enlarging my understanding of Anna Freud. Fox has also pointed out to me how much freer "The Relation of Beating-Phantasies to a Day-Dream" is than her later work.
† In the United States it appeared in 1929 as No. 48 in the Nervous and Mental Disease Monograph Series.

open to any contribution of hers defining the points at issue between her and Anna and generally clearing up the situation. You may well imagine that it never once occurred to me that Anna would claim immunity from criticism of her writings, still less that you would expect any such immunity for her. Extremely important scientific issues were at stake and an open discussion on all sides seemed the obvious course. I certainly could not sympathise with the possibility of one side of the case being artificially blocked, especially when it was the one that seemed to me to be the more progressive and promising of the two.

One cannot help but admire the sturdy way in which Jones here stands up to Freud.

Many years later, long after his death, the British Psycho-Analytical Society held a special centenary on January 17, 1979, in memory of Ernest Jones. Among those paying tribute to Jones was Anna Freud, who ascribed the beginning of scientific differences between the societies in Vienna and London to Melanie Klein's arrival in London. "Ernest Jones disapproved of my early lectures about child analysis," she said, "and complained in a letter to my father about their publication."[21] Anna Freud may have been paying off old scores, but the situation was not quite as she describes it. It was Freud who first wrote to Jones objecting to the criticism of Anna's book that emerged at the May symposium and appeared in the August 1927 edition of the *Journal*.

In her lectures Anna Freud did not merely refer to Klein *en passant* but launched an immediate, frontal attack. Melanie Klein had contended that all children should have analysis as part of their general education, whereas the Viennese group believed it was necessary only in the case of infantile neurosis and was "risky" in normal cases.

Anna Freud drew on her experience in the previous two and a half years when she had conducted ten "long"* analyses of children. Unlike Klein, she believed that children's difficulties were often due to external sources, and that it was the parents, suffering from the child's "naughtiness," who sought relief for themselves as much as for the child. In other words, here at the very outset was an essential difference from adult analysis: in the latter, the adult made a deliberate choice to enter analysis.

Consequently, the analyst had to initiate a gentle, preparatory period, a "creeping into a confidence which was not to be won directly."[22] She then gave a series of examples of ways in which she made herself the child's accessory—in other words, established a state of dependency and a positive transference.

As for Melanie Klein's attempt to make symbolic interpretations of every-

* It is impossible to estimate what she considered a "long" analysis.

thing in the child's play as an expression of aggression or sexual union, could there not be a simple explanation? A reenactment of something the child witnessed in the course of the day, for example?

She then turned again to her own justification for winning children's confidence. She believed that child analysis had an "educational" purpose, and the analyst could guide the child in a certain desirable direction only if he had the child's confidence. Negative impulses towards the analyst are "essentially inconvenient."[23] Unlike Melanie Klein's view that if the child behaves in a hostile way towards the analyst such behavior is a reflection of his feelings towards his mother, Anna Freud believed the contrary—the more tenderly a child is attached to his mother, the more suspicious he will be of outsiders. An interpretable transference is impossible because for the child the analyst is not an empty screen on which the child can inscribe his phantasies, but someone possessing a code of behavior that he communicates to the child.

Furthermore, it is impossible to reach a small child's unconscious because the child is incapable of free association, and cover memories are constructed only in the course of the latency period. The child has not yet had the experience to develop a superego, and what ego-ideal there is turns out only to be an identification with the parents. *"The analyst must succeed in putting himself in the place of the child's Ego-ideal for the duration of the analysis."*[24] The analyst, as the child's mentor, must assume even more authority than the parents.

We can assume that the English group had carefully read Anna Freud's lectures and had come to the meetings on May 4 and 18 with their counterarguments marshaled, although Jones assured Freud that the discussion was "not in any way organised or influenced." The discussion might have used Anna's book as a focal point, but "the whole range of child analysis and cognate problems was widely discussed, and so many definite points of view and considerations were adduced from diverse angles that we thought it worth while to publish the discussions as a whole." He pointed out that Vienna itself had already set a precedent for this kind of ranging discussion.

Anna Freud's book was deliberately provocative; and although Jones admitted that Melanie Klein had pleaded with him to give her an opportunity to refute the charges against her, he not only supported her position but was moved by a British spirit of fair play. Hence he suggested that anyone who wished to submit a contribution to the symposium was welcome to do so. When Freud objected that Jones had rushed to publish the rejoinders in the *Journal* three months later, the latter replied that August seemed the most appropriate time to include the commentaries since there happened to be a dearth of material for that issue, whereas if he had waited until the biennial congress in September he would have been inundated by congress papers. It was a reasonable explanation; but there is no doubt that he also saw the *Journal* as a forum for scientific debate: if Freud complained about points of view that ran counter to his own or those of his daughter, *tant pis.*

Joan Riviere, who had been analyzed by Freud and who for some years had been translating his works into English, translated Melanie Klein's contribution from German into English. The arguments are marshaled so clearly and coherently that she probably had some hand in the organization of the paper as well.

Anna Freud had suggested that the role of the analyst should be confined to educational influence. In the symposium Klein set out to demonstrate that this position was directly contrary to the precedent already established in child analysis. In the earliest recorded case, that of little Hans in 1909, Freud had argued against possible objections that the child might be harmed by being confronted by aspects of his unconscious:

> But I must now inquire what harm was done to Hans by dragging to light in him complexes such as are not only repressed by children but dreaded by their parents. Did the little boy proceed to take some serious action as regards what he wanted from his mother? or did his evil intentions against his father give place to evil deeds? Such misgivings will no doubt have occurred to many doctors, who misunderstand the nature of psycho-analysis and think that wicked instincts are strengthened by being made conscious.[25]

H. Hug-Hellmuth, on the other hand, who deprecated the idea of analyzing very young children, shrank from penetrating at all deeply into the Oedipus complex lest it stir up repressed tendencies that the child was incapable of assimilating, and she also saw the role of the analyst as exerting an educative influence, views that Anna Freud had clearly assimilated.

Klein, however, in her first published paper, "The Development of a Child" (1921), the analysis of a boy aged five and a quarter, had found that it was both possible and salutary to probe the Oedipus complex to its depths.

> I found out that in an analysis so conducted not only was it unnecessary for the analyst to endeavour to exert an educative influence but that the two things were incompatible.[26]

The implied conclusion: she had been following in the tradition of Freud, whereas Anna had abided by the more timid approach of Hug-Hellmuth. Klein was not surprised that in the intervening eighteen years slow progress had been made in child analysis, since the Vienna group seemed convinced that "in analysing children we can discover not only no more, but actually *less* about the early period of life than when we analyse adults."[27] Because of these preconceptions, what had been present, according to Klein, was the inner resistance to finding an adequate technique.

Klein then lists the four principal points of Anna Freud's book and proceeds to demolish them one by one: that no analysis of the child's Oedipus complex was possible, as it might interfere with the child's relations with its parents; child analysis should exert only an educative influence on the child; a transference neurosis cannot be effected because the parents still exert a predominant role in the child's life; and the analyst should exert every effort to gain the child's confidence.

Klein directs her criticism above all at "the elaborate and troublesome means" by which Anna Freud becomes the child's ally—typing letters, making doll's clothes, and so on.* Klein, on the other hand, refrains from all enticements such as gifts or caresses. As she sees it, it is constantly necessary to analyze why the patient must see one as a loved or hated authority figure.

Their most fundamental difference lay in the fact that Anna Freud regarded children as completely different beings from adults, whereas Klein, convinced that children are still very much under the sway of the unconscious, regarded the analysis of the unconscious as her central task. One must accept that suffering is a necessary part of analysis and that anxiety can be alleviated only by forcing suffering and guilt into consciousness; Anna Freud shrank from penetrating the deeper layers of the unconscious lest the child go mad.

What Alix Strachey referred to as the "sentimental" side of Anna Freud asserted that Melanie Klein was unjustified in concluding that if the child reacts in a hostile way it is an indication that a negative transference is at work, for "the more tenderly a little child is attached to his own mother, the fewer friendly impulses are left in him for strangers."[28] In Klein's contrary experience, when hostility was traced back to the mother, the child's anxiety decreased. She had also found that, as with adults, in resolving some part of the negative transference, the positive transference is in turn succeeded by a reemergence of the negative. The reappearance of anxiety is an indication that the unconscious is freer to express itself in phantasy.

Anna Freud had attacked Klein's interpretation of the symbolic content of play, considering that the nature of the play could very likely be occasioned by actual occurrences in daily life. "If a child upsets a lamp-post or one of the figures in the game, she [Melanie Klein] interprets the action probably as due to aggressive tendencies towards the father, while if the child makes two carts collide, it is construed as implying observation of parental coitus."[29] Klein responded indignantly that Anna Freud missed the whole point. If such activities were accompanied by anxiety or guilt, Klein then linked them with the unconscious, her interpretation governed precisely by the same theoretical considera-

* Professor Peter Heller recalls that, during his childhood analysis with Anna Freud from 1929 to 1932, she was "always knitting."

tions as in the analysis of an adult. Her ultimate aim was to lead the child to express himself in speech—to the degree to which he was capable—for the aim of all analysis is to put the patient in touch with reality.

The play technique, she emphasized, is the essential means of reaching the child's unconscious. Utilized properly, it leads inevitably to the Oedipus complex; she declared:

> The analysis of very young children has shown that even a three-year-old child has left behind him the most important part of the development of his Oedipus complex. Consequently he is already far removed, through repression and feelings of guilt, from the objects whom he originally desired. His relations to them have undergone distortion and transformation so that the present love-objects are now *imagos* of the original objects.[30]

Not only was she departing from the orthodox view that the superego is the residue of the resolution of the Oedipus complex, but, from her observations of very young children, she recognized an Oedipus complex of "phantastic severity" deriving from the child's own cannibalistic and sadistic impulses. As she saw it, the Oedipus complex ensues from the experience of weaning—that is, at the end of the first or the beginning of the second year. In later life, when the adult suffers from anxiety of dreaded authorities, it is because "the old conflicts are reactivated or reinforced through the harshness of reality."[31] In the course of development the child will set up all sorts of ego-ideals, but at bottom there is "one super-ego which is firmly rooted in the child and whose nature is immutable."[32]

She compares her own six-year-old patient, Erna, with Anna Freud's "seven-year-old neurotically naughty little girl." Both were suffering from obsessional neurosis. Anna Freud, rather than delve into deep waters, tried to persuade her little patient that she could not possibly hate the mother who clearly loved her so much. For Klein, Erna's compulsive naughtiness was the manifestation of her need for punishment related to her earliest oral and anal-sadistic fixations and her feelings of guilt connected with them. What Anna Freud was doing was attempting to reinforce the superego, whereas Klein was endeavoring to modify its punitive severity.

Melanie Klein's long paper set out not only to refute Anna Freud's criticisms and to discredit her procedure, but to emphasize repeatedly that her own method was *true* psychoanalysis. The other papers contributed to the symposium are relatively short but all very supportive of Klein's views. Joan Riviere's argument is important in that it stresses an aspect of the child's unconscious that was to play a dominant part in Melanie Klein's formulations—namely, the role of phantasy. The objects of pregenital phantasies are not the real parents but unconscious imagos of them which in turn are later transferred to the real parents and worked off on them. Founded on identifications, to begin with they have no moral implications. She ends with a perceptive observation:

> Psycho-analysis is Freud's discovery of what goes on in the imagination of a child—and it still provokes great opposition from us all; this "childishness," these unconscious phantasies are abhorred and dreaded—and unwittingly longed for—by us even yet; and this is why even analysts still hesitate to probe these depths. But analysis has no concern with anything else: it is not concerned with the real world, nor with the child's or the adult's adaptation to the real world, nor with sickness nor health, nor virtue nor vice. It is concerned simply and solely with the imaginings of the childish mind, the phantasied pleasures and the dreaded retributions.[33]

Anna Freud could not have received a gentler rebuke.

Nina Searl, by all accounts a mild woman, testified that after learning Mrs. Klein's methods from the London lectures in 1925, she found it possible to develop a play technique in which she could have confidence, one that took into account the ego differences between child and adult, yet recognized libidinal similarities and was capable of adaptation to different ages. Ella Sharpe was even blunter than Joan Riviere about the resistances of some analysts:

> The problem of child analysis seems more subtly implicated with the analyst's own deepest unexplored repressions than adult analyses. Rationalizations that the child is too young, that the weakness of the child's super-ego makes an admixture of pedagogy with analysis indispensable, and so on, are built upon the alarms of that same infantile super-ego in the analyst that he has to deal with in the child before him.[34]

Edward Glover expressed dismay that while the work on child analysis had been produced almost exclusively by Melanie Klein, other analysts who had no experience felt confident to criticize it; even Anna Freud was in a weak position, since her analytic experience had been confined to the latency period. He saw a similarity between Ferenczi's "forced phantasy" and Melanie Klein's use of toys, and in situations where the analyst found himself at a complete deadlock with a patient, a fresh opening could be made by following Klein's method of direct observation.

Finally, Ernest Jones spoke in generalizations, his own experience having been confined to two youngsters of nine. He was the only contributor not to mention Anna Freud by name; but he stated his view that enough evidence had accumulated "not only to justify the futher pursuit of such investigations with children, but to indicate that the fears of the critics are here as unfounded in fact as they have long been proved to be in respect to adults."[35] Conclusions about the neuroses of the whole spectrum of human life would be proved by experience, not argument, and from the evidence so far accumulated he expressed hope that "we shall experience this last triumph of psycho-analytic theory and practice."

It is not surprising that Freud suspected Jones of organizing "a formal campaign" against Anna, particularly as each of the respondents had addressed himself to one particular aspect of the dispute; yet he could hardly complain that Jones had not kept him abreast of developments in England. Jones had a crafty side to him, which had not been lost on Freud. Freud, on the other hand, was touchy and the kid-glove approach was the only means left open to his colleagues when a disagreement arose. A letter Jones sent him on May 16, 1927, is a model of cunning flattery. He begins by expressing the gratitude he has felt toward Freud through the years; and adds that he feels impelled to express it yet once more because of the wonderful progress both his own children had made in their analyses that had begun the previous September. "The changes already brought about are already so striking and so important as to fill me with thankfulness towards the one who made them possible, namely yourself." He then goes on to describe in great detail the neuroses from which they had been suffering: moodiness, eating problems, temper tantrums, and play inhibitions. "It is plain that they were struggling with infantile conflicts that otherwise could only have ended in an unsatisfactory compromise, at considerable cost to the personality." (He neglects to say that the children were in the prelatency period.)

Ingenuously expressing ignorance of Freud's attitude on the subject, he states his own view that it is preferable to deal with the neuroses when they are

> still in a plastic state, than after the mind has become set and organized on an unhealthy basis and at great cost. I do not know what exactly you think about it, but there are no doubts at all in my own mind. The purely theoretical and academic objections sometimes raised, e.g., about the stability of the child's super-ego, etc. are completely answered by the test of experience, and I wonder if they are not sometimes displaced from a lingering doubt about the *reality* of the phenomena and the richness and capacity of the child's mind. All our experience shows how right were your conclusions in attributing to the infant a far greater maturity than has been suspected.

Jones never once mentions that Melanie Klein was the person analyzing his children.* It is also significant that the letter was written two days before the second of the discussions within the British Society devoted to Anna's book,

* It seems that he never did tell Freud that Klein analyzed his wife as well.

and at this point Jones must have decided that he was going to publish them *in toto* in the *Journal*, knowing full well that they would be highly critical. However, he concludes his letter to Freud in a very straightforward way:

> It is a pain to me that I cannot agree with *some* of the tendencies in Anna's book, and I cannot help thinking that they must be due in part to some imperfectly analyzed resistances;* in fact I think it is possible to prove this in detail. It is a pity she published the book so soon—her first lectures, but I hope she may prove as amenable as her father to further experience. This hope is strengthened by my admiration for all her other qualities—also analytic ones.

Freud's reply to this was that he attempted as far as possible never to take sides. Anna's work was completely independent of his, and any conclusions she drew were based on her own experience. As for his own attitude, "the view of Mrs. Klein about the attitude of the ego ideal in children appears to me completely impossible and stands in contradiction to all my assumptions." Freud was clearly smarting under Jones's insinuation that Anna had not been sufficiently analyzed:

> When the analysts are of different opinion on one point, the assumption is that the erroneous view of one may originate in the fact that he is not completely analyzed so that he allows himself to be influenced by his complexes at a cost to science. But in the practical polemic I consider such an argument is not admissible, because each party can make use of this argument and it does not help to come to a judgment as to which party is in error.

Jones replied blandly that he failed to see why Freud objected so strenuously to Melanie Klein's view of the superego.

> The only [*sic*] difference I was aware of is that she dates both the Oedipus conflict and the genesis of the super-ego a year or two earlier than you have. As one of your chief discoveries has been the fact that young children are much more mature than had been generally supposed both sexually and morally, I had regarded the conclusions reached from Frau Klein's experience as being simply a direct continuation of your own.

Jones therefore requested that Freud tell him directly where their differences lay.

---

* Did Jones suspect that Freud had analyzed Anna? Jones could have reminded Freud that the latter, on May 16, 1926, in a speech to his pupils in the drawing room on the occasion of his withdrawal from participation in the psychoanalytic movement, reminded them that "it is hardly possible to exaggerate the power of inner resistances against acceptance of unconscious tendencies" (Ernest Jones, *The Life and Work of Sigmund Freud* [New York: Basic Books, 1957], III, p. 124).

Freud's reply was evasive. He endorsed Klein's belief that small children were more mature than he had realized; but for a man who refrained from taking sides, he now became remarkably forthright:

I would like to contradict Mrs. Klein in this point, that she regards the super-ego of the children [to be] as independent as that of adults while it appears to me that Anna is right in emphasizing that the infantile super-ego is still under the direct influence of the parents.

That Anna was in a pugnacious mood is attested by her recording years later that "In Vienna from 1927 onward, a group of analysts, later joined by colleagues from Budapest and Prague, held regular meetings with me to discuss the child-analytic technique I had suggested, to report on cases treated with this method, to compare results, and to clarify the theoretical background of our clinical findings."[36] This was the beginning of the annual Four Countries' Conference.

The development of psychoanalytic concepts has usually followed a pattern of response and counterresponse. These letters from Freud to Jones are interesting as a revelation of Freud's reaction to Melanie Klein's views, since he made so few references to her in his published work.* However, while influences are not always easy to detect unconditionally, an argument could be advanced that Klein may have led him to rethink some of his earlier views. It is a question that might be pondered in relation to one of his most important papers, "Inhibitions, Symptoms and Anxiety." First written in July 1925—the very month in which Klein was delivering her lectures in London—it was published early the following year. It was to be his last major statement on anxiety, although he reverted to the subject seven years later in *New Introductory Lectures.*

"Inhibitions, Symptoms and Anxiety" was written as a refutation of Rank's theory of the birth trauma, which Freud had at first been inclined to regard favorably; certainly it contains none of the irritable polemic associated with his attacks on Adler. The tone is ruminative, almost mournful. Not only does he reverse his earlier view that anxiety results from repression, but the latter he now sees as simply one of several defenses employed by the ego. He is willing to admit that the act of birth is the prototype of anxiety, but cannot agree that subsequent attacks of anxiety are simply a repetition of this primal experience, because most anxiety attacks signal approaching danger. Morbid anxiety may emanate from the id or the superego. As in the past, he continued to insist that in males it is the fear of being castrated, in females the fear of loss of love.

* The Index of the S.E. lists three footnote references; but there is actually an important comment in "Female Sexuality" (1931), S.E., 11, p. 242.

Freud seems to be thinking aloud in the note of sad bewilderment with which he poses a series of rhetorical questions:

> . . . a great many people remain infantile in their behavior in regard to danger and do not overcome determinants to anxiety which have grown out of date. To deny this would be to deny the existence of neurosis, for it is precisely such people whom we call neurotics. But how is this possible? Why are not all neuroses episodes in the development of the individual which come to a close when the next phase is reached? Whence comes the element of persistence in these reactions to danger? Why does the affect of anxiety alone seem to enjoy the advantage over all other affects of evoking reactions which are distinguished from the rest in being abnormal and which, through their inexpediency, run counter to the movement of life? In other words, we have once more come unawares upon the riddle which has so often confronted us: whence does neurosis come—what is its ultimate, its own peculiar *raison d'être?* After years of psycho-analytic labours, we are as much in the dark about the problem as we were at the start.[37]

Suffering acute pain from cancer of the jaw, Freud was in a state of pessimism and despair. If he felt that he had come no closer to understanding the origins of anxiety, not so Melanie Klein, who arrived at the Tenth International Congress at Innsbruck at the beginning of September 1927 surrounded for the first time by a circle of loyal and optimistic adherents.

On September 3, Anna Freud traversed the familiar ground of the safe parameters within which to practice child analysis. She pointed out that Melanie Klein had claimed that she—Anna—didn't penetrate the Oedipus complex of her patients. Now she set out to show that she did—within the time-scale and assumptions of the traditional pattern that Freud had set out. Her seven-year-old girl was afraid of loss of love. Anna concluded with two points: the difference between the superego of the child and that of the adult, and the educative role of the analyst. If the demands of the child's superego were lessened (Melanie Klein saw this as her primary goal), the child would be apt to go to extremes and to indulge itself further than even the freest environment would permit. And since the child's superego is so dependent on external factors, it is essential that the analyst should take over the child's upbringing during the period of analysis. In other words, her paper was only a more strongly worded confirmation of her earlier lectures.

On the same day, Melanie Klein delivered "Early Stages of the Oedipus Complex," a paper whose concepts were more challenging than any she had previously presented. Here for the first time she made it clear that on some important issues she differed radically from Freud—on the dating of the Oedipus

complex; on her view of what it constituted; and on the psychic difference between boys and girls, and in the inception of their respective neuroses.

She begins by referring to her earlier Salzburg paper, "The Psychological
Principles of Early Analysis" (1926), in which she had caused shock waves by
adumbrating the following sequence: (1) the Oedipus tendencies are released
as a consequence of the frustration of weaning; (2) they first appear at the end
of the first or the beginning of the second year; (3) they receive reinforcement
through anal frustration experienced during toilet training.

She now turned to the determining influence of the anatomical difference
in the sexes and to the consequent fears experienced by each, a series of reflections distinctly counter to Freud's tenaciously held views of male castration
anxiety and female fear of loss of love.

Guilt had been considered by Ferenczi to relate back to "sphincter-moral-
ity," and by Abraham to the early anal-sadistic phase following the cannibalistic level at which anxiety first makes its appearance. Klein would go further
than this: guilt follows from the Oedipus conflict in which love-objects have
been introjected; and in a child of one "the beginning of the Oedipus conflict
takes the form of a dread of being devoured and destroyed."[38] In other words,
when the baby is still in the oral stage he has formed an imago, a superego who
punishes him in the only way comprehensible to his pregenital experience.*

Freud had agreed with Rank that birth is the prototype of all anxiety. Klein
takes a different tack: oral and anal frustrations form the prototype of all later
frustrations and while they also signify punishment, they give rise to anxiety.

The infant's curiosity is incapable of being expressed verbally and his frustration finds expression in a surprising amount of hate. Hence Klein concluded
that the early connection between the epistemophilic impulse and hate is important for the whole mental development. Since oedipal tendencies have already become operative, the child is curious about the mother's body and
craves to appropriate its contents, a craving that is so linked to its Oedipus
feelings that it gives rise to guilt. Such a pattern is common to both sexes up to
the anal-sadistic phase.

The boy is beginning to turn his mother into a love-object, so that in addition to his guilt over his sadistic phantasies against her, he begins to dread castration by his father. The conclusion Klein drew from this was to have
important consequences for her thinking on mental development: the degree
to which the child surmounts oral frustrations to attain the genital position will
partly depend on his capacity for tolerating this anxiety.

---

* According to Dr. James Lieberman, Rank used the term "preoedipal" in 1927 and possibly earlier. In Rank's
"Literary Autobiography" (1930) he speaks of "the primal source of the super-ego in the preoedipal (maternal) inhibitions. The preoedipal super-ego has since been overemphasized by Melanie Klein (without any reference to me)."[39]

If the baby boy desires to rob his mother's body of its contents, these would be her feces, but as he moves into what she describes as the "femininity-phase," he now wants to rob it of babies as well as the breasts that have provided him with nourishment, and his greed encompasses the father's penis, which he assumes has been absorbed into the mother's body. He phantasizes that his mother will punish him for what he wants to do to her by castrating him. Hence the superego formed at this stage is created from the combined persecutory figures of mother and father.

How does the boy cope with the predicament of his femininity complex? His inability to have a child is overcompensated for by the superiority he assumes by the possession of a penis. His masculine contempt is basically rooted in fear of retaliation. Future neurotic difficulties are often an expression of an inability to resolve the conflicts associated with the femininity phase.

The contribution that Klein made to an explanation of female sexuality has never been sufficiently acknowledged. First, a word about the argument that had been developing over Freud's "phallocentrism," a question much discussed by Freud and Abraham in their correspondence. In Abraham's 1924 paper "Manifestations of the Female Castration Complex," pursuing his interest in the preoedipal period, he makes some interesting observations on the girl's reaction to her recognition that she can never have a penis. What then can she grow or be given? A child. She now begins to envy her mother and crave a child by her father. Ultimately these feelings must be sublimated by the cultivation of a passive feminine receptivity.

Karen Horney very courageously took up the cudgels against her own analyst, Abraham, at the Berlin Congress in 1922 with her paper "On the Genesis of the Castration Complex in Women."* Her paper opens with a summary of Abraham's views. She then proceeds to an account of what really happens in the life of a little girl. Since the lack of a penis puts her at a disadvantage, she identifies with her mother, but her inevitable rejection by her father propels her back to the pregenital phase of penis envy, which means that her future relationships with men will be tinged with revenge and disappointment. Her woman is a rebel, not the passive, submissive type whom Freud and Abraham saw as the "normal" woman.

Helene Deutsch's paper "The Psychology of Women in Relation to the Functions of Reproduction" (1925) echoes the orthodox position, drawing even greater attention to the inferiority of the clitoris in comparison with the penis. In "The Phallic Phase" (1933), Ernest Jones comments that the writers on female sexuality "have been laudably concerned to lay stress on the points of agreement with their colleagues, so that the tendency to divergence of opinion has not always come to full expression."[40] In Melanie Klein's Innsbruck

* Abraham's paper was written in 1919, delivered at The Hague in 1920, and published in 1922. Horney's was delivered in 1922, published in German in 1923, and the *International Journal of Psycho-Analysis* in 1924.

paper, "Early Stages in the Oedipus Complex," she states that she agreed with Helene Deutsch that the woman's genital development finds its completion only with the successful displacement from the oral libido to the genital. However, she believes this process starts with "the first stirrings of the genital impulses and that the oral, receptive aim of the genitals exercises a determining influence in the *girl's turning to her father*."[41] Unlike anyone before her, she states her belief that the girl has an innate knowledge of her vagina. She agrees implicitly with Horney that masturbation does not afford the girl anything like the gratification it does boys, and her frustration is another reason for her difficulties in development. While she does not have to struggle with the castration anxiety experienced by the boy, she has her own problems. Her epistemophilic impulse is first roused during the Oedipus complex when she discovers her lack of a penis, which she blames on her mother, thereby compounding the fear engendered by her impulses to rob and destroy her mother.

According to Freud, the girl, on discovering her lack of a penis, turns to her father. Melanie Klein would agree that this was a reinforcement of her Oedipus complex at this stage of her development, but regards "the deprivation of the breast as the most fundamental cause of the turning to the father."[42] Such identification with her father is less charged with anxiety and, because of her uneasy relationship with her mother, her hatred and envy become strong motives in her desire to possess her father. The mother who frustrates persists in the child's mental life as the mother who is feared. If the girl is able to overcome her sadistic fixations and develop a more positive relation to her mother, eventually her love for her own husband will be strongly reinforced, "since for the woman he always stands at one and the same time for the mother who gives what is desired and for the beloved child."[43]

The woman's maternal capacity, however, may be damaged by anxiety and guilt. Since she has once phantasied destroying the contents of her mother's body, in her unconscious she fears retribution against her own maternal capacities. Hence, behind the constant primping of some women is the motive of *restoring* damaged comeliness. The girl's anxiety about her capacity for motherhood is analogous to the boy's dread of castration; the girl's anxiety is determined by the maternal superego, and the boy's by the paternal superego.

While she would agree with Freud that the girl's superego develops on different lines from the boy's, Melanie Klein sees the paternal superego at work in the unattainable goals an ambitious girl is driven by. When these are combined with the capacity for self-sacrifice and intuitive gifts derived from the mother, the woman is able to reach fulfillment. For the boy, however, it is the paternal superego that is more strongly operative and accounts for "the more sustained and objective creative work of the male."[44] Did she believe that the girl had to struggle harder because for years her own gifts had been held in abeyance because she had been forced into the sacrificial role of model wife and mother, and had failed dismally by conventional standards?

Klein pays tribute to Karen Horney, "who was the first to examine the sources of the castration complex in women insofar as those sources lie in the Oedipus situation."[45] These women analysts could not entirely surmount the attitudes of their time, but it should be remembered that they were remarkable in the questions they were willing to reexamine, and in the very profession to which they were devoting their lives.*

Melanie Klein concludes by stating that she does not believe that she has contradicted Freud essentially in dating the processes of the Oedipus complex earlier than the accepted position or in describing the different phases as merging more freely into one another than was formerly assumed. (Nevertheless, compared to her later conceptions, she was still relatively rooted in Abraham's stratified libidinal stages.) The Oedipus complex may be clearly recognizable between the third and fifth year, but what takes place in that shadowy pregenital period plays a decisive part in determining the development of the super-ego, character formation, and sexuality. In "Infantile Anxiety-Situations" (1929) she reiterated in even more emphatic form that she would go beyond the early anxiety situations described in "Inhibitions, Symptoms and Anxiety," to the little girl's "sadistic desire, originating in the early stages of the Oedipus conflict, to rob the mother's body of its contents, namely, the father's penis, faeces, children, and to destroy the mother herself."[46] However, a recognition of the harm she is doing leads to reparation and to all creative acts, which are in fact forms of sublimation. Klein was tending to a more and more constructive interpretation of the process.

Although Freud did not attend the Innsbruck Congress, his presence overshadowed it. Eitingon, who had taken over as acting president of the International Association after Abraham's death, wished to step down. Freud, fearing that Eitingon might be succeeded by Jones and realizing that his favorite candidate, Ferenczi, would be unacceptable, prevailed upon the dull but reliable Eitingon to continue in the post. After the congress the delegates made the pilgrimage to report and pay homage to the ailing man, who was vacationing at the Semmering.

The meeting between Jones and Freud was marked by cool courtesy, and both avoided controversial subjects. However, the nature of Melanie Klein's paper must have been described to him by Anna,† for within a few days of Jones's departure for London Freud fired off a furious letter to him. All his in-

---

* Deutsch, Klein, and Horney were all analyzed by Abraham, but reached significantly different views on female sexuality.
† As well as Jones's own paper, "Early Development of Female Sexuality," which supported Klein's connections between the oral and oedipal stages.

dignation about the "formal campaign" by the English group against Anna was revived. Freud had never stopped brooding about Jones's suggestion that some of Anna's resistances had not been analyzed sufficiently. "Who is really sufficiently analyzed?" he demanded. "I can assure you Anna has been analyzed longer and more thoroughly than, for instance, yourself. The whole critique rests on a flimsy preconception which one could avoid quite easily with a little benevolence."*

As for Frau Klein's claim that Anna did not analyze a child's Oedipus complex, how did she know? The whole campaign seemed to Freud to be based on this misconception of Melanie Klein's. And Jones apparently wanted to give it the widest possible publicity! He had heard a rumor that Jones wanted to publish the symposium in brochure form. Freud insisted on an explanation.

Jones repeated his feelings of confidence about Melanie Klein:

> There is general confidence in her method and results, which several of us have been able to test at the closest quarters, and she makes the general impression of a sane, well-balanced person. We were somewhat astonished to learn with what little sympathy her work has been regarded on the Continent, but decided to give her work a fair hearing and form our own judgment about it. This has been so favourable that we have come to regard her extension of psycho-analysis into this new field as not only a valuable addition to our powers, but as opening up the most promising avenue to direct investigation of the earliest and deepest problems. Holding such an attitude, we could, as you will well understand, only regard any attempt made to close this avenue as unfortunate.

This confidence was attested to by the fact that Melanie Klein was elected a member of the British Psycho-Analytical Society on October 2, 1927.†

Freud might have talked about a "formal campaign" against Anna; but Anna's "unexpected attack" on Melanie Klein caused dismay among British analysts who found her method highly valuable, despite Anna's repudiation of it as "untrustworthy." "A book issued by Verlag," Jones continued,

> and bearing the name it does could not fail to carry exceptional weight, in spite of the fact, which I well recognize, of Anna's personal independence from yourself; and that it has this weight is shown by the extent to which

---

* Freud was particularly sensitive on this issue because it seems probable that Anna was in her second analysis with him at precisely this time (see Uwe Henrik Peters, *Anna Freud: A Life Dedicated to Children* (London: Weidenfeld & Nicolson, 1985), pp. viii and ix.
† In October 1929 Klein was elected a member of the Institute as well.

Mrs. Klein's work is thought on the Continent to have been discredited by it.

Jones pointed out to Freud that the principles of fair play had not been observed. Radó would allow only a favorable review of Anna's book to appear in the *Zeitschrift*, so he felt it only right to publish other points of view in the *Journal*:

> If there is any illegitimate criticism of Anna in Mrs. Klein's paper I am of course technically responsible, though it happens that I did not read it until after your letter came this week. It seems to me that any question of possible misunderstanding would best be left by us to the two people most directly concerned. Anna must know that any reply or contribution from her would be received with welcome by the "Journal" and esteemed as an honour. I was not myself aware of any *illegitimate* criticism in what Mrs. Klein said at the meeting nor do I observe that any have been inserted into the written account. In saying this I naturally cannot make myself responsible for or defend everything she writes—it is her own affair and all I have as Editor to see to is that the tone and content of such a contribution is within the usual bounds of scientific controversy.

As for the brochure Freud had heard about, Jones felt that Klein's self-defense should be read by German-speaking analysts as well. Radó told him that he had no space for papers on child analysis in the *Zeitschrift*, but offered to publish a two-page abstract of the discussion and suggested that it be published in its complete form by the Internationaler Psychoanalytischer Verlag. Finally, Jones assured Freud that the symposium was motivated only by scientific considerations and that "The mood here is one of entire devotion to your personality and fidelity to the principles of psycho-analysis."

Freud was somewhat mollified by Jones's conciliatory tone. He expressed total ignorance of the fact that Melanie Klein was insufficiently appreciated in Berlin, and assured Jones that he would see to it that she had freedom to publish her opinions in German.

> On the other side I think it is unjust to emphasize in [Anna's] book the character of the attacks on Mrs. Klein. She has only on the basis of her own but very extensive experiences developed her view and only with reluctance did she mention anything polemic. Two points remain unexcused in the behaviour of the English against Anna, namely the accusation which is not usually used and is against all good custom that she has not been suffi-

ciently analyzed,* and the observation by Mrs. Klein that she believed Anna evades the analysis of the Oedipus complex in principle. This misunderstanding could easily have been avoided with a bit of good will.

The discussion continued in a reasonably amicable way, fire being drawn away from Melanie Klein and directed to Joan Riviere's view of the parental imagos introjected by the child, a point discussed in the next chapter.

Freud continued to insist that Anna's views were completely independent of his own, but the true state of the matter was revealed in a letter to Jones dated February 22, 1928:

> Your demand that the analysis of children should be a real one independently of any educative measures appears to me as theoretically unfounded as [it is] unpractical in reality. The more I hear of these things the more I believe that Melanie Klein goes the wrong way and Anna the right one. All that we know of the early feminine development appears to me unsatisfactory and insecure. I only see two points clearly, that the first idea of sexual intercourse is an oral one, the sucking of the penis as previously the mother's breast, and the stopping of the clitoral masturbation because of the painfully recognized inferiority of the clitoris. So far as anything else is concerned I shall have to reserve my judgment.

In March, Jones reported the death of his daughter Gwenith at age seven and a half. In response Freud purred that he and Jones had had only "a slight family quarrel," and assured him that his own griefs had been greater than those of Jones because his daughter and grandson had died when he was too old and frail to absorb the grief. "You and your dear wife are of course young enough to be able to regain serenity in life." To divert him, Freud suggested that he think about Freud's favorite new theory, viz. J. T. Looney's hypothesis that Shakespeare was actually the Earl of Oxford.

On December 12, 1928, Jones announced proudly that his son had completed his analysis, which had taken eighteen months (apart from holidays). He was extremely satisfied with the results. Jones must have known that the news would irritate Freud, since he probably suspected that Mervyn had been analyzed by Klein.

For the moment there was no more discussion about Melanie Klein, but Freud was still brooding about her. In "Female Sexuality" (1931) he wrote ap-

---

* The question of Anna's analysis was never raised, except in a letter from Jones to Freud.

provingly of Otto Fenichel's dismissal of Melanie Klein's displacement of the Oedipus complex back to the beginning of the second year:

> The dating of it, which would also necessarily imply a modification of our view of all the rest of the child's development, does not in fact correspond to what we learn from the analyses of adults, and it is especially incompatible with my findings as to the long duration of the girl's pre-Oedipus attachment to her mother.[47]

CHAPTER TWO

Cock of the Walk

The decade from 1928 until 1938 was, in relative terms, the most peaceful and productive of Melanie Klein's turbulent life. She had emerged from the skirmish with the Freuds in a stronger position. For a time most of the members of the British Society seemed to be solidly behind her. She had custody of Erich, who was at school at St. Paul's. Her practice grew, she was able to employ a cook and a parlor maid and to take summer holidays in Austria and France.

Arthur Klein had custody of Hans, who stayed in Berlin to study chemical engineering and eventually, because of his father's naturalization, did his national service in Sweden. With time the acrimony over the divorce subsided; Hans shared holidays with his mother on the Continent, and Erich made regular trips to Berlin to see his father and to Slovakia to visit his grandparents.

In August 1927 Melitta graduated with distinction from the Friedrich-Wilhelms-Universität in Berlin. But in 1928 she followed her mother to London—leaving her husband behind in Berlin—to write her thesis, *Geschichte der homöopathischen Bewegung in Ungarn* ("The History of Homeopathy in Hungary"). The most obvious explanation would be that she was so dependent on her mother that she was persuaded she needed her for advice in the preparation of her thesis. The following year she returned to Berlin to present her thesis, which was dedicated to her father (*Meinem Vater gewidmet*). This might have merely been a conventional gesture, but it would appear that some form of reconciliation had taken place. In 1929 she was in training analysis with Karen Horney in Berlin, and she attended the Oxford Congress in July. Presumably she then returned to Berlin; but from early May 1930 the minutes of the British Society record her regular attendance at scientific meetings, where she soon began to read papers whose presuppositions were very much in accord with those of her mother. As a member of the British Society, one of her first papers published in the *I.J.P.A.* (1933, 14, 225–260), "Some Unconscious Mechanisms in Pathological Sexuality and Their Relation to Normal Sexual Activity," was based on a paper read to the German Society on November 18, 1930. Among the many references to her mother is a personal communication: "Melanie Klein has found that pregnancy is equated with the introjection of the penis: the child may assume the significance of the 'bad' penis, the dangerous element" (p. 237).

Many of the European analysts were already beginning their exodus abroad, chiefly to the United States. Few came to England, for a combination of reasons: distrust of Jones, who did little to encourage them; the presence of Melanie Klein; and the greater economic possibilities in America. With a Swedish passport, Melitta had no difficulty entering England, but it was a different matter for Walter Schmideberg, whose entry Jones was unable to secure until 1932. Before the arrival of her husband Melitta stayed with her mother and Erich in Linden Gardens, where the waiting room was made into a bedroom for her. It could be argued that when she preceded her husband to England she had no idea that it would take as long as two years to get him into the country. On the other hand, she had spent 1928 away from him; and it is curious that she did not stay in Berlin with Schmideberg until he received his visa.

As for Klein, year by year her patients provided her with ever deeper insights into psychic processes. Some of the papers she delivered to the British Society were eventually incorporated in *The Psycho-Analysis of Children* (1932); other were presented at international congresses. In 1929 she read to the British Society "Personification in the Play of Children," in which she described transference as a complex process whereby splitting and the imagos of inner figures are projected onto the analyst. The paper contains a medley of diverse ideas, a reflection of the creative thinking that was being released in her within a congenial atmosphere. Venturing into hazardous depths, she suggests that psychosis is marked by the ascendancy of a cruelly tormenting early superego, a counterpart of the views she advanced in "Criminal Tendencies in Normal Children" (1927).

Among the children in this paper we meet for the first time the overanxious Rita, aged two and three-quarters, who enacted an elaborate ritual before dropping off to sleep. Her doll had to be tucked up and a stuffed elephant placed by her bed. This watchful animal (the superego) was there to ensure that the child (the id) did not get up in the night to enter her parents' bedroom and inflict harm on them by stealing the babies contained within her mother or injure both parents so that no more children could be produced. In the early stages of the analysis the excessive severity of the superego prevented any sort of phantasy play. Progress was marked by a journey game in which Rita and a toy bear (representing the penis) traveled in a train to visit a good woman whose role was to give them gifts. For months the happy termination of the journey was interrupted by struggles between Rita and the driver of the train, by a bad woman who hindered their progress, or, at the end of the journey, by the transformation of the good woman into a menacing figure.*

One of her most important papers, "The Importance of Symbol-Formation in the Development of the Ego," was delivered to the British Society on February 5, 1930. Ernest Jones had published "The Theory of Symbolism" in 1916. Written in response to Jung's changed views of the libido and the unconscious, it attempted to differentiate between true symbolism and symbolism in its widest sense. The latter can be applied to almost anything in the world, whereas "True symbolism arises as the result of intrapsychical conflict between the repressing tendencies and the repressed." The primary ideas of life—those concerning the body, the family, love and death—retain in the deepest level of the unconscious their original importance; and the energy flowing from them is invested in symbols. "Only what is repressed is symbolised; only what is repressed needs to be symbolised."†[1]

Klein—basing her paper to some degree on Jones's premises and on her own 1923 paper "Early Analysis," in which she drew the conclusion that "symbolism is the foundation of all sublimation"—describes her analysis of a psychotic child, in what was to be the first of her attempts to specify the origin of schizophrenia.

Dick, a four-year-old child, had been brought to her six months previously.‡ By now she had analyzed a wide spectrum of disturbed children, but Dick manifested symptoms she had not encountered before. The child expressed no emotions, no attachment to anyone, and no interest in play. Klein is often accused of paying little heed to a child's environment; but in this case she records that as a baby Dick had had nursing problems and that neither his mother nor his father had given him sufficient attention. At the age of two he spent a considerable time with his grandmother, whose tender love clearly had an effect on him. A new nurse, who otherwise treated him kindly, chastised him for masturbating, which left him feeling guilty. He rejected almost all solid food.

Klein immediately realized that the child was totally incapable of tolerating anxiety and that he had reached the genital level prematurely. After a feeble beginning, his capacity to form symbols had come to a standstill, except for

---

* In *The Psycho-Analysis of Children* other aspects of Rita's obsessionalism are stressed. There is a description of Rita's repeated washing and changing of her doll, and the tightness with which the child had to be tucked in at night. We got a fuller picture of the kaleidoscopic nature of the analysis. The elephant, incidentally, plays a much smaller role than in the original paper: "On one occasion during her analytic session she put a toy elephant into her doll's bed so as to prevent it from getting up and going into her parents' bedroom and 'doing something to them or taking something away from them'" (p. 6).

† Marion Milner finds Jones's view of symbol as defense narrow in contrast to that of Klein. In her own work she has pursued the aesthetic of symbol formation as the basis of talent.[2]

‡ Klein's pocket diary indicates that Dick's analysis started on January 7, 1929.

an interest in trains, stations, doors and handles, and the opening and closing of doors.

Klein's usual procedure, she says, was to refrain from interpreting material until it found expression in various representations; but in Dick's case she had to modify her technique. In order to make contact with his unconscious she immediately set out to activate his repressed anxiety. Unlike her other small patients, Dick regarded the toys set before him with utter indifference. Klein then put two trains side by side, and told him that the larger one was the "Daddy-train" and the smaller one the "Dick-train." Dick picked up the latter and rolled it to the window, saying "Cut." Klein then handed him scissors; but because of his clumsiness she took them from him and cut the coal out of the cart, whereupon the child shut the damaged toy in a drawer, exclaiming, "Gone." She interpreted this to him as cutting feces out of his mother.

The child also manifested irrational fear of water. She saw this as an indication that in his phantasy life feces, water, and penis were objects with which to attack his mother. After receiving these explanations the boy became deeply distressed; and, as she had discovered many years before with Erich, the appearance of anxiety was cause not for concern but an indication that a necessary step in development was being activated. Within six months Dick began to show affection for his parents, as well as a desire to make himself intelligible and to increase his meager vocabulary. Her conclusion marked a radical point in the history of psychoanalysis: "the concept of schizophrenia in particular and of psychosis in general as occurring in childhood must be extended, and I think that one of the foremost tasks of child analysis is the discovery and cure of psychoses in childhood."[3] Dick's illness differed from the usual schizophrenia of childhood in that his problem was an inhibition of development, rather than regression to an earlier fixation point. His ego development, his growing relation to reality, had been arrested by a "defense" against his own sadistic tendencies.

One of the major criticisms of Klein's conclusions has been that she used terms like "schizophrenia" when she did not fully understand the medical nature of the disorder. "Dick" is often referred to by analysts as "the autistic child."* In Charles Rycroft's indispensable *Dictionary of Psychoanalysis* he defines autism as "a childhood psychosis in which the patient lacks any capacity to trust or communicate with anyone whatsoever, is either mute or has complex disturbances of speech, and would be regarded as mentally defective were it not for his ability to handle inanimate objects." In 1943 Leo Kanner's description of the syndrome in "Early Infantile Autism"[4] marked a watershed.

---

* In *The Empty Fortress* (1967) Bruno Bettelheim's position is that the autistic child retreats into withdrawal because he encounters a hostile world. In his view, such children are the victims of their mothers' death wishes towards them.

The characteristic features of an autistic child are "a profound withdrawal from contact with people, an obsessive desire for the preservation of sameness." The child retains a pensive and intelligent physiognomy, but is hindered by "mutism or the kind of language that does not seem intended to serve the purpose of interpersonal communication." Kanner differentiated the syndrome he called "early infantile autism" (a term he coined) from mental deficiency, poor care, or detectible brain damage.

Frances Tustin, an authority on autism, on rereading Klein's paper, believes that she was years ahead of her time: "She was very brave and very farseeing."[5] As Tustin points out, she was perceptive enough to realize that "Dick" was different from the schizophrenic children she had previously analyzed. "Against the diagnosis of dementia praecox is the fact that the essential feature of Dick's case was an inhibition in development and not a regression."[6] Tustin admires Klein for being the first to believe that such a child could be cured; and thinks that while Dick was a relatively mild case, Klein "released him from his autistic trap."

Dick's analysis with Klein continued (with an interruption from 1941 to 1944) until 1946, when he was passed over to Beryl Sandford for three years. According to Sandford, by the time he reached her, he was not autistic but "a terrific talker." His I.Q. had been measured by Ruth Thomas as about 100, and he was obviously fairly split, but at the same time he had an extraordinary memory, he read Dickens, and possessed a great deal of technical knowledge about music, which he had learned from a piano teacher. He once took Sandford to a concert and explained to her all the technicalities about key changes and so forth.

On meeting "Dick," then in his fifties, I found him extremely friendly in a childlike way, well informed, and capable of holding a job that did not exert undue pressure on him. He was the son of one of Klein's colleagues, and it must have been startling to members of the British Society to hear her speak forcefully about his parents' failure to give him the real love he needed.

When asked how he knew he was "Dick," he replied that Klein used to read him the relevant passages from her paper.* He riffled through the pages, exclaiming from time to time, "Oh God!" As for the father's penis being incorporated inside the mother's body, he commented: "I think she could have cut this claptrap out really," and of the attacking penis, "Well, I didn't do that." Klein asserted that she regarded urine as a dangerous substance, and he remarked reflectively, "which is true."† "If Melanie were alive today," he con-

---

*Tustin considers this very "un-Kleinian."

† As a baby "Dick" had great difficulty nursing. "Observations have confirmed," Klein writes in *The Psycho-Analysis of Children* (1932), "that children's phantasies of flooding, and destroying by means of enormous quantities of urine in terms of soaking, drowning, burning and poisoning are a sadistic reaction to their having been deprived of fluid by their mother and are ultimately directed against her breast" (p. 128).

cluded, "I'd ring her and say, 'Enough is enough.' " But he confirmed that he used to lock himself into the cupboard sometimes. Why?" "Out of revenge, I suppose." Against whom? "My parents."

He would set Klein's toys up in rows, and was allowed to bring his own teddy bears. "I used to have imaginary tea parties with them. We used to make paper boats and put them in a bowl."

"I was very fond of Melanie," he told me feelingly. In her symposium reply to Anna Freud, Klein insisted that she refrained from caressing a child but, according to "Dick," she always soothed him when he cried, which he frequently did. "Life is not all that bad," she would say.*

During these years there was more cross-fertilization between Freud's ideas and those of Klein than has been acknowledged, especially regarding the conclusions she was drawing about innate aggression and Freud's *Civilization and Its Discontents* (1930),† in which he connects the superego with the child's own innate aggression.‡ Many Freudians tend to think that this picture of the darker side of man's nature was an expression of the increasing pessimism Freud felt when faced with illness and old age. When Freud describes aggression as "an original, self-subsisting, instinctual disposition in man"[7] against which the ego protects itself by internalizing it into something called a superego or conscience and asserts that guilt arises out of the tension between aggression and the watchful conscience, he might appear to be taking a page out of Klein's book. For Freud there was an irreconcilable antagonism between man's instincts and the demands of civilization. Yet he makes a point of saying that "In the most recent analytic literature a predilection is shown for the idea that any kind of frustration, any thwarted instinctual satisfaction, results, or may result, in a heightening of the sense of guilt. A great theoretical simplification will, I think, be achieved if we regard this as applying only to the *aggressive* instincts, and little will be found to contradict this assumption."[8] In a footnote, he adds: "This view is taken in particular by Ernest Jones, Susan Isaacs and Melanie Klein, and also, I understand, by Reik and Alexander."§[9]

For Freud, guilt begins with the fear of losing love or approval; and Klein associated it further with the fear that one has damaged the loved object. In

---

* Tustin believes that an autistic child needs affection. "Dick" frequently met Eric and Melitta in the hall, and remembers Klein's barking Pekinese, Nanky Poo.

† James Strachey points out that *Civilization and Its Discontents* was actually published before the end of 1929, although it bears the imprint 1930. Klein would have had time to read it before writing her paper "The Importance of Symbol-Formation in the Development of the Ego."

‡ Strachey remarks that as early as 1905, in *Three Essays in Sexuality*, Freud wrote: "One gets an impression from civilized children that the construction of these dams is a product of education, and no doubt education has much to do with it. But in reality this development is organically determined and fixed by heredity, and it can occasionally occur without any help at all from education" (S.E., 7, 177–78).

§ He is referring to Jones's paper "Fear, Guilt and Hate," delivered at the Eleventh International Congress of Psycho-Analysis on July 27, 1929. Theodore Reik's theories on man's voluntary submission to punishment were published in *The Compulsion to Confess and the Need for Punishment* (1925), and Franz Alexander's views in "The Neurotic Character," *J.* (1930), 11:291–311.

discussing the matter of conscience, Freud writes: ". . . the child's revengeful aggressiveness will in part be determined by the amount of punitive aggression which he expects from his father. Experience shows, however, that the security of the super-ego which a child develops in no way corresponds to the severity of the treatment which he himself has met with."[10] To this he adds a footnote: "As has rightly been emphasized by Melanie Klein and by other English writers."[11] Who knows what degree of rapport might have been achieved between Klein and Freud had it not been for the hovering presence of Anna? Ferenczi, on reading the manuscript, was also extremely distressed by Freud's agreement with Klein. "Would it not be more correct," he wrote from Budapest on November 11, 1930, "instead of accepting Melanie Klein's view to adhere to the individually acquired (i.e., traumatic) nature (i.e., origin) of conscience, and to maintain that a conscience which is too strict (i.e., the tendency to self-destruction) is the consequence of a treatment that was relatively speaking too strict—i.e., too strict when set into relationship with the need for love, the strength of which varies individually?"?*[12]

In 1931 Melanie Klein took on her first training analysand, a Canadian, Dr. W. Clifford M. Scott. A graduate in medicine from Toronto in 1927, he went on to study at Johns Hopkins, and moved to Harvard, from which he received a fellowship to study abroad. In 1931 he traveled to London to study neurology and to qualify as an adult and child analyst. On his arrival Jones assigned him to Klein. He was in analysis with her for two years, including the summer of 1931, when he traveled to the Black Forest, where she was holidaying, in order to continue his analysis. He stayed at Bad Wildbad and every day took the Bergbahn from the valley to the top of the Sommerberg for a two-hour session in her hotel room. All through his analysis they agreed, as he says, "to disagree" about primary narcissism, which he believed to have a biological basis. The most moving aspect of the analysis occurred for him one Monday morning when she read out to him a long interpretation she had written over the weekend on material he had given her. "This was proof," he recalls, "that I was in her as well as she was in me."[13] A great talker himself, Scott found that Klein occasionally had to interrupt him in order to make interpretations of her own.

The following summer (1932) an American, Dr. David Slight, also accompanied her on holiday to St. Jean-de-Luz in order to continue his analysis without interruption (also for two-hour sessions). Slight is credited with the remark "Freud made sex respectable, and Klein made aggression respectable." Slight, who had already been analyzed by Franz Alexander, was Clinical Professor of Psychiatry at McGill University in Montreal. His clinical experiences stimulated his interest in developmental processes and he considered going to

---

* Freud does not seem to have followed Ferenczi's advice.

Vienna to work with Anna Freud. Stopping off in London, he talked with Edward Glover, who told him that he need not go to Vienna since "a wonderful person" had recently come to England and was taking on new patients. This was Melanie Klein; and on his return from his analysis with her in France, he worked with two small children in London under her supervision, and was amazed at the results. Dr. Slight was the first practicing psychoanalyst in Canada before moving eventually to Chicago, in 1936.

Slight describes Klein as absolutely devoted to her work. Occasionally when he made a little joke she would smile in a rather prim way and say: "This is a *very* serious matter."[14] Slight found it difficult to accept her leaning towards what he describes as "phylogenetic phantasy." He tried to push her to be precise about the age at which the infant has an image of the father as a man with a penis. How early? Six months? "I tried to explain to her that in the brain the nerves are not covered by various layers that insulate them from each other so that the child could not have formed images in the absence of actual perception." One two-and-a-half-year-old who could not yet speak and had an eating problem was obsessed with washing. She even made Slight take off his socks to wash his feet. "How far does this go?" Slight asked Klein. She replied only with one of her wry smiles. The child also made him go to sleep. Never a word was spoken. "It was real play analysis. It was the most spectacular thing I've ever gone through." The child's improvement was so extraordinary that, for all his skepticism, Slight had to admit, "She opened my mind."*

For some years Klein had been planning to bring out a book incorporating her theories.† In January 1928 she submitted a partial manuscript to Max Eitingon, the director of the Internationaler Psychoanalytischer Verlag, but he wrote back on February 1 insisting firmly that he must have a complete manuscript:

> I have heard from the editorial staff of "Zeitschrift" and "Imago" that you are in the habit of constantly changing your texts even in the proof-read stage and thus have become the most expensive contributor to these journals. With a book this would be totally impossible because the publisher must be able to make very precise calculations . . . I think it is of great value and importance to the entire analytical public that the methods and results of your work will be available in such a collected form as to make a detailed and fertile discussion of it easier.[15]

---

* Scott had a similar experience with a child of twenty-six months whom Klein supervised. "I learned a great deal from the analysis of this child in the next nine months, and the boy never said a word. The boy had come in because he hadn't begun to speak, but during analysis he began to speak very actively to his parents. . . . He would have had to have stayed in analysis for several years before his speech capacity would have come up to being the equivalent of his playing capacity. He could show me far more than he could tell me."
† Based on the lectures she had originally delivered in London in 1925.

For the next three years she worked hard at a theoretical description of the respective sexual development of the boy and the girl, comprising the final section of the book. Translated by Alix Strachey, it was brought out in 1932 by the Hogarth Press in London as *The Psycho-Analysis of Children*, and was published simultaneously by the Verlag as *Die Psychoanalyse des Kindes*.

The book was a milestone in that it incorporated the conclusions derived from years of experience and set out theoretical underpinnings for some of the most dramatic of her future concepts, the paranoid-schizoid and depressive positions. The child's reality is described as an interaction of internalized figures that have been introjected and projected with real objects. As a result of the sadistic impulses experienced towards its objects, the child suffers from anxiety. Anxiety, if excessive, can be inhibitory to development, but, if worked through satisfactorily, it is a spur to growth.

The troubled question of the etiology of homosexuality was explored. In Klein's view, in the development of the boy the oral fixation to the nipple can change to an oral fixation on the father's penis. Too strong a sucking fixation to the penis forms the basis of male homosexuality. If a child goes hungry during the suckling period or is fed only on the bottle or if his feelings towards the breast are excessively sadistic, he cannot satisfactorily introject a good mother imago, and fear of the bad mother will dominate his development. Since, in his phantasy, the mother incorporates the penis, he flees from this mysterious and destructive object to the real and visible penis of another man; and the homosexual act will be used as a reassurance against the father's "bad" penis inside the mother, and also against the father's "bad" penis which the child has introjected into his own body, expressed in the "narcissistic choice of object to the penis of another man."[16]

Here for the first time Klein expressly takes up Freud's notion of the life and death instincts, a dialectical structure of opposites, of love and hate, upon which she later based the paranoid-schizoid and depressive positions. While again and again she refers—more than in earlier papers—to Freud's and Abraham's psycho-sexual stages upon which her work was originally founded, in her more clearly formulated conception of anxiety she is striking off onto paths of her own. She now sees anxiety as originating from the presence and danger of the death instinct within the self.

Jones always insisted that he never accepted Freud's view of the death instinct, which suggests a fundamental difference between him and Klein. However, if one reads Jones's chapter on "Metapsychology" in his life of Freud, he clarifies the way in which he and Klein interpreted the death instinct. Jones points out that at first Freud used the terms "death instinct" and "destructive instinct" indiscriminately, but in a discussion with Einstein he made a distinction that the former is directed against the self and the latter, derived from it, is directed outwards. In *Instincts and Their Vicissitudes* (1915) Freud suggested for the first time that there could be a primary masochism (which he had hitherto regarded as secondary to sadism), and that this self-injuring tendency was the expression of the death instinct. It would in turn be directed outwards to other people as a measure of self-protection.

On March 22, 1935, Jones delivered to the British Psychological Society a paper entitled "Psycho-Analysis and the Instincts." The following month he was in Vienna to lecture on "Early Female Sexuality." While there he left the instinct paper with Freud. On May 2, in reply to a letter of Freud's, he wrote:

> I was glad you liked my instinct paper but was very astonished at your thinking I had made such a mistake as to suppose you had used any of Melanie Klein's work as a starting point for any thoughts of yours. Of course I know very well that your exposition of the matter actually preceded her writing. . . . I do not think I have ever known you to be influenced by anyone else, certainly least of all by Melanie Klein. So I turned with curiosity to my paper and think I have found the sentence that puzzled you. It comes after an exposition of the super-ego and its severity and runs as follows:
>
> "Detailed analytic studies, particularly those carried out on young children by Melanie Klein and others, have thrown a great deal of light on the sources of this severity and have led to the conception of a primitive *aggressive instinct*, non-sexual in character."
>
> To avoid the least chance of ambiguity I will re-write this sentence before publishing it.* It does, it is true, come rather as an interpolation in the argument, but I wanted to deal with all the contributions made by Psycho-Analysis, not only your own. When writing it I was not actually thinking of you because I should not ascribe to you the belief in a primary aggressive instinct (that is rather my view); yours I should describe as a belief in an internal Todestrieb which is *secondarily* exteriorised into an aggressive impulse.
>
> In any case there can hardly be a risk of misunderstanding, since almost the next sentence runs:
>
> "But, strangely enough, it was not by this conception and the studies I have just outlined that *he* arrived at his present view of the duality of mental structure."

Jones speaks of "almost the next sentence," but in actual fact three crucial sentences intervene:

> So here at last is something that could be contrasted with the sexual side of mental conflicts. Before considering it further, however, we shall have to

---

* Jones never changed the wording in either the English or the German version.

retrace our steps. Freud published his illuminating concept of the super-ego in a book that appeared in 1923 [*The Ego and the Id*].[17]

Jones then went on to describe how Freud developed his ideas of death instinct from the *repetition-compulsion*, which seemed to predate the pleasure-pain principle (although Jones implies that he did not work this out fully in the way Klein did). When he reprinted the paper in the fifth edition of *Papers on Psycho-Analysis*, in 1948, Jones inserted the original section on Klein, making it even stronger:

> Detailed analytic studies, *strikingly confirmed by* those carried out on young children by Melanie Klein and others . . . [Italics added.][18]

In his carefully worded letter to Freud, Jones was clearly trying to placate him. By 1930 Freud admitted his long aversion to accepting the independent existence of an aggressive instinct, and in *Civilization and Its Discontents* he finally confessed: "I can no longer understand how we could have overlooked the ubiquity of non-erotic aggressivity and destructiveness and have failed to give it its due place in our interpretation of life."[19]

Most of Freud's colleagues were deeply disturbed by this fundamental change in his thinking. Freud had hoped to convince them by drawing upon the second law of thermodynamics, but it was argued that the law of entropy operated only in a hypothetical closed system, not one to be found in nature, least of all in living beings. Nor could biology be brought in to buttress a *primary* aggressive instinct.

The only analysts who supported the idea, according to Jones, were Karl Menninger, Hermann Nunberg, and Melanie Klein*—but their support was in a *clinical* sense, in which their acceptance was based on observation, not on theoretical deduction.

> Thus we have the purely psychological observations of the infant's aggressive and cannibalistic phantasies, followed later by murderous ones, but one cannot infer from them any active will on the part of the cells of the body to lead the body to death. The very phrase "death wishes," i.e. murderous wishes, unavoidable in psychoanalytic work, seems to have wrought much confusion here through the mere play on the word "death." The fact that in rare cases of melancholia such wishes may, through complicated mechanisms of indentification, etc., result in suicide is again no proof that

---

* Jones might have added Ernst Simmel, who in "Self-Preservation and the Death Instinct" (*PQ*, 1944, 13, 160–75) explained man's destructive energies as an instinct of self-preservation connected with oral cannibalistic impulses in which the object is destroyed by incorporation. His position is somewhere between Freud's and Klein's. Jones is referring to H. Nunberg's "The Sense of Guilt and the Need for Punishment" (*J.* [1926] 7, 420–33) and to Karl Menninger's "Characterologic and Symptomatic Expressions Related to the Anal Phase of Psychosexual Development" (*PQ* [1943], 12, 161–93).

they arose from a primary wish for self-destruction on the part of the body; the clinical evidence points clearly in the opposite direction.[20]

It is understandable that Klein, in her total ignorance of biology, was not troubled by the idea of a "death instinct," and found it a useful term to apply to the child's fear of being damaged, overwhelmed, or annihilated. She in turn related it to the superego, which is in effect the most basic of the defense mechanisms—that is, as protection against the destructive potential of the id. At this point she was still trying to adhere to Freud's notion of the formation of the superego through the introjection of oedipal objects, but it is quite clear that she was finding it increasingly difficult to reconcile this with her own views of the nature of anxiety. She was still regarding omnipotent restitutive impulses as the principal method of allaying anxiety. The imaginative leap to the concept of reparation was soon to flower as her most creative and affirmative contribution to psychoanalysis.

On November 9, 1932, Ernest Jones wrote to congratulate her on the publication of *The Psycho-Analysis of Children*:

Dear Mrs. Klein,
    The book has finally appeared today, a momentous event in the history of psycho-analysis* and particularly in the achievement of our Society among which we are proud to count you as an honoured member. I am writing to congratulate you on the final achievement of what I know has been an enormous task. We shall now look forward to the results it will produce, results which will go on expanding for many, many years to come—probably for ever.
    With kindest regards,
    Yours very sincerely,

                                        Ernest Jones [21]

Klein replied:

. . . I do not know whether I would have written it if I had stayed in Germany! I regard the collaboration with you and with a number of my English colleagues so highly that it makes me proud to be a member of the British Group, and it makes me happy if I am considered by you to be a useful member of our group.

Shortly before the publication of the book, Ernest Jones had managed to get Walter Schmideberg into England. Schmideberg organized a dinner to cel-

* Its initial sales were only slightly more than sales of *The Interpretation of Dreams*. In 1933, 198 copies were sold; in 1934, 159; and in 1935, 108.

ebrate the publication of the book at the Mayfair Hotel. In addition to the Schmidebergs and Klein, the guests included Erich Klein; Edward Glover and his wife, Gladys; Jones and his wife, Katherine; Joan Riviere and her husband; and Alix and James Strachey. Glover designed a charming card with a drawing of a baby scrutinizing an enormous book, under which he wrote "Celebrating the First English Birthday of The Psycho-Analysis of Children by Melanie Klein, 14, XI, 32." The Certificate of Birth was duly witnessed by those present.

The book was the most important work yet published by a member of the British Society, and in a long review in the *International Journal*, Edward Glover emphasized its significance:

> I have no hesitation in stating that in two main respects her book is of fundamental importance for the future of psycho-analysis. It contains not only unique clinical material gathered from first-hand analytic observation of children, but lays down certain conclusions which are bound to influence both the theory and practice of analysis for some time to come. So much may certainly be said at a first reading, that even if her views arouse—as they undoubtedly will—a varying degree of dissent in analytical circles the discussion which is bound to follow publication of her book will help to bring out many divergences in analytic tendency which so far have been obscured by a too ready glossing over of difficult passages in standard theory. And this itself is no mean contribution to psycho-analytical science.[22]

He was particularly enthusiastic about her account of the oedipal conflict and the formation of the superego: "I have again no hesitation in saying that it constitutes a landmark in analytic literature worthy to rank with some of Freud's own classical contributions."[23]

Melanie Klein's writings have often been called turgid, and compared unfavorably to the clarity of Freud; and while Glover attempts to explicate her ideas as clearly as possible, the nature of the material indicates the profound difference between Freud's and Klein's ways of thinking. Her critics often describe her as "intuitive" rather than "scientific," and sometimes as "deductive" rather than "inductive," but the distinction is far more complex than that. Freud tends to describe a model of the mind with clearly differentiated stages of development, while Klein's view of the mind is of a dynamic process in which a number of emotions and mental processes are operating simultaneously—love and hate, projection and introjection, splitting, phantasy interacting with reality. Her problem was not simply to express herself clearly or to cope with a language not native to her. When a number of complicated feelings are being experienced simultaneously within the infant's bewildered ego, the result is a mosaic of turbulence; but the linear structure of language permits contradictory impulses to be described only sequentially, and Glover could not reduce them to simple events. From the observation of very small children Klein had grasped that the infant's mind is a seething mass of conflict, with anxiety as the central problem to be surmounted—and that it is the analyst's task, by forcing anxiety to the surface, to help the child to differentiate reality from phantasy. On a practical level, immediate "deep" interpretations are the only means of reaching these anxieties.

In general, Glover agreed with the theories that up to this date had made Melanie Klein a controversial figure: that anxiety springs from aggression; that oral frustration arouses an unconscious knowledge that the parents enjoy mutual pleasure, and the child's oral envy both makes him push into the mother's body and activates his epistemophilic curiosity; and that in both the boy and the girl impulses of hate bring about the formation of the oedipal situation and the formation of the superego. These phases can form the fixation points for the psychoses. The development of the child depends on the success of the libido in its struggle with destructive impulses.

Glover's caveats were minimal. He felt that Klein had followed too closely Abraham's idea of a preambivalent oral stage, and that even at this early point the child employs various defensive maneuvers. He would describe the early super-ego formation as "mainly primitive ego," and finally, in her attempt not to depart too radically from classical theory, it seemed to him that she adhered too rigidly to "a mainly paternal super-ego."[24] In general, then, Glover was in accord with her theories; but the ultimate test was startling to say the least:

> One gathers that Mrs. Klein is in favour of more extended use of her methods in adult analysis. The test case is, of course, the analysis of the psychotic. And although it is likely that acute divergences of opinion will arise on this matter, the sooner the point is tested the better it will be for technical methods in general.[25]

As for whether adult techniques could be applied to children: "I doubt if the comparison of therapeutic results would be the only valid criterion. I have observed grave cases of infantile regression make remarkable progress under a system of careful environmental influence."[26]

Glover was brilliant, but as an expositor of Klein's ideas he was not as clear as Jones, Riviere, or Susan Isaacs—perhaps because he was already beginning to question them. He was a powerful ally to have. At the time—and in retrospect—Glover endorsed her work in an almost totally unqualified way. And yet there is that curious statement that the ultimate validation of her theories would rest upon her analysis of a psychotic. Were his feelings about her already ambivalent, was he pushing her to the point where he knew he could no longer follow her?

Next to Jones, Glover was the most powerful man in the British Society. It took a strong man to be second-in-command to Jones, who behind his back was referred to by members as "Napoleon." Glover, born in 1888, came from a background of rigid Presbyterianism. His father, a country schoolmaster, adored the older brother, James, who was regarded as the brilliant member of the family, while Edward was rather demeaned. Glover described himself as a schoolboy as "reluctant, rebellious, contumacious and obstinate"[27]—and so he always remained. His life seems to have been a competition to surpass James. Both boys received medical degrees from Glasgow University. Edward followed James's advice to devote himself to psychiatric problems, and went into analysis with Abraham in 1920. He described his analysis as an "apprenticeship" rather than a training analysis (the implication being that he was too "normal" to need analysis), and some of their sessions were held under the olive groves of the Gardone Riviera while Abraham was on holiday. On his return to London, Edward became a member of the British Psycho-Analytical Society, of which his brother was already a member. When James died suddenly in 1926, the intensity of Edward's grief was remarked upon; it manifested all the signs of melancholia rather than mourning. He asked Jones if he could take over all his brother's offices in the British Society, a surrogate role whose implications might be pondered. He stepped into James's shoes as scientific secretary, and later as director of research at the Institute and assistant director of the London Clinic, chairman of the Scientific Committee, followed by the powerful position of secretary of the Training Committee of the International Psycho-Analytic Association. When Jones appointed him to this position in 1934, Glover wrote gratefully, "It has always been a joy to me to act as your lieutenant. I only trust you have felt that you had always a loyal henchman at your elbow."[28] Caustic, brilliant, highly attractive to women, he sustained a great personal tragedy in the birth of a mongoloid daughter in 1926. Many analysts have commented on his seeming refusal ever to accept that there was anything wrong with the child, and she accompanied him even to international congresses.

While *The Psycho-Analysis of Children* marked the height of Klein's influence in the British Society before the Second World War, the book only served to reinforce the antipathy of her opponents. Franz Alexander, who had emigrated to Chicago, reviewed it for the *Psychoanalytic Quarterly*. He chastised her for misinterpreting Freud's death instinct and for her "exaggerated stress on the ideational content."[29] Anna Freud had "incontrovertibly" shown the importance of the home environment, but Klein was like an artist: "Artists usually do not know how they create, yet their creations may be good. Indeed, perhaps the greater the artist, the less he is able to give an account of the nature of his creative activity."[30] He was suspicious that she reported no failures (did Anna Freud or other analysts?), and was convinced of the suggestibility of her approach, her unemotional tone that of a "kind aunt." All he seemed to be able to say in her favor was that she had avoided polemics. The review was followed immediately by praise, in a review by Gregory Zilboorg, for the lucidity of Anna Freud's *Introduction to Psycho-Analysis for Teachers*.[31]

By 1934 Klein was indignant that the Internationaler Psychoanalytischer Verlag had neglected to send her the money it owed her, even though she had paid for all the expenses of the publication of the German edition. Freud's son Martin had taken over as director of the Verlag and, not intimidated by the famous name, she wrote him a strong letter of protest on January 2, 1934:

> On this occasion I also want to tell you how surprised I am that the publisher, as far as I can judge, is not publicizing my book at all. What I have in mind are those prospectuses that are inserted in the analytical journals. As far as I can remember a prospectus was inserted in the journals about my book only shortly before its publication and immediately after. Even then, when all the other youth- and child-analytical books were advertised, mine was left out. As proof of this omission I enclose the prospectuses which were in the last issue of the "Zeitschrift für psychoanalytische Pädogogik" and which advertise for Aichhorn, Anna Freud, Nelly Wolffheim and Bernfeld, but do not mention me.
>
> If I compare the publicity for my book (inasmuch as it is done in this way) with the publicity that is being made, for instance, for Anna Freud's book or (to name just one recently published author) for Reich's book, I can indeed not understand why the publisher is doing so little for me.[32]

Still, 1932 seemed in most ways the year of Melanie Klein's triumph and vindication, reinforced by the fact that Jones became president of the International at the Twelfth Congress in Wiesbaden (the last time a congress was to be held in Germany before the war). Nevertheless, it was the year when everything began to go wrong in Klein's personal life. With the arrival of Walter Schmideberg in England, Melitta moved out of her mother's place in Linden Gardens to her own home in Gloucester Place. The couple held a large housewarming party to which they invited all the members of the British Society. Together the Schmidebergs and Klein bought a secondhand Sunbeam, which they called "Sunny"—and on weekends the three of them often toured around England together. But this was a situation that could not continue indefinitely.

Melitta sent her mother a check* buying out Melanie's share in the car. In the undated letter, probably written at the end of the summer of 1934, she categorically spelled out a declaration of independence. She realized that for the past few years she had been in a state of neurotic dependence on her mother, and now that she had decided to enter analysis with Edward Glover, Klein must face the fact that their relationship was going to change irrevocably; and that if a state of amicability was to be maintained, it could exist only if Klein recognized her not as an appendage but as a colleague on an equal footing. She hoped that her mother would buy a small car for herself, because she and Walter found that the joint ownership restricted their freedom.

> I hope you will therefore also allow me to give you some advice. You do not take it enough into consideration that I am very different from you. I already told you years ago that nothing causes a worse reaction in me than trying to force feelings into me—it is the surest way to kill all feelings. Unfortunately, you have a strong tendency towards trying to enforce your way of viewing, of feeling, your interests, your friends, etc. onto me. I am now grown up and must be independent; I have my own life, my husband; I must be allowed to have interests, friends, feelings and thoughts which are different or even contrary to yours. I do not think that the relationship with her mother, however good, should be the centre of her life for an adult woman. I hope you do not expect from my analysis that I shall again take an attitude towards you which is similar to the one I had until a few years ago. This was one of neurotic dependence. I certainly can, with your help, retain a good and friendly relationship with you, if you allow me enough freedom, independence, and dissimilarity, and if you try to be less sensitive about several things.
>
> Also, don't forget that through our shared profession a difficult situation is created; this could most certainly be solved if you treated me like another colleague and allowed me all the freedom of thinking and expression of opinion, as you do the others.
>
> With love
> yours
>
> *Melitta*[33]

On a first reading, this may seem harsh; but perhaps harshness was the only way Melitta could make her point forcefully enough. She had been in analysis with Ella Sharpe, but had decided to transfer to Edward Glover—in itself a highly significant act. Glover must have been aware of the letter; indeed, he may have helped Melitta compose it, as he is known to have done with later ones she wrote.

* According to Eric Clyne, in the divorce settlement Arthur Klein was obliged to pay Melanie alimony, but she refused to take it. Apparently some money was put aside for the children, and it was probably a portion of this accumulated sum Melitta sent.

By late 1933 it was apparent to other members of the Society that Glover and his analysand had joined forces in what looked increasingly like a campaign to embarrass and discredit Melanie Klein. "Edward Glover and I had agreed to ally to fight," Melitta wrote later.[34] At meeting after meeting Glover and Melitta began to attack Klein openly, and to this day members of the British Society continue to speculate as to the motives for this sudden virulence. Since the attacks coincided with the analysis, there is little question that it was connected either with the material that emerged during the analysis or with the transference and countertransference.

Melanie Klein's world was changing. On May 22, 1933, her first mentor, Ferenczi, died.* The precarious position of Jewish analysts under the Nazi regime was persistently discussed at meetings of the British Society. Jones reported that Drs. Maas, Haas, Cohn, Fuchs, and Jakobsohn would probably settle in England, a group scarcely amenable to Klein's ideas. Among the arrivals after the Reichstag fire in 1933 was Paula Heimann, who was to play an important role in Klein's life. Abraham's widow arrived in straitened circumstances and opened a boardinghouse in Hampstead. It was a difficult situation for the British analysts as well, because there was concern that there would not be enough work to go around. Max Eitingon abruptly left Berlin to settle in Palestine. And Klein's former lover, Kloetzel, who had vainly sought to find work in England, had no recourse but to emigrate in 1933 to Palestine, where he eventually became features editor of the Jerusalem *Post*, the leading English-language newspaper of the country. Melanie Klein was never to see him again.

This same year she moved from the maisonette in Linden Gardens to a substantial house, 42 Clifton Hill, in St. John's Wood. The quiet, shaded streets were a great improvement over the Notting Hill area, which was swarming with prostitutes. Aware of the change in status, she gave Freud's architect son, Ernst, his first commission in England—to design the interior of the house. This turned out to be rather Bauhaus, very attractive in its way, but some people felt it unsuitable for a Regency house. Here in the garden, in early 1939, sculptor Oscar Nemon produced a bust of her, twice life-size, as was his custom. He had already done busts of Freud and Jones, and Klein showed the same alarm Ernest Jones had manifested on being confronted with an enlarged image of himself. "My impression," Nemon recalls, "was that Melanie had a noticeable tendency to pomposity and was easily capable of self-righteous behavior. Maybe these qualities were manifest in my work and caused her some

---

* The only Congress Klein ever missed was Wiesbaden in 1932. Here Ferenczi presented *his* highly controversial paper, "The Confusion of Tongues," which would have forced a confrontation since it was contrary to all that she believed. She knew, to o, that he had invited Anna Freud to Budapest to lecture in 1930 and that in the Circular Letter of November 30, 1930, he had commented publicly: "Without denying in principle the importance of the courage with which M. Klein has tackled these problems [of child analysis], the observations made by our group support in general the Viennese view."

discomfort."[35] Klein loathed the head, which she hid in the attic for some years before destroying it.

In addition to the controversy over child analysis, the debate about medical qualifications continued to exercise analysts at both the local and the international level. The Americans insisted that only those who were medically qualified could practice psychoanalysis. In 1926 Freud had published "The Question of Lay Analysis," written on behalf of Theodor Reik, who was being prosecuted in Vienna as a quack. The matter was of some personal importance to Freud: there was the question of professional standing for Anna as well as for his analysand Marie Bonaparte, who he hoped would gain a foothold for analysis in France through her connections and wealth.

In 1927 a questionnaire was circulated among members of the British Society, who agreed that lay candidates should be "urged to obtain medical qualifications, but that they should not be excluded on the sole grounds of their not obtaining them." Nonmedical psychoanalysts, however, had to agree to medical colleagues' interviewing patients and taking medical responsibility for them before treatment could begin.

In 1926, as a result of a number of complaints about quacks passing themselves off as psychoanalysts, the British Medical Association appointed a subcommittee to conduct an investigation of the subject. Ernest Jones was appointed a member of the committee and, as a result of his persuasive arguments, in 1929 the committee ruled that only those trained by Freud's method at the Institute of Psycho-Analysis had the right to be called psychoanalysts. This recognition of the respectable status of psychoanalysis was a great achievement for Jones. The Viennese Society, in contrast, was subjected to the most humiliating regulations by the medical authorities; and its clinic, which could treat only needy cases, was threatened with closure if lay members joined in its work. This meant that Anna Freud was effectively barred from its activities, although she gave lectures in child analysis at the Institute and was also vicepresident of the Society.

The work of child analysis in England continued to expand, conducted by Melanie Klein, Melitta Schmideberg, Nina Searl, and later D. W. Winnicott. On July 7, 1930, certain conditions were laid down by the Training Committee:

1. Personal analysis and other stages of training should be the same for the child analyst as for other analysts.
2. The first stage of controlled analyses should consist of the analysis of two adults under control for at least a year.
3. After adult controls, the candidate should undertake analysis of child controls as follows: three cases, one in adolescence, one in the prelatency

period, and one in the latency period. The minimum period for this phase would be one year.

On July 4, 1932, the minutes record that "Mrs Klein brought up the question of the conditions for training candidates for child analysis: recommending that emphasis should be laid at the next Congress on the necessity of all candidates coming up to the standards of adult analysis and passing through adult training prior to taking up child analysis." Was this a means of ascertaining whether Anna Freud had actually undergone a training analysis? Melanie Klein had the official endorsement of the British Society, whereas the continental analysts were solidly behind Anna Freud. At the Twelfth International Congress at Wiesbaden in September 1932, a subcommittee of the International Training Commission reported that it "had not discussed the questions of the training of Child Analysts, instructions of pedagogues, and lectures to the general public or any special group of it. They would seem to be outside its scope and they are also in part still too subject to divided opinion for it to be hopeful at present to codify any international rules for them." This could have been an attempt to avoid embarrassment for Anna Freud.

Jones again doggedly stood up for Melanie Klein in his congress paper, which was in effect an endorsement of *The Psycho-Analysis of Children.* "The Phallic Phase" was an even more public pronouncement of his divergence from Freud than his earlier paper, "Early Development of Female Sexuality," delivered at the Innsbruck Congress in 1927, in which he had audaciously declared that "There is a healthy suspicion growing that men analysts have been led to adopt an unduly phallo-centric view of the problems in question, the importance of the female organs being correspondingly underestimated."[36] His own analyses bore out Melanie Klein's observation that there were more direct transitions between the oral and the oedipal stages than had previously been acknowledged; and in this paper he introduced the concept of "aphanisis," a fear he described as "the total, and of course permanent, extinction of the capacity (including opportunity) for sexual enjoyment."[37] This corresponded to the situation Klein described where the girl fears that her mother will rob her of her sexual and maternal capacities.

In Freud's 1931 paper "Female Sexuality" he rejected Jones's suggestion that "the phallic phase represented a secondary solution of psychical conflict, of a defensive nature, rather than a simple and direct developmental process."[38] Now Jones declared that he had other doubts which he had refrained from voicing. According to accepted psychoanalytic theory, castration fear was common to both sexes—and confirmed by clinical data—but "The interpretation of the facts ... is of course another matter and is not so easy."[39] The orthodox view was that the castration complex weakens the boy's oedipal relationship and strengthens the girl's. Jones found that he could not agree with Freud that the phallic phase reaches its peak at the age of four. And what is one to make of cases where the male continues to be obsessional about his penis? Jones cites *The Psycho-Analysis of Children* as maintaining that "the narcissistic exaggeration of phallicism . . . is due to the need of coping with specially large amounts of anxiety."[40] Jones would agree with Klein that the boy's sense of danger arises at a remarkably early age in his unconscious knowledge of the existence of the vulva, his desire to penetrate it, and his terror of the ensuing consequences. Jones believes Melanie Klein provided the explanation ("The Early Stages of the Oedipus Complex")—namely, that the boy's fear stems from his sadistic impulses against the body, independently of any thought of his father or his penis, although the latter certainly heightens his sadism.

Jones admits the difficulty of understanding the transition the child makes (in terms of appearance) from the nipple to the penis; but about the child's ambivalent attitude to the nipple Jones has no doubt, nor about the boy's phantasy or oral annihilation during the oedipal conflict. Certainly he agrees with Klein that the boy passes through a feminine, primarily oral stage in the process of masculine development. "In the boy's imagination the mother's genital is for so long inseparable from the idea of the father's penis dwelling there that one would get a very false perspective if one confined one's attention to his relationship to his actual 'external' father; that is perhaps the real difference between Freud's pre-Oedipal stage and the Oedipus complex proper."[41] In Jones's view, the phallic phase is "a neurotic obstacle to development rather than a natural stage in the course of it."[42]

There are two prevailing views about the girl's sexuality: that she is driven into femaleness by her inability to be a male, or that she is female to begin with. Jones finds himself disagreeing with Freud, and agreeing with the observations of the English child analysts that from a very early stage the girl has a definite idea of a penis derived from the father but incorporated into the mother, a notion that forms the basis of her phantasy about coitus. Following Klein's position in *The Psycho-Analysis of Children,* Jones explains that out of oral frustration the girl conceives of a more gratifying object—namely, the penis. If the mother contains the penis, it must be in the supposed act of fellatio between the parents; and as Klein suggests, the girl's desire to incorporate a penis is connected with her desire to incorporate a valuable possession contained within her mother rather than actually to possess one. The mother is withholding something from the girl—and the deprivation intensifies her envy—but in the contest the girl is the inevitable loser. In "Female Sexuality" (1931) Freud had argued that "It is only in the male child that we find the fateful combination of love for the one parent and simultaneous hatred for the other as a rival."[43] Klein and Jones now appear to be *plus royale que le roi.**

Jones and Klein both saw the girl's envy as directed only against the mother. The mother is apparently suckling the father; and in her phantasy the pair are indulging in incredible mutual satisfaction. If the girl feels powerless without a penis, it is because she also sees it as a weapon of destruction. Such complex feelings lead to a fear of retaliation; and Jones emphasizes that "it seems difficult to overestimate the depth and intensity of fear in infants."[44] Jones shares Klein's skepticism about Freud's conception of sexual development, which ignores the guilt and fear that the child must surmount.

Three women analysts had expressed entirely different views on the girl's role in the Oedipus complex. Helene Deutsch had followed the strictly Freudian line: "My view is that the Oedipus complex in girls is inaugurated by the castration complex."[45] Karen Horney speaks of "these typical motives for flight into the male role—motives whose origin is in the Oedipus complex."[46] Melanie Klein, however, asserts that "in my view the girl's defence against her feminine attitude springs less from her masculine tendencies than from her fear of her mother."[47] The mother in this case is resented because she has thwarted the girl's true feminine needs and threatens to destroy her if she persists in them. No wonder she shudders from the thought of congress with her father. Jones acknowledges that this explanation of the deutero-phallic phase, penis envy, which he adumbrated at the Innsbruck Congress, had first been enunciated by Karen Horney and developed more elaborately by Melanie Klein in *The Psycho-Analysis of Children.* Such penis envy is the most basic defense a girl can muster because, by denying her femininity, she thinks she protects herself from attack either from her mother or from the man's dangerous penis. The process, if carried far enough, can play a major part in the formation of lesbianism. Jones fully endorses Melanie Klein's view that the girl's hate is not resentment at being deprived of a penis, as Freud maintained, but essentially of rivalry over the father's penis.

Finally, Jones observed that in the deutero-phallic stage, the renunciation experienced by both boys and girls is an identical anxiety about protecting their respective sexual organs. Ignorance about the reproductive organs may operate at a conscious level, but what about the importance of what takes place in the unconscious? In conclusion, Jones pays tribute to Freud, yet implies that Freud failed to see the implications of his great discovery for girls.

> We would seem to have warrant for recognising more than ever the value of what perhaps has been Freud's greatest discovery—the Oedipus complex. I can find no reason to doubt that for girls, no less than for boys, the

---

* In his life of Freud, Jones wrote, "I did not wholly agree with some of these conclusions, and this led to considerable discussion between Freud and myself, both in correspondence and in publications. Several of the disputed questions are still not satisfactorily solved." (III, p. 263).

Oedipus situation, in its reality and phantasy, is the most fateful psychical event in life.[48]

Like Huxley with Darwin, Jones continued to act as Melanie Klein's bull-dog; and one can understand Freud's consternation about "the English School" when issue after issue of the *International Journal of Psycho-Analysis* was filled with articles by Riviere, Isaacs, Searl, and Sharpe, all supporting the theoretical positions of Ernest Jones and Melanie Klein on the etiology of anxiety and the nature of female sexuality. Even Freud's own analysand and English translator, James Strachey, found that the epistemophilic instinct of the omnivorous reader corresponded to Klein's emphasis on the sadistic incorporative impulses and the beginnings of intellectual development. In "Some Unconscious Factors in Reading" (1930), he wrote:

> The oral-sadistic basis which I have endeavoured to trace in reading would merely be a continuation and derivation of the processes she has described. But there is an even more complete parallelism, which can be carried into considerable detail, between the unconscious wishes that I have been attributing to persons reading books and the phantasies that Melanie Klein has found in children during the oral- and anal-sadistic phases: phantasies of the child forcing his way into his mother, soiling and laying waste her inside and devouring her contents—among them the father's penis as well as babies and faeces.[49]

Despite such support, Melanie Klein was beginning to be attacked not only for her theories but also for her application of them. Strachey disliked controversy, but was impelled to reply to criticisms by Glover and Schmideberg on Klein's technique,* and on the motives behind a questionnaire Glover was distributing to members on the question of technique. Between 1932 and 1933 Glover, assisted by Marjorie Brierley, conducted an investigation into the various techniques employed by members of the British Society, with the veiled intention of questioning Klein's methods. Since this was not published until 1940, a discussion of its implications will be reserved until its appropriate place. However, while a questionnaire may seem an "objective" way to accumulate information, the partisan conclusions Glover drew from it make clear his intention: he had deliberately set out to show that a much smaller number of analysts supported Klein's technique than was generally supposed. Above all, he sought to undermine her contention that adult techniques could be applied to children and that one must attempt immediately to uncover the

---

* Strachey was specifically criticizing Melitta Schmideberg's paper "Reassurance as a Means of Analytic Technique," delivered to the Society on February 17, 1934, and Glover's "The Therapeutic Effect of Inexact Interpretation" (J., 1931, 12, 397–411).

deepest levels of the psyche. "She went too deep too soon," Marjorie Brierley told me.

In a classic psychoanalytic paper, "The Nature of the Therapeutic Action of Psycho-Analysis,"* Strachey brought his knowledge of the history of Freud's ideas to bear on his argument that Freud failed to come to grips with the deepest levels of anxiety. Freud's discovery of transference was regarded as a *libidinal* phenomenon. In *Group Psychology* (1921), passages suggested that Freud was beginning to see that the analyst could affect his patient through his superego. Taking up this idea, Strachey explains the implications of this in terms of *cure*.

> If, for instance, the patient could be made less frightened of his super-ego or introjected object, he would project less terrifying imagos on the outer object and would therefore have less need to feel hostility towards it; the object which he then introjected would in turn be less savage in its pressure upon the id-impulses, which would be able to lose something of their primitive ferocity. In short, a *benign* circle would be set up instead of a vicious one, and ultimately the patient's libidinal development would proceed to the genital level, when, as in the case of a normal adult, his super-ego will be comparatively mild and his ego will have a relatively undistorted contact with reality.[50]

Strachey suggests a "mutative" interpretation, by which the analyst, by acting as an auxiliary superego, shows the patient the distinction between the "archaic phantasy object and the real external object."[51] This cannot be done suddenly, but only through gradual and deep interpretations, as Klein had shown in *The Psycho-Analysis of Children*. They must be directed to what Klein had described as the "point of urgency,"[52] a moment seized by an analyst possessed of unusual insight, and the "mutative" interpretation must be "detailed and concrete."[53]

In the discussion following Strachey's paper, Klein remarked that a mutative interpretation incorporates the analysis of ego, superego, and id, provided that the interpretation is really complete. Riviere agreed, emphasizing that the attitude to the analyst must be the core and kernel of every analytical situation. Ernest Jones, however, expressed skepticism that emerging id-impulses are always directed at the analyst, and suggested that nontransference interpretations may also be mutative. Glover simply could not accept this centrality of the transference, and objected to the terminological difficulty of "depth." It was a topographical concept, but it could also have dynamic connotations. He claimed that by 1933 he saw that a group, who were beginning to be defined as

* First read to the British Society in June 1933, it appears in expanded form in J. (1934) 15, 127–59.

"Kleinians," were attempting "to pre-empt the use of the word 'deep' implying thereby that other types of interpretation were both superficial and therapeutically ineffective." "Clearly," he concluded drily, "the arrogation of proprietary rights, however effective as a political policy, offends every canon of objectivity. It may intimidate an opponent but it does not dispose of his point of view."[54] This was the beginning of a disputed issue that was to reemerge in the Controversial Discussions in 1942–44. Yet on September 18, 1933, Jones wrote to Freud: "The British Society continues to be one of the bright spots on the horizon, and I do not think Brill exaggerates when he says in a recent letter that it is 'the real bulwark of the psycho-analytic movement.' We have checked any slight tendency to the formation of cliques, and work together very harmoniously."

The "English School" was beginning to be defined far more clearly as the "Kleinian School." The early Freudian members of the Society, Stoddart, Fluegel, and Bryan, took less and less part in the Society. But there were more vocal opponents. From the beginning Barbara Low had not concealed her hostility, and Marjorie Brierley kept a remote distance from the group who seemed to be developing a devoted attachment to Melanie Klein. Among Klein's adherents, Susan Isaacs, who had originally been analyzed by Rank, now went into analysis with Joan Riviere, who in turn had begun to analyze Winnicott. Nina Searl seemed utterly faithful, an alter ego. Jones tried to maintain a politically independent position as president, but was regarded with suspicion by Glover et al., since Klein had analyzed his wife and two of his children, and his views seemed in total accord with hers.

Clearly Freud did not want to confront Melanie Klein in print. In private correspondence with Jones he could express his dissatisfaction with him and with his troublesome colleague. Jones's position can be rationalized. From the outset Freud had been suspicious of him; and after the various scandals in which Jones had been involved, it would have been difficult for him to establish a conventional medical practice for himself in England. Psychoanalysis, Freud seemed to suspect, offered an alternative; and Jones might have unconsciously seized upon Melanie Klein's brand of psychoanalysis, which did not focus primarily on the libidinal element, as his salvation. But what was Freud to make of Joan Riviere, a highly intelligent woman, who had been his own analysand? In letter after letter Freud increasingly concentrated all his indignation and frustration on the figure of Joan Riviere.*

Joan Riviere had one of the most brilliant and incisive minds of the English

---

* There apparently was more to it than this. In a letter to Jones, dated February 14, 1954, Anna Freud, in response to a comment by Jones that Riviere had been one of the women in Freud's life, admits that she had been very jealous of her when she was in Vienna (Jones Archives). Jones was constantly undercutting Riviere to Freud in his anxiety to prove that she was a hysterical woman. Why? Because Riviere (in her analysis with Freud) had undoubtedly told him of her early relationship with Jones.

group. A niece of the great classical scholar A. W. Verrall, she moved easily in the world of the English upper-middle-class intelligentsia. She belonged in the tradition of the gifted amateur who pursued her interests with a seeming casualness that concealed real passion. Her own education was as erratic as that of any other young lady born into her class in 1883. At seventeen she was sent for a year to Germany, where she learned the language proficiently. She married a barrister, Evelyn Riviere. Strachey speculated that she might first have become interested in Freud through the Society of Psychical Research (as he did) after reading a paper Freud contributed to the S.P.R. *Proceedings.** In any event, in 1916 she entered analysis with Ernest Jones and became the first lay analyst in England. She began to translate Freud, particularly the *Introductory Lectures*, so that her importance in introducing Freud to the English-speaking world cannot be overestimated, especially after she became translation editor of the *International Journal of Psycho-Analysis*. As Strachey said, "She possessed the three invaluable gifts—a thorough knowledge of the German language, a highly accomplished literary style, and a penetrating intellect." In 1922 she went to Vienna to be analyzed by Freud. Until 1925 she was mainly responsible for the translation of the four volumes of the collected papers in which the Stracheys devoted themselves to the case histories. After that date Strachey became general editor of the Standard Edition (Riviere translated *The Ego and the Id* and *Civilization and Its Discontents*), but she continued as translation editor of the *Journal* until 1937.[†]

Joan Riviere and Melanie Klein found a meeting of minds at the Salzburg Congress in 1924, although they had met formally at the congress in The Hague in 1920. Riviere began to absorb Klein's ideas the following summer in the Endelberg, where they were both holidaying after the Bad Homburg Congress. Her daughter, Diana Riviere, remembers Klein as always in a dreamy state, so constantly preoccupied with her thoughts that on walks she would appear miles away. If spoken to, she would react as though she had been startled out of a trance. In a snapshot taken of the two women at the Innsbruck Congress in 1927, Klein is the "dowdy bundle," Diana Riviere remembers, in contrast to her mother's easy elegance. Even to a child, Klein seemed "very unsophisticated."

Two such different temperaments coming from two entirely different worlds were hardly likely to be compatible; but Riviere recognized that Klein possessed *le feu sacré*. Melanie Klein was a little in awe of Mrs. Riviere when she first arrived in England and consulted her about such matters as what she would consider an acceptable postal address. Much as Riviere admired Freud,

---

* He is referring to *A Note on the Unconscious in Psycho-Analysis* (1912).

† Whenever Freud voiced complaints about the *Journal*, Jones would attempt to divert the responsibility to Riviere, such as his assertion that she categorically refused to publish any articles by Americans. This was extremely devious on his part, since he was totally responsible for all editorial decisions.

she belonged to a class that was never overawed by anyone, and she took on the assignment as an exchange lecturer in Vienna in 1936 with all the aplomb in the world. She believed that Freud's creative life had come to an end after his major operation for cancer in 1924. If Freud later objected to Riviere's speculations on the unconscious, it was he who first made her reel with its full implications.

> In my analysis he one day made some interpretation, and I responded to it by an objection. He then said: "It is *un-conscious.*" I was overwhelmed then by the realization that I knew nothing about it—I knew nothing about it. In that instant he had created in me his discovery of the powerful unconscious in our minds that we know nothing of, and that yet is impelling and directing us. I have never forgotten this reminder from him of what unconscious means.[55]

He had made her understand what the unconscious was, yet he was unwilling to accept its implications, as their future relationship would make abundantly clear. She had reason to know that he could be "choleric, resentful, and unforgiving."[56] He never forgave her for her espousal of Melanie Klein, for her contribution to the Symposium on Child Analysis, and for her subsequent Klein-oriented papers, which must have seemed particularly insulting to him after he had analyzed her.

Apart from the Melanie-Anna row, Freud told Jones (October 9, 1927), "More painful than these storms in the teacup are the theoretical statements of Mrs. Riviere, particularly as I always had a very high opinion of her understanding. I must accuse you in this connection that you have gone too far with your tolerance."[57] How could Jones have given her the opportunity to disseminate so widely "such erroneous and misleading fundamental views"?

Jones defended her, but—characteristically—not in the most courageous way possible. For some years while they were discussing Joan Riviere, they were also *in fact discussing Melanie Klein by implication.* "She [Riviere] insists," said Jones, "that the child's unconscious picture of the parents to which it reacts in such manifold ways is far from being a photograph of them, but is throughout coloured by entirely individual contributions from the child's own component instincts, e.g. the idea of the parent may be much more sadistic than the reality, etc. etc." This struck Jones as perfectly sound psychoanalytic theory, although "I told her she was making a mistake in dwelling only on what might be called the phantastic half of the picture." Why Freud lent himself to this bizarre fiction of attacking Riviere and ignoring Klein provides interesting matter for speculation.

Freud began to describe Riviere's stance as heretical: "It has an embarrassing similarity to Jung's and represents like his view an important step toward making analysis irreal and impersonal." He could not accept her version of guilt as a defense against internal impulses such as cannibalistic wishes. Undeterred by Freud's criticism, which Jones assured Freud he passed on to her, Riviere continued to publish papers that opposed Freud's views.

Jones, after becoming president of the International Association, felt that a break between the London and Vienna societies might be avoided if they arranged a series of exchange lectures. Partly for this reason he went to Vienna at Easter 1935 to discuss the idea with the vice-president, Paul Federn. In his biography of Freud, Jones writes:

> My own differences were partly doubt about Freud's theory of "death instinct" and partly a somewhat varying conception of the phallic stage in development, in particular in the female. So I read a paper on the latter topic before the Vienna Society on April 24, 1935. Freud never agreed with my views, and perhaps they were wrong; I do not think the matter has been entirely cleared up even yet. More troublesome were the views Melanie Klein had been expounding in contradistinction to Anna Freud's, not always in a tactful manner. In a long discussion with Freud I defended Melanie Klein's work, but it was not to be expected that at a time when he was so dependent on his daughter's ministrations and affections he could be quite open-minded in the matter.[58]

In this passage Jones is writing as Freud's official biographer. He is being crafty and circumlocutory. He had almost totally espoused Klein's ideas; but when he says that he opposed Freud's death instinct, he carefully omits adding that he does not reject Klein's interpretation of it. He also insinuates that Freud, old and ailing and utterly dependent upon Anna, was not likely to entertain a fair-minded view. Nevertheless, it is understandable that another generation of analysts, particularly Americans, express utter astonishment when they hear that Jones was a "Kleinian" sympathizer, most dreaded of heresies. They seem to assume that because Jones was the "official" biographer, he must have been totally "orthodox" in his views. Shortly after Jones returned from Vienna in 1935 he received the following letter from Freud:

> I do not estimate our theoretical differences as slight, but so long as there is no bad feeling behind them they can have no troublesome results. I can say definitely that we in Vienna have not infused any ill will into the contradiction and your amiableness has repaired the way in which Melanie Klein and her daughter erred in this respect toward Anna.* It is true I am of the opinion that your Society has followed Frau Klein on a wrong path, but the

---

* Melitta attacked Anna Freud only indirectly in a review of a book by one of her colleagues. See J. (1934) 15, 470. Her more open criticisms were suppressed, except for oral attacks at congresses.

sphere from which she has drawn her observations is foreign to me so that I have no right to any fixed conviction.

Freud concluded: "With patience and devotion we shall certainly overcome our present theoretical differences. We—London and Vienna—must keep together, as other European societies play scarcely a part and the centrifugal tendencies are at the moment very strong in our international association. It would be a great pity if they would not survive my personal existence." When Freud heard of Adler's death in Aberdeen in 1937, he wrote to Stefan Zweig: "I don't understand your sympathy for Adler. For a Jew boy out of a Viennese suburb a death in Aberdeen is an unheard-of career in itself and a proof of how far he had got on. The world really rewarded him richly for his service in having contradicted psycho-analysis." Was he prepared to say as much about a Jewish woman out of a Viennese suburb who had more or less succeeded in getting the English Society in the palm of her hand?

CHAPTER THREE

Mourning

Opposition had been seething under the surface for some years, but if a date could be set for the eruption of open warfare between Glover and Melitta on one side and Klein, it would be October 18, 1933, when at a board meeting of the British Society Melitta Schmideberg was elected to membership of the Institute. Glover announced that Melitta Schmideberg, the sole competitor, had received the Clinical Essay Prize* for her membership paper, "The Play-Analysis of a Three-Year-Old Girl."

Klein's name is never mentioned in the paper, but Kleinian concepts infuse the discussion. Vivian's difficulties with her mother take the form of an unconscious reproach for failing to give her a penis or for robbing her of one, "a projection of her own sadism and a defence against her own sense of guilt."[1] Nevertheless, Schmideberg does not attribute Vivian's problems in eating to constitutional factors as Klein would have done, but traces them to the strict toilet training to which her mother subjected her at six months.

> The possibility that the conflicts discovered in the analysis of a three-year-old child were already producing symptoms in the infant a few weeks or months old might be regarded as a probability, provided further analytic studies of young children and behaviouristic observations of young infants should indicate similar conclusions.[2]

The child's feeding was made difficult by a sore lip; and Schmideberg sees her neurosis as the outcome of both constitutional elements and external events. Most important of all,

* The prize was instituted by Dr. L. S. Penrose, and the judges were Glover, James Strachey, and Professor A. G. Tansley.

Part of Vivian's distrust of her mother was a direct reaction to the mother's own ambivalent attitude, for indeed it seems to be an important part of the mother's character to lie and make excuses. At the same time, she was devoted to the child and spoilt her a good deal.[3]

The case ends on a note that suggests other factors that might be taken into consideration:

The following observations made by the mother are interesting. While from birth Vivian was a difficult and nervous child the little sister was a happy and satisfied baby showing no nervous symptoms. The mother explains the difference on the ground that while pregnant with Vivian she had several frights and the delivery was difficult.[4]

This open-ended conclusion is consistent with her earlier observation that "behaviouristic observation of young infants" would be necessary for more definite theories to be formulated on the neuroses of babies.

Years later Melitta recalled that she was "rather popular"* at first with members of the British Society: her papers were highly regarded, she was asked to lecture, and was made a training analyst at a relatively early age.

But soon matters became uneasy. I was criticized because I paid more attention to the patients' actual environment and reality situation, and regarded reassurance and a measure of advice as legitimate parts of analytic therapy. But I always felt that the main objection was that I had ceased to toe the Kleinian line (Freud by now was regarded as rather out-dated). Mrs. Klein had postulated psychotic phases and mechanisms in the first months of life, and maintained that the analysis of these phases was the essence of analytic theory and therapy. Her claims were becoming increasingly extravagant, she demanded unquestioning loyalty and tolerated no disagreement.[5]

If Melitta's popularity declined, it was due largely to the embarrassment and anguish she caused her colleagues by the virulence of the vendetta she waged against her own mother. Melitta may have thought she was "rather popular," but members recall her as intense and humorless. While she looked unusually young for her age, she was tense and dogmatic. Diana, Joan Riviere's daughter, was delegated to show her around the colleges at the Oxford Congress in 1929. At the conclusion of the tour, Melitta remarked ungraciously, "It was interesting but unscientific."[6]

The difficulties within the British Society were inconsistent with the

---

* In 1942, Klein wrote to Susan Isaacs: "The fact that in the years until Dr. S. turned against me *her* criticism was *dreaded* in the Society people will remember very well."

image it presented to the world. Ernest Jones took pride in its having been acknowledged as the foremost Society by Freud. On December 19, 1932, Jones, in his annual newsletter to the presidents of the component societies, wrote: "Locally there is little for me to report, and only good. Our Society is working well and harmoniously." When Clifford Scott applied from Boston for training, in 1931, he received a letter from Jones excoriating all American analysts. William Gillespie, returning in 1932 from Vienna, where he had been analyzed by Edward Hitschmann, was asked scathingly by Jones why he had chosen to go to Vienna rather than to London. Gillespie did not realize what Jones meant: that he had chosen Viennese rather than English analysis—and he soon discovered they were very different indeed. Jones also told Gillespie that Freud had genius but not talent. In Vienna Gillespie had never heard of Melanie Klein, but in London he found that her work was regarded as "a Bible" by the members of the British Society. Not comprehending what the issues were all about, he was utterly bewildered by the bitter atmosphere he encountered at meetings. Speaking of Melitta's attacks, he shuddered: "It was horrible at times, *really* horrible."[7]

At a scientific meeting Melitta claimed that her mother had analyzed a child of one year, whereas Klein denied analyzing any children under two and a half. Another time she accused Klein of trying to deprive her of her psychoanalytic practice; and shouted, "Where is the father in your work?" In an unseemly scene she stamped her foot and stormed out of the meeting. Generally Melanie Klein tended to preserve a dignified silence during these onslaughts, leaving the fighting to supporters—Riviere, Isaacs, and, later, Paula Heimann. Gillespie has a memory of a kind of phalanx around her, all dressed in black, sitting in a special place across from the opposition.

Like two avenging furies, Melitta and Glover stalked Klein's life. According to Melitta's later account, Jones proposed that she and Walter emigrate to America. Fanny Wride recalled seeing Glover and Melitta openly holding hands at an international congress.[8] Wride believed that Glover regarded Melitta as the daughter he should have had instead of his own mongoloid child. Melitta's behavior indicates that she had an unresolved father-fixation. Glover, in his deep resentment of Klein, exploited Melitta to wound her mother in the cruelest possible way.

The depth of Melitta's bitterness against her mother was illustrated in her reaction to the death of her brother Hans in April 1934. Hans was working in a paper factory originally founded by his grandfather not far from Ružomberok. He loved to walk in the Tatra Mountains, which had formed the background of his life as a small boy; but on one excursion, the path suddenly crumbled away beneath him and he plunged down the side of a precipice. The funeral was held in Budapest, where Erich was visiting his Aunt Jolan. Arthur Klein arrived from Berlin, but Melanie was so distraught that she was unable to leave London. Eric Clyne maintains that Hans's death was a source of grief to her for the rest of her life.

Melitta's immediate reaction was that it had been suicide, and certainly many members of the British Society retain that impression. Eric Clyne categorically denies the possibility, considering the circumstances of Hans's death, and the fact that shortly after he was killed his mother received a letter from a Czech woman who told her that she and Hans had planned to get married after she obtained a divorce. Eric subsequently met the woman. The relationship also seemed proof that Hans had surmounted his earlier homosexual tendencies after his analysis with Simmel in the late twenties. Nevertheless, in the absence of documentary evidence, everything about Hans remains disturbingly shadowy.

An extant letter from Hans to his mother dated March 22, 1933, indicates that he was having difficulty getting work in Czechoslovakia because of his Swedish nationality. The letter is simple, childlike, and straightforward. He describes in great detail a Cossack costume he had worn to a recent fancy-dress ball in Plesivec. He continues: "I enclose a sample of my writing in verse. It is of course only comprehensible if one knows all the people and events in it. But you are quite imaginative and will be able to piece it together, and at least see a sample of my poetry!"[9]

Klein, who made a point of never missing a scientific meeting, was unable to appear publicly until June 6, when Glover spoke on certain controversial aspects of psychoanalytic technique.* It was remarkably insensitive to choose such a polemical subject for the occasion. On November 21, Melitta delivered a short communication to the scientific meeting on suicide, in which she commented:

> Anxiety and guilt are not the only emotions responsible for suicide. To mention only one other factor, excessive feelings of disgust brought about, for example, by deep disappointments in persons loved or by the breakdown of idealizations prove frequently an incentive towards suicide.[10] †

These remarks were made in response to Melanie Klein's analysis of the impulse towards suicide contained in her crucial paper "The Psychogenesis of Manic-Depressive States," which she read at the Lucerne Congress in August 1934, and to the British Society on January 16, 1935. Her "vurk," as she called it, had proved Melanie Klein's salvation in the past, and so it was to do again in this long, elaborately thought-out paper. For the rest of her life she was to turn

---

* However, Glover claims that he did not come into open opposition until October 3, 1934, when he read a paper, "Some Aspects of Psycho-Analytic Research," in which he stated roundly "that existing research activities in the Society were being 'frozen' by the propagation of dogmatic views on matters concerning which a completely open mind was essential" ("An Examination of the Klein System of Child Psychology," 13).

† It became something of an *idée fixe* with her. On May 18, 1938, she delivered another paper, "Technical Problems in a Suicidal Case."

her attention to the questions of loss, grief, and loneliness, experiences that formed the recurrent pattern of her life. Hans's death was the culmination of a year of sorrows—Melitta's treachery, and now the death of Hans, whose problems she must have felt had been exacerbated by her chronic depression when he was a child. Such devastating grief aroused past sorrows—the preference of her father for Emilie; the death of Sidonie; her anguish and guilt over Emanuel; her breakdown following her mother's death; her ambivalent feelings towards Arthur; her devastation after Abraham's death; and the uneasy course of her relationship with Kloetzel. In "Infantile Anxiety-Situations Reflected in a Work of Art and in the Creative Impulse" (1929), she described the urge to create as arising from the impulse to restore and repair the injured object after a destructive attack. This new paper, on the centrality of the depressive position, allowed her to sublimate her suffering so that she not only came to terms with her own grief but achieved the insight that grief could be a stepping-stone to maturity and development. Just as Freud's greatest work, *The Interpretation of Dreams*, was the outcome of his own self-analysis, so "The Psychogenesis of Manic-Depressive States" is an exploration of Klein's psyche. She realized that she had made a major discovery; and she knew, too, that the only way her work could be disseminated would be through the efforts of devoted and gifted students. Like Freud, she demanded undivided loyalty; and like Freud, she could be ruthless in casting off those who expressed doubts or who appeared to be pursuing lines of thought divergent from her own. As she grew older she appeared to many to be fanatical in her total absorption in her "vurk." "It would have been *quite* impossible to break away from her," Margaret Little told me. "If you went, it was because she fired you from the group."[11]

For years, Klein had attempted to adhere to a view of development in terms of libidinal stages, and as a result expressed herself turgidly or tripped over contradictions in the effort to accommodate a rigid structure to the ego's changing relations to its internalized and externalized objects. The central core of her new theory was that at four or five months a significant developmental change occurs in the infant's life, a change from relating only to a part-object to the recognition of a whole object, from the prototype of the breast to the mother as a person. This change carries with it a whole new set of ambivalent feelings and anxieties. The child is terrified of losing his good object; and at the same time, feeling guilty for the aggressive feelings that might have harmed it, seeks to restore it to wholeness. Was Klein's own earlier breakdown the result of the fact that she herself had not worked through what she was to call "the depressive position"?

Anxiety is now distinguished between paranoid (which she later usually called persecutory) and depressive states. Mental health depends on the internalization of a good object whose preservation is synonymous with the survival of the ego. The failure to create such a situation is the seedbed for later psychotic anxieties. In manic-depressive illness there is a dread that one contains dying or dead objects; and the defense against the recognition of this situation is the denial of value of the internalized object, the rejection of one's psychic reality. The infant seeks protection from these inner persecutors by means of expulsion and projection.

In "A Contribution to the Psychogenesis of Manic-Depressive States" (1935) Klein now simply assumed that the superego is based on the earliest incorporated part-objects. As if that theory were not controversial enough, she went on:

> My own observations and those of a number of my English colleagues have led us to conclude that the direct influence of the early processes of introjection upon both normal and pathological development is very much more momentous, and in some ways differs from what has hitherto been accepted in psycho-analytic circles.[12]

Quite clearly the depressive position has replaced the Oedipus complex as the central problem to be surmounted in development.

To begin with, the infant's world is filled with ideally good objects on the one hand, and abominably bad objects on the other; and the baby seeks to keep them apart in his mind. The situation becomes more complicated with time, when the good and the bad intermingle and the infant fears that the good will be destroyed by the bad. This is the case with depressive suffering when the infant, who by now has identified with his good object, fears that its destruction will mean his destruction as well. Hence the depressive patient may form an idea of perfection in order to reject the possibility of irreparable damage.

> In some patients who had turned away from their mother, in dislike or hate, or used other mechanisms to get away from her, I have found that there existed in their minds nevertheless a beautiful picture of the mother, but one who was felt to be a *picture* of her only, not her real self. The real object was felt to be unattractive—really an injured, incurable and therefore dreaded person. The beautiful picture had been dislocated from the real object but had never been given up, and played a great part in the specific ways of their sublimation.[13]

Was she not asking Melitta indirectly to try to see her as a whole person; and was she not inferring that Melitta had never fully worked through the depressive position? In Melitta's accusations against her mother, such as her suspicion that she was trying to deprive her of patients, she had slipped back into an infantile phase where her "paranoid fears and suspicions were reinforced as a defence against the depressive position."[14] Grief is a compound of sorrow, guilt, and despair. In such a state one begins to doubt the goodness of the loved object. Klein quotes Freud's statement that such doubt is in reality a doubt of one's own love and "a man who doubts his own love may, or rather *must*, doubt every lesser thing."[15]

Suicide can be regarded as a defense mechanism. Abraham had viewed it as an attack against the introjected body, she recalls, "But, while in committing suicide the ego intends to murder its bad objects, in my view at the same time it also aims at saving its loved objects, internal or external. To put it shortly: in some cases the phantasies underlying suicide aim at preserving the internalized good objects, and also at destroying the other part of the ego which is identified with the bad objects and the id. Thus the ego is enabled to become united with its loved object."[16]

Such a passage would suggest that Klein in her unconscious might have suspected that Hans could have committed suicide, consciously or unconsciously. In one of his notes he describes his mental state as "middling to rotten." In her state of mourning over her disturbed children (and the analysis of Felix suggests that Hans was probably a depressive) she was trying to *understand*. Neither Hans nor Melitta, apparently, had worked through the depressive position; and in Klein's own grief, she had reverted to an early manic phase. She knew that the first excruciating loss ever suffered occurs at weaning. The reaction to the deprivation of a libidinal part-object and the acceptance of a whole mother, loved but not idealized, is the necessary condition for normal development and the capacity to love. She was still denying any guilt or responsibility for what had happened to her children; she was in effect still using the defense of "undoing." The notion of reparation—later to play a major part in her work—is introduced as a measure generally impractical in its phantasizing nature. She had not yet fully worked out how one is to achieve inner wholeness, but the very fact that out of her anguish she was creating a development model, a *Weltanschauung*, was an affirmation of her belief in herself and in analysis.

Did she ever hope that Melitta would sink to her knees and ask her forgiveness as she herself had done when Libussa lay dying? Melitta was by now ostentatiously omitting references to her mother's work, but Klein quotes from 1931 and 1932 papers by Melitta and Glover to buttress her case. There are several possible explanations for this: an assertion that science is above petty feuding; and an implication that until very recently—as recently as Melitta's analysis with Glover—they both supported her views.

"A Contribution to the Psychogenesis of Manic-Depressive States" seems to have been written in a state of manic depression during the summer of 1934, and for the next two years she published nothing. Nevertheless, she continued to attend meetings regularly and always to make a contribution to the discussions. Her supporters agree that she was deeply depressed during this period, but deny that it was a clinical depression; yet Sylvia Payne later told Pearl King that Jones was so worried about Klein that he asked Payne to see her professionally.

In Klein's appointment book for 1934, Payne is marked down for two hours every Monday (occasionally an hour and a half) from January until the end of July. (Since the 1933 diary is missing, it is possible that she was seeing Payne prior to 1934.) Yet Hans did not die until *April 1934*. This would suggest that Klein's deep depression was triggered by the departure of Kloetzel for Palestine in late 1933. Their parting was a virtual death, since she knew that she would never see him again, and his symbolic death reactivated the feelings she had experienced after the death of Emanuel, whom he so resembled. Hans also reminded her of Emanuel, so that by the time Hans died mourning must have seemed a continuous burden meted out to her by the fates. That she managed to survive was a triumph of resilience and self-understanding.

The implications of Melanie Klein's controversial views continued to exert an influence in a wider sphere. Jones had tried to pacify Freud during the late twenties, diverting attention from Klein to Joan Riviere as an exponent of her theories. Now, in the thirties, he set about wooing Anna Freud by using Melitta Schmideberg as the scapegoat.

Anna was still smarting because the British had not published her first book. On April 1, 1930, she wrote to Jones that Allen & Unwin would be publishing her *Einführung in die Psychoanalyse für Pädagogen* (translated by her ally, Barbara Low, in 1931 as *Introduction to Psycho-Analysis for Teachers*). Anna added ironically that she felt very strongly that everything that happened in psychoanalysis in England would concern him—even if it was the publication of four little lectures of her own. Gradually a correspondence, sometimes of two letters a week, built up between the two. In March 1934, Jones sent Anna a batch of papers, including some by Klein and Melitta. In the *International Journal* he published a series of reviews on child analysis by figures such as Heinrich Meng and Richard Sterba, in which the emphasis was on the curative pedagogy in which child analysis should be involved. Quite clearly he was trying to mend fences.

At the Lucerne Congress in August, Anna was attacked fiercely by Melitta. Jones reported to Anna that Federn had refused to publish Melitta's paper in the *Zeitschrift* unless she omitted all references to Anna and her work.* "I was at first indignant with him on hearing this," Jones opined,

but on reading the paper I was bound to agree with him. Whether the inferences she draws about your work are correct or not, I certainly do not

---

* He is referring to Schmideberg's paper "The Mode of Operation in Psycho-Analytic Theory." It was published in abridged form as "The Psycho-Analysis of Asocial Children and Adolescents" in *J.* (1935) 16:6, 22–48.

think that was the fashion to expound them. If she wishes to do so, she should write a special essay dealing directly with your writings in a more open manner. I have therefore, with much difficulty, induced her to excise that section of her Congress paper and so it will appear in both the Journal and the Zeitschrift. Possibly the time would be ripe for some symposium on child analysis at the next Congress?[17]

Anna Freud complained that Melitta did not give her the benefit of the doubt as to whether she could distinguish between the conscious and unconscious. A different theory lay at the basis of what she was doing, but Melitta simply assumed that she was a fool. Melanie Klein's name was scrupulously avoided. When Jones reported that her son had died tragically, Anna replied that she felt terribly sorry for her, and passed on to something else.

When Freud and Jones parted in the spring of 1934, they had reached an amicable agreement about a series of Exchange Lectures between Vienna and London. In the interval, the Annual Report of the British Society for 1933–34 announced that its most outstanding event was the expansion of a section of the clinic for training in child analysis; the seminars would be conducted by Melanie Klein. Then came the Lucerne paper, "The Psychogenesis of Manic-Depressive States," which left the Viennese suspicious and uneasy. Ernest Jones went so far as to mention Melanie Klein as a possible replacement for Radó on the International Training Commission, which had been set up to work out the problems of affiliation of those analysts who had been forced for political reasons to emigrate from their home base. The only English possibilities he could suggest to Eitingon were Melanie Klein and Ella Sharpe: "The former, whatever one may think of her theories, has certainly shown the utmost interest in all training problems."[18]

Resuming the question of female sexual development, Jones's Viennese paper, "Early Female Sexuality" (1935), is a model of lucidity. The tone is eminently reasonable, yet he makes no attempt to minimize the London and Vienna differences. He begins by listing their divergences: "the early development of sexuality, especially in the female, the genesis of the superego and its relation to the Oedipus Complex, the technique of child analysis and the conception of the death instinct."[19] Using all his diplomatic skills, he assures his listeners that their varying approaches did not represent irreconcilable differences. The problem was one of inadequate communication because of language and geographic distance, as well as the recent political and economic difficulties. Few English analysts read the Zeitschrift, and even fewer German readers the International Journal of Psycho-Analysis. Indeed, he had the impression that analysts did not read as much as they used to. "I have the impression that nowadays far more psychoanalysis is learnt through the spoken than through the written word."[20]

He reiterates the points raised in his Innsbruck and Wiesbaden papers, which had been substantiated by Klein's child analyses—particularly as far as the development of the girl is concerned. Freud had more or less thrown up his hands about the early girl-mother relationship when he said, "Everything connected with this first mother-attachment seemed to me so elusive, lost in a past so dim and shadowy, so hard to resuscitate that it seemed as if it had undergone some specially inexorable repression."[21]

Melanie Klein showed no uncertainty: the small girl regards the mother as a person who has filled herself with all the liquid and solid things the girl craves. The father is a rival, too, because the mother is depriving the child by giving him these precious substances. The girl has to cope with a good deal more anxiety than the boy because of her phantasies of cutting, robbing, and burning the mother's body with excrement and urine. She envies a penis because she views it as a weapon of destruction and also as a defense weapon. But there is a solution to the impasse. Jones refers in passing to Klein's paper, "The Psychogenesis of Manic-Depressive States," in which she describes an emotional attitude rather than a stage in libidinal development. The girl, in her emerging realization that she cannot have the original objects of her desire and that her sadistic impulses are futile, moves into the Oedipus phase where she is in a state of rivalry with her mother. Her mother has not surrendered her breast or the father's incorporated penis—and so the girl rests temporarily in something that might be called a phallic stage in her difficult path to womanhood. "The ultimate question is whether a woman is born or made."[22]

Jones concludes: "Put more generally, I think the Viennese would reproach us with estimating the early phantasy life too highly at the expense of external reality. And we should answer that there is no serious danger of any analysts' neglecting external reality, whereas it is always possible for them to underestimate Freud's doctrine of the importance of psychic reality."[23]

On November 18, 1935, Robert Waelder, as the representative of the Viennese group, addressed the English Society on "Problems in Ego-Psychology."* Waelder's arrogant, condescending attitude did not appeal to the British; and in 1938, when there was some question as to where Waelder would flee from Vienna, Jones told Anna Freud that "I agree with the others that his personality does not lend itself very easily to assimilation."[25] What is puzzling is that Waelder's original paper was never published. Joan Riviere's reply, "On

---

* In *The Technique of Psycho-Analysis*, Edward Glover included a revealing footnote: "Interestingly enough, the English critics of Klein and her group did not associate themselves with Waelder, probably because they felt that he went too far in minimising everything that took place before the classic Oedipal situation, in particular the importance of pregenital factors. Although differing from the later Klein orientation, they did not object to some of her earlier findings which they felt could be woven into the texture of other analytic reconstructions, and which were based to a large extent on the accepted views of Freud and Abraham."[24]

the Genesis of Psychical Conflict in Earliest Infancy," was delivered to the Vienna Society on May 5, 1936, the eve of Freud's birthday.*

Freud had imposed a strict injunction that his eightieth birthday not be observed. Paying affectionate but mischievous respect to his wishes, the Vienna Institute was opened the day before his birthday, on May 5. The ceremony was attended by analysts from America, France, Czechoslovakia, Holland, and Palestine. Ernest Jones, as president of the International Association, gave the inaugural address, "The Future of Psycho-Analysis." He reminded the Viennese of the loss of many of their members by death, defection, or emigration. He touched on the thorny question of lay analysis, emphasizing that except in gifted cases he favored a medical background in order to gain respectability for psychoanalysis with the general public. He then turned again to the unfortunate problem facing overworked younger analysts who were unfamiliar with the history of psychoanalytic literature, a situation that "gravely diminishes the chance of developing a critical perspective and thus exposes one to numerous fallacies that would otherwise be avoided."[26]

He turned to the future of psychoanalysis: "The commonest risk of the investigator is the temptation to a one-sided exaggeration of whatever elements may have seized his interest."[27] Leaving his audience in no doubt that he was referring to Melanie Klein, he continued: "On the other hand, one should not always assume at once that an investigator opening up a new vein has certainly committed this error."[28] Freud had provided the "scaffolding," said Jones, and he looked forward to "very considerable changes in the course of the next twenty years or so."[29] The speech was dignified, respectful, but by no means obsequious.

Joan Riviere gave the Exchange Lecture to a large audience that evening. She was bitter that Jones had played the role of honest broker while leaving all the controversial material to her. A better English representative could not have been chosen—tall, elegant, completely self-assured. The content of her paper, "On the Genesis of Psychical Conflict in Earliest Infancy," was aggressively Kleinian. Klein and her supporters continued to assert that her work represented a development of Freud's ideas, whereas for the Viennese it was a deviation. The question was, which aspect of Freud? The Viennese had seized upon *Group Psychology and the Analysis of the Ego* (1921), in which Freud turned his attention from the unconscious to the way the ego strives to master and control its unconscious drives, using various mechanisms to defend itself against what was now called the Id. Klein, on the other hand, was attracted to the ideas in *The Ego and the Id* (1923), particularly to Freud's theory of guilt

---

* Riviere's paper was published in the *International Journal* in October 1936, whereas a completely different paper by Waelder, "The Problem of the Genesis of Psychical Conflict in Earliest Infancy," subtitled "Remarks on a Paper by Joan Riviere," appeared in the *International Journal* in 1937 (18, 406–73).

and the death instinct. Consequently, Riviere asserts initially that any claim to understand the ego structure of adults necessitates tracing development genetically back to its earliest roots. Evidence of preverbal feelings appeared in the repetition of certain material in adult analyses. Stressing that helplessness is the deepest anxiety in human beings, she adds: "We have reason to think, since Melanie Klein's latest work on depressive states, that all neuroses are different varieties of defence against this fundamental anxiety, each embodying mechanisms which become successively available to the organism as its development proceeds."[30] The ego requires an object upon which it can project its anxiety. Riviere wrote more effectively than any other member of the British Society; and in a dramatic passage she describes the turbulent phantasy life of the infant:

> Limbs shall trample, hit and kick; lips, fingers and hands shall suck, twist, pinch; teeth shall bite, gnaw, mangle and cut; mouth shall devour, swallow and "kill" (annihilate); eyes kill by a look, pierce and penetrate; breath and mouth hurt by noise, as the child's own sensitive ears have experienced. One may suppose that before an infant is many months old it will not only *feel* itself performing these actions, but will have some kind of *ideas* of doing so.[31]

However, aggression was only part of the story. "Feelings of love bring about the essential difference between part-object and whole-object relations."[32] The internalization of a protecting mother is the nucleus of a helpful superego. The child longs to repair harm it may have inflicted and to restore damaged goodness.

> The significance of the phantasies of reparation is perhaps the most essential aspect of Klein's work; for that reason her contributions to psycho-analysis should not be regarded as limited to the exploration of the aggressive impulses and phantasies.[33]

It would be fascinating to know something of the discussion following Riviere's paper, but unfortunately the minutes of the Vienna Society after 1920 are not accessible.

Waelder's "The Problem of the Genesis of Psychical Conflict in Earliest Infancy" (1937), ostensibly a reply to Riviere, is an exposition of the position of the Viennese school, argued with great lucidity and coherence. The main thrust of his paper is skepticism towards the hypothesis that mental activity takes place during the first year of life. He cites Freud's claim that all the experiences of the preoedipal phase are "hoary with age and shadowy." Brushing aside Riviere's contention that the accumulation of child analyses provides evidence for intense infantile conflict, Waelder will not accept unverifiable, nonbehavioristic data. He rejects the word "phantasy" in favor of impulses.

He adheres firmly to the theory that the superego is formed during the fifth year; and differentiates between the male and female superego as the difference between fixation through the abrupt termination of the Oedipus complex and a rather fragile component subjected to social approval. He is willing to admit that guilt and remorse can predate the resolution of the Oedipus complex, but if reparation is sought it is to restore what has been injured in actuality, and he will not accept that these impulses can occur earlier than the second year, when the ego makes an effort to emancipate itself from the forces of the id.

This explanation, he argues, is infinitely more productive than that of Klein, who appears to equate the recognition of reality with the diminution of anxiety. What Joan Riviere has given is "a practically automatic development of anxiety,"[34] detached from the actual conditions of a child's life.

Waelder reserves his most cogent criticisms for Klein's use of transference. She habitually describes any anxiety children feel in analysis as transference, completely overlooking the understandable fears a child might experience on entering a strange situation where he doesn't know which of his secrets is going to be revealed, whether his parents will be informed, and whether he will be punished. In other words, his anxiety is most likely based on the analysis itself. Anna Freud has been completely misunderstood, he assures his readers, in the way she has been criticized for the pedagogic factor; in her view "an adult cannot avoid being in the position of an educator in relation to a child, for every situation in which adult and child are in contact is a pedagogic situation; it therefore seems advisable to make the best practical use of what cannot be avoided."[35] Waelder believes that the analyst must endeavor to align the healthy part of the ego against the neurotic enemy.

His paper contains two interesting ironies. Although he makes only one reference to the phase of "paranoid anxieties and melancholic depression,"[36] he uses Glover, not Melanie Klein, as his whipping boy. Repeatedly he cites Glover's work during the previous five years, even his contribution to a symposium on therapeutic approaches in analysis at the 1936 Congress in Marienbad, as "repugnant" quasi-biology in which Glover described the so-called psychotic modes of behavior belonging to early childhood, the "psychic, frequently psychotic reactions and mental systems characteristic of infancy and early childhood"; and his description of the "small child passing through its schizophrenic and obsessional phases from the age of about one year onwards."[37] Apparently the Viennese were not yet aware of the division within the British Society.

The other irony is a case Waelder recounts of a mother who also happened to be an analyst (Jenny Waelder?), who observed her own daughter carefully and noted that at the age of three the girl began to exhibit marked anxiety, demonstrably linked to her castration complex and penis envy. Seemingly unaware that Klein's theories had emerged from the analyses of her own children, Waelder comments,

> Surely the analytical observation of the child from its earliest days by one who was at once mother and analyst, together with her intimate knowledge of all the events in the child's life and the discussion, in complete accordance with analytical principles, of what was not as yet understood, provides material equivalent to an analysis by a strange analyst. Perhaps, indeed, the mother would know more than any analyst could easily discover.[38]

At the Fourteenth International Congress, at Marienbad in August 1936, at a Symposium on the Therapeutic Results of Psycho-Analysis, Edward Glover had in effect publicly dissociated himself from Klein (although this apparently was not clear to Waelder!). "Although," he announced, "I have not attempted to give a list of references to standard works on the subject, use has been made of some views recently expressed by Dr. Melitta Schmideberg in the analysis of projection mechanisms, on the importance of instinct refusion, on the role of reassurance."[39]

Other humiliations followed. In 1937 the English translation of Anna Freud's book appeared as *The Ego and the Mechanisms of Defence* and was received with the expected accolades. Jones, after reading the German edition, had written to her on June 28, 1936, telling her that he had greatly enjoyed her book, "agreed with its conclusions and regarded it as beautifully written." "You have the gift of orderly writing without any straining for forced organization of the material. I should like to review the book."[40] This time he bent over backwards to be fair. In the *International Journal*, he wrote a short review (not quite so fulsome as his letter), followed by long, laudatory critiques by Otto Fenichel and Ernest Kris. (In contrast, the review of *Love, Hate and Reparation* by Klein and Riviere received nothing but a very brief notice by Jones.) He commends Anna Freud's book for its moderation, but regrets that she "breaks off her voyage of discovery into the depths where he could have wished for further enlightenment."[41] As for her contention that the infantile ego's fears are based on actual fears from the outside world, Jones comments: "I consider this a very questionable assumption and it is quite possible that the truth will ultimately be found to lie rather in the opposite direction."[42]

The Ego and the Mechanisms of Defence was not an overt attack on Melanie Klein as *Einführung in die Technik der Kinderanalyse* had been in 1927, but a far more mature, thought-out exposition of the resistances to which the analyst must address himself, based firmly on Freud's model of the mind and theory of instincts. Nevertheless, it is an oblique criticism of Klein's premises, aims, and methodology. In the history of Freud's thinking, Anna Freud insisted, the id was only a means to an end; and with *Group Psychology and the Analysis of the Ego* (1921) and *Beyond the Pleasure Principle* (1920), Freud turned decisively in a new direction to the ego institutions and an exploration of its boundaries, functions, and relations to the id, the superego, and the outside world. To concentrate on the id, by interpreting symbolic material as one did in the primordial days of analysis, was a shortcut to the unconscious, but it did not explain how the id content came to assume a specific ego form in its recognition of the distinction between itself and the outside world.

Interpretations of the transference may illuminate the past, but not necessarily contribute to an understanding of the present. She considers transference that uncovers the deepest strata of the mind as dangerous because it diminishes the independence of the observing, appraising ego. In an excellent phrase, Anna Freud describes the analyst as a "disturber of the peace"[43] who forces the patient to abandon the repressions that he has so arduously cultivated. And since the defenses—regression, repression, reaction-formation, isolation, undoing, projection, introjection, turning against the self, and reversal—have been carried out unconsciously, the analyst must reveal them with patient caution by circuitous routes.

In the cases that Anna Freud describes, the patients are all suffering from penis envy, unresolved oedipal conflicts, and pressures from the outside world (Fenichel, in his review, says that he would have emphasized external events even more strongly.)[44] Penis envy is actual penis envy. Little Hans is perfectly all right once things are explained to him in a sensible, avuncular way. Melitta had criticized Klein for ignoring the father, but Anna Freud ignores the mother except for the case she describes of the young woman whose intense hatred of her mother (originating in penis envy) was displaced from time to time onto another female.

Anna Freud refers repeatedly to "*objective* anxiety." For instance, while castration may no longer take place in civilized society, there are enough barbaric punishments in the educational world that the child quite understandably experiences "dim apprehensions and fears, residues handed on by inheritance."[45] Objective anxiety can be removed by changing environmental factors. Primeval fears, related to past events, can be alleviated by demonstrating that defense is unnecessary. She does not consider a third possibility—early anxiety springing from innate aggression. Someone who believes that "A little child's ego still lives in accordance with the pleasure principle" would find it impossible to accept the kind of suffering Melanie Klein describes the infant as experiencing. However,

> Children in the latency period may attach more importance to the avoidance of anxiety and unpleasure than to direct or indirect gratification of instinct. In many cases, if they lack external guidance, their choice of

occupation is determined not by their particular gifts and capacities for sublimation but by the hope of securing themselves as quickly as may be from anxiety and unpleasure. To the surprise of the educator the result of this freedom is, in such cases, not the blossoming of personality, but the impoverishment of the ego.[46]

Anna Freud's and Melanie Klein's premises and technique were very different, but Anna Freud's chapter on "Identification with the Aggressor" contains a description so close to Melanie Klein's later concept of "projective identification" that one wonders if she was unconsciously influenced by it. "The child was identifying himself not with the person of the aggressor but with his aggression,"[47] that is, assimilating projected anxiety, although here again Anna Freud lays more stress on *actual* threat.

The final section on the problems of puberty testifies to Anna Freud's shrewd powers of observation. She attributes the particular anxieties of puberty to the intensification of libidinal impulses. Klein's preconceptions about anxiety and her underemphasis of the libidinal component in neurosis meant that she did not sufficiently investigate this stage in development. For Anna Freud, periods in which there are strong upsurges of libido offer the best opportunity for analysis; while for Melanie Klein, periods of stress, such as mourning, reactivate intense early anxiety.

If we assume that Melanie Klein wrote out of her deep personal experience, it is tenable that Anna Freud is herself the governess in "A Form of Altruism" who "lived in the lives of other people, instead of having an experience of her own."[48] Anna Freud was an expositor of her father's ideas, but only of those ideas that could be scrutinized in clearly lit, well-ventilated places. Sin, cruelty, suffering she shunned. The witches of the night ride on broomsticks and converse with the powers of darkness in Klein's work, but a Viennese spinster creates a tidy, reasonable world by vigorously sweeping away the cobwebs.

Freud evidently felt that he should write something in support of his daughter's book. For the first time in nearly twenty years he published a purely technical work, *Analysis Terminable and Interminable* (1937). Strachey's bewildered introduction reflects the wayward and uncoordinated character of Freud's argument, so unlike his usual firm mastery of his subject.

In the closing sentences of Lecture XXXI of *New Introductory Lectures* (1933), Freud had stated that the intention of psychoanalysis is "to strengthen the ego, to make it more independent of the super-ego, to widen its field of perception and enlarge its organization, so that it can appropriate fresh portions of the id. Where id was, there ego shall be."[49]

However, here he lays stress on the "constitutional" strength of the instincts and the relative weakness of the ego, and fears that psychoanalysis cannot hope to effect any lasting alterations in the defense processes. Where Anna

Freud's book shines with optimism, his paper is threaded with dark despair; and indeed, he points out that the most powerful impeding factor is the death instinct, a subject Anna sedulously avoided. He seems to be haunted by the failure of his analysis of Ferenczi, most beloved of sons, who eventually accused him of failing to analyze his negative transference. Freud seems to be thinking aloud in *Analysis Terminable and Interminable*: How could I have treated him other than the way I did?*

> To activate it the negative transference would certainly have required some unfriendly piece of behaviour in reality on the analyst's part. Furthermore, [I] added, not every good relation between an analyst and his subject during and after analysis was to be regarded as a transference, there were also friendly relations which were based on reality and which proved to be viable.[50]

Freud agrees with Anna about the inadvisability of creating a negative transference, which "would oblige the analyst to behave in an unfriendly way to the patient, and this would have a damaging effect upon the affectionate attitude—upon the positive transference—which is the strongest motive for the patient's taking a share in the joint work of analysis."[51] He argues in favor of a therapeutic alliance, whereas Klein would insist that this might bypass deep anxiety and aggression. For Freud, the danger in stirring up what he would consider an "artificial" conflict would mean that a past conflict may only replace a present one. Finally, in his pessimism that anyone can ever be analyzed permanently and completely, he advises analysts to undergo a new analysis every five years. But he himself rejected Ferenczi's suggestion that he analyze him during one period of depression following the discovery of his cancer, whereas Klein at least turned to Payne for seven months in 1934.

Klein's opponents were mounting a powerful counterattack. At a Four Countries Conference in Budapest in May 1937, Otto Fenichel from Prague spoke on the methodological difficulties of investigating the earliest phases of the ego, and in the ensuing discussion there was an evaluation of the current literature on the topic, which paid special attention to the views of Melanie Klein. Michael Balint from Budapest observed that up to the present, ideas about the earliest stages of the mind were unsatisfactory, particularly those of the London School and their criticism of the Vienna Society. The Budapest analysts, he asserted, based their conclusions on well-observed and easily verifiable primitive object-relations.

---

* In discussing the actual case Freud does not mention Ferenczi by name, but Jones identifies him in his biography and the paper is filled with references to Ferenczi.

Klein delivered a paper on weaning* in the course of public lectures at Caxton Hall in February 1936, published in 1938 in *On the Bringing Up of Children*, a collection edited by John Rickman. All the contributors were known to favor Klein's views—Ella Sharpe, Merrell Middlemore, Nina Searl, and Susan Isaacs. On May 11, 1936, Jones reported to the Training Committee charges made by Melitta Schmideberg that there was plagiarism in the book, and a committee of Jones, Brierley, and Payne was set up to investigate. The findings were to be submitted privately to Dr. Schmideberg and the six contributors to the volume. The minutes do not reveal the specific nature of the charges, but whatever they were, Marjorie Brierley told me that the committee found they could not be substantiated.

Melitta continued her strident campaign. On March 19, 1937, Joan Riviere wrote to James Strachey: "Melitta read a really shocking paper on Wednesday personally attacking 'Mrs. Klein and her followers' and simply saying we were all bad analysts—indescribable."[52] She is referring to "After the Analysis—Some Phantasies of Patients," which was delivered to the British Society on February 17.† It is a scathingly brilliant comparison of the expectations inculcated in patients by certain analysts (apparently "Kleinians" in the original). They are brainwashed to believe that they are incapable of making any decisions or coping with life unless they have undergone "a thorough analysis." They are also led to believe that once they have been "fully analyzed" they will, like the true believer, "be saved from hell and enjoy eternal bliss in the life after death."[53] She draws an ingenious analogy with the rituals and liturgy of the Church.

Analysis is regarded as an atonement, as a cleansing process, as a religious exercise; getting on in the analysis means doing one's duty, obeying one's parents, learning one's prayers, defecating.[54]

Again she reverts to the comparison with the child:

The fully analyzed person is the ideally good child, free from all aggression, pregenital interests, or even the most minute symptom or difficulty. The patient is as intolerant of his symptoms as his parents were of his naughtiness, anxiety, bad habits and crying. The impatient wish to get rid of this neurosis may be a repetition of his parents' impatience with his childhood helplessness or illnesses, or it may be also an over-compensation for the wish to retain them and to enjoy the "gain from illness."[55]

---

* See p. 232.
† Published in watered-down form as "After the Analysis . . ." in *PQ* (1938) 7, 122–42.

As for therapeutic success, Melitta Schmideberg would find it helpful to know what happened to patients in later life.

And what of the situation where the parent is an analyst?

Some analysts seem to assume as a matter of course that analyzed parents are also the best parents. This is definitely not the case. All we can legitimately expect is that a person who has been successfully analyzed will have a better relation to his child than before he was analyzed. But this improved attitude is not necessarily better and is in fact often less good than that of a genuinely good parent. [56]

One can imagine the sensations of the paralyzed British members as they listened to this argument ad hominem.

During the Extraordinary Meetings of 1942, Schmideberg charged that Mary Chadwick, one of the early child analysts, had been pushed out of the Society by "the Kleinian clique."* She then turned to the case of Nina Searl, for years one of Klein's closest supporters.

About 1932 started the campaign against Miss Searl. To give only one of the methods employed, when she gave lectures for candidates Kleinian training analysts and full members attended them in order to attack her concertedly in the subsequent discussion in front of the candidates. This induced the Training Committee to lay down the rule that members should not attend lectures for candidates. In the meetings no occasion was omitted to make a joint attack on her.[57]

One of the few people who has been able to shed any light on Nina Searl's resignation on December 1, 1937, is Dr. Clifford Scott of Montreal. He has described Miss Searl's resignation as one of the most poignant spectacles he ever witnessed: she confessed publicly to the Society that she must resign because she was beginning to share the hallucinations of one of her patients. The reasons Searl gave at the Business Meeting for her decision suggest a deeply troubled woman.

1. She thought the Society was not developing on the best lines to advance the knowledge of truth as first represented by Freud.
2. She considered that an analyst should be able to convey to the patient that the psycho-analyst did not represent the highest ideals, in other words that there was room for the expression of a religious ideal.
3. That she was in touch with a group interested in spiritual healing and wished to be able to send suitable cases for treatment.[58]

* Yet Klein wrote a favorable review of Chadwick's Women's Periodicity in 1933. See Envy and Gratitude and Other Works, p. 318.

According to Dr. William Gillespie, Searl had developed strange interests and beliefs. He remembers attending a party at her house in 1937 at which he was introduced to weird people who had been buried with the pharaohs. "Her resignation (under what pressures I don't know)," he writes, "was received with general relief."[59]

Melanie Klein's great papers during these years—"A Contribution to the Psychogenesis of Manic-Depressive States" (1935), "Weaning" (1936), "Love, Guilt and Reparation" (1937), and "Mourning and Its Relation to Manic-Depressive States" (1940)—emerged out of her own deep personal suffering, but they should not blind us to the fact that she could be intensely partisan and in some respects highly insensitive. Granted that we may accept these aspects of her temperament, it is important first to examine the papers as contributions to the history of ideas without confusing them with the factional disputes that were tearing the British Society to pieces.

CHAPTER FOUR

The Arrival of the Freuds

In 1936, in a course of public lectures, given at Caxton Hall by a group of psychoanalysts, Klein delivered a lecture titled "Weaning"—in effect, a practical guide to baby care. Perhaps the wider audience on this occasion influenced her in ascribing more to the influence of the external world than she had previously done, although she continued to insist that subsequent failure in life to establish trusting relationships can be traced back to the crucial experience of the way in which the child survives the trauma of weaning. If the child succeeds in establishing within himself a kind and helpful mother—that is, an inner feeling of kindness and wisdom—he is building confidence both in himself and in others.

Actually, from the moment of birth, the child is in a constant state of being weaned, since the breast is not always available; but final physical weaning generally takes place between six and nine months. For the first time Klein considered in some detail the ways in which a good mother can ease the situation for the infant. She will regard the baby as a being in his own right, not as a machine or an extension of herself. She learns the patience to insert the nipple gently, to avoid artificial regularity in the nursery schedule, and to establish a good relationship by cuddling, singing, and talking to the child. Klein would even accept the use of a pacifier,* and advises restraint in preventing thumb-sucking or masturbation or in enforcing early toilet training. The mother, in handling the child, should never excite it sexually, and under no circumstances should the child sleep in the parents' bedroom. Bottle-feeding in which the child is held lovingly can be a reasonable substitute for breast-feeding, but even so it can never, even at best, offer the child a high degree of fulfillment.

* Her own children had had them.

In many respects, this advice was the opposite of the early experiences of her own children.

Her paper contains an interesting footnote: "I have to thank Dr. W. Winnicott for many illuminating details on this subject."[1] Since 1923 Donald Winnicott, a Gold Medalist in Paediatrics, had been working at Paddington Green Children's Hospital, where he had gained immense experience in mother-child relationships. Analyzed by James Strachey, he became a qualified psychoanalyst in the mid-thirties.

Strachey suggested to him that he take some of his interesting child cases to Melanie Klein. One case may well have been that of Andrew Malleson (now a psychiatrist in Toronto), who was analyzed by Winnicott twice a week during this period. Malleson was suffering depression following the divorce of his parents. Even though he was only four at the time, Dr. Malleson still has a clear recollection of the sessions with Winnicott, whose methods were apparently very different from those of Klein. He was allowed to wreak absolute havoc in Winnicott's office, creating a tent out of a large canvas screen, peeing through plastic tubes eight inches long, and lighting fires with huge piles of paper. There was very little sexual interpretation, although Winnicott explained the facts of life to him through diagrams. One of the few prohibitions he imposed was his refusal to show Andrew his penis. Not unexpectedly, Malleson remembers these sessions with pleasure. Later Winnicott evolved the famous "squiggle game," in which therapist and child doodle together, and through the child's drawings the therapist attempts to interpret the child's anxieties.

Winnicott was on holiday in Dartmoor when he first read *The Psycho-Analysis of Children*, and was so excited that he immediately reread it from beginning to end. Klein was naturally very interested in the cases Winnicott brought to her and gave him supervision between 1935 and 1940; but he could not agree to what he considered a bizarre proposal on her part: that she supervise his analysis of her son Erich. In 1940 he went into analysis with Joan Riviere for six years. According to his wife, Clare Winnicott, he would have preferred to have had analysis with Klein, but she persuaded him to analyze Erich without her supervision. Despite their initial clash over Erich, Klein accepted Winnicott's independent spirit; and it reflects well on her that she recognized his stature sufficiently to consider selecting him as her son's analyst from 1935 until 1939. At the end of the analysis Klein wrote to Winnicott on July 25, 1939: "I don't know whether I can convey to you how very grateful I feel for all you have done for Eric."[2]

Klein herself acknowledged that she was not a natural-born mother. Winnicott, on the other hand, possessed such a strong maternal identification, even though he had no children of his own, that Katherine Whitehorn in an article in *The Observer* once described him as a "Madonna."'[3] It is interesting that

Ferenczi also "mothered" his patients. Winnicott had had a very happy childhood, but Ferenczi came from a large family and apparently his overworked mother had not had the time to give him the attention he craved.

The year 1937 seems to have been the crisis and turning point in Klein's mourning. (There are no entries in her diary for that year, but it is possible that there is another, now missing diary.) Though generally in good health of late years, she had to go into the hospital in July for a gall bladder operation.* By now Erich was married; and in August she stayed in a cottage in Devonshire with his wife, Judy, who was expecting her first baby. (Michael, born in October, was to become very precious to his grandmother.) For four weeks in September she took a real holiday in Italy, and the enforced rest seemed to revitalize her.

That she was beginning to emerge from the deepest stages of her depression was apparent in the way she again plunged into the struggle to assert the primacy of her views. While Klein could be influenced by her collaborators, she was scathing in her attacks on competitors. She took on Maria Montessori, the Italian progressive educator, whose theories were receiving worldwide attention. At an Inter-Clinic Conference on January 29, 1937, Klein used the occasion to deliver a paper, "Play,"† which demolished a lecture Montessori had recently delivered at the Institute of Medical Psychology. Montessori, she claimed, had entirely failed to understand the part played by phantasy in the child's unconscious. She misinterpreted the significance of repetition in play. Montessori believed that lack of concentration was at the root of unfavorable mental development and that the child blossoms if the teacher puts him in a position in which he can function in a good way. The "play therapist" (Klein's description of Montessori) is not qualified to make interpretations of the child's play, Klein asserted, because he has no inkling of how to interpret the negative transference. The psychoanalyst knows how to utilize both the positive and negative transferences.

> *All* the hate as well as the love which the individual has felt from his earliest days onwards, and which has been partly repressed, [is] transferred onto the analyst. *All* the bad phantasy figures which have existed in the patient's mind . . . *all* these bad phantasy figures, and also the good ones, become related to the person of the analyst and thus may be brought to consciousness. By bringing this to the patient's attention while the feeling is still present, and by the patient's understanding of how his anxieties of

---

* She told Clifford Scott during his analysis in 1931 that she had to have a gall bladder operation. Dame Annis Gillie, her physician, remembers no such operation at either date; but Eric Clyne confirms the 1937 operation.
† Never published. The manuscript is among her papers at the Wellcome Institute for the History of Medicine.

these bad figures came about in the past, these figures now lose some of their power over the mind, and in this it is possible to bring about a diminution or resolution of fundamental and deep-rooted anxieties. The success of an analyst works both with the negative and with the positive transference. By working with the negative transference he releases anxieties of a strength which experience shows can only be grasped by the patient with such help as the specialised technique analysis affords. To illustrate this by an everyday experience of the child analyst: I may discover in a child's mind, while he is in my playroom, that the strong anxiety revealed is due to the fact that in phantasy I, the analyst, am an awful witch who is going to cut him in pieces. Through my interpretation I resolve this special anxiety, the child begins to play happily, and I may then become a nice fairy to him. This would mean that through my interpretation I have been able to resolve the negative transference, and that has resulted in the positive transference coming up.[4]

Writing papers was one thing, but to face the Viennese group in an Exchange Lecture was more than she felt able to cope with. On April 15, 1937, Jones wrote to Anna Freud: "The chief news I have to send is the very regrettable one that Mrs. Klein will not be able to pay her projected visit to Vienna. The reason is an invincible one, her health being such that her doctors have absolutely forbidden the journey. She very much regrets it also. Now can anything be done in the circumstances? Really it was the turn of the Viennese to come to us."[5] Anna Freud assured him that there was great interest in the lectures, and that the atmosphere was altogether more relaxed and receptive than it had been even two years before. "But this," she hastened to add, "of course doesn't change so quickly and there can be a shift in the atmosphere." Bibring and Fenichel might be possible spokesmen to send to London. She considered that Fenichel had a real gift for lecturing, but Bibring was more to the point and not so theoretical. However, she doubted whether either of them could prepare an adequate lecture between May and the autumn, and the whole program was allowed to lapse.

"Love, Guilt and Reparation" (1937) grew out of some public lectures Joan Riviere and Melanie Klein gave in 1936 under the title "The Emotional Life of Civilized Men and Women," from which they published a small volume, *Love, Hate and Reparation*, the following year.* In dividing the subject, Riviere concentrated on hate and aggression, while Klein spoke on love and reparation. However—and Jones seems to suggest this in his brief review—the

---

* Considering the times, the sales were reasonably respectable: 508 copies the first year, and in 1943, during the middle of the war, 136 copies were sold.

lectures were very much rewritten for the book. It is impossible to assign certain ideas to Melanie Klein and others to Joan Riviere, particularly as Riviere's Vienna Exchange Lecture had been the first to elaborate the concept of reparation;* and while Riviere might have worked hard at clarifying the density of Klein's early style, by 1940 Klein was accepting advice from her only on matters such as syntax, as an examination of her manuscripts indicates. In any event, both women were in agreement in their view of the psychic processes.

In Klein's paper she extends the ramifications of the parent-child-sibling relationships to wider fields than she had yet explored. Never before had she discussed what makes a happy marriage—the situation where "the unconscious minds of the love partners correspond"[6]—and again the breast is the source from which the infant learns the process of displacing love. Real joy, beauty, and enrichment can be experienced only when in the unconscious mind the individual feels "the mother's loving and giving breast and the father's creative penis"[7]—the two great affirmative principles of life. The paper is full of autobiographical echoes, and she seems to be referring indirectly to her difficulties with Melitta as stemming from her own relationship to Emanuel and to her older sisters, as well as Arthur's (and her own) expectations of Hans:

> The individuality of the child may not correspond to what the parents wished it to be. Either partner may unconsciously want the child to be like a brother or a sister of the past, and this wish obviously cannot be satisfied in both parents—and may not be fulfilled even in one. Again, if there has been strong rivalry and jealousy in relation to brothers and sisters in either or both partners, this may be repeated in connection with the achievements and the development of their own children.[8]

In one interesting section she discusses the Don Juan syndrome—and quite clearly she had Emanuel, Arthur, and Kloetzel in mind. By persistent infidelity such a man "is proving to himself over and over again that his *one* greatly loved object (originally his mother, whose death he dreaded because he felt his love for her to be greedy and destructive) is not after all indispensable since he can always find another woman to whom he has passionate but shallow feelings."[9] This is not true reparation since, as he is driven from one woman to another, "the other person soon comes to stand again for his mother. His original love object is thus replaced by a succession of different ones."

Genuine reparation occurs when in a love relationship or parental role the

---

* In *The Psycho-Analysis of Children* and in early papers Klein had spoken of "restitution." In "On Criminality" (1934), for instance, she had linked the child's greed and stealing with robbing the mother of her feces and phantasied babies. If the child is not devastated by guilt, he often seeks to make restitution. In the analysis of Richard she often speaks of "restoration," but as Donald Meltzer points out, it was not until *Envy and Gratitude* (1957) that she took up the idea again and developed it into a central concept. (See *The Kleinian Development*, Part II, p. 44.)

adult emulates the love he has received, or repairs the love denied to him by becoming a more loving being. Klein goes on to apply the concept of reparation to the artist and the explorer. This latter may give expression to his aggressive instincts in his exploitation of the natives, but in repopulating a new territory he is expressing the need to make reparation.

It would be reassuring to believe that Klein emerged from her ordeal wise, tolerant, and benign; that she and Melitta were reconciled; and that the British Society turned to do what it was established for in the first place: to help people in deep emotional distress and to pursue rigorous scientific research. Unfortunately, this was the real world, not the world of fantasy (or phantasy), where everything comes right in the end. The divisions within the British Society were now so deep that it could no longer contain both Edward Glover and Melanie Klein. Secondly, Klein's life itself was to be affected deeply, like millions of other lives, by the advent of Adolf Hitler. And, although she had surmounted despair, she was assailed by continuing problems within herself, and by circumstances that made life just as difficult in different ways.

On March 8, 1939, the British Psycho-Analytical Society held its twenty-fifth anniversary dinner at the Savoy (Ernest Jones dated its founding either to 1914 or 1919 as it suited his purposes). Virginia and Leonard Woolf were among the guests; and they dined with Klein on March 15. In her diary Virginia Woolf recorded that she was "a woman of character & force some submerged—how shall I say?—not craft, but subtlety; something working underground. A pull, a twist, like an undertow: menacing. A bluff grey haired lady, with large bright imaginative eyes."[10] It is a marvelous description. It seems inevitable that they should finally have met—these two women, born the same year, from entirely different backgrounds, but with interesting parallels in their lives.

Klein continued to convince herself that she had the complete support of Ernest Jones. Shortly after the dinner she sent him a letter of profound and sincere gratitude.

> *42, Clifton Hill,*
> *St. John's Wood, N.W.8*
> *11th March 1939*

My dear Dr. Jones,

Now that the official celebration is over, I would like to tell you what I personally feel on this occasion.

We all who are identified with Psycho-analysis and more especially with Psycho-analysis in England, owe you so much that it seems futile to try to express one's gratitude in words. What you have done for the development of theory and the growth of our science will endure for always—that is to say if Psycho-analysis survives. If it does, it will again largely be due to your efforts and achievements. You have created the movement in England and carried it through innumerable difficulties and hardships to its present position. You have for years wisely guided the International through troubled times. And it is owing to you that Psycho-analysis and its future is now centralized in London.

Now, I want to thank you for your personal friendship, and for your help and encouragement in what is of infinitely greater importance to us both than personal feelings—namely our work. I shall never forget that it was you who brought me to England and made it possible for me to carry out, and develop, my work in spite of all opposition.

Lastly I would like to tell you how deeply gratified I am by the appreciation of my work which you expressed on Wednesday night. Here again it is not only a case of personal gratification. I have heard from a number of people whose work you established that they feel greatly encouraged by what you have said about my work and I know your words will also prove helpful to all those who look to you for guidance at a critical time for Psycho-analysis.

Wishing you continued success and personal happiness in the future and with kindest regards,
        Yours

                        Melanie Klein[11]

Her reference to the possibility that psychoanalysis might not survive reflected her fear that Anna Freud was destroying it. She would have been horrified if she had known that on June 29, 1938, shortly after the Freuds' arrival in London, Jones had written to Anna Freud:

How I wish I could have a long talk with you about the situation here. At present you have only my confidence to rely on, but I could then show you on what solid ground it is based. You are right in saying that you need a great deal of information about the character and work of many of the members here. For the rest you have mentioned exactly the qualities needed, courage, common sense, tolerance, and above all, Mangel an Empfindlichkeit [a short supply of touchiness]. I think you are richly endowed with these and that is one of the bases of my confidence.[12]

Klein had no idea that Jones was in effect undermining her position. Jones is the most convoluted figure in this complex pattern of relationships. His attitude toward Klein had become increasingly ambivalent. He liked her as a woman, he subscribed to her theories, but was uneasy and envious about the way his protégée had assumed the most prominent place within *his* Society.

The first group of German-Jewish analysts from Berlin had begun arriving in Britain in 1933 after the Reichstag fire—S. H. Fuchs (later Foulkes), Paula Heimann, and Kate Misch (later Friedlander). From the beginning there was worry among the British analysts that there would not be enough work for additional people. To Max Eitingon on July 12, 1933, Jones wrote: "My standpoint is as follows. We cannot recommend that anyone come here because, even if all the great difficulties are overcome, there is not enough work for our own poor people and the prospects of making a living are at present very poor indeed."[13] Through the help of David Eder, Heimann and Misch arrived in England and settled in the East End, where they found it impossible to make ends meet. When Jones learned where they were living he was horrified and suggested more respectable locations. The passing of the monstrous Nuremberg Laws, which deprived Jews of citizenship, forbade marriage between Jews and Aryans, and barred Jews from the liberal professions, made 1935 a crucial year. (On June 2, 1934, Melanie Klein had become a naturalized British subject; in this situation she found her Swedish passport helpful.) The situation had now become so desperate that Jones promised the members of the Berlin Institute that he would secure permits for the members to come to London through his friendship with Sir Samuel Hoare, the Jewish Home Secretary (Jones's wife, Katherine, incidentally, was Jewish). Eva Rosenfeld did not arrive until March 1936, because Freud wanted her to continue at the Tega Sanitorium, which he desperately wanted to remain open. War began to seem imminent; and if there was an invasion of Britain, the Jews knew what their fate would be.

Eitingon had gone to Palestine. Erich's former analyst, Clare Happel, settled in Chicago, as did Hans's analyst, Ernst Simmel, before moving on to California. Melitta's original analyst, Karen Horney, had already moved to New York; and Helene Deutsch, who had always regarded Melanie as a rival, was by 1934 establishing orthodox analysis in Boston. Klein's old enemies in Berlin, Franz Alexander and Sándor Radó, settled respectively in Chicago and New York.

In 1937 Susan Isaacs's husband, Nathan, advised Erich Klein to change his name to Eric Clyne. The following year, Klein stood guarantor for Hermann Deutsch's relatives from Austria, many of whom moved on to America and Australia. Mrs. Hanna Clampitt of Michigan, the daughter of Hermann's son, Emil Deutsch,* feels that Klein's sponsorship was an extremely generous act, since she was in effect making herself financially responsible for all of them.

In 1938 Emilie and Leo arrived as refugees from Vienna.† They moved

---

* Hermann himself had died in Vienna in 1937.

† The Pick family was sponsored by the Society of Friends, according to Emilie's grandson, Walter, now a dentist in Oxford. However, Hertha Pick points out that Walter would have been only three or four when he arrived in England, and his memory would be based on what his mother had told him. Mrs. Pick asserts that the Schmidebergs sponsored the Picks. She also describes the relationship of Emilie and Melanie as "of the love/hate kind."

into a flat around the corner from Clifton Hall, but Klein seldom saw her sister. Emilie's daughter-in-law, Hertha Pick (who had married Willi), recalls that her mother-in-law had great admiration for her brilliant younger sister, but warned Hertha *never* to read her shocking book on children! (It must have been galling to Klein to know that Emilie's son Otto, who had been Freud's dentist in Vienna, was a frequent visitor at Maresfield Gardens after Freud's arrival in England.)

Clifford Scott remembers that during the Munich crisis in 1938 Klein visited him at his place at Hildenborough, south of London, where he was working in a hospital. That weekend people were digging shelters in their gardens. Klein, having spent the first war in Budapest, where life went on comparatively normally, was in a state of agitation about the threat of an invasion. She well remembered the wave of anti-Semitism that had swept Hungary in 1919, forcing her and many others to leave the country, so her fear is understandable.

In 1939 Klein's old friend from Berlin, the child psychologist Nelly Wollfheim, reached England on the guarantee of "an unknown lady." Klein, advised of her arrival, telephoned her on the day she landed. With real regret she told her that she was unable to help her financially as she was already responsible for so many of her own relatives. Ernest Jones received Wollfheim kindly but was able to give her only £15 out of the Society's funds, which had been exhausted by the needs of refugees already among them; still, £15 was a godsend for someone who had arrived in England with only ten shillings.

When Wollfheim first visited Klein one evening at the house in Clifton Hill, she was astonished by what seemed to her the splendor in which Klein now lived, in contrast to the lodgings in Berlin that she remembered. A servant opened the door and took her coat. After a time other guests arrived, including "Erna," now a tall young woman, who embraced her warmly. "Erna" was also a refugee. Klein had prepared the surprise of meeting the child about whose welfare they had both been concerned so many years before. "Erna" was about to emigrate to Australia.

Jones appointed Eva Rosenfeld secretary of the Jones Rehabilitation Fund, and it was she who was responsible for getting many of the analysts out of Austria, a fact not generally known.[14] Jones and Princess Marie Bonaparte devoted all their efforts first to persuading Freud to leave Vienna, and then to the complicated arrangements to secure his exit after the Nazis invaded Austria in March 1938. As Ernest Jones described it,

> A meeting of the Board of the Vienna Society was held on March 13 at which it was decided that everyone should flee the country if possible, and that the seat of the Society should be wherever Freud would settle. Freud

commented: "After the destruction of the Temple in Jerusalem by Titus, Rabbi Jochanan ben Sakkai asked for permission to open a school at Jabnet for the study of the Torah. We are going to do the same."[15]

Ironical words!

By 1938 one-third of the analysts in the British Society were from the Continent. A comparison of the 1937 and 1938 membership lists shows the number of new names that were added—Bibring, Eidelberg, Hitschmann, Hoffer, Isakower, Kris, Lantos, Stengel, Schur, Stross, Sachs, Straub—and of course Sigmund and Anna Freud. Hilda Abraham also arrived from Berlin in 1938 and, although the daughter of Klein's mentor, always remained fiercely opposed to her ideas. In 1939 Ferenczi's successor, Michael Balint, appeared from Budapest and set up practice in Manchester. Many of these Europeans were to move on to the United States, but the climate of the British Society, particularly with the arrival of the Freuds, was to be changed irrevocably. "It will never be the same again," Melanie Klein lamented to Winnicott. "This is a disaster."[16]

Freud arrived in London on June 6. Awaiting him was a letter of welcome from Melanie Klein, expressing the wish to call on him as soon as he was settled. He replied with a brief, courteous note on the 11th, thanking her for her letter and adding that he hoped to see her in the near future. An invitation failed to materialize, although Melitta and Walter Schmideberg were frequent visitors. Klein was in Cambridge when his funeral service took place at Golders Green Crematorium in late September 1939.

It is important at this point to understand the constellation of affiliations. Ernest Jones retreated more and more into the background with the arrival of the Freuds, and consequently delegated most of the administrative work of the Society to Edward Glover. His anxiety not to offend the Freuds accounts for the space he allotted to Anna Freud's *The Ego and the Mechanisms of Defence* in the *International Journal of Psycho-Analysis*, whereas the notice he gave the Klein-Riviere book is almost insulting in its brevity. His determination to stay above the fracas also accounts for the innocuous nature of the papers he published during the rest of his life.

Alix Strachey, Melanie's original supporter, seldom attended meetings. She and James tended to support Klein, but in 1941, in one of her rare papers, "A Note on the Use of the Word 'Internal,'" Alix indicated uneasiness about the direction Klein's thought was taking.[17] Nina Searl had resigned, so the stalwarts comprised Clifford Scott, David Matthew, Joan Riviere, Susan Isaacs, Donald Winnicott, and, increasingly, Paula Heimann. After John Rickman's return from his analysis with Ferenczi he had begun, in 1934, a seven-year analysis with Klein.* For some years he regarded himself as a Kleinian, although Klein always suspected that he did not adhere passionately enough to her ideas, particularly as in the Preface to *On the Bringing Up of Children* (1936) he emphasized the importance of the father in the child's life, even insisting that "in his fantasies the child gives about equal attention to the father and mother figures."[18]

John Bowlby, who was analyzed by Joan Riviere between 1933 and 1937, was beginning to be viewed with distrust. Bowlby says that until 1937 he might have been classified as a Kleinian because "the edges were so blunt," but after the war he was unmistakably an independent.

Paula Heimann and Eva Rosenfeld were two relatively new members in the Kleinian group. Heimann had taken her M.D. in Berlin and had been analyzed by Theodor Reik. Just after she qualified as an analyst, the rise of the Nazis and her separation from her husband, Dr. Franz Heimann, brought her career in Berlin to an end in 1933. She emigrated to London with her small daughter, and in the confused state such deep changes had made in her life, she accepted Melanie Klein's suggestion that she enter analysis with her; she soon developed into the most ardent of Klein's supporters. Their relationship will be discussed in detail in due course.

Like Heimann, Eva Rosenfeld had found the uprooting totally disorienting. She had been very close to the Freud family in Vienna; as a niece of the chanteuse Yvette Guilbert, whom Freud adored, she was particularly welcome in the Freud household. She loved England and her first walk on Hampstead Heath in 1936 was a joyous occasion after the nightmare she had been through in Germany. Nevertheless, resettlement was a tremendously disturbing experience. Klein's paper on depression made a deep impact on her, and after anguished soul-searching she decided to go to Klein for analysis. Before making the decision she wrote to Freud, confessing what she was contemplating; and he replied (in her words): "I am afraid I cannot convince you in four weeks that Mrs. Klein's theories might not be right. So you do what you have got to do, sort out who is better, father or mother." [19] Her analysis proved a very disturbing experience, as at meeting after meeting she witnessed the bizarre spectacle of her analyst being attacked by her own daughter:

> At the meetings I could only see something quite terrible and very un-English happening, and that was a daughter hitting her mother with words and this mother being very composed, quite quiet, never defending herself, but having such power in that society, being so powerful that it really didn't matter what Melitta said. We knew only that we would be

* According to Pearl King, at one point he was invited to the Menninger Clinic, but the invitation was withdrawn when it was discovered he was a Kleinian.

the victims of this quarrel and we were and the society was, there was no doubt about it.[20]

The harassment of Klein by Melitta and Glover continued. Other figures who were overtly hostile to her were Marjorie Brierley, Barbara Low, Ella Sharpe (increasingly so, although she had been one of Klein's earliest supporters), and Adrian and Karin Stephen. The only two truly independent figures at that time seemed to be Sylvia Payne and W. H. Gillespie.

Life was very difficult for the European analysts. At first, as Willi Hoffer recalled, they felt like "bloody immigrants." The Viennese found everything about the English group disturbingly different from what they were accustomed to. In London the chairman sat on a dais facing the members lined up in rows, an arrangement that enabled factions to sit together, whereas in Vienna they were a cozy group gathered around a table. The émigrés were startled to find the English women wearing hats, a small detail but indicative of the prevailing formality.

The Viennese had been totally united in their loyalty to Freud, who would usually join them at the end of a discussion, bringing the issues into perspective, as Willi Hoffer described it. On Saturday evenings Anna Freud had meetings at her home with Hoffer, Bernfeld, Aichhorn, and a friend of hers, Edith Richer, "free discussions, wonderful discussions, on child and adolescent psychology, seeing the child in analysis, in the environment, in society, who interacts with human beings and thus is educated."[21] While these discussions were taking place, Freud was in another room playing cards with his cronies. What the German-speaking analysts found in London was "war, absolute war."[22] No wonder there were tearful reunions at the international congresses in later years, when these exiles, dispersed far and wide, fell into each other's arms!

Naturally all the continental analysts were solidly behind Anna Freud and highly distrustful of Melanie Klein. Anna Freud moved slowly at first. In September 1938 she initiated small fortnightly group meetings at her home, conducted by herself and her Viennese colleagues, at which attendance for trainees was optional. By June 1939 the seminars had been made obligatory; and the following month she declined to take child seminars at the Institute because the candidates for child training "who had been analyzed or otherwise trained by analysts holding different views would not be likely to benefit from her teaching."[23] Mrs. Klein agreed that there was no way in which their teaching could be amalgamated.

Freud was too ill to attend scientific meetings. One can imagine the sort of tension electrifying the room on December 7, 1938, when Anna Freud appeared, flanked by her American friend Dorothy Burlingham and Princess

Marie Bonaparte. Melanie Klein, Melitta Schmideberg, and Edward Glover were also present. On this occasion Susan Isaacs presented a paper, "Temper Tantrums in Early Childhood in Their Relation to Internal Objects." This short, sturdy Lancashire woman exuded confidence, her head tilted back, her eyes sparkling, mischievously relishing the drama of the occasion. Temper tantrums, she claimed, were a part of normal development, and reached their peak of development during the second year. In these situations the child reacts in helplessness to his internal persecutors. These internal objects, first described by Freud and Abraham, had been developed more theoretically by Klein; but, she adds, "This paper is concerned not with the elucidation of the general theory of internal objects, but with the way in which an understanding of the various phantasies connected with internal objects serves to illuminate the phenomena of temper tantrums and helps in their analytic treatment."[24] She presents the case of a child with an epileptic mother.* The circumstances of the child's life enter into the composition of his persecuting internal objects; at the same time, they are phantasies with which the child is fighting "with the utmost extremity of terror." In the subsequent discussion following the paper, her paper was criticized for being too condensed, and that it took for granted many points needing further explication.

Eva Rosenfeld suggested that a small group of Kleinians meet regularly to formulate their ideas for presentation to the Viennese. On January 13, 1939, Susan Isaacs wrote to Clifford Scott: "She feels that we don't make it easy for the Viennese to understand our views, and that one ought to give much more attention to the educational side of our work—to find ways of putting things which will get rid of *intellectual* obstacles at least."[25] And so the I.O. (Internal Object) Group was launched—about five members in all—to hammer out a comprehensible theoretical framework. It was the first step toward making some form of rapprochement with the Viennese.

At the end of June 1939 a joint meeting with the French Psychoanalytical Society gathered in London (probably at the instigation of Marie Bonaparte) for a further clarification of differences. On this occasion Anna Freud delivered a paper, "Sublimation and Sexualization" (apparently never published), to which the respondent was Paula Heimann, with "A Contribution to the Problem of Sublimation and Its Relation to Processes of Internalization," in which Heimann sets out to describe the nature of the inner world and the objects it contains. Her definition of the ego is worth quoting:

[It is not] an organization which is firmly established and demarcated in contrast to other parts of the personality—indeed, Freud has warned us against being dogmatic in this matter—but of the sum-total of an individ-

* According to John Bowlby, Isaacs never disagreed with his emphasis on environmental factors.

ual's feelings, emotions, impulses, wishes, capacities, talents, thoughts and phantasies, in short, all those psychic forces and formations which a person . . . would identify as his own and which would make him feel: "That is I."[26]

She then gives the case of a woman artist, inhibited in her work because she felt persecuted by inner devils roaming around inside her with pitchforks. The hysteric may be haunted by reminiscences, but Heimann reminds her listeners that memory is "a composite superimposed picture" of what Otto Kernberg later called "internal world and external reality." Because the patient was crippled by guilt and anxiety, she was unable to restore her good objects and to effect reparation through creativity. This inhibition was gradually released to give her internal freedom, a relative state that "does not abolish conflicts, but . . . enables the subject to enlarge and unfold his ego in his sublimations."[27]

The year 1939 was one of confusion in every sense. Freud's condition was deteriorating rapidly. On the occasion of the twenty-fifth anniversary of the British Psycho-Analytical Society in early March, Freud had sent Ernest Jones the last letter he would ever write him:

Dear Jones:

I still find it curious with what little presentiment we humans look to the future. When shortly before the war you told me about founding a psychoanalytical society in London I could not foresee that a quarter of a century later I should be living so near to it and to you, and still less could I have imagined it possible that in spite of being so near I should not be taking part in your gathering.

But in our helplessness we have to accept what fate brings. So I must content myself with sending your celebrating Society a cordial greeting and the warmest wishes from afar and yet so near. The events of the past years have brought it about that London has become the main site and center of the psycho-analytical movement. May the Society which discharges this function fulfill it in the most brilliant fashion.

Ihr alter

Sigm. Freud[28]

On September 3, Britain declared war on Germany. On the 23rd, Freud was dead.

Jones considered disbanding the Society for the duration. He returned from his country house near Midhurst for meetings of the Society, which began to be held only monthly; and for a year the British Society was virtually left in the hands of Glover and the continental analysts, who, as aliens from an enemy country, were not allowed to travel out of the London area. Anna Freud and Dorothy Burlingham started the Hampstead Wartime Nurseries for children whose families had been disrupted by war. These were modeled on Siegfried Bernfeld's Kinderheim Baumgarten, which had been established in Vienna after the first war.

All the medical members of the Society joined the forces in one capacity or another. Scott went into the Emergency Medical Service and Winnicott became visiting psychiatrist for the Oxfordshire Hostel Scheme, through which he met his future wife, Clare Britton, a psychiatric social worker. Rickman was posted to a hospital in Sheffield six months after the outbreak of war. Bowlby became an army psychiatrist for the next five years.

In late August 1939 Klein took her holiday in Walberswick, Suffolk. From there she wrote to Winnicott on August 31: "In case of war I shall stay on here until my plans have taken definite shape. I intend in this case to settle down in the country with a few patients and also to do some war work."[29] The moment Germany invaded Poland, she went to Bishop's Stortford to be near Susan Isaacs, and within a week moved in with her. In the middle of August Dr. Sophie Bookhalter, a psychiatrist from Winnipeg, had had an interview with Klein in London, and was accepted for training. However, when she turned up for her first session in September, she was informed that Mrs. Klein had moved to Cambridge for the duration.

PART FOUR

1940-1941
CAMBRIDGE
AND
PITLOCHRY

CHAPTER ONE

Moratorium

It was an ironic twist of fate that Melanie Klein should have been confronted with an alliance of her most intransigent enemies just at a moment when she seemed to be emerging from her long period of depression. Her infantile paranoia was reactivated—a phenomenon she recognized—and she incorporated some of her feelings into the paper on mourning she delivered at the Paris Congress on August 2, 1938.

With the outbreak of war, James Strachey took over the editorship of the *International Journal of Psycho-Analysis* from Jones. On October 28, 1939, he wrote to Klein in Cambridge, pleading with her to submit a paper: "The number of papers from the British Society is very small, and the general level of the other (non-British) papers is very high. So it is really a patriotic duty to send me something."[1] Accordingly, she sent him off a paper on the Don Juan syndrome. It says much for both of them that Strachey, as soon as he had read it at the beginning of November, firmly rejected it as not up to her usual standard, and that Klein accepted his judgment without taking offense. She admitted to Jones that "Anything I could write seemed so utterly unimportant in comparison with world happenings."[2] On November 15, Strachey wrote that he was relieved that she bore him no ill will, and explained that he felt the paper lacked coherence.

With Eric expecting to be called up presently, Klein had been busily looking into the Cambridge area for a safe haven for Judy and Michael. It was the act of a concerned but interfering mother-in-law, for Judy loathed the place she found at Trumpington, missed Eric, and returned to their home in London as quickly as possible.

Emilie became seriously ill and died in London in May 1940, when Klein was in Cambridge—adding one more milestone to her long pattern of bereavements threaded with guilt. Klein was not with Emilie when she died; however, in her Autobiography she says that she saw her sister die "full of anxieties and persecution."*

Klein had heard of other people dying in a state of great anxiety, an experience she quite clearly dreaded. Hence, she possibly fantasized the serenity of her mother's death. At the end of August 1939, Arthur Klein had died in Sion, Switzerland. Jolan traveled from Budapest to the funeral, and was in constant touch with her sister-in-law by telephone and letter about the death, which seemed to distress Klein, according to Jolan's daughter, Maria.† Maria was supposed to come to England the following month to spend a year with her aunt, but when war broke out Klein told Jolan: "London was bombed during the last war, and if you were to read in the papers that there was bombing again, you would worry yourself to death. We had better wait for the end of hostilities." However, after the war Maria emigrated to Australia, and Jolan, whose hat factory was expropriated by the Communists in 1948, eventually left Hungary to live in Sweden with her son, Thomas Vágó. She experienced many years of financial hardship, and Klein paid for her periodic visits to England and helped her in many other ways.

The very ambivalence of Klein's feelings toward Emilie and Arthur enabled her to gain further insight into the process of mourning. She now began to understand the feeling of triumph in one stage of grief that had puzzled Freud in *Mourning and Melancholia*. She spent the winter of 1939 revising her Paris paper, which was in effect a working through of her own feelings.

The paper is so well written that some people have assumed that Joan Riviere was responsible for the final version. Klein relied greatly on Riviere's judgment, but although she sent her drafts of the revisions, Riviere's contribution was confined to editorial suggestions. In the margin she put red pencil marks whenever she had a query.

On April 2, 1940, Riviere wrote:

> I think it is immensely improved by the additions and rewriting. Especially your bringing in the matter of "triumph," which always represented a sort of gap or broken thread in the theory as left us by Freud and Abraham; and also which was clinically so evident in the material of these situations and so characteristic of these types, and which yet seemed to be ignored

---

* Hertha Pick, Emilie's daughter-in-law, contradicts this statement. She says that Emilie contracted pneumonia in September 1939. When X-rays were taken she insisted that the doctor swear that she did not have tuberculosis, which had been the dread of all her family after Emanuel's death. The doctor informed her husband that she had lung cancer. Mrs. Pick does not remember Emilie as being querulous; but she had such great difficulty in breathing that for a time she was put on oxygen. Mrs. Pick does not believe that Klein ever visited her sister during her illness; Melanie would have avoided such a visit, given her own fear of tuberculosis.

† There was some concern about whether Arthur had left her a residue of his estate, as he had implied he would some years earlier (letter to Winnicott, April 1, 1941).

and overlooked in your work on the subject. . . . I feel this paper should really go far to make your new theory about depression become better known and understood.[3]

Again, on April 8, she sent off some further reflections on mourning as a *good* experience:

Naturally, "normal" people take it for granted, both intuitively, and understand it scientifically, that a person *should* be able to feel grief. But we know this was very much disputed before by Melitta and Glover, and there are a lot of people who, consciously or not, have a tendency to agree with their attitude about this. Moreover, they also tend to feel, as M obviously does, that your views represent a wish to force depression on everybody and are quite persecutory in their feelings about it.[4]

The paper is based on both Freud's and Abraham's observations on mourning and melancholia, but departs significantly from Freud and advances further than Abraham. Recalling her earlier postulations about the depressive position, Klein reiterates that it involves two stages: feelings of persecution that the ego is going to be destroyed by internal persecutors, and a "pining" for the lost love-object.

The loss of a loved one in later life reactivates this infantile psychodrama; and the more securely the good internal objects have been incorporated in early life, the more effective the eventual outcome of later mourning will be. When one is in mourning one is actually "ill"—in a "modified and transitory manic-depressive state"—just as the normal child experiences a stage of infantile neurosis in his development.

Freud could not understand the phenomenon of "a phase of triumph" in the course of mourning. "In the first place, normal mourning, too, overcomes the loss of the object, and it, too, while it lasts, absorbs all the energies of the ego. Why, then, after it has run its course, is there no hint in its case of the economic condition for a phase of triumph? I find it impossible to answer this objection straight away."[5] For Klein it is a temporary manic phase, an expression of ambivalent feelings towards the dead person, when the mourner feels that he has triumphed over a persecutor by being still alive himself; and this phase intensifies his sufferings by arousing guilt for such feelings towards the dead person. As illustration, she relates the course of mourning of Mrs. A (quite obviously herself).

In the days immediately following her son's death Mrs. A sorted through letters, retaining some and throwing others out (in other words, keeping him safe inside her while discarding bad feelings). During the first week Mrs. A seldom cried. Some relief was found by seeing one or two intimate friends. During this week she stopped dreaming, but at the end of the week she had the following dream:

> She saw two people, a mother and a son. The mother was wearing a black dress. The dreamer knew that this boy had died, or was going to die. No sorrow entered into her feelings, but there was a trace of hostility towards the two people.[6]

The associations recalled memories of her childhood. Emanuel needed extra coaching, and the mother of one of his schoolfellows came to make arrangements with Libussa about it. The woman's patronizing manner and her mother's air of dejection made the dreamer feel as though a terrible humiliation had descended on the family. The ideal of her brilliant older brother was shattered, and her feelings were complex: she shared her brother's chagrin, yet felt guilty because she had been jealous both of her brother's greater knowledge and of his penis, and also of her mother for possessing such a son. Her first reaction was: "My mother's son died, and not my own"; but this manic unreality was succeeded by compassion. "One death of the kind was enough. My mother lost her son; she should not lose her grandson also."[7] Since none of this material, nor any discussion of Hans's death, appears in her Autobiography, one suspects that she was evading the guilt following the deaths of Sidonie, Emanuel, and her parents—an overwhelming burden reactivated by the death son and the defection of her daughter, and now by Emilie's and Arthur's deaths.

Other dreams gradually indicated a process by which she was regaining satisfaction in being alive. In the second week of her mourning she found some comfort in looking at pleasantly situated houses in the country, and in wanting such a house for herself. At last she was able to find relief in tears, although these alternated with bouts of despair. The houses provided her with the solace of rebuilding her inner world, whereas in other moods she viewed the death of her son as retaliation from those who had already died. Kind friends helped to reinforce her inner and outer worlds. Only a few weeks after Hans's death she had gone for a walk through familiar streets, hoping for reassurance, but then the houses threatened to topple and submerge her, and even the sunshine seemed ominous. In a state of total confusion she retreated into a quiet restaurant, where the people looked blurred and she feared that the ceiling was coming down. This intense suffering was part of the necessary process of grief. Gradually her mourning began to stimulate sublimation, the conviction that the lost object was preserved within herself, and that she had gained enrichment and greater wisdom through her suffering.

As far as the paper was directly connected with Klein's own grief, the letters through which she sorted were clearly those received from Hans. It is curious that few of his letters and none of his case notes have survived, although she described him to Winnicott as the child who showed most concern about her.

Abraham, basing his work on Freud, believed that in working through mourning, the individual succeeds in establishing the lost loved person in his ego. For Freud it was the actual parents (and here Klein reminds us that the processes of introjection in mourning and melancholia led Freud to recognize the existence of the superego in normal development). For Klein it is a far more richly populated inner world, "a complex world-object, which is felt by the individual, in deep layers of the unconscious, to be concretely inside himself, and for which I and some of my colleagues therefore use the term 'internalized objects' and an 'inner world.' "[8] In normal mourning the individual reintrojects the actual person for whom he is grieving as well as the imagos from his earliest part-object-world.

Winnicott paid her a visit in the middle of October 1939 and on the twenty-fifth she wrote to him: "We should be very pleased to see you soon again in Cambridge. I cannot yet promise you that I shall play the piano for you as I need some time to regain the technique I possessed in the past—but I shall do my best for some future visits. In the meantime we would just have a pleasant talk—I find one does want to see more of one's real friends in these beastly times."[9] Since the cessation of Eric's analysis a few months before, they had begun to address each other by their first names. Winnicott sent her a pamphlet he was preparing on the effect on parents when their children are evacuated. In the notes she returned to him on January 19, 1940, she advised him not "to give them too much of the unconscious motives unless you can so describe them that they are not confused with conscious motives . . . I think, as you have put it, that it would not be easy for non-analysts to appreciate the ambivalence in the parent-child relationship . . . you could quite easily bring the various aspects of this relation together, and connect it with the ordinary wishes of the parents to keep their children with them. The separation is a threat to their personal security, and this is perhaps more true in poorer families because it is less easy for them to find other forms of security. . . . The parent has also real grounds for being anxious as to whether his child will accept the standards of his own home when he comes back, and this is worth mentioning together with the more obscure anxieties."[10] These comments indicate that she was very much aware of the environmental factors involved in separation anxiety.

On November 29, 1939, she had written to Glover that she was prepared to take on a clinic case in Cambridge. For the first six months of 1940 John Rickman (who had been in analysis with her since 1934) was assigned by the Emergency Medical Service to a hospital at Bishop's Stortford. The town was filled with refugees (many of whom Rickman accommodated), including some of Klein's relatives. Every two or three days Rickman would travel to Cambridge for an hour or an hour and a half's analysis with Klein. Paula Heimann came up from London most weekends for intensive analysis. By midsummer Rickman was moved to Sheffield and later, in the autumn of 1942, he joined Wilfred Bion at Northfield, a psychiatric hospital near Birmingham.

During the Battle of Britain, "Dick's" parents became increasingly worried about the boy's safety and decided to move him to Pitlochry, a beautiful mountain town in the heart of Scotland; and in July, Klein was persuaded to join them. On July 2 she wrote to Winnicott:

> My dear Donald,
> Scotland surpasses my expectations—that is saying a lot since from a very early time in my life I fancied it as beautiful and romantic.
> I found very good accommodation with nice people in a simple but pleasant house in the most lovely position. I am quite comfortable and do enjoy the rest and the beautiful country in spite of the knowledge—or all the more because of it—that this peaceful time will not last. I am giving myself a rest & holiday for the time being—I have only 2 patients as you know—and the days pass quickly in an easy & pleasant way. I am just reading Churchill's "Great Contemporaries" and enjoy & admire this book very much. What a wise & understanding man he is—besides all his other great qualities as a writer. It really reassures me to see what a statesman he is—now that he is in charge of our so terribly difficult position.[11]

While she loved the surrounding hills, even in the rain, she had mixed feelings about moving so far from London. By July 30 she was telling Winnicott, "I very much want to come back to London in the autumn and shall do so if it is *at all* possible. Though I am thankful for the peaceful surroundings in which I live now, I feel increasingly drawn to be there where my friends are and where I feel my work should be done."[12] She thought vaguely that she might stay until the spring or summer of 1941, depending on the situation of the war. On August 10, 1940, during the Battle of Britain, she wrote to Clifford Scott:

> You seem to assume that I shall stay here indefinitely. Actually I should very much like to return to London and plan to stay here until the situation becomes clearer. We are told that in the next two months we may expect attempts for invasion or wholesale bombing, etc. . . . I am quite well but should be glad to get to know people—especially interesting ones!—in case I stay on. I don't miss company so far, but may do so as time goes on.[13]

On August 15, Klein again wrote to Scott:

> I am not intending an indefinite stay in Scotland but it depends on the development of the situation in the next few weeks or months whether I shall stay here for the winter or return to London.[14]

In this isolated place she had even more time to brood about the fate of the work she had so painstakingly sought to establish in England. She wrote to Ernest Jones of her gratitude for the way he had supported her against Freud in 1927, but it was clear that she felt he had committed a perfidious act in bringing the Freuds to England. "I want to say again," she told him,

> how deeply moved and encouraged I was by the admirable way in which you stood up to Freud on behalf of my work—not on this occasion only but all along. There are other ways in which you helped my work and many occasions in which I felt myself to be in complete agreement with you about matters which both of us had at heart, many occasions too on which you gave evidence of your personal friendship for me.[15]

However, Jones was touched to the quick by her charge that he had done "much harm to psycho-analysis" by providing the Freuds with a refuge. He asserted that he had done nothing for which to reproach himself, and he appealed to her sense of fair play. Freud had always remained his "best personal friend as well as a great man to whom we all owe so much."[16] The urgency of events was such that he had no time to consult any of his colleagues before going to Vienna in March 1938 to organize the flight of the Freud family.

> The first possibility was Holland; but even if Anna herself had been allowed to enter she would not have been allowed to work there, so that the future would have been extremely gloomy. According to the Princess, who also came to Vienna at the time, the situation was even worse in France and there was no other country open at that time of intense xenophobia and anti-Semitism. It was then that I suggested the possibility of going to England, which was eagerly accepted.

Jones left unsaid that the United States was ruled out because Freud loathed America, and as a nonmedical person Anna would have had no professional standing there. He had not in any way encouraged Federn or Waelder, whose presence he knew would not be welcomed in England. He reminded Klein that he had discussed the Viennese applications personally with every member of the Council,* as well as with herself and Joan Riviere.

---

* The policy-making body of the Society.

"The result," he concluded, "has worked out much as I expected, though not altogether what I had wished. Freud, apart from his pain, spent one of the happiest years of his life in London, with all his family and servants gathered round him, including even brother, nephew and grandchildren; all his own children except one were there. The Viennese members behaved pretty well on the whole." Most of them had already left for America, except for the Hoffers, "whom I regard as decent people." As for Anna, "She is certainly a tough, and perhaps indigestible morsel. She has probably gone as far in analysis as she can and she has no pioneering originality. Much worse than that, however, can be said of a good many of our members, and she undoubtedly has many valuable qualities."

Klein was somewhat appeased by his letter: "I also am very glad to think that Freud had a happy year in England in spite of the difficulties to which Anna's presence here gives rise."[17] She also felt impelled to add: "Some of those Viennese who since went to the U.S.A. have very soon volunteered the information to me and others that they had every possibility to go to America and would have done so had you not invited and encouraged them to come to England." Jones glossed over the number of Viennese analysts left in England; but Klein was not willing to let the matter rest. She assured him that she understood the predicament he had been in and would not have raised the matter if she had not been concerned about the fate of psychoanalysis as a result of his decision. Quite clearly she saw the fate of psychoanalysis—and its progressive future—as resting in her hands alone.

Klein had reason to be worried. On April 24, 1940, she had traveled from Cambridge to London for a meeting of the Training Committee, and for the first time was faced with the combined opposition of Glover and the Viennese. Sylvia Payne, who was taking the minutes, was unable to describe the vehemence of the discussion, and on Klein's return to Cambridge she reconstructed the argument in which Anna Freud had asserted that Klein's work was not psychoanalysis but a substitution for it and Glover had contended that controversial matter should be avoided in the teaching of candidates, with particular reference to Klein's work. It was extremely offensive, and the anger spilled out of her in the memo she sent from Susan Isaacs's house in Fen Causeway to all the members of the Training Committee:

> Miss Freud said (speaking about her work and Mrs. Klein's) that her work and that of her collaborators is Freudian analysis, and that Mrs. Klein's work is not psycho-analysis but a substitution for it. The reason she gave for this opinion was that Mrs. Klein's work differs so greatly in theoretical conclusions and in practice from what they know to be psychoanalysis. . . .

Referring to Miss Freud's statement about Mrs. Klein's contributions,

[Dr. Glover] said (refraining from expressing his own opinion) that her work may either turn out to be a development of psycho-analysis or a deviation from it—that it might prove to be the cauliflower growing out of the stalk (or was it stump?) on the side of it. Regarding the body of knowledge which should be taught to candidates, he said that controversial contributions should be excluded, referring to Mrs. Klein's work (but not making clear whether he meant the whole of it or part of it). . . .

Miss Freud referred again to the great differences which have arisen; for instance, the great stress laid in Mrs. Klein's work on the oral impulses influences the whole conception of the actual development [of] the Oedipus complex, furthermore the instincts being personified (or was it animated?). The importance of regression was also diminished. Mrs. Klein agreed about the importance of the differences, but not altogether about the way Miss Freud has defined these differences.

In reference to the advisability of including her work in the body of knowledge to be taught, Mrs. Klein said that she wished to point out that among the English members of the Training Committee it was actually only Dr. Glover who doubted the advisability of this.[18]

James Strachey was unable to attend the meeting because of a feverish cold, but the previous day sent Glover his thoughts about the impending battle between Melanie Klein and Anna Freud:

I'm very strongly in favour of compromise at all costs. The trouble seems to me to be with extremism, on *both* sides. My own view is that Mrs. K. has made some highly important contributions to $\psi\alpha$, but that it's absurd to make out (a) that they cover the whole subject or (b) that their validity is axiomatic. On the other hand I think it's equally ludicrous for Miss F. to maintain that $\psi\alpha$ is a Game Reserve belonging to the F. family and that Mrs. K's ideas are fatally subversive.

These attitudes on both sides are of course purely religious and the very antithesis of science. They are also (on both sides) infused by, I believe, a desire to dominate the situation & in particular the future—which is why both sides lay so much stress on the training of candidates. Actually of course, it's a megalomaniac mirage to suppose that you can control the opinions of people you analyse beyond a very limited point. But in any case it ought naturally to be the aim of a training analysis to put the trainee into a position to arrive at his own decisions upon moot points—not to stuff him with your own private dogmas.

In fact I feel like Mercutio about it. Why should these wretched fascists and communists invade our peaceful compromising island?—(bloody foreigners)[19]

Strachey concluded with the wry remark that he was more feverish than he had thought; but any suggestion of a split should be resisted to the utmost.

The members present at the next meeting on October 30, 1940 (by which time Klein had moved to Pitlochry), included the chairman, Glover, and Payne, Brierley, Ella Sharpe, Anna Freud, and Edward Bibring, an émigré from Vienna. (The absent members, in addition to Klein, were Rickman an Strachey.) Brierley presented two lists of readings drawn up by herself and Bibring for the candidates, and Klein was incensed when she discovered her paper on mourning was not included in Brierley's list. She was even more angered by Bibring's suggestions. In a letter to Brierley, she fumed: "I object to the part he assigns to the bulk of the work done in England (not to the *word* English School) but to his treating it as a minor sideline. . . . This would not have been surprising had he suggested this for the Vienna Group, but considering that he recently joined the British Group,"[20] it was arrogant, to say the least. Brierley indicated little sympathy with her complaints. Those remaining in London were going to run the British Society according to their own theoretical views.

In Scotland Klein missed little Michael, who was now almost three years old. She constantly worried about the safety of her family and wished that they would move further from London. In October Eric received his first call-up papers; and on the fifteenth the Clifton Hill house was hit by a bomb which left a gaping hole in the roof and most of the windows broken. Nevertheless, she longed to spend Christmas in London, where she could resume the interrupted analyses of her regular patients. She expressed her eagerness in a letter of December 5, 1940, to Winnicott: "I shall see most of my patients I left behind and doing whatever work I can with them,—I am very sorry about their having their analyses interrupted. But seeing Michael & my children again —bombs or no bombs in London!—is a prospect at which my heart beats faster!"[21] She was there from the sixteenth until the twenty-first. Winnicott arranged for her to have a consulting room immediately above his at 44 Queen Anne Street (as he also did on her subsequent visits) and filled the room with flowers. Here she analyzed Heimann and Rickman, who was on leave over Christmas.

On her return to Pitlochry she reported to Clifford Scott that "On the last night the sky was red with fires in the City—a gruesome and impressive sight."[22] On the nineteenth of January, 1941, she told Winnicott, "We are nearly snowed in here. Everything is covered with snow and the country is lovely to look at. I wish I could do some winter sports which implies the wish to be 30 years younger. (But I am not so sure whether I'd really like that. It has given me enough trouble to get where I am—meaning to get as old as I am.)"[23]

Apart from her anxiety to be far removed from the bombing, part of her reluctance to leave Pitlochry was based on financial considerations. On November 9, 1940, Sylvia Payne described the very discouraging economic situation in London.

> There is no work in London except a little badly paid training, and an occasional old patient. I am very anxious to carry on and the Clinic is doing a little work, enough to make it worth while continuing. If it does this it is obviously desirable that some British Directors shall be in London as long as it is open.[24]

During the winter Klein considered the possibility of moving to Oxford. She admitted candidly to Payne that part of the uncertainty about the date of her departure was due to the fact that "the fees are very welcome and make things less difficult."[25] At the beginning of December 1940 a general practitioner, Dr. Jack Fieldman (referred by Payne), had moved to Scotland to go into analysis with her. In the New Year her financial situation had improved slightly because in addition to Dr. Fieldman, she had "Dick," "Dick's" brother, and Dr. Matthew as patients. As she saw the situation, she had no alternative but to wait out the duration of the war. In a sense Pitlochry was a haven of rest and recuperation in the way that Abbazia had once been.

Nevertheless, she was fretful that she was losing touch with what was going on in the Training Committee. She continued to keep a close eye on the work of her colleagues, and she exhorted Scott to revise the paper he had given at the 1938 Congress in Paris.* "Of course we have to be very careful with every publication," she advised him, "revising it from the various angles from which it could be misunderstood or misinterpreted, but contributions are urgently needed and it seems a pity not to publish them when they are at hand."[26]

During the early spring she poured her anxieties into long letters to Winnicott. On March 24 she told him that she was "quite thrilled" that he was planning to present a paper to "our poor decrepit society." It brought to mind "happier times, when we left our meetings with a feeling of satisfaction that work and insight were growing and that we had our share in this; that there was hope that a science which might mean so much for mankind was on its way to future achievements." However, all that had been changed six years previously when Glover and Melitta initiated "the New Order." She then launched into a nine-page diatribe about her grievances over the past and her hopes for the future.

> I shall never forgive Jones for having been so weak, so undecided and actually treacherous to a cause he himself values so highly and the possibilities of which he never underrated. Others,—afraid of conflict found it

---

* Eventually published as "On the Intense Affects Encountered in Treating a Severe Manic-Depressive Disorder," *J.* (1947) 38: 139–45.

more convenient to withdraw,—others sit on the fence and feel that to keep the society together at all costs or rather to pretend to the outside world that *this* is *Ps.An.* (in contrast to such inferior beings as Tavistock etc!—) that to do this is more important than to preserve and protect the essence of our work and make it grow.

Does it sound funny that I compare this great struggle we are in for the preservation of freedom in the *world* with such a small thing as the goings on in our Society? Still, the enthusiasm I feel in this great cause, the boundless admiration for the British (and my pride to be one of them) for what they are rescuing from disaster and my feelings about what might be lost when this work goes under—have much in common—both have to do with great irreplaceable values which one wants to protect. It is true—this work may go under and might be rediscovered again;—that has happened before but its very nature, the fact that even each of us, of those who have got most hold of it have to keep great vigil not to let it slip,—& at *this* point or *that*—because it makes such very great demands and there is a constant temptation to cover it up or to turn away from the points where it strikes terror or causes pain,—all this makes one afraid that *if* lost, it might not easily be rediscovered in the entity to which it has progressed in recent years.

In 1927 Jones after his correspondence with Freud about my work told me, It will take you a long time to carry your work to people (obviously he meant analysts)—it might take you 15 years! When I once mentioned this to Glover (at this time he was still trying to assimilate it and in any case still *expressing* belief in and appreciation for it)—he said: "I wonder whether you ever will.—it goes too much to the roots."—However all this is in some ways beside the point! For in spite of my fear that it all might go under—there is very strong determination and hope in me that it *won't*.— This time in Pitlochry has not been lost. Solitude & greater leisure have done quite a lot for me—I have been *taking in* in various ways (how I enjoy now reading history!) and I have been *thinking* a lot. I am sure I have progressed and done better work with myself. I shall be in a better position to write those books which it is my duty—and perhaps privilege too—to write—the book on technique and my collected papers with notes and an explanatory preface in which I shall have much to say.[27]

It was a disadvantage not to have a secretary, but she accepted this philosophically for the time being. She was torn about advising Winnicott to contest the papers that were being given in their absence—"after all people are bound to get bored with always hearing the same fruitless things and they may be all the more interested if they hear again a paper which has really something to give." On the whole, she favored shaking up people who were falling back into superficial and apathetic ways of looking at things, "obsessed with the fear that penetrating deeper in the unc. might leave them as it were in midair—far away from reality and real people."[28]

She advised Winnicott to be on the alert for promising people, adding, "One cannot of course do anything for people who *refuse* to accept as some of the Viennese,—but as I said we should be on the look-out for people who might be induced to learn something." Winnicott, Heimann, and Rosenfeld might consider organizing small group discussions.

> What is going to happen later on with our society—one can't foresee yet. I was thinking that we may very much extend for *certain* discussions the circle of our little meetings and thus have the kind of meetings in which real work could be done and interest revived and increased,—without formally withdrawing from the society. Still,—in the meantime to hear our voices at meetings and to let others hear them seems very desirable and I am delighted to think of you giving a paper.

Quite clearly she regarded Winnicott as a valuable friend and ally on whom she had to count in the future. Her need for friendship breaks through in another long letter of April 1, in which she discusses her anxieties about Eric and gives Winnicott a detailed account of the family constellations—lest he might have been influenced by what Eric could have said about her during his analysis. Future events were to prove that such allies were vitally important to her.

Richard

By April 1941, Klein no longer had time to write long letters. On May 30 she asked Winnicott if he minded if she kept a paper he had sent her for comment until she could put her whole mind to it. The last paragraph reveals that she had something more pressing to think about:

> I have started the analysis of a very unusual boy of ten a month ago & keep full notes including my interpretations from this case. It takes me 1½–2 hours a day to make these full notes,—a drag but well worth while. They should show much about the things we wish most people to understand, also about progress in technique through knowledge of depression. It really gives me pleasure to think what a good paper this should make.[1]

A letter of August 29 to Clifford Scott indicated her continuing interest in the case.

> We are only at the beginning of making people understand the importance and meaning of depression—I am afraid it will be a lengthy and difficult job! Still—it has to be done—I now analyse a boy of ten and keep full notes of this analysis (including interpretations). It is surprising and gratifying to see how much the knowledge of the depressive position has advanced technique and theoretical and practical understanding. The case is not typical though—still it should prove a lot for people who wish to see and learn. I am afraid however that most of our colleagues are extremely reluctant to accept these new things—this may retard progress but should not altogether hold it up.[2]

From the time she left Pitlochry in the late summer of 1941 until she delivered the paper* to the British Psycho-Analytical Society on March 7, 1945, her attention was concentrated almost exclusively on the political turmoil within the British Society—the Extraordinary Meetings of 1942, the Controversial Discussions of 1943–44, the investigation into the power of the Training Committee, and the thorny question of how the British Society could remain intact and yet accommodate the theories of both Melanie Klein and Anna Freud. But she constantly brooded about the projected length and format of the case history of the boy in Pitlochry and when she would have time to assemble it. As early as June 26, 1942, she wrote to Susan Isaacs:

> I am very keen to settle down to the book I have in mind round the case history. . . . It seems a great difficulty that it should be such a large book. There might be difficulty in getting it published. My own impression is that if I left it in its original form and only shortened it in the form of expression, I would not gain very much, because I don't think it could be shortened in that way by more than one-fifth or one-sixth at most. I am convinced more than ever that this is the most urgent thing to do.[3]

Edward Glover had been attacking her theories of the depressive position and manic defenses; and as a consequence, she saw that she would have to emphasize the connection between her theories and those of Freud. "I am sure," she continued in her letter to Isaacs,

> that in the comments on this case history I shall have to lay particular stress on the connection between the depressive position and the Oedipus situation, and possibly will have to make this the central point of these chapters. Of course the connection between castration complex and depressive position etc. would all have to come in. I can see fairly clearly what I want to do about it, and I have the impression that if only I could be left alone and having nothing more to do with those wasteful and horrible discussions, I could get on with it.

Consequently she describes the section on Richard as "Extracts from the Case History Illustrating the Boy's Oedipal Development." The child was brought to her initially because, with a neurotic fear of other children, he was in terror of venturing outdoors. Depressed and hypochondriacal, he was unable to attend school, although he was precocious and gifted. The details she gives about him are adequate but scanty; and she takes more pains to disguise his identity in this earlier version than she does in the later *Narrative of a Child*

* "The Oedipus Complex in the Light of Early Anxieties."

Analysis. In both versions the locale is Wales; in the first paper Richard's older brother was "a few years his senior" and had been sent away to school, whereas in actual fact—as the *Narrative* records accurately—he was eleven years older and had joined the army. Richard's mother, a highly anxious type, clearly preferred his older brother and found Richard's clinging to her tiresome. The father seems to have left most of the boy's upbringing to the mother.

Richard and his mother had been evacuated from their home and had settled temporarily in Pitlochry in April 1941 in order for the boy to be analyzed by Klein. In the early paper Klein does not relate that Richard's home had been hit by a bomb shortly after his departure. "As in every case," she writes,

> we have to take into consideration the internal processes resulting from, and interacting with, constitutional as well as environmental factors; but I am unable to deal here in detail with the interaction of all these factors. I shall restrict myself to showing the influence of certain early anxieties on genital development.[4]

In her account of the analysis Klein concentrates on the seventy-four drawings and the play maneuvers the boy executed with his toy fleet. The drawings were occupied with two themes. In the first of these a starfish (which he explained was a hungry baby) hovered near an underwater plant that it wanted to eat. Soon an octopus with a human face appeared, and this Klein interpreted to him as his father's genital. The four main colors used were black, blue, purple, and red—in Klein's view symbolizing his father, mother, brother, and himself respectively. The territory of his drawings was an empire in which modifications appeared representing the changing course of events in the war. He brought his own ships with him; and the bumping of the ships against each other she interpreted as his parents in sexual intercourse.

Her conclusions in the first paper were based on six selected analytic hours during a resumption of his analysis after a break of ten days, following six initial weeks of analysis. During this period Klein had been in London; and during her absence Richard was extremely worried about the danger to which she was subjected during the air raids.

In the drawings in which he depicted the ships, the octopus, and the starfish, his mother was represented by a patch of blue,* and often in unison with himself as fighting off the dangerous father and brother. In lining up his fleet, the smallest ship was put first, indicating that he had annexed his father's and brother's genitals. By reversing the role of father and son, Richard was made to see his rivalry with his father, but gradually he expressed a desire for reparation

---

* Blue representing the cloudless blue sky he loved. See *Love, Guilt and Reparation*, p. 394.

to him by placing the father between the underwater plants, thus allowing him the position of gratified child. It seemed to Klein that he was recognizing his own potential for increased potency; and he avoided guilt by phantasizing the two male rivals into babies, a situation that would bring relative peace to the family.

Richard also suffered from a paranoid fear of being poisoned and a suspicion that various people were spying on him. Gradually Klein made him see he was imbibing good things, symbolizing the internalization of his good, not his persecuting, mother. With the development of increasing inner peace, the external world began to appear beautiful to him, and there are touching descriptions of his standing at the door delighting in nature.

In drawings of birdlike creatures he depicted a devouring monster with a red and purple beak; gradually the areas of blue enlarged as Richard began to accept that these were prototypes of both the bad, hated breast and the good, proffering breast. Whenever his fear of his internal persecutors was revived, his anxiety was not only for his own safety, but also for his internalized parents. With his growing acceptance that his loved object was also his hated object, the establishment of his feeling for his mother was more firmly secured. He had wanted to destroy the unborn babies within her, but now he began unconsciously to recognize that reproduction was the most important means of combating death.

The significant theoretical conclusion Klein drew from the case (at this point) was her realization that she was wrong in her earlier assumption that the Oedipus complex is associated only with the impulse of hate; she now saw that it is coincident with the onset of the depressive position. Not guilt, but the child's growing awareness and love of his parents bring about the dissolution of the power of the Oedipus complex. Through her observation of Richard's struggles to integrate love and hate, she gained the courage to defy Freud's interpretation of the resolution of the Oedipus complex as emerging from a realistic acceptance of the libidinal structure of the family. In her final remarks she wrote:

> The infant's emotional life, the early defences built up under the stress of the conflict between love, hatred and guilt, and the vicissitudes of the child's identifications—all these are topics which may well occupy analytical research for a long time to come. Further work in these directions should lead us to a fuller understanding of the Oedipus complex and of sexual development as a whole.[5]

Since one of the main objections of her critics was that her conclusions were drawn from inference, she longed to give a full case history, replete with actual detailed material. Klein had not intended to write one on a child as old

as Richard, but the extra time she had in Pitlochry enabled her to compile co-
pious notes after every session. Moreover, in subsequent years she was able to
reappraise the material in light of her new insights into splitting, projective
identification, and breast envy.

In 1956, with the aid of Elliott Jaques,* she began to assemble the masses
of notes into a coherent whole, the longest case history ever recorded. According to Jaques, when he started working with her the manuscript was substantially finished and his contributions lay in elaborating the footnotes in view of
her later theories. They worked on the manuscript from 1956 to 1959; and she
was correcting the proofs while in the hospital just before her death in 1960.
The footnotes indicate her enlarged understanding of the material; but since
the analysis took place in 1941, it is not inappropriate to insert commentary on
it at this juncture.

Narrative of a Child Analysis is an extraordinary book—the account of a
friendship between an elderly Austrian Jewess and a precocious, terrified ten-
year-old Scottish boy, between whom a feeling of a rare and tender sort developed. Melanie Klein always made much of the importance of the negative
transference, and while it is true that she made Richard see, through his projec-
tions onto her, that his attitude to his mother was yearning and ambivalent,
there is little doubt that the relationship was established so securely because
she represented his beloved grandmother who had recently died.

While in Pitlochry, Klein saw her adult patients in the house where she
boarded, but Richard's sessions were held in a hall mainly used by the Girl
Guides. Richard and his mother stayed in a hotel, and on weekends were
usually joined by Richard's father, a professional man who continued to work
in their hometown. At the same time Richard was seeing Mrs. Klein, another
boy "five years Richard's senior"† was also in analysis with her, and Richard
was intensely jealous of him as he was of any other men in her life—the
grumpy old lodger, shopkeepers, men encountered in the street, her son, and
her grandson back in London, whom she obviously longed to see.

The content of Richard's paranoia and unsociability was revealed through
his drawings, his deployment of the toy ships he brought along occasionally,
his conversation, and the alternation of his moods between manic and depressive. The analysis took place against the backdrop of a particularly tense
period of the war—the continuous bombing of London; the fall of Athens to
the Germans on April 27; the bizarre appearance of Hess near Glasgow on
May 10; the invasion of Crete on May 20; the sinking of the *Bismarck* on May
27; and the invasion of Russia on June 22. While Pitlochry seemed a haven of

---

* Jaques was in analysis with her from 1946 until 1954.
† This was Dick, who figures in "The Importance of Symbol-Formation in the Development of the Ego"
(1930). He was Richard's cousin and was actually six years older than Richard.

idyllic peace, Richard was vitally interested in all these disturbing events; and Klein related them to his inner turmoil.* In addition, in the middle of July he opened the bathroom door to find his father slumped on the floor with a heart attack. For a little boy who had severe problems to begin with, these external events could only have exacerbated his anxiety.

Klein emphasizes that when Richard entered the analysis, it was made clear to him and his parents that the analysis had to be limited to a short time. Her pocket diary records that the analysis started on April 28 and ended on August 23, 1941, and covered ninety-six sessions (not ninety-three, as listed in *Narrative of a Child Analysis*). The book is divided into daily sessions, and the analysis was interrupted for eight or ten days: when Klein went to London, when Richard had an occasional cold, and when he returned home for weekends after his father's heart attack.

As early as 1934, Richard's mother had written to Dr. David Matthew that despite the fact that the child was very friendly and loved meeting people, he became genuinely terrified of even a scratch, a phobia she attributed to the effects of a circumcision he had experienced that year. His favorite game was Pretence, in which he assumed different personalities for hours on end. With the passing of the years his condition worsened, and on the advice of Matthew, Richard was sent to Klein. When Klein arrived in Pitlochry, she knew that she was not going to stay there indefinitely; and she did not know that the analysis would occupy exactly four months. Indeed, Richard's mother tried unsuccessfully to persuade her to give a specific estimate of the duration of the analysis. In "The Oedipus Complex in the Light of Early Anxieties" (1945), Klein says,

> I take as my starting point the resumption of the analysis after a break of ten days.† The analysis had by then lasted six weeks. During this break I was in London, and Richard went away on holiday. He had never been in an air-raid, and his fears of air-raids centred on London as the place most in danger. Hence to him my going to London meant going to death and destruction. This added to the anxiety which was stirred up in him by the interruption of the analysis.[6]

Richard may not have experienced an actual air raid, but since his house had been bombed after he left it, London could not have represented the only real source of danger. Secondly, there is no reference to the landing of Rudolph Hess, about which he undoubtedly would have heard. It could be argued that for the sake of confidentiality Klein altered the location of the analysis from Scotland to Wales, and if she mentioned Hess she might have revealed the ac-

---

* It is not mentioned in the *Narrative* that Richard's brother was called up on April 3.
† June 14–24, 1941.

tual area, yet Hess's strange arrival out of the sky would undoubtedly have increased the boy's fears.

By the middle of July, Klein decided that she must return to London in September to resume her normal life. In a letter to Clifford Scott dated September 13, she wrote:

> I am back in the South, and comfortably settled in Harpenden (Herts). I shall see one or two patients here, and travel five times a week to London. I have taken a room at Nottingham Place. It was not easy to arrive at this decision because I had to leave a few patients behind in Scotland. One of them whom you know also came to London and another will, I think, join me at Harpenden.* I had to interrupt a very interesting and promising analysis of a boy which I was sorry for, but felt that I [had to] continue my work in London which I had interrupted.[7]

Part of the sudden urgency of her decision seems to have been based on the fact that Eric was finally called up in the Signal Corps. She was also anxious to keep an eye on political events in the British Society.

For a month prior to her departure Richard was in a state of distress about the separation, fearing her death by bombs and his loneliness without her. As she describes those last sessions, it is definitely understood between them that the analysis is coming to an end. In the Introduction to the book, Klein writes: "I was aware of my positive counter-transference but, being on my guard, I was able to keep to the fundamental principle of analysing consistently the negative as well as the positive transference and the deep anxieties which I encountered." In other words, she does not commit herself to an experiential description or share her inner feelings with us, but the poignancy of the situation breaks through in the private notes she made on the last session.

23rd Aug. 1941

Last day. Let's get the most out of it. — K. sad? — K. very sorry etc. R. pleased. — Is she going to cry? [His eyes watering] — R. pleased. — Should not kiss him, parting. — Some days ago when so clinging, asked to be kissed. — To-day's mood — serious, some depression, but determined & resolved. Last night's film: Sailors three. — Capturing Ger. battleships with help of Austrian etc — (K. — R. uniting with K.= good mum & good dad — to beat bad dad [resolve & consolation from united good purpose and consolation & greater hope of keeping intern. good mum] — Puts electr. train — (K suggested a few days ago) into his case. — Tying up his laces tight (agrees int. keeping K. safely)*

---

* The principal patients were Paula Heimann and John Rickman.

Going through hut to look after flies — pleased that most exterminated.

Will he see hut again? — arranging at end 2 chairs under table [us. R. & K. kept together, — also two breasts] — On road — seeing K. winter after next, — feels confident about this. — quiet when parting — a few days later first pict-post card.

Drawings — [begun when discussing film]

1. the bay the sailors sailed in [remarks looks like hand] — then II his own hand — III K.'s hand drawing contours in II.

*depression to some extent worked off on preceding days.[8]

Richard repeatedly begged her to persuade his mother either to let him have a tutor or to send him to a very small school. This she promised to do. He also pleaded with her to let him accompany her to London. This, she says in parentheses, she believes his mother could have arranged. It would, in fact, have been a terrible decision, and one suspects Klein of rationalizing her own behavior. In a letter of November 10, 1941, in reply to a letter from Richard's mother explaining that she could not possibly endanger the child's life by sending him to London despite the fact that she knows he needs help, Klein writes: "That you cannot for the time being make it possible for him to continue his analysis, I am fully aware. I could not myself take the responsibility of advising you to send him South at present. By the way, as my arrangements are at the moment I would find it extremely difficult to arrange an hour for him."[9] Her commentary on the case study tends to be as critical of Richard's mother as she had been of Dick's.*

More discussion has been devoted to the *Narrative* than to any other of her cases. In J. O. Wisdom's opinion, it "constitutes a milestone in the history of psycho-analysis"; and he contends that even if some of her views do not survive, "no other contribution to psycho-analysis of comparable stature with Mrs. Klein's has been made since Freud."[10]

Such courageous self-exposure naturally left her open to criticism. She even admits strategic mistakes, such as her note to the 65th session where she regrets having "given a very direct reassurance which I on the whole deprecate. What caused me to do this was that the child not only unconsciously feared the end of his analysis but consciously realized his urgent need for it" (p. 325). John Padel, an independent member of the British Society, objected that "mother is never allowed to seem anything but *best*, unless contaminated by father, Richard, or his elder brother." In the last session Daddy is presented as somebody

---

* Incidentally, she also left "Dick" behind in Pitlochry when she returned to London. His condition deteriorated until the analysis was resumed in London in 1943.

nearly as good as Mummy. "Nearly!!!" Padel exclaims. "This is a system which, used unmodified, could imprison both patient and analyst in a matriarch world."[11]

Donald Meltzer has written of the *Narrative* in "Richard Week-by-Week," in Part II of *The Kleinian Development*. Meltzer's work is a remarkable accomplishment in that he uses this particular case as a means of integrating Klein's theories into a coherent psychology. He expresses, in his critique of the case, a certain unease at the rapidity and unequivocal nature of her interpretations. He attributes this to the fact that she was working against time, as she frequently laments in the course of the *Narrative*. Meltzer has an uncanny sense of the ambience of the analysis—the small town set in the mountains, an alien place Richard refers to as a "pig-sty," despite the fact that it is famed for its beauty. He empathizes with Richard's curiosity about how Mrs. Klein spends her time when she is not with him: is she up to unspeakable things or is she lonely? And how can he be sure that Mr. Klein, who fought for the enemy in the last war, is really dead inside her? He is intrigued by her red jacket, which he regards as exotic and continental; but the element of the "enemy" in her (after all, she was Austrian) also increases his anxiety.* Meltzer captures the atmosphere of the hall with its electric fire (which Richard feels compelled to keep alight during Mrs. Klein's absences) and the posters on the wall, distractions that she would have considered totally unsuitable under normal circumstances.

As we read Meltzer we experience with him the boy's initial suspicion, his attempts to ingratiate himself with her, her brilliant insights and occasional fumbles. Meltzer, for example, is puzzled as to why she felt it necessary to inform Richard that he had been weaned very early.

A thoroughly Freudian critique of the *Narrative* was published by Elisabeth R. Geleerd in the *International Journal of Psycho-Analysis* in 1963. It is an extremely fair account of the development of Klein's ideas from "The Psychological Principles of Infant Analysis" in 1926. In discussing Melanie Klein's conviction that anxiety *must* be activated, Geleerd poses a legitimate question: "But how, when anxiety reappears, does Mrs. Klein know whether it is due to the progress of the analysis, or to the anxiety which the direct symbolic interpretation had aroused in the child?"[12]

In a "classical" analysis, the positive transference would have led to interpretations of Richard's positive Oedipus fantasy; and the biting patterns would in turn be linked to an oral fixation responsible for the oral elements in the phantasies of his phallic stage. "Klein's random way of interpreting does not reflect the material but, rather, her preconceived theoretical assumptions regarding childhood development."[13]

---

* The ambivalence of his feelings towards her is reflected in the fact that Richard himself is represented as "red" in the analysis.

Melanie Klein is less concerned with the oedipal fantasy as such. In her theoretical conceptions these fantasies are subordinate to the struggle of the ego to overcome the depression; in the second phase the ego has to restore the love object which was destroyed by the superego in the paranoid phase. Hence she searches in the material for destructive fantasies as well as for indications of the process of reparation. At some points her interpretations and discussion coincide to some extent with those a non-Kleinian analyst would have made: for example, in the discussion of the boy's attempt to control his hostile impulses. But from that point we would again have pursued a different course.[14]

As Geleerd readily admits, "real communication" was established between Klein and Richard. In many ways he was an ideal patient, since he recognized that he needed help and was willing to cooperate. He brought day-to-day material as well as past traumas, such as his circumcision when he was seven (actually three), and confessions of sex play in bed with his dog, Bobbie. He also worked out in his transference his rivalry with the dead Mr. Klein and his suspicion of her as really an enemy since she was an Austrian. He feared a cosmic catastrophe such as a collision between the sun and the earth; and Geleerd points out that Richard's constant worry about helpless little countries like Sweden and "lonely" Rumania was always interpreted as a fear of how long a weak child could resist being overpowered by a stronger force. Klein directs into sexual anxiety his fear that his father would attack his mother and him in the way the Germans might attack England. (It might be pointed out that fear of invasion was a constant anxiety of Klein herself.)

Geleerd is suspicious that the daily events in the boy's life are not reported fully, particularly the illness of his father. The boy seemed to have improved, but unfortunately there was no follow-up study.

All workers in the field know, however, that one cannot expect too great and lasting results from four months of analysis.

But there is no doubt that the boy seemed to have gained a great deal. During these four months he had a chance to analyse partially his Oedipus Complex and his castration fear; he had brought up some homosexual fears and episodes; and had discussed ambivalent feelings; he had also brought up his fear of being poisoned. And Melanie Klein mentions that Richard learned to go out by himself on his bicycle and was willing to accept going to school.[15]

While it is difficult to doubt Richard's improvement, the account of the lessening of his general suspiciousness towards the world seems somewhat precipitous, as though there was an urgency to effect improvement.

One of the most incisive accounts of the *Narrative* was written in 1963 by Hanna Segal and Donald Meltzer in a review-article which followed that of Elisabeth Geleerd.[16] Having been analyzed by Klein, both Segal and Meltzer could speak with authority about her technique. They point out that the detail in the *Narrative* is so overwhelming that it tends to intimidate the novice. They emphasize that at the time of the actual analysis, Klein had not yet worked out her postwar theories about the paranoid-schizoid and the depressive positions, or the schizoid mechanisms. Here they agree that "Some attempt at a retrospective evaluation of the theories and technique in the light of her subsequent experience would have enriched the reading for analysts well acquainted with her more recent findings."[17] For instance, splitting of the parental figures protected the boy from the full impact of his oedipal wishes. Klein did not recognize the importance of the transference as she would have done later in her career. Segal and Meltzer are particularly illuminating in describing how she went about alleviating the child's anxiety—interpretation, mobilization of anxiety, increase of material, further interpretation, relief of anxiety. "Melanie Klein," they say, "always believed that insight was the chief therapeutic agent in analysis and the main line of defence against regression after termination."[18]

I myself met Richard through entirely fortuitous circumstances. From the few details I heard about a man who as a child had had an analysis with Melanie Klein, I hoped that he would prove to be Richard. However, when we met, and I said, "I assume you're Richard?" he replied, "No, I'm X." "Yes, but you're Richard too." He looked puzzled. "I don't know what you're talking about." At first I assumed I had made an awful mistake. Then I had a sudden inspiration: "Do you remember the bus conductress?"* "Do I indeed!" and he then imitated her voice: "Half-fares, stand up!" What was extraordinary was the fact that while he is a man in his fifties, well educated and in comfortable circumstances, he had no idea that he was the subject of a book or that he had been discussed in so many learned articles and lectures. Quite simply, his life does not touch the analytic world at any point. He travels widely, usually to remote places covered most of the year in snow, under which lie extinct volcanoes.

We subsequently had much discussion, and with his permission I reproduce some of his memories and observations that strike me as having significant bearing on the case. I asked him to give me his first recollections of Melanie Klein.

"I remember her as short, dumpy, with big floppy feet. I hope it's not out of context to tell you an anecdote about that subject. My aunt said to my

---

* One of Richard's *bêtes noires* in the *Narrative*.

mother that Melanie had bad feet. My mother, I hasten to add the least anti-Semitic of people, made the sardonic comment in reply, 'Well, if you had been walking in the wilderness for forty years, you would have bad feet too.' Melanie had a rather loose lower lip, I can remember that. It always seemed to hang a bit, and her mouth never seemed to be closed. She had a strong accent. She was always sympathetic."

I inquired why he had originally been sent to Melanie Klein.

"It was David Matthew who persuaded my mother that due to my excessive terror of other children, and I think because of a certain amount of aggressiveness, that I should see Mrs. Klein. I think I'm still a fairly aggressive kind of person."

"Why were you frightened of other children?"

"I don't know. I just was."

"Did you think they were going to hurt you?"

"They would hurt me, or hit me. That's what I feared. The odd thing is, they never did hurt or hit me."

"So you were both timid and aggressive?"

"Yes, a mixture of both. I was always frightened of being hit."

"What was your father like?"

"He was a very upright, honest man. The poor man, the trouble with him was that he was nearly totally deaf,* which was a fearful drawback. At that time hearing aids were extremely primitive. During most of my formative years you couldn't purchase batteries for these things. Consequently, he used the hearing aid that he kept in his office for his clients, and you had to put your mouth to one ear and talk to him that way. The other ear was completely deaf. He was rather cut off in that way. We weren't very alike. My mother and I were much more like each other. We had a much closer bond than I had with my father."

"Can you remember the first time you went to Mrs. Klein, and what it was like? Would you describe it for me?"

"Oh, it's difficult to remember too much. I do recall the Girl Guide hut. There were two rooms, and there must have been a table. We must have had toys. The only toys I can remember were the battleships. I mentioned to you this morning that I remember going on about the fact that we were going to bomb the Germans, and seize Berlin, and so on and so on and then Brest. Melanie seized on b-r-e-a-s-t, which of course was very much her angle. She would often talk about the 'big Mummy genital' and the 'big Daddy genital,' or the 'good Mummy genital' or the 'bad Daddy genital.' I can't remember what other things she had to say. It was very much a strong interest in genitalia."

* A fact not mentioned in the *Narrative*.

"Was that right from the beginning?"

"Yes, very much so."

"Tell me about the bus conductress."

"It wasn't one conductress in particular. There was a fixed rule that all half-fare children stood, and adults sat down. There were no cars in those years, and everybody had to take the bus."

"And you felt aggrieved about this?"

"Oh yes, terribly."

"Why?"

"I suppose I was a self-important little upstart. I don't know. I didn't see why I should be made to stand."

"Did you think it was something unjust, or something that was directed against you personally?"

"I think the latter, probably. I don't know. It is funny you reading through that book, I think that's terribly funny. I really hadn't thought about the bus conductress for thirty-five or forty years."

"What kind of little boy do you think you were at the age of ten?"

"Well, dispassionately, looking back on it, I think I was a pretty appalling sort of kid. I'd cuff his ear if I could get hold of him."

"Why?"

"I always had quite a temper. I think I'm still somewhat like this. I flew into a panic several days ago at the office about something very trivial. Tiny things do rattle me. That's my nature. I've always been very impatient."

Richard continued to suffer from depression and this had led him to visit Klein some years later.

"When did you see her?"

"I must have been sixteen, I think. I was in London for some reason. I rang her up and asked her if I could pay her a visit. She was a bit reluctant to see me, I do remember that. She was a little frosty."

"And what happened when you did see her? Was she frosty to you only on the telephone?"

"She wasn't prepared to make any effort to help me. On the other hand, how could she possibly have benefited me in such circumstances? It was a semi-social chat. She wasn't charging me or anything."

"But let me ask you this. Do you think consciously or unconsciously you thought that she might help you?"

"I think so. I had the feeling that she was brushing me off, in a very polite sort of way. She wasn't prepared to do anything for me. Perhaps that was my feeling about it, but it was the feeling I had at the time.* Looking back on the

---

* Klein says that she saw Richard several times in subsequent years, but in his recollection there was only the one occasion.

episode, I suppose she was getting to be an old and tired woman, and didn't wish to become involved."

Finally, he still has in his possession the maps prominent in the *Narrative*; and he showed me how he had effaced the border of Russia because the lines of advance and retreat changed frequently. He is still deeply interested in international affairs, and is greatly concerned about the prospect of a nuclear holocaust.

When we met on a subsequent occasion, I brought along a copy of *Narrative of a Child Analysis*, which he had never seen before. He gazed at the photograph of Melanie Klein on the back cover. "Dear old Melanie," he murmured. Then he suddenly put the photograph to his lips and kissed it affectionately.

A year later, Richard and I met again. In the meantime he had read the *Narrative*, which he found rather heavy going. In some ways the child he was then was almost unrecognizable, whereas certain aspects of the book triggered his memories. Fears were reawakened: an imbecile on a tricycle who made animal-like noises, and the occasion on which he heard of the invasion of Russia while in his parents' bedroom about a month before his father's heart attack. Reading through the book, he believes that the circumcision performed on him in his parents' bedroom had a profound effect upon him. He was terrified of ether, and felt deceived because his mother had failed to prepare him for this horrifying experience. He also clearly remembers finding his father lying on the bathroom floor, tea dribbling from his mouth. "I can see it now."

Weather affected him far more intensely as a child, and he has always had a "tremendous passion" for landscape. He found the scenery around Pitlochry particularly beautiful.

After Mrs. Klein's departure he was sent to a day school, and his mother watched anxiously as he stood by himself in the schoolyard. He was not really unhappy, he believes, but becoming the "sociable solitary," never lonely, which is how he describes himself. Incidentally, his passion for red has altered to a preference for blue and orange.

As for the boy who was analyzed by Melanie Klein: "The Adagietto from Mahler's Fifth Symphony more perfectly than any words I could use sums up the complete truth of my feelings at that time."

We have the perspective of the analysis from the book itself, from Richard's own recollections, and from various commentators. There is another participant who should not be ignored—Richard's mother. During the analysis she sent frequent notes to Klein. For example, on July 12, 1941, she reported: "I forgot to tell you that he said a little while since that you always spoke to him of genitals and he tried to get you off the subject. Today he announced, 'Mrs. Klein still speaks of genitals, but doesn't have them in her head so much now' or words to that effect. He is killing." For over a year after the end of the analysis she continued to write to Klein about Richard's condition, and her letters give an invaluable insight into Richard's reaction to the termination of the analysis and to the changes within his mother initiated by the analysis. Klein encouraged these letters to a degree, and on two occasions sent her questionnaires to fill out about Richard's progress. At first the mother was filled with gratitude for Richard's improvement, but soon a querulous note begins to intrude, she hints that Klein hadn't got to the root of his real problems* (e.g., the effects of the circumcision), and asserts defiantly that what the boy needs is a "disciplined life." By the beginning of October she complains that the prospect of his future fills her with dismay. On October 24 Klein replied:

> Your two letters, though coming so close together, present a very different picture of Richard. In the first you stress the importance of some of the changes, such as his greater capacity to understand mathematics, his bicycling, and so on—not only as useful things but as denoting some actual changes in his state of mind. This, I think, is very true, and I do believe that in spite of the difficulties which you emphasize in your second letter, something has been done to improve Richard's difficulties. That these have not by any means gone is not surprising, since as you know I stressed from the beginning that there was no prospect of this kind at all, and that I should be glad if I could to a certain extent help him.[19]

His mother continued to find him deceitful, lazy, disobedient, irritable, and at times violently aggressive, especially to animals. Moreover, his fear of other boys had been reactivated. Nevertheless, she conceded that she did not think Klein's efforts had been "entirely wasted" because the boy had begun to gain insight into himself. For the rest of the autumn Klein was bombarded by letters as the woman became frantic in her inability to cope with her child. She was torn between compassion for him and self-pity, especially as she had to cope with her husband's illness as well ("Sometimes I feel discouraged when I reflect that I have devoted so many of the best years of my life to attempting to dealing with Richard, and with so little apparent success. No one can imagine the physical and mental energy I have expended on him, and here he is at ten years quite unable to cope with life"). On November 10 Klein explained that she believed that his more overt aggression was a sign of hope.

> I am quite sure that though this might perhaps be unpleasant for his environment it is kind of a safety valve in him, and in itself a good sign, if only one could have followed up all this through further analytic work. And here I come to the point where I am afraid I must repeat myself: you

---

* Much the same series of reactions Klein had after the termination of Eric's analysis with Winnicott.

give me valuable information about Richard's early upbringing and show me that you wish me to know all about him—anything that could further my handling of the case. But unfortunately I cannot handle the case from a distance, and the help I can give you through advice is unfortunately extremely limited, even if at all valuable. My help could lie in analysing him. By this I do not mean to say that I am not extremely interested to hear about him. You know this, I am sure. But the guidance you expect from me is really not feasible—or at least not feasible in details.

By January 1942 Richard's mother began to accept that she must cope with the situation day by day and not expect instant solutions. She was beginning to see her son as a whole person in his own right, and not the "normal" image she had wanted to impose upon him.

PART FIVE

1942-1944
THE CONTROVERSIAL DISCUSSIONS

CHAPTER ONE

Resumption of Hostilities

Melanie Klein might have been afraid of German bombs, but she was still more afraid of the invasion of German-speaking analysts and their occupation of her territory—not to speak of Quislings.

With Jones's semiretirement to the country, the running of the British Society was virtually left to Edward Glover. An Emergency Committee, consisting of Glover and Sylvia Payne, was set up, but Payne's health broke down under the strain of carrying not only the duties of the scientific secretary, but those of the business secretary, which she had taken over from Rickman. In a letter dated March 16, 1942, she described to Melanie Klein the exhaustion of traveling back and forth to her cottage in Abingdon during the Blitz:

> Travelling has been so awful during the two winters, and worst of all since Xmas as I have had to wait ½–¾ hour at the station, then an unheated train arriving at Paddington ½–¾ hour late—the return journey being often 3 hours.[1]

Even before the outbreak of war a reaction against Jones's autocracy was beginning to appear, especially as many people were greatly concerned about his inability to control the highly charged emotional atmosphere of the meetings. Now that Glover was in effect running the Society, the members began to rebel against a situation that they had endured for years—the reelection, year after year, of the leading officers simply because there was no limitation on tenure of office and no secret ballot.

Jones had a hot temper; and he was incensed when, after traveling up to London from Elsted for a meeting of the Training Committee on April 23,

1940,* he found that Glover had changed the time of the meeting from the afternoon to the evening, when Jones could not possibly attend because he had to return home before the air raids started. To Sylvia Payne, Jones gave vent to his irritation about Glover: "His manner towards me in the past twelve months may have made me unduly suspicious, but I must say that I do not find the matter at all pretty, since it would mean that the President would be excluded from attending meetings."[2]

Apparently this particular misunderstanding was cleared up; but on May 1 Jones wrote again to Sylvia Payne, this time in a rather plaintive, bewildered tone:

> I still feel that I can be of some use as an objective Chairman, ungrateful as the task may be in these days when the meetings are so unrepresentative. Indeed I am very dubious whether the harm done by a talkative clique does not counterbalance any good purpose the meetings may serve in present conditions and should myself prefer to have only quarterly meetings combined with a special effort to get the other people to attend. Of course I thoroughly agree with what you say about the childishness of three or four prominent people who ought to know better. I wonder if there is any hope of remedying this absurd situation, either by open or private discussion, and should very much like an opportunity of talking it over with you as one of the very few people who are sane on the matter.[3]

However, as the bombing increased, only a handful of people remained in London to attend meetings. In Pitlochry during the summer of 1941, Melanie Klein grew anxious about the fate of the Society. She poured out her distress in a letter to Jones, after first making a number of drafts, as she did when an issue was of vital importance to her. Jones had emphasized to her how difficult things had been for him during the past few years, but she reminded him that he could have exerted far stronger leadership when the concerted attacks began against her in May 1935, following her paper on the depressive position. (At this point she inserted the comment that the Viennese had been particularly bewildered by his refusal to check Melitta's outbursts during meetings.) Because Jones was ineffectual, Glover stepped into the breach.

> Can it surprise you that I—and believe me many others, among them some of those who now out of weakness, fear, or opportunism bow to Glover—expected that the lead should have come from you, who were not only in the official position to give guidance but were personally equipped

---

* This was the meeting at which Glover and Anna Freud launched their first concerted attack on Klein. Had Jones been present it would not have been so intemperate, so it seems not unreasonable to assume that Glover deliberately planned to exclude Jones.

with all the necessary authority to do so through your eminent part in the development of Psycho-Analysis in general and in England in particular.[4]

Had he consistently and wholeheartedly checked these "personal attacks and regressive tendencies (thinly veiled by scientific verbiage) you would have had the majority of the members on your side and the whole situation would have developed differently. It is true, the Society is weak and without initiative and many individual members seem to lack more than average discrimination and strength of character—all the more they would have needed a strong lead from you." She reminded him that in 1936 she was proposed for the Council and would probably have been elected if he had supported her; but in a conversation they had at her house in February of that year he told her that she must concentrate on her scientific work. She felt bitter now because, having lacked Jones's support since 1935, she had produced so little in contrast to what she could have done.

Glover was not only scientific secretary of the British Society, secretary of the International Psycho-Analytic Association, and director of the clinic, but also chairman of the Training Committee and, now that Jones was in semiretirement, he was in effect acting president of the British Psycho-Analytical Society. In addition, as director of research he held probably the most powerful position in the Society, and it was in this area that Klein felt that he could exert real harm. She would not agree with Jones that Glover was "the only available successor." If he seemed so to Jones, it was only because Glover was "not prevented from fortifying himself so strongly in this position." What about Rickman and Payne as potential candidates? Jones seemed to regard Rickman as somewhat unstable (especially since his periodic analysis with Ferenczi in Budapest from 1928 until 1931); but Klein reminded Jones of the significant contribution he had made to the Society in recent years and how highly regarded he was by the medical profession. Klein herself was convinced that Sylvia Payne would have an excellent chance of being elected president.

With regard to her own future, her recent insights led her to feel as though she were beginning all over again: "Mind you—I am not despairing and if I have fifteen or twenty more years left to work I should be able to accomplish my task. But I realize how difficult it is and what powers of presentation would be needed to give evidence for the truth and importance of these findings." She had often recalled Jones's "prophetic words" in the spring of 1927 when he had shown her Freud's letter objecting to her conception of the superego.

> You told me then it would be a long time—well, fifteen years—until I would have brought this home to analysts in general. (It is interesting by the way that when I quoted your words to Glover some years later, when the concept of internal objects had further developed, he said with severe

conviction, "You will *never* be able to do so. It goes too much against
Freud's or other people's work," etc.) . . . How often did you point out that
analysts are like fishes and that there is a strong tendency to get away from
the depths!

In considering where her work had received its greatest inspiration, she exclaimed, "My greatest experience in this way was 'Beyond the Pleasure Principle' and 'The Ego and the Id'—and *what* an experience it was!" These works
were illuminations. "I began to understand reparation (in connection with aggression) and the part it played in the structure of the personality and in
human life." She then turned to an even more personal note. During her absence from meetings following Hans's death, Jones had visited her and told her
to transfer her love from Hans and Melitta to "my other child—the work."
    Were the struggles of years, to have her theories accepted and to entrench
her position in the British Society, to vanish overnight? While she was absent
in Pitlochry, Glover and Melitta were leading discussions on the means of assessing the relative validity of widely different interpretations, and the differences between preconscious and deep interpretations, all of which were
intended to undermine Klein's work. ("We had a very pleasant time through
the Blitz," Glover recalled placidly in an interview with Bluma Swerdloff in
1965.)[5] Klein became increasingly aware that it was essential to reestablish her
presence in the London scene, that she must form tight links of communication with her collaborators—and that she must fight.
    After her return late in 1941, the first time that her presence was recorded
at a Society meeting was October 22. On November 20 Sylvia Payne wrote to
her:

> Dear Melanie,
>   Problems connected with the Society seem rather desperate. I feel that
> the best thing I can do is to get a deeper and more complete understanding
> of your work in connection with the depressed position. I have already a
> considerable insight into it but I am aware of limitations and believe I
> should help the Society most (quite apart from personal considerations) by
> being more certain about things.[6]

Payne had heard that Paula Heimann was gathering together a research circle
and wondered if she could join it.
    As 1941 drew to a close, the British Society was entering the most confused
period in its history. Everyone was in a state of repressed panic about the war,
and overt hysteria over affairs in the Society. At Scientific Meetings Melitta
Schmideberg continued to give papers such as "Introjected Objects: An Issue
of Terminology or a Clinical Problem?" in which she questioned Abraham's

linking of incorporation, identification, and introjection as synonymous, whereas for Freud introjection denoted the process of mental intaking of imagos that preceded identification. It was highly confusing to the Viennese, who had always been under the impression that Abraham would not diverge from Freud's teaching in the slightest degree. For Willi Hoffer the papers seemed "centred always on criticism, merely on finding spots which one has overlooked, or where one has a blind spot. The positive side was not important any more. The main thing was that the difference was established."*[7]

On December 17, 1941, the Society spent an evening discussing a paper of Barbara Low's, "The Psychoanalytic Society and the Public." In the subsequent debate—for such it was—John Rickman lost his temper, attacking the officers of the Society for their rudeness to the public and their failure to respond to the needs of the wider community. As a result of this incident, it was decided to hold an Extraordinary Business Meeting to discuss the general affairs of the Society.

The main issue was power. Were the president and other officials to hold office in perpetuity, or should there be periodic elections? With the inevitable wartime decrease in patients, were some people being denied referrals? Which group was responsible for the largest group of students? This last was a vital question because it determined the future orientation of the Society. Finally, were Kleinian ideas a development of or a deviation from those of Freud? If they were the latter, as in Glover's view they were, the Kleinians should be thrown out of the official Society and form a splinter group of their own. There was also an attempt among some of the medically trained analysts to downgrade the status of the lay analysts. (This was never overtly stated, out of consideration for Anna Freud, but this issue was one of the strands in the tangled web.)

Since the majority of the members then lived outside London, an agitated round robin of letters was in constant circulation. People were ill, tired, hungry, and testy in difficult wartime conditions. But Melanie Klein was in her element, fighting for her life, exhorting and deploying her troops, issuing commands, bullying, encouraging, unceasingly vigilant.

On January 1, 1942, she actually telephoned Anna Freud to discuss the crisis and later reported the conversation to Joan Riviere:

> Though it probably won't lead to anything it was interesting and informative. Here are her main points. She is despairing about the state of the Society, but is loath to segregate for a number of reasons, some of which would also apply to us if we segregate. One faint possibility for further cooperation would seem to her to be if the two schools were kept separate as

---

* All had not been sweetness and light with the central Europeans, however. Fenichel, according to Glover, used to bang people over the head if he disagreed with their papers.

far as the training is concerned—a suggestion which both of us made to the Training Committee just years ago. She doubts very much that this would be possible and sufficiently supported. She thinks Glover is the most suitable President, but suggested that to meet me she might support Payne as President if Payne agreed to accept this. She thinks Payne would be objective to both of us because she appreciated my work and its value for analysis, and is yet not hostile to hers. . . .

[Nevertheless] Anna's wish for us to form a group of our own (a wish which no doubt meets Glover's wishes and intention—and it would be extremely convenient for them if we were to commit this mistake) is quite plain.[8]

Rickman, Scott, Winnicott, and Isaacs were to form the vanguard of the Kleinian counterattack. Roger Money-Kyrle and Eva Rosenfeld, as associate members, were not expected to play an active part, she explained—but the truth was that she did not believe they would be effective enough spokesmen. Paula Heimann was expected to be extremely effective behind the scenes.

"I think," Klein continued, "we should avoid a) the impression that we are criticizing or blaming Jones, and b) criticism of particular members of the Board; c) the issue with the Viennese. . . . I feel that if what we say is well put, scientific and unemotional, we may have some effect; of course if at least among ourselves we have a definite policy on which we have agreed beforehand."

Occasionally those members who were in the armed forces obtained leave and joined their Kleinian colleagues for an evening of discussion. For instance, on January 29 Scott and Rickman were able to attend a meeting of the Internal Object group. Klein reported to Susan Isaacs, in her weekly letter: "Scott started a discussion on hallucination and object-representation. What a wide field there is to be explored and discussed in connection with the inner world. There seems to be not one subject in psycho-analysis which does not need extension and revision from these points of view. It was really nice to talk from no other point of view than the scientific one."[9]

The following letter, dated January 3, 1942 (an expansion of her letter to Susan Isaacs), which Klein sent to her collaborators, is a fine example of her tactical skills:

After the last meeting, I came to the conclusion that if we are to have any success in whatever we undertake against such a skilful person as Glover, we should organise our efforts—all the more as the time at our disposal at the General Meeting will necessarily be restricted. I asked Mrs. Riviere whether she would undertake to coordinate our contributions by suggesting, if necessary, alterations, in order to avoid overlapping and unnecessary repetitions. She agreed to do so. (I think it would be best if it were not known to outsiders that she is doing this.)* . . .

I think the contributions fall under two headings:

1) Policy. What suggestions regarding alterations of constitution, etc. are you in favour of? It seems to me essential that we should have an agreed policy on all important points beforehand. I personally think that, whatever we suggest, we should be careful to avoid any impression a) that we are criticizing or blaming Jones; b) or for that matter any particular members of the Board; but criticism or suggestions should be directed to the policy of the Board as a whole. c) I think it would be good strategy to avoid at this juncture antagonizing the Viennese and discussing where we differ from them—so that we may not dissipate whatever strength we possess.

2) You may wish to make a contribution referring to matters other than policy. For instance, I intend to take up the point that Glover mentioned in his recent speech—that he favours our going into seclusion and first putting our house in order. I shall contrast this profession with his attitude in his book on "The Technique of Psycho-Analysis"—the whole book being a flagrant contradiction to this recently avowed policy. Otherwise I shall concern myself only with the way in which Glover has abused his position as Director of Scientific Research within the Society, and shall criticise the book from this point of view.

Another point, for instance, which would deserve a reply by anybody who feels like it: Glover made an extremely clever and subtle attack on us by throwing out in an inconspicuous manner the suggestion that the Society has got very far away from Freud in recent years, and that, after all, the purpose of the Society is Freud's work.

Possibly we may find it necessary to have a meeting later to discuss matters personally; but that would be better at a later date, when we have already put down in writing whatever contributions we wish to make.[10]

As members busily went about drawing up resolutions, Jones grumbled about the idea, but bowed to the inevitable. On January 21, 1942, he wrote an extraordinary letter to Anna Freud in which he assured her that she was

quite wrong in saying that I attach no value to your judgement, and of course I should not have asked for it if that were so. It is true that I consider Mrs. Klein has made important contributions. How many of them are actually new is another matter, for I think one would find broad indications of most of them in earlier psycho-analytical writings; to determine this would be a piece of research well worth while. She undoubtedly magnifies the newness of them, but it is undeniable, in my opinion, that she has forc-

---

* The reason for this was that Riviere considered Sylvia Payne to be very hostile to her.

ibly brought to our attention the great importance of such mechanisms as introjection and projection and has, I think, demonstrated the existence of these and other mechanisms at an earlier age than was generally thought possible. That is how I should sum the matter up. On the other hand she has neither a scientific nor an orderly mind, and her presentations are lamentable. She is also in many ways neurotic and has a tendency, which she is trying to check, to become "verrannt" [stubbornly attached]. It would not be surprising, further, that the danger would exist in such a person to distort the objective reality by emphasizing certain aspects at the expense of others. Some of us consider, for example, that she shows this in respect to the Oedipus complex and of the part played by the father. These are, however, all matters that will work themselves out in the course of time, the more easily if we concentrate on the scientific problems in place of the personal ones.

I should not have said that scientific difficulties are ever at the basis of personal ones. Surely our psychological experience must teach us that the reverse is true. . . .

It is an interesting situation, familiar sociologically, where a mood of rebelliousness—mainly induced in this instance, I think, by economic insecurity—draws into itself all other discontents from the most diverse and uncoordinated sources. The practical problem is how best to cope with the situation and it is just there that I especially hope for your co-operation, both because of our success in working together in the past and because of our supreme devotion to the spirit of union as opposed to disunion, in our psycho-analytical organization. I cannot believe, Anna, that I could appeal to you in vain on this fundamental issue. . . .

Dr. Payne, who has done an enormous amount of hard work in the actual running of things, seems hurt at the signs of lack of appreciation. I can myself honestly say that I am above such reactions and am really only concerned with providing the most favourable opportunity for further co-operative work. Also I am very dissatisfied with the present unproductive activities of the Society, for which I hold Dr. Glover partly, though by no means wholly, to blame. By nature I believe in aristocratic leadership, but I think there are occasions, and I wonder if this is not one, where it is more successful to exert that leadership indirectly instead of overtly. Thus I am inclined to the solution of reducing the responsibility of officials, making their policies or decisions more a matter of business meetings, and having the officials re-elected annually. In this way the voice of those with most weight would come to expression in the general meetings without their having to be hampered by anti-parental complexes. It was for this reason, surely, that your father withdrew so early from direct leadership of the Vienna Society and refused to accept a similar official position in the International Association. I think he was quite right, and for the same reason have been trying for some years to withdraw from my unofficial positions.

The main objection to this solution is the practical difficulty of finding suitable people in London to replace the present officials. Naturally I should hate to be succeeded by a nonentity such as Mrs. Stephen, who is working to obtain the position.

I have expressed my opinions to you quite candidly and should now be very glad to hear yours.[11]

Jones's reference to the derivative nature of Klein's theories might have been a ploy to make Anna Freud see that they were a development or extension of already established psychoanalytic tenets. When he said "some of us" considered that Klein undervalued the part played by the father and the role of the Oedipus complex in development, he seemed to be including himself. Yet in "The Phallic Phase" (1934) he had emphasized his concurrence in Klein's belief that the boy's early fear was unrelated to his father or his penis.

Prior to the Extraordinary Meetings the Kleinians compared notes on the resolutions they would submit. Joan Riviere exhorted Klein to emphasize the discouragement and difficulty Freud confessed to when he was forced to change his views. An example of the way in which Klein operated is contained in a note to Winnicott, in which she apologizes for asking him to tone down the resolution he proposed presenting. She called his attention to the "necessity to take out certain things, though they are true and it is worth while saying them, because we don't wish to say them at the moment. I know from my own experience that this is painful but necessary. I therefore hope you won't mind if I suggest anything without restraint which I think would be best to cut out or alter in your communication. I am sure you will understand it has nothing to do with the truth or value of what you say, but only with the question of what is best at the present time."[12] She sent her comments on Winnicott's resolutions to other members of her group:

> I think the impression which it might give that Freud is more or less history would not only be dangerous, but the fact itself is not true. Freud's writings are very much alive, and still a guide for our work (though much has been done since which goes beyond him, or even contradicts him); and this should definitely be *stressed* both for the sake of truth and tactics. It is in my view important that we should keep in mind also for the discussion that anything which could give the impression that we think that Freud could be put on a shelf is the most dangerous trap we could fall into. It is exactly what the Viennese try to prove, and what Glover will fall back on when he tries to brand us, now or later, as heretics.[13]

The first of five Extraordinary Meetings took place on February 25, 1942.* In all there were sixteen resolutions proposed to deal with different aspects of the members' disquiet. There was the usual muddle of cross-purposes as to the parameters of the discussion—for example, Jones took exception to its being classified as a business meeting—but the meetings were remarkably fruitful: various positions were clarified and important statements about what people believed they were devoting their lives to emerged from the occasion. Naturally there were jibes and innuendos, but the meetings did give members an opportunity to affirm their passionate convictions. Walter Schmideberg's desire to focus on anti-Freudian deviation was ruled out ("As well one could propose to discuss first the distance of the earth from the sun," said Adrian Stephen),[14] and attention was concentrated on the dissatisfaction of the majority of the members that administrative policy had been considered a fiefdom for a tiny minority for too long. There was also a general desire to have individuals representing a range of theoretical positions participate in the running of the Society.

Other grievances were voiced. Karin Stephen was concerned that some patients continued in analysis for years (viz. the Kleinians). "Training analyses go on interminably. Why is this?" she asked. "Are training analysts finding that their methods are not producing the results they aim at? The views of members on how analysis really achieves its aims, when it does do this, are seldom heard." Equally disturbing was the re-analysis of a number of members by Klein and her supporters.†

Sylvia Payne's paper (which was read by Ella Sharpe, since Payne was ill) was the most incisive at getting at the heart of the current tensions. It was not simply scientific differences, she declared, but the anxiety that people's livelihoods were at stake. "When economic fear is added to difference of scientific outlook," she emphasized, "all tolerance is liable to disappear and the struggle becomes principally one for power.

"How can we avoid this menace? We can relieve the anxiety of some members by adopting certain safeguards in connection with our constitution, to ensure that the same members do not hold office too long."

Turning to the basic conceptions of psychoanalysis to which members were supposed to adhere, she added:

The recent work on the unconscious oral aspect of psychological development initiated by Mrs. Klein is of great value and is the road by which we should gain deeper knowledge into the earliest phases of ego development and into psychotic illness. When new work is added to old, especially when

* I am greatly indebted for the material about the Extraordinary Meetings to Pearl King's paper "The Life and Work of Melanie Klein in the British Psycho-Analytical Society," read at the London Weekend Conference of English-Speaking Members of European Psychoanalytical Societies on October 3, 1982.
† E.g., John Rickman, Paula Heimann, Susan Isaacs.

it includes therapy, there is often a tendency to think that past knowledge has been superseded, and it takes time for new knowledge to be put into relation to old. I think we are at the moment struggling with a problem of this kind.

Susan Isaacs reminded her colleagues of the purpose of the International Psycho-Analytic Association as set out in Statute 3: "the mutual support of the members in all endeavours to acquire and disseminate psycho-analytic knowledge." She proposed that no member hold office for more than two years, and not more than one office at a time. She spoke at length on the particular problems faced in such a case by a group with a background in an understanding of unconscious motivation.

First of all, there are those difficulties arising from the very special course of the transference and counter-transference among analysts and analysands in our members. We know that these transferences are more intense and troublesome, far harder to allow for in our judgments, than the influence of relationships, such as teacher and pupil among other scientific workers. In other words, peculiarly strong ambivalent feelings are active.

She ended by stressing the danger of having a scientific secretary who also wielded constitutional powers; and Joan Riviere pleaded for secret balloting.

An acerbic note was bound to intrude. Melitta Schmideberg asked sarcastically why those members who were most strenuously campaigning for change were those who had happened to be out of London during the nine months of the Blitz. "It is possible, of course," she commented caustically, "that this sudden bout of energy is due to the good rest they enjoyed in the country. It is conceivable, however, that there are other reasons. The possibility cannot be excluded that there may be some connection between these attempts and the previous ones of trying to induce us to stop our activities." Ella Sharpe spoke of Walter Schmideberg's cheerful demeanor as a fire-watcher, and Anna Freud's readiness to take on seminars abandoned by those who had left London:* "These are the people who have kept the work of the Institute going for two and a half years, and if heavy bombing returns this Society knows upon whom it can depend."

The Kleinian group was taken aback by this, for Sharpe had, in 1930, praised Klein for having "deepened and galvanized into life our theoretical knowledge of the oral and anal phases of development."[15] As late as 1934 she

---

* At a Training Committee meeting on July 3, 1939, Anna Freud declined to take child seminars because the candidates for child training had been analyzed or otherwise trained by analysts holding different views from her own. However, with the departure of the Kleinian child analysts from the scene, she readily stepped into the breach.

was speaking approvingly of Klein at the Lucerne Conference.[16] After Sharpe's hostile comments at the Extraordinary Meetings, Susan Isaacs made a point of meeting her to ascertain her position; and after their conversation it was clear that Sharpe now belonged in the other camp. In her report of the conversation to Klein, Isaacs wrote:

> The most revealing thing said was re Bowlby. In reply to what she had said about our turning out candidates all in agreement with us, I had instanced Bowlby, as opposing us in one important matter, one in which E.S. too opposed us, viz. the relative importance of environment vs. inner factors. She now says that what she really meant was—if only our candidates would be interested in *different* things—"e.g. *fathers, instead of mothers*"!!! I felt this was a very important indication of a) her personal conflict, and b) the degree of distortion in her judgment, and c) the extent to which she feels herself "Freudian," as against us, and will be on the side of A.F.*[17]

At the next meeting, on March 11, 1942, figures who had not spoken at the previous meeting were heard for the first time—Anna Freud, Donald Winnicott, and Melanie Klein—and the general tone was far less moderate. Anna Freud expressed concern that this was not a suitable time for major changes:

> If we alter the rules before settling the scientific differences it seems that we take neither the rules nor the difficulties very earnestly. . . . It is like renovating the house before we know who wants to live in it. Also the renovation of our training system would perhaps depend on these results. I think we should decide all this after the discussion of the scientific differences and not before.[18]

Winnicott agreed that Anna Freud's point was excellent, but "What would happen if the war goes on for ten years?" He spoke eloquently of the need to push back scientific frontiers: "Freud's work is alive, and we are all guided by it, but we have it in our power to stifle the spirit of it by clinging to the letter, and by losing sight of the fact that to continue his work is to continue to reach out into the unknown in order to gain more knowledge and understanding." Klein seconded his resolution. She emphasized how impressed she had always been by Freud's courage in accepting that he had been wrong about the seduction theory. The foundations of psychoanalysis seemed to have been shaken by the sequence of books following *Beyond the Pleasure Principle* (1920). At the

---

* But Sharpe's principal objection she did not make clear until her remarks on Susan Isaacs's paper "The Nature and Function of Phantasy," in which, commenting on the implication for technique of the internal object—"actual objects inside, breasts, penis, parents, evil and good. Sometimes I get the impression that some analysts who deal with these beliefs, interpret to their patients as if they themselves believed not only their patients' beliefs, but in the actuality of the concrete objects inside" (CD, March 17, 1943).

time Eitingon said to her, "This is putting dynamite to the house; but," he added, "Freud knows what he does."

> In "Inhibitions, Symptoms and Anxiety" [she added] Freud brought together the harvest of the years from 1920 onwards. Some fundamental problems, formerly unresolved, had now found a solution, but here and there we find in his writings pregnant hints thrown out, full of possibilities to be followed up, indications which he himself, however, did not pursue any further. For instance, he put the question: "When does separation from an object produce anxiety, when does it produce mourning, and when does it produce, it may be, only pain?" and replies to it as follows: "Let us say at once that there is no prospect of answering these questions at present. We must content ourselves with drawing certain distinctions and adumbrating certain possibilities. . . . We are in the midst of the second epoch in the history of psycho-analysis, and many questions which in the beginning of this epoch were unanswerable are now nearer solution."

Long-winded Walter Schmideberg went to great lengths to impress his audience that he could speak with authority because of his close contact with Freud—as though he had absorbed the sacred truth by osmosis. He even reverted to the charges of plagiarism he and his wife had made against Klein and some of her colleagues a few years before. With heavy Germanic humor he recounted:

> When I first came to this country some ten years ago, this Society was very much under the influence of Mrs. Melanie Klein. She had greatly stimulated discussion and research. Much attention was paid to introjection and projection mechanisms, to sadism and pre-genital phantasies. True, I met my old friends, ideas of Freud, Ferenczi, Abraham and others under new names. Even "Boehm's hidden penis"* (that is how we used to call the phantasy of the father's penis hidden in the mother) was found—honi soit qui mal y pense—in Mrs. Klein's luggage. Will anybody please, who comes across it, return it to its rightful owner, Dr. Felix Boehm, Berlin, Tiergartenstrasse 10?

Melitta Schmideberg then launched into a series of bitter accusations against the British Society: She recalled that when she arrived some fifteen years before, she had been told that the Society was "friendly but dull." Gradually she realized that part of the developing cooperation was due to shared hostility to Anna Freud by a certain group. She saw for herself how Nina Searl was hounded out of the Society. She believed that there had been an attempt to

---

* He is probably referring to Boehm's "Beitrage zur Psychologie der Homosexualität" in *I.Z.P.* (1926), 66–79.

destroy her own reputation. She went on to describe the atmosphere at meetings. She brought out anecdotal material of cases of students who had been dazzled into believing that Klein was one of the great original psychoanalytic minds, even though her ideas on pregenital phases, projection, and introjection owed much to Freud, Abraham, and Ferenczi. She continued:

> Another candidate took objection to the behaviour of his analyst over a certain matter, and wanted to change to another one. His analyst, a leading Kleinian, used every conceivable method of emotional appeal to dissuade him: she pointed out that he would wreck his career and that there was the danger of his committing suicide as other analysts were probably unable to analyse his depressive position. Nevertheless, he clung to his decision. Then suddenly another Kleinian analyst asked him to come and see her. I do not know how she had learned about the matter, but she expressed her concern about it to him, and eventually wept over his intention to leave his analyst. This decided him and he stayed.*

She talked at some length about the power exercised by the Kleinians through transference and control analyses. At the end of her long diatribe, Ernest Jones remarked dryly, "Dr. Schmideberg has really admirably illustrated the difficulty of discussing these matters without personal attacks."

Anna Freud was then given an opportunity to voice a grievance over which *she* had been smarting for years: "I resented it very much in the past, *not* when this Society criticized my little book on the psycho-analysis of children, but I resented it when the Society refused to have it printed in England. What is the use of criticism, when a member is not allowed to publish his views? In Vienna we published Mrs. Klein's book as a matter of course. We always held the view that the publication of all views is necessary. For instance, we published Rank's 'Trauma of Birth' about which we had great doubts."

Finally Glover identified the heart of the problem: "The issue is: whether so long as this struggle for factional power goes on it is possible to discuss usefully *either* scientific differences *or* the working of the constitution. I think it is not possible: I think that *under the existing conditions* the belief that changes in the constitution can produce a change of heart or head is purely magical. No change for the better can take place, no possibility of free scientific discussion can exist, until this ultimately non-scientific issue of power is brought into the open."

Sylvia Payne was confined to a hotel in Bournemouth, so ill that she had missed the first two meetings. She had lain there for weeks reflecting on the

---

* Dr. John Bowlby has confirmed that he was the candidate Melitta was referring to. He was approached by Susan Isaacs, although he cannot remember the tears.

problems of the Society, thoughts that she shared in her forthright way in a letter to Klein, dated March 16, 1942.

I feel it essential to start with that we should not expect full agreement, but that we should even be able to tolerate doubt and uncertainty without re- lapsing into hopelessness and despair and the conviction that the dis- agreeing party is personally hostile.

I am not such a blind fool as to deny that E.G. is hostile to you, and make no attempt to disguise the fact that you are hostile to him and regard him as a personal enemy. Of course this situation is partly the outcome of the unconscious of the people concerned, but I do not think that you will deny that unfortunate circumstances have played into the present situation and precipitated an actual situation which need not have actually occurred.

I have known from the first day I met E.G. that he feared and defended himself against and was jealous of the successful intellectual, i.e., rival woman. . . . This particular unconscious attitude obviously was going to make cooperation hard but not impossible as long as one's own uncon- scious did not respond.

I do not agree with you that he has for many years been *conspiring* for power. He has of course worked for his position and wanted to have it and it is a pity that he did not have a *limited* tenure of office as President a good many years before these dissentions became so marked. He is afraid of power and expects to have it taken from him all the time, so he trusts no one. At the same time he is now consciously doing all he can to keep what he has had, and in his alarm he is more likely to become unscrupulous. He appears to me to make such obviously gross psychological blunders that I cannot fear his methods very much. He has in many ways a right to expect to replace Jones for a time anyhow. I do not believe it is sound or right for you to feel that his wish is to destroy Ps.An., I do not believe he wishes to destroy the *whole* of your work. I cannot accept the proposition that it is right to speak as if psycho-analysis and your contribution to Ps.An. (which I never deny) are one and the same thing. I think that to do so is equivalent to regarding the *part* as the same as the whole. I am sure you injure your own position by giving this *impression*. I am fully aware of the difficulty in keeping in touch with the unconscious and the ease with which we can slide into superficialities, and I know it is the most important problem of all. I believe however that you tend to increase the tendency rather than diminish it in the Society by ignoring the unconscious work, which is done by workers who are not so profound and have not the insight which you have. . . .

You must see he is also being driven by Melitta, and that brings us back to the tragedy of the personal aspect of the situation. I am not whitewashing E.G. I know him too well to attempt to do so. I am only saying he is not all black. He regards me more as an enemy and a rival than anything else.[19]

Knowing that she was returning to London within a few days, she made a final plea for peace: "I know that we understand one another, and that you know I am *terribly* anxious for your work to receive its proper recognition and that we should be able to work *freely and openly.*"

In Klein's round-robin letter to her troops, she could express herself freely about Glover's attitude (March 26, 1942):

It has recently been urged by several speakers, namely Dr. Brierley, Dr. Payne, etc. that a more friendly atmosphere, greater tolerance, etc. should come about in the Society. The way in which these suggestions were received by members (one might mention Anna Freud) showed how urgently this need was felt. Dr. Schmideberg and Dr. Glover put the blame for the lack of cooperation on to us; we recently seem to have become the villain of the piece, are striving for power, etc. . . . If power policy is mentioned and personal attacks are made, then I think we get much closer to the real causes of the disturbances in our Society which have gone on for years— and that the boot is actually on the other foot.[20]

By the end of the month Payne had recovered sufficiently to return to her home in Abingdon. She had been studying the report of the previous (March) meeting very carefully, and now realized that she had been far too sanguine and optimistic about Glover. From the train she wrote to Klein:

I agree that the attitude taken by G. at the last meeting seems to indicate that he has definitely adopted a certain policy with regard to you and intends to carry it out unscrupulously. This is of course what I have striven to prevent for a very long time. I have never been in his confidence, but of course have known the conflict which was going on. The only hope was that the better side of his nature would succeed in controlling the persecuted side. He is not a strong man and is always aggressive when driven to take action. What has crystallised out and made him consciously and openly organise this line of policy is of course the fear that he will not be president, and will lose other positions. It seems to me from his point of view to be idiotic as the line of attack launched via the Schmidebergs alienates people who might otherwise be friendly. His hostility to you received an initial drive from which it has *never* recovered owing to Jones' grave error of judgment in bringing up his relations to Melitta before the training committee.* The affair should have been dealt with privately, but there again Jones was not strong enough. . . .

She went on to express a general weariness with the whole sordid squabble:

> Like you I am sick of the whole business and long to be left alone to work on cases. My time is continually taken up by these useless clamours. I do not want to be president in such a Society, it is no honour for whatever I do or say I shall meet opposition from someone. . . . As you say, if only we had an "Abraham." I make no claim to wisdom of the quality needed.[21]

Klein generally refrained from commenting on Melitta's behavior, but shortly before the April meeting she considered possible tactics for a counterattack against her daughter's accusations at the previous meeting.

> . . . one can certainly generally refer to the sharpness of her *criticism* of younger members and of people in general, *up to the time she turned against me.* Another of her victims was Anna Freud at the Congress in Lucerne in the summer, 1935, and I am quite sure that Anna Freud *remembers* this paper *very well*—and that is certainly a point that can be mentioned. . . .
>
> From one thing I feel very strongly we must refrain, even though it is quite unfair to ourselves—and that is to make any aspersions or accusations which cannot be at once supported by irrefutable facts, not as they appear to us, but as they appear to the others. That is to say, we seem to have to restrict ourselves to refuting their accusations. And there is even one very obvious fact which I feel quite sure *should not be mentioned,* nor even hinted at by any of us, and that is Melitta's illness. I think it must not even be hinted at by any of us either privately or as an argument in the coming discussions. I am convinced, however true it may be, it will be held against us if it is mentioned.†[22]

The mood of the meeting of April 13 was entirely different. Jones took heart from Sylvia Payne's return and spoke out forcibly against the irresponsibility of Melitta Schmideberg's charges (but failed to mention Glover). Payne's reappearance elicited cheers, and she made a moving plea for British fair play. If such charges continued, she felt that Mrs. Klein would have cause to bring a libel action. She spoke bluntly about the large part economic insecu-

---

* This could be construed as suggesting that Glover and Melitta were having an affair. Pearl King disagrees: she believes Payne is referring to Jones's publicly chastising Glover for not sufficiently analyzing Melitta's aggression so that she was displaying it at meetings.
† There is no indication that Melitta was suffering from any physical ailment. Is she suggesting that Melitta was schizoid?

rity was playing in the discussions; and she pointed out that a meeting like this could not operate in the same unrestrained atmosphere as an analytic session where anything could be said. Restraint had to be exercised. Finally she observed: "The conflict is extraordinarily like that which is taking place in many countries and I feel sure that it is in some way a tiny reverberation of the massive conflict which pervades the world."[23]

Nevertheless, a rather ugly exchange took place between Barbara Low and Joan Riviere—precisely underlining Payne's point—in which Low complained that Riviere would never refer patients to her. Throughout the course of the three meetings and the Controversial Discussions the following year, the behavior of Low and Riviere reached a level of undignified invective. Klein maintained correctly that she herself made a genuine attempt to behave with moderation, but Riviere sometimes reproached her for allowing herself to be intimidated. Glover was right in charging some of Klein's followers with lack of restraint.

The question was raised as to whether an outside arbitrator should be called in. Anna Freud remarked tartly, "If we should be able to solve our own personal problems and those of our patients I cannot see why we should not be able to solve the Society's problems."

Following the meeting, Klein wrote to Sylvia Payne to thank her for the frank and dignified way in which she had approached the problems. An element of optimism had been infused into the atmosphere: "One hopeful aspect of the situation is the greater preparedness on A.F.'s part to cooperate in *scientific* matters. I am sure your influence on her has greatly helped towards this change." However, she added, "I am less hopeful about her attitude towards the acute conflict in which she as matters stand will have an important part to play. I don't think she understands the situation sufficiently and how it all came about."[24] To Jones she also expressed her appreciation: "I am sure that the line you took that the Society is at its greatest crisis and in danger of going under is the one which must be brought home. I am also sure that the only possibility of saving the Society is for you and Dr. Payne to keep this line. Members must not be allowed to delude themselves any longer into thinking that this is a private though very disturbing quarrel; they must be made to see that far greater things are at stake—in fact, that psycho-analysis itself is in danger."[25]

Jones replied that he was resolved "to persevere unflinchingly if I can get adequate support." However, he could not agree with her diagnosis of the problem: "The progress of our work is at stake, in my opinion, essentially because of the disturbances to it brought about by ceaseless attacks of a *personal* nature. If they proceeded from scientific differences only they would not show qualities of personal animosity that they actually do."[26] As he saw it, Melitta and Glover were not interested in scientific truth: "their essential motives are personal." People were deluding themselves if they thought otherwise. "The only hope for peace in the Society," he concluded, "is that this personal rancour be fully exposed and condemned."

Behind the scenes there were further attempts to ease the tension. On May 1 Klein again telephoned Anna Freud and suggested that they hold private meetings on scientific differences. "Anna seemed surprised, though very pleased at this idea of mine," Klein told Susan Isaacs. "It did not seem to her possible at first that I could compromise as regards my work, but I explained to her—which is my conviction—that it should not be impossible to bring in certain of my points of view and for the present lay less emphasis on others. Actually if I can do this, it would be the one way profitable for the Viennese candidates, because as experience has shown, otherwise they don't expect anything."[27] To Sylvia Payne she added further details about the discussion: "She [Anna] is inclined to regard Melitta's attacks more in the way of a naughty child, and certainly underrates the disruptive effect on the Society which was—and here she is quite right—only so bad because the Society did not know how to deal with it. She is also certainly right in stressing Dr. Jones's mistakes as the result of his ambivalence and a fundamentally wrong attitude." In an aside she added: "(By the way—to keep a sense of humour—it is funny, isn't it? to think that Anna Freud may be the decisive factor in the conduct of the affairs of the British Society.)" It was agreed to have their first meeting at Anna's home in Maresfield Gardens, and Anna Freud proposed inviting the Hoffers, Mrs. Burlingham, and a pediatrician, Dr. Josephine Stross, and Klein would bring along some of her friends. Klein urged Payne to join them. "Your part as a kind of umpire would be extremely useful, and I think the whole thing might be quite interesting."[28]

Payne was delighted: "I am sure you are doing the only thing that could help matters and that is approaching Anna F. in a friendly spirit. The truth is there is not the machinery available to deal with these problems and I have not the will, time or strength to talk in a circle for hours on the telephone."[29]

At the same time, Marjorie Brierley suggested a subcommittee consisting of herself, Susan Isaacs, and Anna Freud, to thrash out some of the fundamental points of theoretical difference. Brierley felt very strongly that the clarification and assessment of internal objects was one of the most important scientific tasks facing the Society—hence her position that theoretical discussions should take place before the airing of general grievances. In various papers she wrote on Klein's theories, Brierley emphasizes that people who make considerable use of introjection feel more at home with concepts relating to "internalized objects," just as those who habitually make use of projective mechanisms are not naturally disposed to feel that the inner world matters more than the world outside. Her argument was like that of Coleridge, who had divided men into Aristotelians and Platonists. Such a native bias, in Brierley's view, was apt to distort the viewer's objectivity; and "internal objects" were especially prone to subjective interpretation.[30]

In Brierley's opinion, Melanie Klein's work suffered from lack of precise definition. She found the mixture of the language of phantasy with abstract terminology confusing. As an example she cited Klein's expression "whole object," by which she distinguished a person-object from an organ- or part-object. She also used the term "whole" to denote an undamaged or intact object which a child in a state of anxiety may fear is in shattered pieces. "Now it is quite possible," Brierley argues, "to think of a person being dismembered but it is not possible to conceive of a mental object being literally shattered—one cannot take a hammer to a mental object."[31]

Klein had great respect for Brierley, and at one point invited her to dinner to try to convince her of the validity of her views; but Brierley was not one to be influenced by cajolery, enthusiasm, or good food.

Forty years after these events she talked to me in the house on an isolated Cumbrian fell where she had lived in retirement since 1954. She still believed that the concept of internal objects was the worst mistake Klein ever made: she preferred the term "incompatible identifications." Brierley approved of the fact that Klein had opened up the preoedipal stages, but was extremely doubtful about her conviction that the infant had an innate knowledge of sexual intercourse, although she regarded Klein's views on weaning as highly important. Her own clinical practice had indicated that weaning urges the girl to the father and induces in her a certain hostility to her mother. Nevertheless, it depended very much on how it was done; and Brierley admired Winnicott greatly for his recognition of the importance of the mother-child relationship.

As for Klein's emphasis on the interpretation of the negative transference, in Brierley's opinion she never fully analyzed the positive transference. "She liked it to stay there because she had this liking for control over people." She was convinced that Klein should have broken away and formed her own Society; and she said of Anna Freud, "She's never written anything (apart from child reports) that questioned her father's findings in any essential way. She developed some of his findings, but she never questioned their validity. The whole experience of the public debates was very unsettling for Anna so soon after Freud's death and her settling in England. She was horrified to hear any criticism of Freud, but, of course, poor dear, she just had to get used to it."[32]

Just when progress in cooperation seemed about to develop, Brierley refused to participate in the meetings at Maresfield Gardens. "Just now," she told Klein, "if we want to encourage genuine democracy and keep members alive to their communal power and responsibilities, I do feel strongly that no arrangements, however desirable in themselves, ought to be made without Society knowledge and consent."[33]

Melanie Klein disagreed with her position:

> It is true that according to genuine democratic principles the Society should be made to participate in every effort, but in fact, by insisting that the Society in its present unhealthy state should arrange for this seminar there would have been great danger of again stirring ill-feeling—which, I feel sure, would have happened if certain members had been chosen by the Society and others left out. It is a different matter if Anna Freud asks some people privately to discuss with herself and her friends at her house— which, as I mentioned before, is quite an ordinary procedure, for which there have been many precedents in recent years. You will agree with me that this study group is in itself a very delicate affair, for wh. the best possible atmosphere and conditions are to be provided if it is not to turn out a failure, and that one should avoid getting it mixed up with other causes for conflict which I am afraid are still very far from being solved.[34]

Brierley's legalistic attitude was partly responsible for the cancellation of the seminars. It might seem deeply regrettable that the two groups did not meet privately. If conciliatory efforts had been attempted at this point, it could be argued, the intense emotional atmosphere might have abated to some degree.

Matters became still more serious at the meeting on May 13, which was dominated by Glover. Melitta's shrill accusations, based on innuendo and gossip, had been distressing and embarrassing; but Glover's thundering rhetoric in leveling the gravest of charges against the Kleinian group left everyone at the meeting shaken. Glover essentially accused one group of trying to insinuate its way into power through the training of candidates; and if the situation were allowed to continue, within a very few years the British Society would be entirely dominated by the Kleinians—as though they were "a forbidden sect doing some harmful work, which should be prevented from spreading," Melanie Klein complained ruefully.[35]

Glover used facts and dates to buttress his charges. "Of the 20 training analysts in Britain," he began, "18 are situated in London, where virtually all the training work in this country is carried out. By reason of their position and function these 18 training analysts can make or mar the future of psycho-analysis in Britain."

Glover then proceeded to give a breakdown of the affiliation of the eighteen training analysts: eight, possibly nine, were Kleinians, three were Viennese Freudians. Five to seven were "English Freudians (or, as they have sometimes been labelled, Middle Groupers)."

The active members of the Society in the London area numbered forty-eight. Of these, twelve or thirteen were "out and out adherents of Mrs. Klein's views," twenty-three were English Freudians, and seven Viennese Freudians. Klein's adherents held eight or nine key positions, 60 percent of them, while 22–30 percent belonged to the Middle Groupers, and the Viennese-plus-Berlin contingent accounted for 33 percent.

> In the six years up to 1940 every training analyst appointed (5 in all) was an adherent of Mrs. Klein. True, one non-Kleinian was appointed in 1940 and one Viennese Freudian in 1941. But it should be recalled that after 1938 the Training Committee had a different balance of forces. Jones resigned, Mr. Strachey, Miss Freud and Mrs. Bibring were added and I was appointed Chairman.

Power had shifted from the Council to the Training Committee. Glover claimed that the Kleinians' influence was first manifested in organized bloc votes, a charge Klein particularly resented. The problem was not simply one of controversial theoretical views, but of manipulative strategy. Lest anyone was in doubt about these consequences, Glover hammered home his point:

> Now training committees subject to the very sanction of the International Training Commission have very considerable autonomy of function. The Committee selects candidates, prepares the curriculum, does all the teaching, appoints all the teachers (the training analysts, the control analysts, the seminar leaders, the lecturers) and does all the examining. In other words, *it controls absolutely and without appeal entrance to the Society.* The Society can reject Training Committee nominees but it cannot (nor can any member) train other nominees except through the Training Committee.

What difference did it make, then, to discuss scientific issues if in the long run the Society would consist only of "adherents"?

Glover then turned to the practices that he considered most objectionable:

1. The advancement of candidates because of pre-existing allegiances.
2. The criticism, particularly in control analyses, of candidates who do not hold these allegiances.
3. The canvassing for adherents, particularly by trying to persuade them that they need "deeper" analysis.
4. Most vital of all, the teaching of material or method, on the validity of which the Society has not yet reached any conclusion.
5. The election and advancement of candidates on the strength of their allegiance rather than their scientific or teaching capacities.

6. Private discussions as to the placing and advancement of candidates prior to official Committee meetings.

What Glover was conveying was an atmosphere of secret cabals, hooded glances, furtively passed notes, a foot kicked under the table. Did some of the members recognize a situation familiar to them? Or did they suddenly see themselves as naïve outsiders excluded from the privileged circle?

Glover was noted for his cutting Scottish wit, and in this situation he used it to full advantage. "When the Committee is allocating candidates to training analysts," he mused, "I sometimes am tempted to write a new version of the old Gilbert and Sullivan snatch: Every little boy or girl born in this world alive, is either a little Liberal or else a little Conservative."

Just before the war, when Anna Freud and Melanie Klein agreed that it was impossible for candidates sponsored by one group to be taught or controlled by training analysts drawn from the other, "a deadlock was reached. But then came the Blitz and," Glover recalled nostalgically, "a strange peace descended on the Committee"—because the Kleinian representatives had left London. "During the Blitz winter all discussions were correct and friendly"—naturally, because there was no one to contradict Glover or Melitta. By implication the Kleinians were not only devious and unscrupulous, but cowardly as well. (Of course, the continental analysts were not allowed to travel beyond the London radius; if given the opportunity they, too, might have joined the exodus of thousands of others.)

Anna Freud interjected a worldly point of view:

I really think that if all members of the Training Committee used the most legitimate methods in dealing with the matters now in question, we should still be at the same deadlock. If there are two controversial views in a Society it is not possible to compromise. If we let ourselves be sidetracked in our minds to investigate the methods used we will arrive nowhere. Nowhere in the world do people use only legitimate methods. If someone is convinced of his views he will use all the methods available.

Anna Freud's view is not only worldly, but extraordinarily cynical. Klein, considerably taken aback by her attitude, now realized that Anna had interpreted her willingness to cooperate as "weakness and insincerity."

Glover was immensely pleased with his speech and sent copies of it to absent members, including W. D. Fairbairn in Scotland and Dr. David Slight, who was by now professor of psychiatry at the University of Chicago. Slight had met Glover only once in his life, in the summer of 1932, when the latter advised him to go into analysis with Klein. His immediate reaction to Glover's speech was: "My goodness, what's the matter with Glover?" and he wondered if he were ill.[36]

Glover had overstepped himself at the May meeting. There was a widespread feeling of outrage (not shared by Anna Freud) that his figures were inaccurate and his charges irresponsible. For the first time Melanie Klein began to think seriously about setting up an alternate Society. It was intolerable of Glover to insinuate that she had been using her position on the Training Committee to obtain candidates for her group in a roundabout way, and she objected particularly to his claim that there were eight, possibly nine "Kleinian" training analysts. The charge seemed particularly ludicrous in view of the fact that either Glover or Jones (sometimes Payne) habitually interviewed prospective candidates.

Marjorie Brierley now expressed regret that the idea of private seminars had been abandoned. Shocked by the atmosphere of the May meetings, she suggested a temporary armistice from charges and countercharges. At the same time, she felt impelled to voice her own misgivings about Klein's work:

> It does seem to me a simple fact that, up to now, your own attitude and that of your closest adherents, about your work, has been felt by many members to be a difficulty in the way of getting to grips with the work itself. This statement does not impugn either your work or yourself and is definitely not made with hostile intent. The intent is to make clear what I believe to be a very real source of difficulty and a disadvantage all round. My own relations with you and your friends have always been amicable, and I hope they may remain so, but this has not prevented my feeling profoundly uneasy about this matter of attitude to work, and this uneasiness has certainly not been confined to me. Various labels have been attached to this subtle something in attitude from time to time. They might be summed up in the phrase "inadequately scientific."[37]

Brierley's mind and Klein's could not have been more different: one rigid and analytic, the other intuitive and adventuresome. Never the twain could meet. There was an arrogance about Brierley, a trait Klein herself was later accused of. It is amazing, given the condescending tone of this letter, that Klein did not explode. On the same day Brierley wrote to Klein, the latter had dinner with Sylvia Payne, and reported to Joan Riviere on her impressions of Payne's mood:

> She is tired, exhausted, and very hopeless about the whole situation. . . . I think her mood has changed, not only because as time goes on one gets more tired, but also because the last Business Meeting seemed to her so

catastrophic as regards the situation with the Viennese. I think she was very bucked by my previous wish to cooperate with the Viennese, and had set her hopes on a possible compromise or cooperation with them. She seems very doubtful about that now, and naturally the whole situation then becomes much more difficult—I should say quite hopeless. Dr. Payne told me that Anna Freud had not wished to coalesce with Glover but she agreed with me that A.F. would probably think it the best way if we withdrew, though she still thinks A.F. would not use such methods as Glover does. She was not clear about all this, but it was quite obvious to me that that has contributed much to her despondency as regards the situation in the Society.[38]

"I think we must face the fact that the situation in the Society is incurable," Klein concluded sadly. Overcoming her momentary despair, she was determined that her supporters stay in the Society—especially as she saw little prospect that they would be voted out; but they should consider restricting themselves to a minimal part in its proceedings. "And as regards the Viennese discussions I shall not resist it if they are arranged, but I cannot really see that much can come from them, though I am still willing to try." Looking ahead to the period after the summer holidays, she suggested that their study group meet fortnightly to discuss theoretical questions and those of technique on alternate evenings. "It is absolutely essential that we make ourselves completely independent of the rot in the Society and keep our work alive."

A letter from Payne to Klein, dated May 24, 1942, reflects Payne's disillusionment with Glover:

I have studied Glover's speech. He says that there are 8 or 9 of your adherents among training analysts. The following are the actual names. Klein, Riviere, Rickman, Isaacs, Winnicott, Scott (control of child analysis and lectures). To these names he *must* be adding Wilson and Sheehan-Dare.* I propose to say that his figures are open to argument and must include 2 members who could contend that their technique is the ordinary Freudian except for children or special cases. I do not know who the possible 9th is. I also intend to say, unless something happens to make it inadmissible to go into details, that you have had only 4 candidates since 1929, and other people have had more. Of course this is not at all due to no vacancy, but it shows that you have not been grabbing candidates in order to increase your influence.

It is an extremely difficult thing to decide what the best way to handle

---

* Dr. A. C. Wilson and Helen Sheehan-Dare accepted many Kleinian ideas, but refused to be described as "adherents" of anyone.

this situation is as direct attack on Glover gets you nowhere and alienates all the Viennese.[39]

Klein sent this letter on to Joan Riviere, whose reaction was as intractable as ever:

> I am afraid I can never adopt fully the point of view of such opportunism as seems to come naturally to Payne and in a way to you. I cannot accept that the few odd members, and mostly Viennese, at these meetings, are to determine everything that is done according to what they *want* and what they *like*.[40]

Turning to Brierley's letter: "As for a truce, can she make Melitta or Glover, or some of the Viennese stop being offensive?" Riviere suggested that Klein ask Brierley to define privately what she meant by the "unscientific" approach of their work rather than prolonging the conflict at a meeting—a not unreasonable proposal.

The influence of Riviere in strengthening Klein's backbone is apparent in a long letter Klein wrote in reply to Payne. More important than the fact that she had had only four candidates since 1929 was Glover's "insinuation that I have used all sorts of underhand methods to gain power." As long as these accusations were allowed to stand, she and her friends were being treated like outlaws in the Society. She realized that Payne must feel as though she were a champion of lost causes, "But make no mistake—*this is not a lost cause*. It may be a lost cause to the Society, which seems to prove more and more its incapacity to behave scientifically and to be a judge about the development of psycho-analysis."

> Anna's revulsion and hostility to my work has very deep roots, and only if the situation in the Society had been differently handled might she have felt that she must tread more warily. As it is now, when it seems that the British Society is going to let its affairs be conducted by the Viennese, she has no motive to restrain herself . . . though *I am still willing* to start discussions with her and to be patient, I have never thought that the prospects for these discussions are very good,—all the more as their avowed purpose is now not so much to clarify issues and to further cooperation, but to come to a decision *whether or not my work is to be acknowledged* as psycho-analysis. As the situation must appear to her, I have lost my standing and am unsupported. It is clear that to get rid of me must seem to her by far the simplest way of dealing with the situation. But if the Society is to be ruled by the Viennese and they are going to decide what is right or wrong

in psycho-analytic theory and practice, this is not altogether going to please the English members as much as it may appear now.[41]

Marjorie Brierley tried to explain what she meant by describing Klein's work as "inadequately scientific": "I called it a 'subtle something' because it is intangible. To my mind it is far more a matter of mental attitude and emotional atmosphere than of words and deeds."[42]

If her theories were so lacking in scientific rigor, Klein then demanded of Brierley, why was it that Jones, at the public dinner in his honor on the occasion of his sixtieth birthday, had said that no analyst had done more for Freud's work than Mrs. Klein?

The Extraordinary Meeting of June 10 was well attended, and for the first time Alix Strachey was present, as well as John Bowlby, who had been transferred from Edinburgh to Watford on an Officer Selection Board. So many people (thirty-one) had made an effort to turn out because the crucial question of elections was to be discussed, as well as Brierley's armistice resolution:

1. That the Society immediately pass a self-denying ordinance in respect of all current charges and counter charges, and all activities directed against individual Members or groups of Members.
2. That the Society require all Members to refrain from personal attack or innuendo in discussion, but also, strongly affirm the right of all Members to complete freedom of speech within the limits of common courtesy.[43]

The resolution was passed unanimously.

Adrian Stephen then argued passionately for the necessity of regular election of officers. Yet there were still a number of members arguing that the middle of the war was no time for a change; and John Bowlby addressed himself to this issue as one who had been away in the army for two years. In his experience there was a great deal of interest in Freud's work among military personnel, and he himself had been canvassing for more psychoanalysts in the army. "The Society has been insulated," he stated bluntly. "There is far more demand for psycho-analysis than is appreciated. Psycho-analysis has arrived at a time when the Society was concentrated in a few hands."

A committee was then appointed to look into the matter of the election and length of tenure of officers and to report at the General Meeting in July, although the Emergency Board was to continue for another year. A series of carefully monitored scientific discussions on the theoretical differences within the Society was to be held. Finally, the Training Committee was to consider the effect on the training of candidates of the current scientific controversies and to make recommendations. The public recriminations of the past four months had come to an end; but naturally a great deal of activity continued behind the scenes.

To Dr. David Matthew in Pitlochry, Klein sent a long letter (June 15) outlining the turbulent events of the past months. She spoke of the pride she had taken in contributing to the stature of the Society. She expressed her great uneasiness about the consequences if her group defected from the Society. When Glover and Anna spoke about an "inevitable" split in the Society, Klein's impression was "that I and a handful of people should get out." However, she was convinced that a number of members, who did not necessarily subscribe to her views, would not be happy "to find themselves in one boat with Anna Freud's rigid dictate of what can or cannot be accepted in psycho-analysis."[44]

None of the resolutions attacking her had been passed. As for Klein's reaction to the people who had taken a prominent part in the Extraordinary Meetings, she remarked that "The only person who really was helpful and fair was Dr. Payne." There were times when she could have been more supportive, but Klein appreciated the weight of the burden she was carrying on her shoulders.

And Jones? She found it difficult to define his attitude. At times he was very helpful, particularly when he condemned Melitta, but he remained silent when Payne condemned Glover as well. He would occasionally indicate that he disagreed with Glover, but Klein found him "very weak and wavering."

Moreover, she was not at all hopeful about the outcome of the postponed discussions with the Viennese.

> Anna Freud is extremely dictatorial in what she thinks is right or wrong in psycho-analysis, and does not seem to me willing to accept anything which goes beyond her considered views. There is, however, one comfort—that even if these discussions were not to lead to anything they are fruitful in another way, i.e. the necessity to clarify and work out in detail the connection between the newer work and Freud's work. I have known this for years, but have not been able to do as much on this line as is necessary. It will of course need years, and the cooperation of a number of people, to carry this out.

The papers presented at the study groups had been very encouraging; and she ended on a cheerful note:

> Now I shall ask you not to take these things too much to heart, because though I am conscious of the great seriousness of the situation, of its various risks and dangers, I am not disheartened, as you might think I am, through facing the facts as they are. I have a very strong conviction that this work cannot any more be killed, and though I am not yet sure in which way we are going to proceed, if I remain healthy—as I am—and if I have

some time ahead of me, as I hope I have, I feel quite sure that I shall find one way or another for myself and my collaborators to carry on and to succeed. At present I am looking to a break from all these discussions. I am quite well and already feel a little more rested after the strain of the last meetings.

To Susan Isaacs, with whom Klein was much closer than she was to Matthew, she could speak far more frankly about Jones:

What is one to think of a man like Jones, who rather lets me be accused of something he absolutely knows to be untrue and which he must know is damaging to my reputation, but which he nevertheless wishes to be allowed to stand. He would probably say that it was better to wait for the figures and numbers to be checked, or some other excuse. . . . I am definitely not disappointed in Jones, because I never expected anything from him at this juncture. It was only a pleasant surprise to me when he spoke out after Dr. Schmideberg's speech.[45]

She was looking forward to the resumption of their group discussions: "Not only is it useful and interesting for us to meet, but I really think it is a necessity for all of us to counteract the ugliness of the situation we are in. It obviously also provides us with strength, and I therefore think it is quite essential from every point of view that we should meet as often as we can arrange."

Warring Women

In the agitated correspondence passing from one Klein adherent to another there were repeated references to the dangerous power Glover wielded as director of research to the Institute. Klein believed that the office should be abolished.

When Glover was first appointed to the position in 1932 he attempted to correlate work on the psychoses, but nothing emerged from this project. He then turned his attention to the technique of psychoanalysis by means of a questionnaire circulated among the members. This new preoccupation, it would appear, was more than simply an attempt to compile scientific data, since he had already begun to protest publicly about Mrs. Klein's "deep" interpretations. The collection of the data, organized by Marjorie Brierley, proceeded at a reasonably leisurely pace. Then Glover suddenly decided to publish the findings in 1940 in *An Investigation of the Technique of Psycho-Analysis*, just at a time when his opposition was fortified by the appearance of the Viennese in their group.

The markings in Marjorie Brierley's copy of the book are remarkably interesting.* In the Prefatory Note, Glover writes: "The ideas that suggested themselves were then systematized *and subsequently checked for error by Dr. Brierley. Although Dr. Brierley is in agreement with them*, I feel it desirable to point out that the responsibility for this commentary is mine." The section italicized here is circled, and in the margin someone has inserted a deletion mark and a large question mark.

The entire book, written by Glover, is an insidious attack on Melanie Klein

---

* It is conceivable that Klein had made the markings and shown them to Brierley. One entry—"Klein!"—appears to be in Klein's handwriting. Certainly she protested to Brierley about the content and aim of the book.

and her theories. In the final chapter, "Relation of Theory to Practice," there is a long section (marked heavily) that clearly implicates Klein; yet Glover had so cunningly disguised and distorted the people discussed that there was no way Klein could defend herself.

Glover refers to "a recent meeting of the British Psycho-Analytical Society" in which a certain issue arose over the case of a young man. (Although other discussions are specifically dated, this one is not.)

> Referring to the relation of unconscious phantasies to emotional environmental influences, the speaker stated that in his view the patient's mother had had a bad influence on her son's infantile development and hence on the formation of his symptoms. Combining his analytical observations with information gathered from the patient's memories and from indirect sources (including both hearsay and direct observations made by relatives), he concluded that the mother had aroused considerable hate in the child (who had, he believed, sensed the mother's true character with fair accuracy) and at the same time stimulated his guilt to such an extent that it blocked all direct expression of the hate.[1]

In the subsequent discussion some members (clearly Kleinians) objected that this one case did not justify generalizations without comprehensive investigations into the whole subject of the relations of babies to mothers—"hence, that the reports on this particular case were not sufficiently unbiased and objective." Glover then revealed that he had been the original consultant, and that conclusions were based on reports from relatives.

> Examination of these reports on the mother's character from her daughter, her son-in-law, and some of her friends (including one from a friend who had known her from her childhood) proved fairly conclusively that the analyst and the patient were correct in their estimates. The mother had, in fact, had a consistent policy throughout her life of emotionally exploiting dependents, especially her children, and preventing any exhibition of resentment by making them feel guilty. She had a high opinion of herself as a mother but was, in fact, self-aggrandising, tyrannical, and selfish. People who did not know her well were inclined to fall in with her version of herself and to show considerable devotion to her interests. When they became more intimate they developed strong hostility to her emotional steam-rollering. It should be clear that this proof of the existence of a really "bad" mother does not do away with the necessity for exploring the patient's own sadism, nor does it exclude the part played by his own impulses in creating his pathological anxieties. It does suggest, however, that such anxieties are readily reinforced by external factors. It also throws some light on the way

in which theory may influence practice, for it suggests in no uncertain
manner that, had the case been analysed by one of the more severe critics,
the interpretations would have glossed over the environmental factors and
accentuated the endopsychic factors. Such interpretations would, in this
instance, have been unbalanced, and would have tended to maintain guilt
rather than to ventilate plain hostility. In fact, the analyst would have
continued the mother's own policy of playing an intolerant super-ego
role to the patient's own id. This case may or may not be an exceptional
one. But at least it does underline the risk that preconceived theoretical
views can influence the process of interpretation unfavourably as well as
favourably.[2]

It is not at all unlikely that Glover, by making the patient a man, and using the
supporting evidence of Melitta, Walter Schmideberg, and possibly Melanie's
sister Emilie (who had settled in England by then), was creating a fictitious situation in which the only way Klein could defend herself would be to say that
he was lying or distorting facts.

And what about Jones's possible acquiescence in the publication of the
book? He could have been unaware of its contents or of the plans for its publication. Analysts who remember him describe him as sly, devious, autocratic,
sarcastic, yet it is hard to believe that he would have allowed Glover to humili-
ate Klein in this fashion. Glover, in his powerful position, might not have felt it
necessary to submit the manuscript to Jones, even though it was one of the
Research Supplements to the *International Journal of Psycho-Analysis*. Furthermore, it was published at a time when Jones was spending all his time in
his country house.

During the Extraordinary Meetings some of the members seemed to think
that Klein was carrying her animosity to Glover to extremes. For instance,
when Susan Isaacs approached Ella Sharpe about her position, the latter said,
"You are very angry with Glover, aren't you?" Given wartime conditions, it is
probable that most of the members had not had the opportunity to read
Glover's book. This is apparent from an exchange between Klein and Helen
Sheehan-Dare. Klein wrote to ask her whether she was an "out-and-out" Klein
supporter, as Glover had maintained. This she had to ascertain in her attempt
to prove that Glover's figures were exaggerated.

I should hate you to be labelled this way, because if you do not feel you
have subscribed yourself heart and soul, as it were, to what is now considered a kind of creed, you should be able to say so. It is of course complete
nonsense and unscientific, and only motivated by partisan feelings and political points of view to label people in this way.[3]

From Exeter, where she was teaching in a school, Sheehan-Dare replied on June 24, 1943:

> It is not, as you know well, that I don't appreciate all I have learnt from you, and all the help you have given me; it's the principle of the thing I object to. It's *years* since I read or had the opportunity of reading your article on manic-depressive states . . . haven't even read Dr. Glover's book . . . but even if I fully understood and heartily agreed with every word of it, I should still object to being called an "adherent" of yours! It seems to me so dangerously near to party politics which leave one no real freedom of expression. I'm not an "adherent" of any one person within the Society nor likely to become so!!![4]

Those who accuse Melanie Klein of compelling members to choose which group they sided with should consider that Glover bears much of the responsibility for forcing her into a position where she became more intransigent as the years passed.

Klein was now resolved somehow to get back into the center of London because, despite her incredible stamina, the long trip back and forth between her temporary home in Pinner, north of London, and her consulting rooms in Nottingham Place was tiring and time-consuming. She also wanted to resume child analysis because, except for Dr. Winnicott's supervisions, Anna Freud had carved out for herself a monopoly in that field while Klein was absent.

On June 27, she set down policy for her group: none of them would announce a paper before agreement had been reached on its general lines, and at least two or three people should read it over prior to presentation.

> We are now regarded, at least for the moment, as people who are liable to be quarrelsome. This fiction could I think be disproved, as far as proofs will be accepted, through our attitude. This has in fact been more or less our policy in recent years—apart from occasional lapses, which I think we should avoid. It seems to me that it is of no particular value for us to prove that the others are lacking in knowledge, or go wrong in this or that point, but to show that we have something to convey to them which at least some of them can accept. What counts, I think, is to re-establish our position in the Society in respect to the actual value of our work, and that can only be done patiently by giving them at a time no more than they can digest, and also present it in a way which makes this possible for them. . . . I find it necessary, both for the discussions in the Society and with Anna Freud and for our own sake, to refresh our memory on every word Freud has written. This would be a sure foundation from which our discussions can start, and

then we might even be able among other things to meet the "Viennese Freudians" on their own ground.[5]

Later, during the Controversial Discussions, it was clear how profoundly Isaacs and Heimann had absorbed her advice to study psychoanalytic literature thoroughly.

The Training Committee on June 29, 1942, brought a number of issues to a head. Sylvia Payne produced a table of figures of candidates trained between 1927 and 1942 which completely disproved Glover's charges that the Kleinians dominated the training of candidates.* It was decided that the child seminars for students should be divided between Anna Freud and Melanie Klein in conjunction with Donald Winnicott. Glover wanted further meetings in the autumn to be held in order to ascertain how the differences in training and technique were affecting the students. Anna Freud replied firmly that she did not want any discussion to develop into a conflict between two people; and she certainly did not see why she should be compelled to give an exposition of Freudian technique. To Marjorie Brierley, who had left the meeting before Anna Freud made her statement, Melanie Klein sent the following report:

> She was quite indignant at the T.C. meeting at the idea that people should speak of "her" point of view, or of the "continental" point of view, *because she had no view of her own.* She made it clear that she represented her father's views (which according to her are absolutely binding for all who claim to be psycho-analysts). This is obviously a fallacy. . . . Moreover, even if Freud in his later years had completely agreed with every word Anna now states, that would still not bind those of us who think that we are entitled to continue his findings in the way our work leads us.[6]

Klein then sent around a memorandum stating that she and her friends "cannot cooperate when we are under this cloud," although, as she told Jones, "it is my wish to observe and maintain the spirit of the armistice resolution."[7]

Jones, in his role of impartial chairman, had done nothing to defend Klein at the Extraordinary Meetings. On June 26 he wrote to her that he had read her memorandum with great interest; he assured her that he was

> in a position to be able personally to corroborate every word of it. I am sure most of the Society is heartily sick of the wrangling, which only three or four members enjoy. I hope and expect that the Annual Meeting will go off without any of these indulgences. I feel convinced that if the Society shows a firm front it would be well possible to prevent a few members from holding up our scientific progress which after all is much more interesting.[8]

* See Appendix A.

At the Annual General Meeting on July 29, 1942, it was decided that one Scientific Meeting a month would be devoted to a discussion of scientific differences—a series that have come to be termed the Controversial Discussions. A committee of three members—Glover, Brierley, and James Strachey—was formed to organize the program. The first Scientific Meeting would be held in October 1942.

For a brief period there was a respite. It now proved possible to make the house in Clifton Hill habitable, and Klein spent most of the August break trying to resume a normal home life.

October 21 marked the real beginning of the famous Controversial Discussions. Glover, as chairman, announced that the first topic chosen by the committee for the discussion of scientific differences was the role of introjection and projection of objects in the early years of development, and that Susan Isaacs had been asked to deliver a paper on the subject. He proposed that a year be devoted to the discussions. He then stepped down from the chair and, speaking as a private member, stated that the present controversies centered around the theories of Melanie Klein, and the onus of proof always lay with those advancing new views. Neither Anna Freud nor any of her colleagues had aroused controversy by "advancing heterodox views." As to the method of investigation, he suggested the consideration of the following questions:

a) What is the evidence on which the view is based?
b) Is the view valid?
c) If not yet proven, is it nevertheless a plausible assumption?
d) If valid, is that validity general or does the view in question apply only in certain types of cases?
e) Is it incompatible with accepted Freudian teaching?
f) If it does contradict Freudian teaching, which part does it contradict and what is the more accurate view?
g) Does the new view by overemphasis or shift of emphasis or in some other way in effect contradict Freudian teaching?

Anna Freud thanked Glover for his amplification of the issues, but Glover replied that his remarks did not constitute an amplification of the committee's report, which had already been circulated, but represented his personal views. At this point Klein intervened to point out that her work did not necessarily deviate from Freud's views, to which Anna Freud replied that the two theories could not coexist, and the first aim of the Discussions was to ascertain which was the more accurate. Sylvia Payne made the weary comment that Anna Freud and Glover's attitudes were tantamount to coming to a conclusion before discussion had even taken place. Susan Isaacs declared that she had come to the meeting full of hope, but Dr. Glover had attempted "to queer the pitch." Dr. Brierley stated that Glover had made his speech despite the objections of the other members of the committee.

Anna Freud reminded the Society that she and Glover were not bringing up a new issue. It had been known for years that the views of the English School were different from those of any other psychoanalytic society, to which Klein replied that the British Society had taken pride in her theories and that there were no issues other than the usual theoretical differences.

Isaacs also objected to having the topic of introjection and projection foisted on her, since it covered too much ground for one paper, and suggested as an alternative that she speak on the place of phantasy in relation to the mechanisms of introjection and projection. The suggestion had come from Anna Freud, who considered it the most controversial of Klein's concepts, but Isaacs argued that an exposition of phantasy would provide the most accessible route to Klein's views on the early development of the ego and the superego and the importance of internal objects.

An interesting exchange was then initiated by Dr. Elizabeth Rosenberg, who questioned what "accepted Freudian teaching" really was. Glover did not see any problem here: all one had to do was read Freudian literature. Not at all, Rosenberg replied: Freud's views changed considerably during the course of his life, particularly about the importance of actual sexual experience. Finally, it was suggested that papers be circulated prior to meetings. When Dr. Payne objected that the cost would be prohibitive, Michael Balint proposed that anyone who wanted a paper should contribute a pound, which was about the only arrangement greeted with unanimity.

In the last Scientific Meeting of the year—December 16, 1942—Melitta Schmideberg objected to the introduction of any radical alterations in the Society (viz., voting for new officers, etc.) while so many members were absent, but added that "it is not any more in the power of anybody to stop the avalanche." The Controversial Discussions had got off to an inauspicious start.

The Discussions were dominated by women—and what women they were! Anna Freud, in addition to Dorothy Burlingham, received articulate support from Kate Friedlander, Barbara Lantos, Hedwig Hoffer, Barbara Low, and by now Ella Sharpe. (Melitta Schmideberg refrained from actually allying herself with Anna Freud.) The continental males, like Foulkes, Hoffer, and Walter Schmideberg, were not very effective. The Kleinian position was represented by Heimann, Riviere, and Isaacs, and Sylvia Payne. Eva Rosenfeld tried to remain invisible, which was possible since she spent half the week in Oxford. The male members of the Klein group were often absent because of wartime duties—Money-Kyrle, Rickman, Scott, and Winnicott. James Strachey tried to maintain an absolutely neutral position. Marjorie Brierley cast herself in the role of honest broker. It might seem puzzling why someone as relatively junior as Heimann was chosen to speak rather than Riviere, but the latter made it clear that she would no longer act as a "scapegoat" in the way she felt Jones had allowed her to be in Vienna, where she presented the controversial material while he confined himself to platitudes. Jones conveniently shrank into the heart of the country, excusing his absence with a plea of ill health. During 1943 he suffered a series of psychosomatic illnesses from which he miraculously recovered by the end of the Controversial Discussions. In 1938 he had written to Anna Freud: "Mrs. Klein is very worried. . . . She stands in a small minority in the Society with much opposition. My place as President is to bring about free and useful discussion to prevent unfair prejudice and to bring as much cooperation and harmony as is possible among psycho-analysts."[9] By surrendering leadership to Glover he must have been aware that the cards were being stacked against Klein. Glover was not capable of handling a group of vocal women, especially when his own former analysand, Melitta, the Electra of the piece, was filling the role of shrill chorus of vituperation.

The speakers were Susan Isaacs, Paula Heimann, and Melanie Klein.[10] Their principal endeavor was to demonstrate that their views had been a natural development from those of Freud, and that despite the disclaimers of Anna Freud and Edward Glover at the October 21 meeting, Freudian theories did not form a coherent whole. The rigid Freudians tended to accept the early Freud, while the Kleinians were more amenable to his later work, even accepting the death instinct, which most Freudians passed over in embarrassed silence.

Isaacs's crucial paper, "The Nature and Function of Phantasy," was distributed among the members before the first discussion of it on January 27, 1943. It is among the most important papers in the history of psychoanalysis and amply demonstrates her formidable ability to organize an overwhelming mass of material and to convey the psychodrama of the infant's phantasy life. She set out first to define the enlarged concept of phantasy. Freud's English translators had spelled this word with a "ph" to emphasize the psychoanalytic meaning of the term, as opposed to "fantasy," which refers to conscious daydreams. This they did in accordance with Freud's discovery of the unconscious, of which the psychic reality is phantasy; Isaacs described it as "the mental representative and corollary of instinctual urges." Freud's "hallucinatory wish-fulfilment" and his "primary introjection" are the basis of phantasy life; and Klein's particular contribution had been "to show us in more detail than anyone else, and with more vividness and immediacy of understanding, what a person experiences in regard to his inner objects, what they mean to him and how they affect his development." Unconscious phantasies are the primary content of all mental processes. In a phrase that has often been quoted, she contended that "Phantasy is the mental corollary, the psychic representative of instinct."

Freud had emphasized the relation between phantasy and wish fulfillment, but in Klein's experience phantasy also served other purposes—denial, reassurance, reparation, omnipotent control. In other words, at the beginning of life defense mechanisms are already operating. However, phantasies continue to exert an uninterrupted and omnipresent influence throughout life, both in normal and in neurotic people.

As evidence, Isaacs goes into long descriptions of infantile behavior during the first year of life, indications that the child engages in mental activity before he can formulate his thoughts into words. She reminded her colleagues that even Waelder had accepted the fact that a child of three can nurse aggressive phantasies against its mother's body—"But it will be remembered that not so very long ago the existence of such phantasies was, first, unheard of, and then strongly challenged"—namely, by Anna Freud.

Isaacs contended that in Anna Freud's *Young Children in War Time* (1942), her views seem to have been modified. In her description of disturbances in babies of less than a year when separated from their mothers, and in her references to the "mother-image in the mind," Isaacs finds correspondences to the child's introjection of his mother. Even in *The Ego and the Mechanisms of Defence* (1936) Anna Freud had written:

> According to the theory of the English school of analysis, introjection and projection, which in our view should be assigned to the period after the ego has been differentiated from the outside world, are the very processes by which the structure of the ego is developed . . . the chronology of psychic processes is still one of the most obscure fields of analytical theory. . . . It will probably be best to abandon the attempt so to classify them . . . [namely, in time].[11]

Freud believed that early instinctual drives affect later development only through regression, but Isaacs argues that such a postulate might have been formulated differently if these inferences had not been confined to reconstructions from adults and older children. Moreover, in the first stages of infancy, life is generally far from pleasurable, so that these early "not me" impingements form the basis of persecutory fears. Trying to draw Anna Freud out, Isaacs made a preliminary remark prior to the discussion of her paper:

> What I feel is that if a disinterested and intelligent reader, who knew nothing of the controversies within our Society, were to peruse both Melanie Klein's book and recent papers, and this Report by Anna Freud and Mrs. Burlingham, it would never occur to such a reader that there were or could be such deep and radical differences of underlying theory and view of the child's inner life and development, as is being claimed. I should be extremely interested to hear from Anna Freud whether she does feel that

there are such deep and radical differences, and how these are reconciled in her Report.

Isaacs's paper aroused so much interest that all the Scientific Meetings until May 19 were devoted to it. In the course of the Discussions, it became apparent that on certain issues various members held mutually irreconcilable views; but at least there was an impressive attempt to clarify theoretical concepts, a welcome change from the backbiting of the Extraordinary Meetings the previous year.

Jones did not attend the Discussions, but his statement was read by Glover, who must have found it a very galling experience to have to say that Jones believed Isaacs had succeeded admirably in establishing as nearly as possible a noncontroversial basis in her paper. Jones agreed that the word "phantasy" was appropriate, since it extended the meaning of the original concept, and he saw no difference between phantasy and Freud's hallucinatory wish fulfillment. His only point of disagreement was that she had not stated clearly enough that defense phantasies were not only wish fulfillments but derived from instinctual needs. In other words, he was suggesting that there was nothing here with which Freud would have fundamentally disagreed.

Glover immediately countered with the assertion that Isaacs was erecting a new metapsychology. Anna Freud elaborated on this, contending that emphasis on stages of development was transferred to the very earliest period—an emphasis that would be bound to have dramatic consequences for the technique of psychoanalytic treatment.

Sylvia Payne fully endorsed Isaacs's paper. In her concluding remarks she reminded her colleagues that whereas Freud had regarded the resolution of the Oedipus complex as the most important psychological event in the development of mental health, at the same time he recognized that "developmental difficulties could arise before the Oedipus Conflict was fully developed."

Dorothy Burlingham, Anna Freud's co-worker, objected to Isaacs's interpretation of their report, *Young Children in War Time.* What they had said about the relationship of the child to the mother in the second half of the first year was "purely based on the gratification of bodily needs." A memory image and an introjected object were worlds apart.

Melitta Schmideberg did not appear at the meeting, but in her brief submitted contribution complained that Isaacs had mentioned only her supportive statements of the Kleinian position in the past, with no reference to her numerous criticisms. "Such blatant omission is contrary to scientific tradition and spirit. It is the lack of these that makes it impossible for me to take Dr. Isaacs' paper seriously."

Michael Balint could understand the logic of the term "phantasy," but was deeply disturbed by the content of these phantasies as described by Klein with their "undue emphasis on the role of hatred, frustration, and aggression in the infant."

At the next meeting (February 17, 1943), Glover read a paper sent in by W. D. Fairbairn, the only practicing analyst in Edinburgh. Independently of Klein, Fairbairn was arriving at seemingly compatible conclusions, although with time the emphasis shifted in significant respects. In Fairbairn's view, the ego was not primarily pleasure-seeking, but object-seeking. At this point he considered the word "phantasy" as obsolete and suggested substituting "psychical reality" or "internal objects." In an epoch-making statement, he declared,

> . . . in my opinion the time is now ripe for us to replace the concept of "phantasy" by a concept of an "inner reality" peopled by the Ego and its internal objects. These internal objects should be regarded as having an organised structure, an identity of their own, an endopsychic existence and an activity as real within the inner world as those of any object in the outer world. To attribute such features to internal objects may at first seem startling to some, but, after all, they are only features which Freud has already attributed to the Super-Ego. What has now emerged is simply that the Super-Ego is not the only internal object. The activity of the internal objects like that of the Ego is, of course, ultimately derived from the impulses originating in the Id. Nevertheless, subject to this proviso, these objects must be regarded as having an activity of their own. Inner reality thus becomes the scene of situations involving relationships between the Ego and its internal objects. The concept of "phantasy" is purely functional and can only be applied to activity on the part of the Ego. It is quite inadequate to describe inner situations involving the relationships of the Ego to internal objects possessing an endopsychic structure and dynamic qualities.

In the interval allotted to her for rebuttal, Isaacs focused on Anna Freud's remarks at the previous meeting. Claiming that a great advance in the settling of the differences at issue could be established if the members concentrated on the first year of life, Isaacs quoted from Freud's "Turnings in the Way of Psycho-Analytic Theory" (1919): "You know that we have never been proud of the fullness and finality of our knowledge and capacity; as at the beginning, we are ready now to admit the incompleteness of our understanding, to learn new things and to alter our methods in any way that yields better results."[*][12] Turning directly to Anna Freud, Isaacs reminded her that her father had also said that we *all* have an inveterate prejudice in favor of external reality.

---

* The wording is slightly different in the translation of the paper "Lines of Advance in Psycho-Analytic Therapy" in the Standard Edition.

To Isaacs's disappointment, Anna Freud and Mrs. Burlingham refused to be drawn into any discussion about psychic life prior to the second year. Anna Freud continued to insist that the pleasure principle was "the sole governing principle within the unconscious," yet Freud, in reference to dreams of traumatic neurosis in *Beyond the Pleasure Principle*, had said this:

> They thus afford us an insight into a function of the psychic apparatus, which without contradicting the pleasure-principle, is nevertheless independent of it, and appears to be of earlier origin than the aim of attaining pleasure and avoiding pain.[13]

Again and again Isaacs hammered home that it was Klein, not Freud's own daughter, whose views derived from Freud's; and "Where they differ, they are a necessary development of his own work, arrived at by making use, with very young children, of Freud's own instrument of discovering the transference." Isaacs was saddened by the assumption that Freud's ideas were to be developed no further.

While these discussions on hatred and aggression were taking place an air raid started, but the members were so absorbed in their own battle that they remained glued to their seats. Indeed, Winnicott had to draw their attention to the uproar outdoors: "I should like to point out that there is an air raid going on." Margaret Little, who was a student at the time, recalled, "I wondered what in the world I was getting into."[14] At the next meeting, on March 7, the chairman, Glover, felt that it was expedient to decide what action should be taken if another air raid occurred during the meeting. It was agreed that the meeting should be stopped temporarily to allow members who had responsibilities at home to leave, and the others should carry their chairs to the basement to continue the discussion. In fact there was no decrease in the numbers attending the meetings until the late autumn.

In the discussion of April 7, Anna Freud was finally compelled to state her position. An eloquent speaker, she was always noted for the clarity of her extemporaneous perorations, quite obviously modeled on those of her father. The outstanding difference between Klein's views and her own, she declared, was that the former believed object relations begin soon after birth, whereas she had no reason to alter her view that there is a narcissistic and autoerotic phase of several months' duration preceding object relations. The infant, rather than loving, hating, desiring, attacking, dismembering its mother, "is at this time exclusively concerned with his own well-being. The mother is important so far as she serves or disturbs this well-being. She is an instrument of satisfaction or denial, and as such of extreme importance in the child's narcissistic scheme of things." She then put two questions to Isaacs, questions which were in effect formulations.

1. One of the outstanding differences between Freudian and Kleinian theory is, that Mrs. Klein sees in the first months of life evidence of a wide range of differentiated object-relations, partly libidinal and partly aggressive. Freudian theory on the other hand allows at this period only for the crudest rudiments of object-relationship and sees life governed by the desire for instinct gratification, in which perception of the object is only achieved slowly.

2. The assumption of early object-phantasies in Mrs. Klein's theories is bound up with the theoretical substitution in a very early stage of rich and varied object-relationship, for the early phase of narcissism and auto-erotism as described by Freud.

Then, in what was perhaps the only time she referred to the death instinct, she shrewdly manipulated Freud's theory into an interpretation of her own:

The early phantasies most frequently described in Kleinian theory, are violently aggressive phantasies. This seems logical to the analysts who are convinced of the preponderance of the death-instinct at the beginning of life. The existence of these same phantasies is widely questioned by those to whom the libidinal impulses seem of overwhelming importance for this time of life. Again, the underlying difference of opinion does not refer directly to phantasy-activity but, partly to dating as before, and partly to a divergence of views about instinct-theory.

What is one to make of Anna's intransigence? Freud himself described her as a sort of Antigone, and now the daughter of Oedipus was guarding the sacred ashes. That she was analyzed by her own father must have had an inestimable influence upon an impressionable young woman, and in 1931, in *Female Sexuality*, he acknowledged that he had paid inadequate attention to the child's attachment to its mother. In 1926, in *Inhibitions, Symptoms and Anxiety*, written when he was seventy, Freud gave his first systematic attention to separation anxiety. Anna Freud and Melanie Klein were both aware that they were unwanted children, whose fathers had preferred their older sisters; and this affected them, in different ways, all their lives. The relationship of each woman with her mother is possibly even more important. These personal factors suggest interesting possibilities for the reasons psychoanalysis diverged into two very different directions.

In response to Anna Freud's statement about the infant's narcissism, Sylvia Payne asked her why she did not think the child regarded the mother as an object during its first year. Anna replied that she was referring only to the first half year, and that there were quantitative differences between attitude towards an object in this narcissistic phase and object attitudes at later stages. At this point

Glover seemed to think that he had the right to summarize the question and answer "for the sake of clarity in the records." "Dr. Payne asks whether the varying behaviour of the child when fed by different objects does not imply the existence of an object-relationship in embryo, to which Miss Freud replies that these variations are due to differences in the conditioning and do not imply that an object-relationship exists in the first half-year"—a distortion of what Anna Freud had actually said.

Finally, Glover, whose past statements Isaacs had frequently quoted as endorsing Klein's views, made a public recantation of his former theories: "If any proof were needed that my former belief was much too optimistic if not indeed profoundly mistaken, it is to be found in the present discussions between child analysts in our society."

Melanie Klein had not yet taken any part in the Discussions, but followed every detail with the closest attention. Just before going off to a farm in Warwickshire for the Easter break, she wrote Susan Isaacs a long letter on April 9, full of suggestions for Isaacs's formal reply to her critics to be delivered at the Scientific Meeting on May 19. Since one of the major aims of the Discussions was to clarify what school had the right to represent Freud's views, Klein believed that

> . . . it is quite essential for the whole success of our discussions to show how much has been and *is being accepted* which has already become part of psycho-analysis in the full sense of the word. An instance is the attitude towards Waelder's paper. Everybody who reads this paper must get the impression that at this point Waelder *did not believe* that phantasies are active before the third year of life, and this impression was quite general and supported by other writings of the Viennese, not the least by A.F.'s books. They now *realize* that phantasies start much earlier than they thought, and even though not fully, admit the possibility of their being even active in the first year of life. This means that they gave up the idea that preverbal phantasies are not possible. . . . Now all this amounts to the fact that differences have whittled down to some degree and what they have learnt from us and accepted quite a lot—for instance also the greater emphasis on aggression and aggressive phantasies, and I think even the concept of reparation (though not at the early stage), is now being admitted which some years ago was completely abhorrent to them, sticking as they did to the concept of "reaction formation" only.[15]

Of course Anna Freud would never acknowledge that she had accepted anything from "the English School." Twice she evaded Isaacs's question about the baby's grief at the disappearance of the mother—"*conscious and deliberate dishonesty,*" according to Klein, which must not be allowed to pass. Glover's seemingly frank and sincere regret about his past mistakes was "sheer farce," in Klein's view. By not stating explicitly what he disowned, this vague disclaimer enabled him to retain what suited his purposes. Klein therefore proposed that Isaacs pin him down on what concepts he was abandoning. She doubted that this included his own work on drug addiction, "which was largely based on my work, corroborating and expanding it."

That very day Klein had seen her doctor, "a general practitioner of great experience with children," and asked her at what stage she thought object relations start with the infant. "She replied without a moment's hesitation, 'It is an axiom to me that they start at one month.' "* Klein had also talked with Winnicott the previous day, and he suggested working out the difference between the object relations of a three-week-old mentally deficient child and a normal baby.

She then turned to the manner in which Isaacs could handle Anna Freud:

As we know, A.F. is very touchy that she should be supposed not to lay sufficient stress on the unconscious and on psychic reality. I suggested to you when you wrote your last reply that it is worth while pointing out that obviously if *we are accused of overrating* the unconscious at the expense of the conscious (which we don't agree to, but still that is the accusation) then of course we believe that *we really do lay more stress on the unconscious than they do*, and that after all my work on the earlier layers of the mind is bound up with my conviction that more stress *is* to be laid on the unconscious. In other words, though she does not think that she attributes less importance to psychic reality and to the unconscious—we do. I think it is quite as well to acknowledge this fact and we might find that this would strike a chord with others. There is another point which I think is very much worthwhile putting into relief and that is that we do believe that their concept of psycho-analysis is much more *intellectual than ours* . . . it is all *theoretical* stuff because they actually *never tried it themselves* [i.e., to understand and observe unconscious processes in children].[16]

Other letters followed in rapid succession. On May 1 she spoke about the pleasure of employing irony rather than direct attack. As for one of the points made by Anna Freud, "The idea that the child loves his body because it is handled by the mother would refer to a much more adult way of feeling. I would never attribute it to a young baby; nor do I believe that the baby would feel that it is full of good milk. It has not any conception of what milk is. It would feel though that something good, satisfactory, something which is equated with a good object, has gone into him."[17]

* Dame Annis Gillie has confirmed this conversation.

She fully agreed with Isaacs that Fairbairn's work led to absurd extremes. It is difficult to understand their strong objection to Fairbairn, particularly since he had prefaced his remarks by saying that in his opinion "the explanatory concept of 'phantasy' has now been rendered obsolete by the concepts of 'physical reality' and 'internal objects' which the work of Mrs. Klein and her followers has done so much to develop." Fairbairn seemed to be taking Kleinian theories to their logical conclusion. There are two possible explanations for her hostility to Fairbairn. In the first place, an essential part of her argument was that her theories were an extension of those of Freud, whereas Fairbairn was fearlessly saying that if we are going to a new destination, instead of starting from outworn preconceptions, one should look at the whole psychic apparatus afresh. Klein was undoubtedly resentful that Fairbairn—who had never even been analyzed!—was developing concepts similar to her own, yet was not beholden to her. As John Bowlby sees it, Klein and Anna Freud were mirror images of each other—stubborn women who refused to open up their minds to the ideas of others. Katherine Whitehorn once described them as the Valkyries of the psychoanalytical movement. According to Bowlby, Anna Freud worshipped at the shrine of St. Sigmund, and Klein at the shrine of St. Melanie. American opposition to Kleinian ideas has undoubtedly been fostered above all by Anna Freud's émigré supporters (and by the American medical profession), but since Fairbairn is being readily assimilated into American thought,* Klein's immense contribution might have been acknowledged years earlier by a wider audience if she had at least conducted a dialogue with him. Eric Trist remembers a Saturday afternoon during the forties when a group met, probably at Susan Isaacs's house, and Melanie Klein, in her low, strongly accented monotone, did not even deign to argue with Fairbairn, who vigorously persisted in trying to present his point of view.

Klein attempted to give her close supporters free rein, particularly the fiercely independent Susan Isaacs; but before Isaacs presented her final paper, Klein offered her a series of suggestions, and made it clear that she would like to see it in its final form: "In my own work I am so keen to re-read things after a while, because I have that rather slow way of finding more if I read it after a little while again; and I am so terribly keen that this paper should be as good as it can be."[18] While Isaacs was passionately involved with Klein's ideas, the latter realized that she had to be careful that she did not sound as though she were dictating to Isaacs.

After receiving a draft of the paper and discussing it at length with Heimann and Riviere, Klein sent off an *eighteen-page* letter with suggestions for additions, deletions, and emendations—most of which Isaacs embodied in the

---

* In England, Fairbairn's *Psychoanalytic Studies of the Personality* was published in London in 1952; in 1954 it appeared in the United States as *An Object Relations Theory of the Personality*. It is understandable that Americans have regarded Fairbairn as the father of object relations.

final paper, and some of which she simply ignored, such as Klein's suggestion that she omit an approving reference to Adrian Stephen. This letter provides a crucial insight into the way Klein's mind worked. No one was more impressed with her own findings than Klein was, but her comments reveal that there were many aspects of her theories about which she was still speculating; and in this letter it is almost as though she were thinking aloud, particularly in her remarks about the operation of the death instinct in the infant.

> I have been puzzling and puzzling again recently over the contradiction that the death instinct must contribute to the infant's hostile attitude towards stimuli, and all the negative phenomena towards the external world which he exhibits in the early days. Of course one might think that here the life instinct is at work as well because what he is trying to protect himself against are the stimuli felt as danger to himself. The contradiction seemed to be that thus at the beginning of life, when the infant shows such a hostile attitude towards the outer world—and this is actually the period in which I am convinced the ground is laid for persecution phantasies—yet at this time his libido is of a sucking and less sadistic nature than a few months later. . . . The libido of the new-born infant is directed towards the mother's inside where he came from, and his hostility against the external world, stimuli, etc., is bound up with this desire to be back inside her. The nipple is the nearest thing coming close to this situation, which is so strongly stressed by Freud himself as something so extremely valuable and important. . . . So one would have to say that the distribution of the libido still directed towards this internal situation and the mother's inside is part of this complicated problem according to which the destructive instinct seems less strong in connection with the breast, and yet this does not seem so in connection with the relation to the external world. One might surmise that it takes time, as we know, for the child to adjust itself to the situation outside the mother, for the distribution of the libido to be altered.

Klein wrote to Isaacs in great excitement after reading the first of Freud's Encyclopaedia articles (actually written in 1922), published in the current issue of the *International Journal of Psycho-Analysis*.

> A.F. mentions guilt and reparation in the third year. Apart from the question of reparation about which we have already talked at full length, the point of guilt is of the utmost importance against the background of the classic conception of the super-ego. You will remember that I recently suggested to you that I see a rather puzzling contradiction in Freud's paper of

1922 (last Journal) in which he says that the sexual trends are converging between two and five years, building up the Oedipus situation.* Now this is not so puzzling after all, because I remember that he speaks in other places too of the Oedipus features developing between three and five years. It is true I do not know of any other place where he said "two and five." I don't think this is so very important, because the main stress lies on the fact that the height of the Oedipus complex is between four and five years, and our main point here would be that, according to the classic concept, the super-ego and guilt are the heirs of the Oedipus complex. If guilt is now conceived as developing in the third year, it overthrows this concept. Either the Oedipus complex comes to an end earlier (which is nonsense, because actually one could not say it had arrived at its *height* at this age), or guilt is there while the Oedipus complex develops. That proves that the super-ego is not the heir of the Oedipus complex but develops much earlier. I know that you did not put this into your reply, but I do think that more emphasis, more weight, should be given to this particular point, in connection with the fact (as I have suggested to you already) that tacitly the earlier super-ego is now being accepted.

Isaacs was clearly undergoing a crisis of conscience during the preparation of her papers. To her mentor, she wrote:

One thing I want to say to you, Melanie, is that I have no doubt that you have suffered at the hands of your warmest supporters one way or another. Going over my contributions of recent years, prepared and spontaneous, I can see that my implied attitude has been too much "See how well *I* understand Melanie Klein's work—how well I can use this wonderful instrument." Too much pride of possession, too much display, without appreciating what rivalry and antagonism this would inevitably arouse. Forgive my saying this very personal—(and semi-analytic) thing. But I have been anxious to find out *where* "we" have been at fault—one knows that we must have been in *some* way and in some measure at fault—although one need not exaggerate this and blame oneself too much. But this is only one way in which I certainly have been—and perhaps others of your pupils, too. The important thing is to find out how *not* to make such mistakes and arouse *unnecessary* hostility. Some of the hostility comes simply from the greatness of your work, and would be there if we were all as wise as the serpent and as harmless as the sucking-dove. And some of it, as we know, comes from the very *nature* of your work—the inevitable anxieties it stirs up. But I do want to learn not to add to these by avoidable errors.

* See S.E., 18, p. 245.

Klein replied soothingly: "I am very lucky to have such good friends as I have and don't expect them to be superhuman as little as I can be myself. But we shall all try our best to avoid mistakes for the sake of our work."[19]

On May 9, 1943, Isaacs gave a final response to the criticisms raised during the various discussions following her original paper. Klein had referred to the pleasure of using irony in riposte, and Isaacs exploited not only irony but her capacity for clearly organizing her opponents' objections in sequential order, without sacrificing her passionate adherence to her convictions. Her response is as impressive as her original paper.

Since Melanie Klein's use of the death instinct was one of the most disturbing bones of contention, Isaacs tackled it first. To begin with, "Mrs. Klein has nowhere stated that the death instinct predominates in early infancy, *as a general condition*, and does not hold that view." Klein attributed as much importance to the libidinal as to the aggressive elements in early life. At the present state of knowledge there was no way of differentiating the quantitative fusion from individual to individual. Finally Isaacs quoted numerous examples from Freud of the sadistic character of love impulses. The importance of this was twofold: to remind her listeners that the death instinct did not appear as a sudden aberration on Freud's part in 1920, nor could Melanie Klein be tarred with exclusive concentration on it.

Anna Freud and Dorothy Burlingham assumed that their experience provided verifiable data in contrast to that of the Kleinians, but the conclusions of the latter were based on actual analyses of children. Apart from Klein's own contribution, Isaacs herself had spent her entire career with children, and Winnicott's work was based on more than twenty years as a physician observing young children. During the Discussions Anna Freud had admitted that a child in its second year was capable of phantasies, yet Dr. Waelder, representing the Viennese group, had categorically denied this in his Exchange Lecture of 1937. If the Viennese had changed their minds—as Anna Freud seemed to suggest they had—why, then, had they published nothing to this effect since 1937?

There was another matter that had to be cleared up. Lest the members be in any doubt about Klein's disagreement with Fairbairn, Isaacs asserted:

> I have not declared myself in support of Dr. Fairbairn's notion that the concept of phantasy has been rendered obsolete by the concepts of psychical reality and internal objects. I would not subscribe to such a view. Neither the concept of psychical reality nor that of internal objects is a new one. Both are Freud's discoveries. Dr. Fairbairn, to my mind, over-emphasizes and distorts certain parts of Mrs. Klein's theories to the point of caricature. He over-substantiates internal objects and makes them far too independent, leaving wishes and feelings and the id generally out of ac-

count. . . . Dr. Fairbairn's position is not to be taken as representing Mrs. Klein's work or conclusions.

Isaacs then turned to Glover, and quoted case after case where he had not only supported Klein, but had actually criticized Freud. She went on to object to the labels "Freudians" and "Kleinians" that Glover habitually used, particularly when he was acting as chairman of the Discussions. As a result, a note was attached to the minutes of May 19 noting that Glover had always vacated the chair when making personal statements.

In her concluding statement, Isaacs declared that "Mrs. Klein has been accepted about so many things; she might turn out to be right about her most recent contributions!" This was not an issue on which one side or the other could "win"; but Klein and Isaacs could congratulate themselves that they had come off very well indeed in the first round. Their objection to being termed "Kleinian" was based on their concern that they were being represented as a deviant group. In the most eloquent part of her response, Isaacs set forth a cogent argument:

> Listening to the selective accounts of Freud's theories offered by some of the contributors to this discussion, and noting their dogmatic temper, I cannot help wondering what would have happened to the development of psycho-analytic thought if for any reason Freud's work had not been continued after 1913, before the work on Narcissism and Mourning and Melancholia; or after 1919, before Beyond the Pleasure Principle and The Ego and the Id. Suppose some other adventurous thinker had arrived at these profound truths and had dared to assert them! I fear that such a one would have been treated as a backslider from the strict path of psycho-analytic doctrine, a heretic whose views were incompatible with those of Freud, and subversive of psycho-analysis.

Nevertheless, there were important ideological differences and, increasingly, political differences—so that it was not inappropriate to refer to the group as "Kleinian."

On June 10 Klein complained to Isaacs that "It is infuriating how much they misrepresent our views and how little reciprocity there is in the whole situation. I sometimes feel awfully sick and tired of it, but the one comfort is that really good papers are being produced."[20] In addition, the previous weekend had provided a pleasant respite. She had gone to Manchester, where Michael Balint and Alfred Gross had set up a psychoanalytic group. They had nine candidates who left her with a very favorable impression, and she was enormously encouraged by the organizational work Balint had done since his arrival from Budapest in 1939. She and Balint renewed their friendship of Berlin days.* She was optimistic about his support. "He seems to have strong sympathy not only with our work but also with our position, and seems quite capable of expressing this when occasion arises."[21] She gave a lecture on technique, with particular reference to transference. "I felt quite refreshed after my weekend in Manchester—it reminded me of old times when people got pleasure and benefit from what I had to say."

At a Business Meeting in June 1943 it was suggested that a medical committee be formed to examine the role of psychoanalysis in the postwar world (in view of the impending establishment of a National Health Service). One of the tasks of this committee would be to make recommendations for the future training of medical students. In the subsequent election by open vote, of the list of seven candidates, Payne received the most votes while Glover trailed at the rear. This must have shattered Glover, who regarded himself as a great medical psychiatrist, as it indicated that the nonaligned members had turned against him. John Bowlby believes that Glover resolved to resign from the Society at that moment. There was a feeling of general dissatisfaction with both Glover and Jones over what was considered their failure to do enough to establish contact with official medical bodies. According to the account Klein sent to David Matthew in Scotland, "Bowlby said that it might help the discussions very much if there was a change in the constitution. All that was done without particular emotions, and coming as it did from a different side, impressed, I think, the whole meeting as well as Glover himself. He was rather subdued and did not react, at least not at the time, with any aggression to these statements. It would also be very difficult for him to do so, because as things stand it would really mean his being in opposition to the majority of the members."[22]

At a meeting of June 26, 1943, Bowlby, seconded by William Gillespie, put forward a resolution that "No member who has served as President, Scientific Secretary, Training Secretary, or Business Secretary for three consecutive years shall be elected to the same office until two further years have elapsed." This was to lead to vital changes in the British Society.

Klein ended her letter to David Matthew on an optimistic note: "I really think that our discussions so far have very much improved my position and that of my collaborators, and that it has been very fruitful, particularly since some valuable papers have been produced." Paula Heimann's paper "Some Aspects of the Role of Introjection and Projection in Early Development" was discussed at the meeting of June 23, 1943. By this date the air raids had increased in intensity, but it was decided not to transfer the meetings from the evenings to the daytime since such a change would interfere with the members' practices. Some of the audience objected that Heimann's paper was too com-

---

* She seems to have wanted to forget that Balint had claimed at the Four Countries Conference on child analysis, organized by Anna Freud in Budapest in May 1937, that only the Hungarian School were producing *evidential* data on early object relations, in contrast to the British School.

pressed, so on October 20 she presented a more succinct summary, a rather self-defeating endeavor, as she realized, particularly as the issue had been raised by the opposition in order to convey the impression that the concepts were beyond comprehension.

Where Melanie Klein had in the past talked of an early superego, she was now concentrating on primitive internal objects that served as the nucleus of the ego, formed from projection and introjection. In the unconscious, acquiring is equivalent to devouring, giving appears as spitting or defecating, and guilt and anxiety are the concomitants of these activities. She linked the life and death instincts to these phantasies: the aim of the life instinct is the expulsion of the death instinct, which in effect cannot be expelled since it is an inherent component of the organism; but, as Freud showed, deflection is the ultimate defense against the death instinct.

Where Isaacs had tended to stress that Klein's concepts were a logical development from Freud's ideas, Heimann emphasized the dramatic consequences in technique of an acceptance of the death instinct (a point that Anna Freud had quite legitimately raised at an earlier meeting):

> It is by no means merely an academic question whether we accept the theory of the death instinct, for it cannot fail to influence profoundly our practical work; e.g., our understanding of the negative transference rests on a different basis on the light of this theory, which also holds out a prospect of a fuller comprehension of the difficult problems of projection and persecution symptoms.

In Heimann's opinion, Freud had left unresolved what happens between the time of the experience at the breast as the "unattainable prototype of every later satisfaction" and the autoerotic phase. Klein's great contribution had been to show that the breast is forever retained in the unconscious, and is not given up in the autoerotic phase. "This internalised breast forms a core for all further object relations." Indeed, "the earliest experiences lay the foundations for the type of response to people and events, those who have learned in infancy that frustration and anxiety can be quickly removed approach life with an optimistic attitude, and are capable of recovering from disappointments." The first roots of the superego are derived from the introjected "good" and "bad" breast, to which are added the good and bad parents and the good and bad penis. Consequently, the internal objects can be punitive but they can also be helpful and life-enhancing. This was an important development from Klein's earlier emphasis on a primitive superego that was predominantly terrifying.

Kate Friedlander saw this theory as contradicting one of the fundamental principles of psychoanalysis—that within the id antithetical instincts live side by side without disturbing each other. Mrs. Hedwig Hoffer insisted that the death instinct was a biological, not a psychological, hypothesis. Even Sylvia Payne felt uneasy that "introjection" and "identification" were being used indiscriminately:

> ... it is true that Freud himself and many other analysts have used the terms introjection and identification interchangeably, but Freud obviously did not do this systematically, in fact it is clear that he and other leading analysts such as Abraham came to use "introjection" as applicable to a mechanism characteristic of a primitive oral relationship to an object, while he developed the meaning of the term "identification" and applied it to certain types of relationships [between] not only people but things. At the same time he distinguished between identification and what I shall call full object love.
>
> I do not think that this confusion in the use of terms can be hastily dismissed because it has led to the increase of misunderstanding of Mrs. Klein's work and has retarded the assimilation of new ideas to old.

Susan Isaacs intervened to point out that in the infant's mind, the sense of omnipotence fuses wish and act—in other words, "A phantasy is *both* a 'figment' and a function." It was as though she were trying to explain the difference between metaphor and simile; and Glover proclaimed triumphantly that he knew that the Kleinians would sooner or later be compelled to produce a metapsychology to fit their views.

During the autumn Isaacs and Heimann worked together on their joint paper on regression. Isaacs was very musical, and whenever Heimann felt she was drying up, the former would sit down at the piano and play Bach to her. The name in German means "brook," and she offered to continue playing until Heimann felt that her thoughts were flowing again.

On December 15, 1943, the two women presented their paper. They first examined Freud's theory of regression as the principal mechanism in the establishment of mental illness when the libido is dammed up by fixation. However, they point out that this theory antedated Freud's theory of the duality of the instincts and did not take into consideration the role of aggression or account for object relations. For Klein regression does not necessarily imply the appearance of pregenital material, nor is it simply the result of frustration.

> While some analysts think of repression predominantly in terms of the libido, we see *concurrent* changes in the destructive impulses as well, i.e. they return to earlier, archaic aims. We hold that it is this *recurrence of primitive destructive aims* which is the chief causative factor in the outbreak of mental illness.

On February 16, 1944, Melanie Klein entered the general discussion for the first time. She pointed out that Freud had described the death instinct clinically in terms of aggression turned outwards. If aggression is deflected, there is a different situation from that of an inhibited neurotic who is not able to externalize hostility. Besides, her own conclusions did not stand or fall on the death instinct. Many other analysts had come to the same conclusion without believing in the death instinct. More attention should be directed to the origins of aggression, triggered by frustration, from the moment of birth.

Joan Riviere also joined the discussion in an attempt to correct Payne on her interpretation of the death instinct. Payne seemed to regard it as an instinct to kill, whereas Riviere saw it as an impulse to regain a state of health. The manifest state was an inanimate one, but the instinct must be an urge. Freud had called it a mute and silent force, but not a passive and inert one. Freud believed that aggressive tendencies arose through the deflection of the death instinct outwards into aggression and destructiveness. What Klein had observed in clinical work were the two fused impulses struggling for mastery.

Dr. Payne replied that she considered it a philosophical concept, whereas Riviere countered that it was biological. In John Bowlby's view, whatever speculation had led Freud to this concept, he saw two specific difficulties connected with it: (1) Methodologically, the death instinct was a more complicated concept than that of an aggressive instinct stimulated by frustration, which could explain phenomena fairly simply. (2) The death instinct, as conceived by Freud, was an urge to return to a state of inanimate matter. This urge is experienced and turned into an impulse to destroy things in the outer world. Riviere tried to make him see that a frustration is experienced as a threat of death. A baby who cannot get the breast has the feeling "I am going to die." Dr. Bowlby was not convinced. It could be argued, he replied, that the reason the organism cannot bear the idea of dying is due to a strong life instinct.

On this note the Controversial Discussions came to an end for the time being.

CHAPTER THREE

The Ladies' Agreement

While all the fury was let loose in the Business Meetings and the Controversial Discussions, the real struggle for power was being fought out in the Training Committee.

At the General Meeting of July 29, 1942, the Society had instructed the committee "to consider and report upon the effects of current scientific controversies upon questions of Training." There were some complaints that the Training Committee was dragging its feet because some of the members were awaiting the outcome of the Controversial Discussions.* A year later, at the General Meeting of July 21, 1943, James Strachey presented an Interim Report, in which he emphasized that the problem facing the Training Committee was not a scientific one, but political and administrative: they were dealing with questions of practical expediency that called for flexibility and compromise.

Strachey quoted from Freud's posthumously published Encyclopaedia article in the latest issue of the *International Journal:*

> Psycho-analysis is not, like philosophies, a system starting out from a few sharply defined fundamental concepts, seeking to grasp the whole universe with the help of these and, once it is completed, having no room for fresh discoveries or better understanding. On the contrary, it keeps close to the facts in its field of study, seeks to solve the immediate problems of observation, gropes its way forward by the help of experience, is always incomplete and always ready to correct or modify its theories.[1]

---

* The members of the Training Committee were Edward Glover, Sylvia Payne, Marjorie Brierley, Melanie Klein, James Strachey, John Rickman, Ella Sharpe, and Anna Freud.

Since psychoanalysis does not consist of "a few sharply defined fundamental concepts," Freud had left his followers with an administrative challenge. Strachey pointed out that "Without an omniscient leader who could impose his opinion on us" such difficulties as they were now facing were bound to recur periodically.

Strachey described the attitudes of opposing factions in the following terms:

> "Your views are so *defective* that you are incompetent to carry out a training analysis or for the matter of that any analysis at all," says one protagonist. "Your views are so *false* that you are incompetent to carry out a training analysis or for the matter of that any analysis at all," says the other protagonist.

But surely there are some criteria that can be expected of all analysts? Strachey would have thought that one could refuse the position to a person "who has never heard of the Oedipus Complex or one who believes that claustrophobia is caused by the action of moonbeams on the scalp." With heavy irony, he added that he did not believe anyone should be disqualified because he hadn't read some article of Federn's published in the *Zeitschrift* in 1926, or because he believed that the latency period set in more often during the last half of the fifth year rather than the first half of the sixth year.

Strachey admitted that Freud, despite his protestations of freedom to pursue scientific investigation, had his moments of intransigence. In this same Encyclopaedia article, Freud had said that the fundamental foundations of psychoanalysis are "the assumption that there are unconscious mental processes, the recognition of the theory of resistance and repression, the appreciation of the importance of sexuality and of the Oedipus complex," and adds that "no one who cannot accept them all should count himself a psycho-analyst."[2] Strachey asserted that such an attitude is stultifying to psychoanalytic progress:

> Would all of us regard this as an adequate criterion? Or would some of us think that it needed extension or qualification or precision before it was sufficiently exclusive? Above all, there is the question of date. Freud wrote that passage in 1922. Would he himself have been satisfied with the same test fifteen years later?

In Strachey's view, one could hold a "correct" theory and yet be a lamentable clinician. He himself (speaking for most of the members of the committee) simply could not accept that certain theories led to inevitable conclusions. Strachey was highly doubtful that Dr. Glover's questionnaire had done much to enlighten the members about their colleagues' procedure. Therefore, in the understanding that an attitude of suspended judgment should infuse their conclusions, Strachey proposed that the Training Committee set about the following task:

1. To decide, to the best of their ability, the essentials of a valid psychoanalytic technique.
2. To try to discover whether and in *what* respect the parties in the current controversies diverge from these essentials.
3. With this knowledge, to proceed to the purely political question of whether it is expedient to inhibit any of those concerned from functioning as training analysts or in any other educational capacity.[3]

Unlike Glover, who had drawn up specific questions to be answered in the earlier questionnaire, Strachey left his colleagues free to compile descriptions of their approaches in their own way. Most of the members of the committee submitted memoranda on their methods of technique, and during the latter part of 1943 lengthy discussions on the matter were held at Training Committee meetings. These documents are of remarkable interest, particularly those from the pens of Melanie Klein and Anna Freud. Anna Freud is sometimes accused of not knowing anything about Klein's theories, but this paper makes it explicitly clear that she was under no delusions about the difficulties between them. She herself felt that the criticisms of the Training Committee for being dilatory were unjust because she could not see that any final conclusions could be drawn until the outcome of the Controversial Discussions. However, since the committee was acting under the instructions of the Society, she had to say that she saw the issue in black and white terms:

1. Whether Mrs. Klein's new findings and theories necessarily lead to transformations and innovations of technical procedure and
2. if this should be the case, whether the Training Committee considers it as its task to teach one main analytic theory and technique or whether it desires to create an open forum for the free teaching of all current analytic theories and consequent techniques.

She went on to stress a legitimate point that Strachey had not considered, namely, "that every new step in theory produced changes of the technique and every technical innovation produced new findings which could not have been unearthed by the former methods."

If this were so, one could validly ask: apart from the substitution of free association for hypnosis, did Freud change his technique with each of his discoveries, particularly after his postulation of the death instinct? In fact, Freud had very little to say about his actual technique.*

Anna Freud proceeded to give a historical list of the attempts at revision of "classical" technique:

1. Special valuation of the damming-up of libido as a pathogenic agent was responsible for the so-called "active technique" by Ferenczi and Rank.
2. Rank's birth trauma as a main pathogenic factor resulted in the technical rule of planned termination of analysis.
3. The great significance which Ferenczi ascribed to certain frustrations suffered by the infant in early phases of its mother-relationship led to technical prescriptions concerning an indulgent attitude of the analyst, which was deliberately planned to invite reproduction of a mother-child relationship between analyst and patient.
4. Reich, who attributed the failure of normal development of genital faculties to an early repression of aggressive attitudes, evolved a set of technical rules which were specially designed to reproduce aggressive scenes between analyst and patient, etc.

Turning then to Melanie Klein, Anna Freud noted that Klein had not yet expressly stated what changes had taken place in her technique following her latest theory on neurosis. She reiterated that little profit could be achieved until this had been revealed in the current scientific discussions. Certain differences could be inferred; the most prominent seemed to be "the almost exclusive emphasis given by Mrs. Klein to all transference material, compared with material which emerges in dreams, in verbal associations, in memories and screen-memories." In orthodox analysis an interpretation of transference material occurs only in the later stages, after systematic attempts have allowed the deepest levels to emerge (or, at least, so runs the argument in *The Ego and the Mechanisms of Defence*). By that time, the "transference neurosis" has appeared (Kleinians, such as Elliott Jaques, say that they simply don't know what this term means). Unlike Anna Freud, Klein assumed that transference reactions occur from the very beginning of an analysis, and that it is important to interpret them immediately because the analyst is "still an unknown quantity, i.e. a phantasy object, and that the distortions of such a translation are slowly corrected and diminished by real experience where the object becomes known and familiar."

The aims of the two women were therefore entirely different. The "Freudian" analysis attempts to undo repressions, based on the assumption that the

* Most of his comments are contained in *Studies on Hysteria* (1893–95), *Five Lectures on Psycho-Analysis* (1910), and *The Future Prospects of Psycho-Analysis* (1910).

widening of consciousness enables the ego to gain control over the id. Klein's theory, on the other hand, attributing great significance to the mechanisms of introjection and projection, expects beneficial results from the reductions and transformations of the "so-called internalized objects and their interrelations with outside reality." Anna Freud was quite right in declaring that the same technical devices could not serve both purposes, but she wrongly assumed that they shared the aim of uncovering psychic reality, for Klein's emphasis was on the reduction of anxiety. Anna Freud's approach could be described as more in the tradition of nineteenth-century meliorism, where man can learn to be master of his fate, whereas Klein accepts darker and deeper levels of human consciousness.

Where is all this going to lead? Anna Freud asked. How could a teaching program be established if every new theory is acceptable? Would there not be a situation similar to the wild eclecticism of the Tavistock Clinic? Surely the result would be the dissolution of all psychoanalytic societies, which had been founded expressly in order to teach consistent theory.

Melanie Klein's paper did not in any way disagree with Anna Freud's critique of her method. Her technique with adults had been influenced entirely by her experience with small children, in which she had discovered that right from the beginning a transference occurs. "When the analytic situation has been established, the analyst takes the place of the original objects, and the patient, as we know, deals again with the feelings and conflicts which are being revived, the very defences he used in the original situation." The analyst represents not only actual people, past and present, but internalized objects which from infancy have contributed to the foundation of his superego. The analyst must be on guard to ensure that there is a constant interaction between reality and phantasy so that the distinction does not become blurred. Moreover, in the transference situation, the figures always belong to *specific* situations, and only by perceiving these situations can the analysand understand the nature and content of the transferred feelings. This is not a one-to-one situation, but a *mise en scène* of a complex mosaic of actors and emotions.

As for her preoccupations with anxiety and guilt, Klein's work with children had led her to understand that destructive impulses could be diverted to the loved object—"thus the vicissitudes of the libido are fully comprehensible only in relation to the early anxieties with which they are intimately bound up." Her technique varied from patient to patient, but her approach was always governed by her preoccupation with the origins of anxiety and guilt.

In his submission, Glover reiterated his contention that the training system had broken down. He held Klein responsible for creating a situation of stress during training transferences as well as for the reactivation of old transferences.

As for the teachers, I find it hard to abandon the view that these at least should have sufficient gumption not to make controversial views an essential and binding part of their instruction. It follows therefore that in my opinion the main flaw in our training system has been the selection of teachers who are strictly speaking unqualified to teach the most impressionable creature—the student in training.

According to Marion Milner, a student at the time, Glover himself was largely responsible for making the students uneasy that their freedom was being impaired.[4]

Marjorie Brierley gave an admirably comprehensive account of her own experience, unique in that she made no attempt to minimize past mistakes. Her own technique varied so much from patient to patient that she sometimes felt that she did not have one at all. The aim of analysis for her was "ego-reintegration on a reality basis," reclamation work in which she regarded herself as an auxiliary superego. Through the years she had come to regard herself more and more as an active partner in the process. Research and therapy, she found, make uneasy bedfellows:

> I find the conjunction of therapy and research most disadvantageous because therapeutic anxiety interferes with learning. I should learn more and more quickly if I could think of the patient as a guinea-pig and for all I know the patient himself might do better. But from beginning to end he obstinately remains a fellow human being, whose therapeutic needs demand priority over research interests.

Turning to Klein's theories, Brierley associated the depressive position with (by implication) Ferenczi's sphincter morality; and on the rare occasions when she gave internal object interpretations, Brierley related them to life situations. She also believed that after the termination of the analysis it was highly important to humanize the association between analyst and patient and to weaken the transference bond. Klein had helped her to understand the complicated interrelationships between oral, anal, and genital aspects of experience, but she objected to her ready generalizations: "I think she feels what certain babies feel in certain circumstances. I do not think she necessarily knows what all babies feel like in all circumstances." She was alarmed by the way Klein had in effect mesmerized the Society in the past few years so that almost every member was consulting her about cases. "I felt it to be so far from healthy that I remain one of the few members who [have] never consulted Mrs. Klein in this way." What many members were doing was treating her as an "idealized object." "This is a potentially dangerous situation because the idealised object is forever in danger of becoming its denigrated opposite, unless its goodness is constantly inflated by over-compensatory love and it is constantly sheltered from aggression." If Klein's trainees ended by identifying their analysts with ideal objects, "they would inevitably tend to become follow-my-leader copyists. They would remain under the psychic necessity of swallowing their training whole and never using their teeth upon what they are taught."

Brierley and Ella Sharpe both agreed with Dr. Payne, who wrote that "no analytical technique is sound, however applied, if the analyst regards it as the only method of saving the patient and as an exact method depending on exactitude for its success." Payne was particularly interesting in her recollections of her analysis with James Glover. When she started her training with him in 1919 they sat facing each other and he wrote down every word she said. Then, after he returned from his analysis with Abraham in Berlin, he changed his technique: she lay on the couch, Glover sitting behind her, and he usually gave his interpretations at the end of a session. Transference material interpretations were given only when there was undoubted evidence in the material. "The analyst was very passive," just as she found the highly systematic Sachs in her later analysis with him.

Payne then made a point that has never been sufficiently recognized, that even before Klein's arrival, some English analysts had begun to use transference interpretations very actively. This is interesting, since it is usually assumed that the English group fell under the spell of the transference after the arrival of Klein.* Payne, while tending to increase the amount of transference interpretation in recent years, refrained from active participation unless actual material was presented to her, whereas she observed that Klein apparently considered it expedient to relate every internal and external experience to the transference.

Speaking as a doctor who had practiced suggestion, she was well aware of how interpretation at the beginning of an analysis can reanimate the unconscious imago of the parents. Payne saw several disadvantages in a situation in which a transference situation is actively fostered by direct suggestion:

> I am fully aware that the aim is to resolve ultimately the anxiety situations associated with the primitive object relations in the Ego, but does the resolution brought about in this way tend to promote the persistence of an omnipotent parent imago of a beneficent kind rather than an independent integrated Ego?

* On December 13, 1926, Ferenczi wrote to Jones in English, defending himself against Jones's accusation that his works were "phantastic": "I don't always read your works as well with unmixed pleasure. If my works are wild and phantastic, yours often give the impression of a kind of logical-sadistic violence, especially the works, which, by the way, are equally phantastic, on child analysis [which] have appeared. These works of your English group have not charmed me at all."

There were undoubted differences between the techniques of the British and Viennese analysts; Payne believed such differences to be as inevitable as the differences existing among doctors engaged in any form of therapy. "Therapy cannot be a science."

With the data assembled, Strachey's Draft Report was ready to be presented to the Society on January 24, 1944. The Training Committee had been presented with the argument that with two incompatible sets of theoretical opinions, the effective functioning of the Training Committee was impossible. Most members could not accept this gloomy view; and in order to dispose of it, they had decided to address themselves to an examination of the purposes of training.

The first was that of a training analysis, which they concurred differed in no significant respect from a therapeutic analysis. However, it would be only realistic to acknowledge that in a training analysis there was a far greater temptation to influence the candidate's theoretical views. Therefore it would seem reasonable to exclude people deeply involved in the present controversy to appointment as training analysts. The same held true for control analysts, for whom there was a particular necessity to exercise judgment, balance, and tact, qualities unlikely to be associated with a rigid or extremist viewpoint. There was, to be sure, no reason whatsoever for excluding controversial material from seminars and lectures; indeed, there was much to be said for making candidates aware of it. But when it came to training analyses, a real danger arose.

Consequently, the Training Committee offered four recommendations:

1. That as soon as practicable after the end of the War in Europe, the Society should proceed to the election of a new Training Committee.
2. That, in choosing the members of the new Training Committee, the Society should deliberately bear in mind the undesirability of appointing persons who are prominently involved in acute scientific or personal controversies.
3. That it should so far as possible avoid selecting for the functions of Training or Control Analysts persons whose desire to enforce their own extreme or rigid views shows signs of impairing the correctness of their technical procedure or of interfering with the impartiality of their judgment.
4. That, on the other hand, it should be a definite instruction to the new Training Committee that every Candidate should, by means of attending Seminars and Lectures, be given an opportunity of obtaining the closest and most extensive knowledge of all sections of opinion in the Society, including the most extreme.

Not unexpectedly, Edward Glover expressed himself in profound disagreement with the assumptions informing the Draft Report. Whereas in the past he had complained that the "Klein party" was taking over the Society, he now saw the committee as divided into two equally strong factions. As a way out of the impasse, he himself had suggested abolishing the training staff and letting any qualified analyst do the work of analyzing candidates, a system that would work on a rotation basis. He concluded:

> It seems to me that two alternatives exist. Either the Society adjudicates on the respective validity of opposing views and prohibits the teaching of views that are held to be either invalid or controversial: or the Training Committee organises two or more systems of training whereby candidates can be trained exclusively in any given system.* However absurd such a system might appear to a casual observer, it is the only one that would prevent for a time official splitting in the Society. I came to this conclusion with regret. For a long time I held the view that candidates should have sufficient gumption to see through the idiosyncrasies of their teachers. Evidently this is too much to expect.

This conclusion, it should be noted, seems inconsistent with all he had said about the "dire mastery" of the transference.

At this meeting of the Training Committee on January 24, 1944, Anna Freud asked if she were one of the parties alluded to in Strachey's Draft Report; and, as this appeared to be the case, she considered it an insult and intended to resign from the Training Committee. The other members of the committee pleaded with her not to make up her mind on the spot, but to reconsider the situation. Glover also tendered his resignation, not only from the Training Committee, but from the Society as well. He was not asked to reconsider his decision. It was premeditated, since he had dropped in on the Schmidebergs before the meeting to tell them what he intended to do.

To the members of her group Melanie Klein sent news of the dramatic turn of events:

> . . . As far as I am concerned, this finishes now a feud which has lasted for nine years; and since I have had so much patience in the interest of the work, the Society and the future of Psycho-Analysis, I think we shall now all have to keep for the future to a very careful policy. I have no doubt whatever that Glover is going to try to transfer the feud, which more or less remained an internal one so far, into a feud which will be carried out publicly. He will, I think, attack the Society as non-Freudian and so on, and I

* This, as it happens, was the eventual solution.

have no idea yet what he is going to do about me in his books and other ways. Still, all that is much less unpleasant than to have it inside the Society. He will, most likely, found a new group. . . . I do not know what Anna Freud is going to do. As I said, she retains her membership. Whether this means that she is waiting to see in which way Glover is going to start a new society, or whether she does not wish to join with him, I cannot say. But without Glover she is a much less dangerous and troublesome opponent.[5]

To Jones, Glover wrote a personal letter of reflections on the situation on January 28, 1944:

Looking back on the situation, I see that there was a good deal of intelligent anticipation behind your suggestion that the Society should go out of operation for the duration of the war. But I did not believe it would have made any difference in the long run.

I wonder how much we fundamentally agree. On one thing, I think, certainly that it was a woman ridden Society (your favoured hypothesis). Apart from that I have one unalloyed feeling of satisfaction:—We made a good team together until the Klein imbroglio developed. Without being oversententious, I stuck to the professional tradition of loyalty to you as First in Command and didn't mind taking any raps on that score. I'd do that again.[6]

In an interview with Bluma Swerdloff in 1965, Glover recalled the situation: "Training systems had by then developed into a form of power politics thinly disguised by the rationalizations that however unsatisfactory eclectic policies had proved in general psychotherapy they had somehow acquired virtue when they developed as teaching systems. And I well remember the state of relative euphoria I experienced when once having resigned I was no longer under obligation as an office bearer to restrain criticisms."[7] (How benignly one views one's past behavior!)

An Extraordinary Meeting was called on February 2, 1944, at which Sylvia Payne formally announced Glover's resignation from the Society. During the meeting the air raid alarm sounded but no one moved from his place. Before reading Glover's statement, Payne commented on the changes that must necessarily be put into effect. The Emergency War Committee, consisting of Glover and herself, which had been appointed in 1940, now no longer existed; and at a Council meeting that morning it had been decided that Payne should deputize as president in the absence of Jones, and Brierley should act as scientific secretary in place of Glover. Payne then read Glover's letter of resignation, in which he predicted the future situation of the Society:

... The present situation as I read it is as follows: the Controversial series of Discussions will end in smoke. Indeed it is already pointless to continue them. The Klein group will continue to maintain that their views are either strictly Freudian or legitimate, not to say valuable extensions of Freud's work. The "old middle group" will hedge but will end by saying there is no ground for a split. The unattached members will be puzzled but not see any necessity for a split. Only the Viennese Freudians and a few isolated members will continue to maintain that the Klein views are non-analytical; and these will be out-voted by a combination of the Klein group with whatever younger groups are interested less in the present controversies than in the future administration of the Society, so the outcome is a foregone conclusion. ...

Dr. Payne then explained to the members that at first she had been under the impression that it was a personal letter. Subsequently she had written to Glover expressing her great disappointment about his decision, particularly as they had always worked cooperatively together until the emergence of these acute troubles in the Society. Her aim was for compromise, but he was determined to effect a split. Glover then wrote her a reply, which she proceeded to read to the Society, spelling out his uneasiness about "the Klein deviation":

18 Wimpole St. W1
1st Feb. 1944

Dear Dr. Payne,

... You say that we worked in co-operation until the troubles in the Society became acute, and that thereafter our aims became opposed to each other, in that I "worked for a split" and you "worked for compromise." On the second part of this statement it is naturally not my concern to make any personal comment. I will content myself with saying that scientific compromise must be distinguished from administrative conciliation; also that compromise on matters of principle often ends by accelerating the cleavage it is intended to prevent—as indeed has been the result in this instance. On the other hand your suggestion that I "worked for a split" (although limited as to its time reference) might easily give rise to a false impression. I should like therefore to state categorically that I have never worked for a split, have never asked anyone to split, have refused to split when urged to do so and have consistently refused to be a party to movements behind the scenes such as have frequently occurred in the Society since 1925. I have now simply exercised the privilege of withdrawing from the Society (a) because its general tendency and training has become unscientific and (b) because it is becoming less and less Freudian and has therefore lapsed from its original aims.

It is of course true that I have criticised the Klein deviation with in-creasing vigour and plainness ever since 1934 when the Klein party adopted the theory of a "central depressive position" (together with all that this theory connotes). But this criticism, so far from constituting "working for a split," is a legitimate exercise of scientific criticism. When, shortly after the publication of Rank's "Das Trauma der Geburt," the late James Glover and myself prepared a comprehensive adverse criticism of his Birth Theory . . . it was not suggested that we were working for a split, although in fact we attacked the Birth Theory at a time when many analysts had swallowed it whole. Incidentally it may make the present issue more plain if I point out that Mrs. Klein's latest theories, although differing in content from those of Rank, constitute a deviation from psycho-analysis of the same order. The implications are identical and the theories were unsound for precisely the same reasons as were those of Rank. The resemblance be-tween the two deviations is indeed remarkable.

May I further point out that during what I have called the "first phase" of Mrs. Klein's theorizing (i.e. prior to 1934) I went out of my way to find a common basis for some of her views and classical Freudian teaching. Anyone who attended Psycho-analytical Congresses was perfectly aware that even her early views were not accepted by any branch of the Psycho-Analytical Association except the British Society and, for that matter, not even the whole of the British Society. At the Oxford Congress I devoted a paper to this task of compromise and was roundly taxed with the fact by many of our European colleagues. But already during that "first phase" I was profoundly disturbed by two manifestations that developed in the So-ciety (a) the blanketing of scientific discussion in the Society, where accep-tance or non-acceptance of Mrs. Klein's views became a sort of religious "test." (b) the policy of the Training Committee. May I therefore end this letter with some further comment on the Training situation as it has devel-oped from 1923 to the present day.

I have always held that the power to influence the future of psycho-analysis lies, not in the scientific discussions of the Society, but in the policy of the Training Committee. The operation of training transfer-ences and counter-transferences is the decisive factor. When differences of opinion become acute, these transferences automatically lower the level of training from a scientific to a quasi-religious plane. Unfortunately this fact was never openly admitted in the Training Committee. Instead, lipservice to the myth of the "trained (and therefore unbiased) analyst" developed to a degree that was, in my opinion, little short of conscious hypocrisy. The result of this policy could not be indefinitely delayed: already before the War, the Committee was driven to consider the possibility of having two distinct systems of training, and during the war period has openly countenanced two distinct and opposed systems. Candidates who wish a Kleinian training are given Kleinian analysts and controls. Candidates preferring a purely Freudian training are given Freudian analysts and controls. Those who have no particular preference are given potluck. Yet their future views and professional careers will be finally determined by this haphazard allocation. Even so, until the last few years I held out in the Training Committee against a split. But I see now that the position is an impossible one not only for candidates but for psycho-analysis.

And so when it became clear from its Draft Report that the Committee was still prepared to pretend that this real problem is "an unreal dilemma," I could only conclude that there was no prospect of scientific progress in the Society itself. For if the training is unscientific, what hope is there of establishing scientific standards amongst members whose entry to the Society depends on their conforming to the regulations of the Training Committee. Better by far to scrap the whole system and start again.

Yours sincerely,

Edward Glover

P.S.: Since writing this I hear that Miss Freud has resigned from the Training Committee. I need hardly say that although her decision was taken independently of any action of mine, I am not at all surprised: the phantastic stress laid by Mr. Strachey's Draft Report on the alleged capacity of training analysts to promote objectivity in their candidates is in such glaring contradiction to the facts of the present situation! As I said in my "Comment": if this were really the case candidates would already be more advanced than their training analysts and so be in a position to analyse their training analysts with some benefit to the latter.

E.G.

Melitta Schmideberg and Barbara Low pressed Sylvia Payne to give the reasons for Anna Freud's resignation from the Training Committee. Payne replied that the Training Committee had not yet had an opportunity to discuss this aspect of the situation, particularly since Strachey had withdrawn his draft report and had asked for discussion of it to be postponed until Dr. Glover's resignation was received by the Society, thus reserving the discussion for present members, not departing dissidents. This explanation was unsatisfactory to a number of people, including Kate Friedlander and Adrian Stephen.

"Freud's daughter has had to resign," Barbara Low declared dramatically. "Surely we must have some discussion on it." Dr. George Franklin (an analysand of Melitta Schmideberg's) remarked that he was sure more members would have been present at the meeting had they known Glover's resignation was to be announced, to which Payne replied that she believed the Viennese members were aware of what was taking place, implying that they were deliberately staying away.

Low felt that Glover's resignation was a disaster, since "he represents in this country psycho-analysis. Freudian psycho-analysis." She believed that his resignation would be fatal for the future of the Society, and she begged the members to ask Dr. Glover to reconsider his decision.

At this point Dr. Bowlby interjected a strong statement. He did not wish to discuss whether Dr. Glover was "*the* valuable person" in British psychoanalysis, but the fact of the matter was that he had done harm as well as good. In recent broadcasts in a weekly radio journal, "Cavalcade," he had attacked army psychiatrists, and four members (Rickman, Adrian Stephen, Dr. A. C. Wilson, and himself) strongly objected. The particularly offensive remarks were contained in an interview on "Cavalcade" (Jan. 1, 1944), which *The Listener* had summarized. The question had been put to Glover:

Q. Do you consider that an increase in surface psychology (i.e. selection by vocational tests) is likely to be a feature of postwar industry as the results of the present experiments by Army psychiatrists? Is this a trend likely to affect adversely the rights of the individual?

A. My answer to both parts of the question is yes, because not only will it suit employers and the State to aim at 100 per cent efficiency in their workers, but Army psychiatrists have developed swelled heads over the use of selection tests and are, therefore, likely to push these methods before the authorities in peacetime. This move will no doubt be justified on the plea that it is also good for the individual. It is, of course, good for disordered individuals to have a suitable occupation and if normal people want guidance they should have it, provided it is really good.

DIFFERENCE

But there is a vast difference between therapeutic (or preventive) selection of abnormal persons and selection of normal individuals at the behest of the Ministries of employers' federations. A partial safeguard would be to submit all Army psychiatrists to a course of "rehabilitation" (as it is called when applied by them to others) in order that they may regain a proper perspective regarding the rights of civilians. Without adequate safeguards the system may have the seeds of Nazism in it—whatever the experts say.

Bowlby was extremely angry because these comments had come completely out of the blue and Glover had not had the courtesy to communicate his views to any of the army psychiatrists. "It is *the method and not the matter* which has caused criticism in medical circles," Bowlby concluded. He was concerned that the general public would consider the views representative of the British Psycho-Analytical Society. Winnicott agreed that Glover had committed an indiscretion, but it was a red herring in comparison with the issue under discussion—namely, Glover's resignation from the Society. It was altogether a sobering and eventful gathering.

At the next meeting of the Training Committee on February 9, 1944, Dr. Payne tendered the opinion that it was unclear to her whether Anna Freud's resignation was final, a view with which all the other members, except Melanie Klein, concurred. However, they finally agreed that this must have been Anna Freud's intended wish since she had subsequently communicated it to her colleagues and candidates. It was also agreed that James Strachey should draw up a revised version of his draft report which, after discussion in the Training Committee, would be submitted to the next Business Meeting on March 8.

At that March meeting, the Society passed a resolution regretting Dr. Glover's decision to resign, with one dissenting vote. Strachey then declared that while the draft report had been associated with his name, it did in fact represent the views of all the members of the Training Committee except Anna Freud and Glover. Its main aim had been to prevent future splits within the Society such as were occurring in other countries, particularly the United States. "There are always personal emotional factors involved with which we cannot deal. But we can try to revise the machinery of training and devise a machinery which will as far as possible prevent these splits." The only major differences from the previous report were of a practical nature. For example, it was suggested that at least one of a candidate's control analysts be deliberately chosen as differing from the training analyst in his character, interests, and method of approach to psychoanalysis.

The committee suggested that from time to time some of its members attend case seminars by one or another of the training analysts as a way of obtaining detailed knowledge of the technical methods of other analysts. A good technique, it was generally agreed, was "a good handling of transference and counter-transference"—an innocuous enough description. Finally, the Training Committee recommended that as soon as practicable a new Training Committee should be elected. Of the members of the committee only Marjorie Brierley had one further suggestion: "I personally regard it as desirable that all future practitioners should be educated to take at least individual testing of both observational data and of theory. Verification is a communal responsibility in which all members should be encouraged to share whether or not they are attracted to other aspects of research." The report was then thrown open to discussion.

Melitta Schmideberg asked whether Miss Freud had made a statement, to which Dr. Payne replied that she did not wish to do so. Dr. Friedlander inquired whether it had been the custom in the past few years for candidates to be asked whether they wanted to go to a Freudian or a Kleinian analyst, to which Payne replied: "I will explain the custom. If a candidate is introduced by a training analyst, he or she goes to him or to somebody whom he recommends. It is a reasonable thing for a candidate who has a preference to have the right for it to be regarded. Candidates have never been asked whether they want to go to Freudian or Kleinian analysts."*

Glover was frank about his maneuvers in this area when questioned by Bluma Swerdloff in 1965. "Training was the key to the whole problem," he remarked. "When I observed that training was becoming more and more tendentious and that we were threatened with a Klein Group, I was unscrupulous enough to see that Mrs. Klein had quite a number of 'dark horses' to analyse,† and that candidates of merit were passed on to what we would now call classical Freudians in the hope that they would get classical training. If they wanted to alter their views afterwards good and well, but at any rate they should have a non-controversial training, a standard training."[8] Glover was like a corkscrew: in 1943 he had been accusing Klein of grabbing the largest percentage of the candidates; now he was saying that she was given all the lame ducks.

Michael Balint then made an important statement:

In my view the main issue is that the Committee's recommendations are not far-reaching enough. We have a very old training system. The only difference the report suggests is to exclude a few analysts from training, all analysts that are exposed as partisans should not be training analysts. If we go back to see how this system has developed, we get some idea how the situation came to this impasse. The system came about as a mechanism of defence, so to speak, against the unhealed wounds caused by Jung, Adler and Stekel leaving the Society. To avoid personal ambitions and the acting out of unsolved Oedipus situations against a father figure. The present system achieved this aim as long as we had Professor Freud as a father imago, now he is dead there are splits again, and not only here, we have only to look to the USA., there are as many systems as societies and even more. Here we have something working as long as we have common ideas. As soon, however, as there is no longer a patriarchal organisation but an organisation of equal brothers and sisters with equal rights that their views should be accepted as debatable the whole system breaks down and must because it is not meant to stand up to that. I suggest to return the report to the Training Committee and to regard the situation in this light. Until now we mainly relied on the individual analyst. The training analyst was practically uncontrolled and had an almost autocratic power. Instead of trusting to the

---

* This contradicts Margaret Little's recollection. See p. 361.
† *In senilo veritas?*

single member, we must devise a system now, and of this not one word is in
the training report.

When pressed for practical suggestions by Paula Heimann, Balint replied
that he was shocked to discover that in England candidates had so little choice
in their training analyst, whereas in Budapest they were given a list from which
to make their own selection. Balint suggested that in the interim the report be
accepted "because we have no common super-ego any more and our loyalties
are divided." As if to underline the differences between the continental and
British attitudes, the meeting adjourned for tea.

When the discussion was resumed, it focused on the length of tenure of a
new Training Committee. Strachey favored an election every year. Adrian Stephen advocated frequent changes of officers in order to avoid paternalism and
economic dependency. In a long emotional statement, Stephen described what
he had heard about the attitude of the officers of the Society in his various
postings since 1940—"of condescending aloofness, of superciliousness and
sometimes even, so it was said, of downright insolence that often made friendly
co-operation with them impossible." The cooperation of the Society with the
war effort was lamentable in contrast to that of the Tavistock Clinic,* which
was responsible for the entire organization of Army Psychological Medicine.

On two occasions a few years previously, his wife, Dr. Karin Stephen, had
been asked to deliver some lectures on Freudian psychology at the Tavistock.
Each time Jones told her to refuse; and when Dr. Stephen asserted that she
would deliver such a course to the public on her own initiative, one of the officers of the Society warned her that "her name would be mud." "Can anyone
imagine," Stephen asked, "the officers of any other society that claimed to be
scientific (a society of physicists or chemists, for example) being so jealous of
another society as to try to prevent its members having access to important
knowledge?"

Perhaps even more important was the attitude to prospective candidates.

They should not be twitted about the shape of their cheek-bones, sneers
should not be made about their medical schools or about their official psychiatric teachers; they should not be hauled over the coals for coming a few
minutes late, or a few minutes early, as the case may be. They should not
be told that they have the accent of East End Jews.

All these complaints he had heard from prospective candidates; and as a rem-
edy he suggested that they be interviewed by a Selection Board rather than by
one or two individuals. The sorry situation of the Society was the result of its
being an autocracy. "European history for centuries has shown on the grand

* The Tavistock Clinic was founded in 1920 as one of the first outpatient clinics in psychotherapy, based on a
multidisciplinary approach.

scale what our Society is showing on a microscopic scale—that no man is fit to be an autocrat."

In an interview with Bluma Swerdloff in 1965, Willi Hoffer echoed the views of many other analysts that Glover's resignation was an act of despair and emotion. "I'm not sure," he continued, "but I've always had a suspicion that there was a political idea behind it. I suspect, but I've no proof of it, it was like what the Communists often did in the German pre-Hitler time. They made a step, with the idea: 'If we are now very radical, then the others cannot resist and will do the same.' I have the idea he expected Anna Freud would resign at once; she would not want to stay, would not have the courage to stay on her own in the British Society."[9] If this was indeed the case, Glover lacked psychological insight and an understanding of the strength of Anna Freud's inflexibility. She would not allow herself, Freud's daughter, to be pushed out of the Society and branded as a schismatic. (She sometimes said that she stayed in because she was grateful to Jones for bringing her family to England, but it is possible that she also felt that she could work things to her own advantage if she played her cards right.) Glover later claimed that he actually believed, almost up to the end, that she would be victorious over Klein. According to him, when Freud arrived in England they had a discussion about Klein, and Freud remarked that it was the first time in the history of psychoanalysis that a schismatic had retained membership in the International Association.

It is hard to credit Glover's sincerity when he later claimed that he had never wanted to lead a group, because quite clearly he felt entitled to succeed Jones. When trouble started shortly after Anna's arrival in Britain, Glover told her (he says): "I'll give you three years to make up your mind whether you want to be just a good girl and stay in the Society with your opponents, or whether you will form a group, believing the concepts that you believe and I support. I don't want to lead a group, but if you want me to do it, I will; it's up to you. If you don't, I shan't move a finger, let the Society run on."[10]

Glover claimed that he was delighted to leave that "reserved, monastic Society"—"because I hated this sort of atmosphere and would have nothing to do with its system of training." For a persistent meddler, his reflections on the Training Committee are startling: "I think the most abominable committee I've ever been a member of was the Training Committee of the Society. It was a little oily, a little sanctimonious, it always felt or pretended that it was the right thing. After my resignation I suffered or enjoyed—as the case may be—a state of euphoria for not having to attend the Training Committee and keep my tongue in my cheek." What a burden it had been as an officeholder for sixteen years! "You are not free to express yourself because you have certain functions to perform, such as being chairman or promoting one kind of research or another, stimulating people to think."[11]

When he resigned, Glover did not leave himself high and dry. He had long been interested in drug addiction and delinquency, and in 1931 had helped found the Institute for the Study and Treatment of Delinquency, of which he remained cochairman until it was taken over by the National Health Service in 1948. In 1963 he became chairman of the Scientific Committee of the London Institute of Criminology. Despite these interests he had no intention of abandoning psychoanalysis, and after his resignation from the British Society he joined the Swiss Society so that he could continue as secretary of the International Psycho-Analytic Association;* but Jones tried to block his membership. Apparently there were rumors that Anna Freud would follow Glover's lead, as a letter from Sylvia Payne, dated August 1, 1945, to Jones, indicates:

> I think that Anna Freud has several very weak character traits & I am sure that she will not hesitate to try & get what she wants without considering the opinions of those who differ from her. I fancy that her father was the only person who could prevent this, and as she must have taken over Freud's determination to keep psycho-analysis isolated and to allow no one in who showed character traits of omnipotence I cannot see any hope of compromising in any way. Unfortunately, we have the same omnipotence in Melanie and this is really why her work has made so much trouble; it is her personality.
>
> It is of course gross ingratitude to you, and the world is full of such behaviour.
>
> I am wondering whether it is any solution to our local problem that Glover & Anna are members of the Swiss Society. It will not give them any standing except in the International. Are they honorary members? The only possibility of Anna going to Switzerland is the state of Mrs. Burlingham's health, but I doubt that she would move her old mother. Anna told me that the War nurseries would be closed by October. I have heard also that she hinted at the formation of a group in the future but my information on the latter point is not reliable.[12]

Anna was, it seems, playing politics behind the scenes, apparently to force the British Society to accept her terms for continuing her membership.

On December 11, 1944, Glover sent Jones, as president of the International Association, an angry letter protesting Jones's appointment of Anna Freud as secretary to the International Association. Glover pointed out that he had no legitimate right to do this, since Glover had never resigned his membership from the International nor his post as secretary, an appointment that could be made only by the International Congress. He had resigned from the British Society because it was no longer a Freudian society and was now "offi-

---

* This was the mistake Jacques Lacan made in 1953. He did not realize that his resignation from the Paris Society automatically entailed his loss of membership in the International Association as well.

cially committed to teaching psycho-analytic candidates the Klein system of child psychology as part of psycho-analysis, whereas in fact it constitutes a deviation from psycho-analysis."[13] The International Association existed for the advancement of Freudian psychoanalysis, and he, Glover, continued to be a Freudian psychoanalyst. He therefore formally requested a meeting of the Council to consider the matter. Jones replied wearily on January 8, 1945, expressing surprise that "you are not yet tired of psycho-analytic politics. I hoped that you, like me, were going to enjoy the last period of our lives free from what all our experience has proved to be nothing but poison. How much I regret the time and energy I have wasted on the unpalatable and completely fruitless subject."[14] He went on to remind him that one could become a member of the Association without being a member of one of its constituent branches only "by express permission of the President of the Association." Jones had been given that power originally in order to assist lay analysts in America; but in Glover's circumstances "I had no opening but to revert to the time when the President elected the Secretary instead of, as happened later, asking the Congress to ratify his choice." This suggests that Jones had misused his powers arbitrarily.

Glover, in his interview with Bluma Swerdloff, told her: "Give the devil his due, Jones was a clever little man. He used to say I was a divinely normal person, and when I left the Society he said I was a paranoid character."*[15] One must ponder, too, on the fact that Anna Freud took over the position despite Glover's unwavering loyalty to her. She had been appointed secretary in 1928, but in 1934 at the Lucerne Congress had surrendered the post to Glover because Freud required her care. Glover had been reelected by Council in 1943. William Gillespie describes Jones as determined to keep Glover out at all costs in revenge for attempting to destroy *his* Society.†

In 1945 Melitta Schmideberg moved to New York, where she became involved in work with adolescent delinquents until she returned to England in 1961. In 1950 she founded, with a group of other psychiatrists and social workers, the Association for the Psychiatric Treatment of Offenders (APTO) in New York, on the lines of the Institute for the Scientific Treatment of Delinquency.

What is one to make of the strange relationship between Glover and Melitta? In a discussion of the problems brought on the British Society by Klein's ideas, Glover commented to Swerdloff: "Of course there was a good deal of family feuding behind all this, very difficult to assess, but it certainly took

---

* All who opposed or differed from Jones were described in pathological terms.
† According to Dr. Gillespie, Glover managed to regain his status as a member of the International Psycho-Analytic Association by a clause (C) pertaining to membership introduced at the Sixteenth International Psycho-Analytic Congress in 1949: "Membership of a foreign society instead of to the society of one's own country where there is one shall be subject to the consent of the Central Executive."

effect. I think they were both, herself and her daughter, prejudiced. On the other hand, Dr. Schmideberg, her daughter, made a very good fight for her spiritual liberty, and she had some of that slightly desperate character which made her come right out in the open." When Swerdloff pointed out to him that he had analyzed Melitta immediately prior to the disturbances in the Society, he replied evasively: "She had been [analyzed by me], but of course she had been to a dozen analysts before then . . . well, I don't say a dozen* . . . but she did come to me. Of course the trouble was that they both had something of the same disposition. The daughter in a way was less forceful than the mother. Anyhow I think it was largely by Dr. Schmideberg's instigation that these debates continued. I was very much inclined to let things slide a bit just for the sake of peace, to let it pass, hoping the scientific situation would improve somehow."[16]

In March 1944, Winnicott wrote a tactful letter to Klein expressing his hope that she would leave well enough alone now that Glover had resigned. She replied on March 5.

Dear Donald,

Thank you very much for your letter, I very much appreciate your frankness and the spirit in which your letter was written. I know you are my friend and shall never doubt this.—I have no intention to participate in the discussion about Glover, but this does not mean that I agree with you on a number of points you raise in your letter. It is true, what we are most concerned about is to have as many good analysts as possible, but Glover did not only damage our Society and my work because he is a bad analyst but also because he is crooked and unscrupulous. (I think he is very pathological.) He has in various ways also damaged Ps. An. in the public eye not only through misrepresenting us but also through this strife which was his doing. You will never get him to make a proper statement and to the right people and it would be very desirable for the Soc. to dissociate itself from him publicly. He may still have a lot of attacks in store,—all the better it would be if it were now made known publicly that the Soc. dissociates itself from him.

As far as I am concerned I don't wish to participate in discussions about him.—Many thanks again for writing.

Yours ever

Melanie[17]

Glover's resignation from the Society did not in any way deter his vendetta against Melanie Klein. In pamphlets, articles, reviews, letters, he seized every

* Actually, only Karen Horney and Ella Sharpe.

opportunity to denigrate her and her ideas. In 1945, in the first volume of *The Psychoanalytic Study of the Child* (of which he, Anna Freud, and Willi Hoffer were the English representatives on the editorial board), he published the tendentious "An Examination of the Klein System of Child Psychology," which he had published privately in pamphlet form the previous year. In a book, *Freud or Jung* (1950), he suggested that, with their mystical vaporizing, Kleinian and Jungian ideas had much in common.

He also spread scurrilous stories about Klein. To Bluma Swerdloff he repeated an anecdote "a friend" had repeated to him: Klein had allegedly announced to this person that after Jesus Christ she considered herself perhaps the most important person who had ever lived, and she regarded her theories on child development as so revolutionary that in future she would be placed among the prophets. Melanie Klein took herself very seriously indeed, but it is very doubtful that she ever made such an extravagant statement.

Yet somehow, in the depths of his heart, Glover nourished a certain affection for Klein. After her death, he described her as a blend of humor and sadness, a remark suggesting that he did occasionally recognize her humanity.

Glover's resignation elicited a general feeling of relief, but what Anna Freud might do was a matter of concern—that is, to almost everyone except Melanie Klein. What if she followed Glover's example and tendered her resignation to the Society as well as to the Training Committee? As the other members of the committee saw it, it was essential to find a modus vivendi that would be acceptable to her so that she would again take her place on the Training Committee.

They also had to consider the problem of the election of new officers and the length of tenure. At the Business Meeting on June 26, 1944, revised rules were drawn up. The next month, at the General Meeting, Sylvia Payne was elected president and John Rickman replaced Glover as scientific secretary. A new Training Committee was elected; its first job was to draw up a fresh curriculum providing that during the first two years all students should be taught the fundamental principles of psychoanalysis as laid down by Freud, and in the third year developments arising out of the work of other analysts. Anna Freud, like Achilles in his tent, sulked in her wartime nurseries, which were eventually to be transformed into the Hampstead Child Therapy Clinic, and made plans for the launching of *The Psychoanalytic Study of the Child* as an annual forum for classical Freudian views on child analysis and for attacks on Klein. She knew that if she waited long enough, overtures would be made to her.

This chaotic situation left candidates currently in training in a state of utter bewilderment. Margaret Little recalls the British Society in those days as "an absolute hotbed of crazy fury."[18] Marion Milner says it was very difficult to come to any conclusions because "it was like parents quarreling by post."[19] The analysands of Anna Freud and her colleagues had no contact with the Institute. Apparently Ernest Jones bluntly pointed out to Willi Hoffer that the Freudians had no future unless they achieved a compromise with the established group, to which Hoffer replied, "Hail, Caesar, *morituri salutamus.*"[20] Anna Freud herself realized that the situation was intolerable. Sylvia Payne initiated discussions with her, and on October 8, 1945, she sent the Board her proposal for collaboration in training. A subcommittee consisting of Sylvia Payne, John Bowlby, Adrian Stephen, and Susan Isaacs was set up to explore its terms, and they reported back to the Board a month later.

5 Nov. 1945

MEMORANDUM

of Proposals discussed by Miss Freud and the Committee appointed by the Board to consider the possibility of introducing an alternative curriculum organised by Miss Freud for the training of psycho-analysts.

1. Applicants introduced by Miss Freud and wishing to be trained under her scheme shall be interviewed by her and the Training Secretary before they are considered by the Training Committee. A third interview with the Chairman of the Training Committee shall be obligatory if the applicant applies for financial assistance from the Institute or a reduction in the standard fees for training, or if there is uncertainty as to suitability. Authority to accept applicants for training rests with the Training Committee.

2. Details of the training curriculum arranged by Miss Freud shall be submitted to the Training Committee for consideration and confirmation in order that equal standards of training are maintained and with the purpose of promoting collaboration.

3. Candidates undertaking each scheme of training shall attend the whole of that course for the first two years of their training. In addition they shall be free at their request to attend lectures or seminars given in the appropriate year of the other course.

   In the third year the candidates trained by Miss Freud shall attend the lectures and seminars provided for third-year students by the present Training Committee. To ensure continuity of policy in the training the leaders of third-year practical seminars compulsory to students shall be appropriate to both curricula.

4. The nomination for election to associate membership of candidates trained by the alternative scheme shall be based on the joint opinions of their training analyst, control analyst and teachers after consideration, approval and recommendation of the Training Committee. Their election shall be by the members of the Society.

5. The names of analysts proposed to undertake any branch of training

for the first time should be submitted to the Training Committee for consideration and confirmation.

6. At such a time as the proposed Central Training Fund comes into being the rules and regulations controlling the administration of this fund shall apply equally to the alternative curriculum.

7. A representative of the organisers of the alternative curriculum may by invitation or by request attend meetings of the Training Committee when problems in common to both organisations are under discussion until such a time that the constitution of the Training Committee shall make this unnecessary.

8. The resolution recently passed by the Training Committee in connection with the selection of control analysts shall apply to the alternative scheme of training.

Resolution: "That whilst every endeavour would be made to meet the wishes of a candidate and his training analyst in selecting the supervising analyst for a candidate's first case, the Training Committee reserved to itself more freedom of action in selecting the supervising analyst for the second case; although it was obviously undesirable that a supervisor with markedly different views on technique from the first should be selected."

Miss Freud's amendment (for discussion): "In agreement with the principles laid down in the resolution recently passed by the Training Committee in connection with the selection of control analysts, the organisers of the alternative curriculum shall advise their candidates as to the choice of their second supervising analyst."

9. The scheme of an alternative curriculum of training shall be reviewed in an agreed number of years.

10. At no time shall the two curricula be referred to as representing opposing theories under the names of Freud and Klein.

Addition to be discussed: "They will be regarded and referred to as alternative methods of training students in psycho-analysis."

Susan Isaacs pointed out that items 1, 3, 8 (and particularly 3) were the most important. She was worried that all third-year students would be debarred from hearing views of "inappropriate" analysts. The students themselves would object to this arrangement, and far from healing the split in the Society, it would only perpetuate it. Rickman also noted that Miss Freud was holding scientific meetings of her own, and even though she had absented herself from the Society she now indicated that she wanted to participate in the training and was gradually demanding more and more concessions. The Training Committee agreed unanimously that it could not recognize as training analysts those who had been trained only by Anna Freud. Sylvia Payne then suggested sending a letter to Anna Freud with a counterproposal: (a) second-year practical seminars to be separate, Miss Freud providing her own; (b) third-year practical seminars to be in common, one of three given by a member of the Freudian group to be chosen by the Training Committee; (c) for lectures, (1) there should be two courses on child analysis given by Anna Freud and Melanie Klein, both compulsory, but the order of them left to the option of the student; (2) for other lectures and seminars one of Anna Freud's group would give one lecture course or theoretical seminar in the first year. After the proposal was passed, Klein remarked that the Training Committee should have the final word with regard to the second control analyst.*

The bargaining continued. Payne went personally to discuss the situation with Anna Freud, who told her that she could see no advantage in the second proposal. The need for the situation to be resolved became even more acute in view of the Society's position vis-à-vis the National Health Service, since it was essential that the Institute be recognized as the central training school for psychoanalysis. Throughout these discussions Anna Freud's behavior was that of a shrewd, highly astute politician.

For the first time in two years Anna Freud attended a meeting of the Society when, on June 26, 1946, an Extraordinary Meeting was held in order to present the members with a final proposal hammered out after endless consultations.

(a) Anna Freud would recognize the authority of the Training Committee.
(b) Lecture-seminars other than those in technique would be common to all students, and members of different shades of opinion would be invited to lead them.
(c) Two parallel sets of lecture-seminars on technique would be run, one conducted as at present and the other by Anna Freud's group.

Dr. Bowlby understood that these proposals had the full endorsement of the entire Board, but at the June meeting, matters turned out differently, although the chairman opened the discussion by stating that since the Council had not voted on the proposals, they were to form an outline for discussion.

However, it was soon apparent that the Kleinians were not willing to accept the terms, when Susan Isaacs stood up and suggested the following amendment:

That the responsibility of the Institute of Psycho-Analysis to its students calls for a unified and systematic course of lectures and seminars in which adequate opportunity is given throughout the three years' training for all students to become acquainted with the main trends in current psycho-

---

* Actually, on January 25, 1945, the Training Committee agreed in principle with Klein's suggestion that the control analyst should be described as a "supervising" analyst.

analytic thought. This meeting of members recommends that there should be a single series of theoretical lectures and practical seminars, compulsory for all students throughout the three years' curriculum; and that those psycho-analysts who undertake teaching and training should always include accredited representatives of the two major lines of present-day psycho-analytic thought.

Melanie Klein added that students should have the opportunity from the beginning to become familiar with both points of view. There should be no parallel seminars; instead, attendance at every seminar should be obligatory for all, a proper share being given by each side. Dr. Heimann was convinced that students were stimulated rather than confused when presented with different points of view. Clifford Scott felt that a unified course was essential. It was finally decided to drop the amendment and the vital proposal was put to the members, proposed by Ella Sharpe and seconded by Adrian Stephen. The motion was carried, 29 for and 7 against. The nays were obviously a bloc vote, in Bowlby's view, consisting of Heimann, Klein, Isaacs, Rickman, Elizabeth Rosenberg, Scott, and Thorner. For Bowlby this was "a very black mark"[21] against the Kleinians, who had given no previous indication that the vote would not be unanimous.

The Society had now agreed in principle to the introduction of two parallel courses to be referred to as Course A, which would continue to be organized as formerly, with teachers drawn from all groups, and Course B, which would teach the technique of Anna Freud and her followers. Pearl King has traced the developments in "The Education of a Psycho-Analyst: The British Experience," and in "The Life and Work of Melanie Klein in the British Psycho-Analytical Society."[22] An "Ad Hoc Committee on Training" was set up, consisting of Sylvia Payne (chairman), John Bowlby (secretary), Anna Freud, Willi Hoffer, Melanie Klein, Susan Isaacs, Adrian Stephen, and John Rickman, to work out the details. In the frequent discussions that followed, it was apparent that the Kleinians were becoming increasingly militant and determined not to surrender an inch to Anna Freud's demands.

Finally, in November 1946, it was formally agreed that there would be "two parallel courses to be referred to as Course A, which would continue to be organised as formerly, teachers being drawn from all groups: and Course B, which would teach technique along the lines supported by Miss Freud and her colleagues, although both courses would be under one Training Committee which would be responsible for the selection and qualification of students. The students would come together for lectures and seminars other than those on technique. Only their first supervisor could be chosen from their own group; the second had to be from a non-Kleinian member of Course A, the Middle Group." (Even this requirement was dropped in the 1950s after pressure from both Melanie Klein and Anna Freud.) In this way the Society came to be semiofficially divided into three groups, although for training purposes there were officially only two courses. In addition to this arrangement for training was a gentlemen's agreement—or perhaps it should have been called a ladies' agreement—that there should be representatives of all three groups—Kleinians, Anna Freudians, and independents—on the main committees of the Society—that is, the Council, the Training Committee, and other policymaking bodies.

It was probably the best possible arrangement; but the students, who felt affiliations to their own training analysts, continued to suffer from the situation for many years, as Joseph Sandler recalled in 1982. He was analyzed by Willi Hoffer (Anna Freud's medical adviser, a requirement for every lay analyst) during the fifties, when "There was a lot of hostility between the groups, more than now. This was reflected within the student body. What the Kleinians had to say was incomprehensible to the Freudian group. As a student I felt, along with all the others in the 'B' group, that it was a waste of time listening to the Kleinians." When asked if he would describe it as "active acrimony," he replied: "No, I think sometimes friendships crossed these lines, although if they did, I think it was a very uneasy sort of friendship. But if one took a particular year of students, there would be links with the middle group students or even with those of the Kleinian group. The middle group was very amorphous. . . . I think the students in the middle group were always very muddled. Some tended towards the Kleinians, others towards the Freudians. There was a lot of identification of people with their analysts. Certainly I . . . identified with Hoffer, who was very anti-Kleinian. And then there was Anna Freud, who wouldn't say anything positive about them at all." It was not simply a matter of concepts, but "also very much a personal conflict."[23] Dr. Dinora Pines, a member of the "B" group, admits frankly that she and her colleagues have always felt very much cut off from the life of the Institute.[24]

This was precisely the way Anna Freud wanted things to be. On September 15, 1947, she informed the Board that she and Dr. Kate Friedlander and other like-minded analysts were initiating a training of selected people as therapists in child guidance clinics that was designed to take the place of the present play therapy. They would treat less severe cases than those treated by psychoanalysis.

Most members of the Board were highly disturbed by this development. The scheme meant that in certain respects—and certainly in the eyes of laymen—there were in effect two standards of psychoanalytic training. In Anna Freud's scheme a personal analysis was required as a prerequisite of training, in addition to the therapeutic handling of two cases five times a week under supervision. Furthermore, the fact that the lecture staff and supervisors included training analysts might confuse the public as to who was or was not trained in psychoanalysis. Although the word "analysis" was used rather than "psychoanalysis," the very fact that Anna Freud's name was connected with the scheme would lead the public to think of it, inevitably, as a psychoanalytical one.

Just as one group of devoted women attached themselves to Melanie Klein, another adhered to Anna Freud, who held weekly seminars in her home in Maresfield Gardens to discuss case material. These meetings were particularly important to the émigré analysts as they attempted to duplicate the intimacy of the Viennese meetings.

Freud had never forgiven Eva Rosenfeld, who had been so close to his family in Vienna, for going into analysis with Klein when she arrived in England in 1936. Anna, however, behaved very magnanimously to her:

> She even gave me an evening to explain Melanie Klein's theories to her seminar while the doodlebugs went, and Willi Hoffer got such an attack of fury with what I was saying that I said to him, "Willi, next time we must come in arm-in-arm or people will think we are really cross with each other and they mustn't think that, that isn't our way of being friends. You were cross with me but never mind," and we came in together arm-in-arm. Yes, that was our Viennese tradition; nothing could disturb a personal friendship.[25]

Melanie Klein told Rosenfeld, "You have sacrificed your analysis to Anna Freud"; and on meeting her in a bus one day after the agreement was settled, told her categorically that she would belong in the middle group. Rosenfeld recalled the incident to Pearl King in 1974: "I was so relieved because I thought I could not become a Kleinian, how could she think I wanted to be?"

Yet Anna Freud demanded the same sort of intense loyalty to her person as Melanie Klein did of her collaborators. When Margaret Little applied for training in 1941, she was asked by Sylvia Payne if she wanted an analyst of any particular persuasion. Unaware of the dramatic differences, Dr. Little was placed with Ella Sharpe, and had as her supervisors Anna Freud and Willi Hoffer. Consequently she was entitled to attend Anna Freud's evening groups. On one occasion Dr. Marjorie Franklin reported the case of a boy who had a compulsion to light fires. Dr. Little naively piped up, "Why don't you tell him he's depressed?" Dorothy Burlingham turned to her furiously: "You mean we should tell him he's unhappy?"[26] "Depression" was an unacceptable word; and it was made clear to Dr. Little that her presence would no longer be welcome.

In the early fifties, she asked Klein if she might talk to her about a patient with whom she was having difficulties. Klein did not refuse, but just as Little was leaving she asked her, "You're in Anna Freud's group. What is her organization like, anyway?" Never one to mince words, Dr. Little replied, "In the first place, I'm not. I'm in the middle group. From where I stand, your two organizations look exactly alike." Klein did not conceal her anger, and the interview came to an abrupt end. In Dr. Little's view, both women displayed a strong element of homosexuality, but she doesn't know to what degree it was conscious.

It is disturbing to accept that highly intelligent, well-educated people could succumb to the hysteria that swept through the British Society for some years. But one must realize that all human beings, even psychoanalysts, are subject to the same pressures; when engulfed in groups, they exhibit envy, anger, and competitiveness, whether the group be a trade union or a synod of bishops.

The fact that the British Society did not split is, in the view of many members, evidence both of British hypocrisy and of British determination to compromise. Some analysts feel that a split would have been more honest and certainly more beneficial to the Society. But who would have split from whom? One Kleinian analyst, Claude Wedeles, says that the Society has become "too tame" and he misses the fire of the old days.[27] It could be argued that despite all its vicissitudes, the Society has benefited in the long run by the arrangement. To paraphrase that most worldly of philosophers, Jeremy Bentham, if you try hard enough to love people, you sometimes end up by loving them.

PART SIX

1945-1960
THE
POSTWAR
WORLD

CHAPTER ONE

Mothers and Daughters

The best picture we have of Melanie Klein during this period is contained in the recollections of Hanna (Poznanska) Segal, who, at about the same time as Herbert Rosenfeld, began her analysis with Klein during the Controversial Discussions. On December 6, 1944, Klein told Clifford Scott that the young Polish woman was in her view "one of the most promising people we have ever had in Psycho-Analysis. Dr. Rosenfeld is a very different person; but they have in common that they are both very gifted, and also extremely reliable personalities, with stability and integrity."[1] Segal was beginning to be considered for the role of crown princess presumptive.

She had originally entered medical school in Warsaw with the intention of eventually becoming an analyst. She was in her third year when war broke out, but was fortunate enough to be visiting Paris at that time. She then spent a year at the Faculté de Médecin, and after her escape attended Edinburgh Medical School, which had opened a special section for émigré Polish medical students. While there she approached W. R. D. Fairbairn, who gave her two books to read, Anna Freud's *The Ego and the Mechanisms of Defence* and Klein's *The Psycho-Analysis of Children*. She found Anna Freud's book boring, but fell in love, as she puts it, with Klein's work. As a result she went into analysis with David Matthew because he had been an analysand of Klein's. At the end of the compulsory year in Edinburgh she left for London, determined to have an analysis with Klein.

In 1943 she found a job at the children's hospital at Paddington Green and contacted Winnicott, who arranged for her to have an interview with Klein. From the perspective of youth, Klein seemed to be a very old lady, smaller than Segal had expected, and she noticed her unusual way of walking.

Her shoulders were a bit forward, so was her head, and she walked with rather small steps, giving an impression of great attentiveness. Her head was a little bit forward. Now I think this way of walking, and that again was a purely subjective thing, belonged to the consulting room and waiting room. That's how she wanted to meet one. I don't think she was like that outside when she held herself much straighter and she didn't have the same sort of attentive posture. I noticed that her face was very beautiful. She wasn't white yet but she was greying, and there was a particular sort of slant throughout the interview of repose and seriousness. . . . There was no question of history or what are your parents like or childhood, and it was in no way an admission interview. For instance, I know quite clearly that she didn't ask me anything about, let's say, my neurotic difficulties or anything like that. . . . Of course, looking back, I'm sure it was quite a shrewd assessment going on all the time, but the way one experienced it from the other angle was that it was a very serious, very interesting conversation. She was interested in how I came to analysis, why I chose to have analysis with her, what my current plans were, etc., etc., a kind of conversation I think you would have with some elderly friend or relative who wanted to know where you're at and what you propose to do next.[2]

Two problems arose. Klein did not have a vacancy at the moment and suggested that she go to Dr. Heimann; but Segal, a strong-minded woman, refused. Then there was the problem of fees. Segal was earning £10 a month as a house surgeon, and the average fee for an analysis in those days was a pound a session. They eventually arranged that she should pay four or five shillings per session.

Segal knew nothing about the politics of the Society at the time. She went to see Edward Glover, the training secretary, whose *War and Pacifism* (1936) she greatly admired. The interview progressed quietly enough until Glover asked her with whom she wanted to go into analysis. When she told him that she had already started with Mrs. Klein, he jumped out of his chair. "In that case it's nothing to do with me. They train their people, we train ours"; and he held the door open. Segal sputtered with rage at her next session. "Well," she said bluntly, "somebody's crazy in this outfit, and I'm pretty sure it isn't me." She demanded an explanation. In retrospect, she is amazed at how coolly Klein reacted. She didn't mention the Controversial Discussions or discuss Glover, but linked the bewilderment with "the bewildered childhood situation that was going on in one's parental home which one didn't quite understand." Segal left, still smoldering because she had been offered no explanation, but at the same time imbued with a sense of peace and security in the realization that one's analyst provided a refuge of stability in a world gone mad with V1s and V2s and unaccountable behavior.

Melanie Klein delivered the last of the Controversial Discussions, "The Emotional Life of the Infant," on March 1, 1944. With Glover having resigned and Anna Freud withdrawn from active participation in the Society, this paper was, as John Bowlby recalls it, nothing more than a contribution to a Scientific Meeting.

The paper has never been published—a great pity, since it achieved precisely the intention of the Controversial Discussions, namely, to demonstrate that Melanie Klein's theories were an extension and development of Freud's. While sections of the paper were incorporated into later papers, this one is important because it traces the historical development of her concepts. Klein discusses how in *Civilization and Its Discontents* Freud acknowledged that a sense of guilt pre-dates a conscience and is not derived from a developed superego. She concedes that her theories still required a great deal of reflection, especially in the distinction arising from inner and outer sources. While she maintained that the depressive position was crucial in development, she was willing to accept that the baby has a vague conception of the mother as a whole from the beginning.

The discussion following the paper was a gauge of the change in the emotional climate of the Society. Sylvia Payne continued to insist that the depressive position depends primarily on libidinal frustration, not the aggressive impulses that give rise to anxiety and guilt, as Klein maintained. Ella Sharpe injected the only real note of asperity. "I assume hopefully," she remarked ironically,

a possibility of discussing Mrs. Klein's theory, of being critical in the constructive meaning of that word, of accepting some things without its being interpreted that one has swallowed Mrs. Klein and her work whole, or rejecting or doubting or suspending opinion without the assumption that one rejects everything or has no opinions at all. As long as I am not required to accept a closed system of the Alpha and Omega of human development, no matter by whom formulated, I remain in this Society.[3]

Sharpe could not accept that the depressive position was crucial, but only that it was one element in separation anxiety stemming from the birth trauma to which the organism has to adapt itself gradually—indeed, it seemed to her that the first steps a child takes are even more momentous than weaning. Surely, she argued, the loss of the breast is only symbolic of a lost situation?

Below depression lies outraged impotence and the frustration of the first love-greed. A sense of sin and guilt is associated with aggression, when that aggression is aroused not because of real physical needs but when the hunger is for love, thus involving hatred and aggression towards all rivals, actual or potential.

On May 3, 1944, Melanie Klein gave her formal reply. She reminded Miss Sharpe that she had always emphasized that the loss feared by the child was the *introjected love object*, and that this was in keeping with the views of Freud and Abraham on mourning and melancholia. As she herself said in "Mourning and Its Relation to Manic-Depressive States," the mourner "not only takes into himself (re-incorporates) the person whom he has just lost, but also reinstates his internalized good objects (ultimately his loved parents) who become part of his inner world from the earliest stages of his development onwards. These too are felt to have gone under, to be destroyed, whenever the loss of a loved person is experienced."[4] She concluded with the mild remark that much more thought needed to be applied to the various problems raised.

The Minutes record that Lola Brook was present as a guest that evening. Mrs. Brook, a Lithuanian Jew married to an Englishman, had entered Melanie Klein's life during the previous months as a secretary, and for the rest of her life became something far more—a trusted companion and almost collaborator. Lola Brook had a daughter of two, whose relationship with her mother was so close that she did not need speech for communication. Klein believed that the child had not experienced sufficient separation anxiety to motivate her to struggle to communicate and make contact or to find symbols of replacements for other people and objects in the world around her. Judith Fay, who was in supervision with Klein at the time, was assigned the child, Helen, for observation. A limited separation from her mother had to be effected in order to activate anxiety. While Lola Brook went to Klein's house for a few hours several mornings a week for some months without Helen, Fay tried to play with the impassive child. Fay took her to Hampstead Heath, but Helen showed no interest in anything around her. For that matter, when her mother left her, she remained expressionless. Very gradually she began to take an interest in playing, trying to control the situation, until one day she emptied all the bags of sugar on the kitchen floor. To Judith Fay's astonishment, Klein proved "absolutely right": the child began to exhibit stages of anxiety, protest, naughtiness, then such extreme talkativeness that the family complained. Her mother, as Klein had seen immediately, was too good a mother. The grown-up Helen Brook does not recall this period at all, only of often sitting in the kitchen with the housekeeper, Miss Cutler, in the flat at Bracknell Gardens (where Klein moved in 1953) while her mother was closeted with Mrs. Klein.

Susan Isaacs's house in Primrose Hill was bombed during the winter of 1945, and she fell ill with pneumonia, a prelude to the cancer from which she was to die in 1948. But life was beginning to return to relative normality, with a widespread confidence that the end of the war was in sight. For some, life had changed irreversibly. Without Glover as an ally, there was no longer a place for Melitta in the British Society; and when she left for America she began to detach herself emotionally as well as geographically from psychoanalysis.*

In the mid-thirties Walter Schmideberg became involved in some sort of relationship with the bisexual novelist Winifred Ellerman (Bryher), the lover of the American poet Hilda Doolittle (H.D.). H.D. had gone into analysis with Schmideberg after returning from Vienna, where she had been analyzed by Freud.† Bryher, the daughter of an immensely rich shipping tycoon, had financed the escape of many of the Jewish analysts from the Nazis. She agreed to pay for the training of Austrian candidates in England,‡ with the sole stipulation that the analyst had to be "passed" by Walter Schmideberg first. She also helped many of them during their difficult adjustment to England. Paula Heimann was enabled to get a British medical degree in Edinburgh through a loan from Bryher. At the end of the war Schmideberg and Bryher moved permanently to Switzerland, where Melitta visited them amicably from time to time. No one has been able to understand this strange three-sided relationship. Bryher was in the habit of collecting lame ducks, and one theory is that she took on Schmideberg, whose alcoholism became worse with the passing years. Perdita Schaffner, H.D.'s daughter, was adopted by Bryher. Even after sharing a house with Bryher and Schmideberg for many years, she is still puzzled by the nature of the relationship.

Eric Clyne, who remained on good terms with his sister for some years after her break with their mother, believes that Melitta experienced great feelings of guilt over abandoning Walter. Was she displacing the far more anguished guilt over her mother onto her husband? It is more likely that her departure reactivated the guilt she had experienced when her mother had apparently persuaded her to join her in England before Walter was able to get into the country. While in America, Melitta brought her stepsister, Kristina (the child of Arthur's second marriage), from Sweden to live with her. It was an interesting continuation of the dominant mother role, for Melitta became extremely resentful when Kristina insisted on asserting her independence to live a life of her own.

At the end of the war Melanie Klein's roots were deeply planted in England. When the owner wanted to sell the Clifton Hill house, she bought it for about £3,000—the only house she ever owned. An elegant, graceful struc-

---

* She did not resign formally from the Society until 1962.
† Susan Friedman, who is editing the H.D.–Bryher letters, has recently found a letter dated Oct. 31, 1934, from Vienna, in which H.D. reveals that Freud had told her Schmideberg was a homosexual—"that poor dear charming fellow," Freud described him.
‡ Anna Freud had operated the Bryher Fund for supplementing the fees of training analysts in Vienna for some years prior to 1938.

ture with large rooms and high ceilings, both house and garden gave her a great deal of pleasure and a sense of security.

Klein spent August 1945 on a farm with her daughter-in-law, Judy, and the two grandchildren, Michael and Diana;* but with the war over, she longed to be back at work in London in September. "It will be lovely to work without bombs flying about. And isn't it marvellous to think we shall soon have peace!" she wrote to Clifford Scott.[5]

After the long dissipation of energies during the Controversial Discussions it was necessary to produce some new creative papers. She continued to exhort Scott to expand the paper he had given at the Paris Congress in 1938.

> It should make an excellent link with further scientific papers, which should take us away from these abstract discussions on theory which— though I still think they were of great value—were so much hampered by the constant reference to what Freud said or did not say or meant or did not mean. If we want at last to go back to the real status of a scientific society, we should discuss facts and truths; and I think that your paper, since you speak with the authority of a psychiatrist as well as analyst, should be a very good link for the return to actual scientific work.

While she assured him that the atmosphere in the Society was much less tendentious, peace for Klein could not include the voicing of views to which she was very much opposed. She felt highly indignant about some recent remarks made by Karin Stephen on the hazards of analyzing schizophrenics— "old stuff from the beginning of the twenties, when it was an established thing that schizophrenics are not analysable; and we know the Viennese still keep to the idea that borderline cases should not be touched." This moved her to exert even greater pressure on Scott to produce his paper. Her promising candidate, Herbert Rosenfeld, would in due time contribute something from his experience in analyzing schizoids whose psychotic anxieties could be relieved, he had found, only by constant interpretation. But he was not yet fully prepared; whereas Scott, who had analyzed schizophrenic patients on a daily basis at the Cassel Hospital, was "particularly suited to speak with authority on these matters. I realise how very little time you have got, and I therefore think it would be better to give yourself a longer period to work this paper out very carefully, and with the purpose to make clear the theory of these early stages as well as the technique of dealing with psychotic anxieties."

She, Heimann, and Isaacs planned to bring out a collection of papers in book form. This was to include the papers given during the Controversial Dis-

---

* During the Controversial Discussions, Klein told Isaacs: "One thing which is a great happiness to me are my grandchildren. The little girl [Diana, born Sept. 23, 1942] is *simply lovely* and Michael is a very interesting, promising child. I am also very happy to have such a good relation with Judy."

cussions, two papers she was preparing on the early Oedipus complex, Joan Riviere's paper on early conflict, and perhaps Money-Kyrle's paper "Some Aspects of Political Ethics in the Light of Psycho-Analysis."*

Klein noted—almost casually—that the Edinburgh analyst W. R. D. Fairbairn had published "something" in the last issue of the *International Journal*.† His ideas, developed quite independently, were close enough to her own to cause her some uneasiness: "I have not yet had time to read it carefully, but one glance confirms the view that he sees things out of proportion though he has something interesting to say. Now his views on the origin of schizophrenia, which I gather he presents in this paper, would also make it essential that people's minds should be clarified on the early positions." If Fairbairn had turned his attention to schizophrenia, it was necessary to work quickly in order to anticipate him in any concepts he might develop.

In fact, Fairbairn's paper initiated what was to be the last major creative period of Klein's life. He forced her to trace life from its very first moments rather than select later crucial events in infantile development. Klein had always striven to emphasize her close connection with Freud and Abraham. Fairbairn, however, isolated in Edinburgh, was no respecter of persons. J. D. Sutherland emphasizes that he followed the British tradition of taking joy in ideas for their own sake, outrageous as they might seem to the more doctrinaire continentals. If Freud's instinct theory did not accord with the theory of phases, then the whole matter of development must be reexamined.

In Fairbairn's view, Freud had gone wrong when he abandoned hysteria for melancholia as the seat of the neuroses. (Consequently, Fairbairn was implicitly critical of the central importance Melanie Klein assigned to the depressive position.) Attention should have been devoted to the schizoid position, which involved a splitting of the ego, as opposed to simply antedating the Oedipus complex—which Fairbairn saw as no solution, because it left out of account any possibility of repression occurring in the preoedipal period. Freud saw the libido as directionless, but Fairbairn considers the libido as primarily object-seeking, although he does not emphasize the importance of the breast as the first part-object.

Melanie Klein, in her desire not to appear too radical, had hesitated to say bluntly that her system discarded a state of primary narcissism, although the theory that instincts were object-seeking could admit no other interpretation. She seemed unwilling publicly to disown the concept of narcissism as postulated by Freud, but left it to followers such as Riviere and Heimann to define what she meant.

---

* Only the women mentioned contributed to the first collection of Kleinian papers, *Developments in Psycho-Analysis* (1952). Money-Kyrle's paper later appeared in *New Directions in Psycho-Analysis* (1955).
† "Endopsychic Structure Considered in Terms of Object-Relationships," *J.* (1944), 25: 70–93.

Klein would agree with Fairbairn that repression is highly important because it necessitates not only the splitting of the object but the splitting of the
ego. Fairbairn concluded this from observing the fragmented selves appearing
in dreams. He viewed dreams not as wish fulfillments but as dramatizations of
situations existing in internal reality. The splitting of the ego, so characteristic
of schizoid and hysterical conditions, deserved attention in Fairbairn's view
both as a characteristic of normal development and as a fixation point for later
serious emotional and mental malfunctioning.

Klein could not ignore this challenge, which had to be answered as quickly
as possible. Herbert Rosenfeld, in his work with schizophrenics, had been providing her with interesting case material. In 1946 she asked him very sweetly if
he would mind postponing the presentation of his paper until she had delivered the one she was preparing on schizoid mechanisms. In justification, she
informed him that Abraham had actually withheld interpretations lest they be
used first by his students. Dealing in the counter of ideas, analysts have always
been somewhat paranoid about the primacy of their insights; but Klein's pioneering contributions have not been sufficiently acknowledged. From the early
twenties she had stressed the developmental processes through relationship to
objects, so that she may legitimately be described as the parent of object-relations theory.

Klein's paper "Notes on Some Schizoid Mechanisms" was delivered to the
British Society on December 4, 1946, and in the published paper Klein acknowledged her gratitude to Paula Heimann for stimulating suggestions that
had enabled her to think out the concepts presented in the paper. The material
had been derived from the analyses of both children and adults. She had often,
she emphasized, expressed the view that object relations exist from the beginning of life. In this early phase the destructive impulse is expressed by phantasied oral-sadistic attacks on the mother's breast, which soon develop into
onslaughts on all parts of her body. She still described this as the paranoid
phase; but by the time the paper was published she had changed it to the paranoid-schizoid phase, with due acknowledgment to Fairbairn.

She launched immediately into a discussion of Fairbairn's recent papers.
The major difference between them was that Fairbairn's approach derived
largely from a concern with ego development in relation to objects, whereas her
concern had been with the etiology of anxiety. Nevertheless, she agreed with
his contention that schizoid and schizophrenic disorders cover a much wider
spectrum than had previously been considered, that the schizoid position was a
normal phase of development, and, moreover, that there was a close connection between hysteria and schizophrenia. However, she could not agree with
Fairbairn that only the bad object was internalized, nor with his dismissal
of the role of aggression from the beginning of life. "I suggest," she wrote,

Melanie with grandson Michael in 1938.

In the garden of Clifton Hill with Oscar Nemon, 1939.

Melitta and Walter Schmideberg in 1937.

John Bowlby.

Edward Glover.

John Rickman.

Richard, one of Klein's patients.

Klein's "toys."

Donald Winnicott.

Susan Isaacs, 1947.

Marjorie Brierley at 24.

Paula Heimann at the London Congress,
1953.

Joan Riviere.

Wilfred Bion.

Melanie Klein (left), Anna Freud, and
Ernest Jones in Zurich, 1949.

Sylvia Payne.

Anna Freud (left) and Marie Bonaparte, London, 1953.

Dinner to celebrate Melanie's 70th birthday in 1952. From left: (seated) Marion
Milner, Sylvia Payne, W. Clifford M. Scott, Roger Money-Kyrle, Eric Clyne; (standing) Melanie Klein, Ernest Jones, Herbert Rosenfeld, Joan Riviere, Donald Winnicott; (seated) Paula Heimann, James Strachey, Gwen Evans, Cyril Wilson, Michael
Balint, Judy Clyne.

Melanie Klein and W. Clifford M. Scott at the Paris Congress, 1957.

Melanie Klein and Hanna Segal, 1958.

"that the primary anxiety of being annihilated by a destructive force within, with the ego's specific response of falling to pieces or splitting itself, may be extremely important in all schizophrenic processes."[6]

She then turned to a concept that many analysts consider her greatest contribution to psychoanalysis—projective identification. The infant, by projecting his aggressive impulses into his mother, projects some of his own destructiveness so that in his omnipotent phantasy she becomes his persecutor. Excessive splitting of the ego through projective identification leaves the ego with a sense of fragmentation. In a normal personality an optimal balance is achieved between projection and introjection. "The projection of good feelings and good parts of the self into the mother is essential for the infant's ability to develop good object-relations and to integrate his ego."[7] Anxiety can be deepened by a variety of internal and external stresses, leading to later impotence or claustrophobia. Abnormal splitting of the ego causes an imbalance in the relationship of inner and outer worlds so characteristic of schizophrenics, in whom withdrawal to an inner world occurs through the fear of introjecting a dangerous external world; but such withdrawal brings not peace but heightened fear of internal persecutors. This vicious circle in turn can lead to a state of overdependence on the external representative of one's own good parts, as in situations where the mother becomes the ego-ideal to a point that the ego is weakened and impoverished.

Klein had encountered the developmental connections between schizoid and depressive positions in patients who, filled with self-reproaches and unable to surmount the anxiety of having destroyed their good object, slip back into a state of panic about their inner tormentors. That there is a connection between manic-depressive and schizophrenic disorders she recognized only as a "tentative hypothesis" at this point, and she would welcome evidence supporting her view from "colleagues who have had ample material for psychiatric observations"—namely, Scott and Rosenfeld. Her own conclusions were based on cases such as one in which the patient, anxious that his analyst be spared his destructive impulses, turned them against his own ego, a defense mechanism brought into force under the pressure of anxiety and guilt. Such paranoid-schizoid anxiety is characteristic of the baby's first months. The onset of the depressive position can reinforce regression to schizoid mechanisms. Depending on the intensity of the feeling and the strength of the ego, this will be either a normal part of the developmental process or the basis for later schizophrenic illness. In an Appendix she referred to the Schreber case, in which Freud said: "The dispositional point of fixation must be situated further back than in paranoia, and must lie somewhere at the beginning of the course of development from auto-erotism to object-love."[8] Freud was opening up the possibility of understanding psychoses and the processes underlying them. In other words, here—as in so many other cases—she was simply following a hint dropped from Freud to pursue further research in this area. The only other paper in which Melanie Klein discussed projective identification was "On Identification" (1955), in which she analyzed Julien Green's story *If I Were You.**

One of the major criticisms sometimes directed against her was the contention that she failed to substantiate her concepts. Yet when D. W. Winnicott wrote "The Manic Defence" (1935) and "Hate in the Counter-transference" (1947), replete with evidence which he felt gave her this sub-stantiation, she was silent. On one occasion, when driving Pearl King home after a Scientific Meeting, Winnicott, close to tears, suddenly burst out, "If only Mrs. Klein just once would acknowledge an idea she has borrowed from someone else!" Klein's problem with Winnicott was that he was too indepen-dent, and probably had not discussed the papers with her in advance. She seemed to find it hard to tolerate a situation in which he regarded himself as her equal. She felt that Fairbairn, too, had to be watched carefully, because one never knew what he would come up with next. "Psycho-analysis—hah!" she snorted as, flanked by her supporters, she sailed out of the room after one of his papers.† With Rosenfeld it was a different matter. As her analysand, he could be counted on to buttress her theoretical concepts with empirical data. In his use of projective identification with schizophrenic patients, he was to demonstrate the profound validity of the concept.

Many Kleinians (including Klein herself!) have found the term "projective identification" cumbersome. Claude Wedeles has suggested the substitution of "projective intrusion," although he is not altogether sure whether it is much of an improvement.[9] Hanna Segal, in lectures she delivered at University College London in the winter of 1982, argued for scrapping "projective identification" in favor of "projection"; but the rich specificity of the concept might be lost, since "projection" suggests a process or function rather than a complex psychic state.

In a paper delivered at the International Colloquium on Psychosis in Mon-treal in November 1969, Rosenfeld gave a good working definition of projective identification:

"Projective identification" relates first of all to a splitting process of the early ego, where either good or bad parts of the self are split off from the

---

* On Feb. 2, 1949, she read to the Scientific Meeting of the British Society passages from Conrad's *The Arrow of Gold*, which illustrated the mechanism of introjection and projection in a love relationship.

† Dr. J. D. Sutherland is highly skeptical that she ever behaved with such discourtesy to Fairbairn; but three other analysts recall this as her reaction when he delivered his paper "On the Nature and Aims of Psycho-Ana-lytical Treatment," on June 18, 1958. This was the controversial paper in which he questioned the universal validity of the use of the couch.

ego and are as a further step projected in love or hatred into external objects which leads to fusion and identification of the projected parts of the
self with the external objects. There are important paranoid anxieties related to these processes as the objects filled with aggressive parts of the self
become persecuting and are experienced by the patient as threatening to re-
taliate by forcing themselves and the bad parts of the self which they contain back again into the ego.[10]

Rosenfeld's membership paper, "Analysis of a Schizophrenic State with
Depersonalization," was delivered to the British Society on March 5, 1947. He
based it on the second case he analyzed while in training. The patient, who
turned out to be psychotic, was severely depersonalized. He complained of
having no feelings and was clearly struggling against some schizophrenic state.
One of Rosenfeld's supervisors, Sylvia Payne, told him that she could not supervise the case lest Rosenfeld project into her the patient's persecutory fears.
This he feels was a valid acknowledgment of the existence of projective identification, accompanied by anxiety about the possibility of handling it. Even
Joan Riviere, a supporter of Klein from the beginning, was nervous about "borderline" cases, and turned down a patient Clifford Scott asked her to take on in
1940. "Though I have had many patients who are 'borderline' cases in one
sense, they have all been character cases who had made an adjustment of some
sort to ordinary life; and I am doubtful if my technique would be equal to a
more psychotic type."[11]

Joan Riviere had come a long way with Melanie Klein, but was unwilling to
accompany her on the journey into completely alien territory. Klein, perceiving
this reluctance, realized that Riviere could no longer give her the kind of total
adherence she felt she needed from her supporters. And Rickman, another
supporter, began to find her policy unpalatable. Although Klein backed him
against Adrian Stephen for president in 1947, a coldness developed between
them while he was in office. When Rickman interviewed Pearl King as a training candidate in 1945 he told her that he was a Kleinian; but within a year,
while she was in analysis with him, he informed her that Mrs. Klein had
dropped him from her group. It was becoming increasingly clear that to be a
"Kleinian" meant that Klein had deliberately selected one for this status.

To be a student encouraged by Melanie Klein was both a rare and a wonderful experience, according to Herbert Rosenfeld. Before leaving Germany
Rosenfeld had been analyzed, but his first analysis seemed in retrospect utterly
superficial. Deeply impressed by the ease with which Klein followed the connections in his thoughts, within weeks he exclaimed, "What an experience!"[12]
Both Klein and Rosenfeld were more or less on trial in his membership paper:
"Analysis of a Schizophrenic State with Depersonalization" was a pioneering

venture in that it was one of the first cases recorded of an analysis of a schizophrenic patient.* Freud had believed that patients suffering from narcissistic neuroses were incapable of experiencing transference; but Rosenfeld, stimulated by Klein's work with children, found that the avoidance of reassurance leads to the development of a transference psychosis. While only partial success may be achieved, Rosenfeld believed that the study of schizophrenia reveals much about the paranoid-schizoid aspects of normal development.

At the Sixteenth Congress at Zurich, in August 1949, Rosenfeld and Segal gave two more important papers, "Notes on the Psycho-Pathology of Confusional States in Chronic Schizophrenias" and "Some Aspects of the Analysis of a Schizophrenic."[13] It was at this first postwar Congress that Harold Bridger (an analysand of Paula Heimann's) realized the extent to which Klein was reviled in international circles, and perceived an undercurrent of feeling that her ideas opened up an abyss for psychoanalysis. "One had the feeling that it was far more than just a personal antagonism. It was far more deeply seated in the sense of anxiety and fear about what those ideas would do."[14]

The congress was memorable in many ways. For the first time in four years Klein and Melitta saw each other, although they did not speak. Melitta had traveled from New York to give a paper, "Psychology and Treatment of the Criminal Psychopath." Klein's own paper, "On the Criteria for the Termination of a Psycho-Analysis," compared the emotional state of the patient whose analysis has finished to that of mourning. Analysis can be brought to an end when the patient has worked through his infantile schizoid and depressive states so that his ego has been sufficiently strengthened to endure the inevitable reactivation of these emotions occasioned by the termination of his analysis. In order to ease this trauma, the analyst should set a date several months in advance so that the patient can begin to cope with the reappearance of early anxieties.

It was at this congress that Jacques Lacan delivered his paper "The Mirror Stage as Formative of the Function of the I as Revealed in Psychoanalytic Experience."[15] Lacan, in a paper at the Congrès des Psychanalystes de Langue Française in Brussels in 1948, had drawn a connnection between his "imagos of the fragmented body" and Klein's "internal objects," and for some years his papers referred to her work in favorable terms. Contemporary Kleinian analysts, however, do not appreciate any suggestion of affinity in ideas between Klein and Lacan.

In a letter to Clifford Scott, dated January 28, 1948, Klein told him that Lacan had discussed with her the agenda of the first world Congress of Psychiatry to be held in Paris in 1950.

---

*Clifford Scott was one of the first to analyze schizophrenics on a regular basis.

Dr. Lacan, who as a former head of the Psychiatric Clinic in Paris is very strongly using his influence to interest psychiatrists in psycho-analysis, had done his best to get the vote for the last topic in the progress of psycho-analysis. According to his report, this choice was prevented by the psycho-analytic group in Paris, for what he interprets as their reactionary tendencies.

He asked me to use my influence with my psychiatric colleagues to get in London a vote for the topic "The Progress of Psycho-Analysis," and, if possible, to use my influence in getting the same vote in New York. I myself agree with this matter—if congresses mean anything at all and if there is a wish to instruct psychiatry—is right. I am communicating these facts to you (which, needless to say, are confidential) and suggest to you to use all your influence in this direction.

P.S. As you well know, Dr. Jacques Lacan is a member of the Psycho-Analytical Society in Paris—as far as I can gather, the most progressive member of it. Dr. Lacan also suggested that it would have been important that at a Child Psychiatric Congress this summer the progressive point of view in psycho-analysis should have been represented, and that therefore Anna Freud should not have been the speaker selected.*[16]

How Klein reacted to the obsequious references to Anna Freud in "The Mirror Stage" is not known, but she was delighted when Lacan approached her on this occasion and charmed her into agreeing to let him translate *The Psycho-Analysis of Children* into French. Almost simultaneously a young French-woman, Françoise Girard, also told her that she would be greatly interested in translating the same work; Klein informed her that it had already been entrusted to someone else (she did not specify whom), but suggested that Girard might consider eventually translating *Contributions to Psycho-Analysis*, which had been published the previous year. It was a situation that was to lead to some embarrassment.

Ernest Jones's Introduction to *Contributions to Psycho-Analysis* (1948), which included all Klein's papers to date except those included in *The Psycho-Analysis of Children*, indicated his uneasy public position towards her. He had now embarked on the biography of Freud; and while he described Klein privately to his wife as "a wonderful person," if he wrote too fulsomely about her he might alienate Anna Freud whose cooperation was essential.† In the Introduction he remarked that he had never anticipated the "commotion" that would be aroused when he invited Melanie Klein to England twenty years be-

---

* Klein, as respondent to Anna Freud, claimed that the latter had failed to point out the age at which she felt the ego was sufficiently integrated for the child to experience guilt.
† Compare his preface to *New Directions in Psycho-Analysis* (1955), written when he had almost completed the biography. See p. 412.

fore. She had pursued her ideas with "consistent recklessness" (an odd phrase) that had won her fanatical friends and uneasy enemies. Nevertheless, Jones fully anticipated that the sort of uproar into which the British Society had been plunged recently would be duplicated in societies throughout the world.

In his own view, the claims that Mrs. Klein's theories represented a deviation from Freud were "a gross exaggeration," and that her great contribution lay in going directly to children, a procedure necessitating developing a technique of her own. Furthermore, she went on to apply her investigations into the field of insanity, a step that had infuriated many psychiatrists, but Jones did not see how her researches could have logically stopped short of this troubled area.

A new era was at hand. At the Zurich Congress Ernest Jones after seventeen years resigned the presidency, which was taken over by an American, Leo Bartemeier. Deep changes were also beginning in Klein's close relationship with Paula Heimann. One evening in the late fifties Tom Hayley (an analysand of Roger Money-Kyrle's) drove Melanie Klein home from a meeting. On this occasion she confided in him that she had begged Heimann not to deliver a paper on countertransference at the Zurich Congress,[17] and reported that Paula had replied, "Do you think it gives me such great pleasure to stand in your shadow my whole life long?" These were exactly the words Adler had used to Freud when asserting his right to "a place in the sun."[18] Heimann's paper has been accepted as an essential part of the Kleinian corpus;* but few analysts seem to know that Klein and Heimann had a serious disagreement over it, Klein insisting that countertransference is something that interferes with analysis. If you have feelings about your patient, she told Hayley, you must do an immediate lightning self-analysis; but Paula was elevating subjective feelings into a great virtue. Publicly she did not disavow countertransference; Wilfred Bion emphasized the concept later, and it is generally believed that it originated with Klein. It must be remembered that Klein had been deeply impressed by Freud's views about the dangers of countertransference, which he had expressed in *The Future Prospects of Psycho-Analytic Therapy* (1910).[19]

Heimann claimed that Freud's demand that the analyst must recognize and master his countertransference did not necessarily lead to the conclusion that the analyst should become unfeeling and detached, "but that he must use his emotional response as a key to the patient's unconscious."[20] While her paper is often described as the first explicit statement of the positive value of countertransference and hence a milestone in the history of psychoanalytic ideas, it should not be forgotten that Winnicott had delivered a significant

---

* Curiously, it was never delivered to the British Society. The paper does not contain a single reference to Klein.

paper to the British Society on February 5, 1947—"Hate in the Counter-Transference"—which would scarcely have endeared him to Melanie Klein, particularly since he probably had not discussed it with her in advance. While Winnicott was speaking particularly of psychotics, he emphasized that the analyst's own capacity for hate in general cannot be ignored. "However much he cannot avoid hating them [i.e., psychotics] and fearing them and the better he knows this the less will hate and fear be the motives determining what he does to his patients."[21] Hate has to be kept in abeyance, to be used in the analytic situation when the time is ripe. In order to analyze psychotics, the analyst must face things about himself. Winnicott had come to this conclusion through self-revealing dreams following a period in which "I found I was doing bad work."[22] One of Winnicott's most attractive aspects was the disarming way in which he would publicly acknowledge mistakes.

Heimann's view did not differ substantially from Winnicott's. The analyst must acknowledge and sustain the feelings stirred up in him "in order to *subordinate* them to the analytic task in which he functions as the patient's mirror reflection."[23] There are times when the patient unconsciously forces a role on the analyst, and the latter can provide a deeper insight into the patient's unconscious mental processes. As Sandler, Darc, and Holder have pointed out, "It is of some interest that this extension of the concept of the counter-transference is similar to Freud's change in his view of the function of transference, first regarded only as a hindrance but later seen as an asset to therapy."[24] Was Heimann in some way telling Klein something about the unsatisfactory nature of her own analysis? In Winnicott's paper he had said, "in certain stages of certain analyses the analyst's hate is actually sought by the patient, and what is then needed is hate that is objective. If the patient seeks objective or justified hate he must be able to reach it, else he cannot feel he can reach objective love."[25]

Heimann's paper was an act of independence, and she could have argued that she had as much right to produce original and creative work as Melanie Klein did, but this is certainly not the way Klein would have seen it. By 1949 Heimann was, at fifty, the colleague closest in age to Klein. She was determined to strike out on her own, just as Melitta had done. With the passing of the years Klein increasingly resembled Libussa in her inflexibility, her strength, and her drive to get her own way.

There has always been a great deal of speculation about the break between the two women. Neither of them spoke at length to colleagues about their eventual rift, except for cryptic comments; Heimann's unpublished reminiscences are even more bitter than Nelly Wolffheim's memoir of Klein. Also, by 1974, when Pearl King interviewed Heimann, her memory was beginning to deteriorate. Nevertheless, all her comments were colored by resentment and envy, and whether justified or not, these emotions must be taken into consideration. The querulous tone is such that one wonders if there was an unconscious lesbian attachment between them.

Klein had left for England the year before Heimann joined the Berlin Society, but Paula had known Melitta there, and the Schmidebergs were very kind to her during her first period in England. On hearing of the death of Hans in April 1934, Heimann wrote Klein a letter of condolence; and Walter Schmideberg subsequently told her that Mrs. Klein would like to see her. This seemed to her rather odd, and she began to wonder if all was not well between Melitta and her mother. To Heimann's great surprise, Klein immediately began to pour out her feelings to her—a relative stranger—in German. When Pearl King asked her if Klein was very distressed by the death of Hans, Heimann replied: "I was very surprised because she didn't go to the funeral and she said to me that she didn't go because she didn't want to meet her ex-husband who she felt would attempt a reconciliation, which was all very odd because he had married again." (Actually, by then Arthur Klein had been divorced from his second wife.)

During their discussions Klein was very depressed, and once told Heimann of a dream she had in which she did not know whether to commit suicide or not. When Heimann in later situations reminded her of this dream, Klein denied it, insisting that it was quite clear that she did not want to commit suicide. On one of her visits Heimann asked Klein why she had turned to her rather than, say, Mrs. Riviere, who had known her so much longer. Klein replied, "Ah, these are English people," suggesting that she felt much more at home with Paula, with whom she could speak in German. In her vulnerability she showed Heimann her most precious possessions, Emanuel's poems. At one point she decided to write a paper on her experience of bereavement and mourning. Paula offered to act as her secretary and wrote down her thoughts as she expressed them. Of these Heimann commented, "The ideas she expressed were entirely new to me. They were different from what I had learned in the Berlin Society." She has nothing to say about the profound suffering that infuses the paper on the depressive position, no sympathy at all in her recollection of those early meetings. Yet she must have been the friend who accompanied "Mrs. A" on her memorable walk (described in the paper on mourning) when the houses seemed to be falling on top of her and she had to retreat to a restaurant in a state of terrified bewilderment.

All through the summer of 1934, Paula joined Klein and the Schmidebergs on excursions in their Sunbeam. (The exact year can be established by the fact that in 1935 the Schmidebergs bought a Buick.) This would suggest that for some months in 1934, following Hans's death, there was at least a temporary healing of the growing rift between Melitta and her mother. On one of their excursions they ran into Glover, his elegant wife, Gladys, and their daughter, then about nine, whom Paula described as "a mongol idiot." They sat in a garden restaurant, where Glover calmly cut up a banana for the child. Afterward, in the car, Paula exclaimed, "My God, if I were him I'd shoot the child and I'd shoot the wife and I'd shoot myself"; and later Klein told her, "You mustn't say that, Melitta is in analysis with him [Glover]"[26]—which would suggest that Melitta had already left Ella Sharpe by early 1934 and begun analysis with Glover.

When Paula was about to enter analysis with Klein a short time later, she nervously broke the news to Melitta, adding that she hoped it would not affect their friendship. The strain between mother and daughter was now apparent; and this was probably about the time Melitta wrote the letter in which she asserted her independence from her mother. Melitta told Paula she was not surprised because she had expected this would happen. There is not a word of criticism of Melitta in Paula's recollections. She declares that Melitta was "driven" from England, a gross exaggeration. She makes no reference to Melitta's attacks on her mother, yet Paula came to be known as the fiercest of Klein's defenders. If Melitta had been kind to her, she must have found herself in an awkward situation in the cross-fire between mother and daughter. One passage from her interview with Pearl King should be quoted:

> One day Melanie told me that Melitta had mentioned a dream and that she, Melanie, had interpreted; had said, "Well, no wonder that you can't have a child,"—as if maybe there was something of ambition which she interpreted and Melitta was very angry about it. I really do not know [when] Melitta got so ill—but one must also say she was pushed into it, there's no question in my mind about it.

Not long before her death in 1983, Heimann told Dr. William Gillespie that Melanie had "seduced" her into analysis.[27] Paula Heimann was at that time a woman in her mid-thirties and a free agent. It is true that she felt disoriented after a divorce and being transplanted to a strange country, so it is probable that she felt the need of analysis. As for Melanie Klein's motives, she might quite genuinely have realized Paula's predicament when she suggested that she go into analysis with her. Certainly no one could deny that Klein wanted adherents and that she recognized in Heimann's fine mind someone whom she would like to have as an ally. She also had a deep need for someone who would fill her expectations of a daughter, just as Freud, who was not close to his own sons, needed an ideal son; and both played off their surrogate siblings against each other.

Heimann later told Pearl King that Klein had attributed the origin of Heimann's depression to the fact that "my mother must have had mourning depression all through the pregnancy presumably for it seemed to me I might not have been born if it were not for her need to replace the child and my mother used to say even when I was a child that she clearly preferred me to my elder sister, that I always mothered her, and she said that with great admiration and later I thought in a sense how sad that was. But then I felt well I'm prepared to do something for my mother and not prepared to do it for my analyst. She said nasty things about Sylvia, in fact nobody could analyse except her." This stream-of-consciousness monologue suggests that Heimann had probably not resolved her relationship with her mother, and with Klein she was trying to reenact it the way she wished it had been.

Klein's interpretation is profoundly revealing. She herself had been pregnant with Melitta while mourning for Emanuel, wanting the restoration of her dead brother rather than this unwelcome infant. She was also in a state of mourning for Libussa while Erich was an infant. As Winnicott remarked in "Hate in the Counter-Transference," "the mother hates the baby before the baby hates the mother, and before the baby can know his mother hates him."[28]

Heimann's comments indicate the dangers inherent in an analysis that develops from a social situation and friendship. Paula was expected to act as a daughter, helping Klein to move from the maisonette in Linden Gardens to the house in Clifton Hill just on the eve of her analysis. It is apparent that Heimann sometimes took advantage of the ambiguous situation. During one session she made a mischievous comment about Melitta's "scientific courage" in expressing her own views by reinterpreting Klein's concepts. Her analyst then reproached her. "This wasn't scientific and this wasn't courage," she was told; and didn't Paula see that an intrigue was being conducted against her? Heimann told Pearl King that Klein made many malicious remarks about Joan Riviere and Susan Isaacs, and was injudicious in her revelations about the Society. On the other hand, when Heimann was indiscreet, Klein would berate her indignantly.

Heimann gave her membership paper, "A Contribution to the Problem of Sublimation and Its Relation to Processes of Internalization," to the Society in 1939.* Heimann is deliberately vague about the duration of her analysis—it would appear deliberately so. It began on January 30, 1935, continued for years with intermittent interruptions, and terminated finally in 1953.

The analysis was resumed (according to Heimann, at Klein's instigation) after the war, late in the forties. (The implication that Heimann was always the passive partner in their relationship is completely at variance with the memories her supporters have of her, particularly her analysands, who remember her as an extraordinarily strong-minded, humorous woman.)

When war broke out Klein told Heimann that while it would be more convenient for her to stay in London, she was going to evacuate to Cambridge "in order to preserve psycho-analysis, it wasn't because she personally was afraid

---

* She had been qualified in Berlin in 1928, where she had been analyzed by Theodor Reik.

of the bombs, and I think to some degree she really believed it." While Klein was in Cambridge with Susan Isaacs, Paula would travel there to stay for weekends while she underwent several hours of analysis, but what is surprising is that she does not mention at least one visit to Pitlochry. Heimann's daughter, Mrs. Mertza Peatie, recalls that during this period she was at boarding school, and she remembers spending a holiday with her mother in Pitlochry, probably in the summer of 1940. It is doubtful if Heimann was there for a long period, because she was still technically an alien. She recounts that on one occasion Rickman accompanied her to a police station to argue that she should leave London for a time—possibly to spend a short holiday with her daughter in a safe location. She does not mention either Cambridge or Pitlochry or the duration of the analysis to Pearl King, suggesting that she was embarrassed by the length of time she allowed herself to be under Klein's sway—"full of anger against myself for having been so stupid and having been so exploited by Melanie."

When Klein returned to London, the analysis was resumed erratically at first, and then on a daily basis from October 8, 1942, until the end of the year; but in 1943 and 1944 the sessions were sporadic. Klein warned Heimann against telling anyone that she was in analysis with her. Susan Isaacs approached Heimann about writing a paper on introjection and projection for the Controversial Discussions. Heimann claims to have objected that she was a newcomer and "analytically very young," a feeble excuse for a woman of her age and experience, when she could have reasonably explained that she could not truly be independent so long as she was in analysis. It is a measure of the desperation of Klein's situation that Heimann had to be persuaded (after Joan Riviere refused to participate) and a reflection of the magnitude of Glover's exaggeration about the strength of the Kleinians at that point. Heimann explained the method they followed: "The only concession I could get from her was that first we would do a piece of writing which I would then re-write, etc., and then we would have analysis, the hour of analysis, but it was really a dreadful thing." In the hour before the analysis, Klein would go over Heimann's paper on introjection and projection and also the one on regression Heimann and Isaacs were working on together.

Paula Heimann's daughter's impression is that the analysis resumed because her mother was worried about her painful back. Heimann's recollection was that it took place while she was supervising a general practitioner, Jack Fieldman,* and her account is extremely incoherent:

> . . . she had forced me to keep it secret that I was in analysis with her, and I remember how Fieldman once quite correctly said to me "You are in analy-

---

* Fieldman was in analysis with Klein during 1940 and 1941.

sis and under her direction, I had to deny it—very unpleasant. This came
about, I don't know what it was—I had something, rheumatism or whatever—and Fieldman was then in analysis with her, and she grabbed Fieldman, who was a very good and quite contented G.P. to which as you know
he has gone back and he is a first class G.P., and she tried to make an analyst out of him which she could not.* I remember I had him under supervision and I found it dreadful. She must have told him about me and she got
in touch with me and said, "What you obviously want is more analysis";
and then I went into analysis with her, but she couldn't analyze it. It was
most unpleasant and also the South Americans came over and I was in an
awful situation of pretence. . . .†

Paula Heimann was apparently just as ambitious and competitive as Melanie Klein. Although for years Klein was able to keep her under control by
analysis, it was inevitable that the day would come when Heimann, like Melitta, would rebel and would hate herself for her subservience in a period when
she says that Klein repeatedly stole ideas from her without acknowledgment.
Heimann's countertransference paper was of immense significance in that it
was an area where Klein disagreed with her to such an extent that she could not
borrow any of her ideas. Heimann shed the role of subservient daughter at
Zurich, but was she strong enough to be an independent adult?

Because their supporters knew both women personally, divided loyalties
were aroused by the relationship. More protectiveness seems to be operating,
even today, in this area than in any other aspect of Melanie Klein's life. To the
world both women presented an image of strong-minded independence. Possibly they were both basically frightened, lonely, and vulnerable, and clung to
each other in a state of mutual dependence, although Klein was undoubtedly
the stronger of the two.

Some understanding of Klein's sexuality may lie in the chapter "The Effects of Early Anxiety-Situations on the Sexual Development of the Girl" in
The Psycho-Analysis of Children, an aspect of her work that has been neglected by commentators. In a discussion of the difficulties experienced by the
girl baby for whom the internalized penis is equivalent to a superego with
which she has not come to terms, she also tends to make an equation between
feces and the imaginary children within her.

And the anxiety which she feels on account of her phantasies about her
poisonous and burning excreta, and which, in my opinion, reinforces her
trends to expel, belonging to the earlier anal stage, forms the basis for her
feelings of hatred and fear later on towards the real child inside her.[29]

* Klein's letters to Sylvia Payne indicate that she had grave doubts about Fieldman's ability to be an analyst.
† The time sequence is bizarre. The South American training analysts began to arrive in appreciable numbers
after the war.

Further, if the girl feels that she has incapacitated her sadistic father from making restitution because in her phantasy she has castrated or destroyed him, she will then abandon hope of restoring him to wholeness. If she cannot restore, she must play his part, thus assuming the homosexual position. In a footnote to this passage, she writes:

> If her homosexuality emerges in sublimated ways only, she will, for instance, protect and take care of other women (i.e., her mother), adopting in these respects a husband's attitude towards them, and will have little interest in the male sex.[30]

It is problematic at this stage whether Klein was referring to herself, consciously or unconsciously. Many cultural or emotional connotations could be applied to the word "husband." Does she mean, for instance, a dominant male figure or a "motherer" in Erik Erikson's sense, a nurturer?

She returned to the subject in 1937 in her paper "Love, Guilt and Reparation." Here she is even more explicit about the girl's sexual phantasies and desires towards her mother. In certain cases the girl wants to replace her father in the relationship to the mother:

> . . . besides the love to both of them there are also feelings of rivalry to both, and this mixture of feeling is carried further in her relation to brothers and sisters. The desires and phantasies in connection with mother and sisters are the basis for direct homosexual relationships in later life, as well as for homosexual feelings which express themselves indirectly in friendship and affection between women. In the ordinary course of events these homosexual desires recede into the background, become deflected and sublimated, and the attraction towards the other sex predominates.[31]

Her relationship with Heimann, the break with Melitta, and her own self-analysis had deepened her understanding of the complexities of womanhood. Was Klein, then, the androgynous female whose true children were her concepts?

CHAPTER TWO

The Matriarch

Melanie Klein's life contained a pattern of humiliations, but to the world she presented a face of impassive indifference. While she had effectively triumphed over Anna Freud within the British Society, in the last decade of her life it was made abundantly clear to her that her rival was regarded as the queen bee by the rest of the psychoanalytic world. After the war the Americans emerged as the most influential group; and since the majority of the continental analysts had emigrated to the United States, the Americans adopted their attitude of contempt or distaste for Klein's ideas. Until recently the majority of American analysts went through their entire training without once hearing her name.

Anna Freud was, after all, the daughter of the Master; and the Americans tended to treat her as though she had inherited some of his genius. Many Americans have even been under the impression that she possessed a medical degree. In London she occasionally attended Scientific Meetings at the Institute, but she concentrated her attention almost exclusively on her own candidates and on the Hampstead Nurseries, which were financed by American money.*

About a dozen "normal" children from poor homes attended the nursery school to provide a standard of development for the trainees who were working with sixty or seventy children in full- or part-time treatment. In the late fifties the Developmental Profile (devised in large part by Humberto Nagera) came into operation as a means whereby Anna Freud could monitor and assess every case. Her presiding presence was everywhere. The children were told not to

---

* Including from the film star Marilyn Monroe. Her analysts were Marianne Kris and Ralph Greenson, one of Klein's most vigorous critics in the United States.

touch the curtains because they had been made by Miss Freud! The nurseries were shabby and in need of paint, just as Anna Freud always looked dowdy, her hair frizzed only for important occasions. At meetings of the Hampstead Clinic there was a rigid hierarchy in the order in which people spoke, a far more formal system than that prevailing at meetings of the British Society.

Anna Freud made frequent lecture tours in America, and on April 22, 1950, the degree of Doctor of Laws (*honoris causa*) was conferred on her by Clark University, which had conferred the same honor on her father in 1909. Whenever she appeared at congresses she was flanked by her faithful colleagues, Dorothy Burlingham and Princess Marie Bonaparte. At the London Congress in 1953, Marie Bonaparte managed with Anna Freud's help to set up a tribunal of "safe" people to eject Jacques Lacan from the International on the grounds that he had resigned from the Paris Society without taking the shrewd step Glover had previously done of immediately joining a constituent society. The justification for this action was his increasing practice of short sessions; but in actual fact the French political situation was extremely complicated, and the basic issue was power.*

Like her father, Anna Freud spoke proudly of "our Princess." Marie Bonaparte, a born politician, found it the most natural thing in the world to espouse both sides at the same time, endorsing the work of both Anna Freud and Melanie Klein. In February 1945, when Anna Freud's future within the British Society was still uncertain, the Princess wrote to Jones:

> The work of the so-called "English" school and the work of the "Austrian" Freudian school on the other hand, are more and more two diverging approaches to psychology. You say it yourself when you speak of the latter one as "having no future." So they can only be kept artificially and forcibly together. They will inevitably sooner or later one day go asunder!
>
> And why not? Each scientist is free to work on the lines he believes to be true: that is the liberty and liberalisation of science.
>
> Of course I think it is better to postpone such a moment until things in the world are more settled.[1]

The link between Klein and Marie Bonaparte's Five Copy Books, the first of which appeared in 1950, has never been acknowledged. After the death of Princess Marie's father in 1924, she discovered five copy books in which she had recorded her dreams and fantasies between the ages of seven and ten. She had total amnesia about the existence of these books; and their discovery impelled her to seek out Freud. During the next few years she spent much time in Vienna in analysis with Freud, and invested a great deal of money in the

---

* See Sherry Turkle, *Psychoanalytic Politics* (New York: Basic Books, 1978).

fledgling Paris Psychoanalytic Society. What is not generally known is that her decision eventually to publish the Copy Books (in a limited edition) was based not on Freud's influence (actually he discouraged her) but on the impact of Klein's *The Psycho-Analysis of Children*. Bonaparte waited until the Conclusion of the last volume (1953) to reveal the background of their publication:

> Much of the material of the copy-books . . . remained obscure, and when I discussed with Freud what interest there might be in publishing them he favoured the idea, but said that it would be premature until the latent content lying beneath their manifest content had been completely elucidated.
>
> In 1934 I read Melanie Klein's *The Psycho-Analysis of Children*. The importance, which she so well brings out, of sadistic fantasies relating to the interior of the body suddenly opened my eyes to the significance of a number of obscure passages in my myths, the deep meaning of what had previously seemed inaccessible. Re-reading my copy-books in that light, they yielded more and more consistent evidence of the terror inspired in the little female that I was by the avenging return of the "Comet Cacrabe." But the latent content of my terrified childish fantasies revealed, beneath the moral anxiety, the primary, vital anxiety of the female mammal, who fears the male threat of violent penetration into the interior of her body. This turned out to be even more significant than the fear of the retaliation of the oedipal mother.[2]

She then goes on to say that when in 1934 she started rereading and writing commentary on the copy books she now examined them with fresh eyes. Yet in her summary of the central experience of the copy books, published in the first volume of *The Psychoanalytic Study of the Child* (1945) as "Notes on the Analytic Discovery of a Primal Scene," she concluded: "The value of this case lies in the exceptional coincidence of the internal and the external evidence concerning an analytical reconstruction."[3] Her unnamed analyst (who was generally known to be Freud) had inferred the witnessing of the primal scene from a dream, she says. Yet in the published copy books, she writes that he drew this conclusion from her drawings. In other words, here we have the only known case of Freud interpreting a child's drawings—yet unable to get beyond a specific reality to the latent content—which Marie Bonaparte understood only after reading Klein some years following the termination of her analysis. However, publicly she still seemed to take a completely orthodox line in a fierce attack on Klein's paper "On the Origins of Transference" at the Amsterdam Congress in 1951. Klein was courting trouble by making a deliberately provocative reference to Anna Freud. Referring to Freud's statement that the first years of a girl's life are "grey with age and shadowy," she claimed that her own views were closer to those of Freud than were those of his own daughter:

I do not know Anna Freud's view about this aspect of Freud's work. But, as regards the question of auto-erotism and narcissism, she seems only to have taken into account Freud's conclusion than an auto-erotic and a narcissistic stage precede object-relations, and not to have allowed for the other possibilities implied in some of Freud's statements. . . . This is one of the reasons why the divergence between Anna Freud's conception and my conception of early infancy is far greater than that between Freud's views, taken as a whole, and my views. I am stating this because I believe it is essential to clarify the extent and nature of the differences between the two schools of psycho-analytic thought represented by Anna Freud and myself. Such clarification is required in the interests of psycho-analytic training and also because it could help to open up fruitful discussions between psycho-analysts and thereby contribute to a greater general understanding of the fundamental problems of early infancy.[4]

An interesting exchange occurred in connection with this paper. In his introductory speech Leo Bartemeier, the new president, warned the assembled analysts that they must guard against undue idealization by their patients. When Klein stood up to speak, she reminded Bartemeier that excessive idealization would never be a problem if analysts were careful to analyze the negative transference. It was a defiant, confident statement, but not one likely to endear her to the Americans.

At this congress Dr. Margaret Mahler of New York delivered a paper, "On Child Psychosis and Schizophrenia," in which she stressed that bodily contact, especially cuddling from the mother, was an essential stage in the demarcation of the body ego from the non-self. In the course of her paper she spoke of the "obtrusive explicitness" of the mechanisms described by Klein in disturbed babies. One of Klein's supporters later berated her for not giving sufficient credit to Klein for her conclusions, to which she replied that she did not believe that normal babies go through these psychotic stages. Mahler told Klein that she was "eternally grateful" for her description of psychotic mechanisms; but it continues to be her view that Klein reconstructed these generalizations in retrospect, a view shared by many American analysts.[5] But is not the whole concept of the Oedipus complex reconstructed from memory material?

At the Amsterdam Congress, Klein learned from the French child analyst René Diatkine that Lacan had abandoned the translation of *The Psycho-Analysis of Children* and handed over the German version to Diatkine (his student at the time) to complete. Then at the end of December she heard again from Françoise Girard (a student of Lacan's), now married to a French-Canadian psychiatrist, Jean-Baptiste Boulanger, who was in psychoanalytic training in Paris. As Dr. Boulanger recalls the situation: "In October 1951, Lacan, at the end of a seminar or a group supervision, asked Françoise if her husband was a Canadian, then if he knew English. The reply being yes to both questions, he said that the first half of the book had been translated and that as young analysts we would have much to gain in taking part in the translation of such an important work. We agreed, and, in December, we asked Lacan for the second half in order to compare our rendering and to establish a certain uniformity of style and vocabulary. He went through his two Paris apartments and country home, all in vain. We were becoming suspicious and decided to write directly to Mrs. Klein.

"Françoise wrote on our behalf on 31 December 1951, suggesting a one day return flight to London, on Sunday, 20 January, to meet her and clarify the situation. Mrs. Klein answered on 3 January 1952, and invited us for lunch at her home on the date we had proposed. . . . (It never was officially *revealed* nor admitted by Lacan that he had lost the translation made from the German by Diatkine, who had no copy of his work.) We had always thought that Lacan would take all the credit for himself, granting *perhaps* a footnote to his 'students.'"[6] On January 27, 1952, the Boulangers had lunch with Klein, and the full story was revealed to her. The Boulangers were extremely eager to translate the English version (which had been translated from the German by Alix Strachey), and an immediate rapport was established.

Melanie Klein assigned very precise meanings to certain words and concepts. As was the case when the book was translated from German into English, so now a new vocabulary had to be devised. For example, when Daniel Lagache had translated Klein's paper "On the Origins of Transference" for the *Revue française de psychanalyse*, he had used "esprit" for "mind," but the Boulangers felt that "psychisme" was more correct psychoanalytically. Moreover, on several occasions where the English text was unclear (sometimes erroneous), the German original was consulted and Klein would make the final decision. The French edition also included certain missing fragments, particularly the case history of "Mr. A," which had been omitted from the 1932 edition for reasons of confidentiality, but included in *Writings*, 2.

In a letter of September 19, 1952, Klein gave the Boulangers some explanatory advice:

> I think that the "inside" is not correctly translated by "ventre." In the original I have not chosen the word corresponding to "belly" or "ventre" because it does not reproduce the child's feeling that there is something within the mother's body which, although in some places it refers to inner organs, in the phantastic sense does not—it is just an inside. The mother's body is felt to be a container of unknown things of a phantastic quality, good and bad, although they are linked with actual faeces, etc. I think that

this is one of the occasions where a word has to be introduced with quotation marks (and possibly described?).* [7]

In another letter later that month she explained the connection between Freud's interpretation of dreams and the symbolism of play:

> It is of importance to me to show that there is an analogy between dream elements (Freud) and play elements, that is to say, certain parts of the dream which are considered and certain parts of the play which are considered. In the same way as by analysing the association to dream elements the latent content is revealed, so by analysing the details of the child's play which are equal to associations the latent content of the play elements is revealed. I wonder whether you could change the sentence a little to make that clearer. I find now that it had not become clear enough in the English translation.

She makes an interesting distinction between envy and jealousy:

> You use "jalousait" while in English it is envy. Envy and jealousy are not synonymous and I should be glad if you could indicate this distinction by using "enviat" instead of "jalousait."

They mutually decided on "clivage" for "splitting," rather than "scission." Klein also explained that to the child intercourse meant "hammering into the inside." She reacted strongly to the Boulangers' translation of "femme"—or "mère"—"phallique" (woman/mother with a penis). She explained the difference between Freud's "phallic woman/mother" (who has a phantasied *external penis of her own*) and her "woman/mother with a penis" (*whose phantasied paternal penis is inside her*). Unaware that the concept of reparation was not yet part of the Klein corpus when the book was written, Boulanger wrote to ask whether he could use "réparation" for "restitution"—since "restitution" did not sound right to his French ears. "I believe," Dr. Boulanger says, "this anecdote illuminates a characteristic trait of Mrs. Klein as a theorist. She was adamant on a question of principle (the penis) but could not care less for the preservation of the historical development of her ideas (she was now using 'reparation')." She was delighted with their translation:

> I very much wish that I could have put the work in your hands some years ago when Madame Boulanger first offered, after the Congress in Zurich, to

---

* "Intérieur" was substituted for "ventre"; "l'instinct" was used only in reference to the life and death instincts, and "réparation" replaced "restitution."

translate it. It would have been a much better arrangement for you, and how much worry and trouble I should have saved myself! But, as you know, I could not take it away from Lacan. However—it is no good crying over spilt milk, and I am very happy that the work is at last progressing.

The translation was published in the year before her death, in 1959, and Dr. Boulanger is proud that he and his wife were initially responsible for introducing Kleinian ideas into France. In 1966 Dr. Willy Baranger translated *Developpements de la psychanalyse.*

May 6, 1951, marked the twenty-fifth anniversary of the opening of the London Clinic, and coincided almost exactly with the period Melanie Klein had been associated with the British Psycho-Analytical Society. By now the Institute had found a beautiful new home in a late-eighteenth-century building at 63 New Cavendish Street. On March 30, 1952, Klein celebrated her seventieth birthday. Jones arranged a celebratory dinner for her at Kettner's restaurant, at which a memorable photograph of her was taken with all the colleagues who had been at her side during the years of strife. For her immediate associates and students, there was a party at her home.

Klein was beginning to be poignantly aware of her own mortality. Did she remember one of Emanuel's last letters to her? "Do not think ill of me because of my life," he pleaded with her. "Spread all the tolerance which could prepare you for your seventieth year on this my short life. I am not allowed to live till seventy, so permit me to invent it in poetry."[8] Had she taken his plea too literally and expended all her tolerance on him, so that there was little left over for others? In scientific discussions, according to Joseph Sandler, "she would get angry if she felt that she was being misunderstood or attacked. I think that she had enormous self-confidence, plenty of narcissism, whatever you would like to call it. There were never any indications of insecurity. She simply knew."[9] Some analysts feel that anyone who exuded such enormous self-confidence must have harbored profound self-distrust.

In May she informed Eric that Kloetzel had died in Jerusalem.* At the time she appeared perfectly calm and unemotional, and it was not until years after her death that Eric realized how much the relationship had meant to her. Kloetzel, moreover, had been nine years her junior. Klein was still always immaculately groomed, but had developed an arthritic hip and had begun to walk with a cane. People also began to notice how easily she tired.

Her followers were determined to celebrate her birthday with as much fanfare as Freud had received when he reached seventy. First, they published *Developments in Psycho-Analysis,* the book they had been contemplating for several years. At a meeting of the Publications Committee on September 12,

---

* How she knew remains a mystery. An obituary notice?

1950, some of the members had objected to the title on the grounds that it might imply that the Society had fully accepted its contents. Rickman suggested *New Issues in Psycho-Analysis,* but the group involved dug in their heels and the original title was retained.

Joan Riviere was asked to contribute as the General Introduction her 1936 Vienna Exchange Lecture: She emphasized that she allowed it to be published "with some misgivings," since it antedated the other papers by several years and was of a general nature, rather than dealing with a specific issue.*

The volume contained the papers that had been delivered at the Controversial Discussions, Klein's "Some Theoretical Conclusions Regarding the Emotional Life of the Infant" (drawn from her original paper), as well as "On Observing the Behaviour of Young Infants," "On the Theory of Anxiety and Guilt," and "Some Notes on Some Schizoid Mechanisms." The only new paper was Heimann's "Notes on the Theory of the Life and Death Instincts." At the Publications Committee meeting on May 10, 1951, Jones announced that the book had been delayed because of difficulties raised by his Introduction, but by October the manuscript was at the publishers.

In a footnote to "Some Theoretical Conclusions Regarding the Emotional Life of the Infant," Klein wrote: "I have received valuable assistance in my contributions to this volume from my friend, Lola Brook, who went carefully over my manuscripts and made a number of helpful suggestions both as regards formulations and the arrangement of the material. I am much indebted to her for her unfailing interest in my work."[10] This is the first of several warm tributes to her assistant, praise that in the past had been reserved for Paula Heimann, whose assistance was not mentioned again. In the Preface to the first edition of *The Psycho-Analysis of Children,* Klein had singled out Nina Searl, "whose collaboration with me was based on common conviction [and who] has done lasting service towards the advancement of child analysis in England, both from a practical and a theoretical point of view, and towards the training of child analysts."[11] Had Brook now replaced Heimann as the favorite daughter? Mrs. Brook had no psychoanalytic background of any kind; but some Kleinians have assured me of her outstanding intelligence. Susan Isaacs was now dead, Joan Riviere politely ignored, and Heimann about to be ejected from the inner circle. John Rickman died in 1951 without being reconciled to her, and a coolness towards Winnicott and Scott was perceptible. Alix Strachey had drifted away from her, although she still admired her early work: "[The] technique which has been developed by Mrs. Klein, a psycho-analyst and a pupil of Karl Abraham, has not only proved eminently successful but has been responsible for eliciting much of the psychical material present in the in-

---

* Her paper "The Bereaved Wife," in *Fatherless Children,* ed. S. Isaacs (London: Pouskin, 1945), for example, focused on a more specific subject.

fantile mind which is now accepted as part of . . . analytic theory."[12] It was the end of an era.

In 1950 Roger Money-Kyrle had suggested that the Society publish a *Festschrift*, a volume of papers in honor of Mrs. Klein's birthday in 1952. Jones was very much against the idea. He pointed out that a book of this personal kind had never been published in the International Library Series and he did not consider it a sound procedure. As an alternative he suggested that a double number of the *Journal* be allocated for the purpose.

The birthday issue was edited by Paula Heimann and Roger Money-Kyrle. The list of fourteen contributors, writing on a wide variety of topics, was impressive. All the papers, clinical and applied, were infused with Kleinian ideas, except for that of Michael Balint, who offered a contribution as an old friend from Berlin days. He insisted on the inclusion of a prefatory note in which it was made clear that he did not believe that persecutory anxiety was present from the outset and that he was convinced that in a good home there was no reason why such feelings should arise. He had always been skeptical of the objective validity of Klein's inferences, and in "Individual Differences of Behaviour in Early Infancy and an Objective Method of Recording Them" (1945) he had asserted that only Merrell Middlemore in *The Nursing Couple* (1941) had actually studied babies in their first fortnight of life. But here in "New Beginnings and the Paranoid and the Depressive Syndromes" he generously acknowledged that Melanie Klein's concepts of the paranoid-schizoid and depressive positions had enabled him to understand some difficult cases.[13]

Within the previous decade, Melanie Klein had gained sufficient confidence to state explicitly where she differed from Freud. In "The Emotional Life of the Infant" she added an important footnote stating her divergence from Abraham in respect to the preambivalent stage.* However, it was left to her lieutenant, Paula Heimann, to spell out the differences in an appendix to the paper she had read at Amsterdam. This appendix was originally a paper read before the British Society on January 16, 1952, "The Polymorphous Stage of Instinctual Development." Heimann pointed out that although Abraham's "Development of the Libido" (1924) was published four years after *Beyond the Pleasure Principle*, he did not refer to the death instinct. This suggested that Abraham did not accept the death instinct—hence, the first oral stage, the sucking stage, is free from destructive impulses.

---

* "It is implicit in my argument (as presented here and in former writings) that I do not agree with Abraham's concept of a pre-ambivalent stage in so far as it implies that the destructive (oral-sadistic) impulses first arise with the onset of teething. We have to remember, though, that Abraham has also pointed out the sadism inherent in 'vampire-like' sucking. There is no doubt that the onset of teething and the physiological processes which affect the gums are a strong stimulus for cannibalistic impulses and phantasies; but aggression forms part of the infant's earliest relation to the breast, though it is not usually expressed in biting at this stage" (p. 206).

Melanie Klein's work does not endorse the view of a pre-ambivalent stage as Abraham describes it, but . . . her findings of the early splitting mechanism which create an ideal and a persecutory breast represent an important modification of Abraham's concept of the pre-ambivalent stage.[14]

Furthermore, his scheme did not embrace the polymorphously perverse disposition. For Melanie Klein (as for Freud), the infant from the beginning of life is under the two primary instincts of life and death. The oral does not precede the anal as it does in Abraham's scheme: the two operate simultaneously, the oral incorporating the good, feeding, gratifying breast, while in the phantasies of splitting and projecting—projective identification—the infant projects what he does not want to keep into his mother. These projected parts are predominantly anal, the persecuting object equated with feces, the internal persecutors. Klein had finally (through Heimann) publicly rejected Abraham's rigid compartmentalized structural theory of development, but she was in effect also rejecting her own earliest papers, written while in analysis with Abraham.

The most arresting contribution in the birthday issue came from the pen of W. R. Bion, "Group Dynamics: A Re-View," to a significant degree a refutation of Freud's *Group Psychology and the Analysis of the Ego*,* based on Bion's own extensive experience of groups. What Freud did not recognize in his discussion of groups were the implications of the neurotic symptoms implicit in the individual's relationship with objects:

The understanding of the emotional life of the group . . . is only comprehensible in terms of psychotic mechanisms. For this reason advances in the study of the group are dependent upon the development and implications of Melanie Klein's theories of internal objects, projective identification and failure in symbol formation and their application in the group situation.[15]

This endorsement was to have enormous implications for the future study of groups.

The background of a section of Marion Milner's contribution, "Aspects of Symbolism in Comprehension of the Non-Self," deserves comment. Milner, analyzed by Sylvia Payne, had presented her membership paper in 1943 on a suicidal three-year-old. Her two supervisors were Klein and Riviere. Klein had an extraordinary understanding of the child; in her adult case Milner found Riviere (whom she had gone to on Winnicott's advice) too rigorous. In Milner's view, the patient was totally unsuitable for analysis, but Riviere believed anyone could be analyzed according to certain principles—"the pro-

---

* As Bruno Bettelheim says in *Freud and Man's Soul* (New York: Knopf, 1982), the sense in which Freud uses the word indicates "mass" rather than "group."

tractor method of interpretation," Milner describes it.[16] Like many others, she found Riviere "a bully."

Klein also supervised another case of Milner's—an eleven-year-old boy described in "A Game of War Between Two Villages," a section of Milner's longer paper, "Aspects of Symbolism in Comprehension of the Non-Self."* The child was Klein's own grandson, Michael Clyne. Milner says that, despite her misgivings, "I wouldn't have missed the experience for anything." She is scornful of those who say Klein did not take the environment into consideration, because Milner was told a good deal about the home background. For instance, the material revealed the boy's recognition that all the human qualities in the home emanated from the mother. The analysis was based on a game he devised between two villages; in the game his village possessed the mechanical equipment, whereas the human beings were assigned to Milner's village (Milner symbolized his mother). Milner was troubled about the scornful comments Klein made about her own son Eric during the supervision; and she later wondered whether Eric matured considerably after his mother died. One is inclined also to wonder if Klein was *actually* so critical of Eric, or whether she was imposing her own scheme of the predominance of the mother on the material.† According to Klein's family physician, Dame Annis Gillie, Eric was an unusually humane, considerate son—not at all like the person Klein described. It is also possible that Klein was unconsciously trying to transform Eric's wife, Judy, into an idealized daughter. Michael might have assigned loving maternal qualities to Milner because that is the sort of person he found her to be, and the child himself could have been filled with aggression. Once, in discussing this paper, Klein disapproved of something Milner said, and staring at her with her hooded eyes, she reminded Milner of a vulture peering out of a thundercloud. "After that I wasn't frightened of her anymore." Michael was eventually passed on to Bion; but in 1949 Milner went into further analysis with Clifford Scott, to whom she expressed qualms about Michael's analysis. She was troubled not so much about the relationship (which she does not think as questionable a procedure as Klein's analysis of her own son) but by the scornful things Klein said about Eric. According to Paula Heimann, Klein was angry with Milner for having produced "a very original idea" on the capacity for symbol-making as the basis for creativity; and added that Scott (then director of the clinic) had been strongly opposed to Klein's supervision of her own grandson, but "she then brought to bear on him the whole power of her queenly position and attitude."‡[17]

---

* Published under the title of "The Role of Illusion in Symbol Formation," in *New Directions in Psycho-Analysis* in 1955.
† Klein's letters to Winnicott during 1941 and some later ones to her sister-in-law, Jolan, indicate that there was tension between mother and son for a few years.
‡ Both Scott and Milner are bewildered by Heimann's innuendo.

Scott did not contribute to the birthday issue of the *Journal*, although his paper "A Psycho-Analytic Concept of the Origin of Depression" later appeared in *New Directions in Psycho-Analysis*. Another notable omission from the list of contributors was Winnicott. Until this date Winnicott had regarded himself as a Kleinian, but he and Klein fell out over the paper he wished to include in the volume, "Transitional Objects and Transitional Phenomena," which he had delivered to the Society on May 30, 1951. Among the hundreds of papers Winnicott produced over the years, this is probably the one that is best known.

Melanie Klein was prejudiced against the paper from the start. Fairbairn's book, *Psychoanalytic Studies of the Personality*, emphasized stages of transition, and Winnicott had linked his theory with Fairbairn's quasi-independent stage.* Winnicott's subheading was "A Study of the First *Not-Me* Possession"; but in the original paper he made the error of using the term *not-me-object*, which, Klein pointed out to him, was invariably the breast. In the unpublished paper he referred to many analysts who had used the concept, including Melanie Klein's study of the troubled child Rita, with her obsessional ritual. "It would be interesting to know the early history of this doll, or more especially of its precursor," he wrote to Clifford Scott.[18] That very year Klein, in the "The Origins of Transference," and Rosenfeld, in "Transference phenomena and transference-analysis in an acute catatonic schizophrenic patient," described inanimate objects as usually malignant and terrifying.

For Winnicott the "transitional object" belongs to the area of experience between the thumb and the teddy bear, between oral erotism and true object-relationship. (In a very loose way, it represents the breast.) Winnicott is referring to a corner of a blanket, a bundle of wool, some familiar object that serves as a defense against anxiety. The child becomes attached to such an object some time after the age of four months. It is a defense because it must never change and should be able to survive hating as well as loving. It is not an internal object:

> It is interesting to compare the transitional object concept with Melanie Klein's concept of the internal object. The transitional object is *not an internal object* (which is a mental concept)—it is a possession. Yet it is not (for the infant) an external object either.
>
> The following complex statement has to be made. The infant can employ a transitional object when the internal object is alive and real and good enough (not too persecutory). But this internal object depends for its qualities on the existence and aliveness and behaviour of the external ob-

---

* And yet Winnicott and Masud Khan wrote a fierce denunciation of the book as a travesty of Klein's theories (*J.*, 1953, 34: 329–33).

ject (breast, mother figure, a general environmental care). Badness or failure of the latter indirectly leads to a deadness or to a persecutory quality of
the internal object. After a persistence of failure of the internal object the
internal object fails to have a meaning to the infant, and then, and then
only, does the transitional stage become meaningless too. The transitional
object may therefore stand for the "external" breast, but *indirectly* so,
through standing for an "internal" mother.

The transitional object is never under magical control like the internal
object, nor is it outside control as the real mother is.[19]

The "good enough mother," in Winnicott's famous phrase, starts off allowing the child to be totally dependent upon her, but with time allows him to
accept the frustrations imposed by reality. As the child's interests broaden,
they become diffused so that the transition object—unlike the internal object—is discarded and not mourned. Where persistent attachment to an object
continues, the basis of fetishism is laid.

Winnicott took his paper to the 1951 editorial meeting at which the selection of papers was to be made for the seventieth-birthday issue of the *Journal*.
Klein wanted him to revise the paper so that it more clearly incorporated her
ideas. He refused; and with the manuscript under his arm, he sadly left the
room. As he later told his wife, "Apparently Mrs. Klein no longer considers me
a Kleinian." As far as Melanie Klein was concerned, it was the end of their association; but although Winnicott already disagreed with her literal acceptance
of the death instinct, was disturbed about the paranoid-schizoid position, and
was later violently to reject her concept of innate envy, he retained his affection
and admiration for her to the end. The depressive position (with modifications) formed an intrinsic part of his own thinking.

When Winnicott published the paper the following year, he included a
footnote that must have enraged Klein:

When it is said that the first object is the breast, the word "breast" is used,
I believe, to stand for the technique of mothering as well as for the actual
flesh. It is not impossible for a mother to be a good-enough mother (in my
way of putting it) with a bottle for the actual feeding. If this wide meaning
of the word "breast" is kept in mind, and maternal technique is seen to be
included in the total meaning of the term, then there is a bridge forming
between the wording of Melanie Klein's statement of early history and that
of Anna Freud. The only difference left is one of dates, which is in fact an
unimportant difference which will automatically disappear in the course of
time.*[20]

* Why did Winnicott relegate the fundamental theoretical difference to a footnote? The breast and general
mothering are not synonymous.

He always believed that the differences between the two women could be reconciled, certainly an unreal expectation. John Padel had the impression during the fifties that all of Winnicott's papers were addressed to Klein, as though he were trying to persuade her of his point of view, particularly about "good enough mothering" and the importance of the environment. "I don't think that one can truly understand his papers unless one is aware that they have that secondary aim of getting her to modify something," Padel asserts.[21]

Winnicott's experience with children was vast, his prestige enormous. Although he had no children of his own, his intuitive understanding of youngsters was remarkable. Marion Milner has described hearing him lecture in the late thirties when he explained his famous spatula game:

> He told how he would leave a spatula on the table in front of the mother and baby, well within the baby's reach. Then he simply watched what the baby did with the spatula, watching for variations in the normal pattern of reaching for it, grabbing it, giving it a good suck and then chucking it away. He told how, out of this very simple experimental situation, he could work out, according to the observed blocks in the various stages, a diagnosis of the problems between the mother and the baby. As he talked, I was captivated by the mixture in him of deep seriousness and his love of little jokes, that is, the play aspect of his character, if one thinks of true play as transcending the opposites of serious and nonserious.[22]

Almost everyone uses the word "pixie" to describe him. For Betty Joseph he was "a bit of a Peter Pan." Charles Rycroft has described him as "charismatic." He has also said that while Klein was undoubtedly a prima donna, Winnicott was "a crypto–prima donna,"[23] although he appeared a humble man despite his great experience. At the end of a supervision he would thank a student for helping him; and his widow, Clare Winnicott, said that frequently as he came bounding up the stairs, he exclaimed, "I have learned so much from my patients today!" Some recall that it was a marvelous experience to be in contact with him, but, unlike Klein, he had no theoretical structure to *teach.* As a student, he had learned from Lord Horder to *listen* to his patients. He believed that one could activate negative transferences only when a positive transference had been established. According to John Padel, Winnicott's great strength was that "He always relied on the patient to give the maximum account of himself rather than his own speculation. . . . He recognized that it had to be the patient's achievement when it came to making transference possible."[24]

Clare Winnicott used to tell him that he knew from the moment he opened his eyes on the world that he was loved, and she teased him that he suffered from "benignity." Could two people have been more different than

Donald Winnicott and Melanie Klein? How could he possibly believe in innate aggression and the death instinct? Yet Clifford Scott asserts that Klein, too, in her way was very humble in her realization that she still had much to learn. "I think she loved her ignorance," he says.[25] Perhaps the difference between them was that Winnicott was willing to learn from others, whereas Klein had to learn everything for herself. When Winnicott described her as "a Eureka shrieker," he was alluding to her tendency to regard every insight as the ultimate truth.

Yet, despite their temperamental differences, Winnicott was enormously attracted to her. John Padel has described the British Society in the fifties as a *pas de deux*. Klein was the ballerina to whom Winnicott was constantly offering something, which she rejected with a toss of her head as if to say that she had it already. At one Scientific Meeting Winnicott remarked ruefully that he supposed the term "depressive position" was now firmly established, although he would have preferred "the stage of concern." To this Klein replied that she had waited twenty years for Dr. Winnicott to accept "the depressive position," and she was willing to wait another twenty for him to accept "the paranoid-schizoid position."*

One analyst, who liked Winnicott immensely, told me that he was far more ambitious and contentious than his gentle manner would suggest. Winnicott could not help feeling embittered by the way he was treated as a lightweight by the two leading factions in the Society. On one occasion when Anna Freud gave a paper at a Scientific Meeting, she rather curtly dismissed Winnicott's notion of transitional objects. The meeting was chaired by Winnicott, who, white with anger, exclaimed: "Miss Freud cannot dismiss what I've said in one sentence. It's a whole system that she is dismissing." One evening in 1957 he launched into a long diatribe about his grievances against Klein to a member of the independent group. Suddenly he smiled: "But you know—she really *is* a darling!"

Many of the independents were drawn to Winnicott's ideas of "good enough mothering," "the false self," "the capacity to be alone," and the theory of the container. His simple, direct language and his uncomplicated views strike a chord in the British psyche in contrast to the complexity of Kleinian concepts. Yet John Padel, who might be described as a representative independent or Middle Grouper, has complained that Winnicott adhered too closely to the Kleinian idea of the importance of the mother .

It is sometimes said that many of the Middle Group would have liked

---

* In a letter dated Feb. 26, 1954, Winnicott explained to Clifford Scott his own view of the depressive position: " . . . there is a gradual process in the infant whereby the various capacities come together & make possible the depressive position achievement. By contrast, some of the Klein writings seem to give highly organised processes a place in very early infancy where they can be only present at moments or sporadically without a relationship to the total individual."

Winnicott to have been their leader, but, although he served twice as president of the Society, basically he was a loner. When he became president in 1956, he wrote to Clifford Scott: "I feel odd when in the president's chair because I *don't know my Freud* in the way a president should do; yet I do find I have Freud in my bones."[26] Many of the Kleinians felt that he was too meddlesome. Concerned about the isolation of the "B" Group, he sent Miss Freud frequent notes in an attempt to draw her into greater participation. For example, in June 1958, he warned her that a Kleinian, Elliott Jaques, would probably be elected business secretary, a position that might lead to his eventually becoming scientific secretary or a member of the Board. She replied that she was very much opposed to Jaques's election. "Incidentally," he wrote in response to her objections, "I don't happen to like the man myself, but he is gradually recovering from his phase of pro-Kleinian proclivity, and if in office I am quite sure he will act fairly. I do hope that you will not feel too thwarted if Jaques gets elected; it would seem to be a bad thing to nominate an unsuitable person just to keep Jaques out."*[27]

According to Ilse Hellman, "There has never been a policy of B Groupers staying away from Scientific Meetings, but many preferred to stay home when it was clear from the program that the paper would be about a problem quite remote from one's own approach and out of keeping with one's knowledge of children's thinking in the first months of life."[28] Nevertheless, Winnicott fretted that their absence was due in part to Klein's behavior. At the Paris Congress in the summer of 1957, at a meeting chaired by Willi Hoffer, Klein refused to stop talking despite repeated attempts by Hoffer to indicate that her time was up and other speakers were impatiently waiting their turn.† On October 3 Winnicott wrote to Michael Balint, "Certainly the tension in A and B politics has risen in a dangerous way since the Hoffer episode at the Congress. These things concern me very deeply."[29]

At times he lectured the Kleinians like a Dutch uncle. To Francesca Bion he complained that many members found her husband's work difficult to comprehend, and there was a sense of frustration "because so much is being said in each sentence when your husband talks, and I think he does not go slowly enough either for those who are only just beginning to come to terms with his type of contribution to psychoanalysis."[30] To Donald Meltzer, a rising star in the Kleinian orbit, he complained in a letter of May 21, 1959, that Meltzer spoke too slowly and far exceeded the time allotted to him:

It is unfortunate that the sort of presentation which you gave last night makes people feel that the followers of Mrs. Klein talk more than their pa-

---

* An independent, Geoffrey Thompson, was elected.
† Serge Lebovici has the impression that the incident occurred at a panel discussion on "Contributions of Direct Child Observation to Psycho-Analysis" on July 29.

tients do. . . . In a report of a case . . . if the analyst makes too long an interpretation, the listener gets the impression that the analyst is talking to
himself rather than to the patient . . . you will have realized that last night's
meeting was defective in one special respect, which was that one-third of
the Society was not present. My personal opinion is that B-groupers stay
away from these meetings because if they come they are listening to a language which is foreign to them, and they find this boring. One day you will
be able to state what you are doing in a language which will be understandable to the whole Society.[31]

Another figure who had a problematic relationship with the Kleinians was
the now world-renowned John Bowlby. Charles Rycroft describes Bowlby as "a
nineteenth-century Darwinian liberal."[32] Where Winnicott was charming and
fey, Bowlby was blunt and forthright. Some indication of his feisty independence appeared in January 1935 when, as a promising young man (then in
analysis with Riviere), he was invited to participate in the discussion following
Klein's paper "A Contribution to the Psychogenesis of Manic-Depressive
States." On this occasion he reported that several patients he had seen at the
Maudsley suffering from depression had experienced a recent bereavement.
This, he thought, supplemented the ideas Klein was advancing. She and Riviere thought otherwise, however. "At that time," Bowlby recalls, "I had not
realized that my interest in real-life experiences and situations was so alien to
the Kleinian outlook; on the contrary, I believed my ideas were compatible
with theirs. Looking back on the years 1935–39, I think I was reluctant to recognize the divergence. That became crystal clear only after the war, especially
as I became increasingly shocked by their intransigent attitudes."[33] As he points
out, during the thirties the British Society was quite small, and the Kleinian
group was not clearly differentiated in people's minds until after the arrival of
the Viennese analysts.

In 1936, while working at the London Child Guidance Clinic, Bowlby became greatly concerned about the disturbances of children raised in institutions, and was convinced that some children are unable to love because they
lacked the opportunity to form a solid attachment to a mother figure early in
life. Then, during 1938–39, he had Klein as a supervisor, and the profound differences in their outlooks became apparent. Not allowed to offer help to the
intensely anxious mother of a three-year-old he was treating, he was hardly surprised, he recalls, when he learned that she had been admitted to a mental hospital. Klein, instead of recognizing that the mother's condition was crucial to
the boy's problems, seemed concerned only with the untimely interruption of
the analysis. Bowlby considers that the war saved him from open conflict with
Melanie Klein, for which he would not then have been ready.

In 1942 Bowlby was posted to the Officer Selection Boards, where he worked with a number of psychiatrists and psychologists who also subsequently joined the Tavistock Clinic on leaving the army. At the Tavistock he was appointed director of the Department for Children and Parents.

His membership paper, "The Influence of Early Environment in the Development of Neurosis and Neurotic Character," presented to the British Society in June 1939, had indicated the direction in which he was heading. Resuming his prewar study of the ill effects of maternal deprivation, he appointed as his research assistant James Robertson, a newly qualified social worker who had worked with Anna Freud at the Hampstead Nurseries during the war. Robertson, exasperated by the attitude of professional audiences who refused to believe his accounts of the intense distress shown by young children on admission to an institution, resolved, with Bowlby's support, to make a documentary film.* The result, *A Two-Year-Old Goes to Hospital,* illustrated how, during an eight-day stay, the child undergoes a typical sequence of responses varying from distressful protest through despair to brief episodes of detachment. Bowlby and Robertson showed the film at the Institute on March 5, 1952. Anna Freud approved the observational approach and endorsed the view that the distress was due to the absence of Mother, but the Kleinians disagreed. Bion asserted that it was most likely a result of the mother's pregnancy.

In 1951 Bowlby started to read the work of Konrad Lorenz, and was fascinated by the possible connection between the following reponses of ducklings and goslings and the attachment behavior of infants and young children. More and more he was drawn to the study of ethology. In June 1957 he presented to the Society his theoretical paper "The Nature of the Child's Tie to His Mother," the first of a series in which he applied ethological principles to infant behavior. Reviewing the literature on the child's tie, he listed the traditional theories. The most widely held was the theory of the Secondary Drive (what Anna Freud called "cupboard love"). Other theories postulated an infant's congenital need to relate to the breast, an inbuilt need to cling, or a craving to return to the womb. He traced Freud's changing and developing views on the subject, and pointed out that toward the end of his life Freud was "not only moving away from the theory of the Secondary Drive but developing the notion that special drives built into the infant in the course of evolution underlie this first and unique love relationship."[34]

All Klein's theories, he asserted, were based on ideas current before 1926, especially Abraham's excessive emphasis on orality and food, to the detriment of an understanding and recognition of other aspects of a child's early life. (In

---

* Bowlby had been greatly impressed by René Spitz's 1947 film, *Grief: A Peril in Infancy.*

the subsequent discussion Klein drew Bowlby's attention to the role she attributed to the anal and urethral elements in the child's relation to the mother.)

While Winnicott had placed much less emphasis on orality than Klein,
Winnicott's ideas of the internal dynamic for the infant were unclear, in
Bowlby's view, as was Erik Erikson's concept of "basic trust." In advocating a
theory of primary object relations, Fairbairn had at one time invoked the theory of return-to-womb craving. An alternative approach, Bowlby believed, and
one in keeping with the evidence, was to postulate a primary tendency to keep
proximity to a special person; in other words, to become attached to that person, corresponding to a similar tendency to be seen in infant monkeys. This
theory proposes an innate potential in the infant that is elicited and developed
by life experiences. Smiling, crying, clinging, and following are all ways by
which attachment to the preferred individual can be achieved.

A few days prior to the meeting, Bowlby had given a copy of his paper to a
colleague (whom he refuses to name, saying only that it was a man whom he
had long considered a friend). From the concerted attack that followed, in
which to Bowlby's surprise his colleague joined, Bowlby concluded that the
Kleinians had been alerted. Even his own former analyst, Joan Riviere, felt
compelled to protest, for which Winnicott wrote to thank her: "It was certainly a very difficult paper to appreciate without at the same time giving away
almost everything that has been fought for by Freud."[35] Bowlby's explanation
for the reaction of the Kleinians was that he had played down the role of food
and feeding and that they took exception to his use of animal data; and in any
case they were intolerant of any ideas different from their own. "I am with the
object relations school," Bowlby says, "but I have reformulated it in terms of
modern biological concepts. It is my own independent version."[36] In contrast
to the Kleinians, he objects to the idea that analytic theory should take into
account only what can be learned from treating patients. "On the contrary, the
more sources of data the better," he remarks. This is, perhaps, why some critics
feel that Bowlby has abandoned psychoanalysis, a charge he rejects. Bowlby
believes that his approach represents the future.*

Anna Freud missed the meeting, as she was in bed with influenza, but was
very distressed by the direction of Bowlby's paper and wrote to Winnicott that
"Dr. Bowlby is too valuable a person to get lost to psycho-analysis."[37] She felt
that his paper had sacrificed all the "gains" of psychoanalysis—namely, the
principles of mental functioning and ego psychology—and offered very little in
exchange. "I suppose," she concluded, "he was put off by the antedating of
complex mental events in the Kleinian psychology, but that is no real excuse
for going too far in the other direction."

---

* In an interview on November 23, 1981, Bowlby described Klein as "inspirational, the antithesis of what I try
to be." He went on to say that she was totally unaware of scientific method; and after a momentary pause
added, "Anna Freud doesn't know what science is about either."

The Kleinian response to the paper "The Nature of the Child's Tie to His Mother" was relatively muted in comparison with their reaction to "Separation Anxiety," which Bowlby read to the Society on November 5, 1958. Winnicott wrote to Anna Freud in advance, begging her to speak longer than the requisite ten minutes in order to help clear up the confusion. "At the present moment," he confessed, "I cannot tell whether we are discussing the development of Freud's theory of anxiety, or the clinical effect of separation in the seven months to third birthday period, or the contribution of ethology to the theory of instincts."[38] The paper drew an unusually large audience, and two subsequent evenings were devoted to discussion. The second paper was an extension of the first, emphasizing Robertson's observations on the way young children respond to being in a strange place without Mother, and how they behave after their return home. On this occasion Bowlby spoke at length about Freud's final views on separation anxiety and mourning, and how that formulation had been presented too late in Freud's career to have much influence on the subsequent development of theory. These ideas had never gained the central place in psychoanalytic thinking that Bowlby thought they deserved. Like Freud, Bowlby sees no evidence that separation anxiety is present during the earliest months of life. Unlike Freud (and also Klein), however, he sees no merit in speculating about some children being born with an inherently greater amount of libidinal need than others or a stronger death instinct (he does not believe in the death instinct), "since with our present research techniques there is no way of determining differences in constitutional endowment."[39]

In the ensuing discussion Anna Freud's position was much the same as she was to take in 1960 in her reaction to Bowlby's paper "Grief and Mourning in Infancy"—that biological and behavioral considerations "taken by themselves, not in conjunction with metapsychological thinking . . . do not fulfill the analyst's requirements."[40] Bowlby always found Anna Freud "a very nice modest woman," in contrast to Klein's overweening self-righteousness. "I distinguish between the Klein attack and Anna Freud's criticism," Bowlby recalls. "The mood was different. Anna Freud thought I was mistaken and made no bones about it. But Anna Freud was not destructive. The other group were out to destroy." Bowlby's ultimate criterion for a measure of scientific curiosity and detachment is, "Do you treat a new idea with respect?"[41]

Bowlby regarded the Kleinians as his major opponents,* but the truth of the matter is that the "B" Group and Winnicott were also deeply disturbed about the direction of his ideas.

Winnicott refrained from attacking Bowlby publicly, but to Anna Freud he wrote: "I can't quite make out why it is that Bowlby's papers are building up in

---

* However, a Kleinian analyst, Isabel Menzies Lyth, acknowledges her debt to Bowlby in her work on children's institutions.

me a kind of revulsion although in fact he has been scrupulously fair to me in my writings. . . . "[42] To a Kleinian analyst such as Dr. Susanna Issacs Elmhirst, Bowlby is too mechanistic. He treats humans as though they were animals, which is just what they aren't, she asserts. He ignores love and anguish, the real stuff of human life.[43] "Bowlby?" exclaimed another analyst. "Give us Barabbas!" "He took the poetry out of analysis," says Dr. A. Hyatt Williams.[44]

Despite all his caveats, Bowlby readily recognizes his Kleinian roots. He says that the Kleinian ideas that he has found useful are the emphasis on the early development of "object relations" (a term he dislikes) and the importance Klein attached to mourning in early childhood, although he does not link it to weaning. It would appear, then, that his theoretical position has developed partially as a reaction to her emphasis on the centrality of the depressive position.

T. T. S. Hayley describes the Scientific Meetings during the fifties as slave markets for referrals. The economic pressure became particularly intense during a student's final year. "One had to toe the line in order to get patients."[45] Hayley, who already had a degree in anthropology and had spent time in India with the Civil Service, was disgusted by the arrogance of the young trainees, who would look at each other and wink when someone from the other side was speaking. Hayley had a Kleinian analysis with Money-Kyrle but insisted on being an independent, as he did not want to belong to a group. Alan Tyson, one of Freud's translators, left psychoanalysis to become a musicologist. "I'm not a groupie," he says.[46] Moreover, neither group bothered to read the other's work. The distinguished Jungian Michael Fordham was invited to attend some meetings in the fifties and, contrary to all expectation, found not fireworks but tedium.* [47]

This divisiveness and lack of real discussion were apparent to Charlotte Balkanyi when she arrived from Hungary in 1955. She remembers Anna Freud and Melanie Klein sitting in the front row "with barricades of people between them." She says that she did not come to England to have this "religious feeling"; and she attributes the servility and hypocrisy as a reaction to the quarreling that had preceded it.[48] After one frustrating meeting on April 9, 1952, a group of disaffected analysts (among them Pearl King, Barbara Woodhead, Masud Khan, and Charles Rycroft) adjourned to Miss King's consulting room, disgusted by the lack of real discussion in a society that purported to be "scientific." That very evening they decided to form the "1952 Club," limited to twelve members of different orientations. Their plan was to invite speakers

---

* Dr. Fordham has pointed out to me the connection between Klein's views on phantasies about the mother image and myths described by Jung in *Symbols of Transformation*; and that she was in his view talking about childhood archetypes of the dual mother. He sees Klein as opening up the understanding of infant development, but adds, "She's the innovator, but the innovators always get things wrong. They always overstate their case."

so that a stimulating exchange of ideas would be possible. The club exists to this day, although its membership has expanded.

John Padel believes that there was an improvement in 1956, when Charles Rycroft became scientific secretary.[49] Padel found himself relying on Rycroft, who had a gift for summarizing the points of discussion in an extraordinarily lucid way.

Joseph Sandler recalls: "In the Freudian group people reacted to the complete ignoring by the Kleinians of ego-psychology, of developments of it in the United States and at the Hampstead Clinic. The Kleinians were very dismissive and omnipotent at that time. They had seen the light, and the Freudians were lagging behind. It is rather different now." He is inclined to take a more sanguine view than many other analysts about the fact that the Society did not split:

> Anywhere else in the world the Society would have split. There was something very special about the situation of the Society here, which kept it together. And this was a very good thing because being together made it necessary for people to sharpen their thinking in order to defend their particular point of view. It forced them to engage with those that held opposite opinions. It raised the level of British psycho-analysis enormously, I think. Constant debate strengthened the profession.[50]

Perhaps only death, the great healer, could allow divergent opinions to coexist in a state of disagreement without rancor, once the two women around which they were polarized were no longer present.

CHAPTER THREE

Envy

Fearing for the future of her ideas, Klein concentrated increasingly on building up around her a nucleus of gifted and devoted followers. The group cohesion of the Kleinians was demonstrated in the concerted attack on Bowlby. A series of seminars and small study groups enabled them to exchange and develop ideas within a Kleinian framework, and out of these colloquia emerged a series of brilliant papers. If Klein's ideas were to survive, it was necessary, as she saw it, to discard dead wood or jarring elements.

Klein hoped to spend a May holiday in 1953 in Paris, where she would meet again with her enthusiastic new friends the Boulangers, who were introducing her ideas to the French-speaking world. However, she began to have a series of dizzy spells, which were particularly frightening when they occurred on the stairs.

Her physician, Dame Annis Gillie (recommended originally by Joan Riviere), recalled Klein as an ideal patient. She saw her once a year for a checkup, and Klein was always very cooperative; she would accept, for example, that an infection was something she had contracted, whereas Riviere always looked for a psychogenetic origin. The only disagreement they ever had was over her grandson Michael's circumcision. As a baby he suffered from phimosis (astringency of the foreskin); and Dame Annis insisted that he be circumcised. Klein objected violently; and although the operation was eventually carried out successfully, Dame Annis was puzzled by her reaction, given her Jewish origins. Dame Annis always had the impression that Klein wanted to create an image of herself as thoroughly English. She also remembers that the child's emotions in this case were of less interest to his grandmother than his physical condition.

At the time Klein's disorder appeared, Dame Annis felt that she could no longer look after her. The explanation she gave was that Clifton Hill was too far from her consulting rooms. While Dame Annis had found Klein a model patient, she realized that she might be a difficult one to pass on to another doctor, aware that their relationship would not necessarily be typical. With a certain trepidation she put her in the hands of Dr. George Abercrombie, who, in the early spring of 1953, insisted that Klein enter the Elizabeth Garrett Anderson Hospital, where she could receive proper treatment for the infection of the inner ear that was causing the dizzy spells. Klein, in a state of panic about her condition, and had to be put on tranquilizers to calm her nerves. She became abusive of Dr. Abercrombie, who told Dame Annis, "I simply can't handle this woman."[1] She was then transferred to another doctor, and the fact that she had been hospitalized was completely hushed up. On April 14 she wrote to Dr. Boulanger: "I am sorry to say that my nice plan to come to Paris has miscarried. I have recently not been well (I understand through working more than I should) and I have to keep very quiet for a few months. I shall spend a few days in the country at Whitsun instead of in Paris." Then on May 5 she wrote again that she had much improved: "It appears—so my doctors think— that all that was the matter with me was that I was chronically over-tired, which can't be done at my age. But with the amount of work I am now doing I feel perfectly well and get plenty of rest."[2]

In this period of quiet she did some hard thinking. It was clear that she was not going to be able to present a paper at the London Congress in July. The stairs in the house in Clifton Hill were too much for her, and she would have to move to a flat. And she simply could not continue to handle so many patients.

Paula Heimann was instructed to ask Hanna Segal to visit her during her convalescence. In their conversation Klein told Segal that she was going to have to drop two patients because they were "too destructive." She asked Segal if she would take over one of them, Judith Waterlow, a child psychiatrist at the Chistlehurst Child Guidance Clinic. According to Kathleen Cutler, the housekeeper in Klein's last home in Bracknell Gardens, for a long period an agitated woman would ring at all hours. Waterlow, described by Pearl King as "a very idealistic person," clearly felt that she had been abandoned. Miss Cutler, noticing eventually that the telephone calls had stopped for some time, asked her employer what had happened, and was told that the woman had committed suicide. Hanna Segal takes full responsibility for the tragedy.

The concept of countertransference was gradually coming to assume an important role in the theoretical corpus of the English School, although it was regarded skeptically by Melanie Klein until the end. Margaret Little was already working on countertransference when Heimann delivered her paper at Zurich in 1949. Dr. Little had not attended the congress, but found, on reading the manuscript later, that she and Heimann had reached many of the same conclusions. In 1950, Little went further than Heimann in "Counter-transference and the Patient's Response to It," expressing the view that countertransference was *more* than the signal that Heimann had implied it to be. She believed it to be an essential part of every analysis, as positive a tool as transference. Patients often become aware unconsciously of the analyst's countertransference, and unless its *existence* is acknowledged by the analyst, the patient will not believe in the reality of the transference. In 1956, Little elaborated on this thesis in her paper "R—The Analyst's Total Response to His Patient's Needs." In the discussion following the paper, Klein remarked acidly, "All that this paper shows is that Dr. Little needs further analysis"—"presumably from her!" Dr. Little recalls ruefully.[3] Winnicott interceded angrily from the chair that Mrs. Klein had no right to say that: "We *all* need more analysis. None of us can get more than a certain amount, and the same could be said of anybody."[4]

The events of 1953 culminated in the crucial break between Klein and Heimann, although it did not become publicly known until 1955. Klein was highly agitated about her health and the aggravation of moving house. She found a large, pleasant flat on the first floor of 20 Bracknell Gardens, West Hampstead, and sold the beautiful house in Clifton Hill, in which she had lived for twenty years.

Shortly before the move, Paula Heimann's daughter, Mertza, gave birth to a son. It was a difficult delivery, and Heimann was not permitted to see her grandson for well over a week. During this period Klein wanted Heimann to accompany her in choosing curtains and carpets for the new flat. Heimann was in a state of anguish, fearing that she was barred from seeing the baby because he was mentally deficient, and a shopping expedition was the last thing she felt up to. According to Heimann's daughter, her mother never forgave Klein for her manipulative selfishness and total lack of understanding.

Another issue arose this year. According to the recollections Paula Heimann related to Pearl King, William Gillespie informed Heimann that she was being considered for president when his term of office expired. "When I mentioned that to Melanie, she was beside herself with rage: 'You? Why not me?' and I said, 'You are probably too controversial a figure.'" This is pure fantasy on Heimann's part, although some such conversation between the two women may have taken place. According to Dr. Gillespie, there was a move among certain Kleinians to make Heimann vice-president, but he opposed the appointment because, while he considered her brilliant, he regarded her as too scatterbrained for an administrative post.

Klein had recovered sufficiently to participate in the 1953 London Congress to the extent of being a discussant in a symposium on "The Psychology of Schizophrenia" on July 28; Bion was the principal speaker. The Americans were beginning to be volubly uneasy about the lack of precision in her terminology. Edith Jacobson, for instance, in "On Psychotic Identifications," objected to the possible interpretations of Klein's use of "projection" and "introjection," although in a paper "Metapsychological Differences Between the Manic-Depressive and Schizophrenic Processes of Identification," delivered at the Midwinter Meeting of the American Psychoanalytic Association that year, Jacobson nevertheless expressed views remarkably similar to those of Klein on the intensity of affect in the preoedipal stage.* [5]

Klein had been working on an important paper that she had not been able to finish in time for the London Congress. This was "On Identification," based on Julien Green's novel *If I Were You*. Here she treats the protagonist, Fabian, "almost as if he were a patient," using his story to illustrate the process of projective identification. Fabian makes a pact with the devil by which he gains the power to change himself into other people. This strange wish is motivated by greed, envy, and hatred, the prime movers of aggressive phantasies. Fabian must obtain other people's material and spiritual possessions, he must absorb all the contents of his mother's inexhaustible breast. He is jealous of his father, who, adult and potent, possesses his mother, who is both idealized and devalued in Fabian's eyes.

In the end Fabian recovers his love for his mother and makes peace with her. It is significant that he recognizes her lack of tenderness but feels that she might have been better had *he* been a better son. [6]

Could Klein write about these subjects without relating them constantly to her own children? Fabian resembles Hans in his fluctuation between "a strongly repressed homosexuality and an unstable heterosexuality." [7] She also probably identified the fictional character and the real son in their uncon scious search through life for the ideal mother whom they had lost.

Betty Joseph recalls sitting on a bench outside Bedford College with Klein at the London Congress. Melitta passed them; and mother and daughter pretended not to notice each other. Miss Joseph remembers vividly the pain of the experience. In 1954 when Walter Schmideberg died in Switzerland of an ulcerous condition caused by his alcoholism, Klein wrote a consolatory letter to Melitta in New York, but never received a reply. Mother and daughter were never reconciled, although a photograph of Melitta as a young girl was beside Klein's bed until she died.

One is often inclined to suspect that Klein was displacing her distress about Melitta by reacting in an overdetermined fashion to opponents like Glover and Anna Freud.† During the congress an old colleague from Budapest, Sándor

---

* See also Margaret Mahler's differentiation between the autistic and schizophrenic child in "On Child Psychosis and Schizophrenia, Autistic and Symbiotic Psychoses," *Psychoanalytic Study of the Child* (1952) 7: 286–305.

† Nevertheless, at the Paris Congress in 1957 she did break down in tears to Francesca Bion about her estrangement from her daughter.

Lorand, and his wife, Rhoda, invited Klein to join them and Enid and Michael Balint at the Dorchester for dinner. Klein spent the entire evening in a long diatribe against Anna Freud. Rhoda Lorand felt that she should bring these criticisms to an end by confessing that she was training at the Hampstead Clinic that summer. "But why aren't you training with me?" Klein demanded. The embarrassed young woman stammered something about learning the Anna Freud system first. When she got up to dance with Michael Balint, he expostulated, "You don't tell the Queen that you are learning someone else's system first!"[8]

Through Rhoda Lorand, Klein heard about an interesting American, Judith Kestenberg, who was also studying at the Hampstead Clinic that summer. Kestenberg had been doing innovative work in child analysis and was one of the first to study the psychological state of victims of the Holocaust. Klein invited her to one of her seminars, and Kestenberg found herself utterly bewildered by the talk about reparation and other unfamiliar concepts. Nevertheless, the two women became very friendly for a short time and in one significant talk, Kestenberg told Klein that she felt that her ideas would be more amenable to the Americans if she said that the baby has feelings that he later phantasizes. "Thoughts? Feelings? What's the difference?" Klein replied.[9] She seemed deliberately to ignore the implications Kestenberg was suggesting about the early dating of the phantasies.

For some years Klein had been thinking of establishing a trust to further psychoanalytical research and teaching based on her concepts. In February 1955 the original trustees were chosen: Klein herself, Wilfred Bion, Paula Heimann, Betty Joseph, and Roger Money-Kyrle. Klein donated £600 as a financial base and requested that the contributors to *New Directions in Psycho-Analysis* (1955)* (which included the papers in the birthday issue of the *Journal* in addition to ten others) forgo their royalties in order to establish the fund on a sound basis. Jones wrote an enthusiastic Preface:

> Mrs. Klein's work of the past thirty years has been attacked and defended with almost equal vehemence, but in the long run its value can be satisfactorily estimated only by those who themselves make comparable investigations. As is well known, I have from the beginning viewed Mrs. Klein's work with the greatest sympathy, especially as many of the conclusions coincided with those I reached myself; and I have all along been struck by the observation that many of the criticisms have been close echoes of those with which I had been made familiar in the earliest days of psycho-analysis. A good many of her findings and conclusions had been adumbrated in quite early days by Freud, Rank, and others, but what is so distinctive and

---

* Its first suggested title was *Studies in Psycho-Analysis, Clinical and Applied.*

admirable in her work is the courage and unshakable integrity with which she has quite unsparingly worked out the implications and consequences of those earlier hints, thereby making important fresh discoveries in her course.

It is a matter for wide satisfaction as well as for personal congratulation that Mrs. Klein has lived to see her work firmly established. So long as it was simply deposited in what she herself had published there was always the hope, but by no means the certainty, that it would be taken up by future students. The situation has now moved beyond that stage; her work is firmly established. As a result of her personal instruction, combined with the insights of those who decided to accept it, she has a considerable number of colleagues and pupils who follow her lead in exploring the deepest depths. To the papers that many of them have contributed to *New Directions in Psycho-Analysis* I have the pleasure of adding this *envoi.*

This impressive collection, spanning literature, aesthetics, philosophy, and sociology, contained suggestions for further application of Kleinian ideas. It included a contribution from the painter Adrian Stokes (an analysand of Klein's), whose "Form in Art" was a precursor of many similar studies from his pen. Marion Milner, in "Aspects of Symbolism in Comprehension of the Not-Self," began to question Jones's views of symbolism ("The Importance of Symbol Formation in the Development of the Ego," 1930) as unduly restrictive, whereas she suggested that symbolism formed the basis of creativity, a view she was to develop further in "The Role of Illusion in Symbol Formation" (1955). In "A Psycho-Analytical Approach to Aesthetics" Hanna Segal took up Klein's position in "Infantile Anxiety-Situations Reflected in a Work of Art and in the Creative Impulse" (1929) of art as reparation. Later, in 1957, in "Notes on Symbol Formation," Segal traced the significance of the development from symbolic equations to fully formed symbols.

By the end of July 1955 Klein seemed to have recovered her vigor sufficiently to attend the Geneva Congress. She arrived two days before the congress began and passed the time happily with Elliott Jaques and his wife, the actress Kay Walsh. She sat at a sidewalk café chattering about the passersby, obviously enjoying the relaxing company of a vivacious woman with whom she did not have to talk shop. At one point she exclaimed suddenly, "Ah, how I should love to swim once more!" After the congress Jaques drove her to a hotel on the mountain above Montreux, where she spent a holiday before returning to London. It was here that Emanuel had gambled away all his allowance fifty years before, a crisis she could never have forgotten.

Klein always took an immense pleasure in choosing a special "Congress" hat, and on this occasion she looked more regal than ever. Some of her English colleagues have remarked that she greeted them as though she were the hostess at a very grand garden party.

Klein had always regarded it as a matter of principle to present a paper incorporating a new idea at each congress. For the first time she became unusually guarded about the contents of her own paper. In the past she had always discussed her forthcoming congress paper with close associates, but this time few knew its actual contents until they heard the provocative paper, "A Study of Envy and Gratitude," on the first morning of the congress, July 24. It certainly gave people something to talk about over lunch. During the presentation of the paper Clare Winnicott recalled that her husband, stunned, held his head in his hands, muttering, "Oh no, she *can't* do this!" Paula Heimann later said that this paper marked the irrevocable theoretical break between them.

What did the paper contain that made it so controversial? She begins with a reference to Abraham's "Short History of the Development of the Libido, Viewed in the Light of Mental Disorders" (1924), in which he explored the roots of destructive impulses more deeply than anyone had done before; and although he failed to mention the death instinct that Freud had postulated four years before in *Beyond the Pleasure Principle*, Klein was convinced that had Abraham lived longer, he would have connected the implications of his own findings with Freud's theory.*

She then turns to envy as a basic inborn motivator; and the capacity for envy is linked to the death instinct or, by inference, is the expression of innate aggression. In its primal form its first object is the breast; and while envy is not an original Kleinian concept, primary breast envy was first formulated by Klein (and later, in her own view, worked to death by some of her adherents). As early as *The Psycho-Analysis of Children* (1932) it is clear that she regarded envy as an infantile response to frustration.

She distinguishes carefully between envy, greed, and jealousy. "Envy is the angry feeling that another person possesses and enjoys something desirable— the envious impulse being to take it away or spoil it."[11] Greed is an insatiable craving and, at an unconscious level, it expresses itself in the phantasy of completely devouring the breast. Jealousy derives more from a fear of losing what one has.† Greed differs significantly from envy in that its aim is destructive introjection, whereas envy, at its deepest level, seeks to destroy the creativeness of the object. Envy is excessive when the paranoid-schizoid features are particularly strong.

---

* Was this in answer to Heimann, who, in "The Polymorphous Stage of Instinctual Development" (1952), had suggested that Abraham did not accept the death instinct? Dr. Hyatt Williams remembers Klein saying about Heimann in the late fifties, "I shouldn't have given her that important paper at that particular time."[10]
† The fact that she has so little to say about sexual jealousy is indicative of her emphasis on the introjected object rather than on the tripartite structure of the oedipal relationship.

Primary envy is directed toward the contents of the mother's breast; and in its later developmental manifestations, it is transferred to the mother's incorporation of the penis, her ability to conceive, give birth, and feed babies. Paradoxical though it may seem, it is not only the phantasized withholding breast that is envied, but the satisfactory breast for its unattainable riches. This can be detected in later life in the individual's envy of people who are themselves lacking in envy, who possess a good internalized object which allows them a state of contentment and peace of mind.

But the baby is also capable of gratitude for the goodness and enjoyment received, an emotion essential for the building up of all future relationships. (Freud had described the infant's bliss in being suckled as the prototype of sexual gratification.) In ideal development, gratification and gratitude enlarge the capacity for love, thus absorbing envy into the integrated ego. Unlike Freud, Klein assumes the existence of an ego from the outset, since the functions Freud assigns to the organism she believes can be performed only by an ego, even if in an undeveloped form. One of these functions is the expression of love and gratitude, a manifestation of the life instinct. But the infantile ego is torn by conflict from the beginning of life; and as a defense against anxiety it splits the breast into a good and a bad object. Primal splitting is necessary in order to achieve integration of the good internalized object and to learn to differentiate realistically between good and bad. This process, however, is disturbed if excessive envy interferes with the split between the good and bad breast so that integration cannot be achieved, especially when through excessive projective identification, by which split-off parts of the self are projected into the object, the result is a bewildering confusion of self and object.

Klein gives an effective account of the defenses erected by the ego against the ravages inflicted by envy. People endowed with a high degree of envy tend to idealize their objects; this is followed by an ensuing reaction in which they subsequently fear the idealized person as a persecutor into whom they have projected their envy. Jealousy is also an acceptable compromise as a defense against envy, since it gives rise to far less guilt. In the confused state that characterizes envy, the unfortunate victim often flees from the primal object—the mother—to other idealized people as a means of preserving the mother from envy. Alternate modes of defense are the devaluation of the object, violent possessiveness, and the stirring up of envy in others by emphasizing one's own success and good fortune.

In Klein's experience, penis envy can always be traced back to envy of the breast. The envious relation to the mother in oedipal rivalry is due less to love of the father than to the fact that the father (or his penis) has become an appendage of the mother, which the girl wants to steal from her. This envy can be carried over into later life in situations in which the woman wants a man only if she has taken him from another woman. Homosexuality in women may be based on the need to find an alternative good object instead of the avoided primal object. It would appear to be a defensive position against envy.

If the boy's oral gratification has been frustrated, his anxieties are transferred to the vagina, thus creating a disturbed attitude toward women, which often leads to homosexuality. Guilt towards a loved woman can lead to a flight to homosexuality. There are also many cases of male envy of the female capacity to produce babies.

Earliest envy feelings are conveyed through "memories in feelings," by which the patient again experiences early emotions through the transference in which the analyst sometimes plays the role of father, sometimes mother. Here she gives us some sense of her technique. "In analysis," she says, "we should make our way slowly and gradually towards the painful insights into the divisions in the patient's self."[12] The analyst must resist the temptations of the countertransference, which may increase his identification with the patient and hence fail to uncover the deepest strata of the mind. Was she making an oblique criticism of Winnicott when she spoke of some analysts who "attempt to strengthen feelings of love by taking the role of the good object which the patient had not been able to establish in the past"?[13] The evocation of primary envy feelings is particularly painful when the analysand is confronted with envy and hatred of the breast. The analyst's most challenging task is to enable the patient to recognize and integrate these feelings into a more self-confident image. But for the first time she expressed pessimism about the possibility of being able to help all patients, and especially those with strong paranoid anxieties and schizoid mechanisms.

Klein was here adumbrating a constitutional basis for envy rather than a drive-derivative one, as had been assumed by Freud. Moreover, she ascribed an extremely complex object-related set of conflicting feelings to the infant. The envy paper aroused more criticism than any other she had presented. It confirmed a general attitude, especially prevalent among the Americans, that her views were grotesque. However, the envy concept bound her supporters to her more closely than ever, so that by 1969 Walter G. Joffe, a member of the "B" Group, described the British Society as "a supremely envy-conscious Society."[14] No classical analyst could accept the assumption of an early ego that seemed to ignore the length of time necessary for a process of differentiation between self and object, or the failure to recognize the maturation and development of the psychic apparatus as a whole. Joffe was to write:

In the Kleinian theoretical framework there is in addition no need to discriminate between drives, wishes, fantasies and affects (cf. Isaacs, 1948). There is no place in the scheme as a whole for the maturation and development of the psychic apparatus as a whole, and the perceptual apparatus in particular, as entities distinct from the drives. Perceptual awareness is taken to mature as a result of the interaction of introjective and projective mechanisms.[15]

The main objection seemed to be that her bias had become absurdly minimalist: that the presence of envy in the patient invariably indicated a psychopathology rooted in early oral frustration. But often *real* objections are not voiced: envy has traditionally been regarded as a *female* weakness, one of the horrors that escaped with the opening of Pandora's box,* and the predominantly male group was reluctant to accept the idea that it was an inherent element in themselves.

Winnicott had never been happy with the paranoid-schizoid position; and Klein's account of primal envy seemed to develop it to an even more extreme level. The child, in Winnicott's view, did not exist *in vacuo:* the mother-child relationship preceded any awareness of self. He believed one must allow for a stage preceding a fusion of destructive and erotic impulses. Klein's concept of envy implied extremely complex feelings in the baby; and he simply could not accept any description of the infant that ignored the behavior of the person caring for it. He was prepared to accept envy as one component in a situation in which the mother acted towards the child in a "tantalizing" way.[16] By this he meant a situation in which the mother's behavior was inconsistent and the child, in recognizing that goodness was being withheld from him from time to time, was initiated into a process of disillusionment. Moreover, Klein's account of her present position disturbed Winnicott because he believed that it tended to weaken the concept of oral sadism, which he was willing to accept because it was related to the biological concept of hunger as well as a drive to object relationships. Many Kleinian analysts feel that Winnicott "sentimentalized" the mother-child relationship, that he objected basically to the idea of babies having such distressing feelings. "It's cosy to think that if you are nice to baby," Elinor Wedeles comments, "baby will be nice to you."[17]

While Heimann later said that she broke with Klein theoretically over the concept of breast envy, she never spelled out what her objections were. Betty Joseph, who was in analysis with Heimann between 1951 and 1954, finds it curious in retrospect that she never interpreted splitting or projective identification, two of the cornerstones of Kleinian analysis, and believes that she had already begun to go her own way.

When the envy paper was expanded into book form in 1957† (with the as-

---

* I am indebted to one of my students, Mary Katherine Travers, for this insight.
† The anonymous reviewer in *The Times Literary Supplement* (Sept. 27, 1957) remarked: "Although the theoretical background of her work may seem improbable to many, her understanding of human development is indeed remarkable." It struck a topical chord with Jean Howard in her review in *The Spectator:* "Why are the so-called 'angry young men' so bitter towards a community that has never offered the young so much, if not because of their envy of the giver?"

sistance of Elliott Jaques), case material was added. It is possible that Heimann was one of the case histories in the envy paper, and that she not only resented what was said about her but feared that she would be recognized as the woman with "strong depressive and schizoid features." In the early part of the patient's analysis the complexity and depth of her difficulties were not easily grasped. "Socially, she gave an impression of being a pleasant person, though liable to be depressed. Her reparative tendencies and helpful attitude towards friends were quite genuine."[18] Many people have spoken of Heimann's charm and vivacity. Judith Fay recalls her as having "the best sense of humour of anyone I have ever known."[19]

In the case Klein recounted, the severity of the patient's problem became apparent "partly due to the previous analytic work."[20] The main cause of the appearance of her destructive envy was "an unexpected success in her professional career that brought more to the fore what I had been analysing for some years, namely, the intense rivalry with me and a feeling that she might in her own field become equal, or rather superior to me."[21] Is Klein referring to the countertransference paper and Heimann's subsequent ambition to become vice-president of the Society? When the depth of her envy and of her destructive impulses towards her analyst were examined, "they were felt to be omnipotent and therefore irremediable."[22]

Klein then relates the intensity of the patient's dreams, in one of which an endless strip of blanket represented the endless strip of words in the analysis— woolly and worthless—words that the analyst now had to swallow. The patient was shocked by the interpretation and the revelation of the depth of her envy, especially by a dream of wet pants, which was interpreted as a poisonous urethral attack on the analyst in a desire "to destroy her mental powers and change her into a cow-woman."[23]

The patient had such an idealized conception of herself that it was particularly difficult for her to acknowledge her envy.

> Her guilt and depression focused on her feeling of ingratitude towards the analyst who, she knew, helped her and was helping her, and towards whom she felt contempt and hate: ultimately on the ingratitude towards her mother, whom she unconsciously saw as spoilt and damaged by her envy and destructive impulses.[24]

After a temporary improvement, she was assailed again by deep depression. "The steps towards integration which took place following the analysis of the depression implied regaining these lost parts, and the necessity to face them was the cause of her depression."[25] Klein does not say whether integration was ever achieved. She concludes: "At the present state of our knowledge, I am inclined to take the view that these are the patients, not necessarily of a manifest psychotic type, with whom success is limited, or may not be achieved."[26] One devastating question might arise in response to this dismissal: That it perhaps illuminates something about the analyst's state of mind as much as that of the patient.

It will be remembered that during Klein's convalescence in 1953 she told Hanna Segal that there were two patients whom she had to drop because they were "too destructive"—and one of them turned out to be Heimann. Kleinian analysts have speculated that envy played a strong part in the break between Klein and Heimann. The assumption seems to have been that the envy was Heimann's. There is little doubt that Heimann was ambitious and resented her subservience to Klein—"enslavement," she described it to Pearl King. She felt that she should have been listed as the coauthor of some of Klein's papers, especially "Notes on Some Schizoid Mechanisms." She was deeply jealous of Lola Brook, and even more of Hanna Segal, who was already being regarded as Klein's successor.

But what about Klein's own envy of Heimann? Surely in the countertransference a good deal of projection could have been taking place? Heimann was younger than Klein, widely liked, and regarded as brilliant. Klein was highly critical of Heimann's countertransference paper, which had immediately been hailed as a classic. Heimann was a surrogate daughter; and like Freud with his surrogate sons, daughters were expected to remain in a position of dependency.

Both Klein and Heimann have been described frequently as greedy eaters, and Klein as a "greedy" speaker at congresses. Klein was famous for asking, when leaving a party, if she could take a couple of little cakes with her. One analyst recalled, "If Mrs. Klein was coming for dinner, one always worried whether the food was going to be good enough."

Klein had envied her mother, her sister Emilie, her sister-in-law Jolan, Helene Deutsch, Anna Freud, Marie Bonaparte, her own daughter, and various surrogate daughters. On one occasion, when Tom Main was driving her home from an evening at his house, she asked wistfully, "I think my work will last, don't you? I've done better than Helene Deutsch, haven't I?"[27]

Paula Heimann could easily have interpreted the envy paper as an act of aggression. But Klein might also have detected hostility in Heimann's papers on countertransference at Zurich (1949) and at Geneva (1955). In the former, Heimann had contended that countertransference is effective only when the analyst has worked through his own infantile anxieties so that he will not impute to the patient what belongs to himself. Similarly, at Geneva she stated that any confession of personal matters (and how much Melanie had confided in Paula) could injure the analytic process—an intrusion and projection by the analyst could lead the patient to notice something disturbing in the analyst.

In the envy paper Klein may well be discussing herself in the case of

a woman patient whom I would describe as fairly normal whose envy of her older sister had been held in check by her sense of strong intellectual superiority to her, which was in fact an actuality. The patient, through her dreams, recalled the envy she had experienced towards her sister who was courted while the younger sister was yet a child and of a dress her mother wore which clearly revealed the shape of her breasts. Her ensuing guilt [localized, presumably, in the self-analysis] made her sad that as a child she had loved her sister far more than she thought. Considering herself "fairly normal," the patient was shocked to recognize and acknowledge the residue of paranoid and schizoid feelings and mechanisms. The revision of her earliest relations was bound up with changes in feeling towards her primal introjected objects. The fact that her sister also represented the mad part of herself turned out to be partly a projection of her own schizoid and paranoid feelings on to her sister. It was together with this realization that the split in her ego diminished.[28]

She was finally coming to terms with her envied older sister, both here and in the earlier paper on mourning, even if the mature Klein was not able to do so now with Heimann.

To most of the members of the British Society there was no apparent strain in the relationship; but Bion, Segal, and Elliott Jaques, who took a postgraduate seminar with Heimann, were aware that Heimann was making acerbic references to Klein. The matter was discussed by Klein with her closest associates. On November 24, 1955, she wrote the following brief letter:

Dear Paula Heimann,

This is a painful letter, so I shall make it short. I have been considering the Trust which has been formed to develop my work in the future. I have come to feel that I no longer have confidence in you as one of the people in whom I would wish to place such a trust. I do not wish to have to say this at a meeting of the Trust, and I would therefore ask for your resignation. I would appreciate it if you would let me have it as soon as possible.

I do not consider in a matter of such complexity that any purpose can be served by further personal discussion.

Yours faithfully,

Melanie Klein[29]

On November 27, Heimann replied:

Dear Mrs. Klein,
It is with deep concern that in accordance with the circumstances and your feelings I am herewith resigning from the Melanie Klein Trust Fund. I am sending a copy of this letter of resignation to its Secretary, Elliott Jaques.
Wishing the M.K.T.F. prosperity and success, I am
Yours sincerely,

Paula Heimann[30]

The same day she wrote a letter to Jaques, who had become secretary of the Trust in October.* She went to see Betty Joseph, her recent analysand, to tell her that she was leaving the group, adding, "Will you leave as well? You'll see, others will follow." But, Miss Joseph recalls ruefully, "no one did."[31] Heimann then sent a letter to the members of the Society announcing that she was no longer a member of the Klein group.

People were plunged into a state of stunned bewilderment, and the news quickly spread to the students in the Institute. Heimann's analysands were put in a particularly difficult position. One South American burst into tears. Judith Fay described her own reaction: "At the time it was a shock, and I felt torn in two directions, like a child whose parents get a divorce, and who, inevitably, builds up its own explanations to try to make sense of it, which may be completely wrong."[32] Heimann's own analysands were given no explanation for the break. Since they could not detect any change in her technique or interpretations, what did it mean that she was no longer a "Kleinian"? As one analyst commented wittily, "Did I say 'breast'? Oh sorry, I didn't mean that." Was a Kleinian, then, only someone whom Mrs. Klein designated as such?

It was a period of confusion and loneliness for Heimann. Joan Riviere was sympathetic to her, but refused to be dragged into the political infighting, and Heimann had to form an entirely new set of relationships. Donald Winnicott immediately invited her to his weekly seminar. She was immensely grateful and never missed a single one. But her future depended on her reputation as a bril-

* Jaques inserted a note on the aims of the Trust into the *Journal—J.* (1956) 37, 515–16: "The aims of the Trust are to contribute to psycho-analysis by ensuring the further development of Mrs. Klein's work. The Trustees will endeavour to promote clinical work, training and research, using theory and technique which may subsequently arise.
    "The initial income of the Trust will come from the royalties of the book *New Directions in Psycho-Analysis*, recently published by Tavistock Publications. These royalties have been assigned to the Trust by the sixteen contributors to the book. The Trust is open to receive donations and bequests from individuals and grants from organizations who judge the work of Mrs. Klein to be important for the development of psycho-analysis and the further understanding of human behaviour."

liant clinician—and her charm—for she was no longer going to get Kleinian referrals. In supervision, Judith Fay says she learned more from her than from anyone else. Heimann was strict and expected one to be very precise. "She was very good at hitting the nail on the head, provided you could find the hammer in the first place."[33]

Unlike Klein, Heimann was opposed to a great deal of interpretation. It was possible, Fay contends, to criticize or quarrel with Heimann, who would have laughed, whereas she felt that with Klein one would always have felt in the wrong. Eric Trist, who was analyzed by Heimann for some months in 1944 when his own analyst, Susan Isaacs, contracted pneumonia after her house was bombed, believes that she had "a touch of Ferenczi about her."[34] A passionate person, she *lived* her interpretations, which she generally made in a summation at the end of a session. Every session had a theme. Margret Tonnesmann, who went into training with her in 1959, experienced her as fragile, whereas men (like her analysand Harold Bridger) found her very tough. Tonnesmann, unlike Trist, says that she made many interventions and was extremely concise about verbalizing the negative transference. To her students, she never mentioned her quarrel with Klein, but she did not hide the contempt with which she regarded the envy concept. To those intimate friends whom she could trust, she expressed her anger, not only against Klein but against herself for her subservience over so many years. Her daughter insists that Heimann's intellect was far superior to Mrs. Klein's and, moreover, sees Klein's influence on many people as "malevolent."

Heimann's sympathizers (mostly independents) felt that she had been badly treated. Dr. James Gammill, an American analysand of Heimann's (now practicing in Paris), is saddened that two such brilliant women should have parted in so painful a fashion. A number of Kleinian analysts speak regretfully about the fact that Heimann never again did any real creative work. At the Paris Congress in 1957 she gave a paper in which she attempted to integrate object relations with ego psychology. According to Margaret Tonnesmann, Anna Freud invited her to dinner with the Hoffers to discuss this paper. Anna Freud advised her to withdraw it from publication in the *International Journal*, although it appeared in German in *Psyche* in October 1959.[35]

The split did not help in the dissemination of Kleinian ideas beyond Britain. In 1957 Dr. Marianne Baumann wrote to Klein from Switzerland that a group of analysts were organizing a round-table discussion of Kleinian ideas in the autumn of 1958 in Zurich, and asked her to suggest names of colleagues who could attend. After months passed without a reply, Dr. Baumann wrote to D. W. Winnicott, the president, for help. The latter replied on January 20, 1958, that Klein had passed on Dr. Baumann's letter to him; Klein had suggested Esther Bick, who had the best command of German. He added: "Dr. Heimann has told me that she also has been approached. She may be able to give you other names but you understand at the present time Mrs. Klein does not consider that Dr. Heimann accurately represents her point of view."[36] Apparently plans for the meeting proceeded, but on June 3, 1958, Dr. Baumann again wrote to Winnicott that " . . . we got a little confused about a letter by Dr. Heimann who wrote us about an independent group who split off from the Kleinians. It was then decided by our people that we wanted Dr. Heimann herself. She refused . . . it was decided to cancel. . . . " Winnicott replied immediately: "I think you should not be caught up in our splits, which have no effect on the general situation. Melanie has much to teach us all, and anyone she sends over will be very helpful. I specially recommend Mrs. Bick."[37] However, analysts outside Britain tended to side with Heimann (without knowing anything about the issue), and the American analytic community gleefully gossiped about Melitta's eccentric behavior while she was working in the United States as corroboration that Klein was generalizing about infantile psychotic states from a retrospective view of her own disturbed children.

CHAPTER FOUR

Political Infighting

Many British analysts consider Klein ruthless in the way she discarded people if they did not subscribe wholeheartedly to her person and her ideas—not only Heimann, but also Rickman, Winnicott, Riviere, Eva Rosenfeld, and Clifford Scott. Her relationship to the last presents an interesting case. For some years she took a motherly interest in Scott and his first wife, who was the daughter of the family with whom he boarded in the Black Forest when he accompanied Klein on her 1931 summer vacation in order to continue his analysis. His wife later became godmother to Michael Clyne, Klein's first grandchild.

However, Scott had interests of his own, although the idea of projective identification might have occurred to Klein through the case he reported of a patient who thought she had projected everything good in herself into the figure of Greta Garbo.

He was absorbed in developing a complicated idea, the body scheme, to which he devoted many papers, the first of which was delivered to the Society on March 19, 1947. Many people have had difficulty in understanding it; and to Winnicott, Scott wrote explaining it as simply as he could:

> The body scheme is another name for primary narcissism as Freud used it, but it means much more than that in the sense that there is always a totality which later may be broken into many parts and, of course, the history of the development of the individual is a history to some extent described in a certain way of the way the various parts develop—for instance, the parts which I so frequently mention—the body boundary, the inner world and the outer world.[1]

Scott and Klein were increasingly to disagree over primary narcissism; and while Scott remained loyal to her, she did not disguise the fact that she was distancing herself from him. As one of the first people to analyze a schizophrenic, he was important to her; but now that Segal, Rosenfeld, and Bion were analyzing borderline cases she could afford to dispense with him. (In Scott's view, Kleinians do not sufficiently distinguish between psychosis and schizophrenia.) Scott, a forthright man, did not hesitate to criticize Klein more directly than her other adherents would do:

> When you say that excessive persecutory and depressive anxieties in young infants form the basis of all mental illness, I think if you put it in this way it may be thought that you are boasting that you have discovered the last word—at the same time as putting forward all your new views. I think you should not leave yourself open to the kind of criticism this statement in the form in which it is now would provoke. If you can say "my contention that excessive persecutory and depressive anxieties in young infants form an extremely basic aspect of many mental illnesses which have been previously neglected," I think you would be going as far as you should. Anyway I am sure you yourself want to leave room for the future—if you could work as actively in the next thirty years as in the past, I am wondering how you would look back on a statement like the one I have just quoted.[2]

Klein did not appreciate this kind of bluntness. When Scott contended that the feelings of love and hatred oscillated in the infant, Klein tried to make him see that "anxiety contents which initiate the oscillation and the object-relations, identifications and splitting processes and defences . . . are operative at the moment of oscillation."

> I am afraid [she continued] I cannot believe that your point, so very clinically, provides a better basis for instinct theory. It was always implied in Freud's concept of ambivalence, that the contrasting emotions of love and hatred are experienced at the same time, sometimes one getting the upper hand, sometimes the other. When he arrived at his findings about the life and death instinct, the early concept of ambivalence was not invalidated— I would say it was strengthened. With his views I still fully agree and therefore I do not see that things become clearer by thinking of oscillations in terms of succession or transformation.[3]

In late 1954 Scott returned to Canada to become associate professor in charge of training in psychoanalysis at McGill, and the following year he became founding president of the Canadian Psychoanalytic Society. A number of British analysts believe that his decision to return to Canada was based on his mounting divergence with Klein's views. His departure seemed particularly curious to some people because he had then completed only two years as president. (Sylvia Payne filled in for the intervening year until Winnicott took over.) He and Klein continued to keep in touch, but her notes and Christmas cards became increasingly perfunctory. In 1958 Scott sent her a draft of the paper he was planning to give at the Copenhagen Congress in 1959, "Depression, Confusion and Multivalence." She returned it to him with the following apology:

> I have for many years been forced to refuse to read books or papers or drafts of papers, to which any comment of mine would be expected. This principle has become much more stringent in the last few years, when I have had to reduce my work considerably in order to keep up with what to me is most important. If I overstep my working hours, I get extremely tired, and, under doctor's orders and my own, I know that I must avoid extra work. For me to read a paper and to comment on it is work.
>
> The time I leave for work I select most carefully and divide it between my own writing and still some analysis and supervisions. You must therefore forgive me if I return your draft without the comments you wish me to make. I may add that even my very closest associates refrain now from asking me for advice and comments, because they know how essential it is for me not to overwork.[4]

Those who dropped away were replaced by even more ardent supporters. None was more fervently loyal than Esther Bick, who had a doctorate in psychology from Vienna, where she had worked with Karl and Charlotte Blühler, who, in Bick's view, were more interested in statistics than in children. When she arrived in England she found Anna Freud's methods too superficial and moved on to Manchester to work with Michael Balint. After the war she came to London, where Melanie Klein first supervised her in child analysis and then took her into analysis in 1950. In 1951 Bick initiated a course for child psychotherapists in infant observation at the Tavistock. "I will do Blühler, but properly," she said.[5] Bick was important to Klein because she provided observational data on infant emotions. A leading member of the "B" Group, Ilse Hellman (who had also worked with the Blühlers in Vienna), found it absurd that one could learn from the expression on a baby's face whether it was feeling persecuted or depressed.[6] Elinor Wedeles recalls the famous occasion when a baby "quite clearly" turned from its mother's breast "in terror," and Willi Hoffer's exasperated explanation was that perhaps there was a hair on the nipple!*[7] His wife, Hedwig Hoffer, also once remarked that it was possible that *working class* babies could feel persecuted. The Kleinians, subject to so much criticism themselves, delighted in repeating these stories. Nevertheless, infant observation was introduced into the curriculum of the Institute of Psycho-Analysis in 1960, and has become an established tradition in many centers.

The brightest star in Klein's firmament during the last decade of her life was Wilfred Bion. Born in 1897, he had come to Kleinian theories after a distinguished career—or more precisely, several careers. He had been awarded a D.S.O. in the First World War, was a graduate in history from Oxford, and had received a gold medal in clinical surgery from University College Hospital. For some years before the war, while working at the Tavistock Clinic, he was in analysis with Rickman, and was accepted for training by the British Institute of Psycho-Analysis, but this period of his life was ended by the outbreak of World War II.

During the war he made an enormous impact as a senior psychiatrist by devising new methods for the recruiting and selection of officer candidates. In 1947 his close friend J. D. Sutherland became medical director of the Tavistock Clinic, while Bion was appointed senior psychiatrist. Klein recognized him as a prize catch when he applied to her for analysis after being demobilized.† He insisted that it was to be on the condition that he was his own person when it came to thinking and reacting. She agreed to his terms—probably because she was so anxious to have him as a patient‡—although there were inevitable problems when Bion rejected the literal interpretation that an infant evacuates parts of its personality it doesn't want and shoves them into another body—in other words, an omnipotent phantasy. Nevertheless, he accepted that there was a psychotic core to every individual, and he had been attracted to her work initially through her paper "Notes on Some Schizoid Mechanisms." During the fifties he wrote six brilliant papers, all except one ("On Arrogance") devoted to borderline cases. On one occasion, after a Scientific Meeting, Klein was found weeping in the hall because Bion had failed to give acknowledgment to her. "But Mrs. Klein," someone expostulated, "everyone *knows* his assumptions are based on yours!" Probably as a result of her touchi-

---

* When Hoffer reviewed *Contributions to Psycho-Analysis, 1921–45* in the *British Medical Journal* (1949) 6: 109, he observed: "While [Klein's] theories and observations of [early persecution fantasies] are earnestly discussed among psychoanalysts, they have definitely been accepted only by those who have been working in close co-operation with the author. Without such contact familiarization with her approach seems impossible or, at least, difficult. The likelihood is not remote, however, that one day psychiatry will be able successfully to contact the psychotic, for his benefit, through what it has learned from the psychology of children."

† His membership paper, "The Imaginary Twin," was delivered to the Society in 1950.

‡ Compare the uneasy terms to which she and Clifford Scott agreed when he entered into analysis with her. See p. 189.

ness, Bion says in one of his papers, "even where I do not make specific ac-
knowledgement of the fact, Melanie Klein's work occupies a central position in
my view of the psycho-analytic theory of schizophrenia."[8]

Dr. J. D. Sutherland thinks that Bion went into analysis because he felt he
did not know enough about individuals. While in analysis with Klein he was
writing *Experience in Groups*, based on his own wide and unique background.
Klein did not approve of the book, and on one occasion Bion told her that he
had decided not to become an analyst. The following day she said to him, "Dr.
Bion, I have been thinking over what you said and you are probably quite
right"—undoubtedly gambling on his commitment to analysis. When his
book was published in 1961 he added a concluding "Re-View" in which he
emphasized that in adult life the individual in group situations, through
projective identification, resorts to mechanisms typical of the earliest phases of
mental life.

> The adult must establish contact with the emotional life of the group in
> which he lives; this task would appear to be as formidable to the adult as
> the relationship with the breast appears to be to the infant, and the failure
> to meet the demands of this task is revealed in his regression. The belief
> that a group exists, as distinct from an aggregate of individuals, is an essen-
> tial part of this regression, as are also the characteristics with which the
> supposed group is endowed by the individual.[9]

In 1955 he became director of the clinic, an appointment that delighted Klein.
She was not filled with the same enthusiasm for Winnicott's ascendancy to the
presidency.

In 1950 there were seventy-five practicing analysts in London. By this date,
according to John Bowlby, "it was as clear as a pikestaff that it was advanta-
geous to be a Kleinian."[10] He compared the group to a religious sect* in which,
once one had espoused the doctrine, one was welcomed to the fold. If one deviated, if one did not subscribe totally to the doctrine, one faced the terrible
threat of excommunication. Those who were not medically qualified were particularly vulnerable because of the uncertainty of getting referrals. Some medically qualified members of the Society recall Klein using flattery to court them:
"Dr. ———, you are very promising. I think I could help you." She would
then go on to tell them how her father had been a doctor and how she had
longed to be one. It was important to her to secure as many medically qualified
members as possible, particularly now that she was venturing into areas of
psychosis. Yet, according to Dr. Margaret Little, she could never accept or understand the legal status of doctors in England. She insisted that she be listed

---

* Charles Rycroft describes it as "the Ebenezer Church."

in precisely the same way as doctors were, a proposal the Board of Trade would not consider. She could not comprehend that unless one was a doctor one could not have a patient admitted to a hospital or, as a nonmedical person, attend a coroner's court. While Heimann was still in favor, she supported Klein in her stand, contending that her medical background had done nothing to help her understanding of mental illness. Nevertheless, Rosenfeld, Bion, and Segal, as medically qualified people, were particularly important supporters of her views of the origin of the psychoses.

Not only were the numbers of Kleinians increasing, but, in the opinion of the independents, their efforts to secure converts were being intensified. The postwar memorandum of agreements had attempted to be fair in its endeavor to place two members from each of the three factions on all committees wherever possible. Klein often asked William Gillespie for advice on how to get her associates appointed to committees. Behind the scenes, the struggle for power erupted once more. In June 1953 the Training Committee drew up a revised set of more equitable regulations as a result of complaints by a number of independent members that they were far outnumbered by the Kleinians in the number of teaching events. Melanie Klein took particular exception to the section dealing with Personal Analysis.

D. THE PERSONAL ANALYSIS

14. The personal analysis is on a basis of a session of fifty minutes, five times a week. Only very exceptionally does the Training Committee agree to a temporary period of analysis on a basis of four sessions a week.

15. Students are allotted to analysts by the Training Committee according to the following principles:

    (a) Whenever possible the student is referred to the analyst of his or her choice, provided that the analyst is being used at the time for training purposes.

    (b) If a student has no means of making a choice, or if no definite wish is expressed, then the Committee allots the student to an analyst, taking into consideration the vacancies that exist at the time among analysts of the various groupings.

16. *Trends in the Society*

    Of several trends in the development of psycho-analytic theory, there are two which at the present time differ sufficiently from each other to justify arrangement of the training programme in two parallel courses. The B. Course follows the method of teaching which is sponsored by Miss Anna Freud and her immediate colleagues. The A. Course represents the teaching by analysts not specifically associated with Miss

Freud. The lectures are common to the two courses. Two different courses of seminars are given in the early stages. There are combined seminars, especially in the later stages.* Students are encouraged to attend both A and B courses if their analysts approve. Choice is inevitable when occasionally it proves impossible to avoid holding the parallel courses at the same hour.

Klein fired off an angry letter to the president, Clifford Scott.

Flat 2
20 Bracknell Gardens
N.W.3

15th March 1954

Dear Dr. Scott,

I have been reading the new Training Committee regulations, and I noticed that the committee has made a number of departures from the minutes of the Council of 11th December 1946. . . .

If you will remember, that minute was based on the recommendations of an ad hoc committee representing

1. Miss Freud's views
2. those of the middle group (so-called in the minute)
3. myself.

The object of the recommendations was to ensure that satisfactory development of our work should continue, within the framework of our Society, with the minimum of friction between the groups.

I do not think it a perfect document, but it must not be forgotten that the differences then were deep and serious, and could still become extremely disruptive; it is in the light of the fact that, whatever its defects, it has enabled us to work together without a damaging schism that it should be judged. Any departure from it could easily upset the balance we then achieved.

I am not saying this because I am opposed to change, but because I think that any change should be made only after careful consideration and by the Council. Further changes should only be made when it is clear that the reasonable aspirations of the groups (which were represented on the ad hoc committee by Miss Freud, Dr. Payne and myself) have in the views of the groups themselves, been adequately safeguarded in any new directive

---

* The practice has unfortunately arisen of referring to the group of Mrs. Klein's immediate colleagues as the "A" group, with the result that those analysts who are in an independent position have been said to form a "middle group." There is in fact no group that could be called "middle." It is hoped that the above explanation will help to remove the confusion that has been caused in this manner about the nature of the "A" course of training, which, it will be noted, is not limited to any one school of thought.

that the Council sees fit to promulgate; this could only be done if the Council first sought the advice of another ad hoc committee comparable to the committee of 1946. Any group wishing to make a change should, I think, in view of the serious issues involved be asked to show that its work was being adversely affected by the present arrangements.

Yours sincerely

(sgd.)
Melanie Klein

As a result, at a Council meeting on May 31, 1954, Winnicott, seconded by Bion, proposed that Council appoint an Ad Hoc Committee to reconsider the training regulations. It was feared by some that Klein was trying to form her *own* group and split Course "A." Paula Heimann suggested that Anna Freud, Melanie Klein, and Sylvia Payne be invited to discuss the uneasy matter of training at the meeting scheduled for May 31. At this meeting Bion, seconded by Winnicott, proposed that Mrs. Klein's "draft" be submitted to the Training Committee for further consideration. In the meantime the proportions were readjusted, so that training events taken by the Kleinian training analysts were reduced from eighty-four to sixty-six, and those by the independent analysts were increased to sixty-two events from forty-four.

It was ironic that it should be Sylvia Payne who produced the figures indicating the disproportion; in 1943 she had checked Glover's contention that there was a predominance of Kleinians, only to find at the time that the balance was reversed.

Klein continued to rage; and after months of discussion the Training Committee referred the issue to the Council for arbitration. On March 22, 1957, Klein addressed a memorandum to the Council complaining of unfairness in the new arrangements.

When the matter was raised at Council, it was noted that Mrs. Klein had made "a serious allegation" against the Training Committee—namely, that teaching was not distributed fairly, and that the Training Committee "had arrogated to itself the right to patronage." The chairman, William Gillespie, was particularly angry; and Winnicott suggested that Mrs. Klein be asked to withdraw the memorandum. Council asked him as president of the Society to approach her about reconsidering her charges. At a meeting of Council on May 6, 1957, Rosenfeld and Bion objected that the Council was not competent to deal with the matter, but the objection was overruled. It was decided to set up a subcommittee in the autumn "to clarify and codify the relations between the Council, the Training Committee, and the Society." Winnicott persuaded Klein to withdraw her memorandum, which alienated him even further from the Klein group. The new arrangement prevailed, and Klein began seriously to think of breaking away and forming her own Society; she was dissuaded largely through the efforts of Bion. In response to a letter from Winnicott in which he expressed his misgivings about the Society's political structure, Klein replied:

> The groupings in the Society are, as I see it, predominantly not "political organizations" but the consequence of serious theoretical and technical differences and facts (I am referring to your remark at the Council meeting that it is not scientific to have different groups and courses in our training). As long as these differences remain very considerable, it is only fair that the future analyst should be openly told about their existence and given the choice not of personalities but of technique in which he wishes to be trained.
>
> Your statement that anybody who has been analysed by myself or by one of my analysands automatically becomes or remains a member of my group is factually untrue. As a rule a candidate who chooses my group and becomes qualified is a member of the group. If subsequently his views and technique fundamentally change, he is quite free to leave the group. I have personally analysed (and so have my analysands) a number of candidates and analysts who have never become members of my group or did not remain members. I cannot, of course, quote names; but if you give it some thought, you might yourself remember a few instances [Winnicott himself?]. This applies also to several analysts who either will not occur to you or about whom you do not know.
>
> As regards the future—it will have to look after itself. I do not believe that my influence after my death will be so great as to hamper future developments—and believe me, I do not aim at this either.[11]

The real struggle within the Society had now become centered on the resistance of the independents to a takeover by the Kleinians. Throughout these quarrels Anna Freud and Melanie Klein agreed that no candidate of one could possibly be supervised by a member of the opposite group. In October 1955 the Council decided that the students' preferences should be taken into account in the choice of a second supervisor, and that they would not be required to be supervised by someone from the independent group.

Differences were buried during the Freud Centenary celebrations, at which Jones unveiled a plaque to Freud's memory on May 6, 1956. In a snapshot Dr. Alan Tyson took in the garden of 20 Maresfield Gardens Anna Freud and Melanie Klein appear to be chatting amiably. Klein is standing in a relaxed, queenly pose ("I absolutely was not shy") and Anna Freud appears round-shouldered and diffident, her hands clutched nervously. Both women were short; but Joseph Sandler remembers Klein as "a big person, but whether she was in fact that big is open to question. I don't know. . . . At that time she had striking charisma, this aura of being so important."* [12] Charles Rycroft also remembers that one noticed, when Klein walked into a room, she had "a certain grande dame quality," whereas Anna Freud gave the impression that one was meant to notice that she was self-effacing, that she was "retreating into the limelight."[13]

The ceremony in Freud's honor was one of Jones's last public appearances. He had been operated on earlier in the year for a gall bladder condition, but actually was already suffering from cancer. Still pale and drawn, his reduced energies were devoted to the completion of the Freud biography. In 1953 the first volume appeared, with its dedication:

To Anna Freud

True Daughter of an Immortal Sire

The second volume followed in 1955 and Melanie Klein's name appeared for the first time. In referring to the "Little Hans" case, Jones speaks about how the child's play was interpreted as a reflection of what was going on in the boy's mind: "This feature was seized on later by Hermine von Hug-Hellmuth, and then far more profitably by Melanie Klein, as a cardinal device in the application of psycho-analysis with young children."[14] In a discussion of the Schreber case he refers to a number of subsequent elaborations and interpretations, including that of Melanie Klein, who "correlated Schreber's multiplication of souls with his inner dissociation, and suggests that the reduction of their number is part of a healing process."[15] Jones never believed that psychoanalysis had been codified in Freud's work, and in "Contributions to Theory," in a discussion of *Instincts and Their Vicissitudes* (1915), Jones refers to Freud's view of introjection and projection: "It is noticeable here that Freud spoke only of the absorption of the good and the expulsion of the bad. Some years later Melanie Klein amplified this statement by laying stress on the two opposite processes."[16] Jones does not say whether he agrees or disagrees with Melanie Klein—"amplifies" is a shrewd word—but his reaction to *The Psycho-Analysis of Children* at the time of its publication is a significant indication that he felt Klein had developed Freud's original theory in a fruitful way.

After slowly reading and savoring the first two volumes, Klein wrote to Jones to congratulate him on his mammoth achievement: "I admire very much the way you have presented both the man and his work, the detachment and objectivity you showed in solving such a difficult task which should disarm any opponent. It gives a picture of Freud which was unknown and will together with Freud's work go down to posterity."[17]

---

* The artist, Feliks Topolski, for whom she sat in 1957, was startled to learn that she was not the tall woman he remembered.

The final volume of the Freud biography, covering the years 1919 to 1939, was published in 1957. Jones admits frankly that during the twenties his relationship with Freud was strained, one of the principal reasons being "my support of Melanie Klein's work." Jones's account of the difficulties is equivocal on several points. He does not mention that Anna Freud had initiated the controversy with *Einführung in die Technik der Kinderanalyse*, not does he make a single reference to *The Ego and the Mechanisms of Defence*. Jones explained why he had felt it necessary to arrange Exchange Lectures between London and Vienna in 1935:

> My own differences were partly doubt about Freud's theory of a "death instinct" and partly a somewhat varying conception of the phallic stage in development, particularly in the female. So I read a paper on the latter topic before the Vienna Society on April 24, 1935. Freud never agreed with my views, and perhaps they were wrong; I do not think the matter has been entirely cleared up even yet. More troublesome were the views Melanie Klein had been expounding in contradistinction to Anna Freud's, not always in a tactful manner. In a long discussion with Freud I defended Melanie Klein's work, but it was not to be expected that at a time when he was so dependent on his daughter's ministrations and affections he could be quite openminded in the matter.[18]

His most favorable passage about Klein describes the general drift of her career in a reference to Hug-Hellmuth, who "is remembered for having devised the play technique for child analysis which Melanie Klein was to exploit so brilliantly after the war; incidentally, though it is generally forgotten, Freud himself had as long ago as 1904 given a broad hint of such possibilities."[19]

Jones wished to avoid controversy; but neither Klein nor Anna Freud might have felt satisfied with such muted acclaim. Jones, to be sure, could argue quite legitimately that this was a book about Freud.

CHAPTER FIVE

Last Years

Between 1953 and 1959 Melanie Klein worked intermittently on her autobiography, a document marked by an elderly person's repetitiveness and blocking out of painful memories. Ultimately the autobiography trails off, as though she were preoccupied with her impending death.

That change from strong personal ambition to the devotion to something which is above my own prestige is characteristic of a great deal of change that went on in the course of my psycho-analytic life and work. When I abruptly finished my analysis with Abraham, there was a great deal which had not been analysed and I have continually proceeded along the lines of knowing more about my deepest anxieties and defences. In spite of the scepticism which I said was quite characteristic of a large part of my analytical life, I have never been hopeless, nor am I now. It is a mixture of resignation and some hope that my work will perhaps after all survive and be a great help to mankind. There are, of course, my grandchildren who contribute to this feeling that the world will go on, and when I speak of my having been completely dedicated to my work, this does not exclude my also being completely dedicated to my grandchildren. Even now, when they have become much less close to me, I know that I have been a very important figure in the first few years of their lives and that this must have been of great benefit to them. All three loved me deeply until 6 or 7 years old, and Hazel* even up to 9 or 10, and I believe that they have kept some affection for me, though unfortunately they are far less in contact with me; except Michael, who has in recent years become much closer to me again

*Hazel, her third grandchild, was born on May 18, 1947.

and who I know has at least unconsciously, and perhaps partly consciously, the feeling that I am of great value and also that he can speak freely to me.[1]

Klein and Judy experienced the inevitable tensions between a mother and her son's wife. Judy recalls that she was terrified whenever her mother-in-law held one of the babies because she seemed tense and unnatural with infants. Every Sunday Mrs. Klein came to lunch. Judy Clyne complained that this ritual prevented the family from doing anything else that day; and on one occasion she expostulated: "If you would wait just once to be invited!" Her complaint fell on deaf ears, and Klein continued stolidly to occupy her accustomed place. Not that her grandchildren objected. Diana and Hazel say that she was "a very good kind of gran, always there to listen to whatever we wanted to tell her."

The summer of 1956 she took Michael and Diana on a trip to the Rhine, and the following summer Michael accompanied her on another holiday to the Dolomites.* They often attended concerts together at the Festival Hall. She had a particularly close rapport with Michael. When he was very little he suffered night terrors and his grandmother would hold his head until his feverish phantasies abated. He knew that she understood his terror; and her understanding helped him to realize that his fears were insubstantial.

Before going up to Cambridge in 1956 Michael told her that he would like to be a psychoanalyst. With great frankness she advised him that he still had too many things to sort out and that he would make a fine research scientist. On April 22, 1960, she told Jolan that he enjoyed life and would not develop into "one of those fossilized scientists."[2] She was proven right, for he obtained Firsts in both parts of the Natural Science tripos. He went on to win a worldwide reputation as an atomic scientist and was awarded the Marlow Medal of the Faraday Society in 1970 and the Royal Society of Chemistry's Award for Kinetics and Mechanism in 1980. He died prematurely of cancer on November 6, 1981, mourned by family and colleagues. His oldest daughter is named Melanie.

Melanie Klein seems to have been more relaxed with other babies than with her own—especially the children of her supporters. When Irma Brenman Pick (no relation), then a student, gave birth to a baby boy in April 1960, Mrs. Klein asked if she might come and see him. She arrived with a beautiful shawl, and asked, "How's the baby?" Pick, in order to impress Klein with her knowledge of her theories, announced proudly, "He's very paranoid!" (He wasn't really, she recounts now with amusement.) "Oh no!" Klein looked greatly distressed. "I'm very sorry." Pick describes it as "a blush-making story if there

---

* It is interesting that her son, Eric, following in her steps as the ideal grandparent, takes his children and grandchildren on frequent trips.

ever was one, but it is very touching about Mrs. Klein—and no doubt about the lengths young students would go to be loved by their distinguished elders!"[3] Ilse Hellman, a leading member of Anna Freud's group, recalls how caring Klein was with her child when they once holidayed in the same place in Switzerland. Her husband was a little anxious after all the stories he had heard about Klein, but to his delight she played and told stories to the child. "She had a lovely way with children," Hellman recalls. "She was like a jolly, nice granny." Michael Clyne never forgot an incident that occurred in a hotel dining room while he was on holiday with his grandmother. A disturbed child at the next table was misbehaving, and Klein's expression of sorrowing empathy as she watched him remained with Michael for the rest of his life.

While Klein was living in Clifton Hill she had a series of couples working for her, but the arrangement was never very satisfactory. Shortly after she moved to Bracknell Gardens, through an advertisement she engaged a housekeeper, Kathleen Cutler, who cared for her devotedly until her death. Curiously, Miss Cutler had met her in 1936 when she accompanied her then employer, an analysand of Klein's, to the latter's consulting rooms. "Once you met her, you would always remember her," Miss Cutler says.[4]

Miss Cutler loved those seven years in Bracknell Gardens. The flat was always filled with young people, there was constant entertaining, sometimes a very hectic atmosphere. Klein adored flowers, and on her birthday the kitchen was overflowing with bouquets delivered throughout the day. Miss Cutler attended to all the domestic arrangements because Klein was hopeless about household details. One evening she arrived back to find the kitchen smeared from end to end with a red substance. Fearing that her employer had injured herself, she rushed into Mrs. Klein's bedroom, only to find her calmly reading in bed. It appeared that she had spilled a jar of beets. When Miss Cutler told her that she had thought it was blood, Klein replied coolly, "I didn't think it was like you not to knock before you came in."

One of Miss Cutler's most vivid memories of Klein was her scrupulousness in returning money. "She would remember even if it were a penny halfpenny." This accords with a note Clifford Scott received from her, dated January 1, 1948, in which she reminded him that he still owed £46 for his analysis in June and July 1933!

In some ways these were the best years of her life, surrounded by an adoring extended "family" of her own making. She was still handsome, vivacious, and vain. She began to enjoy the theater and parties as she had never done before. Elinor and Claude Wedeles had steps installed in their minibus so that she could more easily accompany them to the theater. They were impressed by her stamina in the rapt attention with which she followed *The Iceman Cometh* and *Long Day's Journey into Night*, although she could see nothing interesting in "those two old tramps" in *Waiting for Godot*. Elliott Jaques and his actress-wife, Kay Walsh, also often took her to the theater. The latter remembers the approving nod Klein turned to give her with the opening bars of *Tosca*—a far cry from the chatterbox Alix Strachey had to endure through *Così fan Tutte* thirty years before!

In 1957, on her seventy-fifth birthday, the British Society wished to honor her with a gift, and she asked for jewelry that she could leave to her granddaughters. "What would my granddaughters do with a salver or a clock?" she asked jocularly. Ilse Hellman and Charles Rycroft (an Anna Freudian and an independent) were delegated to choose the gift. This was meant as a tactful gesture to demonstrate the solidarity of the Society in recognition of her achievement. She was delighted with their choice of a pretty Victorian gold and garnet bracelet, brooch, and earrings. For her more immediate associates there was a party at her home, where she was presented with a drawing of herself by Feliks Topolski. The artist remembers her as rather overbearing; nevertheless, he felt that she had the sort of confidence of a woman who was once deeply aware of her sexual attractiveness. Her skin, as he describes it, had the pink and white tones of a Viennese who has loved cream and pastry. Some people have objected to the hawklike appearance Topolski gave her, but for Hanna Segal it captures the expression of satisfaction elicited when one has given a particularly perceptive interpretation.

People who knew Klein late in life speak of her ringing laugh, a characteristic seldom evident in her earlier years. Much as she appreciated the devotion, she commented to friends like Enid and Michael Balint that she liked to get away from the Kleinians sometimes. Jung once remarked, "Thank God I am Jung, and not a Jungian"; and Melanie Klein made the same comment about her overzealous supporters, although, as Hedy Schwartz says, she was like a mother hen looking after her chicks. Once when Klein herself protested about being called a "Kleinian," Betty Joseph told her, "You are too late—you are a Kleinian whether you like it or not."[5]

By now Elliott Jaques had become one of her closest associates, working with her on the expanded book version of *Envy and Gratitude*, which appeared in June 1957. Some months prior to publication she boasted to T. T. S. Hayley that it would come out exactly thirty years after *The Ego and the Id*, in precisely the same format.* "This made me think," Hayley recalls, "that she felt it would be just as (if not more) important and that she was being very competitive with Freud."[6] Jaques also worked closely with her, starting in 1956, in organizing *Narrative of a Child Analysis*, a work she probably would never have completed without his energy and suggestions.

---

* *Das Ich und Das Es* had first appeared in German in 1923. The first English translation by Joan Riviere was published in 1927 (thirty years before *Envy and Gratitude*), although another version by James Strachey is the one included in the Standard Edition.

In actual fact, because she had taken so long to assemble the material, the *Narrative* was preceded a year earlier by *Un Cas de Psychose*, which came out in 1960. This was the account of almost a year's analysis* of an American boy of nine and a half conducted in Paris by Joyce McDougall under the supervision of Serge Lebovici. In 1950 Mrs. McDougall had come from New Zealand to England, where she had a year and a half's training at the Family Guidance Clinic in Hampstead before moving to Paris. She began to read Klein's work after her arrival in Paris. She recalls that "it made me dream right away."[7] *The Psycho-Analysis of Children* had an enormous impact on her work.

The McDougall analysis was conducted five times a week without interruptions. The boy was clearly far more disturbed than Richard had been. Winnicott, who enthusiastically read the material, urged that an English translation be published; and this appeared as *Dialogue with Sammy* in 1969. Sammy's fragmentary state corresponded, in McDougall's view, to "that constellation of anxieties described by Melanie Klein as the paranoid-schizoid position." Sammy's use of projective identification was constantly in evidence. Like Richard, Sammy was intensely interested in geography, particularly in the Baltic provinces that had been integrated into the Soviet Union. "Poor Latvia," he would often cry out, "I shall deliver you from the hands of that Holy Mother Russia!" Mrs. McDougall seems to have been able to integrate the ideas of Klein and Winnicott (who contributed the Preface) and her own greater emphasis on the role of the father:

> Psychoanalysis has consistently revealed the cardinal importance of the human relationship in the maturation of the sense of reality—maturation which is the result of the *dialogue*, preverbal and verbal, conscious and unconscious, between mother and child, completed as the child grows older by other dialogues with subsequent love objects, in particular, the father. The latter's influence on the dialogue is, of course, present from the beginning and conveyed to the child through the medium of his mother and *her* relationship to the father.[8]

A number of Klein's colleagues were not altogether happy with the paper she delivered at the Paris Congress in 1957, "The Development of Mental Functioning." Elliott Jaques, for one, did not feel that it was up to her usual standard. Here she emphasized more explicitly than ever that when she referred to the life and death instincts, she was not referring to them as biological processes but as the actual instinctual basis of love and hate. When Freud declared that the unconscious has no knowledge of death, he did not see that this statement was incompatible with his own perception of the dangers of the death instinct working within the organism in the impact of aggression on

---

* Mrs. McDougall says that it actually lasted eight months.

emotional life.* In Klein's view an incipient ego is gradually developed from birth to counteract the death instinct, and the strength of this ego is formed from the internalized good object; the superego, formed by the introjection of the good and bad breast, influences the *subsequent* development of the Oedipus complex.

While she had formerly asserted that mental health depends on the integration of the ego through a minimum of splitting, she now seems to see it as inevitable that the ego projects a part of the death instinct into a split-off, repressed part of the self which surfaces at times of emotional crisis. Mental health depends on the relative strength of the life and death components of the ego. "When development goes well, the super-ego is largely felt as helpful and does not operate as too harsh a conscience."[10] The early superego no longer appears in a necessarily punitive guise.

At the Paris Congress the presidency, held by the Americans since 1949, reverted to a member of the British Society, William Gillespie. The vice-presidents were nominated by an extremely orthodox Nominating Committee, including Anna Freud. In addition to the official slate, Edward Glover and Melanie Klein were proposed from the floor. Glover declined the nomination. Klein, who did not withdraw ("I absolutely was not shy"), was inevitably defeated. The strength of the establishment faction was made apparent when Marie Bonaparte was defeated for the first time. From the floor Serge Lebovici jumped to his feet: "I think it is absolutely essential that [the Princess] remains a member of the Central Executive of the International." His motion was passed unanimously.

One American who Klein felt was not unsympathetic to her views was Maxwell Gitelson. They talked both at this congress and at Geneva; and he respected her work. She always found his papers and remarks in discussions interesting and reflective, and he indicated a real interest in the development of child analysis in America.†

It could be argued that the paper on mental functioning is a continuation of her thinking in the envy paper, in which she expressed pessimism about the hope of integration in some recalcitrant cases. Here she is extending this more modified view to all human beings; and what appears as pessimism—a word often applied to the later theoretical position of Freud—is simply a realistic acceptance of the human condition, and also an acceptance of the limitations of psychoanalysis. She had traversed a long road since the enthusiastic opti-

---

* Probably the clearest Kleinian description of the death instinct is that given by Hanna Segal: "To me the death instinct is not a biological drive to return to the inorganic (as Freud described it) but it is a psychological wish to annihilate this sudden change brought about by birth. So the infant is born into a sort of chaos of contradictory perceptions—pleasant and unpleasant—and of contradictory desires; very soon he starts to sort them out and the sorting out is called 'splitting.' One is assailed by bad things, or one experiences something very ideal."[9]

† See Maxwell Gitelson, "Re-evaluation of the Rôle of the Oedipus Complex," *J.* (1952), 33, 351–54.

mism of her papers in the early twenties; yet her changing views of a kindly, supportive superego (ego) constitute an affirmative statement of hope. She had, after all, always contended that both love and hatred coexist from the beginning of life. Love, the security of one's attitude towards oneself, forms the core of the self.

When Ernest Jones died on February 11, 1958, she forgot her disgruntlement over his occasional duplicity and instead remembered how he had supported her. She genuinely grieved for the man who had done more than anyone else to establish her work, and Jones owed as much to her for her contributions to the distinctive character of the British Society.* Jones suffered a coronary attack in June 1957. Nevertheless, as honorary president of the International Psycho-Analytical Association he addressed the Paris Congress in August 1957, attended Princess Marie Bonaparte's elaborate fête, and danced charmingly. However, people noticed that he was extremely pale, and while in Paris he suffered a hemorrhage in his right eye. After his death his widow was so distraught that she went back into analysis with a Kleinian analyst, Sonny Davidson—so that Jones's substantial adherence to Kleinian ideas persisted beyond the grave.

Winnicott sent Klein his obituary of Jones for comment; she returned it with detailed comments, emphasizing that he had not given a balanced enough picture of the former president. In a letter of June 12, 1958, she wrote:

By stressing more certain points, for instance, the great importance of his principle that every psycho-analyst be analysed (whatever his personal qualities), and his achievement that analysis should only be applied to Freudian teaching, and furthermore, by stressing what you perhaps have not so strongly experienced, that is, a great deal of kindness and helpfulness, as against his at times forbidding approach, the picture of his personality would appear in a different light.

I do not believe that Jones was in principle against giving up his position as president, but that he was rather sensitive on the point that it should not be an expression of dissatisfaction with him personally. . . .

I think the counterpart of Jones's at times sharp and caustic attitude needs much more stressing, that is, the great deal of kindness, which expressed itself in helping so many people, and which had its root in a dislike of falsity and mediocrity, and in a real enthusiasm for the value of psycho-analysis. He hated to see it badly or not genuinely represented. It is true that, with his intellectual brilliance, it was not easy for him to put up with

---

* Anna Freud's tribute to him at the memorial meeting was curiously ambivalent, and James Gammill remembers that at a seminar she mentioned his death almost in passing. Dr. Gammill, who was in supervision with Klein at the time of Jones's death, recalls how deeply moved she was. When he qualified, she asked him, "Aren't you proud to be a member of the Society founded by Ernest Jones?"

stupidity and excessive mediocrity, but this rather sharp attitude was apt to pass over quickly and give way to a real appreciation as soon as he found something interesting, new or true. You were right in mentioning that, in some degree, his defensive attitude was due to a fight with very hostile and stupid opponents in his medical profession, but, as you say, his bitterness did not go deep and there was a good deal of optimism and hope for the future in his personality. If this side of his work is more stressed than you have done, and also the enormous amount of work and devotion which he put into supporting Freud and his work, his personality appears in a different light.... I believe that the nearer we came to the war and during the war, resignation and therefore greater mildness had already set in. However, he showed great courage and devotion in the way in which he saved Freud from Vienna and enabled him to die peacefully.[11]

In a postscript she added that Jones had set aside the writing of his own autobiography in order to write his life of Freud. This she saw as reflecting Jones's characteristic recognition of someone greater than himself ("typical of his attitude towards Freud and his conviction of Freud's greatness"); and she remembered the happy mood he was in at the Paris Congress when he had actually finished the manuscript; she believed that he had been kept alive "by his intense need to finish the biography."

Klein curtailed her activities considerably, yet she occasionally attended private meetings in which her ideas were discussed. She was invited to the 1952 Club on June 23, 1959; and some members were dissatisfied by her failure to speculate about matters on which she had not previously reflected or written. She was far more forthcoming with a group of analysts, all of whom were sympathetic with her views, who held three meetings in October, November, and December of 1958. Tom Hayley taped the discussions, to make the only recording of her slow, heavily accented voice.

She spoke frankly and at length on a wide variety of topics. In the matter of technique, she said that there were a number of things that could be taught and a number that could not. One cannot make hard and fast rules. Her own technique was extremely variable, although from 1926 transference had been its distinguishing feature. There was always a stronger transference with a child, either positive or negative. She had never found that counter-transference helped the patient, only herself. It should be used and controlled only by and for the analyst. She recalled that in Berlin there was a saying: "If you feel like that about your patient, go in a corner and think it out carefully: what is wrong with *you*?" But projective identification, the putting oneself in another's shoes, is vital, she emphasized, as well as linking of material as often as possible.

One cannot always cure everybody, although one can help a great number of people. She believed that Freud tended to overrate the element of curiosity and scientific interest, and, while he wanted to help his patients, his concern was not great enough.

When asked if it was impossible to analyze someone of another culture—for example, an Asian, a Japanese or Chinese—she replied, "I've never tried it. I would have liked it." However, she admitted that it was very difficult to analyze an Orthodox Jew or a Roman Catholic. Her answers to specific questions indicate that her attitude to technique was more flexible than is generally thought. She advised discouraging telephone calls from patients, and felt it usually inadvisable to see a patient after the termination of an analysis.

There was a long discussion about the standard five-times-a-week analysis. Despite the objections of some of her younger colleagues, she was adamant about classical procedure. It is important, she emphasized, to analyze why the patient cannot manage to come five times a week: it might simply be a subterfuge. If he cannot afford to come on a daily basis, then one should reduce one's fees. But suppose, she was asked, owing to other commitments, either the analyst or the patient cannot manage a regular routine. Would it not be heartless, under those circumstances, not to make another arrangement, if the aim was to relieve suffering? She replied that she would describe it as psychotherapy. Well, then, how do you do psychotherapy? Stanley Leigh asked her. "I really couldn't tell you," she answered. "I couldn't do it." Yet she had already admitted that during the war it had been possible to see some patients only on an irregular basis. (She had also told Hanna Segal that during the last part of Paula Heimann's analysis she had seen her three times a week, and Sylvia Payne had seen her only once a week in 1934.)

The third discussion, on December 11, 1958, was devoted almost entirely to the concept of envy. Klein realized, she said, that she had made herself extremely unpopular by her elaboration of envy as well as her espousal of the death instinct. Envy is not only a response to frustration, but a constitutional factor, so that some people are far more envious than others. She had never had a patient whose problems could not be traced back to his relationship with his mother, so that from the beginning there is an object relation with the breast, where it is seen as both good and as persecutory. There is an unconscious knowledge of the breast, and the so-called good mother is really envied because she contains things that are wanted. Paradoxically, it is not the bad object that is envied but the good. The complete primal situation is revealed in the transference. Where envy is very strong, the patient will refuse something (the breast). He cannot accept that the analyst knows more about his unconscious than he does, and this knowledge is very difficult for some patients to bear. Greed is also a constitutional factor to some extent, and the combination of anxiety and greed increases envy. But it is very important not to overlook "positive" envy. Here there is an element of gratitude where something is admired, and the feelings might indeed be called love.

Kleinian ideas were beginning to be discussed in wider contexts. An important group that began to meet regularly during the fifties was the Imago Society, founded by the painter and aesthetician Adrian Stokes. Its aim was to discuss art from a psychoanalytic (Kleinian-oriented) perspective. Stokes had been analyzed by Klein from 1931 until 1936, and resumed analysis again in 1938.* His autobiography, *Inside Out* (1947), gives a fascinating account of how and why he viewed the world as he did, and of his belief that certain infantile phantasies had directed him towards art. He recalls his childhood through the terrors he projected in Hyde Park and the gradual attainment of reparation, achieved through recognition of the beauties of Kensington Gardens. Later his imagination expanded in the wider world of Italy, ultimately coming to rest in contemplation of Cézanne's paintings, undistorted and serene in their own right.

In his review of Stokes's *Greek Culture and the Ego* (1958), Professor Richard Wollheim explains why he believes Kleinian concepts can be applied fruitfully to the study of art:

> . . . By concentrating upon the content of the work of art, Freudian criticism laid itself open to the objection, often urged against it, that it ignored the specifically aesthetic aspect of art; for if products of identical content are treated identically, how do we distinguish between say, a Leonardo and a day-dream or a child's game with the same motivation? Kleinian criticism has deliberately set itself to redress the balance. A work of art is defined in terms of the possession of certain formal characteristics and those characteristics are then analysed as the natural correlates or products of certain ego-processes.[12]

Besides Stokes and Wollheim, other prominent members of the group included Donald Meltzer, Wilfred Bion, Roger Money-Kyrle, J. O. Wisdom, and Stuart Hampshire. The meetings were generally held at the home of Mrs. Ernest Jones.

In 1954 Donald Meltzer joined another ex–Air Force American, James Gammill, in becoming part of the Kleinian group. Meltzer was analyzed by Klein, and Gammill by Heimann. In 1950 while Gammill was working as an intern at the Walter Reed Hospital in Washington, he read "Notes on Some Schizoid Mechanisms." He experienced, he says, "a feeling of wonderment."[13] The following summer, while working at the Topeka State Hospital, under the

---

*These periods are recorded in Klein's pocket diaries. According to Richard Wollheim, Stokes went back into analysis in 1946 when his marriage broke up, but this cannot be verified in the diaries since she had begun to use private symbols for her patients by this date.

direction of Dr. Karl Menninger, Gammill mentioned that he wished to have psychoanalytic training in London. Menninger's reaction was immediate: "You will never be accepted in American psychoanalysis. Mrs. Klein's theories are all wrong and contrary to accepted classical psychoanalysis!" When Gammill later related this incident to Klein, she smiled sadly and responded with a shrug: "Oh, I think he was trained in Chicago, perhaps even analyzed by Franz Alexander.* When I was in Berlin, Franz was one of the most gifted analysts there. But he needed to have colleagues around him to discuss with and hold him in check. Two things seem to have gone to his head. First, there were two or three laudatory references to him in Freud's writings. Second, he was made director of the Chicago Institute. As an analyst, he seems to have been wrecked by too much success in America, where he was idolized in the 1930s. Also, I certainly did not appreciate his reference to my 'kind aunt' technique in the review he wrote of my *Psycho-Analysis of Children*."† Dr. Gammill had the impression that American psychoanalysts had been more favorably disposed toward her before the arrival of European émigré analysts. She tended to see Gammill as courageous in coming to London for his analysis in the face of American psychoanalytic disapproval—"perhaps it was more my Southern stubbornness in holding onto my beliefs and clinical experience in the face of the damned Yankees!"

Between 1957 and 1959, she supervised Gammill's analysis of a child (at this period Klein no longer did child analyses herself). He sometimes found her sitting in the garden in front of the house in Bracknell Gardens, where he went to see her on Thursday afternoons; and she often commented on the Scientific Meeting of the previous evening. He was grateful to her, he says, for giving him a sense of the continuity of the psychoanalytic tradition. Dr. Gammill's experience of the supervision should be quoted in his own words:

> One felt quite at ease in presenting clinical material to her. She listened attentively, but made fewer comments and suggestions than I expected for a first child case. She seemed mainly concerned that the principal themes and the relevant emotions should be detected and deepened, emphasizing that with a highly communicative three-year-old patient one cannot recall and follow through on all the material. However, she did want the material recalled with as much detail as possible, so that the candidate should have a *feel* for the extraordinary complexity of the psychic life at that age. She considered that many analysts working only with adults would not have

---

* Dr. Menninger has confirmed that he was analyzed by Dr. Alexander.
† Alexander gave this as an explanation of her technique: "When the meaning of the game is correctly understood and then conveyed to the child in its own language, the child's anxiety diminishes—because of the fact that the children immediately conceive these interpretations, given to them by a 'kind aunt' in an unemotional tone of voice, to be 'permissions.' "[14]

come to oversimplified conclusions about the first five years of life, if they had given themselves the opportunity of working analytically with very small children. In fact in the late 1950s, she only did supervisions of child analyses of small children, considering that she could offer more from her experience with this age group. She once said that only a few very highly gifted analysts had been able to grasp the essence of her work without having analysed at least one small child (and that much ignorant and misguided criticism of her work might have been altered if these critics had tried child analysis in using her technique which aimed at favouring the whole range of the young child's possibilities of communicating his emotional experience). For instance, she advised explaining to my three-year-old patient that he had dreamed when he said, "Mr. Gammill, last night I opened the curtains and I saw murder inside"; and that the dream experience when told and thought about helped our work together. . . . She emphasized not only getting to know the specific vocabulary of a small child, but also his individual style of self-expression so as to formulate interpretations in a way that they would have the greatest possible chance of being understood and used. She felt that the child had a right to ask the analyst for the *evidence of an interpretation* if the evidence were not made clear in the making of the interpretation; or if something blocked the child's comprehension, he was entitled to another try with the analyst making the evidence as clear as possible.[15]

For Dr. Gammill she was "the only person of genius with whom I have studied in close contact." In 1959, before he left for Paris where he now works, there was a farewell party for him; and Judith Fay's fondest recollection of Mrs. Klein is of her being driven off in Gammill's open car with her hair flying in the wind.

According to Dr. Gammill, she laid great stress on the capacity to respect other people's scientific integrity even if their views differed from her own—"perhaps because I know only too well how hard it is, and have been myself swept by passionate feelings and at certain moments needed unconditional support." This, however, is at variance with R. D. Laing's experience.

Laing, who was on the staff at the Tavistock Clinic, began a training analysis with Charles Rycroft in 1957, and had supervision by Marion Milner and Donald Winnicott. In the course of his training he attended Klein's clinical and theoretical seminars, but never met her socially. "I couldn't stand her," he says bluntly. "I found her an absolutely detestable person."[16] He recoiled from what he describes as her "adamantine dogmatism"; he saw her followers as "beaten down into complete submission." He soon perceived that it was impossible to have a discussion or argument with her or with her followers, such as Rosenfeld and Bion. Totally confident in himself, he was already writing

The Divided Self (1960), which was greatly influenced by Winnicott and does not contain a single reference to Klein, an omission that was not lost on her. "I had already discarded the theoretical principles to which she objected," Laing explains. He sat sullen and silent in seminars; he refused "to demean" himself by arguing with her. He realized, he said, that if one did, she would reply that one needed more analysis or was full of envy of her good breast. He also found her physically repellent with her jewelry and heavy makeup, particularly the combination of vivid lipstick and white powder.

However, Laing had great respect for her ideas, far more than he had for those of Anna Freud, who never ventured beyond the shallows and therefore offered nothing of a theoretical challenge. He respected the depth of *sensibility* in Klein's writings, the way she plowed into very deep, confused waters with complete self-assurance; and while he objected to her dogmatism, he could not help admiring the firm stand she took against those who pooh-poohed the psychic dynamics of mental structure, "undeterred by scorn and contempt." As for her understanding of the unconscious, "If it hadn't come from her, I don't know where it would have come from." She above anybody else was "a witness to psychic reality which most people denied." He speaks of the respect with which Merleau-Ponty had referrred to her in his lectures on child development. She was "a natural empirical phenomenologist" in the sense that she considered what children were actually saying or doing—although she would not have known what phenomenology was. Laing describes her as "someone of calibre, not *trivial.*"

Unlike many Kleinians—and others—Laing sees her "planetarium" as intellectually very easy to get hold of—good and bad objects, projection, introjection, splitting, part-objects, etc. The death instinct is "the minus." In his view, she didn't really need this any more than Freud did. Laing concurs with J. D. Sutherland that it postulates a closed system with which no contemporary biologist could have any way of negotiating, except perhaps in terms of entropy. He approves of the way her work has been utilized by Isabel Menzies with her study of nursing and Elliott Jaques in his attempt to fuse internal and external realities in an understanding of social systems.*

Laing objects to her structural theory of the mind because he believes that it leaves no mediation between the external and internal world, no difference between phantasy and perception. Despite Glover's animus, Laing feels that Glover presented a cogent critique of her work. Laing says that he himself shares the attitude of Payne, Milner, and Winnicott towards Klein: a combination of admiration and irritation.

As for breast envy, she is no more wrong than Freud was about penis envy

---

* Isabel E. P. Menzies, *The Functioning of Social Systems as a Defence Against Anxiety* (Tavistock, 1970), and Elliott Jaques, *The Changing Culture of a Factory* (London: Routledge & Kegan Paul, 1951).

or Margaret Mead about womb envy—it was good that someone pointed these things out. In *Envy and Gratitude* he feels that she carries it "almost to a theological position, a theology without God." Moreover, she applies envy on too universal a scale. Reparation, too, should be put into a larger context of reconciliation, contrition, remorse, repentance, sorrow for one's evil thoughts and actions.

Regarding her technique, Laing believes that by emphasizing anxiety to an enormous degree, she intensified it, creating an indeterminately protracted dependence on the analyst. If one attacks anxiety immediately, the analyst risks leaving the patient completely alone in his paranoia, and every interpretation seems to be another impingement, a critical devaluation of the self that doesn't admit any sympathy, any community of feeling. He considers it an excellent technique for the professional torturer. When asked what he thought about her having analyzed her own children, he threw back his head and laughed. "I'm glad I was spared Melanie Klein as my mother!"

"She's one of those people to whom I'd say, 'Ta-ta and best of luck. I don't want to have anything to do with you and I'm sure you don't want to have anything to do with me either. We'll just go our own ways and let's make a pact, a gentleman's agreement. It's a big world and there's plenty of space for both of us.' "

Laing was not alone in considering her followers a humorless, intense clique. A. S. Neill, the progressive headmaster of Summerhill, in a letter to his friend Wilhelm Reich shared some of Laing's misgivings about Klein's work "full of castration and anal characteristics and mother's penis and what not. To read her is like being in a graveyard with open putrefying bodies; to turn to your function [of the orgasm] is like going out into a meadow in spring." In October 1955 he sent Reich a report of a wedding he had attended:

Filled with followers of Melanie Klein. Interesting to hear their talk. I mentioned your name as a test; their faces clouded with disapproval which amused me. They can't laugh; Melanie has evidently shown them humour is a complex which no normal man should have. To my asking what Klein was doing to prevent complexes there was silence. I said: you can't analyse humanity but you can attempt to get a humanity that won't need analysis. No answer. *Gott*, they were a dull crowd. I couldn't help comparing them with the life and energy of the Orgonon conferences. They depressed me . . . rather like talking to communists with a blank curtain that you couldn't penetrate.[17]

Few of those who were actually analyzed or supervised by Klein share R. D. Laing's bleak view of the effects of her technique. Claude Wedeles was supervised by her once a week at the end of her life. These sessions took place just after her afternoon rest; she was strained and tired, and Dr. Wedeles was very concerned about tiring her even more. He described it as "a humbling experience" and felt "incredibly privileged" to have her as a supervisor. "She was gentle, totally unpersecuting, one of the two marvellous supervisors I've had"[18] (the other was Donald Meltzer). There are numerous stories about comments she would make in supervision. One little boy of three was playing with some water. When he was told by the candidate that he wanted to be a baby at the breast, the child stumped out of the room angrily. "You were quite right," Mrs. Klein told the candidate, "he did want to be a baby, and wanted to have the breast, but you should have said you also want to be a good big boy, and that is why you minded so much." She was sensitive to the abuse of projective identification. In one supervision Sonny Davidson told her that "I interpreted to the patient that he put his confusion into me." Mrs. Klein replied, "No, dear, that's not it, *you* were confused." She was particularly worried about the "fashion" for countertransference she saw developing. If a candidate tended to talk too much about how a patient made him angry or confused, she would remark pithily: "Look, you tell that to your analyst. I really want to know something about your patient." Harold Bridger, now senior consultant at the Tavistock, recalls trying to describe a patient in the best possible technical way. "Yes," Klein replied rather impatiently, "but what is she really like? She sounds like a bit of a manipulator to me."[19]

Hanna Segal describes her analysis as "rigorous," and objects to the "misconceptions" about how Klein worked—misconceptions arising "partly through ill-will, partly wilful distortions, partly through people not understanding."[20] One misunderstanding is that Klein talked a great deal. Both Clifford Scott and Segal are notable talkers themselves, and in Scott's case he and Klein made an agreement to give each other at least equal time. Segal stresses that while it is a common assumption that in a classical analysis the analyst should remain relatively silent, in actual fact Freud talked a great deal.* "She certainly allowed silences," Segal says, "and quite long silences; and silence was a very powerful experience. . . . Actual silence, like interpreting, was a technical tool which I think she used very effectively."

The widely held belief that Klein always analyzed in concrete bodily terms was also contrary to Segal's experience:

My experience is that she analysed and went in very carefully about one's external relations; certainly she would never interpret phantasy before taking the emotional transference situation and whatever was going on, and when she brought it together to an underlying phantasy it again came with a very powerful effect. It wasn't a sort of daily chitchat about urine, faeces, this and that. It was something that would come now and then in an ex-

---

* See Joseph Wortis, *Fragments of an Analysis with Freud* (New York: McGraw-Hill, 1954).

tremely powerful way and I remember very clearly some of those interpretations because of the effect they made.

When she did make an interpretation about, for example, one's relationship with one's mother's body, everything else would fall into place in an integrated way, so that such interpretations were extraordinarily effective.

Then there is the "old chestnut," as Segal calls it, of Klein's neglect of external reality, which did not at all accord with Segal's experience. She thinks that the basis for this is partly that Klein analyzed so many children whose parents were analysts that she had to be extremely careful in describing the cases so that she did not divulge the identity of the participants.

Klein is said to have habitually interpreted aggression at the expense of libido, but what Segal remembers is her "great balance." Segal had no sense that this was a mother envying the brilliant work her students were doing, but rather that Klein was experiencing a sense of bemusement. As Segal puts it, "My God, what have I spawned? Here are all those things happening all around which I started . . . she was so tremendously interested in any work, any advances, and with a kind of modesty about it too. She would sort of say, 'Ah, you've got much further in that direction than I have,' or 'You would analyse the splitting in much more detail than I have done.'"

Segal concludes: "She was an absolutely outstanding psychoanalyst herself," possessing intuition combined with an extreme stability of personality as an analyst, "someone very, very hard to emulate or even to equal."

Klein had three people in analysis with her at the time of her death—A. Hyatt Williams, Clare Winnicott, and Donald Meltzer. Dr. Hyatt Williams had been in analysis with Elizabeth Rosenberg, and later qualified in 1955 after a training analysis with Eva Rosenfeld. He belonged to the Middle Group, but always tended towards the Kleinians, particularly after the help Klein gave him with a difficult case of narcotic addiction. "Simply trust your capacity to listen," she told him. In 1957, while working in prisons, he felt that he did not know enough to cope with the murderers he was seeing, and to his delight, she had a vacancy. He found the quality of the contact quite different from anything he had experienced before. He was impressed by her fine sensitivity in *listening*, and her ability to remember everything one told her. He had heard that she was ruthless, but found her patient, kind, courteous, straightforward, clear. At the Copenhagen Congress in 1959 he gave his paper on a murderer,[*] after which Mrs. Klein came up and shook his hand in congratulation. She had incorporated something he had told her in his analysis into her paper on loneliness, which she gave at the same congress. She had read it out to him in advance and asked him if he wanted anything changed; and the only altera-

---

[*] A. Hyatt Williams, "A Psycho-Analytic Approach to the Treatment of the Murderer," *J.* (1960) 41, 532–39.

tion they agreed upon was the transformation of a hedgehog into a field mouse.

Like Claude Wedeles, Dr. Williams was concerned about her health. Her walk was unsteady and she began to look very pale. He wondered if he was projecting something into her in his attempt to deny to himself that she was ill when he noticed that she looked quite different at meetings, her makeup always immaculate in the face she turned to the world. Only once did she lie to him. Late in the summer of 1960 she confided that she would not be back when term started. He asked her if she had the flu. "Well, something like that," she replied.

The second analysand was Donald Winnicott's wife, whom he had married in 1951. Clare Britton had been director of Child Care Studies in the Home Office, for which she was awarded the O.B.E. In 1949 she went into a training analysis with Clifford Scott until he left for Canada in late 1954. She had been greatly impressed by Klein's paper on mourning and wanted a Kleinian analysis—"but I wouldn't get there in a hundred years with Scott."[21] She recalled that when she related a dream to him, she would sometimes plead, "'You're supposed to be a Kleinian—give me a Kleinian interpretation of it'—but he never could." After Scott's departure, Mrs. Winnicott told her husband that she wanted to have an analysis with Klein herself—"I think she's tough enough for me"—and in retrospect she was bemused and impressed that he raised no objections, in view of the fact that, as he had told her two years before, "I find that she no longer considers me a Kleinian." Nevertheless, Winnicott still regarded her as a genius. He approached her, reminding her that she owed him a favor: he had sacrificed his analysis with her by going to Riviere instead, freeing him to analyze Eric as she had wanted him to do. Surely now she would agree to take on Clare?

After Winnicott's initial visit to her, Klein wrote to him on January 14, 1954, emphasizing strongly that she felt it inadvisable for them to have any further communication, as she wanted nothing to disturb his wife's analysis. She added: "Of course as far as work is concerned we need not agree about everything and as you say no one has a monopoly of the truth."

This analysis was an extraordinary battle of wills; and at one point Winnicott told his wife that he could see no foreseeable end to it: "You'll kill Melanie or she'll kill you." Clare Winnicott recalled its positive aspects: Klein's "fantastic memory for detail" and "She gave you a feeling of strength behind you." But there were aspects of the analysis that troubled her greatly—for instance, the impersonality of the situation which was exemplified in the fact that Klein never greeted her or said good-bye. She found her a brilliant theoretician but not a clinician: "She implanted her own theory on what you gave her. You took it or left it." Mrs. Winnicott was also troubled by her total disregard of the environmental factor. "It's no good your talking about your mother," she was told one day. "We can't do anything about it now." There was not much room for tears on the couch. One crisis occurred after Mrs. Winnicott had been hospitalized for meningitis. On her return, speaking of the helpful nurses, she said: "You have enabled me to trust other people, Mrs. Klein." "No," Klein replied, "this is simply a cover-up for your fear of death." Her illness and dependency were discounted. Clare Winnicott believed that in the analytic situation it was very hard for Klein to accept love and reparation, and she always emphasized the destructive side, so that positive acts were interpreted as a disguise for hate. Mrs. Winnicott felt that hostility emanated from Klein except for one epiphany, when she knew that she had touched a deep chord in the older woman. One day, on entering the room, she was startled by a vase of beautiful red and white tulips. She remarked that it must be Mrs. Klein's birthday, and went on to say that they symbolized the fusion of love and hate. "I shall send red and white flowers like that when you die." Klein did not reply—a period of uncharacteristic silence—and Mrs. Winnicott felt that she was deeply moved. "I shall never forget those tulips—never!!!"

On one occasion, a year before Mrs. Klein's death, Clare Winnicott brought her "a thoroughly Kleinian dream." "Mrs. Klein will be very pleased with this dream," she remembered thinking at the time. Klein then proceeded to analyze it; and her irritated patient timed the interpretation by her watch: twenty-five minutes.* Furiously Mrs. Winnicott exclaimed, "How dare you take my dream and serve it up to me?" and slammed out of the room. Winnicott tried to mediate. He went to see Klein, who told him, "She's too aggressive to analyze." On his return he advised his wife, "If you give it up, she'll never let you qualify." After a week Clare Winnicott returned, still truculent: "I have come back on your terms, Mrs. Klein, not on mine."

Clare Winnicott believed in retrospect that she made a great mistake in going to Klein for analysis, especially as it put her husband in a highly embarrassing position, even though he did nothing to discourage her. After Klein's death she had a further analysis with Lois Munro, about whom she spoke enthusiastically. In extenuation she was aware that Klein was in failing health towards the end of her life. She ventured: "I do use her ideas all the time—*my way.*"

The whole situation seems bizarre. What were the conscious and unconscious motives of the people involved? Mrs. Winnicott went to Klein because she was deeply impressed by her paper on mourning; but why did she not apply to her in the first place, rather than to Clifford Scott, who had analyzed Win-

---

* Clifford Scott believes that her interpretations towards the end of her life became very long because she was so anxious that her ideas be understood. Bion gathered from Meltzer that her constant stream of interpretations was "too coloured by a wish to defend the accuracy of her theories so that she lost sight of the fact that what she was supposed to be doing was interpreting the phenomenon with which she was presented."[22]

nicott's first wife? It is hard not to entertain the conjecture that both Winnicott and Klein, for conscious and unconscious motives, were using her as a stalking horse. And what were Clare Winnicott's own unconscious motives? No wonder the woman was confused, caught as she was in a difficult situation. Occasionally Winnicott would inquire about the analysis. "Does she ever mention sex?" "No." "Did she ever mention the Oedipus complex?" "No." His wife recalled him then asserting, *"That* is because she knows nothing about it!" Nor was it easy for Clare Winnicott to continue the analysis, knowing how strongly Klein disapproved of her husband's famous paper "Classification: Is There a Psycho-Analytic Contribution to Psychiatric Classification?" which he read to a Scientific Meeting on March 18, 1959.

Was Winnicott trying to persuade Klein, through his wife, of some of his ideas, particularly about the importance of environmental factors? In the account other people have given of their analysis with Klein, we have seen how completely she captivated them. Did Klein have enough confidence in her own power to feel that she could make an out-and-out Kleinian out of Clare Winnicott? Had she done so, it would have been her ultimate victory over Winnicott. But her patient proved a handful; and Klein, old, tired, and ailing, simply could not help her. The analysis seemed doomed from the start.

Donald Meltzer is unable to talk about his analysis because he feels that his impressions would be colored by the transference situation. According to many people, he was shattered by Klein's death, but did not heed their advice to go into further analysis with someone else.

In the last year of her life—1959–60—Klein continued to produce papers. "Our Adult World and Its Roots in Infancy" (1959), delivered to a group of sociologists, indicates that her concepts were not so complex that they could not be explained clearly to a wider lay audience. Here she drew a distinction between the ego and the self, an issue that has preoccupied contemporary psychoanalysis:

> The ego, according to Freud, is the organized part of the self, constantly influenced by instinctual impulses but keeping them under control by repression; furthermore it directs all activities and establishes and maintains the relation to the external world. The self is used to cover the whole of the personality, which includes not only the ego but the instinctual life which Freud called the *id.*[23]

Her own work, she asserted, had led her to assume that the ego exists and operates from birth onwards; and she had also come to the conclusion that it had the task of defending itself against anxiety.

Turning to envy, she claimed it was possible to enjoy vicariously the achievements of others so long as one is not in the grip of destructive feelings. She must have been thinking of some of her younger colleagues as she made this statement:

> If gratitude for past satisfactions has not vanished, old people can enjoy whatever is still within their reach. Furthermore, with such an attitude, which gives rise to serenity, they can identify themselves with young people. For instance, anyone who is looking out for young talents and who helps to develop them—be it in his function as teacher or critic, or in former times as patron of the arts and of culture—is only able to do so because he can identify with others; in a sense he is repeating his own life, sometimes even achieving vicariously the fulfilment of aims unfulfilled in his own life.[24]

In the spring of 1960 Jean MacGibbon wrote an article on Klein's work on women and children.* When MacGibbon (who had already reviewed *Envy and Gratitude* in *The Spectator*)† approached Klein about this, she detected "a hint of flatness in her response." While MacGibbon was writing the profile, Klein went to see her "to make sure that my account of her work was accurate, my impression of herself, not too wide of the mark." In some sense she was never "off the job," MacGibbon recalls. In her piece (which eventually appeared in *The Guardian*) MacGibbon wrote that Klein's response was "I have talked about it so often."

> Her mind is on the future, on research into new fields in which her findings, with their wide social and ethical implications, are beginning to be applied.[25]

Her mind continued to seethe with ideas. To colleagues she speculated about intrauterine life. Among her unpublished papers are notes for material she was accumulating for projected papers on religion and memory. One of the notes for the religion paper reads:

> Christ as the good part of God. The harsh and persecuting God was so much mitigated by having a son who is the representative of love and forgiveness but who forms part of him. Christ said "I am in my father and my father is in me"; it may have been unbearable to have this lonely and harsh punishing God who was an internalised figure and therefore increased their own super-ego and anxieties. . . .

---

* The article was originally intended to appear in *The Observer*, but its owner, David Astor (an analysand of Anna Freud's), refused to publish it.
† Klein was extremely pleased with the review, and wrote to thank MacGibbon in a letter MacGibbon describes as "characteristically unassuming, straightforward, warmhearted."

There is another equally interesting comment:

> Of course wish to live on fear of persecutory death, etc.—in connection with life and death instincts: in heaven there is to be no hate, only love—finding again relatives with whom there had been envy hate jealousy—where will be wholesale reparation because only love—religion an expression of life instinct.

Again: "Forgetting somebody is killing them in the unconscious. Therefore any painful situation or person is killed. In the Bible 'his name shall be forgotten' is one of the curses."

Through Jean and James MacGibbon, Klein enlarged her range of interesting friends in the last years of her life. They invited her to parties where they knew there would be people who would interest her—the philosopher Stuart Hampshire, the novelist Angus Wilson, the musician Rosalyn Tureck. Tureck was enchanted with her and asked James MacGibbon to bring her to one of her rehearsals, where Klein positively shone with pleasure.

Hearing that she loved the theater, MacGibbon invited her to the dramatization of E. M. Forster's *Passage to India* in 1959. The poet Henry Reed, a great admirer of her work, longed to meet her, and MacGibbon asked him to join them. They returned to her house for coffee and sticky Viennese-like little cakes. Reed shyly remarked, "Mrs. Klein, I greatly admire your works." She replied, wagging her finger at him, "Young man, people often tell me that, but I usually find they haven't read my books!" As he had a photographic memory, Reed rose to the occasion and was able to point out two misprints he had noticed, with actual page references. It was the high point of the evening, and she beamed with satisfaction, looking very beautiful. It was on occasions like this that she was at her best.

She also invited the MacGibbons to parties, and they were greatly impressed by her younger colleagues' interest in a wide range of subjects, and the fact that they never referred to their work. At one party, Jean MacGibbon sat between Stuart Hampshire and Richard Wollheim while they discussed Walter Pater.

In the last year of her life, Klein asked Jean MacGibbon with almost a hint of wistfulness, "Couldn't you call me Melanie?" to which she replied, "Oh no, Mrs. Klein, I couldn't possibly!" She believes that many people regarded Klein as a kind of ideal mother—her genius, her beauty, her presence—and as a result, she must have felt a little lonely and distanced from intimacy.

A woman doctor, Dinora Pines, who lives at 16 Bracknell Gardens, noticed an old lady who often sat by herself in the sun in front of her house at No. 20. She always wore beautiful hats and used to stop in her walks sometimes to talk to Dr. Pines's children. Dr. Pines at the time was undergoing training at the

Hampstead Clinic. They fell into conversation one day, and on this occasion Mrs. Klein made the famous remark which has often been repeated: "My dear, don't make any mistake. I'm a Freudian, but not an Anna Freudian."

Her devoted colleague Esther Bick was deeply concerned about the lonely holidays she spent by herself at the end of her life, when Eric's children were growing up and had interests of their own to pursue. In 1958 Klein went to Norway, a rather adventurous thing to do; but once having made the decision, she began to develop an old woman's terror of being trapped in her room on the second floor of the hotel if a fire broke out.

She was beginning to exhibit some of an old woman's eccentricities. When William Gillespie's son, Dr. Andrew Gillespie, was married early in January 1958, Margaret Little offered to give her a lift to the wedding. Klein insisted on being picked up far earlier than seemed necessary. As a consequence, they sat in the icy-cold interior of St. Luke's, Chelsea, for nearly an hour.

In 1959 Willi Hoffer, Anna Freud's right-hand man, succeeded Winnicott as president of the British Society—but it didn't seem to matter much anymore. According to Hedy Schwartz, a member of the "B" Group, although Hoffer was always loyal to Anna Freud, he ingratiated himself with Melanie Klein; and she believes that he would never have been made president of the British Society if he had not been liked by the Kleinians. "He played a very clever game. He saw this was the only way of getting on in England."[26]

Nelly Wollfheim, Klein's old friend from Berlin, turned up in her life once more. Wollfheim had moved to Oxford shortly after her arrival in England in 1939, and on her visits to London she and Klein would occasionally see a film together. On March 30, 1952, Wollfheim telephoned that she was in town, but Klein said that she was very busy as it was her seventieth birthday and she was preparing for a large reception at her house that afternoon. Wollfheim was clearly offended that there was no hint of an invitation.

Later that year Wollfheim settled permanently in London in a flat near Clifton Hill, but Klein made it clear that she had no time to meet her. After Klein's move to Bracknell Gardens Wollfheim indicated that she would like to see the new flat, but her hints were pointedly ignored. Whenever Klein acknowledged her existence—for example, by a postcard sent from a continental holiday—Wollfheim assumed that she was simply "a case to confirm her kindness," a perfunctory gesture. At Christmas she always received a carefully chosen little gift until Klein wrote that she was no longer capable of Christmas shopping and was sending her a pound instead. This Wollfheim interpreted as charity, and she tried to impress Klein with the fact that her financial situation had improved. When Klein did not seem to comprehend the hints, Wollfheim began sending her flowers with the exact amount she received. The "donations," as she called them, stopped.

The year before her death, Klein suddenly called on Wollfheim in the old people's home to which she had moved. Klein brought with her a copy of *Envy and Gratitude*, in which she had written a dedication. In this, their last conversation, Klein said something which indicated that Abraham had discussed material from Wollfheim's analysis with her. Since Klein had been in a training analysis with him, Wollfheim realized that he had done nothing unethical, yet she was haunted by a sense of betrayal.

They never saw each other again, and Wollfheim's reminiscences should be accepted with a good deal of caution. She had been fiercely envious of Klein in Berlin and was even more envious of her success in England. Theoretically they had nothing in common, since Wollfheim was committed to a pedagogic approach, and they had drifted apart, as people tend to do when their only bond is a friendship dating back many years. The very fact that Wollfheim wrote what was a veiled attack on Klein which she took to Winnicott after Klein's death does not indicate true friendship on her part. What she did not know was that her name was among the few entries in Klein's pocket diary that she took to Switzerland on her last journey in the summer of 1960.

Klein often said to Miss Cutler, "I do hope I'll live for another ten years in order to do what I want to do." Kind as people were to her, she hated to be alone. Lola Brook was gravely ill and Klein seldom saw her anymore. When Mrs. Brook's son was killed in an airplane crash in August 1959, Klein went into a state of empathetic shock. One evening she wandered into the kitchen and asked Miss Cutler if she ever felt lonely. Cutler replied yes, of course she did, but the important thing was to keep busy. She recalls Mrs. Klein suddenly saying, "You know, I think I'll write a paper on loneliness!"

The idea was not an impulsive one nor based simply on her own feelings in old age. She had clearly pondered D. W. Winnicott's paper "The Capacity to Be Alone," which he had delivered to the British Psycho-Analytical Society on July 24, 1957.

While much had been written in psychoanalytic literature about the fear of being alone, Winnicott pointed out that little consideration had been directed to the ability to be alone. This capacity he traces back to the baby's experience of being alone in the presence of Mother. Turning to Klein's theories, he assumes the existence of a good object in the individual's psychic reality, but, while skillfully managing to avoid disagreement with Klein, adds that a belief in a benign environment depends upon "good-enough mothering."

First there is "I," the unit formed from an organization of ego-nuclei. There follows the stage of "I am," "undefended, vulnerable, potentially paranoid." Finally: "I am alone," a state reached progressively from the infant's early awareness of a reliable mother, a more primitive state than that of the introjected mother, a relationship of ego relatedness.

... theoretically, there is always someone present, someone who is equated ultimately and unconsciously with the mother, the person who, in the early days and weeks, was temporarily identified with her infant, and for the time being was interested in nothing else but the care of her own infant.[27]

On the first morning of the Copenhagen Congress, July 27, 1959, Klein delivered her paper "On the Sense of Loneliness." It is an extraordinary paper, both brilliant and moving in the sense that her 1940 paper on mourning had been. For a woman so reticent about the actual details of her life, she spoke openly—in the interests of scientific understanding—about her deepest experiences: grief, depression, loneliness. From the outset she explained the kind of loneliness with which she was concerned: "By the sense of loneliness I am referring not to the objective situation of being deprived of external companionship. I am referring to the inner sense of loneliness—the sense of being alone regardless of external circumstances, of feeling lonely even among friends or receiving love."[28] This state, she suggests, is the result of a generalized yearning for an unattainable perfect internal state. The relationship with the good mother forms the prototype of the ideal situation which can never again be duplicated. This close contact between the unconscious of the mother and the unconscious of the baby, the understanding without words, never again to be repeated, is the basis for the sense of irretrievable loss in an inassuageable loneliness (p. 301).

The relationship with the mother is inevitably flawed, since persecutory anxiety is bound to arise in the infant; and as integration gradually develops within the child's ego in his perception of his mother as a whole person—that is, her "otherness," as well as "whole" in the sense of being unharmed by destructive impulses—anxiety arises that this good object can be endangered. Integration is achieved at the cost of feeling lonely and deserted in the unwilling acceptance of the bad parts of one's "self." Full and permanent equilibrium is never possible because of the polarity of the life and death instincts that are always threatening to disturb the ego's precarious balance.

Referring to Bion's perception of the universal phantasy of having a twin, she links this to the loneliness of grieving for split-off parts of one's "self," a feeling of pity not only for oneself but for one's lost components.

Integration means facing the destructive aspects of the self, the fear of one's death wishes. At the same time integration implies a loss of idealization of an image of perfection one can never achieve. The girl suffers from penis envy, the boy from breast and womb envy; and in both sexes there is an unrealistic, unconscious longing to contain all these sources of goodness.

Loneliness is an inevitable concomitant of the human condition. In order to combat loneliness, various defenses are employed. A child may become unusually dependent on its mother. Youth idealizes the future. In old age a preoccupation with and idealization of the past is part of the search for idealized inner objects. (Hence, in Klein's Autobiography, she said that she would give anything to return to the peace and security of the lamplit table around which she, Emanuel, and Emilie did their homework. More important, she idealized Libussa, and perhaps the Autobiography trailed off just at the time she was writing this paper because she realized what a reassuring idol she was making of her mother.)

There was a significant difference between Klein's and Winnicott's papers, even though Klein, perhaps more than ever in the past, reverted to the crucial importance of the relationship of infant and mother. Winnicott's paper is optimistic, a reflection of the joys of shared solitude. Klein's paper is tragic, threaded with a longing for a harmony that can never be regained or perhaps never achieved. The words seem to flow from some deep well of sadness, nostalgia, and longing. In some of the photographs taken of Klein during these last years, she has the bewildered expression of a lost little girl.

At the Copenhagen Congress she also participated in a symposium on depression. The rules were that the participants had only five minutes in which to speak. As Klein launched into her contribution, the chairman, Dr. Elizabeth Rosenberg Zetzel, kept trying to interrupt her: "You have been speaking ten minutes." Klein ignored her; and finally Zetzel forced her to stop—"but I have said what I wanted to say," Klein declared triumphantly. According to Herbert Rosenfeld, who was to be the next speaker, Zetzel, out of revenge, ruled that Rosenfeld could have five minutes and no more. Rosenfeld considered this treatment shabby and humiliating. "If it had been Anna Freud, she would have been given half an hour."[29]

Compressed though it was, "A Note on Depression in the Schizophrenic" contains some modifications of previous views in the distinction she draws between schizophrenia and depression. In the past she had emphasized the distinction between paranoid anxiety, centered on the preservation of the ego, and depressive anxiety, focused on the preservation of the internal and external good objects. She had now reached the conclusion that the distinction was too schematic. As she now described it, in the paranoid schizophrenic, the unstable ego possesses a good object differing in nature and strength from that in the manic-depressive in that it is incapable of sufficient identification with its object. But, as in her early paper on tics (1925), she emphasized that schizophrenia, a seemingly narcissistic disorder, is not an objectless state but one that reflects intense relations with internal objects.

Referring to Schreber's capacity to divide himself into sixty souls, she described the schizophrenic as unable to experience guilt and depression since he has been cut off from his deepest feelings. Furthermore, the mechanism of projective identification operates so forcefully in the schizophrenic that he projects it into an object—during the analytic procedure mainly into the analyst.[30] Only by helping schizophrenics to reach deep layers of the mind, as in the recent work of Hanna Segal, had they been able to experience the pain and suffering of relatively normal depression. Until the end Melanie Klein was willing to incorporate into her thinking the work of her younger colleagues.

Her daughter-in-law, Judy, accompanied her to Copenhagen, as she and Eric were concerned about the old woman's stamina. There was a formal dinner at the end of the congress, and Klein by then was almost collapsing from exhaustion. She was confused by the number of people who wanted to speak to her, particularly admirers from South America. Judy took her back to the hotel, and after a good night's sleep Klein was ready for a reception at the town hall given by the city of Copenhagen and the following night a very grand party on the grounds of Marie Bonaparte's palace. Klein seemed to enjoy herself thoroughly. With her amazing resilience she boarded a plane for Sweden to visit her sister-in-law, Jolan, in Göteborg.

In the spring of 1960 Klein was diagnosed as anemic. Miss Cutler noticed that she tired from the slightest exertion. Plans were being made for her to visit the Philadelphia Veterans' Hospital—one of the few invitations she ever received from America—but she canceled them because she did not feel strong enough to undertake the arduous journey, particularly in the face of American hostility. She began to think she ought to take up her Jewish faith again, and a rabbi came to see her. When he told her what would be required of her if she became a practicing Jew, she realized that this had been only a sentimental idea.

She spent Easter of 1960 at Sandridge Park Hotel, Melksham, Wiltshire, where she wrote to Jolan that she was beginning to overcome the great fatigue from which she had suffered all winter. She went on to speak proudly of each of her grandchildren, adding, "Eric is very sweet and caring towards me so that I see Judy and everybody else usually on Sundays now and also during the week." She was confident that she would return "a refreshed person to my beloved work. I am working at present on a book which, though not voluminous, I believe will be interesting."* On June 21 she wrote a final brief note to Jolan in which she complained that

> I find it very tiring to pursue my beloved work. Unfortunately my osteoarthritis is progressive and this, together with progressive old age, makes me very tired. I hardly write any private letters now—the rest is done by Eric and my secretary.
>
> Apart from being tired and finding it difficult to move I am healthy. The children give me much joy. I have just spent a week-end in Cambridge with Michael, it was beautiful.
>
> Much love and kindness,
>
> *Melanie*[31]

---

* This must have been *Narrative of a Child Analysis.*

Almost in desperation to regain her strength, she felt that she would recover if she went away on a holiday to Switzerland, where she had always loved the mountains. Miss Cutler was extremely worried that she was too ill to travel, but she was determined to reach Villars-sur-Ollon, where Eric, who was holidaying elsewhere in Switzerland, visited her. She was later joined by Esther Bick, who was told that her friend was dangerously ill. She found her lying white against the pillows, but there was a dramatic change when Mrs. Pick spoke to her about the papers she had recently read and Klein's eyes glistened with interest.

Somehow Bick managed to get her back to England. An ambulance was called; and Miss Cutler will never forget the ashen face and disheveled hair of the woman who had always been so faultlessly groomed—as she lay helpless, wrapped in a red blanket, while the attendants lifted her into an ambulance. She was taken to University College Hospital, where cancer of the colon was diagnosed. Early in September an operation was performed—apparently successfully.

Most of her colleagues were still away on holiday; but Hanna Segal, Esther Bick, and Betty Joseph came to see her regularly. The latter thinks that Klein wanted to savor every moment of life, and death she intended to experience to the full. She spoke very frankly about her funeral, emphasizing that she wanted it to be totally nonreligious in character. According to Eric, she was greatly preoccupied with a crying baby in another room. She told her colleagues that they were to convey to the Society that Clare Winnicott was now qualified as an analyst.

Michael was distraught at the prospect of his beloved Gran dying. She told him that she was not afraid of death. The only thing that was immortal was what one had achieved; and her strength and courage lay in her belief that one's ideas were carried forward by others.

But the abrasive Melanie was there to the end. She did not like her bossy night nurse—Libussa had also complained about hers!—and refused to allow her to stay in the room with her. As a result she fell out of bed and broke her hip, complications developed, and she died on September 22. It was hard to grasp that the life had been snuffed out of the stormy petrel. At the cremation ceremony at Golders Green a large group of analysts stood silent, tears streaming down their faces while Rosalyn Tureck, a recent and affectionate friend, played the Andante from Bach's Sonata in D Minor. Melitta, unreconciled to the end, gave a lecture in London that day, wearing flamboyant red boots. Eric wrote to her in an attempt at reconciliation, but was "rebuffed."

Klein's old adversary, Marjorie Brierley, wrote to the president, Willi Hoffer: "Though I have never been able to accept her views in toto I have never doubted the importance of her pioneering work." Mrs. Ernest Jones experienced grief and disbelief: "How could she disappear when she had always been there?" At the memorial service Hanna Segal described her as "generous, warm, passionate, even explosive—such defects as she had were defects of her qualities and did not detract from her lovability."[32]

To Eric, Klein bequeathed her worldly effects except for some specific items. To Hanna Segal she left her enameled hunter watch; to Mrs. Lola Brook, her silver-rimmed tortoiseshell cigarette and powder cases;* and to her daughter, Melitta, "my gold flexible bracelet which was given to me by her paternal grandmother, the single stone diamond ring given to me by my late husband, my gold necklace with garnets and the brooch which goes with the said necklace, both of which I received as a present on my 75th birthday and I have no other bequest to my said daughter because she is otherwise well provided for and by her technical qualifications able to provide for herself."

To the rest of us there was a legacy of rich, provocative, and enduring ideas.

---

* She had given her some money a few years earlier to help her buy a house.

CHRONOLOGY

1875 Marriage of Moriz Reizes and Libussa Deutsch, January 19
1876 Birth of Emilie Reizes in Deutsch-Kreutz
1877 Birth of Emanuel Reizes in Deutsch-Kreutz
1878 Birth of Sidonie Reizes in Deutsch-Kreutz
1879 Birth of Ernest Jones in Gowerton, Wales
1882 Birth of Melanie Reizes in Vienna, March 30
1886 Death of Sidonie Reizes
1895 Birth of Anna Freud in Vienna, December 3
1897 Emanuel enters medical school
1900 Emanuel leaves for six months in Italy in January
      Death of Moriz Reizes, April 6
      Emanuel transfers from medical school to Faculty of Arts, University of
          Vienna, in October
      Marriage of Emilie to Leo Pick, December 25
1901 Emanuel leaves for Italy in January
      Melanie Reizes engaged to Arthur Klein in June
      Emilie's first son, Otto, born October 16
1902 Death of Emanuel in Genoa, December 2
1903 Melanie marries Arthur Klein, March 31
1904 Birth of Melitta Klein in Rosenberg, January 19
1905 Melanie and Arthur visit Trieste, Venice, Abbazia
1906 In spring Melanie and Arthur visit Rome, Naples, Florence, and Emanuel's
          grave in Genoa
      Publication of Emanuel's *Aus meinem Leben* in September
1907 Birth of Hans Klein, March 2
1908 Ernest Jones meets Freud at Salzburg Congress in September
      Jones joins faculty of University of Toronto
      Kleins move from Rosenberg to Krappitz
1909 Jones joins Freud in Worcester, Massachusetts, in September
      Kleins move to Hermanetz
1910 Kleins move to Budapest
1913 Jones returns to Europe. Analyzed by Ferenczi during summer
      Jones founds London Psycho-Analytical Society, October 30

1914   Birth of Erich Klein, July 1
        Death of Libussa Deutsch, November 6
        Melanie Klein possibly goes into analysis with Ferenczi
        Melanie Klein reads Freud's _Über den Traum_
        Ferenczi joins Hungarian Medical Corps
        Arthur Klein conscripted into Austro-Hungarian Army
1916   Arthur Klein invalided back to Budapest
1918   Fifth International Psycho-Analytic Congress held in Budapest, September
           28–29. Ferenczi chosen as president
        Klein hears Freud read _Lines of Advance in Psycho-Analytic Therapy_
1919   Jones reorganizes British Psycho-Analytical Society, February 20
        Klein reads first paper, "Der Familienroman in statu nascendi," and is made a
           member of Budapest Society, July
        Arthur Klein moves to Sweden. Klein takes children to Ružomberok during
           "White Terror" in autumn
1920   _International Journal of Psycho-Analysis_ founded by Jones
        Berlin Poliklinic opens, February 14
        Klein's first published paper, "Der Familienroman in statu nascendi," pub-
           lished in _Internationale Zeitschrift für Psychoanalyse_ 6
        Klein attends Sixth International Psycho-Analytic Congress at The Hague in
           September. Meets Hug-Hellmuth and Karl Abraham
1921   Klein moves to Berlin with Erich in January
1922   Klein made an associate member of the Berlin Psychoanalytic Society
        Anna Freud made a member of the Vienna Psychoanalytic Society
        Seventh International Psycho-Analytic Congress held in Berlin September
           22–27 (last congress attended by Freud)
1923   Klein elected to full membership in Berlin Psychoanalytic Society in February
        Reconciliation with Arthur Klein
1924   British Institute of Psycho-Analysis established
        British Society becomes joint publisher with Hogarth Press of International
           Psycho-Analytical Series
        Klein enters analysis with Abraham
        Melitta marries Walter Schmideberg in April
        Eighth International Psycho-Analytic Congress at Salzburg, April 21–23. Abra-
           ham elected president
        Klein gives first congress paper, "The Technique of the Analysis of Young
           Children," at Salzburg
        Final separation of Melanie and Arthur Klein
        Klein meets Alix Strachey in September
        Klein delivers paper, "Psychological basis of psycho-analysis of young chil-
           dren," to Vienna Society on December 17
1925   James Strachey reads abstract of Klein's work to British Society on January 7
        Klein lectures in London for three weeks in July
        Death of Abraham, December 25
1926   Probable year of Kleins' divorce
        London Clinic for Psycho-Analysis opens, May 6
        Klein arrives in England in September
        Klein recorded as "visitor" at British Society, November 17
        Erich Klein arrives in England on December 27

1927 Symposium on child analysis in May
 Klein elected to full membership in British Psycho-Analytical Society on
  October 2
1928 Melitta joins Klein in London
1929 Eleventh International Psycho-Analytic Congress at Oxford, July 27–31
1931 Klein takes on first training analysand, W. Clifford M. Scott
1932 Twelfth International Psycho-Analytic Congress at Wiesbaden, September 4–7
 Arrival of Walter Schmideberg in England
 Publication of Klein's *The Psycho-Analysis of Children*
1933 Death of Ferenczi, May 22
 Paula Heimann arrives in England
 C. Z. Kloetzel settles in Palestine
 Melitta Schmideberg elected to full membership in British Psycho-Analytical
  Society
1934 Death of Hans Klein in April
 Thirteenth International Psycho-Analytic Congress at Lucerne, August 26–31
1935 Beginning of London-Vienna Exchange Lectures
 Publication of Anna Freud's *The Ego and the Mechanisms of Defence* (*Das
  Ich und die Abwehrmechanismen*)
1936 Fourteenth International Psycho-Analytic Congress at Marienbad, August 2–8
1937 Publication of Anna Freud's *The Ego and the Mechanisms of Defence* in
  English
 Death of Hermann Deutsch in Vienna
 Birth of Michael Clyne in London, October 17
 Publication of *Love, Hate and Reparation* by Melanie Klein and Joan Riviere
1938 Germany invades Austria, March 11
 Freud arrives in London, June 6
 Fifteenth International Psycho-Analytic Congress at Paris, August 1–5
1939 Michael Balint arrives in England
 War declared, September 3
 Klein moves to Cambridge with Susan Isaacs
 Death of Freud, September 23
1940 Death of Emilie Reizes Pick, May 13
 Klein settles in Pitlochry in July
1941 Analysis of "Richard"
 Klein returns to London in September
1942 Extraordinary Meetings
1942–44 Controversial Discussions
1944 Edward Glover resigns from British Psycho-Analytical Society, January 24
 Anna Freud resigns from Training Committee, January 24
 Sylvia Payne elected president of British Psycho-Analytical Society
1945 Melitta Schmideberg leaves for America
1946 "A" and "B" programs established in British Society
1947 John Rickman elected president of British Psycho-Analytical Society
 Ernest Jones becomes official Freud biographer
1948 Publication of Klein's *Contributions to Psycho-Analysis*
1949 Sixteenth International Psycho-Analytic Congress at Zurich, August 15–19
 Ernest Jones succeeded by Leo Bartemeier as president of International Association

1950 British Institute of Psycho-Analysis moves to 63 New Cavendish Street
Degree of Doctor of Laws (honoris causa) conferred on Anna Freud by Clark University, April 22

1951 Death of John Rickman, July 1
Seventeenth International Psycho-Analytic Congress at Amsterdam, August 5–9
Death of C. Z. Kloetzel, October 27

1952 Publication of *Developments in Psycho-Analysis*
Special issue of *International Journal of Psycho-Analysis* for Klein's seventieth birthday

1953 Eighteenth International Psycho-Analytic Congress at London, July 26–30
First volume of Jones's life of Freud published

1955 The Melanie Klein Trust founded, February 1
Nineteenth International Psycho-Analytic Congress in Geneva, July 24–28
Paula Heimann resigns from Melanie Klein Trust, November 27
Publication of *New Directions in Psycho-Analysis*

1956 D. W. Winnicott elected president of British Psycho-Analytical Society

1957 Publication of *Envy and Gratitude*
Twentieth International Psycho-Analytic Congress at Paris, July 28–August 1
William Gillespie elected president of International Psycho-Analytic Association
Publication of final volume of Jones's *The Life and Work of Sigmund Freud*

1958 Death of Ernest Jones, February 11

1959 Willi Hoffer elected president of British Psycho-Analytical Society
Twenty-first International Psycho-Analytic Congress at Copenhagen, July 26–30

1960 Death of Melanie Klein, September 22

1961 Publication of *Narrative of a Child Analysis*

APPENDIX A

STATISTICS OF TRAINING
from 1927 to 1942 (June 30).
(*For the information of Members.*)

Candidates			Controls	Seminars	Lectures
DR. JONES	2	1 qualified 1 resigned	10	7 single.	3 courses 1 single
DR. GLOVER	4	2 qualified 1 in training 1 America	6	6 courses of theor. sem. monthly. 4 single.	3 courses.
DR. PAYNE	9	1 advised to resign after 3 weeks. 1 qualified 3 in training 1 transferred 2 training suspended by war 1 resigned.	9	4 single pract. 1 course.	2 courses.
MISS SHARPE	12	2 resigned 1 transferred 1 suspended (war) 5 qualified 3 in training.	15	5 single pract. 3 courses "	3 courses.
MRS. KLEIN	4	1 resigned 1 returned to America 1 qualified 1 suspended (war)	3 adult 6 child	3 single 1 course adult pract. 4 courses child.	4 courses.

Candidates			Controls	Seminars	Lectures
MRS. RIVIERE	4	1 transferred 1 resigned (Amer.) 2 qualified.	6	3 single 1 course.	1 course.
MR. STRACHEY	6	3 qualified 3 resigned.	6	5 courses 1 single.	2 courses.
DR. RICKMAN	7	4 resigned 1 suspend. (war) 1 transferred 1 qualified	6	1 single 1 course pract.	2 courses.
MISS SEARL	3	1 resigned 2 transferred	5 child.	5 single 1 course pract.	2 courses.
DR. BRIERLEY	3	1 qualified 1 suspend. (war) 1 in training	3	3 years theor.	3 courses.
MISS SHEEHAN-DARE	2	1 transferrred 1 qualified.	5 adult 1 child.	2 courses child.	- - -
DR. WILSON		1 suspended (war)	2	- - -	- - -
DR. M. SCHMIDEBERG		1 in training	3 adult 3 child	1 course 1938. (child)	1 course.
MRS. ISAACS		1 transferred (war)	child	1 course 1938. (child)	3 courses.
DR. WINNICOTT		- - -	4 child	1 course (child)	- - -
MISS FREUD	4	1 resigned 1 suspend. (war) 2 in training.	4 adult 1 child	4 courses.	- - -
DR. G. BIBRING	2	2 transferred	4	2 courses.	- - -
DR. E. BIBRING	2	2 transferred	3	1 course.	- - -
DR. W. HOFFER	3	1 in training 1 suspend.(war) 1 qualified.	3	- - -	- - -
MR. E. KRIS		1 transferred	1	- - -	1 course.
MRS. BURLINGHAM	2	1 transferred 1 in training.	3	- - -	- - -

S. M. PAYNE.
Hon. Training Secretary.

July 1942.

APPENDIX B

Among Melanie Klein's unpublished papers is a fragment of a letter (probably written to Jones in 1941) accompanying a draft of some notes on transference technique. The fragment is interesting as a personal evaluation of her place within the history of the psychoanalytic movement.

Though the enclosed pages were written in connection with technique, you can see my main point which is that Freud's discovery of the super-ego if not carried further is in danger of getting lost in its *essence*. I could give you many instances of my observations in this respect made in Berlin, in Vienna in Hungary and in England. In my view P.A. developed in a more or less straightforward way up to these crucial discoveries, and after this turning point was reached regressive tendencies, dissensions and actual notable failures among analysts became much more frequent (Rank, Ferenczi and many others, particularly in America). Freud himself after having reached his climax in "Inhibitions, Symptoms and Anxiety" not only did not go further, but rather regressed. In his later contributions to theory some of his great findings are weakened or left aside, and he certainly did not draw the full conclusions from his own work. That might have had many reasons in himself such as age, his illness and the fact that there might be a point beyond which no person, however great a genius, can go with his own discoveries. I am convinced though that Anna's influence was one of the factors which held him back. This is, however, beside the point. As it happened, Freud's work on the super-ego left these great discoveries, as it were, in mid air. Abraham's big stride towards the exploration of deeper layers of the mind in his contributions about oral sadism and what he called the earlier anal-sadistic level, though it was not brought in connection with Freud's discoveries, tended in the same direction—but Abraham's work too was not carried further, owing to his death. The Viennese group under Anna's leadership has in fact considerably withdrawn from Freud's and Abraham's most important points. Elsewhere, too, strong regressive tendencies could be observed, or quite divergent views developed. The burden of my argument is that these discoveries containing as they do the seed for all further development in P.A., cause danger if they are not further developed, and are also in danger of being discarded. The expansion of Freud's work in the direction I undertook it might keep it alive in its full meaning and possibilities. This is my conviction, and one which is based on many observations, clinical work and the result of much thought. You yourself remarked in your letter on the great danger to every analyst and for analysis in general which comes from the tendency to get away from the depths and to regress. This danger is nowhere greater than where the super-ego and the deeper layers of the unconscious are concerned. This is my reason for saying in my letter to you that if the regressive tendencies in our Society prevail psycho-analysis in its essence might go under. These hostile regressive tendencies, though they are particularly directed against my work, in fact also attack much of what Freud himself found and stated between 1920 and 1926. It is tragic that his daughter, who thinks that she must defend him against me, does not realise that I am serving him better than she.

REFERENCES

List of Abbreviations

BPS:	British Psycho-Analytical Society
CD:	Controversial Discussions
EG:	*Envy and Gratitude*
IZP:	*Internationale Zeitschrift für Psychoanalyse*
Int. Rev. Psycho-Anal:	*International Review of Psycho-Analysis*
J. or Int. J. Psychoanal.:	*International Journal of Psycho-Analysis*
JA:	Jones Archives
LGR:	*Love, Guilt and Reparation*
MKT:	The Melanie Klein Trust
OHC:	Oral History Research Library, Columbia University
PC:	*The Psycho-Analysis of Children*
PQ:	*The Psychoanalytic Quarterly*
PSA. ST. C.:	*Psychoanalytic Study of the Child*
S.E.:	*The Standard Edition of the Complete Psychological Works of Sigmund Freud*
Zbl. Psychoanal:	*Jahrbuch der Psychoanalyse*

I. VIENNA TO BUDAPEST, 1882–1920

Chapter 4: *Crisis*

1 MKT.
2 Interview with Bluma Swerdloff, March 16, 1963 (OHC).
3 Michael Balint, Obituary, J. (1949) 30: 217.
4 "Pioneer of Pioneers," in *Psychoanalytic Pioneers*, p. 17.
5 "Lines of Advance in Psycho-Analytic Therapy," S.E., 17, p. 164.
6 Interview, Dec. 21, 1981.
7 *First Contributions to Psycho-Analysis* (London: Maresfield Reprints, 1954), p. 228.
8 Ibid., p. 247.
9 Copyright Enid Balint.
10 Translation by Eva Harte from IZP. 6, 1920.
11 LGR, p. 18.
12 LGR, p. 35.
13 MKT.
14 Private communication.
15 Strachey Letters.
16 LGR, p. 40.
17 Private communication.
18 EG, p. 122.
19 LGR, p. 27.
20 S.E., 10, p. 5.

II. BERLIN, 1920–1926

Chapter 1: *The Protégée*

1 MKT (Courtesy Mrs. Vroni Gordon).
2 JA.
3 JA.
4 JA.
5 Courtesy of Edith Balint.
6 "Death and the Mid-Life Crisis," *J.* (1965), 46, Part 4, p. 502.
7 MKT.
8 "Early Analysis" (1923), LGR, p. 94.
9 "A Contribution to the Psychogenesis of Tics" (1925), LGR, p. 106.
10 "Early Analysis," LGR, p. 103.
11 "The Psychogenesis of Tics," LGR, p. 121.
12 "The School in Libidinal Development" (1923), LGR, p. 71.
13 "A Contribution to the Psychogenesis of Tics," p. 115.
14 S.E., 9, p. 48.
15 *The Psycho-Analysis of Children* (London: Hogarth, 1975), p. 32.
16 "The Psycho-Analytic Play Technique: Its History and Significance" (1955), EG, p. 128.
17 Ibid.
18 *Inhibitions, Symptoms and Anxiety* (1926), S.E., 10, p. 119.
19 *A Psycho-Analytic Dialogue, The Letters of Sigmund Freud and Karl Abraham, 1906–27* (London: Hogarth Press, 1965), p. 339.
20 Ernest Jones, *The Life and Work of Sigmund Freud*, III (New York: Basic Books, 1957), p. 57.
21 *Selected Papers of Karl Abraham* (London: Maresfield Reprints, 1979), p. 138.
22 S.E., 17, p. 244.
23 Ibid., p. 248.
24 *Abraham*, op. cit., p. 426.
25 S.E., 18, p. 53.
26 MKT.
27 MKT.
28 "The Development of a Child" (1921), LGR, p. 45.
29 Ibid., p. 46.

Chapter 2: *Limbo*

1 Interview with Dr. Bluma Swerdloff, August 5, 1965 (OHC).
2 Interview with Grant Allan, March 28, 1982.
3 *J.* (1924) 6.
4 *The Psycho-Analysis of Children* (London: Hogarth Press, 1975), p. 37.
5 Autobiography (MKT).
6 *The Psycho-Analysis of Children*, op. cit., p. 50.
7 Interview with Dr. Bluma Swerdloff, August 5, 1965 (OHC).
8 Now in the possession of the Melanie Klein Trust.
9 "New Beginning and the Paranoid and the Depressive Syndromes," *J.* (1952) 33, Part II, p. 214.
10 Interview with Dr. Bluma Swerdloff, Feb. 13, 1963 (OHC).
11 Interview with Dr. Bluma Swerdloff, August 5, 1965 (OHC).
12 Strachey Letters (British Library). All subsequent extracts are from same source.

Chapter 3: *Ostracism*

1 Strachey Letters (British Library). All Strachey quotations are from same source.
2 MKT.
3 Sigmund Freud Copyrights.
4 Ibid.
5 MKT. All correspondence between Klein and Kloetzel from same source.

III. LONDON, 1926–1939

Chapter 1: *The British Psycho-Analytical Society*

1 Interview with Dr. Bluma Swerd-loff, August 11, 1965 (OHC).

2 Ernest Jones, *The Life and Work of Sigmund Freud* (New York: Basic Books, 1957), III, p. 129.

3 *The Freud/Jung Letters: The Correspondence Between Sigmund Freud and C. G. Jung*, ed. William McGuire, tr. by Ralph Manheim and R. F. C. Hull, Bollingen Series XCIV (Princeton, N.J.: Princeton University Press, 1974), p. 101.

4 Ibid. (Dec. 8, 1907), p. 102.

5 Ibid. (July 18, 1908), p. 165.

6 Presented at the Canadian Society for the History of Medicine Annual Conference, University of British Columbia, June 8, 1983.

7 Vincent Brome, *Ernest Jones: Freud's Alter Ego* (London: Caliban, 1982), p. 66.

8 *Freud/Jung Letters*, op. cit. (March 7, 1909), p. 208.

9 Jones, *Life*, op. cit., III, p. 58.

10 Ibid., p. 152.

11 Jan. 13, 1911, in Nathan G. Hale, Jr., *James Jackson Putnam* (Cambridge, Mass.: Harvard University Press, 1971), pp. 252–53.

12 *Journal of Abnormal Psychology* (1911), 81–106. It did not appear in the fifth (and final) edition of Ernest Jones, *Papers on Psycho-Analysis* (London: Hogarth Press, 1948), although it appeared in earlier editions.

13 Elizabeth R. Zetzel, "Ernest Jones: His Contribution to Psycho-Analytic Theory," *J.* (1958) 39, p. 314.

14 Ernest Jones, "The Origin and Structure of the Super-Ego," *J.* (1926) 7, p. 304.

15 JA.

16 JA.

17 Copyright Enid Balint.

18 Sigmund Freud Copyrights. All letters between Jones and Freud are from this collection. Translation of Freud's letters by Dr. Hans Thorner.

19 See K. R. Eissler, *Talent and Genius* (New York: Quadrangle Books, 1971), p. 81; also Paul Roazen, *Brother Animal* (New York: Alfred A. Knopf, 1969), p. 100, and *Freud and His Followers* (New York: Alfred A. Knopf, 1975), pp. 438 ff. The most complete account is to be found in Uwe Henrik Peters, *Anna Freud: A Life Dedicated to Children* (London: Weidenfeld & Nicolson, 1985).

20 Anna Freud, *The Psycho-Analytical Treatment of Children* (London: Imago, 1946), p. ix.

21 *J.* (1979) 60, Part 3, p. 286.

22 Anna Freud, op. cit., p. 9.

23 Ibid., p. 31.

24 Ibid., p. 45.

25 S.E., 10, p. 144.

26 *J.* (1927) 8, p. 340.

27 Ibid., p. 342.

28 Ibid., p. 345.

29 Ibid., p. 347.

30 Ibid., p. 352.

31 Ibid., p. 357.

32 Ibid., p. 358.

33 Ibid., p. 376.

34 Ibid., p. 384.

35 Ibid., p. 384.

36 *The Writings of Anna Freud*, Vol. 1 (1922–1935), Introduction, p. viii (New York: International Universities Press, 1974).

37 S.E., 20, p. 148.

38 LGR, p. 187.

39 *Journal of the Otto Rank Society* (1981) 16, 3–38.

40 Ernest Jones, *Papers on Psycho-Analysis* (London: Maresfield Reprints, 1948), 5th ed., p. 452.

41 LGR, p. 192.
42 Ibid., p. 193.
43 Ibid., p. 194.
44 Ibid., p. 196.
45 Ibid.
46 Ibid., p. 217.
47 S.E., 21, p. 242

Chapter 2: *Cock of the Walk*

1 Jones, *Papers on Psycho-Analysis* (London: Maresfield Reprints, 1948), 5th ed., p. 116.
2 Interview, March 15, 1983. See (Joanna Field) *On Not Being Able to Paint* (New York: International Universities Press, 1957), *A Life of One's Own* (London: Chatto and Windus, 1936), and *The Hands of the Living God: An Account of a Psycho-Analytical Treatment* (London and New York: Hogarth and International Universities Press, 1969).
3 LGR, p. 231.
4 See "Autistic Disturbances of Affective Contact," *The Nervous Child* (1943) 2: 217–50.
5 Private communication.
6 LGR, p. 230.
7 S.E., 21, p. 132.
8 Ibid., p. 138.
9 Ibid.
10 Ibid., p. 130.
11 Ibid.
12 Copyright Enid Balint.
13 Interview, October 8, 1981.
14 Interview, November 27, 1982.
15 MKT.
16 *The Psycho-Analysis of Children* (London: Hogarth Press, 1975), p. 260.
17 *Papers on Psycho-Analysis*, op. cit., p. 162.
18 Ibid.
19 S.E., 21, p. 120.
20 Jones, *Life*, III, p. 277.
21 Eric Clyne Collection.
22 *J.* (1933) 14, 119.
23 Ibid.
24 Ibid., p. 124.
25 Ibid., p. 126.

26 Ibid., p. 127.
27 Interview with Dr. Bluma Swerdloff, August 1965 (OHC).
28 JA.
29 *PQ* (1933) 2, 143.
30 Ibid., 145.
31 Gregory Zilboorg, *PQ* (1933) 2, 152–54.
32 MKT.
33 Eric Clyne Collection.
34 "A Contribution to the History of the Psycho-Analytical Movement in Britain," *British Journal of Psychiatry* (Jan. 1971) 118, 63.
35 Private communication.
36 *Papers on Psycho-Analysis*, op. cit., p. 438.
37 Ibid., p. 440.
38 Ibid., p. 452.
39 Ibid., p. 453.
40 Ibid., p. 455.
41 Ibid., p. 463.
42 Ibid., p. 466.
43 S.E., 21, p. 229.
44 *Papers on Psycho-Analysis*, op. cit., p. 475.
45 Helene Deutsch, "The Significance of Masochism in the Mental Life of Women," *J.* (1930) 11, 53.
46 Karen Horney, "The Flight from Womanhood," *J.* (1926) 7, 337.
47 *The Psycho-Analysis of Children*, op. cit., p. 324.
48 *Papers on Psycho-Analysis*, op. cit., p. 484.
49 James Strachey, "Some Unconscious Factors in Reading," *J.* (1930) 11, 330.
50 James Strachey, "The Nature of the Therapeutic Action of Psycho-Analysis," *J.* (1934) 15, 138.
51 Ibid., 143.
52 Ibid., 150.
53 Ibid., 151.
54 Edward Glover, *An Investigation of the Technique of Psycho-Analysis* (London: Balliere, Tindall & Cox, 1940), pp. 280–81.
55 "A Character Trait of Freud's" (p. 356) in *Freud As We Knew Him*, ed. Hendrik M. Ruitenbeek (De-

troit: Wayne State University Press, 1956).

56 Ibid., p. 130.
57 The Jones-Freud correspondence is quoted by permission of the Sigmund Freud Copyrights Ltd.
58 Jones, *Life*, op. cit., III, p. 196.

Chapter 3: *Mourning*

1 "The Play-Analysis of a Three-Year-Old Girl," *J.* (1934) 15, 248.
2 Ibid., p. 258.
3 Ibid.
4 Ibid., p. 264.
5 "A Contribution to the History of the Psycho-Analytical Movement in Britain," *The British Journal of Psychiatry* (Jan. 1971), 118, p. 63.
6 Private communication.
7 Interview, Sept. 24, 1981.
8 Interview, Feb. 22, 1982.
9 Eric Clyne Collection.
10 Minutes, British Institute of Psycho-Analysis.
11 Interview, Sept. 17, 1981.
12 LGR, p. 267.
13 Ibid., p. 270.
14 Ibid., p. 274.
15 *Notes upon a Case of Obsessional Neurosis*, S.E., 10, p. 241.
16 LGR, p. 276.
17 JA.
18 Jan. 11, 1935 (JA).
19 Ernest Jones, *Papers on Psycho-Analysis* (London: Maresfield Reprints, 1948), p. 484.
20 Ibid.
21 *Female Sexuality* (1931), S.E., 21, p. 226.
22 *Papers on Psycho-Analysis*, op. cit., p. 491.
23 Ibid.
24 Edward Glover, *The Technique of Psycho-Analysis* (London: Bailliere, Tindall & Cox, 1940), p. 168.
25 April 29, 1938 (JA).
26 "The Future of Psycho-Analysis," *J.* (1936) 17, 274.
27 Ibid., p. 275.

28 Ibid.
29 Ibid.
30 "On the Genesis of Psychical Conflict in Earliest Infancy," *J.* (1936) 17, 401.
31 Ibid., p. 407.
32 Ibid.
33 Ibid., p. 413.
34 "The Problem of the Genesis of Psychical Conflict in Earliest Infancy," *J.* (1937) 18, 442.
35 Ibid., 447.
36 Ibid., 450.
37 Edward Glover, "Medical Psychology or Academic (Normal) Psychology," *British Journal of Medical Psychology* (1934), 14, pp. 36 and 40.
38 Waelder, op. cit., p. 460.
39 *J.* (1937), 18, 132.
40 JA.
41 *J.* (1938) 19, 115.
42 Ibid., 116.
43 Anna Freud, *The Ego and the Mechanisms of Defence* (London: Hogarth Press, 1979), p. 29.
44 *J.* (1938) 19, 125.
45 Anna Freud, op. cit., p. 58.
46 Ibid., p. 103.
47 Ibid., p. 112.
48 Ibid., p. 125.
49 S.E., 22, p. 80.
50 S.E., 23, p. 222.
51 Ibid., p. 233.
52 Strachey Letters (British Library).
53 Melitta Schmideberg, "After the Analysis . . . ," PQ (1938) 7, 127.
54 Ibid., p. 128.
55 Ibid.
56 Ibid., p. 138.
57 Minutes, British Institute of Psycho-Analysis.
58 Ibid.
59 Private communication.

Chapter 4: *The Arrival of the Freuds*

1 LGR, p. 297.
2 Courtesy Madeleine Davis.

3 *The Observer*, Sept. 25, 1966.
4 MKT.
5 JA.
6 LGR, p. 325.
7 Ibid., p. 336.
8 Ibid., p. 321.
9 Ibid., p. 323.
10 *The Diary of Virginia Woolf*, V: 1936–41. Ed. Anne Olivier Bell (London: Hogarth Press, 1984), p. 209.
11 JA.
12 JA.
13 JA.
14 Interview with Pearl King, 1974.
15 Ernest Jones, *The Life and Work of Sigmund Freud* (New York: Basic Books, 1957), III, p. 221.
16 Interview with Clare Winnicott, Sept. 18, 1981.
17 *J.* (1941) 22, 37–43.

18 *On the Bringing Up of Children*, ed. John Rickman (London: Routledge & Kegan Paul, 1936), p. xii.
19 Interview with Pearl King, 1974.
20 Ibid.
21 Interview with Dr. Bluma Swerdloff, July 28, 1965 (OHC).
22 Ibid.
23 Minutes, British Society of Psycho-Analysis.
24 *J.* (1940) 21, 282.
25 Clifford Scott Collection.
26 Paula Heimann, "A Contribution to the Problem of Sublimation and Its Relation to Processes of Internalization," *J.* (1942) 22, 8.
27 Ibid., p. 17.
28 Jones, *Life*, op. cit., III, p. 243.
29 Courtesy Madeleine Davis.

IV. CAMBRIDGE AND PITLOCHRY, 1939–1941

Chapter 1: *Moratorium*

1 MKT.
2 MKT.
3 MKT.
4 MKT.
5 S.E., 14, p. 255.
6 LGR, p. 356.
7 Ibid.
8 Ibid., p. 362.
9 Courtesy Madeleine Davis.
10 Courtesy Madeleine Davis.
11 Courtesy Madeleine Davis.
12 Courtesy Madeleine Davis.
13 Clifford Scott Collection.
14 Clifford Scott Collection.
15 MKT.
16 MKT.
17 MKT.
18 MKT.
19 BPS.
20 MKT.
21 Courtesy Madeleine Davis.
22 Clifford Scott Collection.
23 Courtesy Madeleine Davis.
24 MKT.

25 MKT.
26 Clifford Scott Collection.
27 Courtesy Madeleine Davis.
28 Courtesy Madeleine Davis.

Chapter 2: *Richard*

1 Courtesy Madeleine Davis.
2 Clifford Scott Collection.
3 MKT.
4 LGR, p. 372.
5 Ibid., p. 419.
6 Ibid., p. 374.
7 Clifford Scott Collection.
8 MKT.
9 MKT.
10 J. O. Wisdom, "Freudian Offspring," *Time & Tide*, 2 March 1961, p. 330.
11 "No Man's Formula," *Bulletin of the European Psychoanalytical Federation* (1977) No. 8, p. 13.
12 Elisabeth R. Geleerd, "Evaluation of Melanie Klein's 'Narrative of a Child Analysis,' " *J.* (1963) 44, 495.

13 Ibid., 506.
14 Ibid., 504.
15 Ibid., 505.
16 "Narrative of a Child Analysis," *J.*

(1963) 44, 507–13.
17 Ibid., 508.
18 Ibid., 512.
19 MKT.

V. THE CONTROVERSIAL DISCUSSIONS, 1942–1944

Chapter 1: *Resumption of Hostilities*

1 MKT.
2 JA.
3 JA.
4 MKT.
5 OHC.
6 MKT.
7 Interview with Bluma Swerdloff,
  July 29, 1965 (OHC).
8 MKT.
9 MKT.
10 MKT.
11 JA.
12 Feb. 17, 1942 (MKT).
13 MKT.
14 Minutes, BPS.
15 Ella Sharpe, "Technique of Psycho-
  Analysis," *J.* (1930) 11, 11.
16 See "Pure Art and Pure Science," *J.*
  (1935) 16. Also *Collected Papers on
  Psycho-Analysis* (London: Hogarth
  Press, 1950).
17 July 13, 1942 (MKT).
18 Minutes, BPS.
19 MKT.
20 MKT.
21 March 30, 1942 (MKT).
22 N.d. (Courtesy Madeleine Davis).
23 Minutes, BPS.
24 MKT.
25 April 18, 1942 (MKT).
26 April 21, 1942 (MKT).
27 May 2, 1942 (MKT).
28 May 2, 1942 (MKT).
29 May 5, 1942 (MKT).
30 See Brierley, " 'Internal Objects'
  and theory," *J.* (1942) 22, 107–12.
31 Ibid., 109.
32 Interview, Dec. 5, 1981.
33 May 7, 1942 (MKT).

34 MKT.
35 MKT.
36 Interview, Nov. 27, 1982.
37 May 22, 1942 (MKT).
38 May 22, 1942 (MKT).
39 MKT.
40 May 28, 1942 (MKT).
41 May 31, 1942 (MKT).
42 June 5, 1942 (MKT).
43 Minutes, BPS.
44 MKT.
45 June 17, 1942 (MKT).

Chapter 2: *Warring Women*

1 *An Investigation of the Technique
  of Psycho-Analysis* (London: Bailliere, Tindall & Cox, 1940), p. 139.
2 Ibid., p. 141.
3 MKT.
4 MKT.
5 MKT.
6 MKT.
7 MKT.
8 MKT.
9 Vincent Brome, *Ernest Jones:
  Freud's Alter Ego* (London: Caliban
  Books, 1982), p. 207.
10 The papers were published in Klein
  et al., *Developments in
  Psycho-Analysis* (1952).
11 Anna Freud, *The Ego and the
  Mechanisms of Defence* (London:
  Hogarth Press, 1979), p. 52.
12 S.E., 17, p. 159.
13 S.E., 18, p. 32.
14 Interview, Sept. 17, 1981.
15 MKT.
16 MKT.

17 MKT.
18 MKT.
19 Courtesy Madeleine Davis.

20 MKT.
21 MKT.
22 MKT.

Chapter 3: *The Ladies' Agreement*

1 S.E., 18, p. 253.
2 Ibid., p. 247.
3 Minutes, BPS.
4 Interview, March 15, 1983.
5 Clifford Scott Collection.
6 JA.
7 Interview, August 1965 (OHC).
8 Ibid.
9 Interview, July 29, 1965 (OHC).
10 Ibid.
11 Ibid.
12 JA.
13 JA.
14 JA.
15 (OHC).
16 (OHC).
17 Courtesy Madeleine Davis.
18 Interview, Sept. 17, 1981.

19 Interview, March 15, 1983.
20 Interview with Dr. Bluma Swerd-loff, July 29, 1965 (OHC).
21 Interview, Nov. 16, 1981.
22 See "The Education of a Psycho-Analyst: The British Experience," *Bulletin of the British Psycho-Analytical Society* (February 1981), 2: 93–107; "The Life and Work of Melanie Klein in the British Psycho-Analytical Society," *J.* (1983), 64: 251–60.
23 Interview, Jan. 17, 1982.
24 Interview, March 12, 1982.
25 Interview with Pearl King, 1974.
26 Interview, Sept. 17, 1981.
27 Interview, Jan. 2, 1982.

VI. THE POSTWAR WORLD, 1945–1960

Chapter 1: *Mothers and Daughters*

1 Clifford Scott Collection.
2 Melanie Klein Centenary Celebration, Tavistock Clinic, July 17, 1982.
3 Minutes, BPS.
4 See LGR, p. 363.
5 Clifford Scott Collection.
6 EG, p. 5.
7 EG, p. 9.
8 S.E. (1911), 12, p. 77.
9 Interview, February 2, 1982.
10 "Contribution to the Psychopathology of Psychotic States: The Importance of Projective Identification in the Ego Structures and the Object Relations of the Psychotic Patient."
11 Clifford Scott Collection.
12 Interview, March 13, 1982.
13 See *The Work of Hanna Segal* (New York and London: Jason Aronson, 1981), 101–20; and Her-

bert Rosenfeld, *Psychotic States* (London: Hogarth Press, 1965), 13–33.
14 Private communication.
15 See Jacques Lacan, *Écrits* (London: Tavistock Publications, 1977), 1–7.
16 Clifford Scott Collection.
17 Interview, March 30, 1982.
18 S.E., "On the History of the Psycho-Analytic Movement" (1914), 14, p. 51.
19 See S.E., 11, p. 145.
20 Heimann, "On Counter-Transference," *J.* (1950) 31, 83.
21 Winnicott, "Hate in the Counter-Transference," *Through Paediatrics to Psycho-Analysis* (London: Hogarth Press, 1978), p. 195.
22 Ibid., p. 197.
23 Heimann, op. cit., 82.
24 Joseph Sandler, Christopher Dare, Alex Holder, *The Patient and the*

Analyst (London: Maresfield Reprints, 1979), p. 66.
25 Winnicott, op. cit., p. 199.
26 Interview with Pearl King, 1974.
27 Interview, March 22, 1983.

Chapter 2: *The Matriarch*

1 JA.
2 Marie Bonaparte, *Five Copy-Books* (London: Imago, 1953) IV, pp. 313–14.
3 *Psychoanalytic Study of the Child* (1945), 1, p. 125.
4 EG, p. 52.
5 Interview, Dec. 16, 1983.
6 Private communication.
7 MKT.
8 Eric Clyne Collection.
9 Interview, Jan. 17, 1982.
10 *Developments*, p. 198.
11 *The Psycho-Analysis of Children*, p. xi.
12 *The Unconscious Motives of War* (London: George Allen & Unwin, 1957), p. 260.
13 J. (1952) 33, Part 2, 214–24.
14 *Developments*, p. 206.
15 Ibid., 90.
16 Interview, March 15, 1983.
17 Interview with Pearl King, 1974.
18 Letter to Clifford Scott, May 30, 1951. (Clifford Scott Collection)
19 J. (1953) 34, Part 2, 94.
20 Ibid., 95.
21 Interview, Dec. 8, 1981.
22 *Between Reality and Fantasy*, eds. Simon A. Grolnick and Leonard Barkin (New York: Jason Aronson. 1978), pp. 38–39.
23 Interview, Dec. 22, 1981.
24 Interview, Dec. 8, 1981.
25 Interview, Oct. 8, 1981.
26 Dec. 26, 1956 (Clifford Scott Collection).
27 Courtesy of the Archives of Psychiatry, New York Hospital, Cornell Medical Center (henceforth referred to as Cornell).
28 Private communication.

28 Winnicott, op. cit., p. 73.
29 *The Psycho-Analysis of Children*, p. 228.
30 Ibid., p. 216.
31 LGR, p. 310.

29 Cornell. I am indebted to Ilse Hellman for background information.
30 Oct. 3, 1957 (Cornell).
31 Ibid.
32 Interview, Dec. 22, 1981.
33 Private communication.
34 "The Nature of the Child's Tie to His Mother," J. (1958) 39, 354.
35 June 21, 1957 (Cornell).
36 Interview, Nov. 30, 1981.
37 June 22, 1957 (Cornell).
38 Nov. 7, 1958 (Cornell).
39 "Separation Anxiety," J. (1960) 41, 106.
40 Anna Freud, "Discussion of Dr. John Bowlby's Paper," *Psychoanalytic Study of the Child* (1960), 15, p. 54.
41 Interview, Nov. 23, 1981.
42 Nov. 5, 1958 (Cornell).
43 Interview, Jan. 24, 1982.
44 Interview, Feb. 12, 1982.
45 Interview, March 30, 1982.
46 Interview, March 30, 1983.
47 Interview, Feb. 20, 1982.
48 Interview, March 17, 1981.
49 Interview, Dec. 8, 1981.
50 Interview, Jan. 17, 1982.

Chapter 3: *Envy*

1 Interview, March 13, 1983.
2 MKT.
3 Private communication.
4 Margaret Little, *Transference Neurosis and Transference Psychosis* (New York: Jason Aronson, 1981), p. 270.
5 *The Annual Survey of Psycho-Analysis* (1953) 4: 91–93.
6 EG, p. 174.
7 Ibid., p. 165.
8 Interview, Dec. 18, 1983.

9 Interview, Dec. 18, 1983.
10 Interview, Feb. 12, 1982.
11 EG, p. 181.
12 EG, p. 225.
13 Ibid.
14 Walter G. Joffe, "A Critical Review of the Status of the Envy Concept," *J.* (1969) 50, 533.
15 Ibid., 538.
16 D. W. Winnicott, "On Envy," Case Conference, Tavistock (1957), p. 178.
17 Interview, Feb. 2, 1982.
18 EG, p. 206.
19 Interview, March 12, 1983.
20 EG, p. 207.
21 Ibid.
22 Ibid.
23 EG, p. 208.
24 EG, p. 209.
25 Ibid.
26 EG, p. 232.
27 Interview, Dec. 21, 1981.
28 EG, p. 210.
29 MKT.
30 MKT.
31 Interview, March 18, 1983.
32 Interview, March 12, 1983.
33 Ibid.
34 Interview, Feb. 14, 1983.
35 See "Bemerkungen zur Sublimierung," *Psyche* (1959) 13: 397–414.
36 Courtesy of the Archives of Psychiatry, New York Hospital, Cornell Medical Center.
37 June 15, 1958 (Cornell).

Chapter 4: *Political Infighting*

1 Dec. 19, 1949 (Clifford Scott Collection).
2 Feb. 14, 1950 (Clifford Scott Collection).
3 N.d. (Clifford Scott Collection).
4 June 19, 1958 (Clifford Scott Collection).
5 Interview, March 12, 1982.
6 Interview, Dec. 17, 1981.
7 Interview, Feb. 2, 1982.

8 Oliver Lyth, Obituary of Bion, *J.* (1980) 61, 271.
9 "Group Dynamics," *Experience in Groups* (London: Tavistock, 1961), p. 141.
10 Interview, Jan. 19, 1982.
11 Courtesy Madeleine Davis.
12 Interview, Jan. 17, 1982.
13 Interview, Dec. 22, 1981.
14 Ernest Jones, *The Life and Work of Sigmund Freud* (New York: Basic Books, 1955), II, p. 261.
15 Ibid., pp. 272–73.
16 Ibid., p. 319.
17 Nov. 12, 1955, JA.
18 *Life*, III, p. 137.
19 Ibid., p. 197.
20 Ibid., p. 290.

Chapter 5: *Last Years*

1 MKT.
2 Courtesy Thomas Vágó.
3 Private communication.
4 Interview, Feb. 10, 1982.
5 [Wilfred Bion,] *Bion in New York and São Paulo* (Perthshire: Clunie Press, 1980), p. 86.
6 Private communication.
7 Interview, Sept. 2, 1982.
8 Joyce McDougall and Serge Lebovici, *Dialogue with Sammy* (London: Hogarth Press, 1969), pp. 4, 5.
9 Jonathan Miller, *States of Mind* (New York: Methuen, 1983), p. 255.
10 EG, p. 240.
11 Courtesy Madeleine Davis.
12 Richard Wollheim, "A Critic of Our Time," *Encounter* (April 1959), 43.
13 Interview, July 1982.
14 PQ (1933) 2, 149.
15 "Quelques souvenirs personnels sur Melanie Klein," paper presented at the conference "Melanie Klein aujourd'hui" by Société Psychanalytique de Paris, Nov. 27, 1982.
16 Interview, March 18, 1982.
17 Beverley R. Placzek, ed., *Record of a Friendship: The Correspondence*

of *Wilhelm Reich and A. S. Neill*
(New York: Farrar, Straus, Giroux,
1981), pp. 398, 399.
18 Interview, Feb. 2, 1982.
19 Interview, Jan. 9, 1982.
20 "Melanie Klein As I Have Known
Her," Celebration of the Centenary
of Melanie Klein's Birth, Tavistock
Clinic, July 17, 1982.
21 Interview, Sept. 18, 1981.
22 *Bion in New York and São Paulo,*
op. cit., p. 37.

23 EG, p. 249.
24 EG, p. 259.
25 *The Guardian,* May 16, 1960.
26 Interview, Feb. 22, 1982.
27 *The Maturational Processes and the
Facilitating Environment* (London:
Hogarth Press, 1965), p. 36.
28 EG, p. 300.
29 Interview, March 14, 1982.
30 EG, p. 266.
31 Courtesy Thomas Vágó.
32 MKT.

BIBLIOGRAPHY

Works of Melanie Klein

1920 Der Familienroman in statu nascendi, *I.Z.P.*, 1920.

1921 Eine Kinderentwicklung, *Imago*, 1921; *J*, 1923.

1922 Hemmungen und Schwierigkeiten im Pubertätsalter, in *Die Neue Erziehung*, vol. IV, 1922.

1923a Die Rolle der Schule für die libidinöse Entwicklung des Kindes, *I.Z.P.*, 1923; The Role of the School in the Libidinal Development of the Child, *J.*, 1924.

1923b Zur Frühanalyse, *Imago*, 1923; Infant Analysis, *J.*, 1926.

1925 Zur Genese des Tics, *I.Z.P.*, 1925; A Contribution to the Psychogenesis of Tics, 1948.

1926 Die psychologischen Grundlagen der Frühanalyse, *Imago*, 1926: The Psychological Principles of Early Analysis, *J.*, 1926.

1927a Criminal Tendencies in Normal Children, *British Journal of Medical Psychology*, 1927.

1927b Symposium on Child Analysis, *J.*, 1927.

1928a Frühstadien des Ödipuskonfliktes, *I.Z.P.*, 1928; Early Stages of the Oedipus Conflict, *J.*, 1928.

1928b Notes on "A Dream of Forensic Interest," by D. Bryan, *J.*, 1928.

1929a Die Rollenbildung im Kinderspiel, *I.Z.P.*, 1929; Personification in the Play of Children, *J.*, 1929.

1929b Infantile Anxiety-Situations Reflected in a Work of Art and in the Creative Impulse, *J.*, 1929.

1930a Die Bedeutung der Symbolbildung für die Ichentwicklung, *I.Z.P.*, 1930; The Importance of Symbol-Formation in the Development of the Ego, *J.*, 1930.

1930b The Psychotherapy of the Psychosis, *British Journal of Medical Psychology*, 1930.

1931a Frühe Angstsituationen im Spiegel künstlerischer Darstellungen, *I.Z.P.*, 1931; tr. Eng. in 1929b.

1931b A Contribution to the Theory of Intellectual Inhibition, *J.*, 1931.

1932 *Die Psychoanalyse des Kindes*, Wien: Internationaler Psychoanalytischer Verlag; *The Psycho-Analysis of Children*, London: Hogarth Press, 1932.

1933 The Early Development of Conscience in the Child, in *Psycho-Analysis Today*, New York: Covici-Friede Publishers, 1933.

1934 On Criminality, *British Journal of Medical Psychology*, 1934.

1935 A Contribution to the Psychogenesis of Manic-Depressive States, *J.*, 1935.

1936   Weaning, in J. Rickman & coll., *On the Bringing Up of Children*, London: Kegan Paul, 1938.

1937   Love, Guilt and Reparation, in Klein, M., & J. Riviere, *Love, Hate, and Reparation*, London: Hogarth Press.

1940   Mourning and Its Relation to Manic-Depressive States, *J.*, 1940.

1942   Some Psychological Considerations, in Waddington & coll., *Science and Ethics*, London: Allen & Unwin, 1942.

1945   The Oedipus Complex in the Light of Early Anxieties, *J.*, 1945.

1946   Notes on Some Schizoid Mechanisms, *J.*, 1946.

1948   *Contributions to Psycho-Analysis*, London: Hogarth Press.

1948b A Contribution to the Theory of Anxiety and Guilt, *J.*, 1948.

1950   On the Criteria for the Termination of a Psycho-Analysis, *J.*, 1950

1952a Some Theoretical Conclusions Regarding the Emotional Life of the Infant, in 1952c.

1952b On Observing the Behaviour of Young Infants, in 1952c.

1952c In coll. with P. Heimann, S. Isaacs, & J. Riviere, *Developments in Psycho-Analysis*, London: Hogarth Press.

1952d The Origins of Transference, *J.*, 1952.

1952e The Mutual Influences in the Development of the Ego and the Id, *The Psycho-Analytic Study of the Child*, 1952.

1955a The Psycho-Analytic Play Technique; Its History and Significance, in 1955b.

1955b In coll. with P. Heimann & R. E. Money-Kyrle, *New Directions in Psycho-Analysis*, London: Tavistock.

1955c On Identification, in 1955b.

1957   *Envy and Gratitude*, London: Tavistock.

1958   On the Development of Mental Functioning, *J.*, 1958.

1959   Our Adult World and Its Roots in Infancy, *Human Relations*, 1959.

1960   On Mental Health, *British Journal of Medical Psychology*, 1960.

Posthumous publications

1961   *Narrative of a Child Analysis*, London: Hogarth Press.

1963a Some Reflections on the Oresteia, in 1963c.

1963b On the Sense of Loneliness, in 1963c.

1963c *Our Adult World*, London: Heinemann.

Critical editions

Money-Kyrle, R. E., *The Writings of Melanie Klein*, ed. in coll. with B. Joseph, E. O'Shaughnessy, and H. Segal, 4 vols., London: Hogarth Press and the Institute of Psycho-Analysis, 1975; New York: Free Press, 1984. These include *Love, Guilt and Reparation and Other Works*, 1921–1945; *The Psycho-Analysis of Children; Envy and Gratitude and Other Works*, 1946–1963; and *Narrative of a Child Analysis*.

General Bibliography

ABRAHAM, HILDA C. "Karl Abraham: An Unfinished Biography," *International Review of Psycho-Analysis* (1974) 17: 17–72.

[ABRAHAM, KARL.] Obituary by Ernest Jones, *International Journal of Psycho-Analysis* (1926) 7: 155–81.

———. *Selected Papers of Karl Abraham*. London: Maresfield Reprints, 1979.

ADLER, ALFRED. *The Pattern of Life*. London: Kegan Paul, Trench, Trebner, 1931.

ALEXANDER, FRANZ. "The Neurotic Character," *International Journal of Psycho-Analysis* (1930) 11: 291–311.

———. "Review of *Die Psycho-Analyse des Kindes*," *Jahrbuch der Psychoanalyse* (1933) 2: 141–52.

———. *The Scope of Psychoanalysis: Selected Papers of Franz Alexander*. New York: Basic Books, 1961.

———, Samuel Eisenstein, and Martin Grotjahn (eds.). *Psychoanalytic Pioneers*. New York: Basic Books, 1966.

BALINT, MICHAEL. "Analytic Training and Training Analysis," *International Journal of Psycho-Analysis* (1954) 34: 157–62.

———. *The Basic Fault*. London: Tavistock, 1968.

———. "Early Developmental States of the Ego. Primary Object Love," *International Journal of Psycho-Analysis* (1949) 30: 265–73.

———. "New Beginnings and the Paranoid and the Depressive Syndromes," *International Journal of Psycho-Analysis* (1952) 33, Part II: 214–24.

———. Obituary by John D. Sutherland, *International Journal of Psycho-Analysis* (1971) 52: 331–33.

———. "On the Psycho-Analytic Training System," *International Journal of Psycho-Analysis* (1948) 29: 163–73.

———. *Primary Love and Psycho-analytic Technique*. London: Hogarth Press, 1952.

———. *Problems of Human Pleasure and Behaviour*. London and New York: Liveright International Psycho-Analytical Library, 1956.

BERNSTEIN, ANNE E., and GLORIA MARMON WARNER. *An Introduction to Contemporary Psycho-analysis*. New York and London: Jason Aronson, 1981.

BERTIN, CELIA. *Marie Bonaparte*. New York: Harcourt Brace Jovanovich, 1982.

BETTELHEIM, BRUNO. *The Empty Fortress: Infantile Autism and the Birth of the Self*. New York: Free Press, 1967.

———. *Freud and Man's Soul*. New York: Knopf, 1982.

BIBRING, E. "The So-called English School of Psychoanalysis," *Psychoanalytic Quarterly* (1947) 16: 69–93.

BICK, ESTHER. "Child Analysis Today" (Symposium on Child Analysis), *International Journal of Psycho-Analysis* (1962) 43: 328–32.

————. "The Experience of the Skin in Early Object-Relations," *International Journal of Psycho-Analysis* (1968) 49: 484–86.

————. "Notes on Infant Observation in Psycho-Analytic Training," *International Journal of Psycho-Analysis* (1964) 45: 558–66.

BION, WILFRED. *Bion in New York and São Paulo.* Perthshire: Clunie Press, 1980.

————. *Experience in Groups.* London: Tavistock, 1961.

————. "Notes on the Theory of Schizophrenia," *International Journal of Psycho-Analysis* (1954) 35: 113–18.

————. "Obituary of W. R. Bion," by Oliver Lyth, *International Journal of Psycho-Analysis* (1980) 61: 269–73.

————. *Second Thoughts: Selected Papers on Psycho-Analysis.* London: Heinemann, 1967 (contains "The Imaginary Twin").

————. "A Theory of Thinking," *International Journal of Psycho-Analysis* (1962) 43: 306–10.

BOEHM, FELIX. "Beitrage zur Psychologie der Homosexualität," *Internationale Zeitschrift für Psychoanalyse* (1926), 66–79.

————. *Über den Ödipuskomplex, drei psychoanalytische Studien.* Wien: Psychoanalytischer Verlag, 1931.

BONAPARTE, MARIE. *Five Copy-Books.* London: Imago, 1950–53.

BOWLBY, JOHN. *Attachment and Loss.* 3 vols. London: Hogarth Press; New York: Basic Books. I: *Attachment,* 1963. II: *Separation: Anxiety and Anger,* 1973. III: *Sadness and Depression,* 1980.

————. "Forty-Four Juvenile Thieves: Their Characters and Home Life," *International Journal of Psycho-Analysis* (1944) 25: 1–57.

————. "Grief and Mourning in Infancy and Early Childhood," *Psychoanalytic Study of the Child* (1960) 15: 3–39.

————. "The Influence of Early Environment in the Development of Neurosis and Neurotic Character," *International Journal of Psycho-Analysis* (1940) 21: 154–78.

————. *The Making and Breaking of Affectional Bonds.* London: Tavistock; New York: Methuen, 1973.

————. "The Nature of the Child's Tie to His Mother," *International Journal of Psycho-Analysis* (1958) 39: 350–73.

————. "Pathological Mourning and Childhood Mourning," *Journal of the American Psychoanalytic Association* (1963) 11: 500–41.

————. "Perspective," *Bulletin of the Royal College of Psychiatry* (Jan. 1981) 5: 2, 3.

————. "Processes of Mourning," *International Journal of Psycho-Analysis* (1961) 42: 317–40.

————. "Separation Anxiety," *International Journal of Psycho-Analysis* (1960) 41: 89–113.

————. "Separation Anxiety: A Critical Review of the Literature," *Journal of Child Psychology and Psychiatry* (1961) 1: 251–65.

————. "Symposium on Psycho-Analysis and Ethology," II: "Ethology and the Development of Object Relations," *International Journal of Psycho-Analysis* (1960) 41: 313–17.

BREGER, LOUIS. *Freud's Unfinished Journey.* London: Routledge & Kegan Paul, 1981.

BRENNER, CHARLES. *The Mind in Conflict*. New York: International Universities Press, 1982.

BRIERLEY, MARJORIE. " 'Internal Objects' and theory," *International Journal of Psycho-Analysis* (1942) 23: 107–12.

———. "Notes on the Metapsychology as Process Theory," *International Journal of Psycho-Analysis* (1944) 25: 97–107.

———. "A Prefatory Note on 'Internalized Objects' and Depression," *International Journal of Psycho-Analysis* (1939) 20: 240–43.

———. "Present Tendencies in Psycho-Analysis," *International Journal of Psycho-Analysis* (1934) 14: 214–29.

———. "Review of *Contributions to Psycho-Analysis 1921–1945*," *International Journal of Psycho-Analysis* (1950) 31: 209–11.

———. "Review of *Developments in Psycho-Analysis*," *International Journal of Psycho-Analysis* (1952) 33: 158–60.

———. "Specific Determinants in Feminine Component," *International Journal of Psycho-Analysis* (1936) 17: 163–80.

———. *Trends in Psycho-Analysis*. London: Hogarth Press, 1951.

BROME, VINCENT. *Ernest Jones: Freud's Alter Ego*. London: Caliban Books, 1982.

BROPHY, BRIGID. "Good and Bad Breast," *New Statesman*, 1 March 1963, p. 308.

BROWN, J. A. C. *Freud and the Post-Freudians*. London: Penguin, 1976.

BROWN, THOMAS E. "Dr. Ernest Jones, Psychoanalysis, and the Canadian Medical Profession, 1908–1913," in S. E. D. Short (ed.), *Medicine in Canadian Society: Historical Perspectives*. Montreal: McGill/Queen's University Press, 1981.

CHADWICK, MARY. *Women's Periodicity*. London: Noel Douglas, 1933.

CLARE, GEORGE. *Last Waltz in Vienna*. London: Macmillan, 1981.

CLARK, RONALD W. *Freud: The Man and the Cause*. London: Jonathan Cape and Weidenfeld & Nicolson, 1980.

CRAIN, WILLIAM C. *Theories of Development—Concepts and Applications*. Englewood Cliffs, N.J.: Prentice-Hall, 1982.

DAVIDSON, AUDREY, and JUDITH FAY. *Phantasy in Childhood*. London: Routledge & Kegan Paul, 1952.

DAVIS, MADELEINE, and DAVID WALLBRIDGE. *Boundary and Space: An Introduction to the Work of D. W. Winnicott*. London: Karnac, 1981.

DELEUZE, GILLES, and FÉLIX GUATTARI. *Anti-Oedipus*. New York: Viking Press, 1977.

DEUTSCH, HELENE. "Absence of Grief," *Psychoanalytic Quarterly* (1937) 6: 12–22.

———. *Confrontations with Myself*. New York: W. W. Norton, 1973.

———. *Psycho-Analysis of the Neuroses*. London: Hogarth Press, 1932.

———. "The Psychology of Women in Relation to the Functions of Reproduction," *International Journal of Psycho-Analysis* (1925) 6: 405–18.

———. "The Significance of Masochism in the Mental Life of Women," *International Journal of Psycho-Analysis* (1930) 11: 48–60.

DRELL, MARTIN J. "Hermine Hug-Hellmuth, A Pioneer in Child Analysis," *Bulletin of the Menninger Clinic* (1982) 42: 139–50.

DYER, RAYMOND. *Her Father's Daughter: The Work of Anna Freud*. New York: Jason Aronson, 1983.

EDER, DAVID. *Memoirs of a Modern Pioneer*, ed. J. B. Hobman. London: Victor Gollancz, 1945.

[EITINGON, MAX.] Obituary by Ernest Jones. *International Journal of Psycho-Analysis* (1943) 24: 190–92.

ELLIS, HAVELOCK. *Studies in the Psychology of Sex.* 4 vols. New York: Random House, 1936.

ELMHIRST, SUSANNA ISAACS. "Developmental Stages of Mother-Daughter Relationship with Particular Emphasis on the Tasks and Changes of Each Stage." Weekend Symposium on Mothers and Daughters, organized by University of California at San Diego, Extension Q. 014, June 10–12, 1977.

ERIKSON, ERIK H. *Identity, Youth and Crisis.* London: Faber & Faber, 1968.

FAIRBAIRN, W. R. D. "Endopsychic Structure Considered in Terms of Object-Relationships," *International Journal of Psycho-Analysis* (1944) 25: 70–93.

————. Obituary by J. D. Sutherland, *International Journal of Psycho-Analysis* (1965) 245–47.

————. *An Object Relations Theory of the Personality.* New York: Basic Books, 1954.

————. "On the Nature and Aims of Psycho-Analytical Treatment," *International Journal of Psycho-Analysis* (1958) 39: 374–85.

————. *Psychoanalytic Studies of the Personality.* London: Tavistock, 1952.

————. "Review of *Psychoanalytic Studies of the Personality,*" by D. W. Winnicott and M. Masud R. Khan, *International Journal of Psycho-Analysis* (1953) 34: 319–33.

FENICHEL, OTTO. "The Pregenital Antecedents of the Oedipus Complex," *International Journal of Psycho-Analysis* (1931) 12: 141–66.

————. "Problems of Psychoanalytic Technique," *Psychoanalytic Quarterly* (1939) 8: 57–87.

————. *The Psychoanalytic Theory of Neurosis.* New York: Norton, 1945.

————. "Review of *The Ego and the Mechanisms of Defence,*" *International Journal of Psycho-Analysis* (1938) 19: 116–36.

FERENCZI, SÁNDOR. *Final Contributions to the Problems and Methods of Psycho-Analysis.* London: Maresfield Reprints, 1955.

————. *First Contributions to Psycho-Analysis.* London: Maresfield Reprints, 1952.

————. *Further Contributions to the Theory of Psycho-Analysis.* London: Maresfield Reprints, 1980.

————. Obituary by Michael Balint, *International Journal of Psycho-Analysis* (1949) 30: 215–19.

————. Obituary by Ernest Jones, *International Journal of Psycho-Analysis* (1933) 14: 463–85.

FLIESS, ROBERT. *The Psycho-Analytic Reader.* London: Hogarth Press, 1950.

FORDHAM, FRIEDA. "Some Views of Individuation," *Journal of Analytic Psychology* (1969) 14: 1–12.

FOREST, IZETTE DE. "The Therapeutic Technique of Sándor Ferenczi," *International Journal of Psycho-Analysis* (1942) 23: 120–39.

FRANKL, LISELOTTE, and ILSE HELLMAN. "The Ego's Participation in the Therapeutic Alliance," *International Journal of Psycho-Analysis* (1962) 43: 333–37.

FREUD, ANNA. "Aggression in Relation to Emotional Development: Normal and Pathological" (1949), *Writings,* IV, 3–38.

————. "Discussion of Dr. John Bowlby's Paper," *Psychoanalytic Study of the Child* (1960) 15: 53–57.

————. *The Ego and the Mechanisms of Defence.* London: Hogarth Press, 1979.

————. *Einführung in die Psychoanalyse für Pädagogen.* Stuttgart und Leipzig: Hippokrates Verlag, 1930.

————. *Einführung in die Technik der Kinderanalyse.* Leipzig: Internationaler Psychoanalytischer Verlag, 1927.

———. *Introduction to Psycho-Analysis for Teachers.* Trans. Barbara Low. London: Allen & Unwin, 1931.

———. *Normality and Pathology in Childhood.* New York: Int. Univ. Press, 1965.

———. "Observations on Child Development," *Psychoanalytic Study of the Child* (1951) 6: 18–30.

———. "On the Theory of Analysis of Children," *International Journal of Psycho-Analysis* (1929) 10: 29–38.

———. *The Psycho-Analytical Treatment of Children.* London: Imago, 1946.

———. "The Relation of Beating-Phantasies to a Day-Dream," *International Journal of Psycho-Analysis* (1923) 3: 89–102.

———. *The Writings of Anna Freud.* 8 vols. New York: International Universities Press, 1964–81.

———. *Young Children in War Time: A Year's Work in a Residential Nursery.* London: Allen & Unwin, 1942.

———, and D. BURLINGHAM. *Infants Without Families.* New York: International Universities Press, 1944.

FREUD, SIGMUND. *The Freud Journal of Lou Andreas-Salomé.* London: Hogarth Press, 1965.

———. *The Freud/Jung Letters: The Correspondence Between Sigmund Freud and Carl Jung.* Ed. William McGuire. Trans. Ralph Manheim and R. F. C. Hull. Bollingen Series XCIV. Princeton, N.J.: Princeton University Press, 1974.

———. *Letters of Sigmund Freud, 1873–1939.* Ed. Ernst L. Freud. London: Hogarth Press, 1970.

———. *The Letters of Sigmund Freud and Arnold Zweig.* London: Hogarth Press, 1969.

———. *The Origins of Psychoanalysis: Letters to Wilhelm Fliess.* Eds. M. Bonaparte, A. Freud, and E. Kris. New York: Basic Books; London: Imago, 1954.

———. *A Psycho-Analytic Dialogue: The Letters of Sigmund Freud and Karl Abraham, 1907–1926.* Eds. Hilda C. Abraham and Ernst L. Freud. London: Hogarth Press, 1965.

———. *The Standard Edition of the Complete Psychological Works of Sigmund Freud.* Ed. James Strachey. 24 vols. London: Hogarth Press, 1953–1964.

GADDINI, EUGENIO. "La Controversia e l'eredità kleiniana" [Kleinian Controversy and Inheritance], Foreword to Hanna Segal, *Introdozione all'Opera de Melanie Klein.* Florence: Martinelli, 1968.

GAMMILL, JAMES. "Quelques souvenirs personnels sur Melanie Klein," paper presented at the conference *Melanie Klein aujourd'hui* by Société Psychanalytique de Paris, Nov. 27, 1982.

GELEERD, ELISABETH R. "Evaluation of Melanie Klein's 'Narrative of a Child Analysis,' " *International Journal of Psycho-Analysis* (1963) 44: 493–506.

GILLESPIE, WILLIAM. "Revieiw of Hanna Segal's *Klein,*" *International Journal of Psycho-Analysis* (1980) 61: 85–88.

GITELSON, MAXWELL. "Re-evaluation of the Rôle of the Oedipus Complex," *International Journal of Psycho-Analysis* (1952) 33: 351–54.

GLOVER, EDWARD. "An Examination of the Klein System of Child Psychology," *Psychoanalytic Study of the Child* (1945) 1: 75–117.

———. *An Investigation of the Technique of Psycho-Analysis.* London: Bailliere, Tindall & Cox, 1940.

———. "Medical Psychology or Academic (Normal) Psychology," *British Journal of Medical Psychology* (1934) 14.

———. *On the Early Development of Mind.* London: Imago, 1956.

———. "The Position of Psycho-Analysis in Great Britain," *British Medical Journal* (1949) 6, No. 1–2: 27–31.

———. "Review of *The Psycho-Analysis of Children*," *International Journal of Psycho-Analysis* (1933) 14: 119–29.

———. "The Therapeutic Effect of Inexact Interpretation," *International Journal of Psycho-Analysis* (1931) 12: 397–411.

———. *War, Sadism and Pacifism: Further Studies on Group Psychology and War.* London: George Allen & Unwin, 1933.

GRAF, MAX. "Reminiscences of Professor Sigmund Freud," *Psychoanalytic Quarterly* (1942) 11: 465–76.

GREENACRE, P. (ed.). *Affective Disorders.* New York: International Universities Press, 1965.

GREENBERG, JAY R., and STEPHEN A. MITCHELL. *Object Relations in Psychoanalytic Theory.* Cambridge, Mass.: Harvard University Press, 1983.

GREENSON, RALPH R. "The Origin and Fate of New Ideas in Psychoanalysis," *International Journal of Psycho-Analysis* (1969) 50: 503–15.

———. "Transference: Freud or Klein," *International Journal of Psycho-Analysis* (1974) 55: 37–48.

GROLNICK, SIMON A., and LEONARD BARKIN (eds.). *Between Reality and Fantasy.* New York and London: Jason Aronson, 1978.

GROTSTEIN, JAMES S. (ed.). *Dare I Disturb the Universe? A Memorial to Wilfred Bion.* London: Maresfield Reprints, 1983.

GUEST, BARBARA. *Herself Defined: The Poet H.D. and Her World.* Garden City, N.Y.: Doubleday, 1984.

GUNTRIP, H. "The Manic-Depressive Problem in the Light of the Schizoid Process," *International Journal of Psycho-Analysis* (1962), 43: 98–112.

———. *Personality Structure and Human Interaction.* London: Hogarth Press, 1977.

———. "A Psychodynamic Theory and the Problem of Psychotherapy," *British Journal of Medical Psychology* (1963) 36: 161–72.

HALE, NATHAN G., JR. *James Jackson Putnam.* Cambridge, Mass.: Harvard University Press, 1971.

HAMILTON, VICTORIA. *Narcissus and Oedipus.* London: Routledge & Kegan Paul, 1982.

HARTMANN, HEINZ. "Psychoanalysis and Developmental Psychology," *Psychoanalytic Study of the Child* (1950) 5: 7–17.

HEIMANN, PAULA. "Bemerkungen zur Sublimierung," *Psyche* (1959) 13: 397–414.

———. "Certain Functions of Introjection and Projection in Early Infancy," in S. Isaacs, M. Klein, and J. Riviere, *Developments in Psycho-Analysis.* London: Hogarth Press, 1952, pp. 122–68.

———. "A Contribution to the Problem of Sublimation and Its Relation to Processes of Internalization," *International Journal of Psycho-Analysis* (1942) 22: 8–17.

———. "Dynamics of Transference Interpretations," *International Journal of Psycho-Analysis* (1956) 37: 303–10.

———. "On Counter-Transference," *International Journal of Psycho-Analysis* (1950) 31: 81–84.

———. "Problems of the Training Analysis," *International Journal of Psycho-Analysis*" (1954) 35: 163–68.

HOFFER, WILLI. "Review of Contributions to Psycho-Analysis, 1921–45," British Medical Journal (1949) 6, p. 109.

HOLROYD, MICHAEL. Lytton Strachey. London: Heinemann. I: The Unknown Years, 1967. II: The Years of Achievement, 1968.

HORNEY, KAREN. "The Denial of the Vagina," International Journal of Psycho-Analysis (1933) 14: 57–70.

———. "On the Genesis of the Castration Complex in Women," International Journal of Psycho-Analysis (1924) 5: 50–65.

HUG-HELLMUTH, H. "Bibliography," International Journal of Psycho-Analysis (1920) 1: 316–18.

ISAACS, SUSAN. "Criteria for Interpretation," International Journal of Psycho-Analysis (1939) 20: 148–60.

——— (ed.). Fatherless Children. London: Pouskin, 1945.

———. "The Nature and Function of Phantasy," International Journal of Psycho-Analysis (1948) 29: 73–97.

———. "Temper Tantrums in Early Childhood in Their Relation to Internal Objects," International Journal of Psycho-Analysis (1940) 21: 280–93.

JACOBSON, EDITH. "Contribution to the Metapsychology of Psychotic Identifications," Journal of the American Psychoanalytic Association (1954) 2: 239–62.

———. "Metapsychological Differences between the Manic-Depressive and Schizophrenic Processes of Identification," Annual Survey of Psycho-Analysis (1953) 4: 91–93.

———. "On Psychotic Identifications," International Journal of Psycho-Analysis (1954) 35: 102–7.

———. The Self and the Object World. New York: International Universities Press, 1964.

JAMES, MARTIN. "Infantile Narcissistic Trauma: Observations on Winnicott's Work in Infant Care and Child Development," International Journal of Psycho-Analysis (1962) 43: 69–78.

JAQUES, ELLIOTT. The Changing Culture of a Factory. London: Routledge & Kegan Paul, 1951.

———. "Death and the Mid-Life Crisis," International Journal of Psycho-Analysis (1965) 46, Part 4: 502–14.

———. "Review of Hanna Segal's Klein," International Journal of Psycho-Analysis (1980) 61: 88, 89.

———. Work, Creativity and Social Justice. London: Heinemann, 1970.

JOFFE, WALTER G. "A Critical Review of the Status of the Envy Concept," International Journal of Psycho-Analysis (1969) 50: 533–44.

JONES, ERNEST. Free Associations. London: Hogarth Press, 1959.

———. "The Future of Psycho-Analysis," International Journal of Psycho-Analysis (1936) 17: 269–77.

———. Hamlet and Oedipus. New York: Norton, 1976.

———. The Life and Work of Sigmund Freud. 3 vols. New York: Basic Books, 1957.

———. "The Oedipus Complex as an Explanation of Hamlet's Mystery: A Study in Motive," American Journal of Psychology Analysis (Jan. 1910) 21: 72–113.

———. "The Origin and Structure of the Super-Ego," International Journal of Psycho-Analysis (1926) 7: 303–11.

———. Papers on Psycho-Analysis. London: Maresfield Reprints, 5th ed., 1948.

———. "The Pathology of Early Anxiety," Journal of Abnormal Psychology (1911) 6.

―――. "Review of *The Ego and the Mechanisms of Defence*," *International Journal of Psycho-Analysis* (1938) 19: 115–16.

JOSEPH, BETTY. "On Understanding and Not Understanding: Some Technical Issues," *International Journal of Psycho-Analysis* (1983) 64: 291–98.

JULIEN, ROBERT M. *A Primer of Drug Action.* 3d ed. San Francisco: W. H. Freeman, 1981.

JUNG, C. G. *Symbols of Transformation.* Princeton, N.J.: Princeton University Press, 1967.

KANNER, LEO. "Autistic Disturbances of Affective Contact," *The Nervous Child* (1943) 2: 217–50.

KENDRICK, WALTER, and PERRY MEISEL (eds.). *Freud/Bloomsbury: The Letters of James and Alix Strachey, 1924–1925.* New York: Basic Books, 1985.

KERNBERG, OTTO F. "A Contribution to the Ego-Psychological Critique of the Kleinian School," *International Journal of Psycho-Analysis* (1969) 50: 317–33.

―――. "Critique of the Kleinian School," in Peter L. Giovacchini (ed.), *Tactics and Techniques in Psychoanalytic Therapy.* New York: Science House; London: Hogarth Press, 1972.

―――. *Internal World and External Reality.* New York and London: Jason Aronson, 1980.

―――. "Structural Derivatives of Object Relationships," *International Journal of Psycho-Analysis* (1966) 47: 236–60.

KING, P. H. M. "The Contributions of Ernest Jones to the British Psycho-Analytical Society," *International Journal of Psycho-Analysis* (1979) 60: 280–84.

―――. "The Education of a Psycho-Analyst: The British Experience," *Bulletin of the British Psycho-Analytical Society* (Feb. 1981) 2: 93–107.

―――. "Identity-Crisis: Splits or Compromises, Adaptive or Maladaptive," in Edward D. Joseph and Daniel Widlocher (eds.), *The Identity of the Psychoanalyst.* New York: International Universities Press, 1980.

―――. "The Life and Work of Melanie Klein in the British Psycho-Analytical Society," *International Journal of Psycho-Analysis* (1983) 64: 251–60.

KLOETZEL, CHESKEL ZWI. *Moses Pipenbrinks Abenteuer.* Berlin: Welt-Verlag, 1920.

KRIS, E. "Review of *The Ego and the Mechanisms of Defence*," *International Journal of Psycho-Analysis* (1938) 19: 136–46.

KÜBLER-ROSS, E. *On Death and Dying.* New York: Macmillan, 1969.

LACAN, JACQUES. *Écrits.* London: Tavistock, 1977.

LAING, R. D. *The Divided Self: A Study of Sanity and Madness.* London: Tavistock, 1960.

―――. *Self and Others.* London: Tavistock, 1962.

LANGS, R. (ed.). *Classics in Psychoanalytic Technique.* New York: Jason Aronson, 1981.

LIEBERMAN, E. JAMES. *Acts of Will: The Life and Work of Otto Rank.* New York: The Free Press, 1985.

LINDON, JOHN A. "Melanie Klein's Theory and Technique: Her Life and Work," in Peter L. Giovacchini (ed.), *Tactics and Techniques in Psychoanalytic Therapy.* New York: Science House; London: Hogarth Press, 1972.

LITTLE, MARGARET. "Counter-Transference and the Patient's Response to It," *International Journal of Psycho-Analysis* (1951) 32: 32–40.

―――. "R—The Analyst's Total Response to His Patient's Needs," *International Journal of Psycho-Analysis* (1957) 38: 240–54.

————. *Transference Neurosis and Transference Psychosis.* New York: Jason Aronson, 1981.

LORENZ, KONRAD. *On Aggression.* London: Methuen, 1966.

LOW, BARBARA. *Psycho-Analysis: A Brief Account of the Freudian Theory.* London: Allen & Unwin, 1920.

LOWENFELD, MARGARET. *The World Technique.* London: Institute of Child Psychology Press, 1977.

LYTH. *See* Menzies.

MCDOUGALL, JOYCE, and SERGE LEBOVICI. *Dialogue with Sammy.* London: Hogarth Press, 1969.

MACGIBBON, JEAN (Jean Howard). "Why Are They Angry?," *The Spectator,* Aug. 30, 1957, 284.

MACKAY, NIGEL. "Melanie Klein's Metapsychology: Phenomenological and Mechanistic Perspective," *International Journal of Psycho-Analysis* (1981) 62: 187–98.

MAHLER, MARGARET. "On Child Psychosis and Schizophrenia, Autistic and Symbiotic Psychoses," *Psychoanalytic Study of the Child* (1952) 7: 286–305.

MATTE-BLANCO, I. "On Introjection and the Processes of Psychic Metabolism," *International Journal of Psycho-Analysis* (1941) 22: 17–36.

MEAD, MARGARET. "Changing Patterns of Parent-Child Relations in an Urban Culture," *International Journal of Psycho-Analysis* (1957) 38: 369–87.

MELTZER, DONALD. "Adhesive Identification," *Contemporary Psychoanalysis* (1975) 11: 289–310.

————. *The Kleinian Development: Part II, Richard Week-by-Week.* Perthshire: Clunie Press, 1978.

————. "The Kleinian Expansion of Freud's Metapsychology," *International Journal of Psycho-Analysis* (1981) 62: 177–85.

————. *The Psycho-Analytic Process.* London: Heinemann, 1967.

————. *Sexual States of Mind.* Perthshire: Clunie Press, 1973.

MENAKER, ESTHER. *Otto Rank: A Rediscovered Legacy.* New York: Columbia University Press, 1982.

MENDELSON, MYER. *Psychoanalytic Concepts of Depression.* Springfield, Ill.: Charles C. Thomas, 1960.

MENNINGER, KARL. "Characterologic and Symptomatic Expressions Related to the Anal Phase of Psychosexual Development," *Psychoanalytic Quarterly* (1943) 12: 161–93.

MENZIES (LYTH), ISABEL E. P. *The Functioning of Social Systems as a Defence Against Anxiety.* London: Tavistock, Pamphlet No. 3, 1970.

————. *Staff Support Systems: Task and Anti-Task in Adolescent Institutions in Therapeutic Communities.* Ed. Hinshelwood and Mannig. London: Routledge & Kegan Paul, 1979.

————. "Thoughts on the Maternal Role in Contemporary Society," *Journal of Child Psychotherapy* (1975), Vol. 4, No. 1.

MIDDLEMORE, M. *The Nursing Couple.* London: Hamish Hamilton, 1941.

MILLER, JONATHAN. *States of Mind.* New York: Methuen, 1983.

MILNER, MARION, "Aspects of Symbolism in Comprehension of the Not-Self," *International Journal of Psycho-Analysis* (1952) 33, Part 2, 181–95.

————. *The Hands of the Living God: An Account of a Psycho-Analytical Treatment.* London: Hogarth Press; New York: International Universities Press, 1969.

———— (Joanna Field). *A Life of One's Own.* London: Pelican, 1952.

————— (Joanna Field). *On Not Being Able to Paint.* New York: International Universities Press, 1957.

MITCHELL, JULIET. *Psychoanalysis and Feminism.* New York: Vintage Books, 1975.

MONEY-KYRLE, R. E. "Melanie Klein and Kleinian Psychoanalytic Theory," *American Handbook of Psychiatry* 3: 225–38.

—————. "Normal Counter-Transference and Some of Its Deviations," *International Journal of Psycho-Analysis* (1956) 37: 360–66.

—————. "Psycho-Analysis and Ethics," in *New Directions in Psycho-Analysis.* London: Tavistock, 1955, 421–39.

—————. *Psychoanalysis and Politics.* London: Duckworth, 1951.

NACHT, S., and P. C. RACAMIER, "Symposium on 'Depressive Illness,'" *International Journal of Psycho-Analysis* (1960) 41: 481–503.

NUNBERG, H. "The Sense of Guilt and the Need for Punishment," *International Journal of Psycho-Analysis* (1926) 7: 420–33.

OGDEN, THOMAS J. "On Projective Identification," *International Journal of Psycho-Analysis* (1979) 60: 357–73.

O'SHAUGHNESSY, E. "A Clinical Study of a Defensive Organization," *International Journal of Psycho-Analysis* (1981) 62: 359–69.

PADEL, JOHN. "No Man's Formula," *Bulletin of the European Psycho-Analytic Federation,* No. 8 (1976), 10–13.

—————. "Positions, Stages, Attitudes, or Modes of Being?," *Bulletin of the European Psycho-Analytic Federation,* No. 12 (1978), 26–31.

—————. "The Uses of Identification," *The Listener,* 17 Nov. 1977, 648–49.

PASKAUSKAS, A. A. "C. K. Clarke and Ernest Jones: The Rise and Fall of a Kraepelin Clinic in Toronto, 1907–1909," unpublished paper presented at Canadian Society for the History of Medicine Annual Conference, University of British Columbia, June 8, 1983.

PETERS, UWE HENRIK. *Anna Freud: A Life Dedicated to Children.* London: Weidenfeld & Nicolson, 1985.

PETOT, JEAN MICHEL. *Mélanie Klein—premières découvertes et premier système, 1919–1932.* Paris: Dunod, 1979.

—————. *Mélanie Klein—le moi et le bon object, 1932–1960.* Paris: Dunod, 1982.

PHILLIPS, J. L., and R. D. WYNNE. *Cocaine: The Mystique and the Reality.* New York: Avon Books, 1980.

PLACZEK, BEVERLEY R. (ed.). *Record of a Friendship: The Correspondence of Wilhelm Reich and A. S. Neill, 1936–1957.* New York: Farrar, Straus, Giroux, 1981.

PONTALIS, J. B. *The Limits of Psychoanalysis.* London: Hogarth Press, 1980.

RANK, OTTO. "Literary Autobiography" (1930), *Journal of the Otto Rank Association* (1981) 16: 3–38.

REED, HENRY. "Richard," *The Listener,* 9 March 1961, 445–46.

REIK, THEODOR. *The Compulsion to Confess and the Need for Punishment.* Leipzig: Internationaler Psychoanalytischer Verlag, 1925.

—————. *Masochism in Modern Man.* New York: Farrar, Straus, 1941.

REISENBERG-MALCOLM, RUTH. "Melanie Klein: Achievements and Problems (Reflections on Klein's Concept of Object Relationship)," *Bulletin of the British Psycho-Analytical Society* (1980), No. 8: 15–26.

RICKMAN, JOHN. "Reflections on the Function and Organization of a Psycho-Analytical Society," *International Journal of Psycho-Analysis* (1951) 32: 218–37.

————. *Selected Contributions to Psycho-Analysis.* London: Hogarth Press, 1957.

RIVIERE, JOAN. "The Bereaved Wife," in S. Isaacs (ed.), *Fatherless Children.* London: Pouskin, 1945.

————. "A Character Trait of Freud's," in Hendrick M. Ruitenbeek (ed.), *Freud as We Knew Him.* Detroit: Wayne State University Press, 1973.

————. "A Contribution to the Analysis of the Negative Therapeutic Reactions," *International Journal of Psycho-Analysis* (1936) 17: 304–20.

————. "General Introduction," in J. Riviere (ed.), *Developments in Psycho-Analysis.* London: Hogarth Press, 1952.

————. "Hate, Greed and Aggression," in M. Klein and J. Riviere (eds.), *Love, Hate, and Reparation.* London: Hogarth Press, 1937.

————. "Jealousy as a Mechanism of Defence," *International Journal of Psycho-Analysis* (1932) 13: 414–24.

————. Obituary by James Strachey. *International Journal of Psycho-Analysis* (1963) 44: 228–35.

————. "On the Genesis of Psychical Conflict in Earliest Infancy," *International Journal of Psycho-Analysis* (1936) 17: 395–422.

————. "Womanliness as a Masquerade," *International Journal of Psycho-Analysis* (1929) 10: 303–13.

ROAZEN, PAUL. *Freud and His Followers.* New York: Knopf, 1975.

ROSENFELD, HERBERT. "An Investigation into the Psycho-Analytic Theory of Depression," *International Journal of Psycho-Analysis* (1959) 40: 105–29.

————. "Notes on the Psycho-Analysis of the Superego Conflict in an Acute Catatonic Patient," *International Journal of Psycho-Analysis* (1952) 33: 111–31.

————. *Psychotic States: A Psycho-Analytic Approach.* London: Hogarth Press, 1950.

————. "Review of *Envy and Gratitude*," *International Journal of Psycho-Analysis* (1959) 40: 64–66.

————. "Transference-phenomena and transference-analysis in an acute catatonic schizophrenic patient," *International Journal of Psycho-Analysis* (1952) 33: 457–64.

ROSOLATO, GUY, et DANIEL WIDLOCHER. *Karl Abraham: Lecture de son oeuvre.* Paris: Presses Universitaires de France, 1958.

ROUSTANG, FRANÇOIS. *Dire Mastery: Discipleship from Freud to Lacan.* Baltimore and London: Johns Hopkins University Press, 1982.

RUITENBEEK, HENDRIK M. (ed.). *Freud as We Knew Him.* Detroit: Wayne State University Press, 1973.

RUSTIN, MICHAEL. "A Socialist Consideration of Kleinian Psychoanalysis," *New Left Review* (Jan. 1982), 69–83.

RYCROFT, CHARLES. *Anxiety and Neurosis.* London: Allen Lane, 1968.

————. *A Critical Dictionary of Psychoanalysis.* London: Penguin, 1979.

————. "Freud and His Heirs," *The Listener,* 27 Oct. 1977, 522–24.

SANDLER, JOSEPH, CHRISTOPHER DARE, and ALEX HOLDER. *The Patient and the Analyst.* London: Maresfield Reprints, 1973.

SCHAFER, ROY. *A New Language for Psychoanalysis.* New Haven and London: Yale University Press, 1976.

SCHMIDEBERG, MELITTA. "After the Analysis . . . ," *Psychoanalytic Quarterly* (1938) 7: 122–42.

————. "Bad Habits in Childhood: Their Importance in Development," *International Journal of Psycho-Analysis* (1935) 16: 455–61.

————. "A Contribution to the History of the Psycho-Analytical Movement in Britain," *British Journal of Psychiatry* (1971) 118: 61–68.

————. "A Contribution to the Psychology of Persecutory Ideas and Delusions," *International Journal of Psycho-Analysis* (1931) 12: 331–67.

————. "A Note on Suicide," *International Journal of Psycho-Analysis* (1936) 17: 1–5.

————. "The Play-Analysis of a Three-Year-Old Girl," *International Journal of Psycho-Analysis* (1934) 15: 245–64.

————. "The Psycho-Analysis of Asocial Children," *International Journal of Psycho-Analysis* (1935) 16: 22–48.

————. "Psychotherapy with Failures of Psycho-Analysis," *British Journal of Psychiatry* (1970) 116: 195–200.

————. "Reassurance as a Means of Analytic Technique," *International Journal of Psycho-Analysis* (1935) 16: 307–24.

————. "Some Unconscious Mechanisms in Pathological Sexuality and Their Relation to Normal Sexual Activity," *International Journal of Psycho-Analysis* (1933) 14: 225–60.

SCOTT, W. CLIFFORD M. "The 'Body Scheme' in Psycho-therapy," *British Journal of Medical Psychology* (1949) 22: 139–50.

————. "Depression, Confusion and Multivalence," *International Journal of Psycho-Analysis* (1960) 41: 497–503.

————. "On the Intense Affects Encountered in Treating a Severe Manic-Depressive Disorder," *International Journal of Psycho-Analysis* (1947) 28: 139–45.

SEGAL, HANNA. *Introduction to the Work of Melanie Klein.* London: Hogarth Press, 1978.

————. *Klein.* London: Fontana, 1979.

————. "Melanie Klein As I Have Known Her," Celebration of the Centenary of Melanie Klein's Birth, Tavistock Clinic, July 17, 1982.

————. *The Work of Hanna Segal.* New York and London: Jason Aronson, 1981.

————, and DONALD MELTZER. "Narrative of a Child Analysis," *International Journal of Psycho-Analysis* (1963) 44: 507–13.

SHARPE, ELLA FREEMAN. *Collected Papers on Psycho-Analysis.* London: Hogarth Press, 1950.

SIMMEL, ERNST. "Self-Preservation and the Death Instinct," *Psychoanalytic Quarterly* (1944) 13: 160–75.

SMIRNOFF, VICTOR. *The Scope of Child Analysis.* London: Routledge & Kegan Paul, 1971.

SOUZA, DECIO SOARES DE. "Novisi desenvolvimentos da psicanálise, segundo a escola inglesa" [New Developments in Psychoanalysis, Following the English School], *Arque bras Neurol Psiquat,* 1955, 1 (1). Preface to *New Directions in Psycho-Analysis.* Rio de Janeiro: Zahar Editores, 1968.

SPILLIUS, ELIZABETH BOTT. "Some Developments from the Work of Melanie Klein," *International Journal of Psycho-Analysis* (1983), Part 3, 64: 321–32.

STERBA, RICHARD F. "Oral Invasion and Self-Defence," *International Journal of Psycho-Analysis* (1957) 38: 204–8.

STOKES, ADRIAN. *Greek Culture and the Ego.* London: Tavistock, 1958.

STRACHEY, ALIX. "A Note on the Use of the Word 'Internal,' " *International Journal of Psycho-Analysis* (1941) 22: 37–43.

————. *The Unconscious Motives of War.* London: George Allen & Unwin, 1957.

STRACHEY, JAMES. "The Nature of the Therapeutic Action of Psycho-Analysis," *International Journal of Psycho-Analysis* (1934) 15: 127–59.

————. Obituary by D. W. Winnicott, *International Journal of Psycho-Analysis* (1963) 44: 228–35.

————. "Some Unconscious Factors in Reading," *International Journal of Psycho-Analysis* (1930) 11: 322–31.

SULLOWAY, FRANK J. *Freud: Biologist of the Mind.* New York: Basic Books, 1979.

SUTHERLAND, JOHN D. "The British Object Relations Theorists: Balint, Winnicott, Fairbairn, Guntrip," *Journal of the American Psychoanalytic Association* (1980) 28: 829–60.

————. "Object-Relations Theory and the Conceptual Model of Psycho-Analysis," *British Journal of Medical Psychology* (1963) 36: 109–20.

————. *Psycho-analysis and Contemporary Thought.* London: Hogarth Press, 1958.

TAFT, JULIAN. *Otto Rank.* New York: The Julian Press, 1958.

TANSLEY, A. G. *The New Psychology and Its Relation to Life.* London: Allen & Unwin, 1921.

TAUSK, VICTOR. "On the Origin of the 'Influencing Machine' in Schizophrenia" (1919), in Robert Fliess (ed.), *The Psycho-Analytic Reader* (London: Hogarth Press, 1950), pp. 31–64.

THOMAS, HUGH. *John Strachey.* London: Eyre Methuen, 1973.

THOMPSON, CLARA. "The Therapeutic Technique of Sándor Ferenczi: A Comment," *International Journal of Psycho-Analysis* (1943) 24: 64–66.

TOROK, MARIA. "The Significance of Penis Envy in Women," in J. Chassequet-Smirgel (ed.), *Female Sexuality* (Ann Arbor: University of Michigan Press, 1984), pp. 135–70.

TURKLE, SHERRY. *Psychoanalytic Politics.* New York: Basic Books, 1978.

TUSTIN, FRANCES. *Autism and Childhood Psychosis.* London: Hogarth Press, 1972.

————. *Autistic States in Children.* London and Boston: Routledge & Kegan Paul, 1981.

WAELDER, ROBERT. *Basic Theory of Psychoanalysis.* New York: Schocken Books, 1970.

————. "The Problem of the Genesis of Psychical Conflict in Earliest Infancy," *International Journal of Psycho-Analysis* (1937) 18: 406–73.

WEININGER, O. *The Clinical Psychology of Melanie Klein.* Springfield, Ill.: Charles C. Thomas, 1984.

WILLIAMS, A. HYATT. "A Psycho-Analytic Approach to the Treatment of the Murderer," *International Journal of Psycho-Analysis* (1960) 41: 532–39.

WINNICOTT, D. W. *The Maturational Processes and the Facilitating Environment.* London: Hogarth Press, 1965.

————. "On Envy," Case Conference, Tavistock, 1957, pp. 177, 178.

————. *Playing and Reality.* London: Penguin, 1980.

————. *Therapeutic Consultations in Child Psychiatry.* London: Hogarth Press, 1971.

————. *Through Paediatrics to Psycho-Analysis.* London: Hogarth Press, 1978.

WISDOM, J. O. "Comparison and Development of the Psycho-Analytical Theories of Melancholia," *International Journal of Psycho-Analysis* (1962) 43: 113–32.

————. "Fairbairn's Contribution on Object Relationship Splitting and Ego Structure," *British Journal of Medical Psychology* (1963) 36: 145–60.

————. "Freudian Offspring," *Time & Tide*, 2 March 1961, 330.

WITTENBERG, J. S. *Psychoanalytic Insight and Relationships: A Kleinian Approach.* London: Routledge & Kegan Paul, 1970.

WOLLHEIM, RICHARD. "A Critic of Our Time," *Encounter*, April 1959, 41–44.

———. *The Thread of Life*. Cambridge, Mass.: Harvard University Press, 1984.

WOLPE, JOSEPH, and STANLEY ROACHMAN. "Psychoanalytic 'Evidence': A Critique Based on Freud's Case of Little Hans," *Journal of Nervous and Mental Disease* (1960) 131: 135–48.

WOOLF, VIRGINIA. *The Diary of Virginia Woolf*. Ed. Anne Olivier Bell. London: Hogarth Press. I: 1915–1919, 1977. V: 1936–41, 1984.

WORTIS, JOSEPH. *Fragments of an Analysis with Freud*. New York: McGraw-Hill, 1954.

YORKE, CLIFFORD. "Some Suggestions for a Critique of Kleinian Psychology," in *Psychoanalytic Study of the Child*. New York: Quadrangle Books, 1971.

ZETZEL, ELIZABETH R. "An Approach to the Relation between Concept and Content in Psychoanalytic Theory (with special reference to the work of Melanie Klein and her followers)," *Psychoanalytic Study of the Child* (1956) 11: 99–121.

———. "Current Concepts of Transference," *International Journal of Psycho-Analysis* (1956) 37: 369–76.

———. "Ernest Jones: His Contribution to Psycho-Analytic Theory," *International Journal of Psycho-Analysis* (1958) 39: 311–18.

ZILBOORG, GREGORY. "Review of *Introduction to Psycho-Analysis for Teachers*," (1933) 2: 152–54.

Acknowledgments

A biography of this scope is dependent for help from a wide variety of sources. The research and writing were made possible by generous fellowships from the Laidlaw Foundation, the Rockefeller Foundation, and the John Simon Guggenheim Foundation. I also wish to express my appreciation to Mrs. Carol Gillen and her staff at the Office of Research Administration, and to Mrs. Mary Ann Hummel of the Department of English, as well as to my chairman, Professor Denton Fox, all of the University of Toronto.

Eric Clyne, the Melanie Klein Trust, and the Wellcome Institute for the History of Medicine have kindly allowed me to quote from the unpublished correspondence of Melanie Klein. I thank Mervyn Jones and the British Society of Psycho-Analysis for permission to quote from the Jones Archives. Enid Balint has allowed me to quote from Ferenczi's correspondence, of which Dr. Judith Dupont has generously sent me relevant passages. Sigmund Freud Copyrights Ltd. have given me permission to quote from the Jones-Freud correspondence. The late Clare Winnicott gave me permission to quote from the letters of her husband, D. W. Winnicott, which were kindly put at my disposal by the New York Hospital–Cornell Medical Center and by Madeleine Davis and the Winnicott Publications Committee.

Dr. W. Clifford M. Scott generously gave me access to his voluminous files, now in the National Archives of Canada. I am also indebted for help of various kinds to the British Library; Embassy of the Hungarian People's Republic, Ottawa; Farrar Library, Clarke Institute of Psychiatry, University of Toronto; Israelitesche Kultusgemunde Wien; the Archives of the *Jerusalem Post*; the Jewish National and University Library, Jerusalem; the Library of Congress; The Abraham A. Brill Library, The New York Psychoanalytic Institute; Oral History Research Office, Butler Library, Columbia University; the Osborne Children's Library, Toronto; "Shalavata" Mental Health Center, Tel Aviv University Medical School; and Stadtbezirksgericht Berlin.

Kate Hamilton and Jane Widdicombe did noble work in the final word-processing and typing. My editors, Robert Gottlieb, Lee Goerner, and Melvin Rosenthal in New York, and Sarah Russell in England, know how much I needed them. The copy-editor, Mary Jane Alexander, did a superlative job. My Canadian and British publishers, Jack McClelland and Ion Trewin, have been stalwart friends. And I had the good fortune to obtain the services of Douglas Matthews, Librarian of the London Library, as compiler of the excellent and comprehensive index.

There is a long list of individuals who have helped me in innumerable ways. Some of them have died in the five years in which I have been engaged in learning about Melanie Klein, but their names are listed here because I shall never forget the privilege of having known them: Grant Allan; Frank Allen; Margaret Vanderhaar Allen; Leon Altman; Natalie Altman; A. Alvarez; Noël Annan; Charlotte Balkanyi; Esther Bick; Francesca Bion; Christopher Bollas; Sophie Bookhalter; J. B. Boulanger; John Bowlby; H. Braham (Schwarz); Eric Brenman; Diana (Clyne) Brimblecombe; Harold Bridger; Marjorie Brierley; Helen Brook; Paul D. Byers; Eric T. Carlsen; J. E. Chamberlin; Hazel (Clyne) Charlwood; Hanna Clampitt; Ronald Clark; Judy Clyne; Lesley Clyne; Michael Clyne; Kathleen Cutler; Madeleine Davis; René Diatkine; Marianne Horney Eckhardt; Susanna Isaacs Elmhirst; Nini Ettlinger; Judith Fay; Maria Fazekas; Trude Feigel; Michael Fordham; Anna Freud; Susan Friedman; James Gammill; Peter Gay; Ernest Gellner; Ellen Gilbert; Beryl Gilbertson; W. H. Gillespie; Dame Annis Gillie; Sander Gilman; M. Glasser; Vroni Gordon; Angela Graf-Nold; Sanford Gifford; J. Groen-Prakken; James Grotstein; Ilse Grubrich-Simitis; Béla Grunberger; Fru Lind af Hageby; Lesley Hall; Stuart Hampshire; Charles Hanly; Martha G. Harris; Eva Harte; Negley Harte; T. T. S. Hayley; Ilse Hellman; H. P. Hildebrand; Michael Holroyd; Marie Jahoda; Martin James; Elliott Jaques; Mervyn Jones; Betty Joseph; Harry Karnac; Cynthia Kee; Otto Kernberg; Judith Kestenberg; Masud Khan; Pearl H. M. King; Martin Kinston; Nick Laidlaw; Peter Lambda; Jeanne Lampl de Groot; W. R. Layland; Serge Lebovici; Stanley Leigh; Ernest Le Pore; L. E. Levine; Paul Levy; E. James Lieberman; Adam Limentani; Margaret Little; Rhoda Lorand; Sándor Lorand; Isabel E. P. Menzies Lyth; Jack McClelland; Joyce McDougall; James MacGibbon; Jean MacGibbon; Veronica Mächtlinger; Bob McMullan; Margaret Mahler; T. F. Main; Andrew Malleson; Margaret Maloney; Steven Marcus; J. Moussaieff Masson; Ronald Mavor; Donald Meltzer; Karl Menninger; Marion Milner; Ann Mully; Humberto Nagera; Oscar Nemon; Edna O'Shaughnessy; John Padel; Allan Parkin; Mertza Peatie; Hertha Pick; Irma Brenman Pick; W. F. Pick; Dinora Pines; Vivien Rackoff; Ruth Reisenberg-Malcolm; George Rink; Diana Riviere; Paul Roazen; Paul Robinson; Norman Rosenblood; Herbert Rosenfeld; Saul Rosenzweig; Charles Rycroft; William St. Clair; Beryl Sandford; J. J. Sandler; Janice de Saussure; Perdita Schaffner; Ann Scott; W. C. M. Scott; Hanna Segal; Paul Segal; Susan Shatto; R. D. Shepherd; David Slight; Victor Smirnoff; David Sorensen; Elizabeth Bott Spillius; Riccardo Steiner; Brenda Sutherland; John D. Sutherland; H. A. Thorner; Margret Tonnesmann; Feliks Topolski; Eric Trist; Rosalyn Tureck; Frances Tustin; Alan Tyson; Thomas Vágó; P. J. Van der Leuw; Michael Wagner; Kay Walsh; C. H. A. Wedeles; Elinor H. Wedeles; Maurice White; Katherine Whitehorn; A. Hyatt Williams; Clare Winnicott; J. O. Wisdom; Richard Wollheim; Fanny Wride; Helena Wright; Clifford Yorke. Finally I wish "Dick," "Richard," and other anonymous analysands to know how greatly I have appreciated the confidence they have placed in me.

Index

Abbazia, 49–52, 54, 68, 84, 259
Abercrombie, George, 409
Abraham, Hilda (KA's daughter), 241
Abraham, Karl, 4, 71, 93–4, 115; MK cites, 73; and 1920 Hague conference, 92–3; and Freud, 93, 95, 105, 118–19; on control analysts, 94; and Berlin Society, 94–5; and MK's analysis of sons, 96, 98; on MK and infantile sexuality, 105; on depression, 106–7; MK on work of, 109; analyzes MK, 109, 113n, 114–15, 119, 178, 435; death, 109, 140, 148, 163, 216; praised as analyst, 114; and Glover, 114, 197; encourages and influences MK, 117–18, 125n, 140, 161, 196; and prophylactic analysis, 121; analyzes Alix Strachey, 123, 133, 139; conducts Berlin Society meetings, 123–4; illness, 136, 138–40, 148; on guilt, 175; and Oedipus complex, 178; on suicide, 218; on mourning, 251, 253; Melitta challenges views on introjection, 284–5; and introjection, 332; withholds interpretations from students, 372; MK's differences with, 394–5; on orality and food, 403; analysis of Wollfheim, 457 WORKS: "Contributions to the Theory of the Anal Character," 98; "Development of the Libido," 394; "Influence of Oral Eroticism on Character Formation," 115n; "Manifestations of the Female Castration Complex," 122, 176; "Notes on the Psychoanalytic Investigation and Treatment of Manic-Depressive Insanity," 106; "A Short Study of the Development of the Libido," 103, 105, 107, 115n, 117, 414; Three Essays on Sexuality, 106
Abraham, Mrs. Karl, 200, 241
active technique, 337
Adler, Alfred, 173, 209, 349, 378
aggressiveness: in child transference, 101–2; Freud and MK on, 108, 188–9, 192–3; Riviere on, 223; and death instinct, 333; Reich provokes, 337; and projection identification, 373

Aichhorn, August, 124, 243
Alexander, Franz, 94, 239; and MK's analysis of child, 95, 97; in Berlin Society, 122, 124; on aggression, 188; reviews Psycho-Analysis of Children, 197; and Menninger, 445
Allan, Grant, 114–15
American Journal of Psychology, 156
American Psycho-Analytical Association, 157, 411
Andreas-Salomé, Lou, 135
anxiety: in children, 99–100, 168, 178; search for prototype of, 127; Freud and Jones on, 158–9, 205; Freud on Rank's ideas of, at birth, 173–5; in MK's patient Dick, 185–6; and MK's idea of reparation, 194; and paranoid and depressive states, 216, 372–3; and helplessness, 223; in analysis situation, 224; Anna Freud on objective, 226–7; activation of, 270; MK's concentration on, 338, 372–3, 448; separation, 405
aphanisis, 202
Arpád (Ferenczi's case), 74, 78
art: Stokes on psychoanalysis and, 444
Association for the Psychiatric Treatment of Offenders (APTO), USA, 353
autism, 186–7

Balint, Alice (née Kóvacs), 72, 122
Balint, Enid, 412, 438
Balint, Michael, 241, 329, 394; and Ferenczi, 72, 75; on MK, 75n, 122; praises Abraham, 123; on earliest stages of mind, 228; at Controversial Discussions, 316, 319; friendship and support for MK, 329–30; on training recommendations, 349–50; Winnicott and, 401; and MK in old age, 438
Balkanyi, Charlotte, 406
Baranger, Willy, 392
Bartemeier, Leo, 378, 389
basic trust, attitude of, 404
Baumann, Marianne, 422
Benedek, Therese, 94
Bentham, Jeremy, 362

Berlin, 90, 94–5, 97, 100, 110
Berlin Psychoanalytic Society and Institute, 93, 94–5, 133; MK delivers papers to, 104–5, 140–1; MK made member of, 105; Wollfheim lectures at, 120; hostility to MK, 121–4; and Rank, 127; Anna Freud at, 164; and exodus of Jewish refugees, 239
Bernfeld, Siegfried, 124, 163, 243, 246
Bettelheim, Bruno, 108*n*, 186*n*, 395*n*
Bibring, Edward, 258
Bibring, Mrs. Edward, 302
Bick, Esther, 422–3, 426, 456, 461
Bion, Francesca, 401, 411*n*
Bion, Wilfred, 396, 410, 427, 444; Rickman and, 254; on countertransference, 378; on child despair, 403; as Klein trustee, 412; on Heimann and MK, 420; and borderline cases, 425; MK analyzes, 427–8; supports MK on origin of psychoses, 429; supports revision of training regulations, 431–2; Laing on, 446; and twin phantasy, 458 WORKS CITED: *Experience in Groups*, 428; "Group Dynamics: A Re-View," 395; "On Arrogance," 427
birth: trauma, 173, 175, 337, 345; as prototype of anxiety, 175
Blühler, Karl and Charlotte, 426
body scheme (Scott), 424–5
Boehm, Felix, 122, 124, 293
Bonaparte, Marie, Princess: Freud and, 73, 387–8; and lay analysts, 201; persuades Freud to leave Vienna, 240, 255, supports Anna Freud, 244, 387; Copy Books, 387–8; relations with MK, 387–8; at congresses, 440–1, 460
Bonhoeffer, Karl, 93
Bookhalter, Sophie, 246
Bornstein, Berta, 119
Boulanger, Jean-Baptiste, 389–91, 408–9; *see also* Girard, Françoise
Bowlby, John, 242, 402; on Isaacs, 244*n*; war service, 246, 307, 403; relations and disagreements with Kleinians, 292, 402–5, 408; at Extraordinary Meeting, 307; on MK and Anna Freud, 325; proposes British Society changes, 330; on Glover, 330, 347; on death instinct, 333; and Anna Freud's proposals for collaboration in training, 356, 358–9; on Ad Hoc Committee on Training, 359; on MK at Controversial Discussions, 367; on professional advantages of being Kleinian, 428 WORKS CITED: "The Influence of Early Environment in the Development of Neurosis and Neurotic Character," 403; "The Nature of the Child's Tie to His Mother," 403–5; "Separation Anxiety," 405
Brandes, Georg, 46–7
breast: feeding, 232; as love source, 236; and object relations, 331, 372, 397–8; and envy, 414–17, 443, 447; and superego, 440
Bridger, Harold, 376, 422, 449
Brierley, Marjorie: asked to translate MK's papers, 135; questionnaire on techniques, 205–6; attitude toward MK, 207, 243, 304;

investigates Melitta's plagiarism charge, 229; and training, 258; and British Society disputes, 296, 299–300, 304, 306–7, 314; professional criticism of MK, 300, 304, 306–7; resolution at Extraordinary Meeting, 307; organizes Controversial Discussions, 315–16; on Training Committee, 334*n*, 339, 348; describes technique, 339–40; scientific secretary of British Society, 343; at MK's death, 461
Brill, A. A., 207
British Institute of Psycho-Analysis, 179*n*, 201, 212, 358
British Medical Association, 201
British Psycho-Analytical Society (*formerly* London Psycho-Analytical Society), 71, 157–8; MK joins, 4, 179; Strachey delivers MK's paper to, 125, 127, 130; and child analysis, 125, 159; and lay analysis, 134, 201–2; MK lectures to, 137, 153; MK's success in, 183–5; and publication of *Psycho-Analysis of Children*, 195; and Glover-MK conflict, 200; questionnaire on techniques, 205; Kleinian "school" and factionalism in, 207, 212–14, 231, 237, 243, 258–60, 281–305, 310–13; child clinic expanded, 220; differences with Vienna, 220; Melitta attacks MK at, 229; 25th anniversary, 237, 245; and German refugees, 238–41, 243, 245, 255; in World War II, 245–6, 281–97, 301, 307, 315; political turmoil in, 263, 268; Emergency Committee, 281; Extraordinary Meetings (1952), 290–2, 302–4, 307–8, 312–14; Glover's numbering of allegiances in, 301–3; election and tenure of officers, 307; medical committee, 330; Ad Hoc Committee on Training, 359; composition of main committees, 360; training groups, 359–60; 1950's Scientific Meetings, 406–7; as "envy-conscious" body, 416; Kleinian dominance in, 428–9; groupings, 431–2; *see also* Controversial Discussions; Training Committee
British Psychological Society, 147, 183
Brook, Helen, 368
Brook, Lola, 368, 393, 419, 457, 462
Bryan, Douglas, 207
Bryher (Winifred Ellerman), 369
Budapest, 58, 60, 64, 69–72, 94
Burlingham, Dorothy: relations with Anna Freud, 243, 299, 387; starts Hampstead Wartime Nurseries, 246; at Controversial Discussions, 316, 319, 321, 328; health, 352; rebukes Margaret Little, 361

castration: infantile fears of, 125–6, 153, 173, 175; in women and girls, 176–8, 204; Jones's doubts on, 202–3
"Cavalcade" (radio series), 347
Chadwick, Mary, 230
Chapuis, Mlle (governess), 14
Chekhov, Anton, 38
Clampitt, Hanna, 239
Clare, George, 17
Clark, Mitchell, *Studies in Hysteria*, 154

Clark University, USA, 387
Clarke, C. K., 155–6
Clyne, Diana (MK's granddaughter), 370, 436
Clyne, Eric (Erich Klein; MK's son), 48, 64, 89, 113, 143, 145; and Jolan, 22; analysis of, and upbringing, 75–81, 91, 95–6, 114, 186; disordered family background, 96–7, 109–10, 113; taunted for Jewishness, 97; analyzed by Winnicott, 99, 233, 253, 261, 276n, 451; body exploration, 104; and Nelly Wollfheim, 139; and Kloetzel, 146n, 150, 153n; and Hans's death, 214–15; marriage, 234; changes name spelling, 239; war service, 249, 258, 268; on Melitta and Walter, 369; MK critical of, 396; concern for MK in old age, 460–1; writes to Melitta at MK's death, 461; bequest from MK, 462
Clyne, Hazel (MK's granddaughter), 435–6
Clyne, Judy (Eric's wife), 234, 249, 370, 396, 436, 460
Clyne, Melanie (MK's granddaughter), 436
Clyne, Michael (Eric's son), 249, 396, 408, 436; relations with MK, 234, 258, 370, 435–7, 460
cocaine, 35
Coleridge, Samuel Taylor, 300
"Committee of the Seven Rings," 93
Conference of German Psychoanalysts, 1st, Würzburg, 1924, 116
Congrès des Psychanalystes de Langue Française, Brussels, 1948, 376
Congress of Psychiatry, 1st, Paris, 1950, 376
Controversial Discussions, 1942–44, 207, 263, 314–33, 344, 367, 370
countertransference, 378–9, 384, 409–10, 416, 418–19, 442, 449
creativity, 216
Cutler, Kathleen (MK's housekeeper), 368, 409, 437, 457, 460–1

Davidson, Sonny, 441, 449
death instinct: Freud postulates, 108, 191, 223, 317, 322, 333, 337; MK's views on, 191, 194, 322, 326, 328, 331–3, 394–5, 398, 439–40; Jones's doubts on, 193, 210, 434; Kleinians accept, 317; disavowed by various analysts, 394, 405, 414, 447; and ego, 440
depressive position: Abraham and Freud on, 106; MK's theories of, 191, 216–17, 223, 262–3, 284, 339, 345, 367–8; Fairbairn criticizes MK on, 371; and schizoid state, 373; Winnicott on, 398, 400
Deutsch, Emil, 239
Deutsch, Felix, 139
Deutsch, Helene, 94, 239; Abraham, 178; on Oedipus complex in girls, 204; MK's jealousy of, 419
   WORKS CITED: *Confrontations with Myself*, 113; "The Psychology of Women in Relation to the Functions of Reproduction," 176–7
Deutsch, Hermann (MK's uncle), 6, 10–11,

42; loans to MK's parents, 9, 20, 29, 43, 48; and Jewish refugees, 239
Deutsch, Karoline (MK's aunt), 7, 61
Deutsch, Rabbi Mandel (MK's maternal grandfather), 7
Deutsche Papierzeitung (journal), 69, 110
Developmental Profile, 386
Developments in Psycho-Analysis (collection), 4, 371n, 392–3
Diaghilev, Sergei, 60
Diatkine, René, 389–90
Dick (MK's patient), 185–8, 254, 259, 266n, 269n
Don Juan syndrome, 236, 249
Doolittle, Hilda (HD), 369
Dora (Freud's patient), 154
dreams, 391

Eckhardt, Marianne Horney, 104–5
Eder, David, 154n, 158, 164, 239
ego: Freud-MK differences over, 222–3, 226, 228, 415; and anxiety, 223; Freud on strengthening, 227; Heimann defines, 244; and introjection/projection, 318; Fairbairn on, as object-seeking, 320, 372–3; and envy, 415–16; and death instinct, 440; MK distinguishes from self, 453; and loneliness, 458
Eitingon, Max, 71, 93, 190; on control analysis, 94; and Schmideberg, 111; kindness to MK, 121; in Berlin Society, 122, 133; as president of International Association, 178; settles in Palestine, 200, 239; and International Training Commission, 229; Jones's letter to, on refugees, 239; on Freud's theories, 293
Ellis, Havelock, 154, 158
Elmhirst, Susanna Isaacs, 406
Emden, E. G. von, 94
envy: and jealousy, 391, 414; innate and primary, 398; MK's Geneva paper on, 414–20; applied to Heimann, 418–20, 422; MK on, 443–4, 447–8, 453–4
Erikson, Erik, 385, 404
Erna (MK's child patient), 116–18, 120, 128, 136, 169, 240

Fabian (Julien Green character), 374, 411
Fackel, Die (journal), 17
Fairbairn, W. R. D., 303, 365; on ego, 320; MK's hostility to, 325, 374; *Psychoanalytical Studies of the Personality*, 325n, 397; Isaacs opposes, 328–9; on schizophrenia, 371–2, 374; on return-to-womb craving, 404
Falconer, Sir Robert, 157
fantasy, 59n, 138, 317
Fay, Judith, 368, 421–2, 446
Fazekas, Maria, 59
Federn, Paul, 90n, 123, 210, 219, 255
Feigel, Trude, 9n, 49
female sexuality, 176–7, 181, 202–4, 220
Fenichel, Otto, 119, 122, 182, 225–6, 228, 285n
Ferenczi, Moriz, 69
Ferenczi, Sándor, 69–72, 82, 92, 93, 114, 156; analyzes MK, 4, 69, 72–3, 75, 114; relations

Ferenczi, Sándor (cont'd)
　with Freud, 69–71, 73, 118, 163, 178, 228;
　techniques and principles, 72–3, 337; influ-
　ence on and relations with MK, 73–4, 82,
　100, 119, 130; and child analysis, 74–5, 96,
　170; on omnipotence, 83; letters from MK
　to, 91; on training analysis, 94; and Berlin
　Society, 94–5; Freud's letter to, on conserva-
　tism, 106; and Schmideberg, 111; as analyst
　for other analysts, 122, 157, 158, 283; on
　MK's influence in Britain, 162; on guilt,
　175; on MK's and Freud's views on aggres-
　sion, 189; death, 200; supports Anna Freud,
　200n; mothers patients, 234; on sphincter
　morality, 339
　WORKS CITED: "The Confusion of Tongues,"
　200n; Entwicklungsziele der Psychanalyse,
　94; "A Little Chanticleer," 74, 78; "Psycho-
　Analytical Observations on Tic," 98; "Stages
　in the Development of Reality," 73; "Tech-
　nical Difficulties in Analysis of a Case of
　Hysteria," 72n
Fieldman, Jack, 259, 383–4
Fliess, Wilhelm, 93, 139
Fluegel, J. C., 207
Fordham, Michael, 406
Foulkes, S. H. (formerly Fuchs), 239, 316
Four Countries' Conferences, 173, 228, 330n
Franklin, George, 346
Franklin, Marjorie, 361
free association, 336
French Psychoanalytical Society, 244
Freud, Anna, 114, 154n, 173, 200n, 308, 369n,
　403, 432–3; and Ferenczi, 70, 74; father ana-
　lyzes, 99n, 179, 322; Alix Strachey on, 124,
　168; relations and differences with MK, 126,
　131, 140, 164–9, 174, 180–1, 189, 210, 225,
　238, 243, 256–7, 322, 388–9, 411; work in
　child analysis, 126, 165–6, 313; relations
　with father, 163–4, 167, 172–3; theories and
　writings, 164–70; and Jones, 165, 171–2,
　179–81, 219, 225, 238, 256, 287–9, 377;
　medically unqualified, 201–2, 285; Melitta
　attacks, 210n, 219–20, 297; on adult rela-
　tionship to child, 224, 226; on objective anx-
　iety, 226–7; and MK's cancelled visit to
　Vienna, 235; settles in Britain, 241, 255;
　meetings with European refugees, 243; starts
　Hampstead Wartime Nurseries, 245–6; dis-
　putes with MK on training, 256–8, 303,
　356–61, 429–32; and British Society wartime
　conflicts, 263, 282n, 285–6, 291–2, 294,
　296, 298, 300–1, 306; takes on seminars,
　291; MK proposes compromises to, 299,
　303–6, 308; defends father's theories, 300,
　314, 322; on Training Committee, 302,
　334n, 336–7, 348; shares child training with
　MK, 314; in Controversial Discussions,
　315–21, 322–4, 328, 331; on death instinct,
　331; aims, 338; and Glover's resignation,
　343, 351–2, 355; resigns from Training
　Committee, 346, 348, 355; appointed secre-
　tary of International Society, 352–3; The
　Psychoanalytic Study of the Child, 355; detachment from British Society, 355, 367;
　proposals for collaboration in training,
　356–60; on Ad Hoc Committee on Training,
　359–60; and training groups, 359–61; holds
　seminars at home, 361; Lacan praises, 377;
　and age of guilt, 377n; status in USA,
　386–7; work at Hampstead Clinic, 386–7;
　Winnicott on bridge to MK, 398–9; dis-
　misses Winnicott's transitional objects, 400;
　and Bowlby, 404–5; and Heimann, 422; and
　revised training regulations, 429–32; at
　Freud centenary celebration, 432; and
　Jones's biography of Freud, 433, 434; at
　1957 Paris Congress, 440; and Jones's death,
　441n; Laing's view of, 447
　WORKS: The Ego and the Mechanisms of
　Defence, 225–8, 241, 318, 337, 365, 434;
　Einführung in die Technik der Kinderana-
　lyse, 163, 225, 434; "A Form of Altruism,"
　227; Introduction to Psycho-Analysis for
　Teachers, 198, 219; The Psycho-Analytical
　Treatment of Children, 164; "The Relation
　of Beating-Phantasies to a Day-Dream," 163,
　164n; "Sublimation and Sexualization" (un-
　published), 244; Young Children in War-
　time, 318–19
Freud, Ernst, 200
Freud, Martin, 198
Freud, Sigmund, 49, 106, 163; prescribes co-
　caine, 35; and Ferenczi, 69–71, 73, 118,
　163, 178, 228; and Wolf Man, 71, 117; MK
　meets, 71, 126; on patient-analyst relation-
　ship, 73; on pleasure-principle, 74; on om-
　nipotence, 84; and 1920 Hague Conference,
　92; and Abraham, 93–4, 105, 118–19; influ-
　ence on MK, 96; on early witnessing of sex,
　98n; analyzes Anna, 99n, 163, 172n; attends
　1922 Berlin Congress, 105; structural theory
　of mind, 105; on depression, 106–7; Jones's
　biography, 108, 154n, 191, 210, 433–4, 442;
　on love, hate, and death instinct, 108, 188–9;
　and Schmideberg, 111; MK moves away
　from, 118, 172; supports prophylactic analy-
　sis, 121n; and MK's theories of child analy-
　sis, 126–7; and Joan Riviere, 135, 207–10;
　and Jones, 138, 154–7, 162–5, 171–3,
　178–81, 202–4, 207, 434; and MK's influ-
　ence in Britain, 138, 162–3, 172, 211; differ-
　ences with MK, 163, 172–4, 189; cancer,
　163, 174, 209; and Anna's theories and writ-
　ings, 164–7, 171–3, 179–81, 227; refutes
　Rank, 173–4; and phallocentrism, 176; and
　Innsbruck Congress, 178; on instincts,
　191–3, 331, 333, 337, 395, 414, 425, 434;
　supports lay analysts, 201; and Kleinian
　school, 207; on girl-mother relationship, 221;
　80th birthday, 222; on impermanence of
　analysis, 228; settles in Britain, 240–1,
　255–6; death and funeral, 241, 245; and
　Vienna group, 243; congratulates British So-
　ciety on 25th anniversary, 245; on mourning,
　250–1, 253; and British Society disputes,
　288–9, 292, 308, 313–21, 349; and phan-
　tasy, 317; attitude toward Anna, 322; on

guilt and superego, 326–7; Isaacs on development of theories, 329; on progress in psychoanalysis, 334–5; on technique, 337; on MK as schismatic, 351; Fairbairn criticizes, 371; on understanding psychoses, 373–4; on narcissistic neuroses, 376; Americans' attitude toward, 386; and Marie Bonaparte, 387–8; and separation anxiety, 405; 1956 centenary celebrations, 432–3; talks during analyses, 449
  WORKS: "Analysis of a Phobia in a Five-Year-Old Boy," 81; *Analysis Terminable and Interminable*, 228; *An Autobiographical Study*, 11; *Beyond the Pleasure Principle*, 102, 107–8, 164, 226, 284, 321, 414; *Civilization and Its Discontents*, 188, 193, 208, 367; *The Ego and the Id*, 105, 193, 208, 222, 284, 438; "Female Sexuality," 173n, 181, 202–3, 322; *Five Lectures on Psycho-Analysis*, 337n; "Fragment of an Analysis of Hysteria," 100; *The Future Prospects of Psychoanalytic Therapy*, 337n, 378; *Group Psychology and the Analysis of the Ego*, 206, 222, 226, 395; "Inhibitions, Symptoms and Anxiety," 81, 100, 118, 173, 178, 293, 322; *Instincts and Their Vicissitudes*, 191, 433; *The Interpretation of Dreams*, 11, 70, 91, 194n, 216; "Lines of Advance in Psycho-Analytic Therapy," 71, 320n; *Mourning and Melancholia*, 206, 250–1; *New Introductory Lectures*, 121n, 208, 227; *A Note on the Unconscious in Psychoanalysis*, 208n; *On Dreams* (*Über den Traum*), 3, 69; *On the Psychopathology of Everyday Life*, 91; "The Question of Lay Analysis," 201; *Studies on Hysteria*, 337n; *Three Essays in Sexuality*, 71, 82, 91, 188n; "Turnings in the Way of Psycho-Analytic Theory," 320
Freud, Sophie, 163
Freund, Anton von, 72, 75 and n, 77–8, 81
Friedlander, Kate (*formerly* Misch), 239, 316, 331, 346, 348, 360
Fuchs, S. H., *see* Foulkes, S. H.

Gammill, James, 126–7, 422, 441n, 444–6
Geheimnisse einer Seelen (film: "The Secrets of a Soul"), 119
Geleerd, Elisabeth R., 270–1
Gilbertson, Beryl, 35
Gillespie, Andrew, 456
Gillespie, William H., 214, 243; on Searl, 231; and election of British Society officers, 330; on Jones and Glover, 353 and n; and Heimann, 381, 410; anger at MK's protest on Training, 431; presides at 1957 Paris Congress, 440
Gillie, Dame Annis, 234n, 324n, 396, 408–9
Girard, Françoise (*later* Boulanger), 377, 389–91, 408
Gitelson, Maxwell, 440
Glover, Edward, 158, 170, 197, 253, 260, 352; at Berlin Society, 94, 123; analyzes Melitta, 99, 199–200, 354, 381; and Abraham, 114–15, 197; on Freud and Abraham, 118;

on MK's personality, 123; and MK's paper at British Society, 130–1; attends MK's first British lectures, 137; and MK's settling in England, 161; and Anna Freud, 164, 170; refers Slight to MK, 190; reviews *Psycho-Analysis of Children*, 195–6; moves away from MK, 196–7, 200, 225; criticism of MK's techniques, 205–6, 215, 310–12; open opposition to MK, 212, 214, 215n, 237, 243, 256–7, 259, 282, 284, 299, 301, 305, 313, 411; at congresses, 224–5, 440; administrative work in British Society, 241, 245, 281–3, 286–9, 295, 304; at meeting with Anna Freud, 244; on grief, 251; and training, 256–8, 302, 314, 345–6, 349; attacks MK on depressive position, 263; at Extraordinary Meetings, 294–5; relationship with Melitta, 297n, 353–4, 369; account of composition and allegiances of British Society, 301–6, 314, 349, 383, 431; as Institute director of research, 310; in Controversial Discussions, 315–17, 319–21, 323, 329, 332; resigns from British Society, 330, 342–4, 346–8, 351–2, 354–5, 367; on Training Committee, 334n, 335, 338–9, 342, 346, 348; questionnaire, 335–6; letter to Payne on Klein deviation, 344–5; broadcast on vocational tests, 347; in International Association, 352–3; continues vendetta against MK, 354–5; and Hanna Segal, 366; Laing on, 447
  WORKS: "An Examination of the Klein System of Child Psychology," 355; *Freud or Jung*, 355; *An Investigation of the Technique of Psycho-Analysis*, 221n, 287, 310–12; *War and Pacifism*, 366
Glover, Gladys, 195, 380
Glover, James, 94, 123, 140, 197, 340, 345
God, 454
Goethe, J. W. von, 17
gratitude, 414–15, 443–4, 454
greed, 414, 443
Green, Julien, 374, 411
Grief: A Peril in Infancy (film), 403n
Grimm, Brothers, 79
Gross, Alfred, 329
group dynamics, 395, 428
Guardian, The (newspaper), 454
Guilbert, Yvette, 242
guilt, 127, 175, 188, 210; and restitution, 236n; and superego, 326–7; MK's preoccupation with, 338

Hampshire, Stuart, 444, 455
Hampstead Wartime Nurseries (*later* Child Therapy Clinic), 246, 355, 386
Happel, Clara, 97, 99, 239
Hartmann, Heinz, 122
hate, 175, 379
Hayley, T. T. S., 378, 406, 438, 442
Heimann, Franz, 242
Heimann, Mertza, 410
Heimann, Paula, 200, 239, 314, 370, 410, 418, 422, 429, 444; on Franz Alexander, 122; supports MK, 214, 242, 261; in British So-

Heimann, Paula (cont'd)
 ciety, 241, 286; in Internal Object Group,
 244–5; MK analyzes, 254, 258, 268n, 290n,
 382–3, 443; forms research circle, 284; at
 Controversial Discussions, 316–17, 325,
 330–2, 383; paper on regression (with
 Isaacs), 332; and training recommendations,
 350, 359, 431; helped by Bryher, 369; and
 MK's disavowal of narcissism, 371; and
 MK's concept of schizophrenia, 372; on
 countertransference, 378–9, 384, 409–10,
 418–19; disagreement and break with MK,
 378–85, 393, 410, 417–22; co-edits MK's
 70th birthday issue of Journal, 394; and
 Abraham's theories, 394–5; and MK's convalescence, 409; MK drops as patient, 409,
 419; as trustee of Klein Fund, 412; and
 MK's Envy paper, 414, 418–20; style as analyst, 422; and Baumann's Zurich meeting,
 422–3
 WORKS CITED: "A Contribution to the Problem of Sublimation," 244, 382; "Notes on
 the Theory of the Life and Death Instincts,"
 393; "The Polymorphous Stage of Instinctual Development," 394, 414n; "Some As-
 pects of the Role of Introjection and
 Projection in Early Development," 330–1
Hellman, Ilse, 401, 426, 437–8
Hermanetz (Silesia), 58, 84
Hess, Rudolph, 266, 267–8
Hitschmann, Edward, 214
Hoare, Sir Samuel, 239
Hoffer, Hedwig, 316, 332, 427
Hoffer, Willi, 243, 256, 361; on critical papers
 at British Society, 285; and Anna Freud,
 299; at Controversial Discussions, 316; on
 Glover, 351; on editorial board of Psycho-
 Analytical Study of the Child, 355; and
 Jones, 356; on Ad Hoc Committee on Train-
 ing, 359; at 1957 Paris Congress, 401; rejects
 Bick's infant emotions, 426; president of
 British Society, 456, 461; at MK's death,
 461
Hogarth Press, 158, 191
Hollós, Stefan, 70
homosexuality, 117, 191, 415–16
Hopkins, Pryns, 158
Horder, Thomas Jeeves, 1st Baron Horder, 399
Horney, Karen, 94, 239; analyzes Melitta, 99,
 111, 183, 354n; on penis envy, 122, 176;
 supports MK, 124; "On the Genesis of the
 Castration Complex in Women," 176; on female sexuality, 176–8, 204
Hug-Hellmuth, Hermine von: "On the Technique of Child Analysis," 92; MK meets,
 92–3; and analyzing child away from home,
 101; murdered, 123, 126; Alix Strachey
 reads, 135; and Anna Freud, 163; deprecates
 analysis of young children, 167, 433; play
 technique, 434
Hungary, 82–3, 89, 93, 122, 240; see also Budapest
hypnosis, 336

id, the, 222–3, 226–7, 453
identification, and introjection, 332
Ignatus, Hugo, 70
Imago 7 (journal), 77, 190
Imago Society, 444
infant observation, 426–7
instincts, 108, 138, 191–4, 227, 317–18, 371,
 425, 433; see also death instinct; life instinct
Institute for the Study and Treatment of Delinquency, 352–3
Internal Object Group, 244, 286
internal objects, 244, 286, 300, 317, 320, 328,
 331, 395, 397–8
International Colloquium on Psychosis, Montreal, 1969, 374
International Congress for Psycho-Analysis:
 2nd (Nuremberg, 1910), 70, 157; 5th (Budapest, 1918), 71, 73; 6th (Hague, 1920), 92,
 106, 122, 208; 7th (Berlin, 1922), 95, 105,
 111, 119, 126; 8th (Salzburg, 1924), 95,
 115–16, 159n, 208; 9th (Bad Homburg,
 1925), 153, 208; 10th (Innsbruck, 1927),
 164, 174, 176; 11th (Oxford, 1929), 188n,
 345; 12th (Wiesbaden, 1932), 198, 200n,
 202; 13th (Lucerne, 1934), 292, 297; 14th
 (Marienbad, 1936), 224–5; 15th (Paris,
 1938), 249, 370; 16th (Zurich, 1949), 353n,
 376, 378, 409, 419; 17th (Amsterdam,
 1951), 388; 18th (London, 1953), 410; 19th
 (Geneva, 1955), 413, 419; 20th (Paris,
 1957), 401, 422, 439–41; 21st (Copenhagen,
 1959), 426, 450, 458–60
International Congress of Neurology, Amsterdam, 1907, 155
Internationaler Psychoanalytischer Verlag, 180,
 191, 198
Internationale Zeitschrift für Psychoanalyse, 75,
 141, 164, 190, 219
International Journal of Psycho-Analysis: MK
 published in, 105, 180; founded, 158; Anna
 Freud and, 166, 172, 225, 241; Jones edits,
 172, 208n, 219, 241; publishes Melitta, 184;
 reviews MK's Psycho-Analysis of Children,
 195; on MK's views on anxiety and female
 sexuality, 205; Joan Riviere and, 208; Strachey edits, 249; Research Supplements, 312;
 MK 70th birthday issue, 394–5, 397–8, 412
International Psycho-Analytical Library series,
 158, 164
International Psycho-Analytic Association:
 Ferenczi presides, 71; American branch, 157;
 British branch, 158; Eitingon as president,
 178; Training Commission, 197, 201–2, 220,
 229, 302; Jones as president, 210; Isaacs on
 purpose of, 291; Anna Freud appointed secretary, 352; Glover as secretary, 352–3
introjection: defined, 100n; Freud on, 107,
 285, 433; MK on, in development, 217; Melitta on, 284–5; as issue in Controversial Discussions, 315–17; and internal objects, 331,
 368; and identification, 332, 374n; Jacobson
 challenges concept, 411
Isaacs, Nathan, 239

Isaacs, Susan, 137, 244, 305, 314, 368, 422; MK meets, 137–8; in British Society, 158, 241, 286, 291, 299; views on aggression, 188; as expositor of MK's ideas, 196; supports MK, 205, 214, 229, 256; Riviere analyzes, 207; and MK's interest in depression, 263; and Sharpe, 292, 312; letter from MK on Jones, 309; presents Kleinian view in Controversial Discussions, 315–21, 323–4, 326–9, 332, 383; on phantasy, 317–18, 332; letters from MK on Controversial Discussions, 323–6; paper on regression (with Heimann), 332; and Anna Freud's proposals for training collaboration, 356–9; on Ad Hoc Committee on Training, 359; plans publication of papers, 370; MK makes malicious remarks about, 382; in Cambridge with MK, 383; death, 393
  WORKS CITED: "The Nature and Function of Phantasy," 292n, 317–19; "Temper Tantrums in Early Childhood in Their Relation to Internal Objects," 244

Jacobson, Edith, 410–11
Jaques, Elliott, 413, 437; on MK's analysis of own children, 79; collaborates with MK in writings, 266, 418, 438; denies transference neurosis, 337; Anna Freud opposes, 401; on Heimann and MK, 420; as secretary of Klein Trust, 421; criticizes MK's "Development of Mental Functioning," 439
  WORKS CITED: *The Changing Culture of a Factory*, 447 & n; "Death and the Mid-Life Crisis," 95
jealousy, 391, 414–15; *see also* envy
Jesus Christ, 454
Jews, Jewishness: disdained, 8n; in MK's upbringing, 13–14; position in Austria-Hungary, 41; and communist takeover in Hungary, 82–3, 90; persecution of, 84; refugees, 239–41
Joffe, Walter G., 416
Jones, Ernest, 154–6, 160–1, 197; invites MK to lecture at British Society, 4; and Ferenczi, 70–1, 95; founds British Psycho-Analytic Society, 71, 157–8; at 1920 Hague Congress, 92; in Committee of 7 Rings, 93; and MK's move to Berlin, 94; publishes MK's papers, 105; praises Abraham and Ferenczi, 114; and MK's Oedipal theories, 116; attends British Society, 125, 130–1, 154; and MK's visit to England, 131–2, 134–5, 137–8, 154; disagreement with Vienna, 140; invites MK to England to analyze children, 150, 159; relations with Freud, 154–7, 162–5, 171–3, 178–9, 202–4, 207, 434; analyzed by Ferenczi, 157; theories and ideas, 158–9; interest in child analysis, 159; relations with MK, 162–3; and Anna Freud, 165–6, 171–2, 179–81, 219–20, 225, 238, 287; 1979 centenary, 165; generalizations on child analysis, 170; supports MK in disputes with Freud, 179–81, 202–5, 210, 237–8, 283–4, 441; dis-

courages Europeans, 184; views on aggression, 188; dispute with Freud on instincts, 191–3; congratulates MK on *The Psycho-Analysis of Children*, 194; as expositor of MK's ideas, 196, 221; as president of International Association, 198, 202, 210, 222, 352–3; and lay analysts, 201–2; on phallocentrism and castration, 202–4; on technique and patient relations, 206; and factionalism in British Society, 207, 214, 282–3; and Joan Riviere, 207n, 209; as biographer of Freud, 210, 433–4, 442; worry over MK's depression, 219; suggests MK for Training Commission, 220; and Freud's 80th birthday, 222; investigates Melitta's "plagiarism" charges, 229; and MK's canceled visit to Vienna, 235; and German refugees, 239–41, 255–6; final letter from Freud, 245; and British Society in war, 245, 281–3, 286–7, 290, 294, 298–9, 308, 314, 343; MK criticizes for bringing Freuds to England, 255; MK's grievances against, 259–60, in semi-retirement, 281, 283; letter to Anna Freud on MK and British Society, 287–9; resigns from Training Committee, 302; interviews prospective British Society candidates, 304; praises MK's work for Freud, 307; MK on weakness, 308–9; and Glover, 312, 343, 352–3; at Extraordinary Meetings, 314; avoids Controversial Discussions, 317, 319; letter from Ferenczi on "phantastic" works, 340n; and Karin Stephen, 350; and Anna Freud's continuing membership in British Society, 351; urges Freudians to compromise, 356; ambiguous views on MK, 377–8; writes introduction to MK's *Contributions*, 377; resigns as International president, 378; letter from Marie Bonaparte, 387; celebrates MK's 70th birthday, 392, 394; and publication of *Developments in Psycho-Analysis*, 393; writes preface to *New Directions*, 412–13; unveils Freud memorial plaque, 432–3; cancer, 433; death, 411–2
  WORKS: "Contributions to Theory," 433; "Early Development of Female Sexuality," 178n, 191, 202, 220; "Fear, Guilt and Hate," 188n; *Free Associations*, 155; "The Future of Psycho-Analysis," 222; "The Importance of Symbol Formation in the Development of the Ego," 413; "The Oedipus Complex as an Explanation of Hamlet's Mystery," 156; "The Origin and Structure of the Superego," 159, 162; *Papers on Psycho-Analysis*, 193; "The Pathology of Early Anxiety," 158; "The Phallic Phase," 176, 202, 289; "Psycho-Analysis and the Instincts," 192; *Sigmund Freud*, 108, 159n, 191, 210, 433–4, 442; "The Theory of Symbolism," 185
Jones, Gwenith (EJ's daughter), 159, 162, 181
Jones, Katherine (EJ's wife), 159–60, 162, 171, 239, 441, 444, 461
Jones, Mervyn (EJ's son), 159, 162, 171, 181

Joseph, Betty, 99, 399, 411, 417, 421, 438, 461
Joyce, James, 66
Jung, Carl Gustav: and Ferenczi, 70; Abraham and, 93, 118; Jones meets, 155–6; and symbolism, 185; Freud on Riviere and, 209; resigns from British Society, 349; on Jungians, 438

Kanner, Leo, "Early Infantile Autism," 186–7
Karolyi, Michael, Count, 82
Kernberg, Otto, 244
Kestenberg, Judith, 412
Khan, Masud, 397n, 406
Kinderheim Baumgarten, Vienna, 246
King, Pearl: and MK's analysis of own children, 79; on Jones's anxiety about MK, 219; and Eva Rosenfeld, 361; and Winnicott, 374; and Rickman, 375; interviews Heimann, 379, 381–3, 410, 419; and 1952 Club, 406; on Judith Waterlow, 409
  WORKS CITED: "The Education of a Psycho-Analyst: The British Experience," 359; "The Life and Work of Melanie Klein in the British Psycho-Analytical Society," 290n, 359
King, Truby, 10
Klein, Arthur Stevan (MK's husband), 9, 29–30, 43–5; courtship and engagement, 19–20, 22–3, 27, 30–1, 34; in America, 20, 27–8; returns from America, 31; retrieves Emanuel's papers at death, 40; marriage, 40–1, 49, 63, 72; relations with Libussa, 43, 51–3, 56–8, 62; moves to work in Krappitz, 48, 54; nervous condition, 49–50, 54; infidelity, 53, 236; transferred to Budapest, 58, 60; war service, 64, 72; in MK's stories, 68–9; critical of psychoanalysis, 72, 99; settles in Sweden, 82–3, 89, 109; converted to Roman Catholicism, 83; divorce from MK, 89–90, 109; relations with sons, 96–9, 183, 236; returns to Berlin, 97, 109–10; subsequent life and death, 113, 250, 252; custody of Hans, 183
Klein, Erich (MK's son), see Clyne, Eric
Klein, Hans (MK's second son), 49–50, 58, 80, 82; with MK after parents' divorce, 89; MK's analysis of, 95, 97–9; relations with father, 98–9, 110, 113, 236; later analysis with Simmel, 99, 110, 215; in father's custody, 183; death, 214–16, 218–19, 252, 284, 380; MK's relations with, 236, 411
Klein, Jakob (Arthur's father), 41, 43n
Klein, Klara (formerly Vágó), 49, 58–60, 62, 83–5
Klein, Kristina (Arthur's daughter), 369
Klein, Melanie: obscurity of past, 3–5; autobiography (unpublished), 4, 9, 11, 14, 40, 42, 46, 48, 65, 92, 126, 140, 435, 459; analysis with Ferenczi, 4, 69, 72–3, 75; marriage, 4–5, 40–1, 49, 63, 72; parents and family, 5–7; born 8; childhood in Vienna, 8–10; schooling, 9, 14; relations with father and mother, 11–13, 15–16, 18, 22, 43, 49–50, 55–9, 62–3, 65, 69; Jewish family influences, 13; governesses, 14; relations with sisters and brothers, 14–16, 18, 21, 23–5, 62, 65; child-

hood intellectual activities, 16–17; beauty, 18–19; courtship, 19–20, 22–3, 27–31, 34; in Rosenberg, 22–8; attachment to Emanuel, 23–34, 39, 41; and dress, 28; and Emanuel's death, 39–40, 252; revulsion to sex, 41, 53; birth of children, 41–2, 48, 64; holiday in Adriatic and Italy, 43–5; and publication of Emanuel's writings, 40, 46–8; depressions, 48–50, 56, 63, 66, 72, 99, 216, 218–19; in Krappitz, 48–9; absences from children, 50–1, 53, 90; bladder complaint, 56–7; Rügen holiday, 58, 62; at mother's death, 65, 216, 250; poetry and writings, 65–9, 84–5; sexual and love experiences, 67–9, 84–5; influenced by Ferenczi, 73–5; and analysis in son Erich's upbringing, 75–81, 91, 95–6, 114; on communist takeover in Hungary, 82–3; children baptized, 83; and religion, 83–4; divorce, 89–90, 109–10, 119n; practices psychoanalysis in Berlin, 91, 94–5, 97, 100; writes to Ferenczi, 91; attends 1920 Hague Congress, 92; analyzes son Hans, 95, 97–9; analyzes Melitta, 95–6, 98–9; effect of analysis on children, 99–100; on discussing sex with children, 100; manner in analysis, 105, 188, 449–52; membership in Berlin Society, 105; on death instinct, 108, 192–4; analysis by Abraham, 109, 113n, 114–15, 119, 178, 435; and Arthur's return to Berlin, 109–10; relations with daughter, 111–12, 200, 212–14, 218, 229–30, 242–3, 380–2, 411, 461; moves to Berlin, 112–13; intuitive leaps, 116; differences with Freud, 118, 172–4, 189, 388–9; and Nelly Wollfheim, 119–21; Berlin Society's hostility to, 121–6; strength of personality, 123, 432–3; at Viennese Society, 126, 131; proposed visit to England, 131, 134–5; and Alix Strachey in Berlin, 131–3, 139–40, 148; spoken English of, 132, 135, 442; attends masked balls and dancing lessons, 133–4, 141, 148, 150; lectures translated into English, 135–7; appearance, 136, 139, 432–3; first visit to British Society, 137–8; and Abraham's death, 140; affair with Kloetzel, 141–50, 216, 219; leaves Berlin for England, 150, 159–61; analyzes Jones's wife and children, 159–60, 171, 181; relations and differences with Anna Freud over child analysis, 164–9, 174, 210, 225, 243, 256, 322; at 1927 Innsbruck Congress, 174; on female sexuality, 176; Jones supports, 179–81, 202–5, 441; success in Britain, 183; seeks origin of schizophrenia, 185–7; accepts training analysands, 189–90; writing style, 195–6; and Melitta in London, 199; Melitta's opposition to, 200, 212–14, 218, 229–30, 242–3, 380–2; Nemon bust of, 200–1; and training of analysts, 202, 256–9, 314, 334n, 336–8, 342, 357–9, 429–31; on penis envy, 203–5; techniques, 205–6, 310–11, 442–3, 448–52; faction in British Society, 207, 211, 231; and death of Hans, 214–16, 218–19, 284; fanatical application to work, 216; on girl-mother

relationship, 220–1; analyzed by Payne, 228; gall-bladder operation, 234; Virginia Woolf on, 237; letter of gratitude to Jones, 237–8; naturalized as British, 239; supports Jewish refugees, 239; in World War II, 246, 253–8; and Training Committee, 256–9, 302–6, 334n, 336, 342, 429–31; house bombed, 258; anxieties over British Society, 259–61; and case of Richard (10-year-old depressive), 262–71; Richard describes, 272–3, 275; and British Society wartime disputes, 281–6, 292–305, 308–13; Jones on, to Freud, 287–8; proposes compromise to Anna Freud, 299, 303–4; and Glover, 302–6, 310–12; shares child training with Anna Freud, 314; Clifton Hill home restored, 315; and Controversial Discussions, 315–17, 323–9; correspondence with Isaacs on Controversial Discussions, 323–8; Anna Freud criticizes in Training papers, 337–8; Brierley on, as idealized object, 339–40; Glover criticizes in resignation letters, 334–5; Glover denigrates, 354–5; and Anna Freud's training proposals, 357–9; serves on Ad Hoc Committee on Training, 359–60; and Margaret Little, 361–2; Hanna Segal describes, 365–6; buys Clifton Hill house, 369; and Fairbairn's theories on schizophrenia, 371–2; relations and split with Paula Heimann, 378–85, 410, 417–23; sexuality, 381–5; on the Freuds' view of auto-eroticism, 388–9; at 1951 Amsterdam Congress, 389; advises on translation of writings, 390–2; 70th birthday, 392, 394; tension with son Eric, 396; and analysis of grandson Michael, 396; and Winnicott's views of bridge to Anna Freud, 398–9; dizzy spells, 408–9; moves to Bracknell Gardens, 410; estrangement from Melitta, 411; establishes Trust, 412; attends 1955 Geneva Congress, 413–14; greed, 419; envy, 419–20; claims equal status with medical doctors, 428–9; protests at Training Committee regulations, 429–31; on political structure and groupings of British Society, 432; Topolski drawing of, 433n, 438; at Freud centenary celebration, 432; in Jones's *Freud*, 433–4; relations with grandchildren, 435–6; and young children, 436–7; theater-going, 437–8; 75th birthday, 438; at 1957 Paris Congress, 439–40; and Jones's death, 441–2; recording of, 442–3; health, 451; extended interpretations, 452 & n; at 1959 Copenhagen Congress, 458–60; anemia, 460; cancer and death, 461
WORKS: "A Contribution to the Psychogenesis of Manic-Depressive States," 217–18, 231, 402; "Contribution to the Psychogenesis of Tics," 110; *Contributions to Psycho-Analysis*, 4, 77, 377, 427n; "Criminal Tendencies in Normal Children," 184; "The Development of a Child," 79, 80n, 81, 95, 105, 111, 167; "The Development of Mental Functioning," 439; "Early Analysis," 96, 185; "Early Stages in the Oedipus Complex," 174, 177, 203; "The Emotional Life of Civilized Men and Women" (with Joan Riviere), 235; "The Emotional Life of the Infant" (unpublished), 367, 394; *Envy and Gratitude and Other Works*, 4, 230n, 236n, 417, 438, 448, 454; "Der Familienroman in statu nascendi," 75; "The Importance of Symbol-Formation in the Development of the Ego," 185, 188n, 266n; "Infantile Anxiety-Situations Reflected in a Work of Art," 178, 216, 413; "Inhibitions and Difficulties in Puberty," 96n; "Life Calls" (story), 40; "Love, Guilt and Reparation" (article), 59, 231, 235–6, 385; *Love, Guilt and Reparation, and Other Works* (book), 95, 264n; *Love, Hate and Reparation* (with Joan Riviere), 225, 235, 241; "Mourning and Its Relation to Manic-Depressive States," 231, 250–1, 368; *Narrative of a Child Analysis*, 4, 263–4, 266–7, 269–72, 275, 438–9; *New Directions in Psycho-Analysis*, 4, 377n; "A Note on Depression in the Schizophrenic," 459; "Notes on Some Schizoid Mechanisms," 115, 372, 419, 427, 444; "An Obsessional Neurosis in a Six-Year-Old Girl," 116, 118; "The Oedipus Complex in the Light of Early Anxieties," 263n, 267; "On Criminality," 236n; "On Identification," 374, 411; "On the Criteria for the Termination of a Psycho-Analysis," 376; "On the Influence of Sexual Enlightenment on the Intellect," 91; "On the Origins of Transference," 390, 397; "On the Sense of Loneliness," 458; "Our Adult World and Its Roots in Infancy," 453; "Personification in the Play of Children," 184; "Play" (unpublished), 234
The Psycho-Analysis of Children: reports cases, 78n, 95–6, 100, 104, 116, 118, 185n, 204; on technique, 115; incorporates earlier papers, 121, 184; publication and reception, 191, 194–8; Jones and, 202–4, 433; and transference, 206; Winnicott reads, 233; Segal reads, 365; Lacan part-translates, 377, 389–90; and MK's sexuality, 384; influence on Marie Bonaparte, 388; and envy, 414; *Psycho-Analytic Play Technique*, 80; "The Psychogenesis of Manic-Depressive States," 215–16, 220–1; "The Psychological Principles of Early Analysis," 175; "The Role of the School in the Libidinal Development of the Child," 96n; "Some Theoretical Conclusions Regarding the Emotional Life of the Infant," 393; "A Study of Envy and Gratitude," 414–20; "Technical Problems in a Suicidal Case," 215n; "The Technique of Early Analysis," 100, 118; "Weaning," 231–2
Klein, Melitta, *see* Schmideberg, Melitta
Klein, Sándor, 85
Kloetzel, Chezkel Zvi: affair with MK, 141–50, 216, 236; emigrates to Palestine, 200, 219; death, 392
Kóvacs, Vilma, 72

Kraepelin, Emil, 155 & *n*, 156
Krappitz (Upper Silesia), 48–9, 54
Kraus, Karl, 17, 40, 47, 66, 83
Kris, Ernest, 225
Kún, Bela, 82
Kurtz, Iren, 43, 55, 61
Kurtz, Karl, 43, 55

La Barre, Weston, 71
Lacan, Jacques, 352*n*, 376–7, 387, 389–90, 392; "The Mirror Stage as Formative of the Function of the I as Revealed in Psychoanalytic Experience," 376
Lagache, René, 390
Laing, R. D., 446–8; *The Divided Self,* 447
Lampl, Hans, 131
Lantos, Barbara, 316
Lasker-Schüler, Else, 66
Lawrence, D. H., 138*n*
Lebovici, Serge, 401*n*, 439–40
Leigh, Stanley, 443
Levy, Lajos, 70
libido: Abraham on, 103, 105, 107, 115*n*, 117; MK on, 108; Freud on, 116, 371; Anna Freud's understanding of, 227; MK on distribution of, 326; Fairbairn on, 371
Lieberman, James, 175*n*
Liebermann, Hans, 122
life instinct, 191, 331, 395, 415, 439; *see also* death instinct
Listener, The (journal), 347
Little, Margaret, 216, 321, 349*n*, 355, 361–2, 409, 428, 456; "Counter-Transference and the Patient's Response to It," 409–10; "The Analyst's Total Response to His Patient's Needs," 410
London, MK's homes in, 153, 200, 258, 369, 410
London Child Guidance Clinic, 402
London Clinic for Psycho-Analysis, 154, 392
London Psycho-Analytical Society, *see* British Psycho-Analytical Society
loneliness, 457–9
Looney, J. T., 181
Lorand, Rhoda, 412
Lorand, Sándor, 72, 411–12
Lorenz, Konrad, 403
love: loss of, as cause of female anxiety, 173–4; doubt of, 218; and life instinct, 415, 440–1; and gratitude, 444
Low, Barbara: opposes Isaacs, 138; abstract and translation of Anna Freud's *Einführung,* 164, 219; hostility to MK, 207, 243; dispute with Joan Riviere, 298; supports Anna Freud, 316; and Anna Freud's resignation from Training Committee, 346; and Glover's resignation, 347
WORKS CITED: *Psycho-Analysis: A Brief Account of the Freudian Theory,* 138; "The Psychoanalytic Society and the Public," 285

McDougall, Joyce, 439
MacGibbon, James, 455
MacGibbon, Jean, 454–5

Mahler, Margaret: "On Child Psychosis and Schizophrenia," 389, 411*n*
Main, F. T. (Tom), 73, 419
Malleson, Andrew, 233
Malting House School, Cambridge, 137–8
Manchester, 329–30
manic-depressive state, 217, 373; *see also* depressive position
marriage, happiness in, 236
masochism, 192
masturbation, 97–8, 177
Matthew, David, 241, 259, 267, 273, 308–9, 330, 365
Mavor, Ronald, 17*n*, 38
Mead, Margaret, 448
melancholia, 106–7, 368; *see also* depression
Melanie Klein Trust Fund, 412, 420–1
Meltzer, Donald: on MK's idea of restoration, 236*n*; on MK's *Narrative,* 270, 272; slow delivery, 401; in Imago Society, 444; Wedeles praises, 449; MK analyzes, 450, 453; on MK's interpretations, 452*n*
Meng, Heinrich, 219
Menninger, Karl, 193, 445
Menzies, Isabel, 447
Merleau-Ponty, Maurice, 447
Middlemore, Merrell, 229; *The Nursing Couple,* 394
Milner, Marion: on symbol function, 185*n*; on Glover and students, 339; on turmoil in British Society, 355; MK supervises, 395–6; analyzes Michael Clyne, 396; on Winnicott, 399; supervises Laing, 446; attitude toward MK, 447; "Aspects of Symbolism in Comprehension of the Non-Self," 395–6, 413; "The Role of Illusion in Symbol Formation," 413
Moll, Albert, 120
Money-Kyrle, Roger, 286, 316, 378, 394, 406, 412, 444; "Some Aspects of Political Ethics in the Light of Psycho-Analysis," 371
Monroe, Marilyn, 386*n*
Montessori, Maria, 234
mourning, 249–52, 368, 406
Müller, Josine, 122–4, 128
Munro, Lois, 452
"mutative" interpretation, 206
Myers, Frederic, *Human Personality,* 154

Nagera, Humberto, 386
narcissism, 371, 389, 424–5
Neill, A. S., 448
Nemon, Oscar, 200
Neue Freie Presse (Vienna newspaper), 47
New Directions in Psycho-Analysis, 80, 371*n*, 396*n*, 397, 412–13, 421*n*
Nietzsche, Friedrich Wilhelm, 17
1952 Club, 406–7, 442
1917 Club, 140 & *n*
Nunberg, Hermann, 193
Nuremberg Laws (German anti-Jewish), 239

object relations: MK on, 98, 321–2, 324, 372–3; Fairbairn and, 325*n*; Hungarian

school and, 330n; and schizophrenia, 372–3; and defense against anxiety, 397; Bowlby on, 406
objects (good and bad), 216–17
Oedipus complex: MK's views on dating onset of, 104–5, 115, 117, 131, 167, 169, 172, 175, 178, 182, 203; and melancholia, 107; Searl on, 125; in young child, 125; Jones on, in *Hamlet*, 156; and superego, 159, 172; Anna Freud on, 174, 179, 181; girl's role in, 202–5; and depressive position, 265; in case of Richard, 271; resolution of, 319; Freud on age of, 326–7
omnipotence of thought, 106
Ophuijsen, Johann H. W. van, 109
oscillations, 425

Pabst, G. W., 119
Padel, John, 269–70, 399–400, 407
paranoid-schizoid position (persecutory state), 191, 216, 372–3, 398, 414, 417, 439, 459
Paris Psychoanalytic Society, 388
part-objects, 216, 218, 300
Paskauskas, A. A., 155n
Payne, Sylvia: and Hanns Sachs, 122; in Berlin, 123; on difficulties of child analysis, 125; attends MK's first English lectures, 137; activities and position in British Society, 158, 256, 281–4, 286, 290, 294–9, 306, 308; and MK's depression, 219; analyzes MK, 228; investigates Melitta's plagiarism charge, 229; independence, 243; opposition to MK, 256; and training, 258; in wartime, 259; health breakdown, 281, 290, 294; hostility to Joan Riviere, 287n; Jones on, 288; interviews British Society candidates, 304; MK on mood of, 304–5; disillusionment with Glover, 305; disproves Glover's figures on training, 314; at Controversial Discussions, 315–16, 319, 322–3; elected to medical committee, 330; on introjection and identification, 332; on death instinct, 333; on Training Committee, 334n, 340, 348–9; analyzed, 340, 443; on techniques, 340–1; announces Glover's resignation, 343–4; and Anna Freud's resignation from Training Committee, 346, 348; on Anna Freud's possible defection to Swiss Society, 352; elected president of British Society, 355; and Anna Freud's proposals for collaboration in training, 356–8; chairs Ad Hoc Committee on Training, 359; on depressive position, 367; supervises Rosenfeld, 375; analyzes Milner, 395; acts as president of British Society, 426; and revised Training regulations, 430–1; attitude toward MK, 447
Peatie, Mertza, 383
penis envy, 122, 176–8, 203–4, 221, 226, 415, 447; *see also* phallocentrism
Penrose, L. S., 212n
persecutory state, *see* paranoid-schizoid position
Peter (child patient), 102–4, 153
phallocentrism, 176, 202–3; *see also* penis envy
phantasy: use as term, 59n, 317, 332; Joan Ri-

viere on role of, 169–70; Ferenczi's "forced," 170; in child unconscious, 234; Isaacs on, at Controversial Discussions, 317–20, 322–3; age of, 323, 412; and Jungian archetypes, 406n
Pick, Emilie (née Reizes; MK's sister), 8, 10, 15, 18, 23; relations with MK, 15, 41, 216, 239–40; marriage, 20, 25; children, 26–7, 35, 42, 48; visits MK in Rosenberg, 42; relations with mother, 43, 56; envy of MK, 45; and Emanuel's book, 47; alleged infidelity, 55–6; marriage decline, 56, 60–1; in wartime Vienna, 64; flees Vienna, 239; death, 249–50, 252; in MK's autobiography, 459
Pick, Hertha (Emilie's daughter-in-law), 17n, 64, 239n, 240, 250n
Pick, Irma Brenman, 436
Pick, Leo (Emilie's husband): marriage, 20, 25, 55–6, 61–2; Emanuel respects, 22; lives in Reizes' home, 23; on Emanuel's health, 26; Libussa and, 56, 61–2; jealousy, 61; gambling, 61; war service and imprisonment, 64; flees Vienna, 239
Pick, Otto (Emilie's eldest son), 27, 35, 44, 49, 60–1, 240
Pick, Walter (Otto's son), 49, 239n
Pick, Wilhelm Emanuel (Emilie's second son), 48, 64
Pines, Dinora, 360, 455
Pitlochry (Scotland), 254, 258–9, 262–7, 275, 383
play: in child analysis, 101–2, 169–70, 434; repetition in, 234; and dreams, 391
pleasure-principle, 74, 102, 127, 193, 321
Prince, Morton, 156
projection, 100n, 411, 433; *see also* introjection
projective identification, 227, 373–5, 395, 411, 417, 424, 428, 442, 449, 459
psychoanalysts, training and qualifications of, 201–2
Psycho-Analytic Quarterly, 197
Psychoanalytic Study of the Child, The, 355
psychoses, 186, 429
psychotherapy, 443
Putnam, James J., 156–7
Pyke, Geoffrey, 137

Radó, Sándor, 94, 239; discussions with Ferenczi, 70; and MK's analysis of child, 95; attacks MK, 121, 141; in Berlin Society, 122, 124; and Freud, 141; edits *Zeitschrift*, 164, 180; on International Training Commission, 220
Rank, Otto, 92, 93; Abraham's wariness of, 126–7; defection, 163; and Freud, on birth trauma, 173, 175, 345; revisions in technique, 337
WORKS CITED: "Literary Autobiography," 175n; *The Trauma of Birth*, 126–7, 294, 345
Reed, Henry, 455
regression, 332
Reich, Wilhelm, 448
Reik, Theodor, 94, 188, 201, 242, 337, 382n

Reizes, Emanuel (MK's brother), 8, 10, 15, 17, 18, 26, 35; on Hermann Deutsch's loans, 9; influence on and relations with MK, 16–17, 21, 23–4, 26–7, 29–35, 39, 41, 236, 392; ill health, 17, 23–4, 26, 29, 31, 35–6; relations with father, 17–19; allowance and finances, 18, 20–2, 29–30, 38; death, 20, 36–40, 216, 219, 252; travels in Italy, 21–4, 32–4; stays in Rosenberg, 25; relations with mother, 26, 30–1; travels in Switzerland, 27–8, 413; self-pity, 30, 34–5; drug-taking, 31, 35–6; boasts of married woman, 32–3; handwriting analyzed, 35; MK preserves letters, 35; in Spain, 35–6; work published (*Aus Meinem Leben*), 40, 46–7; grave, 44–5, 48; Leo's jealousy of, 61; in MK's stories, 68; infidelities, 236; MK shows poems to Paula Heimann, 380; in MK's autobiography, 459

Reizes, Libussa (née Deutsch; MK's mother), 6–7, 9, 20, 49; runs shop in Vienna, 8, 11–12; relations with MK, 12–13, 15–16, 22, 24, 49–51, 55–8, 62–3, 65, 69; religion, 13–14; relations with husband, 13, 18; Leo and Emilie live with, 18, 23, 25; and Emanuel, 24–31, 33, 47; financial cares, 28–30, 43; letters to MK, 37; and Emanuel's death, 37; and MK's pregnancy, 41–2, 57; spa treatments, 42–3, 46; on MK's holiday trip to Italy, 44–5; looks after MK's children, 44, 46, 50, 53–4, 58; health, 46, 64; and Emanuel's book, 47; stays with MK and husband in Krappitz, 48–51; and MK's marriage and husband, 51–3, 56–8, 60, 62; cooking, 54; attacks Emilie, 55–6; breakdown, 59; death, 65, 216, 250; in MK's stories, 69; on Klara Vágó, 84; inflexibility, 379; MK idealizes in autobiography, 459

Reizes, Moriz (MK's father), 5–6, 8; courtship and marriage, 6–7, 13, 18, 20; relations with MK, 11–12, 16; and music hall, 11; decline in health, 17; disagrees with son, 17–18; death, 18–19

Reizes, Sidonie (MK's sister), 8, 10, 15, 39, 216

reparation: in child behavior, 102–3, 218; and love relationships, 236–7; and guilt, 326; Boulanger's use of word, 391; Laing on, 448

Revue française de psychanalyse, 390

Richard (MK's Pitlochry patient), 263–72, 439; own account, 273–5; mother, 275–7

Richer, Edith, 243

Rickman, John: at British Society, 125, 130, 158, 281, 283, 285–6; and payment for MK, 136; attends MK's first English lectures, 137; edits Kleinian work, *On the Bringing Up of Children*, 229; analyzed by MK, 241, 253–4, 258, 268n, 290n; views of Kleinian ideas, 242; wartime duties, 246, 253–4, 316; and training, 258; numbered as Kleinian, 305; and Controversial Discussions, 316; on Training Committee, 334n; objects to Glover broadcast, 347; appointed scientific secretary of British Society, 355; and Anna Freud's training proposals, 357, 359; on Ad

Hoc Training Committee, 359; decline in relations with MK, 375, 393, 424; helps Paula Heimann, 383; death, 393

Rita (MK's patient), 100–1, 103, 184–5, 397

Riviere, Diana (Joan's daughter), 208, 213

Riviere, Evelyn (Joan's husband), 208

Riviere, Joan, 207–8; on Oedipus complex, 125, 130; translates MK's papers, 135, 167; attends MK's first English lectures, 137; membership in British Society, 158; and MK's settling in England, 160–1, 208; and Anna Freud, 164, 170; supports MK, 169; on projection by child on parental imagos, 181; at MK publication party, 195; as expositor of MK's ideas, 196, 205–6, 219, 221–3; analyzes Isaacs and Winnicott, 207, 451; relations and differences with Freud, 207–10; translates Freud, 208, 438n; relations with MK, 208–9, 214; presents Kleinian views in Vienna, 221–4, 236, 317; on Melitta's attacks on MK, 229; in British Society, 241, 286–7, 289, 291, 298, 306; and Viennese refugees, 255; and Freud's difficulties in changing views, 289; Barbara Low complains of, 298; MK reports on Payne to, 304; numbered as Kleinian, 305; in Controversial Discussions, 316, 325; on death instinct, 333; and MK's disavowal of narcissism, 371; declines "borderline" cases, 375; MK's malicious remarks about, 382; writes Introduction to *Developments in Psycho-Analysis*, 393; MK ignores, 393, 424; supervises Milner, 395–6; relations with Bowlby, 402, 404; and Heimann's isolation, 421

WORKS CITED: "The Bereaved Wife," 393n; "On the Genesis of Psychical Conflict in Earliest Infancy," 221, 371

Robertson, James, 403, 405

Róheim, Géza, 71, 82

Rosenberg, Austria (now Ružomberok), 20, 22–30, 40–2, 46, 48–9, 79, 82, 90

Rosenberg, Elizabeth, 316, 359, 450

Rosenfeld, Eva: arrival in Britain, 239–40, 242; supports MK, 242, 244, 261; and British Society factionalism, 286; and Controversial Discussions, 316; analyzed by MK, 361; MK discards, 424; and Hyatt Williams, 450

Rosenfeld, Herbert: on Abraham, 115; MK analyzes, 365; and schizophrenia, 370, 372–3, 375–6, 425; on projective identification, 374–5; devotion to MK, 375; supports MK on origin of psychoses, 429; and revised Training regulations, 431; Laing on, 446; at 1959 Copenhagen Congress, 459

WORKS CITED: "Analysis of a Schizophrenic State with Depersonalization," 115, 375; "Notes on the Psycho-Pathology of Confusional States in Chronic Schizophrenias," 376; "Transference Phenomena and Transference-Analysis," 397

Rügen, 58, 62

Rycroft, Charles: on instinct and drive, 108n; on Winnicott, 399; on Bowlby, 402; helps form 1952 Club, 406; as scientific secretary of British Society, 407; describes Kleinians as "Ebenezer Church," 428n; on MK's presence, 433; chooses MK's 75th birthday gift, 438; analyzes Laing, 446; *A Critical Dictionary of Psychoanalysis*, 100n, 186

Sachs, Hanns, 93–4, 119n, 122, 133–4, 138n, 340
sadism, 103–4, 108, 126, 192, 205, 209
Sammy (Joyce McDougall's patient), 439
Sandford, Beryl, 187
Sandler, Joseph, 360, 379, 392, 407, 432
Schaffner, Perdita, 369
Schiller, Johann Friedrich von, 17
schizophrenia: MK seeks origin of, 185–6, 371–3, 376, 459–60; Scott and, 370, 425; Fairbairn and, 371–2; Rosenfeld and, 372–3, 375–6; 1953 symposium on, 410; Segal on, 460
Schlesinger, Professor (Vienna doctor), 46
Schling, Bruni, 66–7, 159n
Schmideberg, Melitta (née Klein; MK's daughter), 42, 54, 79, 213–14; Libussa on, as child, 44–6; dislikes grandmother, 53; attends Budapest Psycho-Analytical Society meetings, 72; with MK after parents' divorce, 89–90; matriculation, 89–90, 112; MK analyzes, 95–6, 98, 111–12, 183; later analyses, 99, 111, 199, 381; in Berlin, 110; studies, 110–12; romance and marriage with Schmideberg, 110–12, 183; graduation and thesis, 183; joins mother in London, 183–4; delivers papers and lectures to British Society, 184, 212–13; at MK's publication party, 195; husband joins, in London, 198–9; opposition to mother, 200, 212–14, 218, 229–30, 236, 242–3, 259, 284, 295, 297; work in child analysis, 201; attacks Anna Freud, 210n, 219–20, 226; elected to London Institute, 212; and death of Hans, 215; and MK's theory of depressive position, 217–18; son's death, 220; accuses Kleinians of plagiarism, 229; visits Freud in Britain, 241; at meeting with Anna Freud, 244; on grief, 251; in British Society wartime disputes, 291, 293, 298, 301, 306; MK refers to "illness," 297; relations with Glover, 297n, 353–4, 369; and Controversial Discussions, 316–17, 319; and Anna Freud's resignation from Training Committee, 346, 348; moves to New York, 353, 369; and Bryher's relations with Walter, 369; final resignation from British Society, 369n; at 16th Zurich Congress, 376; Paula Heimann and, 380–2; ignores mother, 411; ignores mother's death, 461; bequest from MK, 462
WORKS: "After the Analysis," 229–30; "Introjected Objects," 284; "The Mode of Operation in Psycho-Analytic Theory" (*abridged as* "The Psycho-Analysis of Asocial Children and Adolescents"), 219n; "The Play-Analysis of a Three-Year-Old Girl," 212; "Psychology and Treatment of the Criminal Psychopath," 376; "Reassurance as

a Means of Analytic Technique," 205n; "Some Unconscious Mechanisms in Pathological Sexuality and Their Relation to Normal Sexuality, 184
Schmideberg, Walter (Melitta's husband): romance and marriage, 110–12; entry to England, 184, 194, 198; criticizes MK's techniques, 205; visits Freud, 241; at Extraordinary Meetings, 290–1, 293, 296; at Controversial Discussions, 316; relations with Bryher, 369; and Paula Heimann, 380; death, 411
Schnitzler, Arthur, 17, 66
Schonfeld, Irma, 21, 23, 46–8
Schott, Ada, 74, 95, 122–4, 142
Schreber case, 373, 433, 459
Schwartz, Hedy, 438, 456
Scott, W. Clifford M.: in training analysis with MK, 189, 190n, 214, 427n; on Nina Searl's resignation, 230; on anti-Semitism and German refugees, 240; in British Society, 286; and Viennese in London, 244; in wartime, 246, 254–5, 258–9, 316; and MK's interest in depression, 262; numbered as Kleinian, 305; and Controversial Discussions, 316; advocates unified training, 359; MK praises Hanna Segal to, 365; letter from MK at war's end, 370; and schizophrenia, 370, 373, 425; and Joan Riviere's declining borderline case, 375; letter from MK on Lacan, 376; decline in relations with MK, 393, 424–6; and Milner, 396; and Winnicott, 397, 400n, 401; on MK's learning, 400; body scheme, 424–5; return to Canada, 425–6; MK protests to, on Training Committee regulations, 430; MK requests payment from, 437; analyzes Clare Winnicott, 451; on MK's interpretations, 452n
WORKS CITED: "Depression, Confusion and Multivalence," 426; "On the Intense Affects Encountered in Treating a Severe Manic-Depressive Disorder," 259n; "A Psycho-Analytic Concept of the Origin of Depression," 397
Searl, Nina: analyzes Eric, 99; "A Question of Technique in Child Analysis in Relation to the Oedipus Complex," 125; translates MK's lecture, 136–7; and Anna Freud, 164; influenced by MK, 170; work in child analysis, 201; supports MK's ideas, 205, 207, 229; resigns from British Society, 230–1, 241, 293; MK praises, 393
Secondary Drive ("cupboard love"), 403
"Secrets of a Soul, The," see *Geheimnisse einer Seelen*
Segal, Hanna, 365; MK tells of Arthur's infidelities, 53; on word *Trieb*, 108n; reviews MK's *Narrative*, 272; analyzed by MK, 365; on projection, 374; and MK's dropped patients and death of Judith Waterlow, 409, 419; Heimann's jealousy of, 419; on Heimann and MK, 420; and borderline cases, 425; supports MK on origin of psychoses, 429; on Topolski drawing of MK, 438; on

Segal, Hanna (*cont'd*)
    death instinct, 440n; and MK's irregular
    analysis of Heimann, 443; on MK's tech-
    niques in analysis, 449–50; on schizophrenia,
    460; visits dying MK, 461; at MK's memo-
    rial service, 462; bequest from MK, 462
    WORKS CITED: "Notes on Symbol Forma-
    tion," 413; "Some Aspects of the Analysis of
    a Schizophrenic," 376
self, and ego, 453
Sharpe, Ella: analyzes Melitta, 99, 199, 354n,
    381; in Berlin Society, 123; asked to trans-
    late MK's papers, 135; offers rooms for MK's
    visit to England, 135–6; membership in Brit-
    ish Society, 158; and Anna Freud, 164; in-
    fluenced by MK, 170; supports MK's ideas,
    205, 229; suggested for International Train-
    ing Commission, 220; hostility to MK, 243,
    292, 312; on Training Committee, 258,
    334n, 340, 359; reads Sylvia Payne's paper at
    British Society, 290; at Extraordinary Meet-
    ing, 290–2; supports Anna Freud in Contro-
    versial Discussions, 316, 367; analyzes
    Margaret Little, 361; on depressive position,
    367–8
Shaw, George Bernard, *Back to Methuselah*,
    142
Sheehan-Dare, Helen, 305, 312–13, 379
Simmel, Ernst, 94, 133, 239; work on war neu-
    roses, 71; on control analysis, 94; analyzes
    Hans, 99, 110, 215; and anal eroticism, 122;
    presents poor paper, 123; as president of Ber-
    lin Society, 141; "Self-Preservation and the
    Death Instinct," 193n
Slight, David, 189–90, 303
Society of Psychical Research, 208
sphincter morality, 339
splitting, 417, 440 and n
Stekel, Wilhelm, 349
Stephen, Adrian, 137, 243, 290, 326, 346–7,
    350, 356, 359
Stephen, Karin, 137, 243, 289–90, 350, 370
Sterba, Richard, 219
Stokes, Adrian, 413, 444; *Greek Culture and
    the Ego*, 444; *Inside Out*, 444
Strachey, Alix: on Hug-Hellmuth's *Neue
    Wege*, 79; and Berlin Society and Institute,
    94, 123–5, 127, 132; analyzed by Abraham,
    123, 133, 139; and Anna Freud, 124, 168;
    requests MK's clarification on theories,
    125–30; with MK in Berlin, 131–5, 139–40,
    148; and MK's proposed visit to England,
    131–2; translates MK, 135–7, 191, 390;
    James Glover analyzes, 140; in British So-
    ciety, 158; at MK's publication party, 195;
    "A Note on the Use of the Word 'Inter-
    nal,'" 241; unease at MK's ideas, 241; at
    Extraordinary Meeting, 307; moves away
    from MK, 393
Strachey, James: letter from Alix on Hug-Hell-
    muth, 79; and Berlin Society, 123–4; reads
    MK paper at British Society, 125, 127, 130;
    and Alix's conversations with MK, 132; and
    MK's proposed visit to England, 134–5;

    translates MK paper, 135, 137; in British So-
    ciety, 158; on Freud's *Civilization and Its
    Discontents*, 188; at MK's publication party,
    195; on Joan Riviere, 208; and Melitta's at-
    tacks on MK, 229; analyzes Winnicott, 233;
    edits *International Journal*, 249; on Anna
    Freud–MK conflict, 257–8; organizes Con-
    troversial Discussions, 315–16; Reports on
    Training Committee findings, 334–6, 341–2,
    346, 348; on elections to Training Commit-
    tee, 350; translates Freud, 438n
    WORKS CITED: "The Nature of Therapeutic
    Action of Psycho-Analysis," 206; "Some Un-
    conscious Factors in Reading," 205
Strachey, Lytton, 123n
Stross, Josephine, 299
sublimation, 185
suicide, 215, 218
superego: in children, 103, 174; Jones on, 159,
    162, 171–2; MK on, 162, 169, 172, 174,
    177, 194, 283, 441; Ella Sharpe on, 170;
    pre-Oedipal, 175n, 176, 224; paternal, 177;
    and anxiety in Rita, 184; and aggression,
    188–9; effect of analyst's on patient, 206;
    and part-object, 217; Waelder on age of de-
    velopment of, 224; Fairbairn on, 320; and
    guilt, 326–7; and "good" and "bad" breast,
    331, 440
Sutherland, J. D., 371, 374n, 427–8, 447
Sweden, Arthur Klein in, 82–3, 89, 109
Swerdloff, Bluma, 94n, 154, 284, 343, 351,
    353–5
Swiss Psycho-Analytical Society, 352
Sylvester, Constance, 14, 84
symbolism, 185, 413
Symposium on Child Analysis, 209

Tansley, A. G., 130, 212n
Tavistock Institute and Clinic, London, 260,
    338, 350, 403
Tega Sanatorium, 239
Therapy (journal), 70
Thomas, Ruth, 187
Thorner, Hans, 84n, 359
toilet training, 175, 232
Tonnesmann, Margaret, 422
Topolski, Feliks, 433n, 438
Toronto, 155–7
toys, 101–4, 170, 186, 188
Training Committee (of British Society),
    256–9, 263, 286, 302–4, 307, 314; Re-
    ports, 334–41, 346, 348, 350; Anna Freud
    resigns from, 346, 348; election to, 350, 355;
    and Anna Freud's proposals for collabora-
    tion, 356–9; revised regulations (1953–4),
    429–31
transference: in children, 101, 168; Freud's dis-
    covery and exposition of, 206, 228; Waelder
    criticizes MK's use of, 224; Anna Freud on,
    226, 337; negative, 228, 234–5, 266, 300,
    331; importance to MK, 337–8, 340, 442;
    after analysis, 339; interpretation, 340; *see
    also* countertransference
"transference neurosis," 337

transition, 397–8, 400
Trieb, as term, 108n
Trist, Eric, 325, 422
Trotter, Wilfred, 154
Trude (MK's patient), 100, 103
Tureck, Rosalyn, 455, 461
Turkle, Sherry, *Psychoanalytic Politics*, 387n
Tustin, Frances, 187, 188n
Two-Year-Old Goes to Hospital, A (film), 403
Tyson, Alan, 406, 432

unconscious, 209, 324, 439
Unitarian Church, 83
urine, 187n

Vágó, Gyula, 49, 59–60
Vágó, Jolanthe (née Klein; Jolan; MK's sister-in-law): relations with MK, 22, 33; and MK's mother, 27; visits Emanuel's grave, 44–5; in Budapest, 48, 60, 85; marriage, 49, 85; and Arthur's death, 250; settles in Sweden, 250, 460; and Michael Clyne, 436
Vágó, Maria (Jolanthe's daughter), 250
Vágó, Thomas (Jolanthe's son), 250
Verrall, A. W., 208
Viennese Psychoanalytical Society: MK delivers paper to, 126–8, 131; and Anna Freud, 163–4; and professional qualifications, 201; Jones visits and addresses, 210; differences with London, 220–2; Riviere addresses, 221–3; Jewish refugees from, 240–1, 243, 255–6
Vivian (Melitta's patient), 212–13

Waelder, Robert, 221–5, 255, 318, 323, 328; "The Problem of the Genesis of Psychical Conflict in Earliest Infancy," 222n, 223–4
Wagner, Michael, 9n, 22n
Waidhofer Resolution, 1882, 8n
Walsh, Kay (Mrs. Elliott Jaques), 413, 438
Waterlow, Judith, 409
weaning, 229, 232, 300, 406
Wedeles, Claude, 362, 374, 437, 448–9, 451
Wedeles, Elinor, 417, 426, 437
Whitehorn, Katherine, 233, 325
Williams, A. Hyatt, 406, 414, 450–1
Wilson, A. C., 305, 347
Wilson, Angus, 455
Winnicott, Clare (née Britton): and MK's relations with mother, 59; relations with patients, 73; and Donald, 246, 399; and MK's paper at Geneva Congress, 414; MK analyzes, 450–2; Lois Munro analyzes, 452–3; qualifies as analyst, 461
Winnicott, Donald W., 258, 399–401; analyzes Eric, 99, 233, 253, 261, 276n, 451; and

Wolfheim's account of MK, 119; on MK's "discoveries," 121, 400; on Jones, 158; expands child analysis, 201; analyzed by Riviere, 207; on mother-child relationship, 233, 300, 417; analyzed by James Strachey, 233; "maternal" feelings, 233–4; and Jewish refugees in British Society, 241; activities in British Society, 241, 286, 289; wartime duties, 246; and MK's mourning, 253; MK confides in, 259–61; and MK's interest in depression, 262; at Extraordinary Meetings, 292; numbered as Kleinian, 305; supervises child analysis, 313–14; and Controversial Discussions, 316, 321, 328; and age of object relations, 324; and Glover's resignation, 348, 354; and Segal, 365; MK refuses to acknowledge evidence from, 374; MK's coolness to, 393, 398, 424; attitude toward MK, 398–400, 447, 451; intuitive understanding of young, 399; as president of British Society, 401–2, 404–5, 410, 426, 428; unclear ideas on internal dynamic, 404; and Bowlby, 404–6; rebukes MK, 410; and MK's paper at Geneva Congress, 414, 416; supports Heimann, 421; and Baumann's Zurich discussion, 422–3; proposes revised Training regulations, 431; misgivings on British Society's political structure, 432; and McDougall's *Dialogue with Sammy*, 439; obituary of Jones, 441; supervises Laing, 446–7; and wife's analysis with MK, 452–3; WORKS CITED: "The Capacity to Be Alone," 457, 459; "Classification: Is There a Psycho-Analytic Contribution to Psychiatric Classification?," 453; "Hate in the Counter-transference," 374, 379, 382; "The Manic Defence," 374; "Transitional Objects and Transitional Phenomena," 397–8
Wisdom, J. O., 269, 444
wish fulfillment, 317, 319
Wolf Man, the, 71, 117
Wollfheim, Nelly, 119–21, 138–9, 240, 379, 456–7
Wollheim, Richard, 444, 456
Woodhead, Barbara, 406
Woolf, Leonard, 140n, 158, 237
Woolf, Virginia, 237
Wride, Fanny, 214

Zeitschrift, see *Internationale Zeitschrift für Psychoanalyse*
Zetzel, Elizabeth Rosenberg, 159, 459
Zilboorg, Gregory, 198
Zweig, Stefan, 211

Grateful acknowledgment is hereby made to the following institutions and individuals for permission to use illustrations:

For photographs following page 148:

PAGES 1–4: The Melanie Klein Trust / Wellcome Institute
PAGE 5: The National Portrait Gallery
PAGE 6: The British Institute of Psychoanalysis
PAGE 7: top—The New York Psychoanalytic Institute
PAGE 7: bottom—Grant Allan
PAGE 8: top—Mary Evans / Sigmund Freud
PAGE 8: bottom—Melanie Klein Trust / Wellcome Institute

For photographs following page 372:

PAGE 1: top—Eric Clyne; center—Oscar Nemon; bottom—Melanie Klein Trust / Wellcome Institute
PAGE 2: top—John Bowlby; center and bottom—British Institute of Psychoanalysis
PAGE 3: top—anonymous; center—Melanie Klein Trust / Wellcome Institute; bottom—Jane Bown
PAGE 4: top—Vroni Gordon; center—British Institute of Psychoanalysis; bottom—Melanie Klein Trust / Wellcome Institute
PAGE 5: top—Melanie Klein Trust / Wellcome Institute; bottom—Mrs. Francesca Bion
PAGE 6: top—Eric Clyne; bottom—British Institute of Psychoanalysis
PAGE 7: top—Vroni Gordon; bottom—Melanie Klein Trust / Wellcome Institute
PAGE 8: top—Dr. Hans Thorner; bottom—Dr. Hanna Segal